Bloodlands

Bloodlands

Europe Between Hitler and Stalin

TIMOTHY SNYDER

THE BODLEY HEAD
LONDON

Published by The Bodley Head 2010

6 8 10 9 7 5

First published in Great Britain in 2010 by
The Bodley Head
Random House, 20 Vauxhall Bridge Road,
London SW1V 2SA

www.bodleyhead.co.uk
www.rbooks.co.uk

Addresses for companies within The Random House Group Limited can be found at:
www.randomhouse.co.uk/offices.htm

The Random House Group Limited Reg. No. 954009

A CIP catalogue record for this book
is available from the British Library

ISBN 9780224081412

The Random House Group Limited supports The Forest Stewardship
Council (FSC), the leading international forest certification organisation. All our titles
that are printed on Greenpeace approved FSC certified paper carry the FSC logo.
Our paper procurement policy can be found at:

CONTENTS

your golden hair Margarete
your ashen hair Shulamit

Paul Celan
"Death Fugue"

Everything flows, everything changes.
You can't board the same prison train twice.

Vasily Grossman
Everything Flows

A stranger drowned on the Black Sea alone
With no one to hear his prayers for forgiveness.

"Storm on the Black Sea"
Ukrainian traditional song

Whole cities disappear. In nature's stead
Only a white shield to counter nonexistence.

Tomas Venclova
"The Shield of Achilles"

PREFACE: EUROPE

"Now we will live!" This is what the hungry little boy liked to say, as he toddled along the quiet roadside, or through the empty fields. But the food that he saw was only in his imagination. The wheat had all been taken away, in a heartless campaign of requisitions that began Europe's era of mass killing. It was 1933, and Joseph Stalin was deliberately starving Soviet Ukraine. The little boy died, as did more than three million other people. "I will meet her," said a young Soviet man of his wife, "under the ground." He was right; he was shot after she was, and they were buried among the seven hundred thousand victims of Stalin's Great Terror of 1937 and 1938. "They asked for my wedding ring, which I. . . ." The Polish officer broke off his diary just before he was executed by the Soviet secret police in 1940. He was one of about two hundred thousand Polish citizens shot by the Soviets or the Germans at the beginning of the Second World War, while Nazi Germany and the Soviet Union jointly occupied his country. Late in 1941, an eleven-year-old Russian girl in Leningrad finished her own humble diary: "Only Tania is left." Adolf Hitler had betrayed Stalin, her city was under siege by the Germans, and her family were among the four million Soviet citizens the Germans starved to death. The following summer, a twelve-year-old Jewish girl in Belarus wrote a last letter to her father: "I am saying good-bye to you before I die. I am so afraid of this death because they throw small children into the mass graves alive." She was among the more than five million Jews gassed or shot by the Germans.

In the middle of Europe in the middle of the twentieth century, the Nazi and Soviet regimes murdered some fourteen million people. The place where all of the victims died, the bloodlands, extends from central Poland to western Russia, through Ukraine, Belarus, and the Baltic States. During the consolidation of National Socialism and Stalinism (1933–1938), the joint German-Soviet occupation of Poland (1939–1941), and then the German-Soviet war (1941–1945), mass violence of a sort never before seen in history was visited upon this region. The victims were chiefly Jews, Belarusians, Ukrainians, Poles, Russians, and Balts, the peoples native to these lands. The fourteen million were murdered over the course of only twelve years, between 1933 and 1945, while both Hitler and Stalin were in power. Though their homelands became battlefields midway through this period, these people were all victims of murderous policy rather than casualties of war. The Second World War was the most lethal conflict in history, and about half of the soldiers who perished on all of its battlefields all the world over died here, in this same region, in the bloodlands. Yet not a single one of the fourteen million murdered was a soldier on active duty. Most were women, children, and the aged; none were bearing weapons; many had been stripped of their possessions, including their clothes.

Auschwitz is the most familiar killing site of the bloodlands. Today Auschwitz stands for the Holocaust, and the Holocaust for the evil of a century. Yet the people registered as laborers at Auschwitz had a chance of surviving: thanks to the memoirs and novels written by survivors, its name is known. Far more Jews, most of them Polish Jews, were gassed in other German death factories where almost everyone died, and whose names are less often recalled: Treblinka, Chełmno, Sobibór, Bełżec. Still more Jews, Polish or Soviet or Baltic Jews, were shot over ditches and pits. Most of these Jews died near where they had lived, in occupied Poland, Lithuania, Latvia, Soviet Ukraine, and Soviet Belarus. The Germans brought Jews from elsewhere to the bloodlands to be killed. Jews arrived by train to Auschwitz from Hungary, Czechoslovakia, France, the Netherlands, Greece, Belgium, Yugoslavia, Italy, and Norway. German Jews were deported to the cities of the bloodlands, to Łódź or Kaunas or Minsk or Warsaw, before being shot or gassed. The people who lived on the block where I am writing now, in the ninth district of Vienna, were deported to Auschwitz, Sobibór, Treblinka, and Riga: all in the bloodlands.

The German mass murder of Jews took place in occupied Poland, Lithuania, Latvia, and the Soviet Union, not in Germany itself. Hitler was an anti-Semitic politician in a country with a small Jewish community. Jews were *fewer than one percent* of the German population when Hitler became chancellor in 1933,

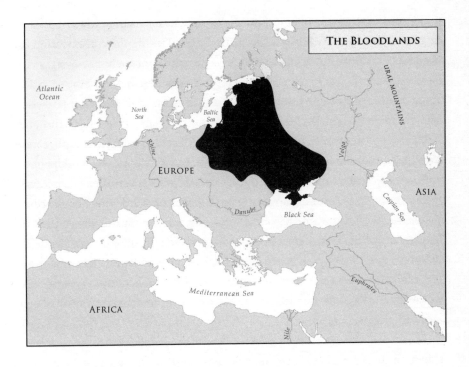

and *about one quarter of one percent* by the beginning of the Second World War. During the first six years of Hitler's rule, German Jews were allowed (in humiliating and impoverishing circumstances) to emigrate. Most of the German Jews who saw Hitler win elections in 1933 died of natural causes. The murder of 165,000 German Jews was a ghastly crime in and of itself, but only a very small part of the tragedy of European Jews: fewer than three percent of the deaths of the Holocaust. Only when Nazi Germany invaded Poland in 1939 and the Soviet Union in 1941 did Hitler's visions of the elimination of Jews from Europe intersect with the two most significant populations of European Jews. His ambition to eliminate the Jews of Europe could be realized only in the parts of Europe where Jews lived.

The Holocaust overshadows German plans that envisioned even more killing. Hitler wanted not only to eradicate the Jews; he wanted also to destroy Poland and the Soviet Union as states, exterminate their ruling classes, and kill tens of millions of Slavs (Russians, Ukrainians, Belarusians, Poles). If the German war against the USSR had gone as planned, thirty million civilians would have been starved in its first winter, and tens of millions more expelled, killed, assimilated,

or enslaved thereafter. Though these plans were never realized, they supplied
the moral premises of German occupation policy in the East. The Germans
murdered about as many non-Jews as Jews during the war, chiefly by starving
Soviet prisoners of war (more than three million) and residents of besieged cities
(more than a million) or by shooting civilians in "reprisals" (the better part of a
million, chiefly Belarusians and Poles).

The Soviet Union defeated Nazi Germany on the eastern front in the Second
World War, thereby earning Stalin the gratitude of millions and a crucial part
in the establishment of the postwar order in Europe. Yet Stalin's own record of
mass murder was almost as imposing as Hitler's. Indeed, in times of peace it
was far worse. In the name of defending and modernizing the Soviet Union,
Stalin oversaw the starvation of millions and the shooting of three quarters of a
million people in the 1930s. Stalin killed his own citizens no less efficiently than
Hitler killed the citizens of other countries. Of the fourteen million people deliberately murdered in the bloodlands between 1933 and 1945, a third belong
in the Soviet account.

This is a history of political mass murder. The fourteen million were all victims
of a Soviet or Nazi killing policy, often of an interaction between the Soviet
Union and Nazi Germany, but never casualties of the war between them. A quarter of them were killed before the Second World War even began. A further two
hundred thousand died between 1939 and 1941, while Nazi Germany and the
Soviet Union were remaking Europe as *allies*. The deaths of the fourteen million
were sometimes projected in economic plans, or hastened by economic considerations, but were not caused by economic necessity in any strict sense. Stalin
knew what would happen when he seized food from the starving peasants of
Ukraine in 1933, just as Hitler knew what could be expected when he deprived
Soviet prisoners of war of food eight years later. In both cases, more than three
million people died. The hundreds of thousands of Soviet peasants and workers
shot during the Great Terror in 1937 and 1938 were victims of express directives
of Stalin, just as the millions of Jews shot and gassed between 1941 and 1945
were victims of an explicit policy of Hitler.

War did alter the balance of killing. In the 1930s, the Soviet Union was the
only state in Europe carrying out policies of mass killing. Before the Second
World War, in the first six and a half years after Hitler came to power, the Nazi
regime killed no more than about ten thousand people. The Stalinist regime

had already starved millions and shot the better part of a million. German policies of mass killing came to rival Soviet ones between 1939 and 1941, after Stalin allowed Hitler to begin a war. The Wehrmacht and the Red Army both attacked Poland in September 1939, German and Soviet diplomats signed a Treaty on Borders and Friendship, and German and Soviet forces occupied the country together for nearly two years. After the Germans expanded their empire to the west in 1940 by invading Norway, Denmark, the Low Countries, and France, the Soviets occupied and annexed Lithuania, Latvia, Estonia, and northeastern Romania. Both regimes shot educated Polish citizens in the tens of thousands and deported them in the hundreds of thousands. For Stalin, such mass repression was the continuation of old policies on new lands; for Hitler, it was a breakthrough.

The very worst of the killing began when Hitler betrayed Stalin and German forces crossed into the recently enlarged Soviet Union in June 1941. Although the Second World War began in September 1939 with the joint German-Soviet invasion of Poland, the tremendous majority of its killing followed that second eastern invasion. In Soviet Ukraine, Soviet Belarus, and the Leningrad district, lands where the Stalinist regime had starved and shot some four million people in the previous eight years, German forces managed to starve and shoot even more in half the time. Right after the invasion began, the Wehrmacht began to starve its Soviet prisoners, and special task forces called Einsatzgruppen began to shoot political enemies and Jews. Along with the German Order Police, the Waffen-SS, and the Wehrmacht, and with the participation of local auxiliary police and militias, the Einsatzgruppen began that summer to eliminate Jewish communities as such.

The bloodlands were where most of Europe's Jews lived, where Hitler and Stalin's imperial plans overlapped, where the Wehrmacht and the Red Army fought, and where the Soviet NKVD and the German SS concentrated their forces. Most killing sites were in the bloodlands: in the political geography of the 1930s and early 1940s, this meant Poland, the Baltic States, Soviet Belarus, Soviet Ukraine, and the western fringe of Soviet Russia. Stalin's crimes are often associated with Russia, and Hitler's with Germany. But the deadliest part of the Soviet Union was its non-Russian periphery, and Nazis generally killed beyond Germany. The horror of the twentieth century is thought to be located in the camps. But the

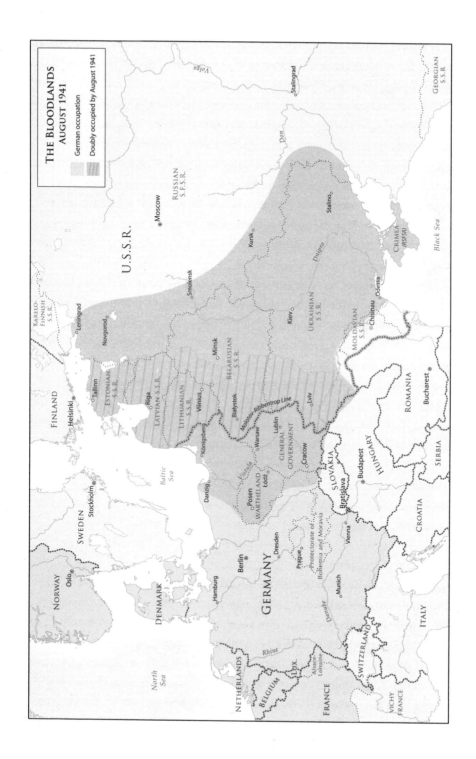

concentration camps are not where most of the victims of National Socialism and Stalinism died. These misunderstandings regarding the sites and methods of mass killing prevent us from perceiving the horror of the twentieth century.

Germany was the site of concentration camps liberated by the Americans and the British in 1945; Russian Siberia was of course the site of much of the Gulag, made known in the West by Alexander Solzhenitsyn. The images of these camps, in photographs or in prose, only suggest the history of German and Soviet violence. About a million people died because they were sentenced to labor in German concentration camps—as distinct from the German gas chambers and the German killing fields and the German starvation zones, where *ten million* people died. Over a million lives were shortened by exhaustion and disease in the Soviet Gulag between 1933 and 1945—as distinct from the Soviet killing fields and the Soviet hunger regions, where some *six million* people died, about *four million* of them in the bloodlands. Ninety percent of those who entered the Gulag left it alive. Most of the people who entered German concentration camps (as opposed to the German gas chambers, death pits, and prisoner-of-war camps) also survived. The fate of concentration camp inmates, horrible though it was, is distinct from that of those many millions who were gassed, shot, or starved.

The distinction between concentration camps and killing sites cannot be made perfectly: people were executed and people were starved in camps. Yet there is a difference between a camp sentence and a death sentence, between labor and gas, between slavery and bullets. The tremendous majority of the mortal victims of both the German and the Soviet regimes never saw a concentration camp. Auschwitz was two things at once, a labor camp and a death facility, and the fate of non-Jews seized for labor and Jews selected for labor was very different from the fate of Jews selected for the gas chambers. Auschwitz thus belongs to two histories, related but distinct. Auschwitz-as-labor-camp is more representative of the experience of the large number of people who endured German (or Soviet) policies of concentration, whereas Auschwitz-as-death-facility is more typical of the fates of those who were deliberately killed. Most of the Jews who arrived at Auschwitz were simply gassed; they, like almost all of the fourteen million killed in the bloodlands, never spent time in a concentration camp.

The German and Soviet concentration camps surround the bloodlands, from both east and west, blurring the black with their shades of grey. At the end of the Second World War, American and British forces liberated German concentration camps such as Belsen and Dachau, but the western Allies liberated *none* of the important death facilities. The Germans carried out all of their major killing policies on lands subsequently occupied by the Soviets. The Red Army liberated Auschwitz, and it liberated the sites of Treblinka, Sobibór, Bełżec, Chełmno, and Majdanek as well. American and British forces reached *none* of the bloodlands and saw *none* of the major killing sites. It is not just that American and British forces saw none of the places where the Soviets killed, leaving the crimes of Stalinism to be documented after the end of the Cold War and the opening of the archives. It is that they never saw the places where the *Germans* killed, meaning that understanding of Hitler's crimes has taken just as long. The photographs and films of German concentration camps were the closest that most westerners ever came to perceiving the mass killing. Horrible though these images were, they were only hints at the history of the bloodlands. They are not the whole story; sadly, they are not even an introduction.

———————

Mass killing in Europe is usually associated with the Holocaust, and the Holocaust with rapid industrial killing. The image is too simple and clean. At the German and Soviet killing sites, the methods of murder were rather primitive. Of the fourteen million civilians and prisoners of war killed in the bloodlands between 1933 and 1945, more than half died because they were denied food. Europeans deliberately starved Europeans in horrific numbers in the middle of the twentieth century. The two largest mass killing actions after the Holocaust— Stalin's directed famines of the early 1930s and Hitler's starvation of Soviet prisoners of war in the early 1940s—involved this method of killing. Starvation was foremost not only in reality but in imagination. In a Hunger Plan, the Nazi regime projected the death by starvation of tens of millions of Slavs and Jews in the winter of 1941–1942.

After starvation came shooting, and then gassing. In Stalin's Great Terror of 1937–1938, nearly seven hundred thousand Soviet citizens were shot. The two hundred thousand or so Poles killed by the Germans and the Soviets during their joint occupation of Poland were shot. The more than three hundred thousand Belarusians and the comparable number of Poles executed in German "reprisals" were shot. The Jews killed in the Holocaust were about as likely to be shot as to be gassed.

For that matter, there was little especially modern about the gassing. The million or so Jews asphyxiated at Auschwitz were killed by hydrogen cyanide, a compound isolated in the eighteenth century. The 1.6 million or so Jews killed at Treblinka, Chełmno, Bełżec, and Sobibór were asphyxiated by carbon monoxide, which even the ancient Greeks knew was lethal. In the 1940s hydrogen cyanide was used as a pesticide; carbon monoxide was produced by internal combustion engines. The Soviets and the Germans relied upon technologies that were hardly novel even in the 1930s and 1940s: internal combustion, railways, firearms, pesticides, barbed wire.

No matter which technology was used, the killing was personal. People who starved were observed, often from watchtowers, by those who denied them food. People who were shot were seen through the sights of rifles at very close range, or held by two men while a third placed a pistol at the base of the skull. People who were asphyxiated were rounded up, put on trains, and then rushed into the gas chambers. They lost their possessions and then their clothes and then, if they were women, their hair. Each one of them died a different death, since each one of them had lived a different life.

The sheer numbers of the victims can blunt our sense of the individuality of each one. "I'd like to call you all by name," wrote the Russian poet Anna Akhmatova in her *Requiem*, "but the list has been removed and there is nowhere else to look." Thanks to the hard work of historians, we have some of the lists; thanks to the opening of the archives in eastern Europe, we have places to look. We have a surprising number of the voices of the victims: the recollections (for example) of one young Jewish woman who dug herself from the Nazi death pit at Babi Yar, in Kiev; or of another who managed the same at Ponary, near Vilnius. We have the memoirs of some of the few dozen survivors of Treblinka. We have an archive of the Warsaw ghetto, painstakingly assembled, buried and then (for the most part) found. We have the diaries kept by the Polish officers shot by the Soviet NKVD in 1940 at Katyn, unearthed along with their bodies. We have notes thrown from the buses taking Poles to death pits during the German killing actions of that same year. We have the words scratched on the wall of the synagogue in Kovel; and those left on the wall of the Gestapo prison in Warsaw. We have the recollections of Ukrainians who survived the Soviet famine of 1933, those of Soviet prisoners of war who survived the German starvation campaign of 1941, and those of Leningraders who survived the starvation siege of 1941–1944.

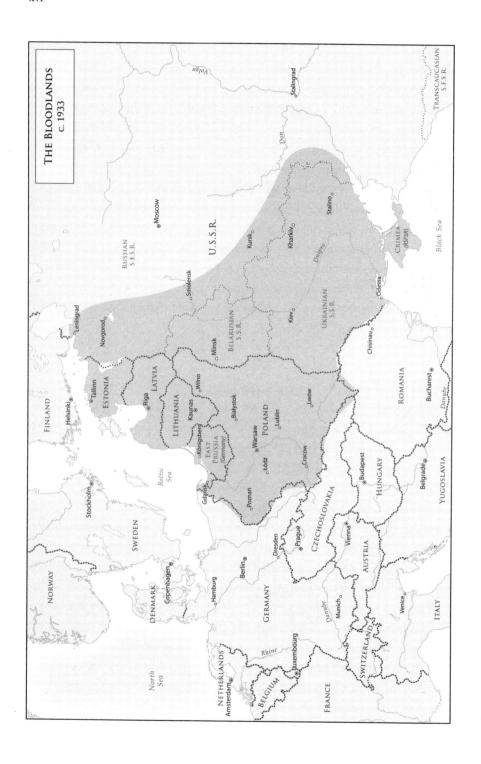

THE BLOODLANDS
c. 1933

We have some of the records of the perpetrators, taken from the Germans because they lost the war, or found in Russian or Ukrainian or Belarusian or Polish or Baltic archives after the collapse of the Soviet Union in 1991. We have reports and letters from German policemen and soldiers who shot Jews, and of the German anti-partisan units who shot Belarusian and Polish civilians. We have the petitions sent by the communist party activists before they enforced famine in Ukraine in 1932–1933. We have the death quotas for peasants and national minorities sent down from Moscow to regional NKVD offices in 1937 and 1938, and the replies asking that these quotas be increased. We have the interrogation protocols of the Soviet citizens who were then sentenced and killed. We have German death counts of Jews shot over pits and gassed at death facilities. We have Soviet death counts for the shooting actions of the Great Terror and at Katyn. We have good overall estimates of the numbers of killings of Jews at the major killing sites, based upon tabulations of German records and communications, survivor testimonies, and Soviet documents. We can make reasonable estimates of the number of famine deaths in the Soviet Union, not all of which were recorded. We have Stalin's letters to his closest comrades, Hitler's table talk, Himmler's datebook, and much else. Insofar as a book like this one is possible at all, it is thanks to the achievements of other historians, to their use of such sources and countless others. Although certain discussions in this book draw from my own archival work, the tremendous debt to colleagues and earlier generations of historians will be evident in its pages and the notes.

Throughout, the work will recall the voices of the victims themselves, and those of their friends and families. It will cite the perpetrators as well, those who killed and those who ordered the killing. It will also call as witnesses a small group of European writers: Anna Akhmatova, Hannah Arendt, Józef Czapski, Günter Grass, Vasily Grossman, Gareth Jones, Arthur Koestler, George Orwell, and Alexander Weissberg. (It will also follow the career of two diplomats: the American Russia specialist George Kennan, who found himself in Moscow at crucial moments; and the Japanese spy Chiune Sugihara, who took part in the policies that Stalin saw as justifying mass terror, and then saved Jews from Hitler's Holocaust.) Some of these writers recorded one policy of mass killing; others, two or even more. Some of them provided lucid analyses, others jarring comparisons, others unforgettable images. What they have in common is a sustained attempt to view Europe between Hitler and Stalin, often in disregard of the taboos of their day.

In a comparison of the Soviet and Nazi regimes, the political theorist Hannah Arendt wrote in 1951 that factuality itself "depends for its continued existence upon the existence of the nontotalitarian world." The American diplomat George Kennan made the same point in simpler words in Moscow in 1944: "here men determine what is true and what is false."

Is truth nothing more than a convention of power, or can truthful historical accounts resist the gravity of politics? Nazi Germany and the Soviet Union sought to master history itself. The Soviet Union was a Marxist state, whose leaders proclaimed themselves to be scientists of history. National Socialism was an apocalyptic vision of total transformation, to be realized by men who believed that will and race could slough off the burden of the past. The twelve years of Nazi and the seventy-four years of Soviet power certainly weigh heavily on our ability to evaluate the world. Many people believe that the crimes of the Nazi regime were so great as to stand outside history. This is a troubling echo of Hitler's own belief that will triumphs over facts. Others maintain that the crimes of Stalin, though horrible, were justified by the need to create or defend a modern state. This recalls Stalin's view that history has only one course, which he understood, and which legitimates his policies in retrospect.

Without a history built and defended upon an entirely different foundation, we will find that Hitler and Stalin continue to define their own works for us. What might that basis be? Although this study involves military, political, economic, social, cultural, and intellectual history, its three fundamental methods are simple: insistence that no past event is beyond historical understanding or beyond the reach of historical inquiry; reflection upon the possibility of alternative choices and acceptance of the irreducible reality of choice in human affairs; and orderly chronological attention to all of the Stalinist and Nazi policies that killed large numbers of civilians and prisoners of war. Its form arises not from the political geography of empires but from the human geography of victims. The bloodlands were no political territory, real or imagined; they are simply where Europe's most murderous regimes did their most murderous work.

For decades, national history—Jewish, Polish, Ukrainian, Belarusian, Russian, Lithuanian, Estonian, Latvian—has resisted the Nazi and Soviet conceptualizations of the atrocities. The history of the bloodlands has been preserved, often intelligently and courageously, by dividing the European past into national parts, and then by keeping these parts from touching one another. Yet attention to any single persecuted group, no matter how well executed as history, will fail as an account of what happened in Europe between 1933 and 1945. Perfect knowledge of the Ukrainian past will not produce the causes of the famine. Following the history of Poland is not the best way to understand why so many Poles were killed in the Great Terror. No amount of knowledge of Belarusian history can make sense of the prisoner-of-war camps and the anti-partisan campaigns that killed so many Belarusians. A description of Jewish life can include the Holocaust, but not explain it. Often what happened to one group is intelligible only in light of what had happened to another. But that is just the beginning of the connections. The Nazi and Soviet regimes, too, have to be understood in light of how their leaders strove to master these lands, and saw these groups and their relationships to one another.

Today there is widespread agreement that the mass killing of the twentieth century is of the greatest moral significance for the twenty-first. How striking, then, that there is no history of the bloodlands. Mass killing separated Jewish history from European history, and east European history from west European history. Murder did not make the nations, but it still conditions their intellectual separation, decades after the end of National Socialism and Stalinism. This study brings the Nazi and Soviet regimes together, and Jewish and European history together, and the national histories together. It describes the victims, and the perpetrators. It discusses the ideologies and the plans, and the systems and the societies. This is a history of the people killed by the policies of distant leaders. The victims' homelands lay between Berlin and Moscow; they became the bloodlands after the rise of Hitler and Stalin.

HITLER AND STALIN

The origins of the Nazi and the Soviet regimes, and of their encounter in the bloodlands, lie in the First World War of 1914–1918. The war broke the old land empires of Europe, while inspiring dreams of new ones. It replaced the dynastic principle of rule by emperors with the fragile idea of popular sovereignty. It showed that millions of men would obey orders to fight and die, for causes abstract and distant, in the name of homelands that were already ceasing to be or only coming into being. New states were created from virtually nothing, and large groups of civilians were moved or eliminated by the application of simple techniques. More than a million Armenians were killed by Ottoman authorities. Germans and Jews were deported by the Russian Empire. Bulgarians, Greeks, and Turks were exchanged among national states after the war. Just as important, the war shattered an integrated global economy. No adult European alive in 1914 would ever see the restoration of comparable free trade; most European adults alive in 1914 would not enjoy comparable levels of prosperity during the rest of their lives.

The essence of the First World War was the armed conflict between, on the one side, the German Empire, the Habsburg monarchy, the Ottoman Empire, and Bulgaria ("the Central Powers") and, on the other side, France, the Russian Empire, Great Britain, Italy, Serbia, and the United States ("the Entente Powers"). The victory of the Entente Powers in 1918 brought an end to three European land empires: the Habsburg, German, and Ottoman. By the terms of the postwar settlements of Versailles, St. Germain, Sèvres, and Trianon, multinational

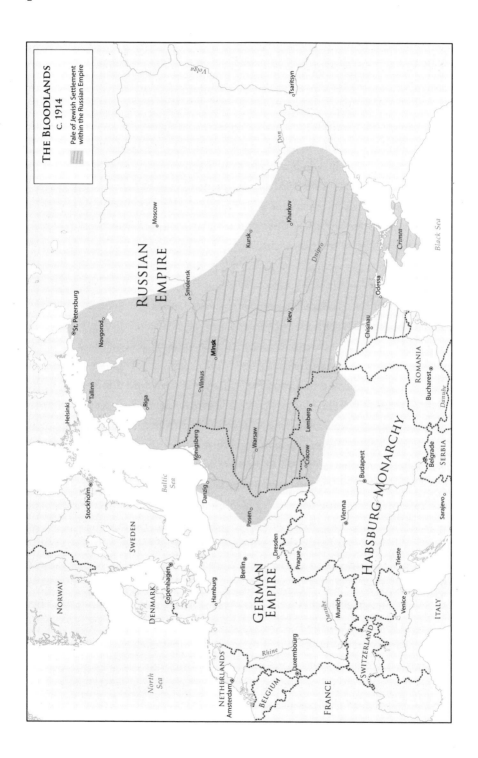

THE BLOODLANDS
C. 1914

Pale of Jewish Settlement
within the Russian Empire

domains were replaced by national states, and monarchies by democratic republics. The European great powers that were not destroyed by the war, Britain and especially France, were substantially weakened. Among the victors, the illusion after 1918 was that life might somehow return to its course before the war. Among the revolutionaries who hoped to lead the defeated, the dream was that the bloodshed could legitimate further radical transformations, which could impart meaning to the war and undo its damage.

The most important political vision was that of communist utopia. At war's end, it had been seventy years since Karl Marx and Friedrich Engels had penned their most famous lines: "Workers of the World Unite!" Marxism had inspired generations of revolutionaries with a summons to political and moral transformation: an end of capitalism and the conflict that private property was thought to bring, and its replacement by a socialism that would liberate the working masses and restore to all of humanity an unspoiled soul. For Marxists, historical progress followed from a struggle between rising and falling classes, groups made and remade by changes in the modes of economic production. Each dominant political order was challenged by new social groups formed by new economic techniques. The modern class struggle was between those who owned factories and those who worked in them. Accordingly, Marx and Engels anticipated that revolutions would begin in the more advanced industrial countries with large working classes, such as Germany and Great Britain.

By disrupting the capitalist order and weakening the great empires, the First World War brought an obvious opportunity to revolutionaries. Most Marxists, however, had by then grown accustomed to working within national political systems, and chose to support their governments in time of war. Not so Vladimir Lenin, a subject of the Russian Empire and the leader of the Bolsheviks. His voluntarist understanding of Marxism, the belief that history could be pushed onto the proper track, led him to see the war as his great chance. For a voluntarist such as Lenin, assenting to the verdict of history gave Marxists a license to issue it themselves. Marx did not see history as fixed in advance but as the work of individuals aware of its principles. Lenin hailed from largely peasant country, which lacked, from a Marxist perspective, the economic conditions for revolution. Once again, he had a revolutionary theory to justify his revolutionary impulse. He believed that colonial empires had granted the capitalist system an extended lease on life, but that a war among empires would bring a general revolution. The Russian Empire crumbled first, and Lenin made his move.

The suffering soldiers and impoverished peasants of the Russian Empire were in revolt in early 1917. After a popular uprising had brought down the Russian monarchy that February, a new liberal regime sought to win the war by one more military offensive against its enemies, the German Empire and the Habsburg monarchy. At this point Lenin became the secret weapon of Germany. The Germans dispatched Lenin from Swiss exile to the Russian capital Petrograd that April, to make a revolution that would take Russia from the war. With the help of his charismatic ally Leon Trotsky and his disciplined Bolsheviks, Lenin achieved a coup d'état with some popular support in November. In early 1918, Lenin's new government signed a peace treaty with Germany that left Belarus, Ukraine, the Baltics, and Poland under German control. Thanks in part to Lenin, Germany won the war on the eastern front, and had a brief taste of eastern empire.

Lenin's peace came at the price of German colonial rule of what had been the west of the Russian Empire. But surely, reasoned the Bolsheviks, the German Empire would soon collapse along with the rest of the oppressive capitalist system, and Russian and other revolutionaries could spread their new order westward, to these terrains and beyond. The war, Lenin and Trotsky argued, would bring inevitable German defeat on the western front and then a workers' revolution within Germany itself. Lenin and Trotsky justified their own Russian revolution to themselves and other Marxists by their expectation of imminent proletarian revolt in the more industrial lands of central and western Europe. In late 1918 and in 1919, it seemed as if Lenin just might be right. The Germans were indeed defeated by the French, British, and Americans on the western front in autumn 1918, and so had to withdraw—undefeated—from their new eastern empire. German revolutionaries began scattered attempts to take power. The Bolsheviks picked up the spoils in Ukraine and Belarus.

The collapse of the old Russian Empire and the defeat of the old German Empire created a power vacuum in eastern Europe, which the Bolsheviks, try as they might, could not fill. While Lenin and Trotsky deployed their new Red Army in civil wars in Russia and Ukraine, five lands around the Baltic Sea— Finland, Estonia, Latvia, Lithuania, and Poland—became independent republics. After these losses of territory, the Russia of the Bolsheviks was less westerly than the Russia of the tsars. Of these new independent states, Poland was more populous than the rest combined, and strategically by far the most

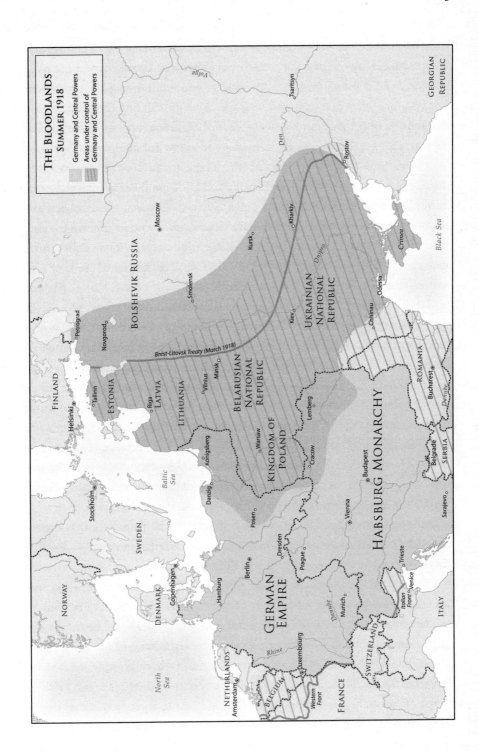

THE BLOODLANDS
SUMMER 1918

Germany and Central Powers

Areas under control of
Germany and Central Powers

Volga

GEORGIAN
REPUBLIC

Tsaritsyn○

Don

Rostov○

○Moscow

Kharkiv○

BOLSHEVIK RUSSIA

Kursk○

Black Sea

Crimea

Smolensk○

Dnipro

UKRAINIAN
NATIONAL
REPUBLIC

○Petrograd

Novgorod○

Kiev○

Odessa○

Brest-Litovsk Treaty (March 1918)

Chisinau○

Tallinn○

ESTONIA

Riga○

Vilnius○

Minsk○

BELARUSIAN
NATIONAL
REPUBLIC

ROMANIA

Bucharest⊛

Danube

FINLAND

LATVIA

LITHUANIA

Helsinki⊛

Lemberg○

Belgrade○

SERBIA

Königsberg○

Warsaw○

KINGDOM OF
POLAND

Cracow○

Budapest⊛

Sarajevo○

Stockholm○

*Baltic
Sea*

Danzig○

Posen○

Vienna⊛

HABSBURG MONARCHY

SWEDEN

Dresden○

Prague○

Trieste○

NORWAY

Copenhagen⊛

Hamburg○

Berlin⊛

GERMAN
EMPIRE

Munich○

*Italian
Front*

Venice○

Danube

ITALY

DENMARK

*North
Sea*

NETHERLANDS

Amsterdam⊛

Rhine

Luxembourg○

BELGIUM

Western
Front

SWITZERLAND

FRANCE

important. More than any of the other new states that came into being at war's
end, Poland changed the balance of power in eastern Europe. It was not large
enough to be a great power, but it was large enough to be a problem for any
great power with plans of expansion. It separated Russia from Germany, for the
first time in more than a century. Poland's very existence created a buffer to both
Russian and German power, and was much resented in Moscow and Berlin.

Poland's ideology was its independence. There had been no Polish state since
the late eighteenth century, when the Polish-Lithuanian Commonwealth had
been partitioned out of existence by its imperial neighbors. Polish politics had
continued under imperial rule throughout the nineteenth century, and the idea
of a Polish nation had, if anything, consolidated. The declaration of Polish independence in November 1918 was only possible because all three of the partition-
ing powers—the German, Habsburg, and Russian Empires—disappeared after
war and revolution. This great historical conjuncture was exploited by a Polish
revolutionary, Józef Piłsudski. A socialist in his youth, Piłsudski had become a
pragmatist capable of cooperating with one empire against the others. When all
of the empires collapsed, he and his followers, already organized into military le-
gions during the war, were in the best position to declare and defend a Polish
state. Piłsudski's great political rival, the nationalist Roman Dmowski, made
Poland's case to the victorious powers in Paris. The new Poland was founded as
a democratic republic. Endorsed by the victorious Entente Powers, Warsaw could
count on a more or less favorable boundary with Germany, to the west. But the
question of Poland's eastern border was open. Because the Entente had won no
war on the eastern front, it had no terms to impose in eastern Europe.

In 1919 and 1920, the Poles and the Bolsheviks fought a war for the borderlands between Poland and Russia that was decisive for the European order. The
Red Army had moved into Ukraine and Belarus as the Germans had withdrawn,
but these gains were not acknowledged by the Polish leadership. Piłsudski saw
these lands between as independent political subjects whose history was linked
to that of Poland, and whose leaders should wish to restore some version of the
old Commonwealth in Belarus and Lithuania. He hoped that Polish armies, supported by Ukrainian allies, could help create an independent Ukrainian state.
Once the Bolsheviks had brought Ukraine under control in 1919, and halted a
Polish offensive there in spring 1920, Lenin and Trotsky thought that they would
bring their own revolution to Poland, using the bayonet to inspire workers to
fulfill their historical role. After Poland's fall, German comrades, assisted by the

new Red Army, would bring to bear Germany's vast resources to save the Russian revolution. But the Soviet forces on their way to Berlin were halted by the Polish Army at Warsaw in August 1920.

Piłsudski led a counterattack that drove the Red Army back into Belarus and Ukraine. Stalin, a political officer with the Red Army in Ukraine, was among the defeated. His own misjudgments there prevented the proper coordination of Bolshevik forces, leaving the Red Army vulnerable to Piłsudski's maneuver. The Polish military victory did not mean the destruction of Bolshevik power: Polish troops were too exhausted to march on Moscow, and Polish society too divided to support such an adventure. In the end, territories inhabited by Belarusians and Ukrainians were divided between Bolshevik Russia and Poland. Poland was thus established as a multinational state, its population perhaps two-thirds Polish reckoned by language, but including some five million Ukrainians, three million Jews, one million Belarusians, and somewhere between half a million and a million Germans. Poland was constitutionally a state "for the Polish nation," but it held the largest population of Jews in Europe and the second-largest (after Bolshevik Russia) population of Ukrainians and Belarusians. It shared all three of its large national minorities—the Jews, the Ukrainians, and the Belarusians—with its eastern neighbor.

As east European borders were being decided on the battlefields of Ukraine, Belarus, and Poland, the victors in the First World War were dictating terms in central and western Europe. While Poland and the Bolsheviks were fighting on what had been the eastern front of the First World War, defeated Germany sought to present a pacific face to the victors. Germany declared itself a republic, the better to negotiate terms with the French, British, and Americans. Its major Marxist party, the Social Democrats, rejected the Bolshevik example and made no revolution in Germany. Most German social democrats had been loyal to the German Empire during the war, and now saw the declaration of a German republic as progress. But these moderating choices helped Germany little. The postwar settlements were dictated rather than discussed; in violation of long European tradition, the defeated were denied a place at the table at the Paris peace talks. The German government had no choice but to sign the Treaty of Versailles of June 1919, but few German politicians felt bound to defend its terms.

Because the treaty was drafted by moralizing victors, it could easily be attacked as hypocritical. While fighting a war against continental empires, the Entente Powers had declared themselves to be supporters of the liberation of the nations of central Europe. The Americans in particular characterized their participation in the war as a crusade for national self-determination. But the French, who had suffered more than any power, wanted the Germans punished and France's allies rewarded. The Treaty of Versailles indeed contradicted the very principle for which the Entente Powers had claimed to fight the war: national self-determination. At Versailles, as at Trianon (June 1920) and Sèvres (August 1920), the peoples considered allies by the Entente (Poles, Czechs, Romanians) got more territory and accordingly more numerous ethnic minorities within their frontiers. The nations considered enemies (Germans, Hungarians, Bulgarians) got less territory and accordingly larger diasporas of their own people within the borders of other states.

The Polish-Bolshevik War was fought in the period between the opening of discussions at Versailles and the signing of the treaty at Sèvres. Because Europe was still at war in the east while these treaties were being negotiated and signed in the west, the new postwar order was a bit ethereal. It seemed vulnerable to revolution from the left, inspired or even brought by the Bolsheviks. So long as the Polish-Bolshevik war was underway, revolutionaries in Germany could imagine that help was coming from the Red Army. The new German republic also seemed vulnerable to revolution from the right. German soldiers returning from the eastern front, where they had been victorious, saw no reason to accede to what they regarded as the humiliation of their homeland by the new republic and the Treaty of Versailles that it had signed. Many veterans joined right-wing militias, which fought against left-wing revolutionaries. The German social democratic government, in the belief that it had no alternative, used some of the right-wing militias to suppress communist attempts at revolution.

The Polish victory over the Red Army at Warsaw in August 1920 brought an end to hopes for a European socialist revolution. The treaty between Poland and Bolshevik Russia signed in Riga in March 1921 was the true completion of the postwar settlement. It established Poland's eastern border, ensured that divided Ukrainian and Belarusian lands would be a bone of contention for years to come, and made of Bolshevism a state ideology rather than an armed revolution. The Soviet Union, when established the following year, would be a state with borders—in that respect, at least, a political entity like others. The end of large-scale armed conflict was also the end of hopes on the Right that revolution could lead to counterrevolution. Those who wished to overturn the new German republic, whether from the Far Right or the Far Left, would have to count on their own forces. German social democrats would remain supporters of the republic, while German communists would praise the Soviet model and follow the Soviet line. They would take their instructions from the Communist International, established by Lenin in 1919. The German Far Right would have to reimagine the end of the postwar order as a goal of Germany alone, to be achieved after Germany itself was rebuilt and remade.

The rebuilding of Germany seemed more difficult than it really was. Germany, blamed for the war, lost not only territory and population but the right to normal armed forces. It suffered in the early 1920s from hyperinflation and political chaos. Even so, Germany remained, at least potentially, the most powerful country in Europe. Its population was second only to that of the Soviet Union, its industrial potential second to none, its territory unoccupied during the war, and its possibilities for expansion sketched implicitly in the logic of the peace settlements. Once the fighting in Europe had ceased, the German government quickly found common ground with the Soviet Union. After all, both Berlin and Moscow wanted to change the European order at the expense of Poland. Each wished to be less isolated in international politics. Thus it was a democratic German government that signed the Treaty of Rapallo with the Soviet Union in 1922, restoring diplomatic relations, easing trade, and inaugurating secret military cooperation.

For many Germans, self-determination was both persecution and promise. About ten million speakers of the German language, former subjects of the Habsburg monarchy, remained beyond Germany's borders. Some three million such people inhabited the northwestern rim of Czechoslovakia, right at the border of Czechoslovakia and Germany. There were more Germans in Czechoslovakia than there were Slovaks. Almost the entire population of Austria, resting between Czechoslovakia and Germany, were German speakers. Austria was nevertheless required by the Treaty of St. Germain to exist as a separate state, although much of its population would have preferred accession to Germany. Adolf Hitler, the leader of the National Socialist German Workers Party established in 1920, was an Austrian and an advocate of an Anschluss: a unification of Austria and Germany. Such goals of national unity, dramatic as they were, actually concealed the full measure of Hitler's ambitions.

Later, Hitler would be the German chancellor who signed the treaty with the Soviet Union that divided Poland. In taking this step, he would be taking to an extreme an idea that many Germans held: that Poland's borders were illegitimate and its people unworthy of statehood. Where Hitler stood apart from other German nationalists was in his view of what must come next, after the unification of Germans within Germany and the mastery of Poland: the elimination of the European Jews, and the destruction of the Soviet Union. Along the way Hitler would offer friendship to both Poland and the Soviet Union, and disguise his more radical intentions from Germans until it was too late. But the catastrophic visions were present in National Socialism from the beginning.

When the cataclysm of war finally ended in eastern Europe in 1921, Lenin and his revolutionaries had to regroup and think. Deprived by the Poles of their European triumph, the Bolsheviks had no choice but to douse the revolutionary conflagration and build some sort of socialist state. Lenin and his followers took for granted that they should hold power; indeed, the failure of the European revolution became their justification for extraordinary aspirations to political control. Power had to be centralized so that the revolution could be completed, and so that it could be defended from its capitalist enemies. They quickly banned other political parties and terrorized political rivals, dismissing them as reactionary. They lost the only competitive elections that they held, and so held no others. The Red Army, though defeated in Poland, was more than sufficient to defeat all armed rivals on the territory of the old empire. The Bolsheviks' secret service, known as the Cheka, killed thousands of people in the service of the consolidation of the new Soviet state.

It was easier to triumph in violence that it was to make a new order. Marxism was of only limited help as a program for a multicultural country of peasants and nomads. Marx had assumed that revolution would come first to the industrial world, and had devoted only sporadic attention to the peasant question and the national question. Now the peasants of Russia, Ukraine, and Belarus and the nomads of Central Asia would have to somehow be induced to build socialism for a working class that was concentrated in Russian-speaking cities. The Bolsheviks had to transform the preindustrial society that they had inherited in order to build the industrial society which history had not yet brought; only then could they alter that industrial society so that it favored workers.

The Bolsheviks had first to perform the constructive work of capitalism before they could really begin the transformative work of socialism. As the state created industry, they decided, it would draw members of the Soviet Union's countless cultures into a larger political loyalty that would transcend any national difference. The mastery of both peasants and nations was a grand ambition indeed, and the Bolsheviks concealed its major implication: that they were the enemies of their own peoples, whether defined by class or by nation. They believed that the society that they governed was historically defunct, a bookmark to be removed before a page was turned.

To consolidate their power when the war was over, and to gain loyal cadres for the economic revolution to come, the Bolsheviks had to make some compromises. Nations under their control would not be allowed independent statehood, of course, but nor were they condemned to oblivion. Though Marxists generally thought that the appeal of nationalism would decline with modernization, the Bolsheviks decided to recruit the nations, or at least their elites, to their own campaign to industrialize the Soviet Union. Lenin endorsed the national identity of the non-Russian peoples. The Soviet Union was an apparent federation of Russia with neighboring nations. Policies of preferential education and hiring were to gain the loyalty and trust of non-Russians. Themselves subjects of one and then rulers of another multinational state, the Bolsheviks were capable of subtle reasoning and tact on the national question. The leading revolutionaries themselves were far from being Russians in any simple way. Lenin, regarded and remembered as Russian, was also of Swedish, German, Jewish, and Kalmyk background; Trotsky was Jewish, and Stalin was Georgian.

The nations were to be created in a new communist image; the peasants were to be consoled until they could be overcome. The Bolsheviks made a compromise with their rural population that they knew, and the peasants feared, was only temporary. The new Soviet regime allowed peasants to keep land that they had seized from their former landlords, and to sell their produce on the market. The disruptions of war and revolution had brought desperate food shortages; the Bolsheviks had requisitioned grain to the benefit of themselves and of those loyal to them. Several million people died of hunger and related diseases in 1921 and 1922. The Bolsheviks learned from this experience that food was a weapon. Yet once the conflict was over, and the Bolsheviks had won, they needed reliable food supplies. They had promised their people peace and bread, and would have to deliver a minimum of both, at least for a time.

Lenin's state was a political holding action for an economic revolution still to come. His Soviet polity recognized nations, although Marxism promised a world without them; and his Soviet economy permitted a market, although communism promised collective ownership. When Lenin died in January 1924, debates

12

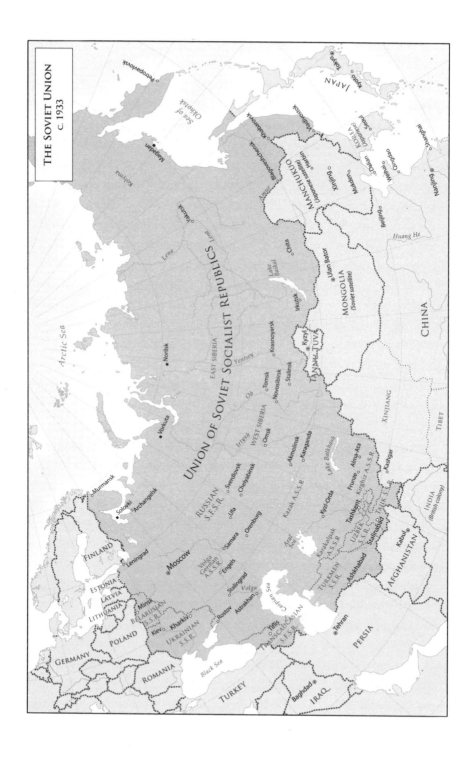

THE SOVIET UNION
C. 1933

were already underway about when and how these transitional compromises should yield to a second revolution. And it was precisely discussion, in the new Soviet order, that determined the fate of the Soviet population. From Lenin the Bolsheviks had inherited the principle of "democratic centralism," a translation of Marxist historiosophy into bureaucratic reality. Workers represented the forward flow of history; the disciplined communist party represented the workers; the central committee represented the party; the politburo, a group of a few men, represented the central committee. Society was subordinate to the state which was controlled by party which in practice was ruled by a few people. Disputes among members of this small group were taken to represent not politics but rather history, and their outcomes were presented as its verdict.

Stalin's interpretation of Lenin's legacy was to be decisive. When Stalin spoke of "socialism in one country" in 1924, he meant that the Soviet Union would have to build its worker's paradise without much help from the workers of the world, who had not united. Though communists disagreed about the priorities of agricultural policy, all took for granted that the Soviet countryside would soon have to finance its own destruction. But where to find the initial capital for the traumatic transition from an agrarian to an industrial economy? A way would have to be found to extract a "surplus" from the peasant, which could be sold for the foreign currency needed to import machinery—and used to fill the bellies of a growing working class. In 1927, as state investment shifted decisively in favor of industry, this discussion entered the critical phase.

The debate over modernization was, above all, a duel between Trotsky and Stalin. Trotsky was the most accomplished of Lenin's comrades; Stalin, however, had been placed in charge of the party bureaucracy as general secretary of the Communist Party of the Soviet Union (Bolsheviks). Stalin's control of personnel and his practical genius in committee meetings brought him to the top. He did not dazzle in theoretical discussions, but he knew how to assemble a coalition. Within the politburo, he allied first with those who favored a slower course of economic transformation and eliminated those who seemed more radical; then he radicalized his own position and purged his previous allies. By the end of 1927, his former rivals from the Left—Trotsky, Grigory Zinoviev, and Lev Kamenev—had been expelled from the party. By the end of 1929, Stalin had associated himself with the policies of those purged rivals, and rid himself of his main ally on the Right, Nikolai Bukharin. Like Zinoviev and Kamenev, Bukharin remained in the Soviet Union, stripped of his previous authority. Stalin found loyal supporters within the politburo, notably Lazar Kaganovich and Viacheslav Molotov. Trotsky left the country.

Dexterous though he was in defining Soviet policy, Stalin now had to ensure that it fulfilled its promise. By 1928, by the terms of his first Five-Year Plan, Stalin proposed to seize farmland, force the peasants to work it in shifts under state control, and treat the crops as state property—a policy of "collectivization." Land, equipment, and people would all belong to the same collective farm, large entities that would (it was assumed) produce more efficiently. Collective farms would be organized around Machine Tractor Stations, which would distribute modern equipment and house the political agitators. Collectivization would allow the state to control agricultural output, and thus feed its workers and keep their support, and to export to foreign countries and win some hard currency for investment in industry.

To make collectivization seem inevitable, Stalin had to weaken the free market and replace it with state planning. His ally Kaganovich proclaimed in July 1928 that peasants were engaging in a "grain strike," and that requisitioning their crops was the only solution. Once peasants saw that their produce could be taken, they hid it rather than selling it. Thus the market appeared even more unreliable—although the state was really to blame. Stalin could then argue, as he did, that market spontaneity was the fundamental problem, and that the state had to control food supplies.

The coming of the Great Depression seemed to prove Stalin right about the unreliability of the market. On Black Tuesday, 29 October 1929, the American stock market crashed. On 7 November 1929, the twelfth anniversary of the Bolshevik Revolution, Stalin described the socialist alternative to the market that his policies would quickly bring to the Soviet Union. He promised that 1930 would be "the year of the great transformation," when collectivization would bring security and prosperity. The old countryside would cease to exist. Then the revolution could be completed in the cities, where the proletariat would grow great on food produced by the pacified peasantry. These workers would create the first socialist society in history, and a powerful state that could defend itself from foreign enemies. As Stalin made his case for modernization, he was also staking his claim to power.

While Stalin worked, Hitler inspired. Whereas Stalin was institutionalizing a revolution and thereby assuring himself a place at the top of a one-party state, Hitler made his political career by rejecting the institutions around him. The

Bolsheviks inherited a tradition of debate-then-discipline from years of illegal work in the Russian Empire. The National Socialists (Nazis) had no meaningful traditions of discipline or conspiracy. Like the Bolsheviks, the Nazis rejected democracy, but in the name of a Leader who could best express the will of the race, not in the name of a Party that understood the dictates of history. The world order was not made by capitalist imperialists, as the Bolsheviks believed, but rather by conspiratorial Jews. The problem with the modern society was not that the accumulation of property led to the domination of a class; the problem was that Jews controlled *both* finance capitalism and communism, and thus America, Great Britain, and the Soviet Union. Communism was just a Jewish fairy tale of impossible equality, designed to bring naive Europeans under Jewish thrall. The answer to heartless Jewish capitalism and communism could only be national socialism, which meant justice for Germans at the expense of others.

Nazis tended to emphasize, in the democratic years of the 1920s, what they had in common with other Germans. Hitler's National Socialists were like most other German parties of the 1920s in their revulsion at the terms of the Treaty of Versailles. The Nazis had a certain obsession with their manifest destiny in the East: where German soldiers had been victorious in the field in the First World War, and where Germany had ruled a large occupation zone in Poland, Belarus, Ukraine, and the Baltic region in 1918. Unlike European rivals such as France and Great Britain, Germany had no vast world empire; it had surrendered its modest overseas possessions after losing the war. Thus the east European frontier beckoned all the more. The Soviet Union, seen as an illegitimate and oppressive Jewish regime, would have to fall. Poland, which lay between Germany and its eastern destiny, would have to be overcome along the way. It could not be a buffer to German power: it would have to be either a weak ally or a defeated foe in the coming wars for the east.

Hitler tried and failed to begin a German national revolution in Munich in November 1923, which led to a brief spell in prison. Though the substance of his National Socialism was his own creation, his coup d'état was inspired by the success of the Italian fascists he admired. Benito Mussolini had taken power in Italy the previous year after the "March on Rome," which Hitler imitated without success in Munich. Italian fascists, like Hitler and his Nazis, offered the glorification of the national will over the tedium of political compromise. Mussolini, and Hitler following him, used the existence of the Soviet Union within domestic politics. While admiring the discipline of Lenin and the model of the one-party state, both men used the threat of a communist revolution as an argument for their own rule. Though the two men differed in many respects, they both represented a new kind of European Right, one which took for granted that communism was the great enemy while imitating aspects of communist politics. Like Mussolini, Hitler was an outstanding orator and the one dominant personality in his movement. Hitler had little trouble regaining the leadership of the Nazi party after his release from prison in December 1924.

Stalin rose to power in the second half of the 1920s in large measure because of the cadres whom he appointed and could trust to support him. Hitler drew support by way of personal charisma, and expected his associates and supporters to devise policies and language that corresponded to his rhetoric and imagination. Stalin interpreted Marxist thought as necessary to hasten his rise and defend his policies, but at least until 1933 he was never free to interpret Marxism exactly as he liked. Hitler, on the other hand, inspired others to do his practical thinking for him. In prison Hitler had written the first volume of his biographical manifesto, *Mein Kampf* (*My Struggle*). This and his other writings (especially his so-called *Second Book*) expressed his plans clearly, but they were not part of a canon. Stalin was at first constrained by what his comrades might do, and later concerned by what they might say. Hitler never had to maintain even an appearance of dialogue or consistency.

Hitler made a certain compromise with the German republic after his release from prison. He practiced parliamentary politics as the leader of his National Socialist party, if only as a means of spreading propaganda, identifying enemies, and approaching the institutions of power. He tried to stay out of prison, even as Nazi paramilitaries engaged in brawls with left-wing enemies. In 1928, after the German economy had shown several consecutive years of growth, the Nazis took only twelve seats in parliament, with 2.6 percent of the votes cast. Then came the Great Depression, a greater boon to Hitler than even to Stalin. The collapse of the German economy summoned the specter of a communist revolution; both helped Hitler come to power. The international economic crisis seemed to justify radical change. The seeming possibility of a revolution led by the large Communist Party of Germany generated fears that Hitler could channel toward nationalism. In September 1930 the Nazis won 18 percent of the vote and 107 seats—and then won the elections of July 1932, with no less than 37 percent of the vote.

By 1932, German parliamentary elections were a demonstration of popular support rather than a direct route to power, since democracy in Germany existed only in form. For the previous two years, heads of government (chancellors) had induced the president to issue decrees that had the force of law. The parliament (Reichstag) convened only thirteen times in 1932. Hitler was appointed chancellor in January 1933 with the help of conservatives and nationalists who believed that they could use him to keep the large German Left from power. To their surprise, Hitler called snap elections, and used his new position to assert his party's hegemony over German society. When the results were announced on 5 March 1933, the Nazis had defeated the social democrats and the communists in dramatic fashion: with 43.9 percent of the vote, and 288 of 647 seats in the Reichstag.

Hitler was remaking the German political system in spring 1933—at the same time that Stalin was asserting his own personal authority in the Soviet Union.

In 1933, the Soviet and Nazi governments shared the appearance of a capacity to respond to the world economic collapse. Both radiated dynamism at a time when liberal democracy seemed unable to rescue people from poverty. Most governments in Europe, including the German government before 1933, had believed that they had few means at their disposal to address the economic collapse. The predominant view was that budgets should be balanced and money supplies tightened. This, as we know today, only made matters worse. The Great Depression seemed to discredit the political response to the end of the First World War: free markets, parliaments, nation-states. The market had brought disaster, no parliament had an answer, and nation-states seemingly lacked the instruments to protect their citizens from immiseration.

The Nazis and Soviets both had a powerful story about who was to blame for the Great Depression (Jewish capitalists or just capitalists) and authentically radical approaches to political economy. The Nazis and Soviets not only rejected the legal and political form of the postwar order but also questioned its economic and social basis. They reached back to the economic and social roots of postwar Europe, and reconsidered the lives and roles of the men and women who worked the land. In the Europe of the 1930s, peasants were still the majority in most countries, and arable soil was a precious natural resource, bringing energy for economies still powered by animals and humans. Calories were counted, but for rather different reasons than they are counted now: economic planners had to make sure that populations could be kept fed, alive, and productive.

Most of the states of Europe had no prospect of social transformation, and thus little ability to rival or counter the Nazis and the Soviets. Poland and other new east European states had tried land reform in the 1920s, but their efforts had proven insufficient. Landlords lobbied to keep their property, and banks and states were miserly with credit to peasants. The end of democracy across the region (except in Czechoslovakia) at first brought little new thinking on economic matters. Authoritarian regimes in Poland, Hungary, and Romania had less hesitation about jailing opponents and better recourse to fine phrases about the nation. But none seemed to have much to offer in the way of a new economic policy during the Great Depression.

In 1933, the Soviet and Nazi alternatives to democracy depended on their rejection of simple land reform, now the discredited pabulum of the failed democracies. Hitler and Stalin, for all of their many differences, presumed that one root of the problem was the agricultural sector, and that the solution was drastic state intervention. If the state could enact a radical economic transformation, that would then undergird a new kind of political system. The Stalinist approach, public since the beginning of Stalin's Five-Year Plan in 1928, was collectivization. Soviet leaders allowed peasants to prosper in the 1920s, but took the peasants' land away from them in the early 1930s, in order to create collective farms where peasants would work for the state.

Hitler's answer to the peasant question was just as imaginative, and just as well camouflaged. Before and even for a few years after he came to power in 1933, it appeared that Hitler was concerned above all with the German working class, and would address Germany's lack of self-sufficiency in foodstuffs by means of imports. A policy of rapid (and illegal) rearmament removed German men from the unemployment rolls by placing them in barracks or in arms factories. Public works programs began a few months after Hitler came to power. It even appeared that the Nazis would do *less* for German farmers than they had indicated. Though the Nazi party program promised the redistribution of land from richer to poorer farmers, this traditional version of land reform was quietly tabled after Hitler became chancellor. Hitler pursued international agreements rather than redistributive agrarian policy. He sought special trade arrangements with east European neighbors, by which German industrial goods were in effect exchanged for foodstuffs. Hitler's agricultural policy of the 1930s was a bit like Lenin's of the 1920s: it was political preparation for a vision of almost unimaginably radical economic change. Both National Socialism and Soviet socialism baited peasants with the illusion of land reform, but involved far more radical plans for their future.

The true Nazi agricultural policy was the creation of an eastern frontier empire. The German agricultural question would be resolved not within Germany but abroad: by taking fertile land from Polish and Soviet peasants—who would be starved, assimilated, deported, or enslaved. Rather than importing grain from the east, Germany would export its farmers to the east. They would colonize the lands of Poland and the western Soviet Union. Although Hitler spoke generally about the need for greater "living space," he never made quite clear to German farmers that he expected them to migrate in large numbers to the east—any more than the Bolsheviks had made clear to Soviet peasants that they expected them to concede their property to the state. During collectivization in the early 1930s, Stalin treated the campaign against his own peasants as a "war" for their grain; Hitler counted on victory in a future war to feed Germany. The Soviet program was made in the name of universal principles; the Nazi plan was for massive conquest in eastern Europe for the benefit of a master race.

Hitler and Stalin rose to power in Berlin and Moscow, but their visions of transformation concerned above all the lands between. Their utopias of control overlapped in Ukraine. Hitler remembered the ephemeral German eastern colony of 1918 as German access to the Ukrainian breadbasket. Stalin, who had served his revolution in Ukraine shortly thereafter, regarded the land in much the same way. Its farmland, and its peasants, were to be exploited in the making of a modern industrial state. Hitler looked upon collectivization as a disastrous failure, and presented it as proof of the failure of Soviet communism as such. But he had no doubt that Germans could make of Ukraine a land of milk and honey.

For both Hitler and Stalin, Ukraine was more than a source of food. It was the place that would enable them to break the rules of traditional economics, rescue their countries from poverty and isolation, and remake the continent in their own image. Their programs and their power all depended upon their control of Ukraine's fertile soil and its millions of agricultural laborers. In 1933,

Ukrainians would died in the millions, in the greatest artificial famine in the history of world. This was the beginning of the special history of Ukraine, but not the end. In 1941 Hitler would seize Ukraine from Stalin, and attempt to realize his own colonial vision beginning with the shooting of Jews and the starvation of Soviet prisoners of war. The Stalinists colonized their own country, and the Nazis colonized occupied Soviet Ukraine: and the inhabitants of Ukraine suffered and suffered. During the years that both Stalin and Hitler were in power, more people were killed in Ukraine than anywhere else in the bloodlands, or in Europe, or in the world.

CHAPTER 1

THE SOVIET FAMINES

Nineteen thirty-three was a hungry year in the Western world. The streets of American and European cities teemed with men and women who had lost their jobs, and grown accustomed to waiting in line for food. An enterprising young Welsh journalist, Gareth Jones, saw unemployed Germans in Berlin rally to the voice of Adolf Hitler. In New York he was struck by the helplessness of the American worker, three years into the Great Depression: "I saw hundreds and hundreds of poor fellows in single file, some of them in clothes which once were good, all waiting to be handed out two sandwiches, a doughnut, a cup of coffee and a cigarette." In Moscow, where Jones arrived that March, hunger in the capitalist countries was cause for celebration. The Depression seemed to herald a world socialist revolution. Stalin and his coterie boasted of the inevitable triumph of the system they had built in the Soviet Union.[1]

Yet 1933 was also a year of hunger in the Soviet cities, especially in Soviet Ukraine. In Ukraine's cities—Kharkiv, Kiev, Stalino, Dnipropetrovsk—hundreds of thousands of people waited each day for a simple loaf of bread. In Kharkiv, the republic's capital, Jones saw a new sort of misery. People appeared at two o'clock in the morning to queue in front of shops that did not open until seven. On an average day forty thousand people would wait for bread. Those in line were so desperate to keep their places that they would cling to the belts of those immediately in front of them. Some were so weak from hunger that they could not stand without the ballast of strangers. The waiting lasted all day, and sometimes for two. Pregnant women and maimed war veterans had lost their right to buy out of turn, and had to wait in line with the rest if they wanted to eat. Somewhere in line a woman would wail, and the moaning would echo up and down the line, so that the whole group of thousands sounded like a single animal with an elemental fear.[2]

People in the cities of Soviet Ukraine were afraid of losing their place in breadlines, and they were afraid of starving to death. They knew that the city offered their only hope of nourishment. Ukrainian cities had grown rapidly in the previous five years, absorbing peasants and making of them workers and clerks. Ukrainian peasant sons and daughters, along with the Jews, Poles, and Russians who had inhabited these cities for much longer, were dependent upon food they obtained in shops. Their families in the country had nothing. This was unusual. Normally in times of hunger city dwellers will make for the countryside. In Germany or the United States the farmers almost never went hungry, even during the Great Depression. Workers and professionals in cities were reduced to selling apples, or stealing them; but always somewhere, in the Altes Land or in Iowa, there was an orchard, a silo, a larder. The city folk of Ukraine had nowhere to go, no help to seek from the farms. Most had ration coupons that they would need to present in order to get any bread. Ink on paper gave them what chance to live that they had, and they knew it.[3]

The proof was all around. Starving peasants begged along the breadlines, asking for crumbs. In one town, a fifteen-year-old girl begged her way to the front of the line, only to be beaten to death by the shopkeeper. The city housewives making the queues had to watch as peasant women starved to death on the sidewalks. A girl walking to and from school each day saw the dying in the morning and the dead in the afternoon. One young communist called the peasant children he saw "living skeletons." A party member in industrial Stalino was distressed by the corpses of the starved that he found at his back door. Couples strolling in parks could not miss the signs forbidding the digging of graves. Doctors and nurses were forbidden from treating (or feeding) the starving who reached their hospitals. The city police seized famished urchins from city streets to get them out of sight. In Soviet Ukrainian cities policemen apprehended several hundred children a day; one day in early 1933, the Kharkiv police had a quota of two thousand to fill. About twenty thousand children awaited death in the barracks of Kharkiv at any given time. The children pleaded with the police to be allowed, at least, to starve in the open air: "Let me die in peace, I don't want to die in the death barracks."[4]

Hunger was far worse in the cities of Soviet Ukraine than in any city in the Western world. In 1933 in Soviet Ukraine, a few tens of thousands of city dwellers actually died of starvation. Yet the vast majority of the dead and dying in Soviet Ukraine were peasants, the very people whose labors had brought what bread there was to the cities. The Ukrainian cities lived, just, but the Ukrainian countryside was dying. City dwellers could not fail to notice the destitution of peasants who, contrary to all seeming logic, left the fields in search of food. The train station at Dnipropetrovsk was overrun with starving peasants, too weak even to beg. On a train, Gareth Jones met a peasant who had acquired some bread, only to have it confiscated by the police. "They took my bread away from me," he repeated over and over again, knowing that he would disappoint his starving family. At the Stalino station, a starving peasant killed himself by jumping in front of a train. That city, the center of industry in southeastern Ukraine, had been founded in imperial times by John Hughes, a Welsh industrialist for whom Gareth Jones's mother had worked. The city had once been named after Hughes; now it was named after Stalin. (Today it is known as Donetsk.)[5]

Stalin's Five-Year Plan, completed in 1932, had brought industrial development at the price of popular misery. The deaths of peasants by railways bore a frightful witness to these new contrasts. Throughout Soviet Ukraine, rail passengers became unwitting parties to dreadful accidents. Hungry peasants would make their way to the cities along railway lines, only to faint from weakness on the tracks. At Khartsyszk, peasants who had been chased away from the station hanged themselves on nearby trees. The Soviet writer Vasily Grossman, returning from a family visit to his hometown Berdychev, encountered a woman begging for bread at the window of his train compartment. The political emigré Arthur Koestler, who had come to the Soviet Union to help build socialism, had a similar experience. As he recalled much later, outside Kharkiv station peasant women held up "to the carriage windows horrible infants with enormous wobbling heads, sticklike limbs, and swollen, pointed bellies." He found that the children of Ukraine looked like "embryos out of alcohol bottles." It would be many years before these two men, now regarded as two of the moral witnesses of the twentieth century, wrote about what they had seen.[6]

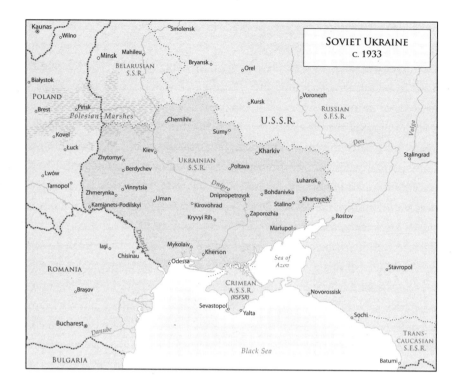

City dwellers were more accustomed to the sight of peasants at the market-place, spreading their bounty and selling their wares. In 1933, peasants made their way to familiar city markets, but now to beg rather than to sell. Market squares, now empty of both goods and customers, conveyed only the disharmonies of death. Early in the day the only sound was the soft breathing of the dying, huddled under rags that had once been clothes. One spring morning, amidst the piles of dead peasants at the Kharkiv market, an infant suckled the breast of its mother, whose face was a lifeless grey. Passersby had seen this before, not just the disarray of corpses, not just the dead mother and the living infant, but that precise scene, the tiny mouth, the last drops of milk, the cold nipple. The Ukrainians had a term for this. They said to themselves, quietly, as they passed: "These are the buds of the socialist spring."[7]

The mass starvation of 1933 was the result of Stalin's first Five-Year Plan, implemented between 1928 and 1932. In those years, Stalin had taken control of the heights of the communist party, forced through a policy of industrialization and collectivization, and emerged as the frightful father of a beaten population. He had transformed the market into the plan, farmers into slaves, and the wastes of Siberia and Kazakhstan into a chain of concentration camps. His policies had killed tens of thousands by execution, hundreds of thousands by exhaustion, and put millions at risk of starvation. He was still rightly concerned about opposition within the communist party, but was possessed of immense political gifts, assisted by willing satraps, and atop a bureaucracy that claimed to see and make the future. That future was communism: which required heavy industry, which in turn required collectivized agriculture, which in turn required control of the largest social group in the Soviet Union, the peasantry.[8]

The peasant, perhaps especially the Ukrainian peasant, was unlikely to see himself as a tool in this great mechanization of history. Even if he understood entirely the final purposes of Soviet policy, which was very unlikely, he could hardly endorse them. He was bound to resist a policy designed to relieve him of his land and his freedom. Collectivization had to mean a great confrontation between the largest group within Soviet society, the peasantry, and the Soviet state and its police, then known as the OGPU. Anticipating this struggle, Stalin had ordered in 1929 the most massive deployment of state power in Soviet history. The labor of building socialism, said Stalin, would be like "raising the ocean." That December he announced that "kulaks" would be "liquidated as a class."[9]

The Bolsheviks presented history as a struggle of classes, the poorer making revolutions against the richer to move history forward. Thus, officially, the plan to annihilate the kulaks was not a simple decision of a rising tyrant and his loyal retinue; it was a historical necessity, a gift from the hand of a stern but benevolent Clio. The naked attack of organs of state power upon a category of people who had committed no crime was furthered by vulgar propaganda. One poster—under the title "We will destroy the kulaks as a class!"—portrayed a kulak under the wheels of a tractor, a second kulak as an ape hoarding grain, and a third sucking milk directly from a cow's teat. These people were inhuman, they were beasts—so went the message.[10]

In practice, the state decided who was a kulak and who was not. The police were to deport prosperous farmers, who had the most to lose from collectivization. In January 1930 the politburo authorized the state police to screen the peasant population of the entire Soviet Union. The corresponding OGPU order of 2 February specified the measures needed for "the liquidation of the kulaks as a class." In each locality, a group of three people, or "troika," would decide the fate of the peasants. The troika, composed of a member of the state police, a local party leader, and a state procurator, had the authority to issue rapid and severe verdicts (death, exile) without the right to appeal. Local party members would often make recommendations: "At the plenums of the village soviet," one local party leader said, "we create kulaks as we see fit." Although the Soviet Union had laws and courts, these were now ignored in favor of the simple decision of three individuals. Some thirty thousand Soviet citizens would be executed after sentencing by troikas.[11]

In the first four months of 1930, 113,637 people were forcibly transported from Soviet Ukraine as kulaks. Such an action meant about thirty thousand peasant huts emptied one after another, their surprised inhabitants given little or no time to prepare for the unknown. It meant thousands of freezing freight cars, filled with terrified and sick human cargo, bound for destinations in northern European Russia, the Urals, Siberia, or Kazakhstan. It meant gunshots and cries of terror at the last dawn peasants would see at home; it meant frostbite and humiliation on the trains, and anguish and resignation as peasants disembarked as slave laborers on the taiga or the steppe.[12]

The Ukrainian peasantry knew about deportations to prison camps, which had touched them from the mid-1920s onward. They now sang a lament that was already traditional:

> Oh Solovki, Solovki!
> Such a long road
> The heart cannot beat
> Terror crushes the soul.

Solovki was a prison complex on an island in the Arctic Sea. In the minds of Ukrainian peasants Solovki stood for all that was alien, repressive, and painful in exile from the homeland. For the communist leadership of the Soviet Union, Solovki was the first place where the labor of deportees had been transformed into profit for the state. In 1929, Stalin had decided to apply the model of Solovki across the entire Soviet Union, ordering the construction of "special settlements" and concentration camps. The concentration camps were demarcated zones of labor, usually surrounded by fences and patrolled by guards. The special settlements were new villages purpose-built by the inmates themselves, after they were dropped on the empty steppe or taiga. All in all, some three hundred thousand Ukrainians were among the 1.7 million kulaks deported to special settlements in Siberia, European Russia, and Kazakhstan.[13]

Mass deportations of peasants for purposes of punishment coincided with the mass use of forced labor in the Soviet economy. In 1931, the special settlements and the concentration camps were merged into a single system, known as the Gulag. The Gulag, which the Soviets themselves called a "system of concentration camps," began alongside the collectivization of agriculture and depended upon it. It would eventually include 476 camp complexes, to which some eighteen million people would be sentenced, of whom between a million and a half and three million would die during their periods of incarceration. The free peasant became the slave laborer, engaged in the construction of the giant canals, mines, and factories that Stalin believed would modernize the Soviet Union.[14]

Among the labor camps, the Ukrainian peasant was most likely to be sent to dig the Belomor, a canal between the White Sea and the Baltic Sea that was a particular obsession of Stalin. Some 170,000 people dug through frozen soil, with picks and shovels and sometimes with shards of pottery or with their hands, for twenty-one months. They died by the thousand, from exhaustion or disease, finding their end at the bottom of a dry canal that, when completed in 1933, turned out to be of little practical use in water transport. The death rates at the special settlements were also high. Soviet authorities expected five percent of the prisoners in the special settlements to die; in fact, the figure reached ten to fifteen percent. An inhabitant of Archangelsk, the major city on the White Sea, complained of the senselessness of the endeavor: "it is one thing to destroy the kulak in an economic sense; to destroy their children in a physical sense is nothing short of barbaric." Children died in the far north in such numbers that "their corpses are taken to the cemetery in threes and fours without coffins." A group of workers in Vologda questioned whether "the journey to world revolution" had to pass "through the corpses of these children."[15]

The death rates in the Gulag were high, but they were no higher than those that would soon attend parts of the Ukrainian countryside. Workers at the Belomor were given very poor food rations, some six hundred grams of bread (about 1,300 calories) a day. Yet this was actually better nutrition than what was available in Soviet Ukraine at about the same time. Forced laborers at Belomor got twice or three times or six times as much as the peasants who remained in Soviet Ukraine would get on the collective farms in 1932 and 1933—when they got anything at all.[16]

In the first weeks of 1930, collectivization proceeded at a blinding pace in Soviet Ukraine and throughout the Soviet Union. Moscow sent quotas of districts to be collectivized to capitals of the Soviet republics, where party leaders vowed to exceed them. The Ukrainian leadership promised to collectivize the entire republic in one year. And then local party activists, with an eye to impressing their own superiors, moved even more quickly, promising collectivization in a matter of nine to twelve weeks. Threatening deportation, they coerced peasants into signing away their claims to land and joining the collective farm. The state police intervened with force, often deadly force, when necessary. Twenty-five thousand workers were shipped to the countryside to add numbers to police power and overmaster the peasantry. Instructed that the peasants were responsible for food shortages in the towns, workers promised to "make soap out of the kulak."[17]

By the middle of March 1930, seventy-one percent of the arable land in the Soviet Union had been, at least in principle, attached to collective farms. This meant that most peasants had signed away their farms and joined a collective. They no longer had any formal right to use land for their own purposes. As members of a collective, they were dependent upon its leaders for their employment, pay, and food. They had lost or were losing their livestock, and would depend for their equipment upon the machinery, usually lacking, of the new Machine Tractor Stations. These warehouses, the centers of political control in the countryside, were never short on party officials and state policemen.[18]

Perhaps even more so than in Soviet Russia, where communal farming was traditional, in Soviet Ukraine peasants were terrified by the loss of their land. Their whole history was one of a struggle with landlords, which they seemed finally to have won during the Bolshevik Revolution. But in the years immediately thereafter, between 1918 and 1921, the Bolsheviks had requisitioned food from the peasants as they fought their civil wars. So peasants had good reason to be wary of the Soviet state. Lenin's compromise policy of the 1920s had been very welcome, even if peasants suspected, with good reason, that it might one day be reversed. In 1930, collectivization seemed to them to be a "second serfdom," the beginning of a new bondage, now not to the wealthy landowners, as in recent history, but to the communist party. Peasants in Soviet Ukraine feared the loss of their hard-won independence; but they also feared starvation, and indeed for the fate of their immortal souls.[19]

The rural societies of Soviet Ukraine were still, for the most part, religious societies. Many of the young and the ambitious, those swayed by official communist atheism, had left for the big Ukrainian cities or for Moscow or Leningrad. Though their Orthodox Church had been suppressed by the atheist communist regime, the peasants were still Christian believers, and many understood the contract with the collective farm as a pact with the devil. Some believed that Satan had come to earth in human form as a party activist, his collective farm register a book of hell, promising torment and damnation. The new Machine Tractor Stations looked like the outposts of Gehenna. Some Polish peasants in Ukraine, Roman Catholics, also saw collectivization in apocalyptic terms. One Pole explained to his son why they would not join the collective farm: "I do not want to sell my soul to the devil." Understanding this religiosity, party activists propagated what they called Stalin's First Commandment: the collective farm supplies first the state, and only then the people. As the peasants would have known, the First Commandment in its biblical form reads: "Thou shalt have no other God before me."[20]

Ukrainian villages had been deprived of their natural leaders by the deportations of kulaks to the Gulag. Even without the deported kulaks, peasants tried to rescue themselves and their communities. They tried to preserve their own little plots, their small patches of autonomy. They endeavored to keep their families away from the state, now physically manifest in the collective farms and the Machine Tractor Stations. They sold or slaughtered their livestock, rather than lose it to the collective. Fathers and husbands sent daughters and wives to do battle with the party activists and the police, believing that women were less likely to be deported than men. Sometimes men dressed as women just for the chance to put a hoe or a shovel into the body of a local communist.[21]

Crucially, though, the peasants had few guns, and poor organization. The state had a near monopoly on firepower and logistics. Peasants' actions were recorded by a powerful state police apparatus, one that perhaps did not understand their motives but grasped their general direction. The OGPU noted almost one million acts of individual resistance in Ukraine in 1930. Of the mass peasant revolts in the Soviet Union that March, almost half took place in Soviet Ukraine. Some Ukrainian peasants voted with their feet, walking westward,

across the frontier into neighboring Poland. Whole villages followed their example, taking up church banners, or crosses, or sometimes just black flags tied
to sticks, and marching westward toward the border. Thousands of them
reached Poland, where knowledge of famine conditions in the Soviet Union
spread.[22]

The flight of peasants to Poland was an international embarrassment and
perhaps a source of real concern for Stalin and the politburo. It meant that Polish
authorities, who at the time were trying to stage a political rapprochement with
their own large Ukrainian national minority, learned about the course and consequences of collectivization. Polish border guards patiently interviewed the
refugees, gaining knowledge of the course and the failure of collectivization.
Some of the peasants begged for a Polish invasion to halt their misery. The
refugee crisis also provided Poland with a major propaganda weapon to use
against the Soviet Union. Under Józef Piłsudski, Poland never planned an aggressive war against the Soviet Union, but it did prepare contingency plans for
the disintegration of the Soviet Union along national lines, and did take some
steps designed to hasten such a course of events. Even as Ukrainians were fleeing
Soviet Ukraine, Poland was dispatching its own spies in the opposite direction,
to encourage the Ukrainians to revolt. Their propaganda posters called Stalin a
"Hunger Tsar" who exported grain while starving his own people. In March
1930, politburo members feared that "the Polish government might intervene."[23]

Collectivization was a general policy, the Soviet Union was a vast state, and insta-
bility in one borderland had to be considered in light of general scenarios for war.

Stalin and the Soviet leaders regarded Poland as the western part of an international capitalist encirclement, and Japan as the eastern. Polish-Japanese relations were rather good; and in spring 1930, Stalin seemed most troubled by the
specter of a joint Polish-Japanese invasion. The Soviet Union, by far the largest
country in the world, extended from Europe to the Pacific Ocean, and Stalin
had to attend not only to European powers but also to the Asian ambitions of
Japan.

Tokyo had made its military reputation at the expense of Russians. Japan had
emerged as a world power by defeating the Russian Empire in the Russo-Japanese
War of 1904–1905, seizing the railways built by the Russians to reach Pacific ports.
As Stalin well knew, both Poland and Japan took an interest in Soviet Ukraine,
and in the national question in the Soviet Union. Stalin seemed to feel the history

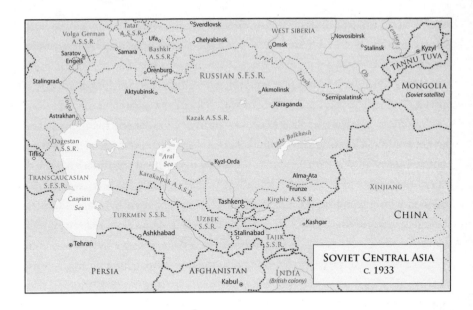

Tatar A.S.S.R. — °Sverdlovsk — WEST SIBERIA — °Novosibirsk — Yenisey — TANNU TUVA

Volga German A.S.S.R. — Ufa° — °Chelyabinsk — °Omsk — °Stalinsk — ⊙Kyzyl

Saratov° Engels — °Samara — Bashkir A.S.S.R. — Irtysh — MONGOLIA (*Soviet satellite*)

Stalingrad° — °Orenburg — RUSSIAN S.F.S.R. — °Akmolinsk — Ob

Astrakhan° — Aktyubinsk° — °Semipalatinsk — °Karaganda

Dagestan A.S.S.R. — Kazak A.S.S.R. — Lake Balkhash

Tiflis° — °Aral Sea — °Kyzl-Orda

TRANSCAUCASIAN S.F.S.R. — Karakalpak A.S.S.R. — Alma-Ata — XINJIANG

Caspian Sea — °Frunze

TURKMEN S.S.R. — Tashkent° — Kirghiz A.S.S.R. — CHINA

UZBEK S.S.R. — °Kashgar

⊙Tehran — Ashkhabad° — Stalinabad° — TAJIK S.S.R.

PERSIA — AFGHANISTAN — INDIA (*British colony*)

Kabul ⊙

SOVIET CENTRAL ASIA
c. 1933

of Russian humiliation in Asia quite deeply. He was fond of the song "On the Hills of Manchuria," which promised bloody vengeance upon the Japanese.[24]

So just as chaos brought by collectivization in the western Soviet Union gave rise to fears of a Polish intervention, disorder in the eastern Soviet Union seemed to favor Japan. In Soviet Central Asia, especially in largely Muslim Soviet Kazakhstan, collectivization brought even greater chaos than in Soviet Ukraine. It required an even more drastic social transformation. The peoples of Kazakhstan were not peasants but nomads, and the first step in Soviet modernization was to make them settle down. Before collectivization could even begin, the nomadic populations had to become farmers. The policy of "sedentarization" deprived the herdsmen of their animals and thus of their means of supporting themselves. People rode their camels or horses across the border into the Muslim Xinjiang (or Turkestan) region of China, which suggested to Stalin that they might be agents of the Japanese, the dominant foreign power amidst Chinese internal conflicts.[25]

All was not going as planned. Collectivization, which was supposed to secure the Soviet order, seemed instead to destabilize the borderlands. In Soviet Asia as in Soviet Europe, a Five-Year Plan that was supposed to bring socialism had brought instead enormous suffering, and a state that was supposed to represent justice responded with very traditional security measures. Soviet Poles were deported from western border zones, and the border guard was strengthened everywhere. The world revolution would have to take place behind closed borders, and Stalin would have to take steps to protect what he called "socialism in one country."[26]

Stalin had to delay foreign adversaries and rethink domestic plans. He asked Soviet diplomats to initiate discussions with Poland and Japan on nonaggression pacts. He saw to it that the Red Army was ordered to full battle readiness in the western Soviet Union. Most tellingly, Stalin suspended collectivization. In an article dated 2 March 1930 under the brilliant title "Dizzy with Success," Stalin maintained that the problem with collectivization was that it had been implemented with just a little too much enthusiasm. It had been a mistake, he now asserted, to force the peasants to join the collective farms. The latter now disappeared just as quickly as they had been created. In spring 1930, peasants in Ukraine harvested the winter wheat, and sowed the seeds for the autumn crops, just as if the land belonged to them. They could be forgiven for thinking that they had won.[27]

Stalin's withdrawal was tactical.

Given time to think, Stalin and the politburo found more effective means to subordinate the peasantry to the state. In the countryside the following year, Soviet policy preceded with much greater deftness. In 1931, collectivization would come because peasants would no longer see a choice. The lower cadres of the Ukrainian branch of the Soviet communist party were purged, to ensure that those working within the villages would be true to their purpose, and understand what would await them if they were not. The independent farmer was taxed until the collective farm became the only refuge. As the collective farms slowly regrouped, they were granted indirect coercive power over neighboring independent farmers. They were allowed, for example, to vote to take the seed grain away from independent farmers. The seed grain, what is kept from one crop to plant the next, is indispensible to any working farm. The selection and preservation of the seed grain is the basis of agriculture. For most of human history, eating the seed grain has been synonymous with utter desperation. An individual who lost control of the seed grain to the collective lost the ability to live from his or her own labor.[28]

Deportations resumed, and collectivization proceeded. In late 1930 and early 1931, some 32,127 more households were deported from Soviet Ukraine, about the same number of people as had been removed during the first wave of deportations a year before. Peasants thought that they would die either of exhaustion in the Gulag or of hunger close to home, and preferred the latter. Letters from exiled friends and family occasionally escaped the censor; one included the following advice: "No matter what, don't come. We are dying here. Better to hide, better to die there, but no matter what, don't come here." Ukrainian peasants who yielded to collectivization chose, as one party activist understood, "to face starvation at home rather than banishment to the unknown." Because collectivization came more slowly in 1931, family by family rather than whole villages at once, it was harder to resist. There was no sudden attack to provoke a desperate defense. By the end of the year, the new approach had succeeded. About seventy percent of the farmland in Soviet Ukraine was now collectivized. The levels of March 1930 had been reached again, and this time durably.[29]

After the false start of 1930, Stalin had won the political victory in 1931. Yet the triumph in politics did not extend to economics. Something was wrong with the grain yields. The harvest of 1930 had been wonderfully bountiful. Farmers deported in early 1930 had sown their winter wheat already, and that crop could be harvested by someone else that spring. The months of January and February, when most of the country had been collectivized on paper in 1930, is a time when farmers are idle in any case. After March 1930, when the collectives were dissolved, peasants had the time to put down their spring crops as free men and women. The weather was unusually fine that summer. The crop of 1930 in Ukraine set a standard that could not be met in 1931, even if collectivized agriculture were as efficient as individual farming, which it was not. The bumper crop of 1930 provided the baseline number that the party used to plan requisitions for 1931. Moscow expected far more from Ukraine than Ukraine could possibly give.[30]

By autumn 1931 the failure of the first collectivized harvest was obvious. The reasons were many: the weather was poor; pests were a problem; animal power was limited because peasants had sold or slaughtered livestock; the production of tractors was far less than anticipated; the best farmers had been deported; sowing and reaping were disrupted by collectivization; and peasants who had lost their land saw no reason to work very hard. The Ukrainian party leader, Stanisław Kosior, had reported in August 1931 that requisition plans were unrealistic given low yields. Lazar Kaganovich told him that the real problem was theft and concealment. Kosior, though he knew better, enforced this line on his subordinates.[31]

More than half of the (nonspoiled) harvest was removed from Soviet Ukraine in 1931. Many collective farms met their requisition targets only by handing over their seed grain. Stalin ordered on 5 December that collective farms that had not yet fulfilled their annual requirements must surrender their seed grain. Stalin perhaps believed that peasants were hiding food, and thought that the threat of taking the seed grain would motivate them to hand over what they had. But by this time many of them truly had nothing. By the end of 1931, many peasants were already going hungry. With no land of their own and with little ability to resist requisitions, they simply had no way to ensure that a sufficient number of calories reached their households. Then in early 1932 they had no seed grain with which to plant the fall crop. The Ukrainian party leadership asked for seed grain in March 1932, but by that time the planting was already delayed, meaning that the harvest that fall would be poor.[32]

In early 1932 people asked for help. Ukrainian communists requested that their superiors in the Ukrainian party ask Stalin to call in the Red Cross. Members of collective farms tried writing letters to state and party authorities. One of these, after several paragraphs of formal administrative prose, closed with the plaintive "Give us bread! Give us bread! Give us bread!" Ukrainian party members bypassed Kosior and wrote directly to Stalin, taking an angry tone: "How can we construct the socialist economy when we are all doomed to death by hunger?"[33]

The threat of mass starvation was utterly clear to Soviet Ukrainian authorities, and it became so to Stalin. Party activists and secret police officers filed countless reports of death by starvation. In June 1932 the head of the party in the Kharkiv region wrote to Kosior that starvation had been reported in every single district of his region. Kosior received a letter from a member of the Young Communists dated 18 June 1932, with a graphic description that was probably, by then, all too familiar: "Collective farm members go into the fields and disappear. After a few days their corpses are found and, entirely without emotion, as though this were normal, buried in graves. The next day one can already find the body of someone who had just been digging graves for others." That same day, 18 June 1932, Stalin himself admitted, privately, that there was "famine" in Soviet Ukraine. The previous day the Ukrainian party leadership had requested food aid. He did not grant it. His response was that all grain in Soviet Ukraine must be collected as planned. He and Kaganovich agreed that "it is imperative to export without fail immediately."[34]

Stalin knew perfectly well, and from personal observation, what would follow. He knew that famine under Soviet rule was possible. Famine had raged throughout Russia and Ukraine during and after the civil wars. A combination of poor harvests and requisitions had brought starvation to hundreds of thousands of peasants in Ukraine, especially in 1921. Scarcity of food was one of the reasons Lenin had made his compromise with peasants in the first place. Stalin was well aware of that history, in which he had taken part. That Stalin's own policy of collectivization could cause mass starvation was also clear. By summer 1932, as Stalin knew, more than a million people had already starved to death in Soviet Kazakhstan. Stalin blamed the local party leader Filip Goloshchekin, but he must have understood some of the structural issues.[35]

Stalin, a master of personal politics, presented the Ukrainian famine in personal terms. His first impulse, and his lasting tendency, was to see the starvation of Ukrainian peasants as a betrayal by members of the Ukrainian communist party. He could not allow the possibility that his own policy of collectivization was to blame; the problem must be in the implementation, in the local leaders, anywhere but in the concept itself. As he pushed forward with his transformation in the first half of 1932, the problem he saw was not the suffering of his people but rather the possibility that the image of his collectivization policy might be tarnished. Starving Ukrainian peasants, he complained, were leaving their home republic and demoralizing other Soviet citizens by their "whining."[36]

Somewhat inchoately, Stalin seemed to think in spring and summer 1932 that if starvation could somehow just be denied then it would go away. Perhaps he reasoned that Ukraine was in any case overpopulated, and that the deaths of a few hundred thousand people would matter little in the long run. He wanted local Ukrainian officials to meet grain procurement targets despite the certain prospect of lower yields. Local party officials found themselves between Stalin's red hammer and the grim reaper's sickle. The problems they saw were objective and not soluble through ideology or rhetoric: lack of seed grain, late sowing, poor weather, machinery insufficient to replace animal labor, chaos from the final push toward collectivization in late 1931, and hungry peasants unable to work.[37]

The world as local party activists had to see it, in the Ukrainian countryside, was described far better by this Ukrainian children's song than by the terse orders and propaganda conceits coming from Moscow:

> Father Stalin, look at this
> Collective farming is just bliss
> The hut's in ruins, the barn's all sagged
> All the horses broken nags
> And on the hut a hammer and sickle
> And in the hut death and famine
> No cows left, no pigs at all
> Just your picture on the wall
> Daddy and mommy are in the kolkhoz
> The poor child cries as alone he goes
> There's no bread and there's no fat
> The party's ended all of that
> Seek not the gentle nor the mild
> A father's eaten his own child
> The party man he beats and stamps
> And sends us to Siberian camps[38]

Around the local party activists was death, and above them was denial. Starvation was a brute fact, indifferent to words and formulas, deportations and shootings. Beyond a certain point, the starving peasant could no longer productively work, and no amount of ideological correctness or personal commitment could change this. Yet as this message traveled upward through institutional channels it lost its force. True reports of hunger from below met political pressure from the top at a Ukrainian party central committee plenum of 6–9 July 1932 in Kharkiv. Ukrainian speakers complained of the impossibility of meeting the annual targets for grain requisitions. Yet they were silenced by Lazar Kaganovich and Viacheslav Molotov, politburo members and Stalin's emissaries from Moscow. Stalin had instructed them to defeat the "Ukrainian destabilizers."[39]

Molotov and Kaganovich were Stalin's loyal and trusted allies, and with him dominated the politburo and thus ruled the Soviet Union. Stalin was not yet an unrivalled dictator, and the politburo was still in principle a kind of collective dictatorship. Yet these two men, unlike some of his previous allies in the politburo, were unconditionally loyal. Stalin manipulated them ceaselessly, but he did not really have to. They served the revolution by serving him, and tended not to distinguish between the two. Kaganovich was already calling Stalin "our father." In July 1932 in Kharkiv, they told Ukrainian comrades that talk of starvation was just an excuse for laziness on the part of peasants who did not wish to work and activists who did not wish to discipline them and requisition grain.[40]

By this time, Stalin was on vacation, having traveled in a train well stocked with fine provisions south from Moscow through the starving Ukraine to the pretty resort town of Sochi on the Black Sea. He and Kaganovich wrote to each other, confirming their shared view of the famine as a plot directed against them personally. Stalin managed a nice reversal, imagining that it was the peasants, not him, who were using hunger as a weapon. Kaganovich reassured Stalin that talk of Ukrainians as "innocent victims" was just a "rotten cover-up" for the Ukrainian party. Stalin expressed his fear that "we could lose Ukraine." Ukraine would have to be made into a "fortress." The two of them agreed that the only reasonable approach was to hold tight to a policy of requisitions, and to export the grain as quickly as possible. By now Stalin seemed to have worked out, at least to his own satisfaction, the connection between starvation and the disloyalty of Ukrainian communists: hunger was a result of sabotage, local party activists were the saboteurs, treacherous higher party officials protected their subordinates—all in the service of Polish espionage.[41]

Perhaps as late as 1931, Stalin might indeed have interpreted Polish and Japanese policies as heralding an encirclement of the Soviet Union. The year 1930 was a peak time for Polish espionage in the Soviet Union. Poland had secretly founded a Ukrainian army on its own soil, and was training dozens of Ukrainians and Poles for special missions inside the Soviet Union. Japan was indeed ever more threatening. In 1931, the Soviets had intercepted a note from the Japanese ambassador in Moscow, in which he advocated preparations for an offensive war to conquer Siberia. That year Japan had invaded Manchuria, a northeastern Chinese region with a long border with Soviet Siberia.[42]

In fall 1931, according to a Soviet intelligence report, Poland and Japan had signed a secret agreement concerning a joint attack on the Soviet Union. This was not the case; and insofar as there had been an incipient Polish-Japanese alliance, it was prevented by an adept Soviet foreign policy. Though Japan had declined to negotiate a nonaggression pact with Moscow, Poland had agreed. The Soviet Union wanted a treaty with Poland so that its economic transformation could be pursued in peace; Poland never had any intentions of starting a war, and was now experiencing economic depression. Its largely unreformed agrarian economic system could not support increasing military spending at a time of economic collapse. Soviet military budgets, comparable to Poland's for many years, were now far greater. The Soviet-Polish agreement was initialed in January 1932.[43]

In 1932 and 1933, there could be no serious thought of Poland as a threat by itself. The Polish army had suffered massive budget cuts. The Soviet police and border guards had captured a large number of Polish spies. Polish agents had not hindered collectivization during the chaos of 1930, and were helpless to rouse a starving population in 1932. They tried, and they failed. Even the most enthusiastic Polish proponents of an aggressive policy saw summer 1932 as a time for calm. If the Soviets promised peace, it seemed best to make no provocative moves. Polish diplomats and spies were witnesses to the famine. They knew that "cannibalism has become a habit of sorts" and that "entire villages have died out completely." But they had nothing to do with the famine's origins, and could do nothing to help the victims. Poland did not publicize to the world what its diplomats knew about the famine. In February 1932, for example, an anonymous letter reached the Polish consulate in Kharkiv, pleading with the Poles to inform the world of the famine in Ukraine. But by then the nonaggression pact with the Soviet Union had been initialed, and Warsaw would take no such step.[44]

Stalin now had won far more room for maneuver in his western borderlands than he had had in 1930. Poland had accepted the status quo by signing the nonaggression pact in July 1932, and so the Ukrainian peasants were at his mercy. With pedantic enthusiasm, Stalin in August (still on vacation) offered his closest collaborators the theory that collectivization was missing only the correct legal basis. Socialism, he claimed, just like capitalism, needed laws to protect property. The state would be strengthened if all agricultural production was declared to be state property, any unauthorized collection of food deemed theft, and such theft made punishable by immediate execution. Thus a starving peasant could be shot if he picked up a potato peel from a furrow in land that until recently had been his own. Perhaps Stalin really did think that this could work; the result, of course, was the removal of any legal protection that peasants may have had from the full violence of the triumphant state. The simple possession of food was presumptive evidence of a crime. The law came into force on 7 August 1932.[45]

Soviet judges usually ignored the letter of the law, but the rest of the party and state apparatus understood its spirit. Often the most enthusiastic enforcers of the law were younger people, educated in the new Soviet schools, who believed in the promise of the new system. Members of the official youth organization were told that their "main task" was "the struggle against theft and the hiding of grain as well as kulak sabotage." For the young generation in the cities, communism had offered social advance, and the world demonized in this agitation was one that they had left behind. The communist party in Soviet Ukraine, though disproportionately Russian and Jewish in its membership, now included many young Ukrainians who believed that the countryside was reactionary and were eager to join in campaigns against peasants.[46]

Watchtowers went up in the fields to keep peasants from taking anything for themselves. In the Odessa region alone, more than seven hundred watchtowers were constructed. Brigades went from hut to hut, five thousand youth organization members among their members, seizing everything they could find. Activists used, as one peasant recalled, "long metal rods to search through stables, pigsties, stoves. They looked everywhere and took everything, down to the last little grain." They rushed through the village "like the black death" calling out "Peasant, where is your grain? Confess!" The brigades took everything that resembled food, including supper from the stove, which they ate themselves.[47]

Like an invading army the party activists lived off the land, taking what they could and eating their fill, with little to show for their work and enthusiasm but misery and death. Perhaps from feelings of guilt, perhaps from feelings of triumph, they humiliated the peasants wherever they went. They would urinate in barrels of pickles, or order hungry peasants to box each other for sport, or make them crawl and bark like dogs, or force them to kneel in the mud and pray. Women caught stealing on one collective farm were stripped, beaten, and carried naked through the village. In one village the brigade got drunk in a peasant's hut and gang-raped his daughter. Women who lived alone were routinely raped at night under the pretext of grain confiscations—and their food was indeed taken from them after their bodies had been violated. This was the triumph of Stalin's law and Stalin's state.[48]

Raids and decrees could not create food where there was none. Of course peasants will hide food, and hungry people will steal food. But the problem in the Ukrainian countryside was not theft and deceit, which might indeed have been solved by the application of violence. The problem was starvation and death. Grain targets were not met because collectivization had failed, the harvest of autumn 1932 was poor, and requisition targets were too high. Stalin sent Molotov to Ukraine to urge comrades forward in the "struggle for grain." But the enthusiasm of Stalin's servants could not change what had already happened. Even Molotov was forced to recommend on 30 October that quotas for Ukraine be reduced somewhat. Stalin accepted the recommendation, but soon he was more categorical than ever. As of November 1932 only about one third of the annual target had been met.[49]

As reports about failed requisitions were delivered to the Kremlin, Stalin's wife killed herself. She chose 7 November 1932, the fifteenth anniversary of the October Revolution, to shoot herself in the heart. Just what this meant to Stalin can never be entirely clear, but it seems to have been a shock. He threatened to kill himself as well. Kaganovich, who found Stalin a changed man, had to give the funeral oration.[50]

The next day Stalin approached the problem of the famine with a new degree of malice. He placed the blame for problems in Ukraine at the feet of Ukrainian comrades and peasants. Two politburo telegrams sent out on 8 November 1932 reflected the mood: individual and collective farmers in Soviet Ukraine who failed to meet requisition targets were to be denied access to products from the rest of the economy. A special troika was created in Ukraine to hasten the sentencing and execution of party activists and peasants who, supposedly, were responsible for sabotage. Some 1,623 kolkhoz officials were arrested that month. Deportations within Ukraine were resumed: 30,400 more people were gone by the end of the year. The activists told the peasants: "Open up, or we'll knock down the door. We'll take what you have, and you'll die in a camp."[51]

As Stalin interpreted the disaster of collectivization in the last weeks of 1932, he achieved new heights of ideological daring. The famine in Ukraine, whose existence he had admitted earlier, when it was far less severe, was now a "fairy tale," a slanderous rumor spread by enemies. Stalin had developed an interesting new theory: that resistance to socialism increases as its successes mount, because its foes resist with greater desperation as they contemplate their final defeat. Thus any problem in the Soviet Union could be defined as an example of enemy action, and enemy action could be defined as evidence of progress.[52]

Resistance to his policies in Soviet Ukraine, Stalin argued, was of a special sort, perhaps not visible to the imperceptive observer. Opposition was no longer open, for the enemies of socialism were now "quiet" and even "holy." The "kulaks of today," he said, were "gentle people, kind, almost saintly." People who appeared to be innocent were to be seen as guilty. A peasant slowly dying of hunger was, despite appearances, a saboteur working for the capitalist powers in their campaign to discredit the Soviet Union. Starvation was resistance, and resistance was a sign that the victory of socialism was just around the corner. These were not merely Stalin's musings in Moscow; this was the ideological line enforced by Molotov and Kaganovich as they traveled through regions of mass death in late 1932.[53]

Stalin never personally witnessed the starvations that he so interpreted, but comrades in Soviet Ukraine did: they had somehow to reconcile his ideological line to the evidence of their senses. Forced to interpret distended bellies as political opposition, they produced the utterly tortured conclusion that the saboteurs hated socialism so much that they intentionally let their families die. Thus the wracked bodies of sons and daughters and fathers and mothers were nothing more than a facade behind which foes plotted the destruction of socialism. Even the starving themselves were sometimes presented as enemy propagandists with a conscious plan to undermine socialism. Young Ukrainian communists in the cities were taught that the starving were enemies of the people "who risked their lives to spoil our optimism."[54]

Ukrainians in Poland gathered money for food donations, only to learn that the Soviet government categorically rejected any assistance. Ukrainian communists who asked for food relief from abroad, accepted by Soviet authorities in the early 1920s during the previous famine, got no hearing at all. For political reasons, Stalin did not wish to accept any help from the outside world. Perhaps he believed that if he were to remain atop the party, he could not admit that his first major policy had brought famine. Yet Stalin might have saved millions of

lives without drawing any outside attention to the Soviet Union. He could have
suspended food exports for a few months, released grain reserves (three million
tons), or just given peasants access to local grain storage areas. Such simple measures, pursued as late as November 1932, could have kept the death toll to the
hundreds of thousands rather than the millions. Stalin pursued none of them.[55]

In the waning weeks of 1932, facing no external security threat and no challenge
from within, with no conceivable justification except to prove the inevitability
of his rule, Stalin chose to kill millions of people in Soviet Ukraine. He shifted
to a position of pure malice, where the Ukrainian peasant was somehow the aggressor and he, Stalin, the victim. Hunger was a form of aggression, for
Kaganovich in a class struggle, for Stalin in a Ukrainian national struggle,
against which starvation was the only defense. Stalin seemed determined to display his dominance over the Ukrainian peasantry, and seemed even to enjoy the
depths of suffering that such a posture would require. Amartya Sen has argued
that starvation is "a function of entitlements and not of food availability as such."
It was not food shortages but food distribution that killed millions in Soviet
Ukraine, and it was Stalin who decided who was entitled to what.[56]

Though collectivization was a disaster everywhere in the Soviet Union, the
evidence of clearly premeditated mass murder on the scale of millions is most
evident in Soviet Ukraine. Collectivization had involved the massive use of executions and deportations everywhere in the Soviet Union, and the peasants
and nomads who made up the bulk of the Gulag's labor force hailed from all of
the Soviet republics. Famine had struck parts of Soviet Russia as well as much
of Soviet Ukraine in 1932. Nevertheless, the policy response to Ukraine was
special, and lethal. Seven crucial policies were applied only, or mainly, in Soviet
Ukraine in late 1932 or early 1933. Each of them may seem like an anodyne administrative measure, and each of them was certainly presented as such at the
time, and yet each of them had to kill.

1. On 18 November 1932, peasants in Ukraine were required to return grain
advances that they had previously earned by meeting grain requisition targets.
This meant that the few localities where peasants had had good yields were deprived of what little surplus they had earned. The party brigades and the state
police were unleashed on these regions, in a feverish hunt for whatever food
could be found. Because peasants were not given receipts for the grain that they

did hand over, they were subject to endless searches and abuse. The Ukrainian party leadership tried to protect the seed grain, but without success.[57]

2. Two days later, on 20 November 1932, a meat penalty was introduced. Peasants who were unable to make grain quotas were now required to pay a special tax in meat. Peasants who still had livestock were now forced to surrender it to the state. Cattle and swine had been a last reserve against starvation. As a peasant girl remembered, "whoever had a cow didn't starve." A cow gives milk, and as a last resort it can be slaughtered. Another peasant girl remembered that the family's one pig was seized, and then the family's one cow. She held its horns as it was led away. This was, perhaps, the attachment that teenaged girls on farms feel for their animals. But it was also desperation. Even after the meat penalty was paid, peasants still had to fulfill the original grain quota. If they could not do this under the threat of losing their animals, they certainly could not do so afterward. They starved.[58]

3. Eight days later, on 28 November 1932, Soviet authorities introduced the "black list." According to this new regulation, collective farms that failed to meet grain targets were required, immediately, to surrender fifteen times the amount of grain that was normally due in a whole month. In practice this meant, again, the arrival of hordes of party activists and police, with the mission and the legal right to take everything. No village could meet the multiplied quota, and so whole communities lost all of the food that they had. Communities on the black list also had no right to trade, or to receive deliveries of any kind from the rest of the country. They were cut off from food or indeed any other sort of supply from anywhere else. The black-listed communities in Soviet Ukraine, sometimes selected from as far away as Moscow, became zones of death.[59]

4. On 5 December 1932, Stalin's handpicked security chief for Ukraine presented the justification for terrorizing Ukrainian party officials to collect the grain. Vsevolod Balytskyi had spoken with Stalin personally in Moscow on 15 and 24 November. The famine in Ukraine was to be understood, according to Balytskyi, as the result of a plot of Ukrainian nationalists—in particular, of exiles with connections to Poland. Thus anyone who failed to do his part in requisitions was a traitor to the state.[60]

Yet this policy line had still deeper implications. The connection of Ukrainian nationalism to Ukrainian famine authorized the punishment of those who had taken part in earlier Soviet policies to support the development of the

Ukrainian nation. Stalin believed that the national question was in essence a peasant question, and as he undid Lenin's compromise with the peasants he also found himself undoing Lenin's compromise with the nations. On 14 December Moscow authorized the deportation of local Ukrainian communists to concentration camps, on the logic that they had abused Soviet policies in order to spread Ukrainian nationalism, thus allowing nationalists to sabotage the grain collection. Balytskyi then claimed to have unmasked a "Ukrainian Military Organization" as well as Polish rebel groups. He would report, in January 1933, the discovery of more than a thousand illegal organizations and, in February, the plans of Polish and Ukrainian nationalists to overthrow Soviet rule in Ukraine.[61]

The justifications were fabricated, but the policy had consequences. Poland had withdrawn its agents from Ukraine, and had given up any hope of exploiting the disaster of collectivization. The Polish government, attempting to be loyal to the Soviet-Polish nonaggression pact signed in July 1932, declined even to draw international attention to the worsening Soviet famine. Yet Balytskyi's policy, though it rode the coattails of phantoms, generated local obedience to Moscow's policy. The mass arrests and mass deportations he ordered sent a very clear message: anyone who defended the peasants would be condemned as an enemy. In these crucial weeks of late December, as the death toll in Soviet Ukraine rose into the hundreds of thousands, Ukrainian activists and administrators knew better than to resist the party line. If they did not carry out requisitions, they would find themselves (in the best case) in the Gulag.[62]

5. On 21 December 1932, Stalin (through Kaganovich) affirmed the annual grain requisition quota for Soviet Ukraine, to be reached by January 1933. On 27 November, the Soviet politburo had assigned Ukraine a full third of the remaining collections for the entire Soviet Union. Now, hundreds of thousands of starvation deaths later, Stalin sent Kaganovich to hold the whip hand over the Ukrainian party leadership in Kharkiv. Right after Kaganovich arrived on the evening of 20 December, the Ukrainian politburo was forced to convene. Sitting until four o'clock the next morning, it resolved that requisition targets were to be met. This was a death sentence for about three million people. As everyone in that room knew in those early morning hours, grain could not be collected from an already starving population without the most horrific of consequences. A simple respite from requisitions for three months would not have

harmed the Soviet economy, and would have saved most of those three million lives. Yet Stalin and Kaganovich insisted on exactly the contrary. The state would fight "ferociously," as Kaganovich put it, to fulfill the plan.[63]

Having achieved his mission in Kharkiv, Kaganovich then traveled through Soviet Ukraine, demanding "100 percent" fulfillment of the plan and sentencing local officials and ordering deportations of families as he went. He returned to Kharkiv on 29 December 1932 to remind Ukrainian party leaders that the seed grain was also to be collected.[64]

6. As starvation raged throughout Ukraine in the first weeks of 1933, Stalin sealed the borders of the republic so that peasants could not flee, and closed the cities so that peasants could not beg. As of 14 January 1933 Soviet citizens had to carry internal passports in order to reside in cities legally. Peasants were not to receive them. On 22 January 1933 Balytskyi warned Moscow that Ukrainian peasants were fleeing the republic, and Stalin and Molotov ordered the state police to prevent their flight. The next day the sale of long-distance rail tickets to peasants was banned. Stalin's justification was that the peasant refugees were not in fact begging bread but, rather, engaging in a "counterrevolutionary plot," by serving as living propaganda for Poland and other capitalist states that wished to discredit the collective farm. By the end of February 1933 some 190,000 peasants had been caught and sent back to their home villages to starve.[65]

Stalin had his "fortress" in Ukraine, but it was a stronghold that resembled a giant starvation camp, with watchtowers, sealed borders, pointless and painful labor, and endless and predictable death.

7. Even after the annual requisition target for 1932 was met in late January 1933, collection of grain continued. Requisitions went forward in February and March, as party members sought grain for the spring sowing. At the end of December 1932, Stalin had approved Kaganovich's proposal that the seed grain for the spring be seized to make the annual target. This left the collective farms with nothing to plant for the coming fall. Seed grain for the spring sowing might have been drawn from the trainloads bound at that very moment for export, or taken from the three million tons that the Soviet Union had stored as a reserve. Instead it was seized from what little the peasants in Soviet Ukraine still had. This was very often the last bit of food that peasants needed to survive until the spring harvest. Some 37,392 people were arrested in Soviet Ukrainian villages that month, many of them presumably trying to save their families from starvation.[66]

This final collection was murder, even if those who executed it very often believed that they were doing the right thing. As one activist remembered, that spring he "saw people dying from hunger. I saw women and children with distended bellies, turning blue, still breathing but with vacant, lifeless eyes." Yet he "saw all this and did not go out of my mind or commit suicide." He had faith: "As before, I believed because I wanted to believe." Other activists, no doubt, were less faithful and more fearful. Every level of the Ukrainian party had been purged in the previous year; in January 1933, Stalin sent in his own men to control its heights. Those communists who no longer expressed their faith formed a "wall of silence" that doomed those it surrounded. They had learned that to resist was to be purged, and to be purged was to share the fate of those whose deaths they were now bringing about.[67]

In Soviet Ukraine in early 1933, the communist party activists who collected the grain left a deathly quiet behind them. The countryside has its own orchestra of sound, softer and slower than the city, but no less predictable and reassuring for those born to it. Ukraine had gone mute.

Peasants had killed their livestock (or lost it to the state), they had killed their chickens, they had killed their cats and their dogs. They had scared the birds away by hunting them. The human beings had fled, too, if they were lucky; more likely they too were dead, or too weak to make noise. Cut off from the attention of the world by a state that controlled the press and the movements of foreign journalists, cut off from official help or sympathy by a party line that equated starvation with sabotage, cut off from the economy by intense poverty and inequitable planning, cut off from the rest of the country by regulations and police cordons, people died alone, families died alone, whole villages died alone. Two decades later, the political philosopher Hannah Arendt would present this famine in Ukraine as the crucial event in the creation of a modern "atomized" society, the alienation of all from all.[68]

Starvation led not to rebellion but to amorality, to crime, to indifference, to madness, to paralysis, and finally to death. Peasants endured months of indescribable suffering, indescribable because of its duration and pain, but also indescribable because people were too weak, too poor, too illiterate to chronicle what was happening to them. But the survivors did remember. As one of them recalled, no matter what peasants did, "they went on dying, dying, dying." The death was slow, humiliating, ubiquitous, and generic. To die of starvation with some sort of dignity was beyond the reach of almost everyone. Petro Veldii showed rare strength when he dragged himself through his village on the day he expected to die. The other villagers asked him where he was going: to the cemetery to lay himself down. He did not want strangers coming and dragging his body away to a pit. So he had dug his own grave, but by the time he reached the cemetery another body had filled it. He dug himself another one, lay down, and waited.[69]

A very few outsiders witnessed and were able to record what happened in these most terrible of months. The journalist Gareth Jones had paid his own way to Moscow, and, violating a ban on travel to Ukraine, took a train to Kharkiv on 7 March 1933. He disembarked at random at a small station and tramped through the countryside with a backpack full of food. He found "famine on a colossal scale." Everywhere he went he heard the same two phrases: "Everyone is swollen from starvation" and "We are waiting to die." He slept on dirt floors with starving children, and learned the truth. Once, after he had shared his food, a little girl exclaimed: "Now that I have eaten such wonderful things I can die happy."[70]

Maria Łowińska traveled that same spring through Soviet Ukraine, accompanying her husband as he tried to sell his handiworks. The villages they knew from previous treks were now deserted. They were frightened by the unending silence. If they heard a cock crow they were so happy that they were alarmed by their own reaction. The Ukrainian musician Yosyp Panasenko was dispatched by central authorities with his troupe of bandura players to provide culture to the starving peasants. Even as the state took the peasants' last bit of food, it had the grotesque inclination to elevate the minds and rouse the spirits of the dying. The musicians found village after village completely abandoned. Then they finally came across some people: two girls dead in a bed, two legs of a man protruding from a stove, and an old lady raving and running her fingernails through the dirt. The party official Viktor Kravchenko entered a village to help with the harvest one evening. The next day he found seventeen corpses in the marketplace. Such scenes could be found in villages throughout Soviet Ukraine, where in that spring of 1933 people died at a rate of more than ten thousand a day.[71]

Ukrainians who chose not to resist the collective farms believed that they had at least escaped deportation. But now they could be deported because collective farming did not work. Some fifteen thousand peasants were deported from Soviet Ukraine between February and April 1933. Just east and south of Soviet Ukraine, in parts of the Russian republic of the Soviet Union inhabited by Ukrainians, some sixty thousand people were deported for failing to make grain quotas. In 1933 some 142,000 more Soviet citizens were sent to the Gulag, most of them either hungry or sick with typhus, many of them from Soviet Ukraine.[72]

In the camps they tried to find enough to eat. Since the Gulag had a policy of feeding the strong and depriving the weak, and these deportees were already weak from hunger, this was desperately difficult. When hungry prisoners poisoned themselves by eating wild plants and garbage, camp officials punished them for shirking. At least 67,297 people died of hunger and related illnesses in the camps and 241,355 perished in the special settlements in 1933, many of them natives of Soviet Ukraine. Untold thousands more died on the long journey from Ukraine to Kazakhstan or the far north. Their corpses were removed from the trains and buried on the spot, their names and their numbers unrecorded.[73]

Those who were starving when they left their homes had little chance of survival in an alien environment. As one state official recorded in May 1933: "When traveling, I often witnessed administrative exiles haunting the villages like shadows in search of a piece of bread or refuse. They eat carrion, slaughter dogs and cats. The villagers keep their houses locked. Those who get a chance to enter a house drop on their knees in front of the owner and, with tears, beg for a piece of bread. I witnessed several deaths on the roads between villages, in the bathhouses, and in the barns. I myself saw hungry, agonized people crawling on the sidewalk. They were picked up by the police and died several hours later. In late April an investigator and I passed by a barn and found a dead body. When we sent for a policeman and a medic to pick it up, they discovered another body inside the barn. Both died of hunger, with no violence." The Ukrainian countryside had already exported its food to the rest of the Soviet Union; now it exported some of the resulting starvation—to the Gulag.[74]

Children born in Soviet Ukraine in the late 1920s and early 1930s found themselves in a world of death, among helpless parents and hostile authorities. A boy born in 1933 had a life expectancy of seven years. Even in these circumstances, some younger children could manage a bit of good cheer. Hanna Sobolewska, who lost her father and five brothers and sisters to starvation, remembered her youngest brother Józef's painful hope. Even as he swelled from hunger he kept finding signs of life. One day he thought he could see the crops rising from the ground; on another, he believed that he had found mushrooms. "Now we will live!" he would exclaim, and repeat these words before he went to sleep each night. Then one morning he awoke and said: "Everything dies." Schoolchildren at first wrote to the appropriate authorities, in the hope that starvation was the result of a misunderstanding. One class of elementary school students, for example, sent a letter to party authorities asking "for your help, since we are falling down from hunger. We should be learning, but we are too hungry to walk."[75]

Soon this was no longer noteworthy. In eight-year-old Yurii Lysenko's school in the Kharkiv region, a girl simply collapsed in class one day, as if asleep. The adults rushed in, but Yurii knew that she was beyond hope, "that she had died and that they would bury her in the cemetery, like they had buried people yesterday, and the day before yesterday, and every day." Boys from another school pulled out the severed head of a classmate while fishing in a pond. His whole family had died. Had they eaten him first? Or had he survived the deaths of his parents only to be killed by a cannibal? No one knew; but such questions were commonplace for the children of Ukraine in 1933.[76]

The duties of parents could not be fulfilled. Marriages suffered as wives, sometimes with their husbands' anguished consent, prostituted themselves with local party leaders for flour. Parents, even when alive and together and acting in the best of faith, could hardly care for children. One day a father in the Vynnitsia region went to bury one of his two children, and returned to find the other dead. Some parents loved their children by protecting them, locking them in cottages to keep them safe from the roving bands of cannibals. Other parents sent their children away in the hope that they could be saved by others. Parents would give their children to distant family or to strangers, or leave them at train stations. The desperate peasants holding up infants to train windows were not necessarily begging for food: often they were trying to give their children away to someone aboard a train, who was likely from the city and therefore not about to starve to death. Fathers and mothers sent their children to the cities to beg, with very mixed results. Some children starved on the way, or at their destination.

Others were taken by city police, to die in the dark in a strange metropolis and be buried in a mass grave with other small bodies. Even when children returned, the news was rarely good. Petro Savhira went with one of his brothers to Kiev to beg and returned to find his other two brothers already dead.[77]

In the face of starvation, some families divided, parents turning against children, and children against one another. As the state police, the OGPU, found itself obliged to record, in Soviet Ukraine "families kill their weakest members, usually children, and use the meat for eating." Countless parents killed and ate their children and then died of starvation later anyway. One mother cooked her son for herself and her daughter. One six-year-old girl, saved by other relatives, last saw her father when he was sharpening a knife to slaughter her. Other combinations were, of course, possible. One family killed their daughter-in-law, fed her head to the pigs, and roasted the rest of her body.[78]

In a broader sense, though, it was politics as well as starvation that destroyed families, turning a younger generation against an older. Members of the Young Communists served in the brigades that requisitioned food. Still, younger children, in the Pioneers, were supposed to be "the eyes and ears of the party inside the family." The healthier ones were assigned to watch over the fields to prevent theft. Half a million preadolescent and young teenage boys and girls stood in the watchtowers observing adults in Soviet Ukraine in summer 1933. All children were expected to report on their parents.[79]

Survival was a moral as well as a physical struggle. A woman doctor wrote to a friend in June 1933 that she had not yet become a cannibal, but was "not sure that I shall not be one by the time my letter reaches you." The good people died first. Those who refused to steal or to prostitute themselves died. Those who gave food to others died. Those who refused to eat corpses died. Those who refused to kill their fellow man died. Parents who resisted cannibalism died before their children did. Ukraine in 1933 was full of orphans, and sometimes people took them in. Yet without food there was little that even the kindest of strangers could do for such children. The boys and girls lay about on sheets and blankets, eating their own excrement, waiting for death.[80]

In one village in the Kharkiv region, several women did their best to look after children. As one of them recalled, they formed "something like an orphanage." Their wards were in a pitiful condition: "The children had bulging stomachs; they were covered in wounds, in scabs; their bodies were bursting. We took them outside, we put them on sheets, and they moaned. One day the children suddenly fell silent, we turned around to see what was happening, and they were eating the smallest child, little Petrus. They were tearing strips from him and eating them. And Petrus was doing the same, he was tearing strips from himself and eating them, he ate as much as he could. The other children put their lips to his wounds and drank his blood. We took the child away from the hungry mouths and we cried."[81]

Cannibalism is a taboo of literature as well as life, as communities seek to protect their dignity by suppressing the record of this desperate mode of survival. Ukrainians outside Soviet Ukraine, then and since, have treated cannibalism as a source of great shame. Yet while the cannibalism in Soviet Ukraine in 1933 says much about the Soviet system, it says nothing about Ukrainians as a people. With starvation will come cannibalism. There came a moment in Ukraine when there was little or no grain, and the only meat was human. A black market arose in human flesh; human meat may even have entered the official economy. The police investigated anyone selling meat, and state authorities kept a close eye on slaughterhouses and butcher shops. A young communist in the Kharkiv region reported to his superiors that he could make a meat quota, but only by using human beings. In the villages smoke coming from a cottage chimney was a suspicious sign, since it tended to mean that cannibals were eating a kill or that families were roasting one of their members. Police would follow the smoke and make arrests. At least 2,505 people were sentenced for cannibalism in the years 1932 and 1933 in Ukraine, though the actual number of cases was certainly much greater.[82]

People in Ukraine never considered cannibalism to be acceptable. Even at the height of the famine, villagers were outraged to find cannibals in their midst, so much so that they were spontaneously beaten or even burned to death. Most people did not succumb to cannibalism. An orphan was a child who had not been eaten by his parents. And even those who did eat human flesh acted from various motivations. Some cannibals were clearly criminals of the worst kind. Bazylii Graniewicz, for example, lost his brother Kolya to a cannibal. When the cannibal was arrested by the militia, Kolya's head was among eleven found in his house. Yet cannibalism was, sometimes, a victimless crime. Some mothers and fathers killed their children and ate them. In those cases the children were clearly victims. But other parents asked their children to make use of their own bodies if they passed away. More than one Ukrainian child had to tell a brother or sister: "Mother says that we should eat her if she dies." This was forethought and love.[83]

One of the very last functions that the state performed was the disposal of dead bodies. As a Ukrainian student wrote in January 1933, the task was a difficult one: "The burial of the dead is not always possible, because the hungry die in the fields of wandering from village to village." In the cities carts would make rounds early in the mornings to remove the peasant dead of the night before. In the countryside the healthier peasants formed brigades to collect the corpses and bury them. They rarely had the inclination or the strength to dig graves very deeply, so that hands and feet could be seen above the earth. Burial crews were paid according to the number of bodies collected, which led to certain abuses. Crews would take the weak along with the dead, and bury them alive. They would talk with such people along the way, explaining to the starving that they would die soon anyway, so what difference could it make? In a few cases such victims managed to dig their way out of the shallow mass graves. In their turn the gravediggers weakened and died, their corpses left where they lay. As an agronomist recalled, the bodies were then "devoured by those dogs that had escaped being eaten and had gone savage."[84]

In fall 1933, in villages across Soviet Ukraine the harvest was brought in by Red Army soldiers, communist party activists, workers, and students. Forced to work even as they died, starving peasants had put down crops in spring 1933 that they would not live to harvest. Resettlers came from Soviet Russia to take over houses and villages, and saw that first they would have to remove the bodies of the previous inhabitants. Often the rotten corpses fell apart in their hands. Sometimes the newcomers would then return home, finding that no amount of scrubbing and painting could quite remove the stench. Yet sometimes they stayed. Ukraine's "ethnographic material," as one Soviet official told an Italian diplomat, had been altered. As earlier in Soviet Kazakhstan, where the change was even more dramatic, the demographic balance in Soviet Ukraine shifted in favor of Russians.[85]

———————————

How many people were killed by famine in the Soviet Union, and in its Ukrainian republic, in the early 1930s? We will never know with precision. No good records were kept. Such records as do exist confirm the mass scale of the event:

public health authorities in Kiev oblast, for example, recorded that 493,644 people were going hungry in that region alone in the month of April 1933. Local authorities feared to record deaths by starvation and, after a while, were in no position to record anything at all. Very often the only instance of state power that had any contact with the dead were the brigades of gravediggers, and they kept nothing like systematic records.[86]

The Soviet census of 1937 found eight million fewer people than projected: most of these were famine victims in Soviet Ukraine, Soviet Kazakhstan, and Soviet Russia, and the children that they did not then have. Stalin suppressed its findings and had the responsible demographers executed. In 1933, Soviet officials in private conversations most often provided the estimate of 5.5 million dead from hunger. This seems roughly correct, if perhaps somewhat low, for the Soviet Union in the early 1930s, including Soviet Ukraine, Soviet Kazakhstan, and Soviet Russia.[87]

One demographic retrojection suggests a figure of about 2.5 million famine deaths for Soviet Ukraine. This is too close to the recorded figure of excess deaths, which is about 2.4 million. The latter figure must be substantially low, since many deaths were not recorded. Another demographic calculation, carried out on behalf of the authorities of independent Ukraine, provides the figure of 3.9 million dead. The truth is probably in between these numbers, where most of the estimates of respectable scholars can be found. It seems reasonable to propose a figure of approximately 3.3 million deaths by starvation and hunger-related disease in Soviet Ukraine in 1932–1933. Of these people, some three million would have been Ukrainians, and the rest Russians, Poles, Germans, Jews, and others. Among the million or so dead in the Soviet Russian republic were probably at least two hundred thousand Ukrainians, since the famine struck heavily in regions where Ukrainians lived. Perhaps as many as a hundred thousand more Ukrainians were among the 1.3 million people who died in the earlier famine in Kazakhstan. All in all, no fewer than 3.3 million Soviet citizens died in Soviet Ukraine of starvation and hunger-related diseases; and about the same number of Ukrainians (by nationality) died in the Soviet Union as a whole.[88]

Rafał Lemkin, the international lawyer who later invented the term *genocide*, would call the Ukrainian case "the classic example of Soviet genocide." The fabric of rural society of Ukraine was tested, stretched, and rent. Ukrainian peasants were dead, or humbled, or scattered among camps the length and breadth of the Soviet Union. Those who survived carried feelings of guilt and helplessness, and sometimes memories of collaboration and cannibalism. Hundreds of thousands of orphans would grow up to be Soviet citizens but not Ukrainians, at least not in the way that an intact Ukrainian family and a Ukrainian countryside might have made them. Those Ukrainian intellectuals who survived the calamity lost their confidence. The leading Soviet Ukrainian writer and the leading Soviet Ukrainian political activist both committed suicide, the one in May and the other in July 1933. The Soviet state had defeated those who wished for some autonomy for the Ukrainian republic, and those who wished for some autonomy for themselves and their families.[89]

Foreign communists in the Soviet Union, witnesses to the famine, somehow managed to see starvation not as a national tragedy but as a step forward for humanity. The writer Arthur Koestler believed at the time that the starving were "enemies of the people who preferred begging to work." His housemate in Kharkiv, the physicist Alexander Weissberg, knew that millions of peasants had died. Nevertheless, he kept the faith. Koestler naively complained to Weissberg that the Soviet press did not write that Ukrainians "have nothing to eat and therefore are dying like flies." He and Weissberg knew that to be true, as did everyone who had any contact with the country. Yet to write of the famine would have made their faith impossible. Each of them believed that the destruction of the countryside could be reconciled to a general story of human progress. The deaths of Ukrainian peasants were the price to be paid for a higher civilization. Koestler left the Soviet Union in 1933. When Weissberg saw him off at the train station, his parting words were: "Whatever happens, hold the banner of the Soviet Union high!"[90]

Yet the end result of the starvation was not socialism, in any but the Stalinist sense of the term. In one village in Soviet Ukraine, the triumphal arch built to celebrate the completion of the Five-Year Plan was surrounded by the corpses of peasants. The Soviet officials who persecuted the kulaks had more money than their victims, and the urban party members far better life prospects. Peasants had no right to ration cards, while party elites chose from a selection of food at special stores. If they grew too fat, however, they had to beware the roving "sausage makers," especially at night. Rich women in Ukrainian cities, usually the wives of high officials, traded their food rations for peasant embroidery and ornaments stolen from country churches. In this way, too, collectivization robbed the Ukrainian village of its identity, even as it destroyed the Ukrainian peasant morally and then physically. Hunger drove Ukrainians and others to strip themselves and their places of worship before it drove them to their deaths.[91]

Although Stalin, Kaganovich, and Balytskyi explained the repressions in Soviet Ukraine as a response to Ukrainian nationalism, Soviet Ukraine was a multi-national republic. The starvation touched Russians, Poles, Germans, and many others. Jews in Soviet Ukraine tended to live in towns and cities, but those in the countryside were no less vulnerable than anyone else. One day in 1933 a staff writer for the party newspaper *Pravda*, which denied the famine, received a letter from his Jewish father. "This is to let you know," wrote the father, "that your mother is dead. She died of starvation after months of pain." Her last wish was that their son say kaddish for her. This exchange reveals the generational difference between parents raised before the revolution and children raised thereafter. Not only among Jews, but among Ukrainians and others, the generation educated in the 1920s was far more likely to accept the Soviet system than the generations raised in the Russian Empire.[92]

German and Polish diplomats informed their superiors of the suffering and death of the German and Polish minorities in Soviet Ukraine. The German consul in Kharkiv wrote that "almost every time I venture into the streets I see people collapsing from hunger." Polish diplomats faced long lines of starving people desperate for a visa. One of them reported: "Frequently the clients, grown men, cry as they tell of wives and children starving to death or bursting from hunger." As these diplomats knew, many peasants in Soviet Ukraine, not only Poles and Germans, hoped for an invasion from abroad to release them from their agony. Until the middle of 1932, their greatest hope was Poland. Stalin's propaganda had been telling them for five years that Poland was planning to invade and annex Ukraine. When the famine began, many Ukrainian peasants hoped that this propaganda was true. As one Polish spy reported, they clung to the hope that "Poland or for that matter any other state would come and liberate them from misery and oppression."[93]

When Poland and the Soviet Union signed their nonaggression pact in July 1932, that hope was dashed. Thenceforth the peasants could only hope for a

German attack. Eight years later, those who survived would be in a position to compare Soviet to German rule.

The basic facts of mass hunger and death, although sometimes reported in the European and American press, never took on the clarity of an undisputed event. Almost no one claimed that Stalin meant to starve Ukrainians to death; even Adolf Hitler preferred to blame the Marxist system. It was controversial to note that starvation was taking place at all. Gareth Jones did so in a handful of newspaper articles; it seems that he was the only one to do so in English under his own name. When Cardinal Theodor Innitzer of Vienna tried to appeal for food aid for the starving in summer and autumn 1933, Soviet authorities rebuffed him nastily, saying that the Soviet Union had neither cardinals nor cannibals— a statement that was only half true.[94]

Though the journalists knew less than the diplomats, most of them understood that millions were dying from hunger. The influential Moscow correspondent of the *New York Times*, Walter Duranty, did his best to undermine Jones's accurate reporting. Duranty, who won a Pulitzer Prize in 1932, called Jones's account of the famine a "big scare story." Duranty's claim that there was "no actual starvation" but only "widespread mortality from diseases due to malnutrition" echoed Soviet usages and pushed euphemism into mendacity. This was an Orwellian distinction; and indeed George Orwell himself regarded the Ukrainian famine of 1933 as a central example of a black truth that artists of language had covered with bright colors. Duranty knew that millions of people had starved to death. Yet he maintained in his journalism that the hunger served a higher purpose. Duranty thought that "you can't make an omelette without breaking eggs." Aside from Jones, the only journalist to file serious reports in English was Malcolm Muggeridge, writing anonymously for the *Manchester Guardian*. He wrote that the famine was "one of the most monstrous crimes in history, so terrible that people in the future will scarcely be able to believe that it happened."[95]

In fairness, even the people with the most obvious interest in events in Soviet Ukraine, the Ukrainians living beyond the border of the Soviet Union, needed months to understand the extent of the famine. Some five million Ukrainians lived in neighboring Poland, and their political leaders worked hard to draw international attention to the mass starvation in the Soviet Union. And yet even they grasped the extent of the tragedy only in May 1933, by which time most of the victims were already dead. Throughout the following summer and autumn, Ukrainian newspapers in Poland covered the famine, and Ukrainian politicians in Poland organized marches and protests. The leader of the Ukrainian feminist organization tried to organized an international boycott of Soviet goods by appealing to the women of the world. Several attempts were made to reach Franklin D. Roosevelt, the president of the United States.[96]

None of this made any difference. The laws of the international market ensured that the grain taken from Soviet Ukraine would feed others. Roosevelt, preoccupied above all by the position of the American worker during the Great Depression, wished to establish diplomatic relations with the Soviet Union. The telegrams from Ukrainian activists reached him in autumn 1933, just as his personal initiative in US-Soviet relations was bearing fruit. The United States extended diplomatic recognition to the Soviet Union in November 1933.

The main result of the summer campaign of Ukrainians in Poland was skillful Soviet counterpropaganda. On 27 August 1933, the French politician Édouard Herriot arrived in Kiev, on an official invitation. The leader of the Radical Party, Herriot had been French prime minister three times, most recently in 1932. He was a corpulent man of known physical appetites, who compared his own body shape to that of a woman pregnant with twins. At the receptions in the Soviet Union, Herriot was kept away from the German and the Polish diplomats, who might have spoiled the fun with an untoward word about starvation.[97]

The day before Herriot was to visit the city, Kiev had been closed, and its population ordered to clean and decorate. The shop windows, empty all year, were now suddenly filled with food. The food was for display, not for sale, for the eyes of a single foreigner. The police, wearing fresh new uniforms, had to disperse the gaping crowds. Everyone who lived or worked along Herriot's planned route was forced to go through a dress rehearsal of the visit, demonstrating that they knew where to stand and what to wear. Herriot was driven down Kiev's incomparable broad avenue, Khreshchatyk. It pulsed with the traffic of automobiles—which had been gathered from several cities and were now driven by party activists to create the appearance of bustle and prosperity. A woman on the street muttered that "perhaps this bourgeois will tell the world what is happening here." She was to be disappointed. Herriot instead expressed his astonishment that the Soviet Union had managed so beautifully to honor both "the socialist spirit" and "Ukrainian national feeling."[98]

On 30 August 1933, Herriot visited the Feliks Dzierżyński Children's Commune in Kharkiv, a school named after the founder of the Soviet secret police. At this time, children were still starving to death in the Kharkiv region. The children he saw were gathered from among the healthiest and fittest. Most likely they wore clothes that they had been loaned that morning. The picture, of course, was not entirely false: the Soviets had built schools for Ukrainian children, and were on the way to eliminating illiteracy. Children who were alive at the end of 1933 would very likely become adults who could read. This is what Herriot was meant to see. What, the Frenchman asked, entirely without irony, had the students eaten for lunch? It was a question, posed casually, on which the image of the Soviet Union depended. Vasily Grossman would repeat the scene in both of his great novels. As Grossman would recall, the children had been prepared for this question, and gave a suitable answer. Herriot believed what he saw and heard. He journeyed onward to Moscow, where he was fed caviar in a palace.[99]

The collective farms of Soviet Ukraine, Herriot told the French upon his return, were well-ordered gardens. The official Soviet party newspaper, *Pravda*, was pleased to report Herriot's remarks. The story was over. Or, perhaps, the story was elsewhere.

CHAPTER 2

CLASS TERROR

Stalin's second revolution in the Soviet Union, his collectivization and the famine it brought, was overshadowed by Hitler's rise to power in Germany. Many Europeans, distressed by the nazification of Germany, looked hopefully to Moscow for an ally. Gareth Jones was one of the few to observe the two systems in early 1933, as both Hitler and Stalin were consolidating power. On 25 February 1933, he flew with Adolf Hitler from Berlin to Frankfurt, as the first journalist to travel by air with the new German chancellor. "If this aeroplane should crash," he wrote, "the whole history of Europe would be changed." Jones had read *Mein Kampf*, and he grasped Hitler's ambitions: the domination of Germany, the colonization of eastern Europe, the elimination of the Jews. Hitler, already chancellor, had dissolved the Reichstag and was in the midst of an electoral campaign, aiming to gain a greater mandate for himself and a stronger presence for his party in the German parliament. Jones saw how Germans reacted to their new chancellor, first in Berlin and then at a rally in Frankfurt. He felt the "pure primitive worship."[1]

When Jones made for Moscow he was traveling from, as he put it, "a land where dictatorship has just begun" to "the dictatorship of the working class." Jones understood an important difference between the two regimes. Hitler's rise meant the beginning of a new regime in Germany. Stalin, meanwhile, was securing his hold on a one-party state with a powerful police apparatus capable of massive and coordinated violence. His policy of collectivization had required the shooting of tens of thousands of citizens and the deportations of hundreds of thousands, and had brought millions more to the brink of death by starvation—as Jones would see and report. Later in the 1930s, Stalin would order the shooting of hundreds of thousands more Soviet citizens, in campaigns organized by social class and ethnic nation. All of this was well beyond Hitler's capabilities in the 1930s, and probably beyond his intentions.[2]

For some of the Germans and other Europeans who favored Hitler and his enterprise, the cruelty of Soviet policy seemed to be an argument for National Socialism. In his stirring campaign speeches, Hitler portrayed communists and the Soviet state as the great enemies of Germany and Europe. During the very first crisis of his young chancellorship, he exploited fears of communism to gather more power to himself and his office. On 27 February 1933, two days after Hitler and Jones had landed in Frankfurt, a lone Dutchman set fire to the German parliament building. Though the arsonist was caught in the act and confessed, Hitler immediately seized the occasion to demonize opposition to his new government. Working himself up into a theatrical display of rage, he shouted that "anyone who stands in our way will be butchered." Hitler blamed the Reichstag fire on German communists who, he claimed, were planning further terrorist attacks.[3]

For Hitler, the timing of the Reichstag fire could not have been better. As head of government, he could move against his political opponents; as a candidate running for election, he could turn fear to his advantage. On 28 February 1933 a decree suspended the rights of all German citizens, allowing their "preventive detainment." In an atmosphere of insecurity, the Nazis decisively won the elections on 5 March, with 43.9 percent of the vote and 288 seats in the Reichstag. In the weeks and months that followed, Hitler used German police and Nazi paramilitaries to crush the two parties he grouped together as "Marxists": the communists and the social democrats. Hitler's close ally Heinrich Himmler established the first Nazi concentration camp, at Dachau, on 20 March. Himmler's SS, a paramilitary that had arisen as Hitler's bodyguard, provided the staff. Although the concentration camp was not a new institution, Himmler's SS meant to use it for intimidation and terror. As an SS officer said to the guards at Dachau: "Any of the comrades who can't see blood should resign. The more of these bastards go down, the fewer of them we'll have to feed."[4]

After his electoral victory, Hitler the chancellor quickly became Hitler the dictator. On 23 March 1933, with the first prisoners already incarcerated at Dachau, the new parliament passed an enabling act, which allowed Hitler to rule Germany by decree without reference to either the president or the parliament. This act would be renewed and would remain in force so long as Hitler lived. Gareth Jones returned to Berlin from the Soviet Union on 29 March 1933, a month after he had left Germany for the Soviet Union, and gave a press conference about the starvation in Soviet Ukraine. The worst political famine in history seemed like a minor news item compared to the establishment of a new dictatorship in the German capital. Indeed, the suffering in the Soviet Union had already become, during Jones's absence, part of the story of Hitler's rise to power.[5]

Hitler had used the Ukrainian famine in his election campaign, making the event a matter of furious ideological politics before it was established as historical fact. As he raged against the "Marxists," Hitler used the starvation in Ukraine as an indictment of Marxism in practice. To a gathering at the Berlin Sportpalast on 2 March 1933, Hitler proclaimed that "millions of people are starving in a country that could be a breadbasket for a whole world." With a single word (*Marxists*) Hitler united the mass death in the Soviet Union with the German social democrats, the bulwark of the Weimar Republic. It was easier for most to reject (or accept) his entire perspective than it was to disentangle the true from the false. For people lacking close familiarity with Soviet politics, which meant almost everyone, to accept Hitler's assessment of the famine was to take a step toward accepting his condemnation of left-wing politics, which in his rhetoric was mixed with the rejection of democracy as such.[6]

Stalin's own policies made it easier for Hitler to make this case, because they offered a similarly binary view of the political world. Stalin, his attention focused on collectivization and famine, had unwittingly performed much of the ideological work that helped Hitler come to power. When Stalin had begun to collectivize agriculture in the Soviet Union, the Communist International had instructed fraternal communist parties to follow the line of "class against class." Communists were to maintain their ideological purity, and avoid alliances with social democrats. Only communists had a legitimate role to play in human progress, and others who claimed to speak for the oppressed were frauds and "social fascists." They were to be grouped together with every party to their right, including the Nazis. In Germany, communists were to regard the social democrats, not the Nazis, as the main enemy.

In the second half of 1932 and the first months of 1933, during the long moment of Stalin's provocation of catastrophe, it would have been difficult for him to abandon the international line of "class against class." The class struggle against the kulak, after all, was the official explanation of the horrible suffering and mass death within the Soviet Union. In German domestic politics, this line prevented the German left from cooperating against Hitler. The crucial months for the famine, however, were also critical time for the future of Germany. The insistence of German communists on the need for immediate class revolution gained the Nazis votes from the middle classes. It also ensured that clerks and the self-employed voted Nazi rather than social democratic. Even so, the communists and the social democrats together had more popular support than the Nazis; but Stalin's line ensured that they could not work together. In all of these ways, Stalin's uncompromising stand in foreign policy during collectivization and famine in the Soviet Union helped Hitler win the elections of both July 1932 and March 1933.[7]

Whereas the true consequences of Stalin's economic policies had been hidden from foreign reporters, Hitler deliberately drew attention to the policies of redistribution that were among his first policies as dictator. At the very moment that starvation in the Soviet Union was peaking, the German state began to steal from its Jewish citizens. After the Nazis' electoral victory of 5 March 1933, they organized an economic boycott of Jewish businesses throughout Germany. Like collectivization, the boycotts indicated which sector of society would lose the most in coming social and economic transformations: not the peasants, as in the USSR, but the Jews. The boycotts, although carefully managed by Nazi leaders and Nazi paramilitaries, were presented as a result of the "spontaneous anger" of the people at Jewish exploitation.[8]

In this respect Hitler's policies resembled Stalin's. The Soviet leader presented the disarray in the Soviet countryside, and then dekulakization, as the result of an authentic class war. The political conclusion was the same in Berlin and Moscow: the state would have to step in to make sure that the necessary redistribution was relatively peaceful. Whereas Stalin had achieved by 1933 the authority and gathered the coercive power to force through collectivization on a massive scale, Hitler had to move far more slowly. The boycott had only a limited effect;

the main consequence was the emigration of some 37,000 German Jews in 1933. It would be five more years before substantial transfers of property from Jews to non-Jewish Germans—which the Nazis called "Aryanization"—took place.[9]

The Soviet Union began from a position of international isolation, and with the help of many sympathizers abroad was able with some success to control its image. By many, Stalin was given the benefit of the doubt, even as his policies moved from shooting to deportation to starvation. Hitler, on the other hand, had to reckon with international opinion, which included voices of criticism and outrage. Germany in 1933 was full of international journalists and other travelers, and Hitler needed peace and trade for the next few years. So even as he called an end to the boycott, Hitler used unfavorable attention in the foreign press to build up a rationale for the more radical policies to come. The Nazis presented European and American newspapers as controlled by Jews, and any foreign criticism as part of the international Jewish conspiracy against the German people.[10]

An important legacy of the March 1933 boycotts was thus rhetorical. Hitler introduced an argument that he would never cease to use, even much later, when his armies had conquered much of Europe and his institutions were killing millions of Jews. No matter what Germany or Germans did, it was because they were defending themselves from international Jewry. The Jews were always the aggressor, the Germans always the victims.

At first, Hitler's anti-communism was more pertinent to domestic politics than his anti-Semitism. To control the German state, he would have to break the communists and the social democrats. Over the course of 1933, some two hundred thousand Germans were locked up, most of them men seen as left-wing opponents of the regime. Hitler's terror in 1933 was meant to intimidate rather than eliminate: most of these people were released after short periods in what the Nazis euphemistically called "protective custody." The communist party was not allowed to take up the eighty-one seats that it had won in the elections; soon all of its property was seized by the state. By July 1933 it was illegal in Germany to belong to any other political party than the Nazis. In November the Nazis staged a parliamentary election in which only their candidates could run and win. Hitler had very quickly made of Germany a one-party state—and certainly not the sort of one-party state that Stalin might have expected. The German communist party, for years the strongest outside the Soviet Union itself, was broken in a matter of a few months. Its defeat was a serious blow to the prestige of the international communist movement.[11]

At first, Stalin seemed to hope that the Soviet-German special relationship could be preserved, despite Hitler's rise to power. Since 1922, the two states had engaged in military and economic cooperation, on the tacit understanding that both had an interest in the remaking of eastern Europe at the expense of Poland. The 1922 agreement at Rapallo had been confirmed by the neutrality pact of the Treaty of Berlin, signed in 1926 and extended for another five years in 1931. The clearest sign of good relations and common purpose were the German military exercises on Soviet soil. These came to an end in September 1933. In January 1934, Nazi Germany signed a nonaggression declaration with Poland. This surprise move seemed to signal a basic reorientation in German foreign policy. It seemed that Warsaw had replaced Moscow as Berlin's favored partner in the East. Might the Germans and the Poles now fight together against the Soviet Union?[12]

The new German relationship with Poland likely meant more to Stalin than the oppression of the German communists. Stalin himself always conducted foreign policy at two levels: the diplomatic and the ideological, one directed at states, the other at societies, including his own. For the one he had his commissar for foreign affairs, Maxim Litvinov; for the other he had the Communist International. He probably assumed that Hitler's approach was much the same, and thus that overt anti-communism need not prevent good relations between Berlin and Moscow. But the approach to Poland added what looked like anti-Soviet diplomacy to an anti-communist ideology. As Stalin correctly suspected, Hitler was trying to enlist Poland as a junior ally in a crusade against the Soviet Union. While the German-Polish negotiations were underway in late 1933, Soviet leaders rightly worried that the Germans were trying to buy Polish territory in the west with the promise that Poland could later annex territories from Soviet Ukraine. Poland, however, never showed any interest in Germany's propositions to extend the accord in such a way. The German-Polish declaration did not in fact include a secret protocol on military cooperation against the USSR, despite what Soviet intelligence and propaganda claimed. Yet Hitler did wish to use the German-Polish declaration as the beginning of a rapprochement with

Warsaw that would culminate in a military alliance against the USSR. He wondered aloud in spring 1934 about the necessary inducements.[13]

In January 1934, the Soviet Union seemed to be in a dreadful position. Its domestic policies had starved millions of its own citizens to death. Its foreign policies had contributed to the rise of a threatening anti-communist dictator, Hitler, who had made peace with the previous common German-Soviet enemy, Poland.

Stalin found the rhetorical and ideological escape route. At the Soviet communist party congress of January-February 1934, known as "The Congress of Victors," Stalin claimed that a second revolution had been completed within the Soviet Union. The famines, the most unforgettable experience of the Soviet peoples, went unmentioned. They blurred into a general story of how Stalin and his loyal retinue had overcome the resistance of enemies to implement the Five-Year Plan. Lazar Kaganovich praised his master Stalin as the creator of "the greatest revolution that human history has ever known." The rise of Hitler, despite appearances, was a sign of the coming victory of the Soviet system in the world. The brutality of the Nazis revealed that capitalism would soon collapse under its own contradictions, and that a European revolution was around the corner.[14]

This interpretation could only make sense to revolutionaries by conviction, to communists already bound to their leader by faith and fear. It took a special sort of mind to truly believe that the worse things appeared, the better they actually were. Such reasoning went by the name *dialectics*, but by this time that word (despite its proud descent from the Greeks through Hegel and Marx) meant little more than the psychic capacity to adjust one's own perceptions to the changing expressions of Stalin's will.[15]

For his part, Stalin knew that rhetoric was not enough. Even as he proclaimed that Hitler's revolution was a sign of the coming socialist victory, Stalin hastened to change his domestic policy. He did not take revenge on the Ukrainian peasant year after year. The peasants had to live on, frightened and intimidated, but productive of the foodstuffs needed by the Soviet state. Soviet policy now allowed all peasants to cultivate a small plot, the equivalent of a private garden, for their own use. Requisition quotas and export targets ceased their unreasoning climb. Starvation within the Soviet Union came to an end in 1934.[16]

INTERWAR EUROPE
c. 1933

The rise of Hitler was indeed an opportunity to present the Soviet Union as the defense of European civilization. Stalin, after more than a year, finally took it in June 1934. According to the new line of the Communist International, propagated then, politics was no longer a matter of "class against class." Instead, the Soviet Union and communist parties around the world would unite the Left in a camp of "anti-fascists." Rather than engaging in uncompromising class struggle, communists would rescue civilization from the rising tide of fascism. Fascism, the term popularized by Mussolini in Italy, was presented by the Soviets as a general corruption of late capitalism. Though fascism's spread signified the end of the old capitalist order, its vicious hatred of the Soviet Union (went the argument) justified Soviet and communist compromises with other capitalist forces (in the interest of defending the Soviet Union). European communists were to restyle themselves as "anti-fascists," and to cooperate with social democrats and other parties of the Left. Communists in Europe were expected to join "Popular Fronts," electoral alliances and win election victories with social democrats and other parties of the Left. For the time being, communists were to work within democracies, rather than toward their destruction.[17]

This came too late for German communists and social democrats, of course. But throughout western and southern Europe, people concerned with halting the spread of Hitler and fascism celebrated the new Soviet approach. By presenting the Soviet Union as the homeland of "anti-fascism," Stalin was seeking after a monopoly of the good. Surely reasonable people would want to be on the side of the anti-fascists, rather than that of the fascists? Anyone who was against the Soviet Union, was the suggestion, was probably a fascist or at least a sympathizer. During the period of the Popular Front, from June 1934 through August 1939, about three quarters of a million Soviet citizens would be shot to death by order of Stalin, and still more deported to the Gulag. Most of the repressed would be peasants and workers, the people whom the Soviet social system was supposed to serve. The others would generally be members of national minorities. Just as Hitler's rise had obscured the Soviet famine of 1933, Stalin's response would distract attention from the Great Terror.[18]

The Popular Front enjoyed the greatest chances for success in the west European democracies furthest from the Soviet Union, France, and Spain. The greatest triumph was in Paris, where a Popular Front government indeed came to power in May 1936. Left-wing parties (including Herriot's Radicals) won elections, and the socialist Léon Blum became prime minister. The French communists, part of a victorious electoral coalition, did not formally join the government, but they did provide the parliamentary majority and influence policy. The votes could thus be found for reforms—although the communists were chiefly concerned with ensuring that French foreign policy was friendly to the Soviet Union. In Paris, the Popular Front was seen as a triumph of native traditions of the Left. But many, not least the political refugees from Nazi Germany, saw it as a Soviet success, and even a confirmation that the Soviets supported democracy and freedom. The Popular Front in France made it far more difficult for some of the most impressive European intellectuals to criticize the Soviet Union.[19]

In Spain, a coalition of parties also formed a Popular Front, and won the elections of February 1936. There, events took a rather different turn. In July army officers, supported by far-right groups, tried to overturn the elected government in a coup d'état. The government resisted, and the Spanish Civil War began. Though for Spaniards this was an essentially domestic struggle, the ideological enemies of the Popular Front era took sides. The Soviet Union began to supply arms to the embattled Spanish Republic in October 1936, while Nazi Germany and fascist Italy supported the right-wing forces led by General Francisco Franco. The Spanish Civil War occasioned closer relations between Berlin and Rome, and became the center of attention of Soviet policy in Europe. Spain was on the front pages of major Soviet newspapers every day for months.[20]

Spain became the rallying cry of European socialists who came to fight for the side of the endangered republic, many of whom took for granted that the Soviet Union was on the side of democracy. One of the more perceptive of the European socialists, the English writer George Orwell, was dismayed by the struggle of Stalinists within Spain to dominate the Spanish Left. As he saw it, the Soviets exported their political practices along with their weapons. Stalin's assistance to the Spanish republic came with a price: his right to carry out factional struggles on Spanish territory. Stalin's greatest rival, Trotsky, was still alive (if in distant Mexican exile), and many of the Spaniards defending their republic were more attached to Trotsky's person than to Stalin's Soviet Union. Soon communist propaganda was presenting the Spanish Trotskyites as fascists, and Soviet NKVD officers were sent to Spain to shoot them for their "treason."[21]

The enemies of the Popular Front presented it as a conspiracy of the Communist International to rule the world. The Popular Front provided Japan and Germany with a convenient pretext to solidify their own relations. On 25 November 1936, Germany and Japan signed the Anti-Comintern Pact, which obliged the two states to consult with each other if either was attacked. An agreement between Japanese and German intelligence agencies of 11 May 1937 provided for the exchange of intelligence on the USSR, and included a plan for both to use national movements in the Soviet borderlands against the Soviet Union.[22]

From the Soviet perspective, the Japanese threat was more immediate than the German. During the first half of 1937, Germany appeared to be an addendum to a Japanese threat, rather than the other way around. Japanese politics was dominated by dueling visions of empire, one in the south and one in the

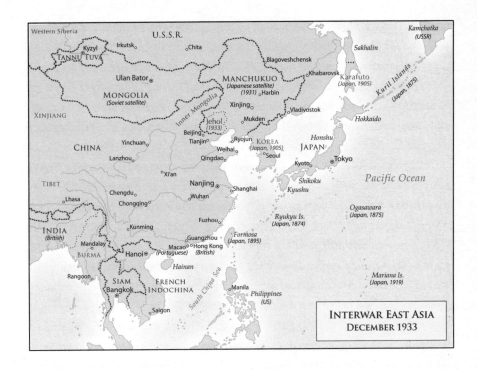

INTERWAR EAST ASIA
DECEMBER 1933

north. An important clique in the Japanese military believed that Siberian resources were the key to the country's future economic development. Japan's Manchurian satellite, Manchukuo, had a long border with Soviet Siberia, and looked ever more like a launching pad for an invasion. The Japanese were toying with the idea of establishing a puppet Ukrainian state on Soviet territory in eastern Siberia, based on the million or so Ukrainians who lived there as deportees or settlers. As Tokyo understood, Ukrainians deported to the Gulag might well oppose Soviet power, given the assurance of foreign backing. Polish spies who knew of the idea referred to it as "Manchukuo Number Two."[23]

The Japanese certainly seemed to have a long-term interest in Siberia. A special Japanese academy in Manchukuo, in the city of Harbin, had already trained a first generation of young, Russian-speaking imperialists, such as Chiune Sugihara. He was one of the negotiators of an agreement whereby the Soviets, in 1935, sold their rights to the railway in Manchuria to the Japanese. Sugihara was also in charge of the foreign policy office of Manchukuo. A convert to the Russian Orthodox religion and husband to a Russian wife, Sugihara called himself Sergei and spent most of his time in the Russian quarter of

Harbin. There he befriended Russian exiles, and recruited them for espionage missions within the Soviet Union. The drama of the Soviet-Japanese duel in east Asia attracted the attention of Gareth Jones, who traveled to Manchuria that same year. The Welshman, with his uncanny instinct for news, was right to see this region as the crucial theater in the global conflict between "fascism" and "anti-fascism." In somewhat mysterious circumstances, he was abducted by bandits and murdered.[24]

Stalin had to be concerned not only with a direct Japanese attack on Soviet Siberia but also with the consolidation of a Japanese empire in east Asia. Manchukuo was one Japanese colony taken from historically Chinese territory; perhaps more were to come. China had the longest border with the Soviet Union, and an unstable polity. China's nationalist government had the upper hand in an ongoing civil war with the Chinese communist party. In the "Long March," Chinese communist troops, led by Mao Zedong, had been forced to withdraw into the north and west of the country. Neither side, however, seemed able to achieve anything resembling a monopoly of force in the country. Even in regions where the nationalists had the upper hand, they were reliant upon local warlords. Perhaps most importantly for Stalin, the nationalists and communists were unable to cooperate against the advance of the Japanese.

Soviet foreign policy had to balance between support for fraternal communist parties (less important) and concerns of Soviet state security (more important). While in principle the Communist International supported the Chinese communists, Stalin armed and funded the nationalist government, in the hope of pacifying the border. In the largely Muslim Chinese province of Xinjiang, which had a long border with Soviet Kazakhstan, Stalin took an equally unideological approach. He supported the local warlord Sheng Shicai, sending engineers and miners to exploit natural resources, and NKVD men to ensure security.[25]

Globally, the German-Japanese rapprochement could be seen as completing an encirclement of the Soviet homeland by Japan, Germany, and Poland. These were the three most important neighbors of the Soviet Union; they were also three states that had defeated the Soviet Union (or the Russian Empire) in the wars of Stalin's lifetime. Even though Germany had lost the First World War, its troops had defeated the Russian Army on the eastern front in 1917. Japan had humiliated the Russian Army and Navy in the Russo-Japanese War of 1904–1905. Poland had defeated the Red Army as recently as 1920. Now, after the German-Polish and the German-Japanese agreements, these three powers appeared to be arrayed against the Soviet Union. If the Anti-Comintern Pact and the German-Polish nonaggression declaration had indeed included secret protocols concerning an offensive war on the Soviet Union, then Stalin would have been right about encirclement. In fact, neither did; and an offensive alliance between Tokyo, Warsaw, and Berlin was highly unlikely, if not impossible. Although Poland's relations with Japan were good, Warsaw wished to take no step that could be interpreted as hostile to the Soviet Union. Poland declined Germany's invitation to join the Anti-Comintern Pact.[26]

Part of Stalin's political talent was his ability to equate foreign threats with failures in domestic policy, as if the two were actually the same thing, and as if he were responsible for neither. This absolved him of blame for policy failures, and allowed him to define his chosen internal enemies as agents of foreign powers. As early as 1930, as problems of collectivization became apparent, he was already speaking of international conspiracies between supporters of Trotsky and various foreign powers. It was obvious, Stalin proclaimed, that "as long as the capitalist encirclement exists there will continue to be present among us wreckers, spies, saboteurs and murderers." Any problem with Soviet policies was the fault of reactionary states that wished to slow the proper course of history. Any seeming flaws of the Five-Year Plan were a result of foreign intervention: hence the harshest of penalties was justified for traitors, and the blame always resided in Warsaw, Tokyo, Berlin, London, or Paris.[27]

In these years, Stalinism thus involved a kind of double bluff. The success of the Popular Front depended on a record of progress toward socialism that was largely a matter of propaganda. Meanwhile, the explanation of famine and misery at home depended upon the idea of foreign subversion, which was essentially without merit. Atop the Soviet party apparatus and atop the Communist International, Stalin was making these two bluffs simultaneously, and he knew just how they could be called: by a foreign military intervention by a state crafty enough to enlist Soviet citizens who had suffered under his policies. The power of the combination of foreign war and domestic opposition was, after all, the first lesson of Soviet history. Lenin himself had been a German secret weapon in the First World War; the Bolshevik Revolution itself was a side effect of the

German foreign policy of 1917. Twenty years later, Stalin had to fear that his opponents within the Soviet Union would use a coming war to overthrow his own regime. Trotsky was in emigration, just as Lenin had been in 1917. During a war Trotsky might come back and rally his supporters, just as Lenin had done twenty years before.[28]

By 1937 Stalin faced no meaningful political opposition within the Soviet communist party, but this only seemed to convince him that his enemies had learned political invisibility. Just as he had during the height of the famine, he argued again that year that the most dangerous enemies of the state appeared to be harmless and loyal. All enemies, even the invisible ones, would have to be unmasked and eradicated. On 7 November 1937, the twentieth anniversary of the Bolshevik Revolution (and the fifth anniversary of his wife's suicide), Stalin raised a toast: "We will mercilessly destroy anyone who, by his deeds or his thoughts—yes, his thoughts!—threatens the unity of the socialist state. To the complete destruction of all enemies, themselves and their kin!"[29]

Unlike Hitler, Stalin had at his disposal the tool to effect such a policy: the state police once known as the Cheka and the OGPU, and by this time called the NKVD. The Soviet state police had arisen during the Bolshevik Revolution itself, when it was known as the Cheka. Its mission at the beginning had been more political than legal: the elimination of opponents of the revolution. Once the Soviet Union was established, the Cheka (OGPU, NKVD) became a massive state police force that was charged with the enforcement of Soviet law. In situations regarded as exceptional, such as collectivization in 1930, normal legal procedures were suspended, and OGPU officers (leading troikas) in effect served as judges, juries, and executioners. This was a return to the revolutionary tradition of the Cheka, and was justified by the presence of a revolutionary situation: either an advance toward or a threat to socialism. In order to be in a position to crush the enemies of his choice in the second half of the 1930s, Stalin would need the NKVD to recognize that some sort of crisis was under way, one that required this sort of special measure.[30]

A dramatic murder gave Stalin the opportunity to assert control over the NKVD. In December 1934 one of Stalin's closest comrades, Sergei Kirov, was assassinated in Leningrad. Stalin exploited the Kirov assassination much as Hitler had used the Reichstag fire the previous year. He blamed internal political opponents for the murder, and claimed that they planned further terrorist attacks against Soviet leaders. Although the assassin, Leonid Nikolaev, was arrested the day the crime was committed, Stalin would not be satisfied with a simple police action. He forced through a special law allowing for the swift execution of "terrorists." Emphasizing the threat of terrorism, he declared that his former politburo opponents on the left plotted the murder of the Soviet leadership and the overthrow of Soviet power.[31]

Stalin's interpretation of the Leningrad murder was a direct challenge to the Soviet state police. His was not a theory that the NKVD was inclined to accept, not least because there was no evidence. When the NKVD chief Genrikh Yagoda dared to make inquiries of Stalin, he was told that he should beware, lest he be "slapped down." Stalin found a confederate, Nikolai Yezhov, who was willing to propagate Stalin's version of events. Yezhov, a diminutive man from the Polish-Lithuanian borderlands, was already known for his view that opposition was simultaneous with terrorism. In February 1935 he took charge of a "control commission" that collected compromising information about members of the central committee for the benefit of the politburo. Stalin and Yezhov seemed to reinforce each other's beliefs in ubiquitous conspiracies. Stalin came to rely on Yezhov, even going so far, in a rare sign of intimacy, as to express concern about Yezhov's health. Yezhov first became Yagoda's deputy, then his replacement. In September 1936 Yezhov become commissar of internal affairs, chief of the NKVD. Yagoda was first appointed to another post, then executed two years later.[32]

Beginning in August 1936, Yezhov charged Stalin's former political opponents with fantastic offenses in public show trials. The confessions of these famous men drew the attention of the world. Lev Kamenev and Grigory Zinoviev, once Trotsky's allies and Stalin's opponents, were tried between 19 and 24 August. They confessed to participation in a terrorist plot to murder Stalin and, along with fourteen other men, were sentenced to death and executed. These old Bolsheviks had been intimidated and beaten, and were doing little more than uttering lines from a script. But their confessions, which were widely believed, provided a kind of alternative history of the Soviet Union, one in which Stalin had always been right. In the show trials to come, Stalin even followed the rhythm of the late 1920s: having dealt with his one-time opponents from the left, Kamenev and Zinoviev, he turned against his one-time opponent from the right, Nikolai Bukharin. Back when debate had still been possible, in 1928, Bukharin threatened to call Stalin an organizer of famine. Though he never fulfilled this threat, he died anyway. Trotsky, who could not be show-tried because he was abroad, was supposedly the ringleader. The party newspaper, *Pravda*, made the connection clear in a headline of 22 August 1936: "Trotsky-Zinoviev-Kamenev-Gestapo." Could the three Bolsheviks in question, men who had built the Soviet Union, truly be paid agents of capitalist powers? Were these three communists of Jewish origin likely agents of the secret state police of Nazi Germany? They were not, but the charge was taken seriously, even outside the Soviet Union.[33]

For many Europeans and Americans, the show trials were simply trials, and confessions were reliable evidence of guilt. Some observers who were sympathetic to the Soviet Union saw them as a positive development: the British socialist Beatrice Webb, for example, was pleased that Stalin had "cut out the dead wood." Other Soviet sympathizers no doubt suppressed their suspicions, on the logic that the USSR was the enemy of Nazi Germany and thus the hope of civilization. European public opinion was so polarized by 1936 that it was indeed difficult to criticize the Soviet regime without seeming to endorse fascism and Hitler. This, of course, was the shared binary logic of National Socialism and the Popular Front: Hitler called his enemies "Marxists," and Stalin called his "fascists."[34] They agreed that there was no middle ground.

Stalin appointed Yezhov just as he decided to intervene in Spain; the show trials and the Popular Front were, from his perspective, the same policy. The Popular Front allowed for the definition of friends and enemies, subject of course to the changing line from Moscow. Like any opening to noncommunist political forces, it demanded great vigilance, both at home and abroad. For Stalin, the Spanish Civil War was simultaneously a battle against armed fascism in Spain and its foreign supporters, and a struggle against left-wing and internal enemies. He believed that the Spanish government was weak because it was unable to find and kill enough spies and traitors. The Soviet Union was both a state and a vision, both a domestic political system and an internationalist ideology. Its foreign policy was always domestic policy, and its domestic policy was always foreign policy. That was its strength and its weakness.[35]

As Orwell perceived, the public Soviet story of a clash with European fascism coincided with the blood purge of past or potential opponents at home. Soviet missions were installed in Barcelona and Madrid just as the show trials began. The encounter with fascism in Spain justified vigilance in the Soviet Union, and the purges in the Soviet Union justified vigilance in Spain. The Spanish Civil War revealed that Stalin was determined, despite the Popular Front rhetoric of pluralism, to eliminate opposition to his version of socialism. Orwell watched as the communists provoked clashes in Barcelona in May 1937, and then as the Spanish government, beholden to Moscow, banned the Trotskyite party. As Orwell wrote of that skirmish in Barcelona: "This squalid brawl in a distant city is more important than might appear at first." He was exactly right. Stalin thought that Barcelona had revealed a fascist fifth column. The event revealed the single powerful Stalinist logic, defying geography and local political reality. It was the subject of a moving chapter in his *Homage to Catalonia*, the war memoir that taught at least some Western leftists and democrats that fascism was not the only enemy.[36]

Within the Soviet Union, the confessions of the show trials seemed to create evidence of organized conspiracies, which Yezhov called "centers," backed by foreign intelligence agencies. In late June 1937 in Moscow, Yezhov informed the central committee of the party of the conclusions that he had drawn. There was, Yezhov announced to the party elite, one master conspiracy, a "Center of Centers," that embraced all of the political opponents, the armed forces, and even the NKVD. Its aim was nothing less than the destruction of the Soviet Union and the restoration of capitalism on its territories. The agents of the "Center of Centers" would stop at nothing, including the castration of prize sheep—an act of sabotage Yezhov specifically mentioned. All of this justified purges within the party, the army, and the NKVD. Eight high commanders of the armed forces were show-tried that same month; about half of the generals of the Red Army would be executed in the months to come. Of the 139 members of the central committee who took part in the party congress of 1934 (the Congress of Victors), some 98 were shot. All in all, the purification of the armed forces, state institutions, and the communist party led to about fifty thousand executions.[37]

During these same years, 1934–1937, Hitler was also using violence to assert his control over the institutions of power: the party, the police, and the military. Like Stalin, he revisited his own rise to power, and visited death upon some of the people who had aided him. Although the scale of the murder was far smaller, Hitler's purges clarified that the rule of law in Germany was subject to the whims of the Leader. Unlike Stalin, who had to subordinate the NKVD to his own authority, Hitler ordered terror as a way to develop his own favored paramilitary, the SS, and assert its superiority over the various German state police forces. Whereas Stalin used his purges to intimidate the Soviet armed forces, Hitler actually drew the German generals closer to his person by killing a Nazi that the army high command regarded as a threat.

The most prominent target of Hitler's purge was Ernst Röhm, the leader of one of the Nazi paramilitaries, the SA brownshirts. The SA had helped Hitler assert his personal authority, to intimidate opponents (and voters), and to come to power in 1933. The streetfighting of the SA was less useful to Hitler as chancellor than it had been for Hitler as politician. Röhm spoke in 1933 and 1934 of the need for a second revolution, an idea that Hitler rejected. Röhm also nurtured personal ambitions that ill fit Hitler's plans to rebuild the German military. Röhm portrayed his SA as a better reflection of the Nazi spirit than the German armed forces, which he wished to control himself. His three million SA brownshirts far outnumbered the hundred thousand soldiers permitted to the German armed forces by the Treaty of Versailles. Hitler meant to break those treaty obligations, but by rebuilding the German army rather than by replacing or merging it with a paramilitary.[38]

In late June 1934 Hitler ordered the SS to murder Röhm and several dozen of his associates, as well as other rivals within the Nazi movement and a few other politicians. The SS was led by Heinrich Himmler, who emphasized racial purity, ideological training, and personal loyalty to Hitler. In what came to be known as the "Night of the Long Knives," Hitler was using one of the Nazi paramilitaries, the SS, to master the other, the SA. He was endorsing Himmler's work, and putting an end to Röhm—and dozens of other people. Hitler told the parliament on 14 July 1935 that seventy-four men had been killed; the true number was at least eighty-five, several of whom were (Nazi) parliamentary deputies. He claimed, naturally, that Röhm and the others had been planning a coup against his legitimate government, and had to be stopped in advance. In addition to the SA leadership, Hitler's blood purge had reached conservatives and former heads of government. Of the three chancellors who had preceded him, one was murdered, one was arrested, and the third fled.[39]

Because the SS was the chosen instrument of the murder campaign, Himmler moved closer to the center of power. The SS, now separated institutionally from the SA, became the most powerful institution within the National Socialist party. After the Night of the Long Knives, its task would be to subordinate the many German police institutions to Nazi ideology. Himmler would seek to merge his SS with Germany's established police forces by way of rotation of personnel and institutional centralization under his personal command. In 1936 Hitler named Himmler the Chief of German Police. This placed him in charge of the uniformed men of the Order Police, the detectives of the Criminal Police, and the operatives of the Secret State Police (Gestapo). The police was a state institution (or rather comprised a number of different state institutions) and the SS was a Nazi party institution; Himmler sought to bring the two together. In 1937, Himmler established the office of Higher SS and Police Leaders, regional chiefs who in theory commanded both SS and police forces, and unified the hierarchy of command.[40]

Just as important as the elevation of the SS over the SA was the improvement of relations between Hitler and the generals. The execution of Röhm earned Hitler a debt of gratitude from the army high command. Until 1934, the army had been the only important state institution that Hitler had not fully mastered. Once Hitler showed that he planned to rebuild the army rather than overwhelm it with the SA, this quickly changed. When the German president died a few weeks later, the military endorsed Hitler's elevation to head of state. Hitler would never claim the title "president"; he preferred "Leader." From August 1934, German soldiers swore an unconditional oath of personal loyalty to Hitler, and thenceforth addressed him as "My Leader." Later that month Hitler's titles as "Leader and Reich Chancellor" were confirmed by national plebiscite. In March 1935, Hitler publically renounced Germany's commitments under the Versailles Treaty, reintroduced military conscription, and began to rebuild the German armed forces.[41]

Like Stalin, Hitler showed himself to be the master of the organs of power, presenting himself as the victim of plots, and then ridding himself of real or imagined rivals. Simultaneously, however, Hitler was creating the kinds of instruments of coercion that Stalin had inherited from Lenin and the Bolshevik Revolution. The SS and the German police would never be capable of organized terror within Germany on the scale of the NKVD in the Soviet Union. The Night of the Long Knives, with its dozens of victims, was dwarfed by the Soviet purges of the party, armed forces, and NKVD, in which tens of thousands of people were executed. That was far more people than the Nazi regime would kill before the Second World War. The SS would need time and practice before it could rival the NKVD. Himmler saw his charges as "ideological soldiers," but they would fulfill their mission of racial conquest and domination only at the backs of true soldiers: behind the lines in Poland after 1939, or in the Soviet Union after 1941.[42]

The logic of Hitler's domestic terror was of a future offensive war: fought by an expanded Wehrmacht loyal to Hitler, transformed into a war of destruction by the SS and the police. In this one sense, Stalin's fears of war were perfectly justified. The Germans, however, were not counting on help from the Soviet population in that coming war. In this respect, Stalin's scenario of threat, the union of foreign enemies with domestic opponents, was quite wrong. Thus the still greater terror that Stalin would unleash upon his own population in 1937 and 1938 was entirely fruitless, and indeed counterproductive.

The Soviet purges within the army, party, and NKVD were the prelude to Stalin's Great Terror, which in 1937 and 1938 would take the lives of hundreds of thousands of people for reasons of class and nation. The interrogations of tens of thousands of people during the purges generated a multitude of "organizations," "plots," and "groups"—categories into which more and more Soviet citizens could fall. The executions of communist party members no doubt gave rise to fears within the communist party; but the party would generally be spared, if its members followed Stalin's lead in summer 1937 and agreed to pursue the true enemies within the mass of Soviet society. The purges also tested the loyalty of the NKVD, as its leadership was changed at the whim of Stalin, and its officers were forced to watch as their colleagues were purged. Yet in summer 1937 the besieged NKVD would be turned against social groups that many of its officers were ready to define as enemies. For months the top leadership of the Soviet Union had been plotting a blow against a group that they perhaps did fear: the kulaks.[43]

The kulaks were peasants, the stubborn survivors of Stalin's revolution: of collectivization and famine, and very often of the Gulag. As a social class, the kulak (prosperous peasant) never really existed; the term was rather a Soviet classification that took on a political life of its own. The attempt to "liquidate the kulaks" during the first Five-Year Plan had killed a tremendous number of people, but it created rather than destroyed a class: those who had been stigmatized and repressed, but who had survived. The millions of people who were deported or who fled during collectivization were forever after regarded as kulaks, and sometimes accepted the classification. What Soviet leaders had to consider was the possibility that the revolution itself had created its own opponents. At the plenum of the central committee of the communist party in February and March 1937, several speakers drew the logical conclusions. "Alien elements" were corrupting the pure proletariat of the cities. The kulaks were "impassioned enemies" of the Soviet system.[44]

To be a kulak was not only to have suffered, it was to have survived movement across vast distances. Collectivization had forced millions of kulaks into the Gulag or into the cities. This meant journeys of hundreds or even thousands of miles. Some three million peasants, at least, had become paid laborers during the first Five-Year Plan. That, after all, was the Plan: that the Soviet Union would be transformed from an agrarian to an industrial country. Perhaps two hundred thousand people who would have been stigmatized as kulaks had made for the cities before they could be executed or deported. About four hundred thousand kulaks had managed to flee the special settlements, some for the cities, more for the countryside. Tens of thousands more had been allowed to leave concentration camps and the special settlements after serving their terms. Five-year Gulag sentences in 1930, 1931, and 1932 meant mass releases of Gulag survivors in 1935, 1936, and 1937.[45]

The optimistic assumption had been that the movement and the punishment would strip the kulak of his harmful social origins, and make of him a Soviet person. By the second half of the 1930s, Stalinism had shed any such expectations of progress. The very social mobility intrinsic to his policy of industrialization was now unsettling. Kulaks were rejoining the collective farms: perhaps they would lead rebellions, as other peasants had done in 1930. The kulaks were returning to a social order that was traditional in many ways. Stalin knew, from the 1937 census that he suppressed, that a majority of adults still defied the atheism of the Soviet state and believed in God. Twenty years after the Bolshevik Revolution, religious faith was perplexing, and perhaps unnerving. Could the kulaks rebuild the society that once had been?[46]

The kulaks sentenced later or to longer terms in the Gulag were still in exile in Siberia or Kazakhstan, in Soviet east or central Asia: might not such people support a Japanese invasion? The NKVD reported in June 1937 that exiled kulaks in Siberia constituted a "broad base on which to build an insurgent rebellion." Surely, given the support of a foreign power and the cover of war, the kulaks would fight against Soviet power. In the meantime, they were the enemy within. One repressive policy created the foundations for another: exiled kulaks did not love the Soviet system; and their place of exile, so far from their homes, was close to a source of foreign threat, the expanding Japanese empire.[47]

Reports from the NKVD in the Far East provided the scenario for an alliance between internal opponents and a foreign power. In April 1937 riots had broken out against the Soviet presence in the Chinese province of Xinjiang. In the Japanese puppet state Manchukuo, the Japanese were recruiting Russian émigrés, who were making contact with kulaks in exile throughout Siberia. According to the NKVD, a "Russian General Military Union," backed by Japan, planned to incite exiled kulaks to rebel when Japan invaded. In June 1937 the regional NKVD received permission to carry out mass arrests and executions of people suspected of collaborating with the "Russian General Military Union." The targets of the operation were to be exiled kulaks and the former Russian imperial officers who supposedly commanded them. Naturally, the former were in much greater supply than the latter. And so began the killing of the kulaks, in their Siberian exile.[48]

Soviet leaders always regarded the Japanese threat as the eastern half of a global capitalist encirclement involving Poland and Nazi Germany. Preparations for a war against Japan in Asia were also preparations for a war in Europe. Precisely because many kulaks were returning home at this time from Soviet Asia to Soviet Europe, it was possible to imagine networks of enemies that extended from one end of the Soviet Union to the other. Though the shooting of peasants began in Siberia, Stalin apparently decided to punish kulaks not only in eastern exile but throughout the Soviet Union.

In a telegram entitled "On Anti-Soviet Elements," Stalin and the politburo issued general instructions on 2 July 1937 for mass repressions in every region of the Soviet Union. The Soviet leadership held kulaks responsible for recent waves of sabotage and criminality, which meant in effect anything that had gone wrong within the Soviet Union. The politburo ordered the provincial offices of the NKVD to register all kulaks who resided in their regions, and to recommend quotas for execution and deportation. Most regional NKVD officers asked to be allowed to add various "anti-Soviet elements" to the lists. By 11 July the polit-buro already had a first round of lists of people to be repressed. At Stalin's ini-tiative, these initial numbers were rounded up, adding "an extra thousand." This raised the stakes of the operation, sending a clear signal to the state police that they were to do more than simply sentence all of the people on whom they al-ready had files. In order to demonstrate their diligence in a climate of threats and purges, NKVD officers would have to find still more victims.[49]

Stalin and Yezhov wanted "the direct physical liquidation of the entire counter-revolution," which meant the elimination of enemies "once and for all." The revised quotas were sent back down from Moscow to the regions as part of Order 00447, dated 31 July 1937, "On the Operations to Repress Former Kulaks, Criminals, and Other Anti-Soviet Elements." Here Stalin and Yezhov anticipated the execution of 79,950 Soviet citizens by shooting and the sentencing of 193,000 more to eight to ten years in the Gulag. It was not that the politburo or the NKVD central office in Moscow had 272,950 particular people in mind for repression. Just which Soviet citizens would fulfill these quotas remained to be seen; the local NKVD branches would decide that.[50]

The killing and imprisonment quotas were officially called "limits," though everyone involved knew that they were meant to be exceeded. Local NKVD offi-cers had to explain why they could not meet a "limit," and were encouraged to exceed them. No NKVD officer wished to be seen as lacking élan when con-fronting "counter-revolution," especially when Yezhov's line was "better too far than not far enough." Not 79,950 but five times as many people would be shot in the kulak action. By the end of 1938, the NKVD had executed some 386,798 Soviet citizens in fulfillment of Order 00447.[51]

Order 00447 was to be implemented by the same institution that had brought ter-ror to the Soviet countryside in the early 1930s: the three-person commission, or troika. Composed of a regional NKVD chief, a regional party leader, and a regional prosecutor, the troikas were responsible for transforming the quotas into execu-tions, the numbers into bodies. The overall quota for the Soviet Union was divided among sixty-four regions, each with a corresponding troika. In practice, the troikas were dominated by the NKVD chiefs, who usually chaired the meetings.

Prosecutors had been ordered to ignore legal procedures. Party chiefs had other responsibilities, were not experts on security matters, and were afraid that they might themselves be targeted. NKVD chiefs were in their element.[52]

The fulfillment of Order 00447 began with the emptying of the file cabinets. The NKVD had some sort of material on kulaks, since *kulak* was a category created by the state. Criminals, the second group mentioned in the order, were by definition people who had an encounter with the judicial system behind them. In practical terms, the other "anti-Soviet elements" named in the order were simply the people on whom the local NKVD had a file. Local NKVD officers, helped by police, carried out investigations in "operational sectors" within each of the sixty-four zones. An "operational group" assembled a list of people to be interrogated. Those targeted were arrested, forced to confess, and encouraged to implicate others.[53]

Confessions were elicited by torture. The NKVD and other police organs applied the "conveyer method," which meant uninterrupted questioning, day and night. This was complemented by the "standing method," in which suspects were forced to stand in a line near a wall, and beaten if they touched it or fell asleep. Under time pressure to make quotas, officers often simply beat prisoners until they confessed. Stalin authorized this on 21 July 1937. In Soviet Belarus, interrogating officers would hold prisoners' heads down in the latrine and then beat them when they tried to rise. Some interrogators carried with them draft confessions, and simply filled in the prisoner's personal details and changed an item here or there by hand. Others simply forced prisoners to sign blank pages and then filled them in later at leisure. In this way Soviet organs "unmasked" the "enemy," delivering his "thoughts" to the files.[54]

The numbers came down from the center, but the corpses were made locally. The troikas who fulfilled Order 00447 were responsible for sentencing the prisoners, with no need for any confirmation from Moscow, and no possibility for appeal. The three members of a troika would meet at night with investigating officers. For each case they would hear a very brief report, along with a recommendation for sentencing: death or the Gulag. (Only a very few of those arrested were not sentenced at all.) The troikas would almost always accept these recommendations. They handled hundreds of cases at a time, at a pace of sixty per hour or more; the life or death of an individual human was decided in a minute or less. In a single night the Leningrad troika, for example, sentenced to death 658 prisoners of the concentration camp at Solovki.[55]

Terror prevailed in the Gulag, as everywhere else. It might be difficult to see how concentration camp inmates could threaten the Soviet state: but like the regions of the USSR, the Gulag system had its own death quota, to be met or exceeded. Just as people who had been defined as kulaks might be dangerous, so might people who were incarcerated as kulaks—so went the logic. The camps of the Gulag had an initial quota of ten thousand executions, though in the end 30,178 of its prisoners were shot. Omsk, a southwest Siberian city whose environs were full of special settlers deported during collectivization, was the site of some of the most vicious campaigns. Its NKVD chief had already requested an additional quota of eight thousand executions on 1 August 1937, before Order 00447 even went into effect. His men once sentenced 1,301 people in a single night.[56]

This kulak operation was carried out in secret. No one, including the condemned, was told of the sentences. Those sentenced would simply be taken, first to some sort of prison, and then either to a freight car or an execution site. Execution facilities were built or chosen with an eye to discretion. Killings were always carried out at night, and in seclusion. They took place in soundproofed rooms below ground, in large buildings such as garages where noise could cover gunshots, or far from human settlement in forests. The executioners were always NKVD officers, generally using a Nagan pistol. While two men held a prisoner by his arms, the executioner would fire a single shot from behind into the base of the skull, and then often a "control shot" into the temple. "After the executions," one set of instructions specified, "the bodies are to be laid in a pit dug beforehand, then carefully buried and the pit is to be camouflaged." As the winter of 1937 came and the ground froze, the pits were prepared using explosives. Everyone who took part in these operations was sworn to secrecy. Only a very few people were directly involved. A team of just twelve Moscow NKVD men shot 20,761 people at Butovo, on the outskirts of Moscow, in 1937 and 1938.[57]

The kulak operation involved shooting from the beginning to the end: Yezhov reported to Stalin, with evident pride, that 35,454 people had been shot by 7 September 1937. During the year 1937, however, the number of Gulag sentences exceeded the number of death sentences. As time passed, new allocations tended to be for executions rather than exile. In the end, the number of people killed in the kulak operation was about the same as the number sent to the Gulag (378,326 and 389,070, respectively). The overall shift from exile to execution was for practical reasons: it was easier to kill than to deport, and the camps quickly filled to capacity—and had little use for many of the deportees. One investigation in Leningrad led to the shooting (not the deportation) of thirty-five people who were deaf and dumb. In Soviet Ukraine, the NKVD chief Izrail Leplevskii ordered his officers to shoot rather than exile the elderly. In such cases, Soviet citizens were killed because of who they were.[58]

Soviet Ukraine, where "kulak resistance" had been widespread during collectivization, was a major center of the killing. Leplevskii expanded the framework of Order 00447 to include supposed Ukrainian nationalists, who since the famine had been treated as a threat to the territorial integrity of the Soviet Union. Some 40,530 people in Soviet Ukraine were arrested on the charge of nationalism. In one variant, Ukrainians were arrested for supposedly having requested food aid from Germany in 1933. When the (already-twice-increased) quotas for Soviet Ukraine were fulfilled in December 1937, Leplevskii asked for more. In February 1938 Yezhov added 23,650 to the death quota for the republic. All in all, in 1937 and 1938, NKVD men shot 70,868 inhabitants of Soviet Ukraine in the kulak operation. The ratio of shootings to other sentences was especially high in Soviet Ukraine during the year 1938. Between January and August, some 35,563 people were shot, as against only 830 sent to camps. The troika for the Stalino district, for example, met seven times between July and September 1938, and sentenced to death every single one of the 1,102 people accused. The troika in Voroshilovgrad, similarly, sentenced to death all 1,226 people whose cases it reviewed in September 1938.[59]

These tremendous numbers meant regular and massive executions, over enormous and numerous death pits. In Soviet Ukrainian industrial cities, workers with real or imagined kulak backgrounds were sentenced to death for some sort of sabotage, and typically killed the same day. In Vinnytsia, people sentenced to death were tied, gagged, and driven to a car wash. There a truck awaited, its engine running to cover the sound of the gunshots. The bodies were then placed in the truck and driven to a site in the city: an orchard, perhaps, or a park, or a cemetery. Before their work was done, the NKVD men had dug no fewer than eighty-seven mass graves in and around Vinnytsia.[60]

Like the show trials, the kulak operation allowed Stalin to relive the years of the late 1920s and early 1930s, the period of his true political vulnerability, this time with a predictable outcome. The former political opponents, representing the moment of political debate over collectivization, were physically eliminated. So were the kulaks, standing for the moment of mass resistance to collectivization. Just as the murder of party elites confirmed Stalin's succession of Lenin, so the murder of kulaks confirmed his interpretation of Lenin's policies. If collectivization had led to mass starvation, that had been the fault of those who starved and the foreign intelligence agencies who somehow arranged the whole thing. If collectivization had given rise to a sense of grievance among the population, that too was the fault of the very people who had suffered and their supposed foreign sponsors. Precisely because Stalin's policy was so disastrous in the first place, its defense seemed to require such tortured logic and massive death. Once these measures had been taken, they could be presented as the verdict of history.[61]

Yet even as Stalin presented his own policies as inevitable, he was abandoning (without admitting anything of the kind) the Marxism that allowed leaders to discuss and pretend to know the future. Insofar as Marxism was a science of history, its natural world was the economy, and its object of investigation the social class. Even in the harshest of Leninist interpretations of Marxism, people opposed the revolution because of their class background. Yet with Stalinism something was changing; normal state security concerns had infused the Marxist language and changed it unalterably. The accused in the show trials had supposedly betrayed the Soviet Union to foreign powers. Theirs was a class struggle, according to the accusation, only in the most indirect and attenuated sense: they supposedly had aided states that represented the imperialist states that encircled the homeland of socialism.

Although the kulak action was at first glance a class terror, the killing was sometimes directed, as in Soviet Ukraine, against "nationalists." Here, too, Stalinism was introducing something new. In Lenin's adaptation of Marxism, nationalities were supposed to embrace the Soviet project, as their social advance coincided with the construction of the Soviet state. Thus the peasant question was initially linked to the national question in a positive way: people rising from the peasantry into the working or clerical or professional classes would come to national awareness as loyal Soviet citizens. Now, under Stalin, the peasant question was linked to the national question in a negative sense. The attainment of Ukrainian national consciousness by Ukrainian peasants was dangerous. Other, smaller national minorities were more threatening still. Most of the victims of Order 00447 in Soviet Ukraine were Ukrainians; but a disproportionate number were Poles. Here the connection between class and nation was perhaps most explicit. In a kind of operational shorthand, NKVD officers said: "Once a Pole, always a kulak."[62]

The Nazi terror of 1936–1938 proceeded along somewhat similar lines, usually punishing members of politically defined social groups for what they were, rather than individuals for anything that they might have done. For the Nazis the most important category were the "asocials," groups that were thought to be (and sometimes truly were) resistant to the Nazi worldview. These were homosexuals, vagrants, and people who were thought to be alcoholic, addicted to drugs, or unwilling to work. They were also Jehovah's Witnesses, who rejected the premises of the Nazi worldview with strikingly greater clarity than most other German Christians. The Nazi leadership regarded such people as racially German but corrupt, and thus to be improved by confinement and punishment. Like the Soviet NKVD, the German police carried out organized raids of districts in 1937 and 1938, seeking to meet a numerical quota of specified sectors of the population. They, too, often overfulfilled these quotas in their zealous desire to prove loyalty and impress superiors. The outcome of arrests, however, was different: almost always confinement, very rarely execution.[63]

The Nazi repression of these undesirable social groups required the creation of a network of German concentration camps. To the camps at Dachau and Lichtenberg, both established in 1933, were added Sachsenhausen (1936), Buchenwald (1937), and Flossenberg (1938). By comparison with the Gulag, these five camps were rather modest. While more than a million Soviet citizens toiled in the Soviet concentration camps and special settlements in late 1938, the number of German citizens in the German concentration camps was about twenty thousand. When the difference in population size is taken into account, the Soviet system of concentration camps was about twenty-five times larger than the German one at this time.[64]

Soviet terror, at this point, was not only on a far greater scale; it was incomparably more lethal. Nothing in Hitler's Germany remotely resembled the execution of nearly four hundred thousand people in eighteen months, as under Order 00447 in the Soviet Union. In the years 1937 and 1938, 267 people were sentenced to death in Nazi Germany, as compared to 378,326 death sentences within the kulak operation alone in the Soviet Union. Again, given the difference in population size, the chances that a Soviet citizen would be executed in the kulak action were about seven hundred times greater than the chances that a German citizen would be sentenced to death in Nazi Germany for any offense.[65]

After a purge of the leadership and an assertion of dominance over the key institutions, both Stalin and Hitler carried out social cleansings in 1937 and 1938. But the kulak action was not the entirety of the Great Terror. It could be seen, or at least presented, as class war. But even as the Soviet Union was killing class enemies, it was also killing ethnic enemies.

By the late 1930s, Hitler's National Socialist regime was well known for its racism and anti-Semitism. But it was Stalin's Soviet Union that undertook the first shooting campaigns of internal national enemies.

CHAPTER 3

NATIONAL TERROR

People belonging to national minorities "should be forced to their knees and shot like mad dogs." It was not an SS officer speaking but a communist party leader, in the spirit of the national operations of Stalin's Great Terror. In 1937 and 1938, a quarter of a million Soviet citizens were shot on essentially ethnic grounds. The Five-Year Plans were supposed to move the Soviet Union toward a flowering of national cultures under socialism. In fact, the Soviet Union in the late 1930s was a land of unequalled national persecutions. Even as the Popular Front presented the Soviet Union as the homeland of toleration, Stalin ordered the mass killing of several Soviet nationalities. The most persecuted European national minority in the second half of the 1930s was not the four hundred thousand or so German Jews (the number declining because of emigration) but the six hundred thousand or so Soviet Poles (the number declining because of executions).[1]

Stalin was a pioneer of national mass murder, and the Poles were the preeminent victim among the Soviet nationalities. The Polish national minority, like the kulaks, had to take the blame for the failures of collectivization. The rationale was invented during the famine itself in 1933, and then applied during the Great Terror in 1937 and 1938. In 1933, the NKVD chief for Ukraine, Vsevolod Balytskyi, had explained the mass starvation as a provocation of an espionage cabal that he called the "Polish Military Organization." According to Balytskyi, this "Polish Military Organization" had infiltrated the Ukrainian branch of the communist party, and backed Ukrainian and Polish nationalists who sabotaged the harvest and then used the starving bodies of Ukrainian peasants as anti-Soviet propaganda. It had supposedly inspired a nationalist "Ukrainian Military Organization," a doppelganger performing the same fell work and sharing responsibility for the famine.[2]

This was a historically inspired invention. There was no Polish Military Organization during the 1930s, in Soviet Ukraine or anywhere else. It had once existed, back during the Polish-Bolshevik War of 1919–1920, as a reconnaissance group for the Polish Army. The Polish Military Organization had been overmastered by the Cheka, and was dissolved in 1921. Balytskyi knew the history, since he had taken part in the deconspiracy and the destruction of the Polish Military Organization back then. In the 1930s Polish spies played no political role in Soviet Ukraine. They lacked the capacity to do so even in 1930 and 1931 when the USSR was most vulnerable, and they could still run agents across the border. They lacked the intention to intervene after the Soviet-Polish nonaggression pact was initialed in January 1932. After the famine, they generally lost any remaining confidence about their ability to understand the Soviet system, much less change it. Polish spies were shocked by the mass starvation when it came, and unable to formulate a response. Precisely because there was no real Polish threat in 1933, Balytskyi had been able to manipulate the symbols of Polish espionage as he wished. This was typical Stalinism: it was always easier to exploit the supposed actions of an "organization" that did not exist.[3]

The "Polish Military Organization," Balytskyi had argued back in summer 1933, had smuggled into the Soviet Union countless agents who pretended to be communists fleeing persecution in their Polish homeland. In fact, communism was marginal and illegal in Poland, and Polish communists saw the Soviet Union as their natural place of refuge. Although Polish military intelligence doubtless tried to recruit Polish communists, most of the Polish leftists who came to the Soviet Union were simply political refugees. The arrests of Polish political émigrés in the Soviet Union began in July 1933. The Polish communist playwright Witold Wandurski was jailed in August 1933, and forced to confess to participation in the Polish Military Organization. With this link between Polish communism and Polish espionage documented in interrogation protocols, more Polish communists were arrested in the USSR. The Polish communist Jerzy Sochacki left a message in his own blood before jumping to his death from a Moscow prison in 1933: "I am faithful to the party to the end."[4]

The "Polish Military Organization" provided a rationale for the scapegoating of Poles for Soviet policy failures. After the signing of the German-Polish nonaggression declaration in January 1934, Poles were blamed not only for the famine but also for the worsening of the Soviet international position. That month Balytskyi blamed the "Polish Military Organization" for the continuation of Ukrainian nationalism. In March 1934 in Soviet Ukraine, some 10,800 Soviet citizens of Polish or German nationality were arrested. In 1935, as the level of NKVD activity decreased in the Soviet Union as a whole, it continued to increase in Soviet Ukraine, with special attention to Soviet Poles. In February and March 1935, some 41,650 Poles, Germans, and kulaks were resettled from western to eastern Ukraine. Between June and September 1936, some 69,283 people, for the most part Soviet Poles, were deported from Ukraine to Kazakhstan. Polish diplomats were confused by these developments. Poland was pursuing a policy of equal distance between the Soviet Union and Nazi Germany: nonaggression agreements with both, alliances with neither.[5]

The "Polish Military Organization," conjured up during the famine in 1933, was sustained as pure bureaucratic fantasy in Soviet Ukraine, then adapted to justify a national terror of Poles throughout the Soviet Union. Stalin gave a first cue in December 1934, asking that the Pole Jerzy Sosnowski be removed from the NKVD. Sosnowski, long before a member of the Polish Military Organization, had been turned by the Cheka and had worked productively for the Soviets for more than a decade. In part because the Soviet state police had been founded by a Polish communist, Feliks Dzierżyński, many of its most prominent officers were Poles, often people recruited in those early days. Yezhov, the NKVD chief, seems to have been threatened by these veteran Polish officers; he was certainly obsessed with Poles generally. Inclined to believe in intricate plots orchestrated by foreign intelligence agencies, he gave pride of place to Poland because Poles, in his view, "know everything." The investigation of Sosnowski, who was arrested in December 1936, might have brought the historical Polish Military Organization to Yezhov's attention.[6]

Yezhov followed Balytskyi's anti-Polish campaign in Soviet Ukraine, and then reconceptualized it. As the show trials began in Moscow in 1936, Yezhov drew his subordinate Balytskyi into a trap. While prominent communists confessed in Moscow, Balytskyi was reporting from Kiev that the "Polish Military Organization" had been re-created in Soviet Ukraine. No doubt he simply wished to claim attention and resources for himself and his local apparatus at a time of security panic. Yet now, in a turn of events that must have surprised Balytskyi, Yezhov declared that the "Polish Military Organization" was an even *greater* danger than Balytskyi claimed. It was a matter not for the regional NKVD in Kiev but for the central NKVD in Moscow. Balytskyi, who had invented the plot of the "Polish Military Organization," now lost control of the story. Soon a confession was extracted from the Polish communist Tomasz Dąbal, who claimed to have directed the "Polish Military Organization" in the entire Soviet Union.[7]

Thanks to Yezhov's initiative, the "Polish Military Organization" lost any residue of its historical and regional origins, and became simply a threat to the Soviet Union as such. On 16 January 1937 Yezhov presented his theory of a grand Polish conspiracy to Stalin, and then with Stalin's approval to a plenum of the central committee. In March Yezhov purged the NKVD of Polish officers. Although Balytskyi was not Polish but Ukrainian by nationality, he now found himself in a very awkward position. If the "Polish Military Organization" had been so important, asked Yezhov, why had Balytskyi not been more vigilant? Thus Balytskyi, who had summoned up the specter of the "Polish Military Organization" in the first place, became a victim of his own creation. He yielded his Ukrainian position in May to his former deputy, Izrail Leplevskii—the NKVD officer who carried out the kulak operation in Soviet Ukraine with such vigor. On 7 July Balytskyi was arrested on charges of espionage for Poland; a week later his name was removed from the stadium where Dynamo Kiev played its soccer matches—to be replaced by Yezhov's. Balytskyi was executed that November.[8]

In June 1937, when Yezhov introduced the imaginary "Center of Centers" to explain the kulak action and the continuing show trials, he also announced the threat of the equally unreal "Polish Military Organization." The two, supposedly, were connected. Like the justification for the kulak action, the justification for the Polish action permitted the rewriting of the entirety of Soviet history, so that responsibility for all policy problems could be placed upon enemies, and those enemies clearly defined. In Yezhov's account, the "Polish Military Organization" had been active in the Soviet Union from the beginning, and had penetrated not only the communist party but the Red Army and the NKVD. It had been invisible (went Yezhov's argument) precisely because it was so important; it had agents in high places who were able to mask themselves and their works.[9]

On 11 August 1937, Yezhov issued Order 00485, mandating that the NKVD carry out the "total liquidation of the networks of spies of the Polish Military Organization." Though issued shortly after the beginning of the kulak operation, Order 00485 notably radicalized the Terror. Unlike Order 00447, which targeted familiar categories of enemies definable at least theoretically by class, Order 00485 seemed to treat a national group as an enemy of the state. To be sure, the kulak order also specified criminals, and was applied to nationalists and political enemies of various kinds. But there was at least a faltering aureole of class analysis. Kulaks as a group could at least be described in Marxist terms. The enmity of the nations of the Soviet Union toward the Soviet project was something else. It looked like an abandonment of the basic socialist premise of the fraternity of peoples.[10]

Soviet influence in the world, in these years of the Popular Front, depended upon an image of toleration. Moscow's major claim to moral superiority, in a Europe where fascism and National Socialism were on the rise, and for American southerners journeying from a land of racial discrimination and lynchings of blacks, was as a multicultural state with affirmative action. In the popular Soviet film *Circus* of 1936, for example, the heroine was an American performer who, having given birth to a black child, finds refuge from racism in the Soviet Union.[11]

Internationalism was not hypocrisy, and ethnic killing was a shock to the Soviet system. The NKVD was composed of many nationalities, and represented a kind of internationalism. When the show trials began in 1936, the heights of the NKVD were dominated by men whose own origins were within the Soviet national minorities, Jews above all. About forty percent of high-ranking NKVD officers had Jewish nationality recorded in their identity documents, as did more than half of the NKVD generals. In the climate of the day, Jews had perhaps more reason than others to resist policies of ethnic destruction. Perhaps to counter the internationalist (or self-preservation) instinct of his officers, Yezhov sent out a special circular assuring them that their task was to punish espionage rather than ethnicity: "On the Fascist-Insurgent, Sabotage, Defeatist, and Terrorist Activity of the Polish Intelligence Service in the USSR." Its thirty pages expanded upon the theory that Yezhov had already shared with the central committee and with Stalin: that the Polish Military Organization was connected to other espionage "centers" and had penetrated every key Soviet institution.[12]

Even if the idea of a deep Polish penetration of Soviet institutions persuaded Yezhov and Stalin, it could not serve as the evidentiary basis for individual arrests. There simply was nothing resembling a vast Polish plot in the Soviet Union. NKVD officers had too few leads to follow. Even with a great deal of ingenuity, connections between the Polish state and events in the Soviet Union would be hard to document. The two most obvious groups of Polish citizens, diplomats and communists, were clearly inadequate for a mass killing action. The heyday of Polish espionage in the Soviet Union was long past, and the NKVD knew what there was to be known about what the Poles had tried to do in the late 1920s and early 1930s. To be sure, Polish diplomats still tried to gather intelligence. But they were protected by diplomatic immunity, not very numerous, and under constant surveillance already. For the most part, they knew better by 1937 than to contact Soviet citizens and thereby endanger their lives—this was a time when they themselves were furnished with instructions on how to behave when arrested. Yezhov told Stalin that Polish political émigrés were major "suppliers of spies and provocateur elements in the USSR." Leading Polish communists were often already in the Soviet Union, and sometimes already dead. Some sixty-nine of the hundred members of the central committee of the Polish party were executed in the USSR. Most of the rest were behind bars in Poland, and so were unavailable for execution. And in any case, these numbers were far too small.[13]

Precisely because there was no Polish plot, NKVD officers had little choice but to persecute Soviet Poles and other Soviet citizens associated with Poland, Polish culture, or Roman Catholicism. The Polish ethnic character of the operation quickly prevailed in practice, as perhaps it was bound to from the beginning. Yezhov's letter authorized the arrest of nationalist elements, and of "Polish Military Organization" members *who had yet to be discovered.* These categories were so vague that NKVD officers could apply them to almost anyone of Polish ethnicity or with some connection to Poland. NKVD officers who wished to show the appropriate zeal in carrying out the operation would have to be rather vague about the charges against individual people. Balytskyi's previous actions against Poles had created a pool of suspects sufficient for a few purges, but this was far from enough. Local NKVD officers would have to take the initiative— not in looking up the card files, as in the kulak operation, but in creating a new paper trail to follow. One Moscow NKVD chief understood the gist of the order:

his organization should "destroy the Poles entirely." His officers looked for Polish names in the telephone book.[14]

Soviet citizens would have to "unmask" themselves as Polish agents. Because the groups and scenarios of the ostensible Polish plot had to be generated from nothing, torture played an important role in the interrogations. In addition to the traditional conveyer method and the standing method, many Soviet Poles were subjected to a form of collective torture called the "conference method." Once a large number of Polish suspects had been gathered in a single place, such as the basement of a public building in a town or village of Soviet Ukraine or Soviet Belarus, a policeman would torture one of them in full view of the others. Once the victim had confessed, the others would be urged to spare themselves the same sufferings by confessing as well. If they wanted to avoid pain and injury, they would have to implicate not only themselves but others. In this situation, each person had an incentive to confess as quickly as possible: it was obvious that everyone would be implicated eventually anyway, and a quick confession might at least spare the body. In this way, testimony that implicated an entire group could be assembled very quickly.[15]

The legal procedures were somewhat different than in the kulak operation, but no less scanty. In the Polish operation, the investigating officer would compose a brief report for each of the prisoners, describing the supposed crime—usually sabotage, terrorism, or espionage—and recommending one of two sentences, death or the Gulag. Every ten days he would submit all of his reports to the regional NKVD chief and a prosecutor. Unlike the troikas of the kulak operation, this two-person commission (a "dvoika") could not sentence the prisoners by itself, but had to ask for approval from higher authorities. It assembled the reports into an album, noted its recommended sentence for each case, and sent them on to Moscow. In principle, the albums were then reviewed by a central dvoika: Yezhov as the commissar for state security and Andrei Vyshynskii as state prosecutor. In fact, Yezhov and Vyshynskii merely initialed the albums after a hasty review by their subordinates. On a single day, they might finalize two thousand death sentences. The "album method" gave the appearance of a formal review by the highest Soviet authorities. In reality, the fate of each victim was decided by the investigating officer and then more or less automatically confirmed.[16]

Biographies became death sentences, as attachment to Polish culture or Roman Catholicism became evidence of participation in international espionage. People were sentenced for the most apparently minor of offenses: ten years in the Gulag for owning a rosary, death for not producing enough sugar. Details of everyday life were enough to generate a report, an album entry, a signature, a verdict, a gunshot, a corpse. After twenty days, or two cycles of albums, Yezhov reported to Stalin that 23,216 arrests had already been made in the Polish operation. Stalin expressed his delight: "Very good! Keep on digging up and cleaning out this Polish filth. Eliminate it in the interests of the Soviet Union."[17]

In the early stages of the Polish operation, many of the arrests were made in Leningrad, where the NKVD had large offices and where thousands of Poles lived within easy reach. The city had been a traditional place of settlement of Poles since the days of the Russian Empire.

Janina Juriewicz, then a young Polish girl in Leningrad, saw her life altered by these early arrests. The youngest of three sisters, she was very attached to Maria, the eldest. Maria fell in love with a young man called Stanisław Wyganowski, and the three of them would go for walks together, little Janina serving as chaperone. Maria and Stanisław, married in 1936, were a happy couple. When Maria was arrested in August 1937, her husband seemed to know what this meant: "I will meet her," he said, "under the ground." He went to the authorities to make inquiries, and was arrested himself. In September the NKVD visited the Juriewicz family home, confiscated all of the Polish books, and arrested Janina's other sister, Elżbieta. She, Maria, and Stanisław were all executed by a shot to the back of the neck, and buried anonymously in mass graves. When Janina's mother asked the police about them, she was told the typical lie: her daughters and son-in-law had been sentenced to "ten years without the right to correspondence." Because this was another possible sentence, people believed it and hoped. Many of them kept hoping for decades.[18]

People such as the Juriewiczes, who had nothing to do with Polish espionage of any kind, were the "filth" to which Stalin was referring. The family of Jerzy Makowski, a young Leningrad student, suffered a similar fate. He and his brothers were all ambitious, wishing to build careers for themselves in the Soviet Union, and fulfill their deceased father's wish that they master a trade. Jerzy, the youngest of the brothers, wanted to be a shipbuilder. He studied each day with his older brother Stanisław. One morning the two of them were awakened by three NKVD men, who had come to arrest Stanisław. Though he tried to reassure his little brother, he was so nervous that he could not tie his shoes. This was the last Jerzy saw of his brother. Two days later, the next brother, Władysław, was also arrested. Stanisław and Władysław Makowski were executed, two of the 6,597 Soviet citizens shot in the Leningrad region in the Polish operation. Their mother was told the typical lie: that her sons had been sent to the Gulag without the right of correspondence. The third brother, Eugeniusz, who had wished to be a singer, now took a factory job to support the family. He contracted tuberculosis and died.[19]

The Russian poet Anna Akhmatova, then living in Leningrad, lost her son to the Gulag during the Terror. She recalled an "innocent Russia" that writhed "beneath the bloody boots of the executioners, beneath the wheels of the black marias." Innocent Russia was a multinational country, Leningrad was a cosmopolitan city, and its national minorities were the people most at risk. In the city of Leningrad in 1937 and 1938, Poles were thirty-four times more likely to be arrested than their fellow Soviet citizens. Once arrested, a Pole in Leningrad was very likely to be shot: eighty-nine percent of those sentenced in the Polish operation in this city were executed, usually within ten days of the arrest. This was only somewhat worse than the situation of Poles elsewhere: on average, throughout the Soviet Union, seventy-eight percent of those arrested in the Polish operation were executed. The rest, of course, were not released: most of them served sentences of eight to ten years in the Gulag.[20]

Leningraders and Poles had little idea of these proportions at the time. There was only the fear of the knock on the door in the early morning, and the sight of the prison truck: called the black maria, or the soul destroyer, or by Poles the black raven (nevermore). As one Pole remembered, people went to bed each night not knowing whether they would be awakened by the sun or by the black raven. Industrialization and collectivization had scattered Poles throughout the vast country. Now they simply disappeared from their factories, barracks, or homes. To take one example of thousands: in a modest wooden house in the town of Kuntsevo, just west of Moscow, lived a number of skilled workers, among them a Polish mechanic and a Polish metallurgist. These two men were arrested on 18 January 1938 and 2 February 1938, and shot. Evgenia Babushkina, a third victim of the Polish operation in Kuntsevo, was not even Polish. She was a promising and apparently loyal organic chemist. But her mother had once been a washer-woman for Polish diplomats, and so Evgenia was shot as well.[21]

Most Soviet Poles lived not in Soviet Russian cities, such as Leningrad or Kuntsevo, but in westerly Soviet Belarus and Soviet Ukraine, lands Poles had inhabited for hundreds of years. These districts had been part of the old Polish-Lithuanian Commonwealth in the seventeenth and eighteenth centuries. Over the course of the nineteenth century, when these territories were western regions of the Russian Empire, Poles had lost a great deal of their status, and in many cases had begun to assimilate with the surrounding Ukrainian and Belarusian pop-ulations. Sometimes, though, the assimilation was in the other direction, as speakers of Belarusian or Ukrainian who regarded Polish as the language of civilization presented themselves as Poles. The original Soviet nationality policy of the 1920s had sought to make proper Poles of such people, teaching them literary Polish in Polish-language schools. Now, during the Great Terror, Soviet policy distinguished these people once again, but negatively, by sentencing them to death or to the Gulag. As with the contemporary persecution of Jews in Nazi Germany, the targeting of an individual on ethnic grounds did not mean that this person actually identified himself strongly with the nation in question.[22]

In Soviet Belarus the Terror coincided with a massive purge of the party lead-ership in Minsk, carried out by NKVD commander Boris Berman. He accused local Belarusian communists of abusing Soviet affirmative action policies and fomenting Belarusian nationalism. Later than in Ukraine, but with much the same reasoning, the NKVD presented the Polish Military Organization as the mastermind behind supposed Belarusian disloyalty. Soviet citizens in Belarus were accused of being "Belarusian national fascists," "Polish spies," or both. Be-cause Belarusian lands, like Ukrainian lands, were divided between the Soviet Union and Poland, such arguments could easily be made. To be concerned with Belarusian or Ukrainian culture as such involved attention to developments on the other side of a state border. The mass killing in Soviet Belarus included the deliberate destruction of the educated representatives of Belarusian national culture. As one of Berman's colleagues later put it, he "destroyed the flower of the Belarusian intelligentsia." No fewer than 218 of the country's leading writers were killed. Berman told his subordinates that their careers depended upon their rapid fulfillment of Order 00485: "the speed and quality of the work in discovering and arresting Polish spies will be the main consideration taken into account in the evaluation of each leader."[23]

Berman and his men took advantage of economies of scale, killing at one of the largest murder sites in the Soviet Union. They carried out executions in the Kurapaty Forest, twelve kilometers north of Minsk. The woods were known for their white flowers—*Kurasliepy* in literary Belarusian, *Kurapaty* in the local dialect. The black ravens drove through the white flowers day and night, in such numbers that they flattened the narrow gravel alley into what the locals called "the road of death." Within the forest, fifteen hectares of pine had been cleared, and hundreds of pits dug. After condemned Soviet citizens were driven through the gates, they were escorted by two men to the edge of a pit. There they were shot from behind, and pushed into the ditch. When bullets were in short supply, NKVD men would force their victims to sit side by side, their heads in a line, so that a single bullet could be fired through several skulls at once. The corpses were arranged in layers and covered with sand.[24]

Of the 19,931 people arrested in the Polish operation in the Belarusian republic, 17,772 were sentenced to death. Some of these people were Belarusians, and some were Jews. But most were Poles, who were also subject to arrest in Belarus in the kulak action and in the other purges. All in all, as a result of executions and death sentences the number of Poles in Soviet Belarus fell by more than sixty thousand during the Great Terror.[25]

The Polish operation was most extensive in Soviet Ukraine, which was home to about seventy percent of the Soviet Union's six hundred thousand Poles. Some 55,928 people were arrested in Soviet Ukraine in the Polish operation, of whom 47,327 were shot. In 1937 and 1938, Poles were twelve times more likely than the rest of the Soviet Ukrainian population to be arrested. It was in Soviet Ukraine that the famine had generated the theory of the Polish Military Organization, here that Balytskyi had persecuted Poles for years, and here that his former deputy, Izrail Leplevskii, had to prove his vigilance after his former superior was removed from the scene. It did Leplevskii little good: he too was arrested, in April 1938, and executed before the Polish operation in Ukraine was even completed. (His successor A. I. Uspenskii was wise enough to disappear in September 1938, but was eventually found and executed.)[26]

One of Leplevskii's deputies, Lev Raikhman, provided categories of arrest that could be applied to the large Polish population of Soviet Ukraine. One of the suspect groups, interestingly enough, was that of Soviet police agents working among the Soviet Poles. This recreated the dilemma of vigilance facing Balytskyi, Leplevskii, and NKVD officers generally. Once it had been "established" that the "Polish Military Organization" was and had been ubiquitous in Soviet Ukraine and powerful throughout the Soviet Union, the NKVD could always argue that policemen and informers had failed to show sufficient vigilance at an earlier moment. Although many of these police agents were themselves Soviet Poles, some were Ukrainians, Jews, or Russians.[27]

Jadwiga Moszyńska fell into this trap. A Polish journalist working for a Polish-language newspaper, she informed on her colleagues to the police. As her colleagues were arrested and charged as Polish spies, she was left in an impossible position. Why had she not told the authorities that the entire Polish community was a nest of foreign agents? Czesława Angielczyk, an NKVD officer of Polish-Jewish origin who reported on teachers of the Polish language, suffered a similar fate. Once the Polish operation was in full swing and teachers were routinely arrested, she too was vulnerable to the accusation that she had not previously been sufficiently diligent in her work. Both women were executed and buried at Bykivnia, a huge collection of mass graves northeast of Kiev. At least ten thousand Soviet citizens were executed at that site during the Great Terror.[28]

In the Ukrainian countryside the Polish operation was, if anything, even more arbitrary and ferocious than in Kiev and the cities. "The black raven flew," as Polish survivors remembered, from town to town, village to village, visiting grief upon the Poles. The NKVD would bring crews to cities in the hopes of completing the business of arresting and executing Poles in a few weeks, or even days. In Zhmerynka, an important railway junction, the NKVD appeared in March 1938, rounded up hundreds of Poles, and tortured them to produce confessions. In Polonne, the dvoika of the NKVD chief and prosecutor commandeered the desecrated Roman Catholic church building. Poles from Polonne and surrounding villages were arrested and locked in the church basement. Some 168 people were killed in the Polonne church.[29]

In the smallest settlements, it was difficult to discern even the emptiest of judicial formalities. NKVD task forces appeared suddenly, with instructions to

THE GREAT TERROR IN THE
WESTERN SOVIET UNION
1937–1938

● *Major Soviet killing and burial sites*

arrest and execute a certain number of people. They would begin from the assumption that an entire village, factory, or collective farm was guilty, surround the place by night, and then torture the men until they got the results they needed. Then they would carry out the executions and move on. In many such cases the victims were long dead by the time that the albums with their case files were assembled and reviewed in Moscow. In the countryside, the NKVD task forces were death squads. In Cherniivka the NKVD waited until 25 December 1937 (Christmas for Roman Catholic Poles, not for Orthodox Ukrainians) and then arrested whoever attended church. Those arrested simply disappeared, as a local woman remembered: "a stone in the water."[30]

Those arrested were almost always men, and their arrests left families in despair. Zeferyna Koszewicz saw her father for the last time as he was arrested at his factory and taken to Polonne for interrogation. His last words to her were: "listen to your mother!" Yet most mothers were all but helpless. In the Ukrainian countryside, as throughout the Soviet Union, wives would ritually visit the prison each day, bringing food and clean undergarments. Prison guards would give them soiled undergarments in exchange. Since these were the only sign that husbands still lived, they were received with joy. Sometimes a man would manage to smuggle out a message, as did one husband in the underwear he had passed to his wife: "I suffer and I am innocent." One day the undergarments would be soiled by blood. And the next day there would be no undergarments, and then there would be no husband.[31]

In October and November 1937, before the camps and special settlements were full, wives were exiled to Kazakhstan after their husbands were shot. During these weeks the NKVD often abducted Polish children over the age of ten and took them to orphanages. That way they would certainly not be raised as Poles. From December 1937, when there was no longer much room in the Gulag, women were generally not exiled, but were left alone with their children. Ludwik Piwiński, for example, was arrested while his wife was giving birth to their son. He could not tell her his sentence, as he was never allowed to see her, and only learned it himself on the train: ten years felling trees in Siberia. He was one of the lucky ones, one of those relatively few Poles who was arrested but who survived. Eleanora Paszkiewicz watched her father being arrested on 19 December 1937, and then watched her mother giving birth on Christmas Day.[32]

The Polish operation was fiercest in Soviet Ukraine, in the very lands where deliberate starvation policies had killed millions only a few years before. Some Polish families who lost men to the Terror in Soviet Ukraine had already been horribly struck by the famine. Hanna Sobolewska, for example, had watched five siblings and her father die of starvation in 1933. Her youngest brother, Józef, was the toddler who, before his own death by starvation, had liked to say: "Now we will live!" In 1938 the black raven took her one surviving brother, as well as her husband. As she remembered the Terror in Polish villages in Ukraine: "children cry, women remain."[33]

In September 1938, the procedures of the Polish operation came to resemble those of the kulak operation, as the NKVD was empowered to sentence, kill, and deport without formal oversight. The album method, simple as it was, had become too cumbersome. Even though the albums had been subject to only the most cursory review in Moscow, they nevertheless arrived more quickly than they could be processed. By September 1938 more than one hundred thousand cases awaited attention. As a result, "special troikas" were created to read the files at a local level. These were composed of a local party head, a local NKVD chief, and a local prosecutor: often the same people who were carrying out the kulak operation. Their task was now to review the accumulated albums of their districts, and to pass judgment on all of the cases. Since the new troikas were usually just the original dvoika plus a communist party member, they were just approving their own previous recommendations.[34]

Considering hundreds of cases a day, going through the backlog in about six weeks, the special troikas sentenced about 72,000 people to death. In the Ukrainian countryside, the troikas also operated now as they had in the kulak operation, sentencing and killing people in large numbers and in great haste. In the Zhytomyr region, in the far west of Soviet Ukraine near Poland, a troika sentenced an even 100 people to death on 22 September 1938, then another 138 on the following day, and then another 408 on 28 September.[35]

The Polish operation was in some respects the bloodiest chapter of the Great Terror in the Soviet Union. It was not the largest operation, but it was the second largest, after the kulak action. It was not the action with the highest percentage of executions among the arrested, but it was very close, and the comparably lethal actions were much smaller in scale.

Of the 143,810 people arrested under the accusation of espionage for Poland, 111,091 were executed. Not all of these were Poles, but most of them were. Poles were also targeted disproportionately in the kulak action, especially in Soviet Ukraine. Taking into account the number of deaths, the percentage of death sentences to arrests, and the risk of arrest, ethnic Poles suffered more than any other group within the Soviet Union during the Great Terror. By a conservative estimate, some eighty-five thousand Poles were executed in 1937 and 1938, which means that one-eighth of the 681,692 mortal victims of the Great Terror were Polish. This is a staggeringly high percentage, given that Poles were a tiny minority in the Soviet Union, constituting fewer than 0.4 percent of the general population. Soviet Poles were about forty times more likely to die during the Great Terror than Soviet citizens generally.[36]

The Polish operation served as a model for a series of other national actions. They all targeted diaspora nationalities, "enemy nations" in the new Stalinist terminology, groups with real or imagined connections to a foreign state. In the Latvian operation some 16,573 people were shot as supposed spies for Latvia. A further 7,998 Soviet citizens were executed as spies for Estonia, and 9,078 as spies for Finland. In sum, the national operations, including the Polish, killed 247,157 people. These operations were directed against national groups that, taken together, represented only 1.6 percent of the Soviet population; they yielded no fewer than thirty-six percent of the fatalities of the Great Terror. The targeted national minorities were thus more than twenty times as likely to be killed in the Great Terror than the average Soviet citizen. Those arrested in the national actions were also very likely to die: in the Polish operation the chances of execution were seventy-eight percent, and in all of the national operations taken together the figure was seventy-four percent. Whereas a Soviet citizen arrested in the kulak action had an even chance of being sentenced to the Gulag, a Soviet citizen arrested in a national action had a three-in-four chance of being shot. This was perhaps more an accident of timing than a sign of especially lethal intent: the bulk of the arrests for the kulak action was earlier than the bulk of the arrests for the national actions. In general, the later in the Great Terror that a citizen was arrested, the more likely he was to be shot, for the simple reason that the Gulag lacked space.[37]

Although Stalin, Yezhov, Balytskyi, Leplevskii, Berman, and others linked Polish ethnicity to Soviet security, murdering Poles did nothing to improve the international position of the Soviet state. During the Great Terror, more people were arrested as Polish spies than were arrested as German and Japanese spies together, but few (and very possibly none) of the people arrested were in fact engaged in espionage for Poland. In 1937 and 1938, Warsaw carefully pursued a policy of equal distance between Nazi Germany and the Soviet Union. Poland harbored no plans for an offensive war with the Soviet Union.[38]

But perhaps, Stalin reasoned, killing Poles could do no harm. He was right to think that Poland would not be an ally with the Soviet Union in a war against Germany. Because Poland lay between Nazi Germany and the Soviet Union, it could not be neutral in any war for eastern Europe. It would either oppose Germany and be defeated or ally with Germany and invade the Soviet Union. Either way, a mass murder of Soviet Poles would not harm the interests of the Soviet Union—so long as the interests of the Soviet Union had nothing to do with the life and well-being of its citizens. Even such cynical reasoning was very likely mistaken: as puzzled diplomats and spies noted at the time, the Great Terror diverted much energy that might usefully have been directed elsewhere. Stalin misunderstood the security position of the Soviet Union, and a more traditional approach to intelligence matters might have served him better in the late 1930s.

In 1937 Japan seemed to be the immediate threat. Japanese activity in east Asia had been the justification for the kulak operation. The Japanese threat was the pretext for actions against the Chinese minority in the Soviet Union, and against Soviet railway workers who had returned from Manchuria. Japanese espionage was also the justification for the deportation of the entire Soviet Korean population, about 170,000 people, from the Far East to Kazakhstan. Korea itself was then under Japanese occupation, so the Soviet Koreans became a kind of diaspora nationality by association with Japan. Stalin's client in the western Chinese district of Xinjiang, Sheng Shicai, carried out a terror of his own, in which thousands of people were killed. The People's Republic of Mongolia, to the north of China, had been a Soviet satellite since its creation in 1924. Soviet troops entered allied Mongolia in 1937, and Mongolian authorities carried out their own terror in 1937–1938, in which 20,474 people were killed. All of this was directed at Japan.[39]

None of these killings served much of a strategic purpose. The Japanese leadership had decided upon a southern strategy, toward China and then the Pacific. Japan intervened in China in July 1937, right when the Great Terror began, and would move further southward only thereafter. The rationale of both the kulak action and these eastern national actions was thus false. It is possible that Stalin feared Japan, and he had good reason for concern. Japanese intentions were certainly aggressive in the 1930s, and the only question was about the direction of expansion: north or south. Japanese governments were unstable and prone to rapid changes in policy. In the end, however, mass killings could not preserve the Soviet Union from an attack that was not coming.

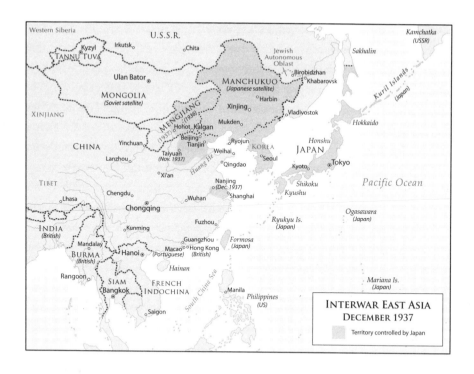

INTERWAR EAST ASIA
DECEMBER 1937

Territory controlled by Japan

Perhaps, as with the Poles, Stalin reasoned that mass killing had no costs. If Japan meant to attack, it would find less support inside the Soviet Union. If it did not, then no harm to Soviet interests had been done by preemptive mass murder and deportation. Again, such reasoning coheres only when the interests of the Soviet state are seen as distinct from the lives and well-being of its population. And again, the use of the NKVD against internal enemies (and against itself) prevented a more systematic approach to the actual threat that the Soviet Union faced: a German attack without Japanese or Polish assistance and without the help of internal opponents of Soviet rule.

Germany, unlike Japan and Poland, was indeed contemplating an aggressive war against the Soviet state. In September 1936, Hitler had let it be known to his cabinet that the main goal of his foreign policy was the destruction of the Soviet Union. "The essence and the goal of Bolshevism," he claimed, "is the elimination of those strata of mankind which have hitherto provided the leadership and their replacement by world Jewry." Germany, according to Hitler, would have to be ready for war within four years. Thus Hermann Göring took command in 1936 of a Four-Year Plan Authority, which would prepare the public and private sectors for an aggressive war. Hitler was a real threat to the Soviet Union, but Stalin seems not to have abandoned hope that Soviet-German relations could be improved. For this reason, perhaps, actions against Soviet Germans were milder than those against Soviet Poles. Some 41,989 people were shot in a German national operation, most of whom were not Germans.[40]

In these years of the Popular Front, the Soviet killings and deportations went unnoticed in Europe. Insofar as the Great Terror was noticed at all, it was seen only as a matter of show trials and party and army purges. But these events, noticed by specialists and journalists at the time, were not the essence of the Great Terror. The kulak operations and the national operations were the essence of the Great Terror. Of the 681,692 executions carried out for political crimes in 1937 and 1938, the kulak and national orders accounted for 625,483. The kulak action and the national operations brought about more than nine tenths of the death sentences and three quarters of the Gulag sentences.[41]

The Great Terror was thus chiefly a kulak action, which struck most heavily in Soviet Ukraine, and a series of national actions, the most important of them the Polish, where again Soviet Ukraine was the region most affected. Of the 681,692 recorded death sentences in the Great Terror, 123,421 were carried out in Soviet Ukraine—and this figure does not include natives of Soviet Ukraine shot in the Gulag. Ukraine as a Soviet republic was overrepresented within the Soviet Union, and Poles were overrepresented within Soviet Ukraine.[42]

The Great Terror was a third Soviet revolution. Whereas the Bolshevik Revolution had brought a change in political regime after 1917, and collectivization a new economic system after 1930, the Great Terror of 1937–1938 involved a revolution of the mind. Stalin had brought to life his theory that the enemy could be unmasked only by interrogation. His tale of foreign agents and domestic conspiracies was told in torture chambers and written in interrogation protocols. Insofar as Soviet citizens can be said to have participated in the high politics of the late 1930s, it was precisely as instruments of narration. For Stalin's larger story to live on, their own stories sometimes had to end.

Yet the conversion of columns of peasants and workers into columns of figures seemed to lift Stalin's mood, and the course of the Great Terror certainly confirmed Stalin's position of power. Having called a halt to the mass operations in November 1938, Stalin once again replaced his NKVD chief. Lavrenty Beria succeeded Yezhov, who was later executed. The same fate awaited many of the highest officers of the NKVD, blamed for the supposed excesses, which were in fact the substance of Stalin's policy. Because Stalin had been able to replace Yagoda with Yezhov, and then Yezhov with Beria, he showed himself to be at the top of the security apparatus. Because he was able to use the NKVD against the party, but also the party against the NKVD, he showed himself to be the unchallengeable leader of the Soviet Union. Soviet socialism had become a tyranny where the tyrant's power was demonstrated by the mastery of the politics of his own court.[43]

The Soviet Union was a multinational state, using a multinational apparatus of repression to carry out national killing campaigns. At the time when the NKVD was killing members of national minorities, most of its leading officers were themselves members of national minorities. In 1937 and 1938, NKVD officers, many of whom were of Jewish, Latvian, Polish, or German nationality, were implementing policies of national killing that exceeded anything that Hitler and his SS had (yet) attempted. In carrying out these ethnic massacres, which of course they had to if they wished to preserve their positions and their lives, they comprised an ethic of internationalism, which must have been important to some of them. Then they were killed anyway, as the Terror continued, and usually replaced by Russians.

The Jewish officers who brought the Polish operation to Ukraine and Belarus, such as Izrail Leplevskii, Lev Raikhman, and Boris Berman, were arrested and executed. This was part of a larger trend. When the mass killing of the Great Terror began, about a third of the high-ranking NKVD officers were Jewish by nationality. By the time Stalin brought it to an end on 17 November 1938, about twenty percent of the high-ranking officers were. A year later that figure was less than four percent. The Great Terror could be, and by many would be, blamed on the Jews. To reason this way was to fall into a Stalinist trap: Stalin certainly understood that Jewish NKVD officers would be a convenient scapegoat for national killing actions, especially after both the Jewish secret policemen and the national elites were dead. In any event, the institutional beneficiaries of the Terror were not Jews or members of other national minorities but Russians who moved up in the ranks. By 1939 Russians (two thirds of the ranking officers) had replaced Jews at the heights of the NKVD, a state of affairs that would become permanent. Russians became an overrepresented national majority; their population share at the heights of the NKVD was greater than their share in the Soviet population generally. The only national minority that was highly overrepresented in the NKVD at the end of the Great Terror were the Georgians—Stalin's own.[44]

This third revolution was really a counterrevolution, implicitly acknowledging that Marxism and Leninism had failed. In its fifteen or so years of existence, the Soviet Union had achieved much for those of its citizens who were still alive: as the Great Terror reached its height, for example, state pensions were introduced. Yet some essential assumptions of revolutionary doctrine had been abandoned. Existence, as the Marxists had said, no longer preceded essence. People were guilty not because of their place in a socioeconomic order but because of their ostensible personal identities or cultural connections. Politics was no longer comprehensible in terms of class struggle. If the diaspora ethnicities of the Soviet Union were disloyal, as the case against them went, it was not because they were bound to a previous economic order but because they were supposedly linked to a foreign state by their ethnicity.[45]

The link between loyalty and ethnicity was taken for granted in the Europe of 1938. Hitler was using this very argument, at this very time, to claim that the three million Germans of Czechoslovakia, and the regions they inhabited, must be allowed to join Germany. In September 1938 at a conference in Munich, Britain, France, and Italy had agreed to let Germany annex the western rim of Czechoslovakia, where most of those Germans lived. British Prime Minister Neville Chamberlain declared that the arrangement had brought "peace for our time." French Prime Minister Edouard Daladier believed nothing of the sort, but he allowed the French people to indulge the fancy. The Czechoslovaks were not even invited to the conference, and were simply expected to accept the result. The Munich agreement deprived Czechoslovakia of the natural protection of mountain ranges and the fortifications therein, leaving the country vulnerable to a future German attack. Stalin interpreted the settlement to mean that the Western powers wished to make concessions to Hitler in order to turn the Germans toward the East.[46]

In 1938, Soviet leaders were concerned to present their own nationality policy as something very different from that of the racism of Nazi Germany. A campaign of that year devoted to this goal included the publication of children's stories, including one called "A Tale of Numbers." Soviet children learned that Nazis were "rummaging through all kinds of old documents" to establish the nationality of the German population. This was, of course, true. Germany's Nuremberg laws of 1935 excluded Jews from political participation in the German state and defined Jewishness according to descent. German officials were indeed using the records of synagogues to establish whose grandparents were Jews. Yet in the Soviet Union the situation was not so very different. The Soviet internal passports had a national category, so that every Soviet Jew, every Soviet Pole, and indeed every Soviet citizen had an officially recorded nationality. In principle Soviet citizens were allowed to choose their own nationality, but in practice this was not always so. In April 1938 the NKVD required that in certain cases information about the nationality of parents be entered. By the same order, Poles and other members of diaspora nationalities were expressly forbidden from changing their nationality. The NKVD would not have to "rummage around in old documents," since it already had its own.[47]

In 1938, German oppression of Jews was much more visible than the national operations in the USSR, though its scale was much smaller. The Nazi regime began a program of "Aryanization," designed to deprive Jews of their property. This was overshadowed by the more public and spontaneous theft and violence that followed the German annexation of Austria that same month. In February Hitler issued an ultimatum to the Austrian chancellor, Kurt von Schuschnigg, demanding that he make of his country a German satellite. Schuschnigg at first accepted the terms, then returned to Austria and defied Hitler by calling a referendum on independence. On 12 March, the German army entered Austria; the next day, Austria ceased to exist. About ten thousand Austrian Jews were deported to Vienna that summer and fall. Thanks to the energetic efforts of Adolf Eichmann, they were among the many Austrian Jews who left the country in the coming months.[48]

In October 1938, Germany expelled seventeen thousand Jews of Polish citizenship from the Reich into Poland. These Jews were arrested at night, placed in train cars, and dumped unceremoniously on the Polish side of the border. A Polish Jew in France whose parents had been expelled decided to take revenge. He assassinated a German diplomat—a deed unfortunate in itself, and unfortunate in its timing: the shooting took place on 7 November, the anniversary of the Bolshevik Revolution; its victim died the next day, the anniversary of Hitler's Beer Hall Putsch of 1923. The murder gave German authorities the pretext for Kristallnacht, the first large open pogrom in Nazi Germany. Pressure had been building in the Reich, especially in Vienna, where in the previous weeks there had been at least one attack every day on Jewish property. Between the ninth and eleventh of November 1938, a few hundred Jews were killed (the official count was ninety-one), and thousands of shops and hundreds of synagogues destroyed. This was generally regarded in Europe, except by those who supported the Nazis, as a sign of barbarism.[49]

The Soviet Union benefited from the public violence in Nazi Germany. In this atmosphere, supporters of the Popular Front counted on the Soviet Union to protect Europe from the descent into ethnic violence. Yet the Soviet Union had just engaged in a campaign of ethnic murder on a far larger scale. It is probably fair to say that no one beyond the Soviet Union had any notion of this. A week after Kristallnacht, the Great Terror was brought to an end, after some 247,157 Soviet citizens had been shot in the national operations. As of the end of 1938, the USSR had killed about a thousand times more people on ethnic grounds than had Nazi Germany. The Soviets had, for that matter, killed far more Jews to that point than had the Nazis. The Jews were targeted in no national action, but they still died in the thousands in the Great Terror—and for that matter during the famine in Soviet Ukraine. They died not because they were Jews, but simply because they were citizens of the most murderous regime of the day.

In the Great Terror, the Soviet leadership killed twice as many Soviet citizens as there were Jews living in Germany; but no one beyond the Soviet Union, not even Hitler, seemed yet to have grasped that mass shootings of this kind were possible. Certainly nothing of the kind was carried out in Germany before the war. After Kristallnacht, Jews entered the German concentration camp system in large numbers, for the first time. Hitler wished at this point to intimidate German Jews so that they would leave the country; the vast majority of the twenty-six thousand Jews who entered the concentration camps at this time left them again soon thereafter. More than one hundred thousand Jews left Germany in late 1938 or 1939.[50]

The violence and motion did stimulate the Nazi imagination about the fate of European Jews generally. A few days after Kristallnacht, on 12 November 1938, Hitler had his close collaborator Hermann Göring present a plan for the removal of European Jews: they were to be sent by boat to the island of Madagascar, in the southern Indian ocean, off the southeastern coast of Africa. Although Hitler and Göring would no doubt have liked to see German Jews worked to death on some sort of SS reservation on the island, such grand imaginative plans really pertained to some future scenario wherein Germany controlled a large population of Jews. The Madagascar scheme was most applicable to a future in which Germany had mastered a large Jewish population. Jews at the time comprised no more than one half of one percent of the German population, and even this total was shrinking with emigration. There had never been very many Jews in Germany; but insofar as they were regarded as a "problem," the "solution" had already been found: expropriation, intimidation, and emigration. (German Jews would have departed even faster than they did had the British allowed them to go to Palestine, or the Americans seen fit to increase—or even fill—immigration quotas. At the Evian Conference of July 1938, only the Dominican Republic agreed to take more Jewish refugees from Germany.)[51]

Madagascar, in other words, was a "solution" for a Jewish "problem" that had not yet really arisen. Grand deportation schemes made a kind of sense in 1938, when leading Nazis could still delude themselves that Poland might become a German satellite and join in an invasion of the Soviet Union. More than three million Jews lived in Poland, and Polish authorities had also investigated Madagascar as a site for their resettlement. Although Polish leaders envisioned no policies toward their large national minorities (five million Ukrainians, three million Jews, one million Belarusians) that were remotely comparable to Soviet realities or Nazi plans, they did wish to reduce the size of the Jewish population by voluntary emigration. After the death of the Polish dictator Józef Piłsudski in 1935, his successors had taken on the position of the Polish nationalist right on this particular question, and had established a ruling party that was open only to ethnic Poles. In the late 1930s, the Polish state supported the aims of the right-wing or Revisionist Zionists in Poland, who wished to create a very large State of Israel in the British Mandate of Palestine—if necessary, by means of violence.[52]

So long as Warsaw and Berlin thought in terms of a Jewish "problem" and some distant territorial solution, and so long as the Germans were still courting

the Poles for an eastern alliance, the Germans could imagine some arrangement to deport east European Jews involving Polish support and infrastructure. But there would be no alliance with Poland, and no common German-Polish plan for the Jews. Piłsudski's heirs in this respect followed Piłsudski's line: a policy of equal distance between Berlin and Moscow, with nonaggression pacts with both Nazi Germany and the Soviet Union, but no alliance with either. On 26 January 1939 in Warsaw, the Poles turned down the German foreign minister, Joachim von Ribbentrop, one last time. In five years of trying, the Germans had failed to convince the Poles that it was in Poland's interests to fight a war of aggression for Soviet territory—while granting Germany Polish territory and becoming a German satellite. This meant a German war not with Poland but against Poland—and against Poland's Jews.[53]

Though the Madagascar plan was not abandoned, it seemed to yield now in Hitler's mind to a vision of a Jewish reservation in a conquered Poland. If Poland would not cooperate in war and deportation, then Poland itself could become a colony where other European Jews could be gathered, perhaps pending some other final removal. It was just after Ribbentrop's return from Warsaw, when Hitler realized that his first war would be against Poland, that he made an important speech on the Jewish issue. On 30 January 1939, Hitler promised the German parliament that he would destroy the Jews if they brought Germany into another world war: "I want to be a prophet once more today: if international finance Jewry in Europe and beyond should succeed once more in plunging the peoples of the world into a world war, then the result will not be the Bolshevization of the earth and thus the victory of Jewry, but the annihilation of the Jewish race in Europe." At the moment of Hitler's oration, about ninety-eight percent of the Jews of Europe lived beyond the borders of Germany, most of them in Poland and the western Soviet Union. Just how they could be annihilated was unknown, but war would have to be the first step.[54]

By early 1939, Hitler had reached a turning point: his foreign policy of gathering in Germans had succeeded in Czechoslovakia and Austria, and his attempts to recruit Poland for an eastern war had failed. He had rearmed Germany and extended its borders as far as possible without war. The annexation of Austria had brought in six million more citizens and extensive reserves of hard currency. Munich brought Hitler not only three million more citizens but also the bulk of the Czechoslovak armaments industry, perhaps the best in the world at the time. In March 1939 Hitler destroyed Czechoslovakia as a state, thus removing any illusions that his goals were limited to ethnic Germans. The Czech lands were added to the Reich as a "protectorate"; Slovakia became a nominally independent state under Nazi tutelage. On 21 March, the Germans tried to intimidate the Poles into an arrangement, and were again rebuffed. On 25 March Hitler gave the instructions for the Wehrmacht to prepare for an invasion of Poland.[55]

As Hitler's power grew, the nature of Stalin's diplomacy changed. The weaknesses of the Popular Front against fascism were evident. Munich had meant the end of a Czechoslovak democracy friendly to the Soviet Union, and Czechoslovakia itself had been dismantled in March 1939. The reactionaries of Francisco Franco won the Spanish Civil War in April 1939. The Popular

Front government in France had already fallen. The relationships between Moscow and the European powers would have to be mainly military and diplomatic, since Stalin lacked the political levers to influence their behavior from within.

In spring 1939, Stalin made a striking gesture toward Hitler, the great ideological foe. Hitler had pledged not to make peace with Jewish communists; Nazi propaganda referred to the Soviet commissar for foreign affairs, Maxim Litvinov, as Finkelstein. Litvinov was indeed Jewish—his brother was a rabbi. Stalin obliged Hitler by firing Litvinov on 3 May 1939. Litvinov was replaced by Stalin's closest ally, Molotov, who was Russian. The indulgence of Hitler was not as strange as it might appear. Stalinist ideology answered all of its own questions. From one day to the next in June 1934, the Popular Front had transformed social democrats from "social fascists" into allies. If "social fascists" could be the friends of the Soviet Union, why not fascists themselves? Fascism, after all, was nothing more (in the Soviet analysis) than a deformation of capitalism; and the Soviet Union had enjoyed good relations with capitalist Germany between 1922 and 1933.[56]

In purely political terms, the arrangement with Germany had a certain logic. The alternative to a German orientation, an alliance with Great Britain and France, seemed to offer little. London and Paris had granted security guarantees to Poland in March 1939 to try to deter a German attack, and tried thereafter to bring the Soviet Union into some kind of defensive coalition. But Stalin was quite aware that London and Paris were unlikely to intervene in eastern Europe if Germany attacked Poland or the Soviet Union. It seemed wisest to come to terms with the Germans and then watch the capitalist powers fight in western Europe. "Destroy the enemies by their own hands," was Stalin's plan, "and remain strong to the end of the war."[57]

Stalin could see, as he later put it, that he and Hitler had a "common desire to get rid of the old equilibrium." In August 1939 Hitler responded to Stalin's opening. Hitler wanted his war that year; he was far more flexible about the possible allies than about the issue of timing. If the Poles would not join in a war against the Soviet Union, then perhaps the Soviets would join in a war against Poland. From Hitler's perspective, an accord with Moscow would prevent a complete encirclement of Germany if the British and French did declare war after the coming German attack on Poland. On 20 August 1939, Hitler sent a personal message to Stalin, asking him to receive Ribbentrop no later than the twenty-third. Ribbentrop made for Moscow, where, as both Orwell and Koestler noted, swastikas adorned the airport of the capital of the homeland of socialism. This, the final ideological shock that separated Koestler from communism, was really a sign that the Soviet Union was no longer an ideological state.[58]

The two regimes immediately found common ground in their mutual aspiration to destroy Poland. Once Hitler had abandoned his hope of recruiting Poland to fight the Soviet Union, Nazi and Soviet rhetoric about the country were difficult to distinguish. Hitler saw Poland as the "unreal creation" of the Treaty of Versailles, Molotov as its "ugly offspring." Officially, the agreement signed in Moscow on 23 August 1939 was nothing more than a nonaggression pact. In fact, Ribbentrop and Molotov also agreed to a secret protocol, designating areas of influence for Nazi Germany and the Soviet Union within eastern Europe: in what were still the independent states of Finland, Estonia, Latvia, Lithuania, Poland, and Romania. The irony was that Stalin had very recently justified the murder of more than one hundred thousand of his own citizens by the false claim that Poland had signed just such a secret codicil with Germany under the cover of a nonaggression pact. The Polish operation had been presented as preparation for a German-Polish attack; now the Soviet Union had agreed to attack Poland along with Germany.[59]

On 1 September 1939, the Wehrmacht attacked Poland from the north, west, and south, using men and arms from annexed Austria and Czechoslovakia. Hitler had begun his war.

In August and September 1939, Stalin was reading maps not just of east Europe but of east Asia. He had found an opportunity to improve the Soviet position in the Far East. Stalin could now be confident that no German-Polish attack was coming from the west. If the Soviet Union moved against Japan in east Asia, there would be no fear of a second front. The Soviets (and their Mongolian allies) attacked Japanese (and puppet Manchukuo) forces at a contested border area (between Mongolia and Manchukuo) on 20 August 1939. Stalin's policy of rapprochement with Berlin of 23 August 1939 was also directed against Tokyo. The Molotov-Ribbentrop Pact between Germany and the Soviet Union, signed three days after the Soviet offensive, nullified the Anti-Comintern Pact between Germany and Japan. Even more than the battlefield defeat, the Nazi-Soviet alliance brought a political earthquake in Tokyo. The Japanese government fell, as would several more in the coming months.[60]

Once Germany seemed to have chosen the Soviet Union rather than Japan as its ally, the Japanese government found itself in an unexpected and confusing situation. The consensus among Japanese leaders was already to expand southward rather than northward, into China and the Pacific rather than into Soviet Siberia. Yet if the union between Moscow and Berlin held, the Red Army would be able to concentrate its forces in Asia rather than in Europe. Japan would then be forced to keep its best troops in the north, in Manchukuo, in simple self-defense, which would make the advance into the south much more difficult. Hitler had given Stalin a free hand in east Asia, and the Japanese could only hope that Hitler would soon betray his new friend. Japan established a consulate in Lithuania as an observation point for German and Soviet military preparations. The consul there was the russophone spy Chiune Sugihara.[61]

When the Red Army defeated the Japanese, on 15 September 1939, Stalin had achieved exactly the result that he wanted. The national actions of the Great Terror had been aimed against Japan, Poland, and Germany, in that order, and against the possibility of encirclement by these three states working together. The 681,692 killings of the Great Terror did nothing to make encirclement less likely, but diplomacy and military force did. By 15 September Germany had practically destroyed the Polish Army as a fighting force. A German-Polish attack on the Soviet Union was obviously out of the question, and a German-Japanese attack on the Soviet Union also looked very unlikely. Stalin had replaced the phantom of a German-Polish-Japanese encirclement of the Soviet Union with a very real German-Soviet encirclement of Poland, an alliance that isolated Japan. Two days after the Soviet military victory over Japan, on 17 September 1939, the Red Army invaded Poland from the east. The Red Army and the Wehrmacht met in the middle of the country and organized a joint victory parade. On 28 September, Berlin and Moscow came to a second agreement over Poland, a treaty on borders and friendship.

So began a new stage in the history of the bloodlands. By opening half of Poland to the Soviet Union, Hitler would allow Stalin's Terror, so murderous in the Polish operation, to recommence within Poland itself. Thanks to Stalin, Hitler was able, in occupied Poland, to undertake his first policies of mass killing. In the twenty-one months that followed the joint German-Soviet invasion of Poland, the Germans and the Soviets would kill Polish civilians in comparable numbers for similar reasons, as each ally mastered its half of occupied Poland.

The organs of destruction of each country would be concentrated on the territory of a third. Hitler, like Stalin, would choose Poles as the target of his first major national shooting campaign.

CHAPTER 4

MOLOTOV-RIBBENTROP EUROPE

The German terror began in the sky. At 4:20 in the morning on 1 September 1939, the bombs fell, without warning, on the central Polish city of Wieluń. The Germans had chosen a locality bereft of military significance as the site of a lethal experiment. Could a modern air force terrorize a civilian population by deliberate bombing? The church, the synagogue, the hospital all went up in flames. Wave after wave of munitions fell, seventy tons of bombs in all, destroying most of the buildings, and killing hundreds of people, mostly women and children. The population fled the city; when a German administrator arrived, there were more corpses than live people. Throughout western Poland, scores of towns and villages met a similar fate. As many as 158 different settlements were bombed.[1]

In the Polish capital, Warsaw, people saw the planes race across the clear blue sky. "Ours," people said to themselves, hopefully. They were wrong. The tenth of September 1939 marked the first time a major European city was bombed systematically by an enemy air force. There were seventeen German raids on Warsaw that day. By mid-month the Polish Army was all but defeated, but the capital still defended itself. On 25 September Hitler declared that he wanted the surrender of Warsaw. Some 560 tons of bombs were dropped that day, along with seventy-two tons of firebombs. In all, some twenty-five thousand civilians (and six thousand soldiers) were killed, as a major population center and historic European capital was bombed at the beginning of an undeclared war. Throughout the month, the columns of refugees were already streaming east, away from the Wehrmacht. German fighter pilots took their pleasure in strafing them.[2]

Poland fought alone. France and Britain declared war on Germany, as promised, but took no meaningful military action during the campaign. (The French advanced a few miles into the Saar region and then withdrew again.) The Polish Army rushed to take defensive positions. The Polish military had been trained to expect an attack either from the east or the west, from either the Red Army or the Wehrmacht. In the war plans and war games of the 1920s and 1930s, both variants had been taken into account. Now all available forces, some thirty-nine divisions (about nine hundred thousand men) were thrown against the fifty German divisions (1.5 million troops). Even so, Polish forces were outnumbered, outgunned, and outflanked by the motorized assault from the north, west, and south. Yet resistance in some places was stiff.

The Wehrmacht had become used to strolling into countries that had already given themselves up, such as Austria and Czechoslovakia. Now German soldiers were actually facing hostile fire. Not everything went their way. In Danzig, the free city on the Baltic coast that Hitler wanted for Germany, Poles defended their post office. German firemen poured gasoline in the basement, and burned out the defenders. The director of the post office left the building waving a white handkerchief. He was immediately shot. Eleven people died of burn wounds. The Germans denied them medical treatment. Thirty-eight men were sentenced to death and shot for the supposedly illegal defense of the building. One of them, Franciszek Krause, was the uncle of a boy named Günter Grass, who later became the great novelist of West Germany. Thanks to his novel *The Tin Drum*, this particular war crime became widely known. It was one of many.[3]

German soldiers had been instructed that Poland was not a real country, and that its army was not a real army. Thus the men resisting the invasion could not be real soldiers. German officers instructed their troops that the death of Germans in battle was "murder." Since resisting the German master race was, in Hitler's terminology, "insolence," Polish soldiers had no right to be treated as prisoners of war. In the village of Urycz, Polish prisoners of war were gathered into a barn, where they were told they would spend the night. Then the Germans burned it down. Near the village of Śladów, Germans used prisoners of war as human shields as they engaged the remnants of a cavalry unit. After the Germans had killed the cavalrymen, who were unwilling to shoot at their fellow

Poles, they made the prisoners bury the bodies of their comrades. Then they lined up the prisoners against a wall at the bank of the Vistula River and shot them. Those who tried to escape by jumping into the river were shot—as the one survivor remembered, like ducks. Some three hundred people died.[4]

On 22 August 1939, Hitler had instructed his commanders to "close your hearts to pity." The Germans killed prisoners. At Ciepielów, after a pitched battle, three hundred Polish prisoners were taken. Despite all the evidence, the German commander declared that these captured soldiers were partisans, irregular fighters unprotected by the laws of war. The Polish officers and soldiers, wearing full uniform, were astonished. The Germans made them disrobe. Now they looked more like partisans. All of them were gunned down and thrown in a ditch. In the short Polish campaign, there were at least sixty-three such actions. No fewer than three thousand Polish prisoners of war were murdered. The Germans also murdered the Polish wounded. In one case, German tanks turned to attack a barn marked with a red cross. It was a Polish first-aid station. If it had not been marked with a cross, the tank commanders would likely have ignored it. The tanks fired on the barn, setting it aflame. The machine gunners fired at people who tried to escape. Then the tanks ran over the remnants of the barn, and any survivors.[5]

Wehrmacht officers and soldiers blamed Polish civilians for the horrors that now befell them. As one general maintained, "Germans are the masters, and Poles are the slaves." The army leadership knew that Hitler's goals for the campaign were anything but conventional. As the chief of staff summarized, it was "the intention of the Leader to destroy and exterminate the Polish people." Soldiers had been prepared to see the Polish civilian population as devious and subhuman. One of them was so convinced of Polish hostility that he interpreted a Pole's death grimace as the expression of irrational hatred for Germans. The soldiers quickly took to taking out their frustrations on whomever they happened to see. As a rule, the Germans would kill civilians after taking new territories. They would also kill civilians after losing ground. If they took casualties at all, they would blame whoever was at hand: men in the first instance, but also women, and children.[6]

In the town of Widzów, the Germans summoned the men, who, fearing nothing because they had done nothing, answered the call. One pregnant wife had a sense of foreboding, but she was torn away from her husband. All of the men of the town were lined up against a fence and shot. In Longinówka, forty Polish citizens were locked in a building, which was then set aflame. Soldiers fired on people as they leapt from windows. Some of the reprisal actions were unthinkably casual. In one case a hundred civilians were assembled to be shot because someone had fired a gun. It turned out that the gun had been fired by a German soldier.[7]

Poland never surrendered, but hostilities came to an end on 6 October 1939. Even as the Germans established their civilian occupation authorities that autumn, the Wehrmacht continued to kill Polish citizens in large numbers in quite arbitrary reprisal actions. In December, after two German soldiers were killed by known Polish criminals, the Germans machine-gunned 114 men who had nothing to do with the incident. In January the Germans shot 255 Jews in Warsaw after the Jewish community had failed to turn over someone whom the Germans, judging by his last name, thought to be Jewish. The person in question had nothing to do with the Jewish community.[8]

German soldiers had been instructed to regard the Jews as eastern barbarians, and in Poland they did encounter something that they never would have seen in Germany: large communities of religious Jews. Though Hitler raged on about the destructive role of Jews in German society, the Jews were an extremely small proportion of the German population. Among the German citizens defined by the Nuremberg laws as Jewish, most were secular, and many did not identify strongly with the Jewish community. Jews in Germany were highly assimilated, and very often married non-Jews. For historical reasons, Jewish life in Poland was very different. Jews had been expelled from Germany in the late middle ages, as they had been from most of central and western Europe. Poland had been for centuries a haven for Jews, and became and remained the center of European Jewish settlement. In 1939 about ten percent of the Polish population were Jews, and most of these were religiously observant and traditional in dress and custom. They generally spoke Yiddish, which Germans tended to hear as a deformed version of their own language. In Warsaw and Łódź, the most important Jewish cities in Poland, Jews were about one third of the population.

Judging by their correspondence, German officers and soldiers saw Polish Jews as living stereotypes rather than as human beings, a special blight on an already benighted Polish land. Germans wrote to their wives and girlfriends to describe an inhuman assemblage of disorder and filth. In their image of Poland, everything that was beautiful was the work of previous German settlers, while everything ugly was the result of Jewish corruption and Polish laziness. Germans seemed to feel an uncontrollable urge to neaten the appearance of the Jews. Again and again, soldiers would surround Jewish men and shave their sidecurls, while others would laugh and take photographs. They would also rape Jewish women, casually, as though this were not an offense for which they could be punished. When they were caught, they were reminded of German laws against racial mixing.[9]

In the town of Solec, Jews were taken as hostages and locked in a cellar. After an escape attempt, soldiers threw grenades into the cellar, killing everyone. In Rawa Mazowiecka, a German soldier asked a Jewish boy for some water. When the boy ran away, the soldier took aim and shot. He hit one of his own comrades instead. The Germans then gathered hundreds of people in the town square and killed them. In Dynów, some two hundred Jews were machine-gunned one night in mid-September. In all, Jews were about seven thousand of the forty-five thousand or so Polish civilians killed by the Germans by the end of 1939, somewhat more than the Jewish share of the Polish population.[10]

Even more than a Polish soldier, a Jewish soldier posed a problem for the Nazi worldview in which German soldiers and officers had been indoctrinated. Jews had been purged from the German armed forces since 1935. Yet Polish Jews, like all male Polish citizens, were subject to military service in the Polish Army. Jews, especially Jewish doctors, were well represented among officers. Germans separated Jews from their units and sent them to special punitive labor camps.

Germany had all but won the war by the time the Soviets entered it on 17 September. On that day the German air force was bombing Lwów (today Lviv), the most important Polish city in the southeast, as the Red Army approached it. The crossing of half a million Soviet soldiers into Poland had elicited both fear and hope. Poles wanted to believe that the Soviets had come to fight the Germans. Some confused Polish soldiers, driven eastward by the German attack, could believe for a moment that they had found allies. The Polish armed forces were desperate for support.[11]

The Soviets claimed that their intervention was necessary because the Polish state had ceased to exist. Since Poland could no longer protect its own citizens,

went the argument, the Red Army had to enter the country on a peacekeeping mission. Poland's large Ukrainian and Belarusian minorities, went the Soviet propaganda, were in particular need of rescue. Yet despite the rhetoric the Soviet officers and soldiers were prepared for war, and fought one. The Red Army disarmed Polish units, and engaged them wherever necessary. Half a million men had crossed a frontier that was no longer defended, to fight an enemy that was all but defeated. Soviet soldiers would meet German soldiers, demarcate the border, and, in one instance, stage a joint victory march. Stalin spoke of an alliance with Germany "cemented in blood." It was mainly the blood of Polish soldiers, more than sixty thousand of whom died in combat.[12]

In cities like Lwów where both the Wehrmacht and the Red Army were nearby, Polish soldiers had a difficult choice: to whom should they surrender?

The Soviet military promised them safe passage back home after a brief interview. Nikita Khrushchev, who had accompanied the Soviet soldiers, repeated the assurance. The artist Józef Czapski, a Polish reserve officer, was among those who were betrayed by this lie. His unit had been beaten back by the Germans, and then surrounded by Soviet armor. He and his men were promised that they would be taken to Lwów and released there. Instead, they were all packed into trucks on the city's market square. Tearful women threw them cigarettes. A young Jewish man bought apples from a stand and tossed them to the prisoners in the truck. Near the post office, women took the notes that the soldiers had written for their families. The prisoners were taken to the train station, and sent east.[13]

As they crossed the Soviet border they had the feeling of entering, as Czapski recalled, "another world." Czapski sat with a botanist friend, another reserve officer, who marveled at the tall grasses of the Ukrainian steppe. In another train, Polish farmers looked through the cracks at Soviet collective farms, and shook their heads in distress at the disorder and neglect they saw. At a stop in Kiev, the capital of Soviet Ukraine, Polish officers met an unexpected reception. Ukrainians were saddened to see Polish officers under Soviet guard. Some of them, it seems, still believed that it would be the Polish Army that would liberate Ukraine from Stalin. Instead, about fifteen thousand Polish officers were taken to three Soviet prison camps, run by the NKVD: one in the eastern part of Soviet Ukraine, in Starobilsk, and two more in Soviet Russia, at Kozelsk and Ostashkov.[14]

The removal of these men—and all but one of them were men—was a kind of decapitation of Polish society. The Soviets took more than one hundred thousand prisoners of war, but released the men and kept only the officers. More than two thirds of these officers came from the reserves. Like Czapski and his botanist companion, these reserve officers were educated professionals and intellectuals, not military men. Thousands of doctors, lawyers, scientists, professors, and politicians were thus removed from Poland.[15]

Meanwhile, Soviet occupying forces in eastern Poland placed the lower orders of society in the vacated heights. Prisons were emptied, and political prisoners, usually communists, were put in charge of local government. Soviet agitators urged peasants to take revenge on landlords. Though most people resisted the call to criminality, chaos reigned as thousands did not. Mass murders with axes were suddenly frequent. One man was tied to a stake, then had some of his skin peeled off and his wound salted before being forced to watch the execution of his family. Usually the Red Army behaved well, though sometimes soldiers joined in the violence, as when a pair killed a local official and then took his gold teeth.[16]

In the background, the NKVD entered the country, in force. In the twenty-one months to come it made more arrests in occupied eastern Poland than in the entire Soviet Union, seizing some 109,400 Polish citizens. The typical sentence was eight years in the Gulag; about 8,513 people were sentenced to death.[17]

West of the Molotov-Ribbentrop line, where Germany ruled, methods were even less subtle. Now that the Wehrmacht had defeated a foreign army, the methods of the SS could be tried against an alien population.

The tool of persecution, the Einsatzgruppe, was the creation of Heinrich Himmler's right-hand man, Reinhard Heydrich. The Einsatzgruppen were special task forces led by Security Police and including other policemen, whose apparent mission was to pacify the rear areas after military expansion. As of 1939 they were subordinate to Heydrich's Reich Security Main Office, which united the Security Police (a state institution) with the Sicherheitsdienst, or SD (the intelligence service of the SS, a Nazi party institution). Einsatzgruppen had been deployed in Austria and Czechoslovakia, but met little resistance in these countries and had no special mission to kill selected groups. It was in Poland that the Einsatzgruppen were to fulfill their mission as "ideological soldiers" by eliminating the educated classes of a defeated enemy. (They were in some sense killing their peers: fifteen of the twenty-five Einsatzgruppe and Einsatzkommando commanders had doctorates.) In Operation Tannenberg, Heydrich wanted the Einsatzgruppen to render "the upper levels of society" harmless by murdering sixty-one thousand Polish citizens. As Hitler put it, "only a nation whose upper levels are destroyed can be pushed into the ranks of slavery." The ultimate goal of this decapitation project was to "destroy Poland" as a functioning society. By killing the most accomplished Poles, the Einsatzgruppen were to make Poland resemble the German racist fantasy of the country, and leave the society incapable of resisting German rule.[18]

The Einsatzgruppen approached their task with murderous energy, but lacked the experience and thus the skills of the NKVD. They killed civilians, to be sure, often under the cover of retaliatory operations against supposed partisans. In Bydgoszcz the Einsatzgruppen killed about nine hundred Poles. In Katowice they killed another 750 in a courtyard, many of them women and girls. All in all, the Einsatzgruppen probably killed about fifty thousand Polish citizens in actions that had nothing to do with combat. But these were not, it seems, the first fifty thousand on their list of sixty-one thousand. They were very often groups selected on the spur of the moment. Unlike the NKVD, the Einsatzgruppen did not follow protocols carefully, and in Poland they did not keep careful records of the people they killed.[19]

The Einsatzgruppen were more successful in missions against Jews, which required much less discrimination. One Einsatzgruppe was tasked with terrorizing Jews so that they would flee east from the German occupation zone to the Soviet side. As much of this as possible was to be accomplished in September 1939, while military operations were still taking place. So in Będzin, for example, this Einsatzgruppe burned down the synagogue with flamethrowers, killing about five hundred Jews in two days. Einsatzkommandos (smaller detachments) fulfilled similar missions. In the city of Chełm one of them was tasked to rob wealthy Jews. The Germans carried out strip-searches of women who looked Jewish on the street, and cavity searches in private. They broke fingers to get at wedding rings. In Przemyśl between the sixteenth and the nineteenth of September Einsatzkommandos shot at least five hundred Jews. As a result of such actions, hundreds of thousands of Jews fled to the Soviet occupation zone. In the vicinity of the city of Lublin more than twenty thousand Jews were simply expelled.[20]

After the conquest of Poland was complete, the Germans and their Soviet allies met once again to reassess their relations. On 28 September 1939, the day Warsaw fell to the Germans, the allies signed their treaty on borders and friendship, which changed the zones of influence somewhat. It assigned Warsaw to the Germans and Lithuania to the Soviets. (It is this border that appears on the maps as the "Molotov-Ribbentrop line.") It also obliged the two sides to suppress any Polish resistance to the regime of the other. On 4 October Nazi Germany and the Soviet Union agreed to a further protocol, defining their new common border. Poland had ceased to exist.

A few days later Germany formally annexed some of the territories in its zone, leaving the rest as a colony known as the General Government. This was

to be a dumping ground for unwanted people, Poles and Jews. Hitler thought
that Jews could be held in some eastern district in a kind of "nature preserve."
The general governor, Hitler's former lawyer Hans Frank, clarified the position
of the subject population in two orders issued in late October 1939. One specified that order was to be maintained by the German police; the other, that the
German police had the authority to issue a death sentence to any Pole who did
anything that might appear to be against the interests of Germany or Germans.
Frank believed that Poles would soon realize the "hopelessness of their national
fate" and accept the leadership of the Germans.[21]

East of the Molotov-Ribbentrop line, the Soviets were extending their own system. Moscow enlarged its Ukrainian and Belarusian republics to the west, forcing their new populations, the residents of what had been eastern Poland, to
participate in the annexation of their own homeland. When the Red Army entered Poland, it presented Soviet power as the great liberator of the national minorities from Polish rule, and the great supporter of the peasants against their
masters. In eastern Poland, the population was about forty-three percent Polish,
thirty-three percent Ukrainian, and eight percent each Jewish and Belarusian,
with a small number of Czechs, Germans, Russians, Roma, Tatars, and others.
But now everyone from every nation and every class would have to express a rit-
ualized support of the new order. On 22 October 1939, all adults in what the Soviets called "Western Belarus" and "Western Ukraine" had to vote in elections to
two assemblies, whose provisional character was revealed by their one legislative
undertaking: to request that the lands of eastern Poland be incorporated by the
Soviet Union. By 15 November, the formalities of annexation were complete.[22]

The Soviet Union was bringing its own institutions and practices to eastern
Poland. Everyone now had to register for an internal passport, which meant that
the state had a record of all of its new citizens. With the registration of citizens
came the military draft: some 150,000 young men (Poles, Ukrainians, Belarusians, Jews) soon found themselves in the Red Army. Registration also allowed
for the smooth pursuit of a major Soviet social policy: deportation.[23]

On 4 December 1939 the Soviet politburo ordered the NKVD to arrange the
expulsion of certain groups of Polish citizens deemed to pose a danger to the
new order: military veterans, foresters, civil servants, policemen, and their fam-

ilies. Then, on one evening in February 1940, in temperatures of about forty below zero, the NKVD gathered them all: 139,794 people taken from their homes at night at gunpoint to unequipped freight trains bound for special settlements in distant Soviet Kazakhstan or Siberia. The entire course of life was changed before people knew what had happened to them. The special settlements, part of the Gulag system, were the forced-labor zones to which the kulaks had been sent ten years before.[24]

Because the NKVD defined *family* very expansively, the trains were full of aged parents as well as the children of people who were thought to be dangerous. At halts on the journey east, guards would go from car to car, asking if there were any more dead children. Wiesław Adamczyk, an eleven-year-old child at the time, asked his mother if the Soviets were taking them to hell. Food and water were given very irregularly, and the cattle cars were without facilities and extremely cold. As time passed, the children learned to lick the frost from metal nails, and watched as the elderly began to freeze to death. Now the adult dead would be taken out and thrown into a hastily dug mass grave. Another boy looked out and tried to remember them, writing later that even as the dead disappeared, "in our thoughts remained their dreams and their wishes."[25]

During the passage alone, some five thousand people would die; about eleven thousand more would perish by the following summer. One little Polish girl in a Siberian school described what happened to her family: "My brother got sick and in a week died from hunger. We buried him in a hill on the Siberian steppe. Mom from worry also got sick from hunger swelled up and lay in the barrack for two months. They didn't want to take her to the hospital until it was the end. Then they took her mama lay in the hospital for two weeks. Then her life ended. When we learned this we were seized by a great despair. We went to the burial twenty-five kilometers away we went to the hill. You could hear the sound of the Siberian forest where two of my family were left."[26]

Even more than the kulaks who had preceded them, these Poles were alien and helpless in central Asia or the Russian north. They usually did not speak Russian, let alone Kazakh. The locals, especially in central Asia, saw them as one more imposition coming from the center. "The natives," as one Pole recalled Kazakhstan, "spoke little Russian and greatly resented the whole arrangement and the new mouths to feed; and would at first sell us nothing, nor help in any way." Poles could not have known that a third of the population of Kazakhstan had starved to death only a decade before. One Polish father of four was murdered for his boots on a collective farm. Another father died of starvation in Siberia. As his son remembered, "He swelled up. They wrapped him in a sheet and threw him in the ground." A third father died of typhus in Vologda, the north Russian city of death. His son, age twelve, had already learned a kind of philosophy: "A man is born once and dies only once. And so it happened."[27]

Deported Polish citizens had probably never heard the Russian word *kulak* before, but now they were discovering its history. In one Siberian settlement Poles found the skeletons of kulaks deported in the 1930s. In another, a sixteen-year-old Pole realized that the foreman at his work camp was a kulak. "He told me frankly," the boy remembered, "what was in his heart": faith in God. Because Poles were thought to be Roman Catholics and thus Christian believers, their presence elicited such confessions of faith from Ukrainians and Russians. But even in the distant east the Soviet authorities reacted with great hostility to any sign of Polishness. A Polish boy who came to town to sell his clothes for food met a policeman who struck the cap from his head. The cap had a white eagle, the symbol of the Polish state. The policemen would not let the boy pick it up from the ground. As Soviet journalists kept writing and teachers kept saying, Poland had fallen and would never rise again.[28]

With calculation, classification, and practiced violence, the Soviets could force Poles into a system that already existed. After a few weeks of chaos, they had extended their state westward, and dispensed with the most dangerous of possible opponents. In the western half of Poland, west of the Molotov-Ribbentrop line, the Germans could take no such approach. Hitler had enlarged his Reich very recently, into Austria and Czechoslovakia, but never into territories populated by quite so many non-Germans. Unlike the Soviets, the Nazis could not even claim to be bringing justice and equality to oppressed peoples or classes. Everyone knew that Nazi Germany was for the Germans, and the Germans did not bother to pretend otherwise.

The premise of National Socialism was that Germans were a superior race, a presumption that, when confronted by the evidence of Polish civilization, the Nazis had to prove, at least to themselves. In the ancient Polish city of Cracow, the entire professoriate of the renowned university was sent to concentration camps. The statue of Adam Mickiewicz, the great romantic poet, was pulled down from its pedestal on the Market Square, which was renamed Adolf-Hitler-Platz. Such actions were symbolic as well as practical. The university at Cracow was older than any university in Germany. Mickiewicz had been respected by the Europeans of his day as much as Goethe. The existence of such an institution and such a history, like the presence of the Polish educated classes as such, was a barrier to German plans, but also a problem for Nazi ideology.[29]

Polishness itself was to disappear from these lands, to be replaced by "Germandom." As Hitler had written, Germany "must seal off these alien racial elements, so that the blood of its people will not be corrupted again, or it must without further ado remove them and hand over the vacated territory to its own national comrades." In early October 1939, Hitler conferred a new responsibility upon Heinrich Himmler. Already the leader of the SS and the chief of the German police forces, Himmler now became the "Reich Commissar for the Strengthening of Germandom," a kind of minister for racial affairs. In the regions that Germany annexed from Poland, Himmler was to remove the native population and replace it with Germans.[30]

Although Himmler embraced the project with enthusiasm, it was a difficult assignment. These were Polish territories. There had not been a large German minority in independent Poland. When the Soviets said that they were entering eastern Poland to defend Ukrainians and Belarusians, this had at least a demographic plausibility: there were about six million such people in Poland. There were, by contrast, fewer than a million Germans. In Germany's newly annexed territories, Poles outnumbered Germans by about fifteen to one.[31]

By now Hitler's propaganda minister Joseph Goebbels had mastered the German press, so Germans (and those who believed their propaganda) had the impression that there were massive numbers of Germans in western Poland, and that they had been subject to horrible repressions. The reality was quite different. It was not just that the nine million or so Poles massively outnumbered the Germans in the new districts of the Reich. Hitler had just added significantly more *Jews* (at least 600,000) to his Reich than he had added Germans, and for that matter nearly tripled the population of Jews in Germany (from about 330,000 to nearly a million). If the General Government (with its 1,560,000 Jews) was included, he had added well over two million Jews to Berlin's dominions. There were more Jews in the city of Łódź (233,000), which was added to Germany, than in Berlin (82,788) and Vienna (91,480) combined. There were more Jews in Warsaw, now in the General Government, than there had been in all of Germany. Hitler had added more Poles to the Reich in this annexation than he had added Germans in this and all previous annexations, including Austria and the border regions of Czechoslovakia. Taking into account the General Government and the Protectorate of Bohemia-Moravia annexed from dissembled Czechoslovakia, Hitler had added about twenty million Poles, six million Czechs, and two million Jews to his empire. There were now more Slavs in Germany than in any other European state, except the Soviet Union. On a crusade for racial purity, Germany had become by the end of 1939 Europe's second-largest multinational state. The largest, of course, was the Soviet Union.[32]

Arthur Greiser, placed in charge of the largest of Germany's new regions, known as the Reichsgau Wartheland, was particularly receptive to the idea of "strengthening Germandom." His province extended west to east from the major Polish city Poznań to the major Polish city Łódź. It was home to about four million Poles, 366,000 Jews, and 327,000 Germans. Himmler proposed to deport one million people by February 1940, including all of the Jews and several hundred thousand Poles. Greiser began the project of "strengthening Germandom" by emptying three psychiatric hospitals and having the patients shot. Patients from a fourth psychiatric hospital, at Owińska, met a different fate. They were taken to the local Gestapo headquarters in October and November 1939 and gassed by carbon monoxide released from canisters. This was the first German mass murder by this method. Some 7,700 Polish citizens found in mental institutions were murdered, beginning a policy of "euthanasia" that would soon be followed within the boundaries of prewar Germany as well. Over the course of the next two years, more than seventy thousand German citizens would be gassed as "life unfit for life." Strengthening Germandom had an internal and an external dimension; aggressive war abroad allowed for the murder of German citizens. So it began and so it would continue.[33]

The goal of removing the Jews from Germany clashed with another ideological priority, that of resettling Germans from the Soviet Union. Once the Soviet Union had extended its borders west by taking eastern Poland, Hitler had to be concerned about the Germans (formerly Polish citizens) who then fell under Soviet rule. Hitler arranged for these people to be sent to Germany. They would live in the Wartheland, on the homesteads vacated by deported Poles. But this meant that Polish farmers, rather than Jews, had to be deported in the first instance, to make room for these incoming Germans. But even if Jews were allowed, for the time being, to remain in their homes, they faced enormous suffering and humiliation. In Kozienice, Orthodox Jews were forced to dance next to a pile of burning books and chant that "the war is our fault." In Łowicz on 7 November 1939, the entire male Jewish population was forced to march to the prison, to be ransomed by the Jewish community.[34]

In the first deportation from the Wartheland to the General Government, carried out from 1–17 December 1939, the vast majority of the 87,883 people expelled were Poles. The police chose in the first instance Poles who "represent an immediate danger to German nationhood." In a second deportation, carried out between 10 February and 15 March 1940, another 40,128 people were sent away, again most of them Poles. The journey was rather short. In normal times, the journey from Poznań, the capital city of the Wartheland, to Warsaw, the largest city of the General Government, would take a few hours. Nevertheless, thousands of people froze to death on the trains, which were often left idle on side tracks for days. Commented Himmler: "It's just the climate there." The weather in Poland, needless to say, was essentially the same as the weather in Germany.[35]

The winter of 1939–1940 in Poland and Germany was unusually cold. The winter in Ukraine, Russia, and northern Kazakhstan was even colder. As the days shortened in the Soviet special settlements, thousands of Polish citizens fell ill and died. In the three camps in Soviet Russia and Soviet Ukraine where the Soviets held the Polish prisoners of war, the men followed their own political and religious calendar. In Kozelsk, Ostashkov, and Starobilsk, people found ways to commemorate the 11th of November, Polish independence day. In all three camps, the men planned to celebrate Christmas Day. These prisoners were generally Roman Catholics, with a considerable admixture of Jews, Protestants, Orthodox Christians, and Greek Catholics. They found themselves in desecrated Orthodox monastic complexes, praying or taking communion in quiet corners of crumbling cathedrals.[36]

The prisoners saw the signs of what had happened to the Orthodox monks and the nuns during the Bolshevik Revolution: skeletons in shallow graves, outlines of human bodies traced in bullets against the walls. One prisoner at

Starobilsk could not help but notice the clouds of black ravens that never seemed to leave the monastery. Nevertheless, prayer seemed to bring hope, and the people of various faiths worshipped together—until 24 December 1939, when the priests, pastors, and rabbis were taken away, from all three camps, never to be seen again.[37]

The three camps were a sort of laboratory for observing the behavior of the Polish educated classes. Kozelsk, Ostashkov, and Starobilsk became Polish in appearance. The prisoners had no other clothes but their army uniforms, with white eagles on their caps. Needless to say, no one wore that particular emblem in public in the former eastern Poland, where the public space was now graced by the hammer, sickle, and red star. Even as Polish universities were closed on the German side or made Ukrainian and Russian on the Soviet, camp inmates organized lectures led by the prominent Polish scientists and humanists who were among the reserve officers. Officers organized modest credit unions, so that poorer officers could borrow from richer. They declaimed by heart the poetry that they had learned at school. Some of them could recite from memory the massively long novels from the period of Polish realism. Of course, the prisoners also disagreed, fought, and stole. And a few people—as it turned out, a very few—agreed to cooperate with the Soviets. The officers disagreed about how to comport themselves during the long nighttime interrogations. Yet the spirit of national solidarity was palpable, perhaps to the Soviets as well.[38]

The men were nevertheless lonely. They could write to their families, but could not discuss their situation. Knowing that the NKVD read everything they wrote, they had to be discreet. One prisoner at Kozelsk, Dobiesław Jakubowicz, entrusted to his diary the letters he wished to write to his wife, his dreams of watching her dress, and of playing with their daughter. The prisoners had to give a sanatorium as their return address, which led to much painful confusion.[39]

The prisoners befriended the dogs who served as sentries, and the dogs from nearby towns. Dogs would visit the camps, entering through the gate past the guards or through holes in or under the barbed-wire fences too small for a man. One of the reserve officers at Starobilsk was Maksymilian Łabędź, the most famous veterinarian in Warsaw. An older gentleman, he had barely survived the transport. He looked after the dogs, and occasionally even performed surgeries. His special pet was a mutt that the officers called Linek, which was short for Stalinek—"Little Stalin" in Polish. The favorite among the dogs that visited was called Foch, after the French general who was supreme commander of the allied armies that defeated Germany in 1918. This was a time, in late 1939 and early 1940, when a Polish government in exile had established itself in Paris, and when Poles generally hoped that France could defeat Germany and rescue Poland. They attached their own hopes for contact with the outside world to the little dog Foch, who seemed to have a home in town. They would tuck notes under his collar, hoping for a response. One day, in March 1940, they got one: "People say that soon you'll be released from Starobilsk. People say that you'll go home. We don't know if that's true."[40]

It was not true. That month in Moscow, Stalin's secret police chief Lavrenty Beria had come to a conclusion, perhaps inspired by Stalin. Beria made clear in writing that he wanted the Polish prisoners of war dead. In a proposal to the politburo, and thus really to Stalin, Beria wrote on 5 March 1940 that each of the Polish prisoners was "just waiting to be released in order to enter actively into the battle against Soviet power." He claimed that counterrevolutionary organizations in the new Soviet territories were led by former officers. Unlike the claims about the "Polish Military Organization" a couple of years before, this was no fantasy. The Soviet Union had occupied and annexed half of Poland, and some Poles were bound to resist. Perhaps twenty-five thousand of them took part in some kind of resistance organization in 1940. True, these organizations were quickly penetrated by the NKVD, and most of these people arrested: but the opposition was real and demonstrable. Beria used the reality of Polish resistance to justify his proposal for the prisoners—"to apply to them the supreme punishment: shooting."[41]

Stalin approved Beria's recommendation, and the mechanisms of the Great Terror began again. Beria established a special troika to deal rapidly with the files of all of the Polish prisoners of war. It was empowered to disregard the recommendations of the previous interrogators, and to issue verdicts without any contact with the prisoners themselves. It seems that Beria established a quota for the killings, as had been done in 1937 and 1938: all of the prisoners at the three camps, plus six thousand people held in prisons in western Belarus and western Ukraine (three thousand in each), plus especially dangerous elements among noncommissioned officers who were not in captivity. After a quick examination of the files, ninety-seven percent of the Poles in the three camps,

THE KATYN MASSACRES
APRIL 1940

■ Soviet prison camps   • Soviet killing sites

→ Transports, April 1940

about 14,587 people, were sentenced to death. The exceptions were a few Soviet agents, people of ethnic German or Latvian background, and people with foreign protection. The six thousand from the prisons were also condemned to death, along with 1,305 other people who were arrested in April.[42]

The prisoners of the three camps were expecting that they would be allowed to return home. When, in April 1940, the first groups were taken from the camp at Kozelsk, there were given a farewell reception by their comrades. Fellow officers formed, as best as they could without their weapons, an honor guard as they walked to the buses. In groups of a few hundred at a time, the prisoners were taken by rail through Smolensk to the smaller station at Gniazdovo. There they found themselves disembarking from the train into a cordon of NKVD soldiers with bayonets fixed. About thirty of them at a time entered a bus, which took them to the Goat Hills, at the edge of a forest called Katyn. There, at an NKVD resort, they were searched and their valuables taken. One officer, Adam Solski, had been keeping a diary up to this moment: "They asked about my wedding ring, which I. . . . " The prisoners were taken into a building on the complex, where they were shot. Their bodies were then delivered, probably by truck in batches of thirty, to a mass grave that had been dug in the forest. This continued until all 4,410 prisoners sent from Kozelsk had been shot.[43]

At Ostashkov, a band played as the prisoners left the camp, to lift their spirits. They were taken by train, in groups of about 250–500, to the NKVD prison at Kalinin (today Tver). All were held briefly while their data were checked. They waited, not knowing what would come next, probably not suspecting until the very last moment. An NKVD officer asked one of the waiting prisoners, alone then with his captors, how old he was. The boy was smiling. "Eighteen." What did you do? Still smiling. "Telephone operator." How long had you worked? The boy counted on his hands. "Six months." Then he, like all of the 6,314 prisoners who passed through this room, was handcuffed and led to a soundproofed cell. Two men held him by the arms as a third shot him from behind in the base of the skull.[44]

The chief executioner at Kalinin, whom the prisoners never saw, was Vasily Blokhin. He had been one of the main killers during the Great Terror, when he had commanded an execution squad in Moscow. He had been entrusted with some of the executions of high-profile defendants of show trials, but had also shot thousands of workers and peasants who were killed entirely in secret. At Kalinin he wore a leather cap, apron, and long gloves to keep the blood and gore from himself and his uniform. Using German pistols, he shot, each night, about two hundred and fifty men, one after another. Then the bodies were driven, in a truck, to nearby Mednoe, where the NKVD had some summer houses. They were thrown into a large pit dug earlier by a backhoe.[45]

From the camp at Starobilsk, the prisoners made the trip by rail, a hundred or two hundred at a time, to Kharkiv, where they were held at the NKVD prison.

Though they could not have known this, they had been brought to one of the main killing centers of Poles in the Soviet Union. Now it was their turn, and they went to their deaths ignorant of the past, ignorant of what was happening to their comrades in other camps, ignorant of what would happen to them. After a day or so in prison they were taken to a room where their details were checked. Then they were led to another room, this one dark and without windows. A guard would ask "May I?" and then lead in the prisoner. As one of the NKVD men remembered, "there was a clack, and that was the end." The bodies were piled onto trucks. Jackets were pulled over the heads of the corpses so that the truck platform would not be stained by the blood. The bodies were loaded head first, then feet first, so they would stack.[46]

In this way 3,739 prisoners of Starobilsk were killed, including all of Józef Czapski's friends and acquaintances: the botanist whom he remembered for his calm, but also an economist who tried to hide his fears from his pregnant wife, a doctor who was known in Warsaw for visiting cafés and supporting artists, the lieutenant who recited plays and novels by heart, the lawyer who was an enthusiast for a European federation, all the engineers, teachers, poets, social workers, journalists, surgeons, and soldiers. But not Czapski himself. He, like a few others from each of the three camps, was sent on to another camp, and survived.[47]

Fyodor Dostoevsky had set a crucial scene of *The Brothers Karamazov* at the Optyn Hermitage in Kozelsk, which in 1939 and 1940 became the site of the Soviet prisoner-of-war camp. Here took place the most famous exchange in the book: a discussion between a young nobleman and a monastery elder about the possibility of morality without God. If God is dead, is everything permitted? In 1940, the real building where this fictional conversation took place, the former residence of some of the monks, housed the NKVD interrogators. They represented a Soviet answer to that question: only the death of God allowed for the liberation of humanity. Unconsciously, many of the Polish officers provided a different answer: that in a place where everything is permitted, God is a refuge. They saw their camps as churches, and prayed in them. Many of them attended Easter services before they were dispatched to their deaths.[48]

The prisoners in the three camps, or at least many of them, guessed that they were being filtered, selected for some role that they might play in the Soviet

Union. They had little or no idea, however, that when they failed this test they would be killed. They knew nothing of the Polish operation of the Great Terror, in which tens of thousands of Soviet Poles had been shot only two years before. Even had they understood the stakes, it seems hard to imagine that very many of them could have demonstrated any sort of believable loyalty to the Soviets. In the camps they had to see Soviet newspapers, watch Soviet propaganda films, and listen to Soviet news broadcasts over loudspeakers. They generally found it all ridiculous, and insulting. Even those who informed on their comrades found the system absurd.[49]

The two cultures did not communicate well, at least not without some obvious shared interest. During this period, when Stalin was Hitler's ally, no such common ground could easily be imagined. The possibilities for misunderstanding, on the other hand, were enormous. Collectivization and industrialization had modernized the Soviet Union, but without the attention to the population, or rather to consumers, that characterized the capitalist West. The Soviet citizens who ruled eastern Poland were falling off bicycles, eating toothpaste, using toilets as sinks, wearing multiple watches, or bras as earmuffs, or lingerie as evening gowns. Polish prisoners were also ignorant, and about more fundamental matters. Unlike Soviet citizens in their position, the Poles believed that they could not be sentenced or killed without a legal basis. It was a sign of the great civilizational transformation of Stalinism that these Soviet and Polish citizens, many of whom had been born in the same Russian Empire, now understood each other so poorly.

The chief interrogator at Kozelsk, the man who inherited the residence of Dostoevsky's monastic elder, put this delicately: it was a matter of "two divergent philosophies." In the end, the Soviets could extend and enforce theirs. Jokes at the expense of the Soviets in eastern Poland could be answered with the easy retort: what is the country called now? The Poles in the camps would not be made to fit Soviet civilization. They did not live like Soviet people: this was the recollection of the Russian and Ukrainian peasants who saw them, who decades later recalled their neatness, cleanliness, and proud bearing. They could not be made to live like Soviet people, at least not on such short notice, and not in these circumstances: but they could be made to die like them. Many of the Polish officers were stronger and better educated than the NKVD captors. But disarmed, confused, and held by two men, they could be shot by a third, and buried where no one, it seemed, would ever find them. In death, it seemed, they could join the silence of the citizens of Soviet history.[50]

In all, this lesser Terror, this revival of the Polish operation, killed 21,892 Polish citizens. The vast majority of them, though not all, were Poles by nationality. Poland was a multinational state, with a multinational officer corps, and so many of the dead were Jews, Ukrainians, and Belarusians. Some eight percent of the victims were Jews, corresponding to the proportion of Jews in eastern Poland.[51]

As in the Great Terror, the families of the repressed were to be punished as well. Three days before proposing that all of the prisoners in these camps be shot, Beria had ordered that their families be deported. The Soviets knew who these people were: this was why they had allowed the prisoners to correspond with their loved ones, to collect names and addresses. Operational troikas in western Belarus and western Ukraine prepared the names of 60,667 people to be sent to special settlements in Kazakhstan. Most of them were family members of what one order called "former people." These were usually families without husbands and fathers. Wives were told, in a typical Soviet lie, that they were being sent to join their husbands. In fact, families were dropped on the Siberian taiga ("the eternal mud and snow" as one thirteen-year-old Polish boy remembered it) as the men were being shot at Katyn, Kalinin, Kharkiv, Bykivnia, and Kurapaty. Some Polish children wrote to Stalin on 20 May 1940, promising to be good Soviet citizens, complaining only that "it's hard to live without our fathers." The following day NKVD men were given cash awards for having cleared out the three camps without allowing a single escape.[52]

Because the men were absent, this deportation was even harder on its victims than the one in February. Women were dropped with their children, and often with their aged parents-in-law, in Kazakhstan. Departing in April on a moment's notice, most women had inadequate clothing. The clothes they brought they often had to sell to buy food. Women survived the following winter by learning to collect and burn dung for heat. Thousands of women died. Many of them had to decide how to keep their children alive. They wished to raise them as Poles, but often realized that they had to give them to Soviet institutions if they were to be fed and to survive. One woman left five of her six children at an NKVD office, and disappeared with the sixth at her breast, never to be seen again. The pregnant wife of the worried economist held at Starobilsk and killed at Kharkiv gave birth to their child in exile. The infant died.[53]

At the same time, in March 1940, NKVD chief Beria had ordered a deportation of people who had declined to accept a Soviet passport. This meant a rejection of the Soviet system, and also a practical problem for Soviet bureaucrats. Polish citizens who refused to allow their identities to enter Soviet records could not be observed and punished with desirable efficiency. As it happened, the vast majority of people who had rejected the Soviet passport were Jewish refugees from western Poland. These people had fled the Germans, but had no wish to become Soviet citizens. They feared that, if they accepted Soviet documents, they would not be allowed to return to Poland—once it was restored. So, in this way, Jews proved to be loyal citizens of Poland, and became victims of both of the regimes that had conquered their homeland. They had fled the depredations of the SS, only to be deported by the NKVD to Kazakhstan and Siberia. Of the 78,339 people deported in the June 1940 action that targeted refugees, about eighty-four percent were Jewish.[54]

Usually people who had no experience in the countryside, Polish Jews were at least as helpless as the Poles who had gone before them. Artisans and cobblers were sent to the far Russian north to fell trees. A Jewish boy called Joseph remembered that the Jews in his hometown had been forced to burn down their own synagogue as the Germans laughed. His family fled to the Soviet zone, but refused the Soviet passport. His brother, father, and mother all died in exile.[55]

In western Europe, this period was known as the "phony war": nothing seemed to be happening. France and Britain were at war with Germany as of September 1939. But that autumn, winter, and the following spring, as Poland was defeated, destroyed, and divided, and tens of thousands of its citizens murdered and hundreds of thousands deported, there was no western front in the war. The Germans and their Soviet allies were free to do as they liked.

The Germans invaded Denmark and Norway in April 1940, thereby securing access to mineral reserves in Scandinavia and preventing any British intervention in northern Europe. But the phony war was well and truly over when Germany attacked the Low Countries and France on 10 May. By 14 June about a hundred thousand French and sixty thousand British soldiers were dead, and the Germans were in Paris. France had fallen, far more quickly than anyone expected. That same month, June 1940, the Soviet Union also extended its

MOLOTOV-RIBBENTROP EUROPE
JULY 1940

empire to the west, annexing all three of the independent Baltic States: Estonia, Latvia, and Lithuania.

The largest and most populous Baltic State, Lithuania, was also the one with the most complicated nationalities issues and international relations. Throughout the interwar period Lithuania had claimed the city of Vilnius and its environs, which lay in northeastern Poland. Though these territories were inhabited mainly by Poles, Jews, and Belarusians, Lithuanians regarded Vilnius as their rightful capital, since the city had been the capital of an important medieval and early-modern state known as the Grand Duchy of Lithuania. In the 1920s and 1930s, the leaders of the independent Lithuanian state had used Kaunas as an administrative center, but regarded Vilnius as their capital. Stalin played on such emotions in 1939. Rather than annexing Vilnius to the Soviet Union, he granted it to still-independent Lithuania. The price, not surprisingly, was the establishment of Soviet military bases on Lithuanian territory. Soviet forces, already installed in Lithuania, stood at the ready as a political revolution, even more hasty and artificial than in eastern Poland, was imposed in summer 1940. Much of the Lithuanian political elite escaped to Nazi Germany.[56]

All of this was carefully observed by the Japanese consul in Lithuania, Chiune Sugihara, who was in Kaunas to monitor German and Soviet military movements. In summer 1940 the Japanese leadership had set a clear course: it would seek a neutrality pact with the Soviet Union. With the north thus secured, the Japanese could plan a move southward for 1941. Sugihara was one of the relatively few Japanese officials in a position to follow German-Soviet relations after the fall of France. Lacking a staff of his own, he used as his informers and assistants Polish military officers who had escaped arrest by the Soviets and the Germans. He rewarded them with Japanese passports and the use of the Japanese diplomatic post. Sugihara helped the Poles find an escape route for their officer comrades. The Poles realized that it was possible to arrange a trip across the Soviet Union to Japan with a certain kind of Japanese exit visa. Only a very few Polish officers escaped by this route, though at least one of them reached Japan and filed intelligence reports about what he had seen while crossing the USSR.[57]

At the same time, Jewish refugees began to visit Sugihara. These Jews were Polish citizens who had originally fled the German invasion of September 1939, but who now feared the Soviets. They had heard of the June 1940 deportation of Jews, and feared the same for themselves. They were right to do so: a year later, the Soviets would deport about 17,500 people from Lithuania, 17,000 from Latvia, and 6,000 from Estonia. With the help of the Polish officers, Sugihara helped several thousand Jews escape Lithuania. They made the long trip across the Soviet Union by rail, then to Japan by ship, and then onward to Palestine or the United States. This action was the coda, silent but firm, of decades of Polish-Japanese intelligence cooperation.[58]

In 1940 the Nazi leaders would have liked to rid themselves of the two million or so Jews in their half of Poland, but could not agree among themselves as to how this was to be achieved. The original wartime plan had been to create some sort of reservation for Jews in the Lublin district of the General Government. But since the area of German conquest in Poland was relatively small, and Lublin not much further from Berlin (seven hundred kilometers) than the two great cities from which Jews would have to be deported, Warsaw (six hundred kilometers) and Łódź (five hundred kilometers), this had never been a satisfying solution. Hans Frank, the general governor, objected to the arrival of more Jews in his terrain. In late 1939 and 1940 Himmler and Greiser continued to dump Poles from the Wartheland into the General Government—some 408,525 in all, similar to the number of Polish citizens deported by the Soviets. This brought enormous suffering to the people in question, but did little to change the national balance in Germany. There were simply too many Poles, and moving them from one part of occupied Poland to another brought little more than chaos. It hardly fulfilled Hitler's grand dreams of living space in the east.[59]

A specialist on deportation, Adolf Eichmann, was recruited in autumn 1939 to improve the efficiency of the operation. Eichmann had already shown his skills by speeding the emigration of Austrian Jews from Vienna. Yet the problem of deporting Jews to the General Government, as Eichmann found, was not so much inefficiency as senselessness. Eichmann learned that Hans Frank, the general governor, had no wish to see any more Jews in his colony. Eichmann managed to send about four thousand Austrian and Czech Jews to the General Government in October 1939 before this policy was halted. Eichmann then drew what must have seemed like the obvious conclusion: that the two million Jews under German power should be deported east to the vast territory of Germany's ally, the Soviet Union. Stalin, after all, had already created a zone of Jewish settlement: Birobidzhan, deep in Soviet Asia. As the Germans noted (and would have occasion to note again), the Soviet regime, unlike their own, had the state capacity and sheer terrain required for effective mass deportations. The Germans proposed a transfer of European Jews in January 1940. Stalin was not interested.[60]

If the General Government was too near and too small to resolve what Nazis saw as the racial problem, and the Soviets were not interested in taking Jews, what was to be done with the racial enemies who made up its native population? They were to be held under control and exploited until the time for the Final Solution (still seen as deportation) came. The model came from Greiser, who ordered the creation of a ghetto for the 233,000 Jews of Łódź on 8 February 1940. That same month Ludwig Fischer, the German mayor of Warsaw, entrusted the lawyer Waldemar Schön with the task of designing a ghetto. In October and November more than a hundred thousand non-Jewish Poles were cleared out of the northwesterly district of Warsaw that the Germans declared to be the ghetto, and more than a hundred thousand Warsaw Jews moved in from elsewhere in the city. Jews were forced to wear a yellow star to identify themselves as Jews, and to submit to other humiliating regulations. They lost property outside the ghettoes, in the first instance to Germans, and then sometimes to Poles (who often had lost their own homes under German bombs). If Warsaw Jews were caught outside the ghetto without permission, they were subject to the death penalty. The fate of the Jews in the rest of the General Government was the same.[61]

The Warsaw ghetto and the other ghettos became improvised labor camps and holding pens in 1940 and 1941. The Germans selected a Jewish council, or Judenrat, usually from among people who had been prewar leaders of the local Jewish community. In Warsaw the head of the Judenrat was Adam Czerniaków, a journalist and prewar senator. The task of the Judenrat was to mediate between the Germans and the Jews of the ghetto. The Germans also created unarmed Jewish police forces, in Warsaw headed by Józef Szerzyński, which were to maintain order, prevent escapes, and carry out German policies of coercion. It was not at all clear what these would be, although with time Jews were able to see that life in the ghetto could not be sustained indefinitely. In the meantime, the Warsaw ghetto became a tourist attraction for visiting Germans. The ghetto historian Emanuel Ringelblum noted that the "shed where dozens of corpses lie awaiting burial is particularly popular." The Baedeker guide to the General Government would be published in 1943.[62]

The Germans themselves returned in summer 1940, after the fall of France, to the idea of a distant Final Solution. The Soviets had rejected a deportation of Jews to the Soviet Union, and Frank had prevented their massive resettlement in his General Government. Madagascar was a French possession; with France subdued, all that stood in the way of its recolonization was the Royal Navy. Himmler mused along those lines: "I trust that thanks to a great journey of Jews to Africa or to some other colony I will see the complete extirpation of the concept of Jews." That, of course, was not the end of the ambition, as Himmler continued: "Over a somewhat longer period of time it must be possible to cause the disappearance on our territory of the national conceptions Ukrainians, Górals, Lemkos. And what has been said about these clans applies, on an appropriately greater scale, also to the Poles. . . . "[63]

Jews were dying at high rates, especially in the Warsaw ghetto, where well over four hundred thousand Jews were assembled. The ghetto comprised an area of only about two square miles, so the population density was about two hundred thousand people per square mile. For the most part, however, the Jews dying in Warsaw were not Warsaw Jews. In the Warsaw district, as elsewhere in the General Government, the Germans drove Jews from smaller settlements into the larger ghettoes. Jews from beyond Warsaw were usually poorer to begin with, and lost what they had as they were deported. They were sent to Warsaw with little time to prepare, and often unable to carry what they had. These Jews from the Warsaw district became the vulnerable ghetto underclass, prone to hunger and disease. Of the perhaps sixty thousand Jews who died in the Warsaw ghetto in 1940 and 1941, the vast majority were resettlers and refugees. It was they who suffered most from harsh German policies, such as the decision to deny any food to the ghetto for the entire month of December 1940. Their death was often a hungry one, after long suffering and moral degradation.[64]

Parents often died first, leaving their children alone in a strange city. Gitla Szulcman remembered that after the death of her mother and her father she "wandered aimlessly through the ghetto and became entirely swollen with hunger." Sara Sborow, whose mother died with her in bed, and whose sister then swelled and starved and died, wrote: "Inside myself I know everything, but I can't say it." The very articulate teenager Izrael Lederman understood that there were "two wars, a war of bullets and a war of hunger. The war of hunger is worse, because then a person suffers, from bullets you die at once." As a doctor remembered, "ten-year-old children sold themselves for bread."[65]

In the Warsaw ghetto, Jewish community organizations established shelters for orphans. Some children, in their desperation, wished for their parents to die so that they could at least get their food allotment as orphans. Some of the shelters were awful spectacles. As one social worker remembered, the children "curse, beat each other, jostle each other around the pot of porridge. Critically ill children lie on the floor, children bloated from hunger, corpses that have not been removed for several days." She worked hard to bring order to a shelter, only to see the children catch typhus. She and her charges were blockaded inside, in quarantine. The shelter, she wrote in her diary with uncanny foresight, "now serves as a gas chamber."[66]

Whereas the Germans preserved prewar Polish-Jewish elites, choosing from among them a Judenrat to implement German policies in the ghetto, they tended to regard non-Jewish Polish elites as a political threat. In early 1940,

Hitler came to the conclusion that the more dangerous Poles in the General Government should simply be executed. He told Frank that Polish "leadership elements" had to be "eliminated." Frank drew up a list of groups to be destroyed that was very similar to that of Operation Tannenberg: the educated, the clergy, the politically active. By an interesting coincidence, he announced this plan to "liquidate" groups regarded as "spiritual leaders" to his subordinates on 2 March 1940, three days before Beria initiated the terror actions against the Polish prisoners in the Soviet Union. His basic policy was the same as Beria's: to kill people already under arrest, and to arrest people regarded as dangerous and kill them too. Unlike Beria, Frank would use the opportunity to execute common criminals as well, presumably to clear prison space. By the end of summer 1940, the Germans had killed some three thousand people they regarded as politically dangerous, and about the same number of common criminals.[67]

The German operation was less well coordinated than the Soviet one. The AB Aktion (Ausserordentliche Befriedungsaktion, Extraordinary Pacification Action), as these killings were known, was implemented differently in each of the various districts of the General Government. In the Cracow district prisoners were read a summary verdict, although no sentence was actually recorded. The verdict was treason, which would have justified a death sentence: but then, contradictorily, everyone was recorded as having been shot while trying to escape. In fact, the prisoners were taken from Montelupi prison in Cracow to nearby Krzesawice, where they dug their own death pits. A day later they were shot, thirty to fifty at a time. In the Lublin district people were held at the town castle, then taken to a site south of the city. By the light of the headlamps of trucks, they were machine-gunned in front of pits. On one night, 15 August 1940, 450 people were killed.[68]

In the Warsaw district prisoners were held at the Pawiak prison, then driven to the Palmiry Forest. There the Germans had used forced labor to dig several long ditches, three meters wide by thirty meters long. Prisoners were awakened at dawn and told to collect their things. In the beginning, at least, they thought that they were being transferred to another camp. Only when the trucks turned into the forest did they understand their fate. The bloodiest night was 20–21 June 1940, when 358 people were shot.[69]

In the Radom district, the action was especially systematic and brutal. Prisoners were bound, and read a verdict: they were a "danger to German security." As in the other cities, Poles did not usually understand that this was supposed to have been a judicial procedure. They were taken away in large groups in the afternoon, according to a schedule: "3:30 binding, 3:45 reading of verdict, 4:00 transport." The first few groups were driven to a sandy area twelve kilometers north of Częstochowa, where they were blindfolded and shot. The wife of one of the prisoners, Jadwiga Flak, was later able to find her way to the killing site. She found in the sand the unmistakable signs of what had happened: shards of bone and bits of blindfold. Her husband Marian was a student who had just turned twenty-two. Four prisoners who were members of the city council had survived. Himmler's brother-in-law, who happened to be the man who ran the city for the Germans, believed that he needed them to construct a swimming pool and a brothel for Germans.[70]

Later groups from Częstochowa were taken to the woods. On 4 July 1940 the three Glińska sisters, Irena, Janina, and Serafina, were all shot there. All three of them had refused to disclose the whereabouts of their brothers. Janina called German rule "laughable and temporary." She said that she would never betray "her brother or another Pole." She did not.[71]

On the way to the killing sites, prisoners would throw notes from the truck, in the hope that passersby would find them and convey them to their families. This was something of a Polish custom, and the notes would surprisingly often find their way to their destination. The people who wrote them, unlike the prisoners in the three Soviet camps, knew that they were going to die. The prisoners at Kozelsk, Ostashkov, and Starobilsk also threw notes from the buses as they left the camps, but they said things like: "We can't tell where they are sending us."[72]

Thus a difference between Soviet and German repression. East of the Molotov-Ribbentrop line, the Soviets wished for secrecy, and barring some extraordinary accident they preserved it. West of the Molotov-Ribbentrop line, Germans did not always want discretion, and were poor at maintaining it even when they so wished. So the victims of the AB Aktion were reconciling themselves, or trying to reconcile their families, to a fate they foresaw. The people awaiting death disagreed about the meaning of it all. Mieczysław Habrowski wrote that: "The blood shed on the Polish land will enrich her and raise the avengers of a free and great Poland." Ryszard Schmidt, who had physically attacked his interrogators, wanted to discourage revenge: "Let the children not take revenge, for revenge breeds more revenge." Marian Muszyński simply bade farewell to his family: "God be with you. I love you all."[73]

Some of the people going to their deaths in the AB Aktion were thinking of family who had been taken prisoner by the Soviets. Although the Soviets and the Germans did not coordinate their policies against the Polish educated classes, they targeted the same sorts of people. The Soviets acted to remove elements that they regarded as dangerous to their system, on the pretext of fighting a class war. The Germans were also defending their territorial gains, though also acting on their sense that the inferior race had to be kept in its place. In the end, the policies were very similar, with more or less concurrent deportations and more or less concurrent mass shootings.

In at least two cases, the Soviet terror killed one sibling, the German terror the other. Janina Dowbor was the only female among the Polish officers taken prisoner by the Soviets. An adventurous soul, she had learned as a girl to hang glide and parachute. She was the first woman in Europe to jump from a height of five kilometers or more. She trained as a pilot in 1939, and enlisted in the Polish air force reserve. In September 1939 she was taken prisoner by the Soviets. According to one account, her plane had been shot down by the Germans. Parachuting to safety, she found herself arrested by the Soviets as a Polish second lieutenant. She was taken to Ostashkov, and then to Kozelsk. She had her own accommodations, and spent her time with air force comrades with whom she felt safe. On 21 or 22 April 1940, she was executed at Katyn, and buried there in the pits along with 4,409 men. Her younger sister Agnieszka had remained in the German zone. Along with some friends, she had joined a resistance organization in late 1939. She was arrested in April 1940, at about the time that her sister was executed. She was killed in the Palmiry Forest on 21 June 1940. Both sisters were buried in shallow graves, after sham trials and shots to the head.[74]

The Wnuk brothers, who hailed from a region that had once been in east-central Poland but was now quite close to the German-Soviet border, met the same fate. Bolesław, the older brother, was a populist politician who had been elected to the Polish parliament. Jakub, the younger brother, studied pharmacology and designed gas masks. Both married in 1932 and had children. Jakub, along with the other experts from his institute, was arrested by the Soviets and killed at Katyn in April 1940. Bolesław was arrested by the Germans in October 1939, taken to Lublin castle in January, and executed in the AB Aktion on 29

June 1940. He left a farewell note on a handkerchief: "I die for the fatherland with a smile on my lips, but I die innocent."[75]

In spring and summer 1940, the Germans were extending their small system of concentration camps so that they could intimidate and exploit Poles. In late April 1940, Heinrich Himmler visited Warsaw, and ordered that twenty thousand Poles be placed in concentration camps. At the initiative of Erich von dem Bach-Zelewski, Himmler's commissar for the Strengthening of Germandom for the Silesia region, a new concentration camp was established at the site of a Polish army barracks close to Cracow: Oświęcim, better known by its German name, Auschwitz. As the AB Aktion came to a close, prisoners were no longer executed, but sent to German camps, very often Auschwitz. The first transport to Auschwitz was made up of Polish political prisoners from Cracow; they were sent on 14 June 1940 and given the numbers 31–758. In July transports of Polish political prisoners were sent to Sachsenhausen and Buchenwald; in November followed two more to Auschwitz. On 15 August began mass roundups in Warsaw, where hundreds and then thousands of people would be seized on the streets and sent to Auschwitz. In November 1940 the camp became an execution site for Poles. At around the same time it attracted the attention of investors from IG Farben. Auschwitz became a giant labor camp very much on the Soviet model, although its slave labor served the interests of German companies, rather than Stalin's dream of planned industrialization.[76]

Unlike the Germans, who wrongly believed that they had eliminated the Polish educated classes in their part of Poland, the Soviets in considerable measure actually had. In the General Government the Polish resistance was growing, whereas in the Soviet Union networks were quickly broken and activists arrested, exiled, and sometimes executed. Meanwhile, a new challenge to Soviet rule from Ukrainians was in view. Poland had been home to about five million Ukrainians, almost all of whom now inhabited Soviet Ukraine. They were not necessarily satisfied by the new regime. Ukrainian nationalists, whose organizations had been illegal in interwar Poland, knew how to work underground. Now that Poland no longer existed, the focus of their labors naturally changed. Soviet policy had made some local Ukrainians receptive to the nationalists' message. While some Ukrainian peasants had initially welcomed Soviet rule and its gifts of farmland, collectivization had quickly turned them against the regime.[77]

The Organization of Ukrainian Nationalists now began to take action against the institutions of Soviet power. Some leading Ukrainian nationalists had inter-war connections with German military intelligence and with Reinhard Hey-drich's SS intelligence service, the Sicherheitsdienst. As Stalin knew, several of them were still gathering intelligence for Berlin. Thus a fourth Soviet deporta-tion from the annexed territories of eastern Poland chiefly targeted Ukrainians. The first two operations had targeted mainly Poles, and the third mainly Jews. An action of May 1941 moved 11,328 Polish citizens, most of them Ukrainians, from western Soviet Ukraine to the special settlements. The very last deporta-tion, on 19 June, touched 22,353 Polish citizens, most of them Poles.[78]

As a little Polish boy from Białystok remembered, "They took us under bombs and there was fire because people began to burn up in the cars." Germany invaded the Soviet Union in a surprise attack on 22 June, and its bombers caught up with the Soviet prison trains. About two thousand deportees died in the freight cars, victims of both regimes.[79]

In purging his new lands, Stalin had been preparing for another war. But he did not believe that it would come so soon.

When Germany invaded the Soviet Union in a surprise attack on 22 June 1941, Poland and the Soviet Union were suddenly transformed from enemies to allies. Each was now fighting Germany. Nevertheless, it was an awkward situation. In the previous two years, the Soviets had repressed about half a million Polish cit-izens: about 315,000 deported, about 110,000 more arrested, and 30,000 exe-cuted, and about 25,000 more who died in custody. The Polish government knew about the deportations, but not about the killings. Nevertheless, the Sovi-ets and the Poles began to form a Polish Army from the hundreds of thousands of Polish citizens now scattered across Soviet prisons, labor camps, and special settlements.[80]

The Polish high command realized that several thousand Polish officers were missing. Józef Czapski, the Polish officer and artist who had survived Kozelsk, was sent to Moscow by the Polish government with the mission of finding the missing men, his former campmates. A sober man, he nevertheless understood his task as a calling. Poland would now have a second chance to fight the Germans, and Czapski was to find the officers who would lead men into battle. As he journeyed to Moscow, to his mind came snatches of Polish romantic poetry, first the deeply masochistic reverie of Juliusz Słowacki, asking God to keep Poland on the cross until she had the strength to stand by herself. Then, speaking to an appealingly honest fellow Pole, Czapski recalled the most famous lines of Cyprian Norwid's poem of desire for the homeland, written in exile: "I long for those who say yes for yes and no for no / For a light without shadow." An urbane, sophisticated man from a nationally mixed family, Czapski found solace by understanding his own nation in the terms of Romantic idealism.[81]

Czapski was indirectly invoking scripture, for Norwid's poem cites the Book of Matthew: "let your communication be, Yea, yea; Nay, nay: for whatsoever is more than these cometh of evil." This was the very same verse with which Arthur Koestler had just ended *Darkness at Noon*, his own novel of the Great Terror. Czapski was on his way to the Lubianka prison in Moscow, the setting of that novel; this was also the very place where Koestler's friend, Alexander Weissberg, had been interrogated before his release in 1940. Weissberg and his wife had both been arrested in the late 1930s; their experiences were one source of Koestler's novel. Czapski was intending to ask one of the Lubianka interrogators about his own friends, the missing Polish prisoners. He had an appointment with Leonid Reikhman, an NKVD officer who had interrogated Polish prisoners.[82]

Czapski passed Reikhman a report, describing the known movements of the thousands of missing officers. Reikhman seemed to read it from beginning to end, following each line with a pencil, but marking nothing. He then spoke some noncommittal words, and promised to call Czapski at his hotel after he had informed himself about the matter. One night at about midnight the phone rang. It was Reikhman, who claimed that he had to leave the city on urgent business. He had no new information. He provided Czapski with some names of other officials with whom to speak, all of whom had already been approached by the Polish government. Czapski even now did not suspect the truth, that all of the missing officers had been murdered. But he understood that something was being concealed. He decided to leave Moscow.[83]

The next day, returning to his hotel room, Czapski felt a pair of eyes staring at him. Weary of the attention that his Polish officer's uniform drew in the

Soviet capital, he paid no attention. An elderly Jew approached him as he reached the elevator. "You're a Polish officer?" The Jew was from Poland, but had not seen his homeland in thirty years, and wished to see it again. "Then," he said, "I could die without regrets." On the spur of the moment, Czapski invited the gentleman to his room, with the intention of giving him a copy of a magazine published by the Polish embassy. On the first page happened to be a photograph of Warsaw—Warsaw, the capital of Poland, the center of Jewish life, the locus of two civilizations, and the site of their encounter. The castle square was destroyed, the famous column of King Zygmunt broken. This was Warsaw after the German bombing. Czapski's companion slumped against a chair, put his head down, and wept. When the Jewish gentleman had gone, Czapski himself began to weep. After the loneliness and mendacity of official Moscow, a single moment of human contact had changed everything for him. "The eyes of the poor Jew," he remembered, "rescued me from a descent into the abyss of unbelief and utter despair."[84]

The sadness the two men shared was of a moment that had just passed, the moment of the joint German-Soviet occupation of Poland. Together, between September 1939 and June 1941, in their time as allies, the Soviet and German states had killed perhaps two hundred thousand Polish citizens, and deported about a million more. Poles had been sent to the Gulag and to Auschwitz, where tens of thousands more would die in the months and years to come. Polish Jews under German occupation were enclosed in ghettos, awaiting an uncertain fate. Tens of thousands of Polish Jews had already died of hunger or disease.

A particular wound was caused by the intention, in both Moscow and Berlin, to decapitate Polish society, to leave Poles as a malleable mass that could be ruled rather than governed. Hans Frank, citing Hitler, defined his job as the elimination of Poland's "leadership elements." NKVD officers took their assignment to a logical extreme by consulting a Polish "Who's Who" in order to define their targets. This was an attack on the very concept of modernity, or indeed the social embodiment of Enlightenment in this part of the world. In eastern Europe the pride of societies was the "intelligentsia," the educated classes who saw themselves as leading the nation, especially during periods of statelessness and hardship, and preserving national culture in their writing, speech, and behavior. The German language has the same word, with the same meaning; Hitler ordered

quite precisely the "extermination of the Polish intelligentsia." The chief interrogator at Kozelsk had spoken of a "divergent philosophy"; one of the German
interrogators in the AB Aktion had ordered an old man to be killed for exhibiting a "Polish way of thinking." It was the intelligentsia who was thought to em-
body this civilization, and to manifest this special way of thinking.[85]

Its mass murder by the two occupiers was a tragic sign that the Polish intelligentsia had fulfilled its historical mission.

CHAPTER 5

THE ECONOMICS OF APOCALYPSE

The twenty-second of June 1941 is one of the most significant days in the history of Europe. The German invasion of the Soviet Union that began that day under the cryptonym Operation Barbarossa was much more than a surprise attack, a shift of alliances, or a new stage in a war. It was the beginning of a calamity that defies description. The engagement of the Wehrmacht (and its allies) with the Red Army killed more than ten million soldiers, not to speak of the comparable number of civilians who died in flight, under bombs, or of hunger and disease as a result of the war on the eastern front. During this eastern war, the Germans also deliberately murdered some ten million people, including more than five million Jews and more than three million prisoners of war.

In the history of the bloodlands, Operation Barbarossa marks the beginning of a third period. In the first (1933–1938), the Soviet Union carried out almost all of the mass killing; in the second, during the German-Soviet alliance (1939–1941), the killing was balanced. Between 1941 and 1945 the Germans were responsible for almost all of the political murder.

Each shift of stages poses a question. In the transition from the first stage to the second, the question was: How could the Soviets make an alliance with the Nazis? In the transition from the second to the third, the question is: Why did the Germans break that alliance? The Molotov-Ribbentrop Europe made by Moscow and Berlin between 1939 and 1941 meant occupation or loss of territory for Belgium, Denmark, Estonia, Finland, France, Latvia, Lithuania,

Luxembourg, the Netherlands, Norway, Poland, and Romania. It also meant
mass deportations and mass shootings for the citizens of Poland, Romania, and
the Baltic States. But for the Soviet Union and Nazi Germany, it meant fruitful
economic cooperation, military victories, and expansion at the expense of these
countries. What was it about the Nazi and Soviet systems that permitted mutually advantageous cooperation, between 1939 and 1941, but also the most destructive war in human history, between 1941 and 1945?

Very often the question of 1941 is posed in a more abstract way, as a matter of
European civilization. In some arguments, German (and Soviet) killing policies
are the culmination of modernity, which supposedly began when Enlightened
ideas of reason in politics were practiced during the French Revolution and the
Napoleonic Wars. The pursuit of modernity in this sense does not explain the
catastrophe of 1941, at least not in any straightforward way. Both regimes rejected the optimism of the Enlightenment: that social progress would follow a
masterly march of science through the natural world. Hitler and Stalin both accepted a late-nineteenth-century Darwinistic modification: progress was possible, but only as a result of violent struggle between races or classes. Thus it
was legitimate to destroy the Polish upper classes (Stalinism) or the artificially
educated layers of Polish subhumanity (National Socialism). Thus far the ideologies of Nazi Germany and the Soviet Union permitted a compromise, the
one embodied in the conquest of Poland. The alliance allowed them to destroy
the fruits of the European Enlightenment in Poland by destroying much of the
Polish educated classes. It allowed the Soviet Union to extend its version of
equality, and Nazi Germany to impose racial schema upon tens of millions of
people, most dramatically by separating Jews into ghettos pending some "Final
Solution." It is possible, then, to see Nazi Germany and the Soviet Union as representing two instances of modernity, which could emanate hostility to a third,
the Polish. But this is a far cry from their representing modernity as such.[1]

The answer to the question of 1941 has less to do with the intellectual heritage
of the Enlightenment and more to do with the possibilities for imperialism, less
to do with Paris and more to do with London. Hitler and Stalin both confronted
the two chief inheritances of the British nineteenth century: imperialism as an
organizing principle of world politics, and the unbroken power of the British
Empire at sea. Hitler, unable to rival the British on the oceans, saw eastern Eu-

rope as ripe for a new land empire. The East was not quite a tabula rasa: the Soviet state and all of its works had to be cleared away. But then it would be, as Hitler said in July 1941, a "Garden of Eden." The British Empire had been a central preoccupation of Stalin's predecessor Lenin, who believed that imperialism artificially sustained capitalism. Stalin's challenge, as Lenin's successor, was to defend the homeland of socialism, the Soviet Union, against a world where both imperialism and capitalism persisted. Stalin had made his concession to the imperialist world well before Hitler came to power: since imperialism continued, socialism would have to be represented not by world revolution but by the Soviet state. After this ideological compromise ("socialism in one country"), Stalin's alliance with Hitler was a detail. After all, when one's country is a fortress of good surrounded by a world of evil, any compromise is justified, and none is worse than any other. Stalin said that the arrangement with Germany had served Soviet interests well. He expected it to end at some point, but not in 1941.[2]

Hitler wanted the Germans to become an imperial people; Stalin wanted the Soviets to endure the imperial stage of history, however long it lasted. The contradiction here was less of principle than of territory. Hitler's Garden of Eden, the pure past to be found in the near future, was Stalin's Promised Land, a territory mastered at great cost, about which a canonical history had already been written (Stalin's *Short Course* of 1938). Hitler always intended to conquer the western Soviet Union. Stalin wanted to develop and strengthen the Soviet Union in the name of self-defense against just such imperialist visions, although his fears involved Japan and Poland, or a Japanese-Polish-German encirclement, more than an invasion from Germany. The Japanese and the Poles took more trouble than the Germans to cultivate national movements within the boundaries of the Soviet Union. Stalin assumed that anyone who would assay an invasion of his vast country would first cultivate an ally within its boundaries.[3]

The contradiction was not a matter of ideas acting on their own. Hitler wanted a war, and Stalin did not—at least not the war of 1941. Hitler had a vision of empire, and it was of great importance; but he was also courting the possibilities and rebelling against the constraints of a very unusual moment. The crucial period was the year between 25 June 1940 and 22 June 1941, between the unexpectedly swift German victory in France and the invasion of the Soviet Union that was supposed to bring a similarly rapid triumph. By the middle of 1940, Hitler had conquered much of central, western, and northern Europe, and had only one enemy: Great Britain. His government was backed by Soviet wheat and oil, and his army was seemingly unbeatable. Why, given the very real gains to Germany of the Soviet alliance, did Hitler choose to attack his ally?

In late 1940 and early 1941, the Soviet Union and Nazi Germany were the only great powers on the European continent, but they were not the only two European powers. Germany and the Soviet Union had remade Europe, but Great Britain had made a world. The Soviet Union and Nazi Germany influenced each other in certain ways, but both were influenced by Great Britain, the enemy that defied their alliance. Britain's empire and navy structured a world system that neither the Nazis nor the Soviets aimed, in the short run, to overturn. Each instead accepted that they would have to win their wars, complete their revolutions, and build their empires, despite the existence of the British Empire and the dominance of the Royal Navy. Whether as enemies or as allies, and despite their different ideologies, the Soviet and Nazi leaderships faced the same basic question, posed by the reality of British power. How could a large land empire thrive and dominate in the modern world without reliable access to world markets and without much recourse to naval power?[4]

Stalin and Hitler had arrived at the same basic answer to this fundamental question. The state must be large in territory and self-sufficient in economics, with a balance between industry and agriculture that supported a hardily conformist and ideologically motivated citizenry capable of fulfilling historical prophecies—either Stalinist internal industrialization or Nazi colonial agrarianism. Both Hitler and Stalin aimed at imperial autarky, within a large land empire well supplied in food, raw materials, and mineral resources. Both understood the flashy appeal of modern materials: Stalin had named himself after steel, and Hitler paid special attention to its production. Yet both Stalin and Hitler understood agriculture as a key element in the completion of their revolutions. Both believed that their systems would prove their superiority to decadent capitalism, and guarantee independence from the rest of the world, by the production of food.[5]

As of late 1940 and early 1941, war factored into this grand economic planning very differently for the Soviets than it did for the Nazis. By then Stalin had an economic revolution to defend, whereas Hitler needed a war for his economic transformation. Whereas Stalin had his "socialism in one country," Hitler had in mind something like National Socialism in several countries: a vast German empire arranged to assure the prosperity of Germans at the expense of others. Stalin presented collectivization itself both as an internal class war and as a preparation for the foreign wars to come. Hitler's economic vision could be realized only after actual military conflict—indeed, after a total military victory over the Soviet Union. The secret of collectivization (as Stalin had noted long before) was that it was an alternative to expansive colonization, which is to say a form of internal colonization. Unlike Stalin, Hitler believed that colonies could still be seized abroad; and the colonies he had in mind were the agrarian lands of the western Soviet Union, as well as the oil reserves in the Soviet Caucasus. Hitler wanted Germany, as he put it, to be "the most autarkic state in the world." Defeating Britain was not necessary for this. Defeating the Soviet Union was. In January 1941 Hitler told the military command that the "immense riches" of the Soviet Union would make Germany "unassailable."[6]

The willingness of the British to fight on alone after the fall of France in June 1940 brought these contradictions to the fore. Between June 1940 and June 1941, Britain was Germany's lone enemy, but stronger than it appeared. The United States had not joined the war, but President Franklin D. Roosevelt had made his commitments clear. In September 1940 the Americans traded fifty destroyers to the British for basing rights in the Caribbean; as of March 1941 the president had the authority (under the "Lend-Lease" act) to send war matériel. British troops had been driven from the European continent when France had fallen, but Britain had evacuated many of them at Dunkirk. In summer 1940 the Luftwaffe engaged the Royal Air Force, but could not defeat it; it could bomb British cities, but not intimidate the British people. Germany could not establish air superiority, a major problem for a power planning an invasion. Though an amphibious assault upon the British Isles would have involved a major crossing of the English Channel with men and matériel, Germany lacked the ships necessary to control the waters and effect the transport. In summer 1940 the Kriegsmarine had three cruisers and four destroyers: no more. On 31 July 1940, even as the Battle of Britain was just beginning, Hitler had already decided to invade his ally, the Soviet Union. On 18 December he ordered operational plans for the invasion to "crush Soviet Russia in a rapid campaign."[7]

Hitler intended to use the Soviet Union to solve his British problem, not in its present capacity as an ally but in its future capacity as a colony. During this crucial year, between June 1940 and June 1941, German economic planners were working hard to devise the ways in which a conquered Soviet Union would make Germany the kind of superpower that Hitler wanted it to become. The key planners worked under the watchful eye of Heinrich Himmler, and under the direct command of Reinhard Heydrich. Under the general heading of "Generalplan Ost," SS Standartenführer Professor Konrad Meyer drafted a series of plans for a vast eastern colony. A first version was completed in January 1940, a second in July 1941, a third in late 1941, and a fourth in May 1942. The general design was consistent throughout: Germans would deport, kill, assimilate, or enslave the native populations, and bring order and prosperity to a humbled frontier. Depending upon the demographic estimates, between thirty-one and forty-five million people, mostly Slavs, were to disappear. In one redaction, eighty to eighty-five percent of the Poles, sixty-five percent of the west Ukrainians, seventy-five percent of the Belarusians, and fifty percent of the Czechs were to be eliminated.[8]

After the corrupt Soviet cities were razed, German farmers would establish, in Himmler's words, "pearls of settlement," utopian farming communities that would produce a bounty of food for Europe. German settlements of fifteen to twenty thousand people each would be surrounded by German villages within a radius of ten kilometers. The German settlers would defend Europe itself at the Ural Mountains, against the Asiatic barbarism that would be forced back to the east. Strife at civilization's edge would test the manhood of coming generations of German settlers. Colonization would make of Germany a continental empire fit to rival the United States, another hardy frontier state based upon exterminatory colonialism and slave labor. The East was the Nazi Manifest Destiny. In Hitler's view, "in the East a similar process will repeat itself for a second time as in the conquest of America." As Hitler imagined the future, Germany would deal with the Slavs much as the North Americans had dealt with the Indians. The Volga River in Russia, he once proclaimed, will be Germany's Mississippi.[9]

Here ideology met necessity. So long as Britain did not fall, Hitler's only relevant vision of empire was the conquest of further territory in eastern Europe. The same held for Hitler's intention to rid Europe of Jews: so long as Britain remained in the war, Jews would have to be eliminated on the European continent, rather than on some distant island such as Madagascar. In late 1940 and early 1941, the Royal Navy prevented Hitler's oceanic version of the Final Solution. Madagascar was a French possession and France had fallen, but the British still controlled the sea lanes. The allied Soviet Union had rejected Germany's proposal to import two million European Jews. So long as the Soviet Union and Nazi Germany were allies, there was little that the Germans could do but accept the Soviet refusal and bide their time. But if Germany conquered the Soviet Union, it could use Soviet territories as it pleased. Hitler had just ordered preparations for the Soviet invasion when he proclaimed to a large crowd at the Berlin Sportpalast in January 1941 that a world war would mean that "the role of Jewry would be finished in Europe." The Final Solution would not follow the invasion of Britain, plans for which were indefinitely postponed. It would follow the invasion of the Soviet Union on 22 June 1941. The first major shooting actions would take place in occupied Soviet Ukraine.[10]

The Soviet Union was the only realistic source of calories for Germany and its west European empire, which together and separately were net importers of food. As Hitler knew, in late 1940 and early 1941 ninety percent of the food shipments from the Soviet Union came from Soviet Ukraine. Like Stalin, Hitler tended to see Ukraine itself as a geopolitical asset, and its people as instruments who tilled the soil, tools that could be exchanged with others or discarded. For Stalin, mastery of Ukraine was the precondition and proof of the triumph of his version of socialism. Purged, starved, collectivized, and terrorized, it fed and defended Soviet Russia and the rest of the Soviet Union. Hitler dreamed of the endlessly fertile Ukrainian soil, assuming that Germans would extract more from the terrain than the Soviets.[11]

Food from Ukraine was as important to the Nazi vision of an eastern empire as it was to Stalin's defense of the integrity of the Soviet Union. Stalin's Ukrainian "fortress" was Hitler's Ukrainian "breadbasket." The German army general staff concluded in an August 1940 study that Ukraine was "agriculturally and industrially the most valuable part of the Soviet Union." Herbert Backe, the responsible civilian planner, told Hitler in January 1941 that "the occupation of Ukraine would liberate us from every economic worry." Hitler wanted Ukraine "so that no one is able to starve us again, like in the last war." The conquest of Ukraine would first insulate Germans from the British blockade, and then the colonization of Ukraine would allow Germany to become a global power on the model of the United States.[12]

In the long run, the Nazis' Generalplan Ost involved seizing farmland, destroying those who farmed it, and settling it with Germans. But in the meantime, during the war and immediately after its (anticipated) rapid conclusion, Hitler needed the locals to harvest food for German soldiers and civilians. In late 1940 and early 1941 German planners decided that victorious German forces in the conquered Soviet Union should use the tool that Stalin had invented for the control of food supply, the collective farm. Some German political planners wished to abolish the collective farm during the invasion, believing that this would win Germany the support of the Ukrainian population. Economic planners, however, believed that Germany had to maintain the collective farm in order to feed the army and German civilians. They won the argument. Backe, Göring's food expert in the Four-Year-Plan Authority, reputedly said that the "Germans would have had to introduce the collective farm if the Soviets had not already arranged it."[13]

As German planners saw matters, the collective farm should be used again to starve millions of people: in fact, this time, the intention was to kill tens of millions. Collectivization had brought starvation to Soviet Ukraine, first as an unintended result of inefficiencies and unrealistic grain targets, and then as an intended consequence of the vengeful extractions of late 1932 and early 1933. Hitler, on the other hand, *planned in advance* to starve unwanted Soviet populations to death. German planners were contemplating the parts of Europe already under German domination, requiring imports to feed about twenty-five million people. They also regarded a Soviet Union whose urban population had grown by about twenty-five million since the First World War. They saw an apparently simple solution: the latter would die, so that the former could live. By their calculations, the collective farms produced just the right amount of food to sustain Germans, but not enough to sustain the peoples of the East. So in that sense they were the ideal tool for political control and economic balance.[14]

This was the Hunger Plan, as formulated by 23 May 1941: during and after the war on the USSR, the Germans intended to feed German soldiers and German (and west European) civilians by starving the Soviet citizens they would conquer, especially those in the big cities. Food from Ukraine would now be sent not north to feed Russia and the rest of the Soviet Union but rather west to nourish Germany and the rest of Europe. In the German understanding, Ukraine (along with parts of southern Russia) was a "surplus region," which produced more food than it needed, while Russia and Belarus were "deficit regions." Inhabitants of Ukrainian cities, and almost everyone in Belarus and in northwestern Russia, would have to starve or flee. The cities would be destroyed, the terrain would be returned to natural forest, and about thirty million people would starve to death in the winter of 1941–1942. The Hunger Plan involved the "extinction of industry as well as a great part of the population in the deficit regions." These guidelines of 23 May 1941 included some of the most explicit Nazi language about intentions to kill large numbers of people. "Many tens of millions of people in this territory will become superfluous and will die or must emigrate to Siberia. Attempts to rescue the population there from death through starvation by obtaining surpluses from the black earth zone can only come at the expense of the provisioning of Europe. They prevent the possibility of Germany holding out until the end of the war, they prevent Germany and Europe from resisting the blockade. With regard to this, absolute clarity must reign."[15]

Hermann Göring, at this time Hitler's most important associate, held overall responsibility for economic planning. His Four-Year-Plan Authority had been charged with preparing the German economy for war between 1936 and 1940. Now his Four-Year-Plan Authority, entrusted with the Hunger Plan, was to meet and reverse Stalin's Five-Year Plan. The Stalinist Five-Year Plan would be imitated in its ambition (to complete a revolution), exploited in its attainment (the collective farm), but reversed in its goals (the defense and industrialization of the Soviet Union). The Hunger Plan foresaw the restoration of a preindustrial Soviet Union, with far fewer people, little industry, and no large cities. The forward motion of the Wehrmacht would be a journey backward in time. National Socialism was to dam the advance of Stalinism, and then reverse the course of its great historical river.

Starvation and colonization were German policy: discussed, agreed, formulated, distributed, and understood. The framework of the Hunger Plan was established by March 1941. An appropriate set of "Economic Policy Guidelines" was issued in May. A somewhat sanitized version, known as the "Green Folder," was circulated in one thousand copies to German officials that June. Just before the invasion, both Himmler and Göring were overseeing important aspects of the postwar planning: Himmler the long-term racial colony of Generalplan Ost, Göring the short-term starvation and destruction of the Hunger Plan. German intentions were to fight a war of destruction that would transform eastern Europe into an exterminatory agrarian colony. Hitler meant to undo all the work of Stalin. Socialism in one country would be supplanted by socialism for the German race. Such were the plans.[16]

Germany did have an alternative, at least in the opinion of its Japanese ally. Thirteen months after the Molotov-Ribbentrop Pact had alienated Tokyo from Berlin, German-Japanese relations were reestablished on the basis of a military alliance. On 27 September 1940, Tokyo, Berlin, and Rome signed a Tripartite Pact. At this point in time, when the central conflict in the European war was the air battle between the Royal Air Force and the Luftwaffe, Japan hoped that this alliance might be directed at Great Britain. Tokyo urged upon the Germans an entirely different revolution in world political economy than the one German planners envisioned. Rather than colonizing the Soviet Union, thought the Japanese, Nazi Germany should join with Japan and defeat the British Empire.

The Japanese, building their empire outward from islands, understood the sea as the method of expansion. It was in the interest of Japan to persuade the Germans that the British were the main common enemy, since such agreement would aid the Japanese to conquer British (and Dutch) colonies in the Pacific. Yet the Japanese did have a vision on offer to the Germans, one that was broader than their own immediate need for the mineral resources from British and Dutch possessions. There was a grand strategy. Rather than engage the Soviet Union, the Germans should move south, drive the British from the Near East, and meet the Japanese somewhere in South Asia, perhaps India. If the Germans and the Japanese controlled the Suez Canal and the Indian Ocean, went Tokyo's case, British naval power would cease to be a factor. Germany and Japan would then become the two world powers.[17]

Hitler showed no interest in this alternative. The Germans told the Soviets about the Tripartite Pact, but Hitler never had any intention of allowing the Soviets to join. Japan would have liked to see a German-Japanese-Soviet coalition against Great Britain, but this was never a possibility. Hitler had already made up his mind to invade the Soviet Union. Though Japan and Italy were now Germany's allies, Hitler did not include them in his major martial ambition. He assumed that the Germans could and should defeat the Soviets themselves. The German alliance with Japan would remain limited by underlying disagreements about goals and enemies. The Japanese needed to defeat the British, and eventually the Americans, to become a dominant naval empire in the Pacific. The

Germans needed to destroy the Soviet Union to become a massive land empire in Europe, and thus to rival the British and the Americans at some later stage.[18]

Japan had been seeking a neutrality pact with the Soviet Union since summer 1940; one was signed in April 1941. Chiune Sugihara, the Soviet specialist among Japanese spies, spent that spring in Königsberg, the German city in East Prussia on the Baltic Sea, trying to guess the date of the German invasion of the Soviet Union. Accompanied by Polish assistants, he made journeys through eastern Germany, including the lands that Germany had seized from Poland. His estimation, based upon observations of German troop movements, was mid-June 1941. His reports to Tokyo were just one of thousands of indications, sent by intelligence staffs in Europe and around the world, that the Germans would break the Molotov-Ribbentrop Pact and invade their ally in late spring or early summer.[19]

Stalin himself received more than a hundred such indications, but chose to ignore them. His own strategy was always to encourage the Germans to fight wars in the west, in the hope that the capitalist powers would thus exhaust themselves, leaving the Soviets to collect the fallen fruit of a prone Europe. Hitler had won his battles in western Europe (against Norway, Denmark, Belgium, Luxembourg, the Netherlands, and France) too quickly and too easily for Stalin's taste. Yet he seemed unable to believe that Hitler would abandon the offensive against Great Britain, the enemy of both Nazi and Soviet ambitions, the one world power on the planet. He expected war with Germany, but not in 1941. He told himself and others that the warnings of an imminent German attack were British propaganda, designed to divide Berlin and Moscow despite their manifest common interests.

Apart from anything else, Stalin could not believe that the Germans would attack without winter gear, which none of the espionage reports seemed to mention.[20]

That was the greatest miscalculation of Stalin's career. The German surprise attack on the Soviet Union of 22 June 1941 looked at first like a striking success. Three million German troops, in three Army Groups, crossed over the Molotov-Ribbentrop line and moved into the Baltics, Belarus, and Ukraine, aiming to take Leningrad, Moscow, and the Caucasus. The Germans were joined in the invasion by their allies Finland, Romania, Hungary, Italy, and Slovakia, and by a division of Spanish and a regiment of Croatian volunteers. This was the largest offensive in the history of warfare; nevertheless, unlike the invasion of Poland, it came only from one side, and would lead to war on one (very long) front. Hitler had not arranged with his Japanese ally a joint attack on the Soviet Union. Japan's leaders might have decided to attack the USSR on their own initiative, but instead decided not to break the neutrality pact. A few Japanese leaders, including Foreign Minister Yōsuke Matsuoka, had urged an invasion of Soviet Siberia. But they had been overruled. On 24 June 1941, two days after German troops had entered the Soviet Union, the Japanese army and navy chiefs had adopted a resolution "not to intervene in the German-Soviet war for the time being." In August, Japan and the Soviet Union reaffirmed their neutrality pact.[21]

German officers had every confidence that they could defeat the Red Army quickly. Success in Poland, and above all in France, had made many of them believers in Hitler's military genius. The invasion of the Soviet Union, led by armor, was to bring a "lightning victory" within nine to twelve weeks. With the military triumph would come the collapse of the Soviet political order and access to Soviet foodstuffs and oil. German commanders spoke of the Soviet Union as a "house of cards" or as a "giant with feet of clay." Hitler expected that the campaign would last no more than three months, probably less. It would be "child's play." That was the greatest miscalculation of Hitler's career.[22]

Ruthlessness is not the same thing as efficiency, and German planning was too bloodthirsty to be really practical. The Wehrmacht could not implement the Hunger Plan. The problem was not one of ethics or law. The troops had been relieved by Hitler from any duty to obey the laws of war toward civilians, and German soldiers did not hesitate to kill unarmed people. They behaved in the first days of the attack much as they had in Poland. By the second day of the invasion, German troops were using civilians as human shields. As in Poland, German soldiers often treated Soviet soldiers as partisans to be shot upon capture, and killed Soviet soldiers who were trying to surrender. Women in uniform, no rarity in the Red Army, were initially killed just because they were female. The problem for the Germans was rather that the systematic starvation

SWEDEN

FINLAND

KARELO-
FINNISH
S.S.R.

Finnish
Army

Helsinki

Lake
Ladoga

Leningrad

*Leningrad
besieged from
September 8, 1941*

Tallinn

Baltic
Sea

ESTONIAN
S.S.R.

Volga

Riga

LATVIAN
S.S.R.

PANZER 4

U.S.S.R.

Dvinsk

Nevel

Rzhev

Klin

Moscow

Danzig

18th

XXXXX
Einsatzgruppe A   NORTH
LEEB

16th

LITHUANIAN
S.S.R.

Vilnius

Smolensk

RUSSIAN
S.F.S.R.

Ryazan

Oka

GERMANY

9th

PANZER 3

Minsk

Roslavl

Tula

Einsatzgruppe B   CENTER
BOCK

Łódź

Warsaw

PANZER 2

Babruisk

BELARUSIAN
S.S.R.

Bryansk

Orel

Yelets

Pinsk

Pripet

2ND ARMY

Homel

GENERAL
GOVERNMENT

Polesian Marshes

Chernihiv

PANZER 2

Kursk

Voronezh

Cracow

XXXXX
Einsatzgruppe C   SOUTH
RUNDSTEDT

6th

Lutsk

Sept. 1, 1941

Rivne

Molotov-Ribbentrop Line

PANZER 1

Kiev

*Front line
Oct. 1, 1941*

Lviv

SLOVAKIA

17TH ARMY

UKRAINIAN
S.S.R.

Dnipro

Poltava

Kharkiv

Dniester

Vinnytsia

PANZER 1

HUNGARY

Hungarian
mechanized
army corps

Uman

Kremenchuk

17TH ARMY

Dnipropetrovsk

Stalino

Romanian
3rd Army

Pervomaisk

German
11th Army

Chișinău

Rostov

Romanian
4th Army

Mykolaiv

Melitopol

ROMANIA

Einsatzgruppe D   XXXX
ROMANIAN
CONSTANTINESCHU

MOLDAVIAN
S.S.R.

Odessa

Sea of
Azov

Belgrade

Danube

Crimea

Kerch

SERBIA

Bucharest

Sevastopol

Sofia

BULGARIA

Black Sea

GREECE

Istanbul

TURKEY

THE GERMAN ADVANCE
22 JUNE – 1 OCTOBER 1941

→ German armor
(Panzergruppen)

→ Movements of
other Axis units

of a large civilian population is an inherently difficult undertaking. It is much easier to conquer territory than to redistribute calories.[23]

Eight years before, it had taken a strong Soviet state to starve Soviet Ukraine. Stalin had put to use logistical and social resources that no invading army could hope to muster: an experienced and knowledgeable state police, a party with roots in the countryside, and throngs of ideologically motivated volunteers. Under his rule, people in Soviet Ukraine (and elsewhere) stooped over their own bulging bellies to harvest a few sheaves of wheat that they were not allowed to eat. Perhaps more terrifying still is that they did so under the watchful eye of numerous state and party officials, often people from the very same regions. The authors of the Hunger Plan assumed that the collective farm could be exploited to control grain supplies and starve a far larger number of people, even as Soviet state power was destroyed. The idea that any form of economic management would work better under Soviet than German control was perhaps unthinkable to the Nazis. If so, German efficiency was an ideological assumption rather than a reality.[24]

The German occupiers never had the ability to starve when and where they chose. For the Hunger Plan to be implemented, German forces would have had to secure every collective farm, observe the harvest everywhere, and make sure that no food was hidden or went unrecorded. The Wehrmacht was able to maintain and control the collective farms, as were the SS and local assistants, but never so effectively as the Soviets had done. Germans did not know the local people, the local harvest, or the local hiding places. They could apply terror, but less systematically than the Soviets had done; they lacked the party and the fear and faith that it could arouse. They lacked the personnel to seal off cities from the countryside. And as the war continued longer than planned, German officers worried that organized starvation would create a resistance movement behind the lines.[25]

Operation Barbarossa was supposed to be quick and decisive, bringing a "lightning victory" within three months at the latest. Yet while the Red Army fell back, it did not collapse. Two weeks into the fighting, the Germans had taken all of what had been Lithuania, Latvia, and eastern Poland, as well as most of Soviet Belarus and some of Soviet Ukraine. Franz Halder, chief of staff of the German army, confided to his diary on 3 July 1941 that he believed that the war had been won. By the end of August, the Germans had added Estonia, a bit more of Soviet Ukraine, and the rest of Soviet Belarus. Yet the pace was all wrong, and the fundamental objectives were not achieved. The Soviet leadership remained in Moscow. As one German corps commander noted pithily on 5 September 1941: "no victorious Blitzkrieg, no destruction of the Russian army, no disintegration of the Soviet Union."[26]

Germany starved Soviet citizens anyway, less from political dominion than political desperation. Though the Hunger Plan was based upon false political assumptions, it still provided the moral premises for the war in the East. In autumn 1941, the Germans starved not to remake a conquered Soviet Union but to continue their war without imposing any costs on their own civilian population. In September Göring had to take stock of the new situation, so disastrously different from Nazi expectations. Dreams of a shattered Soviet Union yielding its riches to triumphant Germans had to be abandoned. The classic dilemma of political economy, guns or butter, was supposed to have been resolved in a miraculous way: guns would make butter. But now, three months into the war, the men carrying the guns very much needed the butter. As the war continued beyond the planned twelve weeks, German soldiers were competing with German civilians for limited food supplies. The invasion itself had halted the supply of grain from the Soviet Union. Now three million German soldiers simply had to be fed, without reducing food rations within Germany itself.[27]

The Germans lacked contingency plans for failure. The troops had a sense that something was wrong; after all, no one had given them any winter coats, and their night watches were getting cold. But how could the German population be told that the invasion had failed, when the Wehrmacht still seemed to be pushing forward and Hitler still had moments of euphoria? But if the Nazi leadership could not admit that the war was going badly, then German civilians would have to be spared any negative consequences of the invasion. Grumbling of stomachs might lead to the grumbling of citizens. Germans could not be allowed to make a sacrifice for the troops on the front, at least not too much, and not too soon. A change in domestic food policy might allow them to see the truth: that the war, at least as their leaders had conceived of it, was already lost. Backe, Göring's food specialist, was sure about what had to be done: the Soviets would have to be deprived of food so that Germans could eat their fill.[28]

It was Göring's task to spare the German economy while supplying the German war machine. His original scheme to starve the Soviet Union after a clear victory now gave way to an improvisation: German soldiers should take whatever food they needed as they continued to fight a war that was already supposed to be over. On 16 September 1941, just as the timeline for the original "lightning victory" was exceeded, Göring ordered German troops to live "off the land." A local commanding general was more specific: Germans must feed themselves "as in the colonial wars." Food from the Soviet Union was to be allocated first to German soldiers, then to Germans in Germany, then to Soviet citizens, and then to Soviet prisoners of war. As the Wehrmacht fought on, in the shorter days and longer nights, as solid roads gave way to the mud and muck of autumn rains, its soldiers had to fend for themselves. Göring's order allowed their misconceived war to continue, at the price of the starvation of millions of Soviet citizens, and of course the deaths of millions of German and Soviet and other soldiers.[29]

Hitler's henchman Göring in September 1941 behaved strikingly like Stalin's henchman Kaganovich had in December 1932. Both men laid down instructions for a food policy that guaranteed death for millions of people in the months that followed. Both also treated the starvation their policies brought not as a human tragedy but as enemy agitation. Just as Kaganovich had done, Göring instructed his subordinates that hunger was a weapon of the enemy, meant to elicit sympathy where harshness was needed. Stalin and Kaganovich had placed the Ukrainian party between themselves and the Ukrainian population in 1932 and 1933, forcing Ukrainian communists to bear the responsibility for grain collection, and to take the blame if targets were not met. Hitler and Göring placed the Wehrmacht between themselves and the hungry Soviet population in 1941 and 1942. During the summer of 1941, some German soldiers had shared their rations with hungry Soviet civilians. A few German officers had tried to ensure that Soviet prisoners of war were fed. In autumn this would have to cease. If German soldiers wanted to eat, they were told, they would have to starve the surrounding population. They should imagine that any food that entered the mouth of a Soviet citizen was taken from the mouth of a German child.[30]

German commanders would have to continue the war, which meant feeding soldiers, which meant starving others. This was the political logic, and the moral trap. For the soldiers and the lower-level officers, there was no escape but insubordination or surrender to the enemy, prospects as unthinkable for German troops in 1941 as they had been for Ukrainian communists in 1932.[31]

In September 1941, the three Wehrmacht Army Groups, North, Center, and South, greeted the new food policy from rather different positions. Army Group

North, tasked to conquer the Baltic States and northwestern Russia, had laid siege to Leningrad in September. Army Group Center raced through Belarus in August. After a long pause, in which some of its forces assisted Army Group South in the battle for Kiev, it advanced again toward Moscow in early October. Army Group South meanwhile made its way through Ukraine toward the Caucasus, much more slowly than anticipated. Platoons of German soldiers resembled the communist brigades of a decade before, taking as much food as they could as quickly as possible.

Army Group South starved Kharkiv and Kiev, the two cities that had served as capitals of Soviet Ukraine. Kiev was taken on 19 September 1941, much later than planned, and after much debate about what to do with the city. Consistent with Generalplan Ost, Hitler wanted the city to be demolished. The commanders on site, however, needed the bridge over the river Dnipro to continue their advance east. So in the end German soldiers stormed the city. On 30 September the occupiers banned the supply of food to Kiev. The logic was that the food in the countryside was to remain there, to be collected by the army and then later by a German civilian occupation authority. Yet the peasants around Kiev found their way into the city, and even ran markets. The Germans were unable to seal the city as the Soviets had done in 1933.[32]

The Wehrmacht was not implementing the original Hunger Plan but rather starving where it seemed useful to do so. The Wehrmacht never intended to starve the entire population of Kiev, only to ensure that its own needs were met. Yet this was nevertheless a policy of indifference to human life as such, and it killed perhaps as many as fifty thousand people. As one Kievan recorded in December 1941, the Germans were celebrating Christmas, but the locals "all move like shadows, there is total famine." In Kharkiv a similar policy killed perhaps twenty thousand people. Among them were 273 children in the city orphanage in 1942. It was near Kharkiv that starving peasant children in 1933 had eaten each other alive in a makeshift orphanage. Now city children, albeit in far smaller numbers, suffered the same kind of horrible death.[33]

Hitler's plans for Leningrad, the old capital of imperial Russia, exceeded even Stalin's darkest fears. Leningrad lay on the Baltic Sea, closer to the Finnish capital Helsinki and the Estonian capital Tallinn than to Moscow. During the Great Terror, Stalin had made sure that Finns were targeted for one of the deadliest of the national actions, believing that Finland might one day lay claim to Leningrad. In November 1939 Stalin had ensured for himself the enmity of the Finns by attacking Finland, which was within his area of influence according to the terms of the Molotov-Ribbentrop Pact. In this Winter War, the Finns inflicted heavy losses and damaged the reputation of the Red Army. They finally had to concede about a tenth of their territory in March 1940, giving Stalin a buffer zone around Leningrad. So in June 1941 Hitler had a Finnish ally, since the Finns naturally wanted to retake land and take revenge in what they would call the "Continuation War." But Hitler did not want to take Leningrad and give it to the Finns. He wanted to remove it from the face of the earth. Hitler wanted the population of Leningrad exterminated, the city razed to the ground, and then its territory handed over to the Finns.[34]

In September 1941, the Finnish Army cut off Leningrad from the north, as the Army Group North began a campaign of siege and bombardment of the city from the south. Though German commanders had not all known about Hitler's most radical plans for Soviet cities, they agreed that Leningrad had to be starved. Eduard Wagner, the quartermaster general of the German army, wrote to his wife that the inhabitants of Leningrad, all 3.5 million of them, would have to be left to their fate. They were simply too much for the army's "provision packet," and "sentimentality would be out of place." Mines were laid around the city to prevent escapes. The surrender of the city was not forthcoming, but had it come it would not have been accepted. The German goal was to starve Leningrad out of existence. At the very beginning of the siege of Leningrad, on 8 September 1941, German shells destroyed the city's food warehouses and oil tanks. In October 1941 perhaps 2,500 people died of starvation and associated diseases. In November the number reached 5,500; in December, 50,000. By the end of the siege in 1944, about one million people had lost their lives.[35]

Leningrad was not starved completely because local Soviet authority functioned within the city and distributed what bread there was, and because the Soviet leadership took risks to provision the population. Once the ice froze over Lake Ladoga, there was an escape and supply route. That winter the temperature would fall to forty below, and the city would face the cold without food stockpiles, heat, or running water. Yet Soviet power within the city did not collapse. The NKVD continued to arrest, interrogate, and imprison. Prisoners were also dispatched across Lake Ladoga; Leningraders were among the 2.5 million or so people whom the NKVD transported to the Gulag during the war. The police and fire departments performed their duties. Dmitrii Shostakovich was a volunteer for a fire brigade when he wrote the third movement of his Seventh Symphony. Libraries remained open, books were read, doctoral dissertations written and defended.[36]

Within the great city Russians (and others) faced the same dilemmas that Ukrainians and Kazakhs (and others) had faced ten years before, during the collectivization famines. Wanda Zvierieva, a girl in Leningrad during the siege, later remembered her mother with great love and admiration. She "was a beautiful woman. I would compare her face to the Mona Lisa." Her father was a physicist with artistic inclinations who would carve wooden sculptures of Greek goddesses with his pocketknife. Late in 1941, as the family was starving, her father went to his office, in the hope of finding a ration card that would allow the family to procure food. He stayed away for several days. One night Wanda awakened to see her mother standing over her with a sickle. She struggled with and overcame her mother, or "the shadow that was left of her." She gave her mother's actions the charitable interpretation: that her mother wished to spare her the suffering of starvation by killing her quickly. Her father returned with food the following day, but it was too late for her mother, who died a few hours later. The family sewed her in blankets and left her in the kitchen until the ground was soft enough to bury her. It was so cold in the apartment that her body did not decompose. That spring Wanda's father died of pneumonia.[37]

In the Leningrad of the day, such stories could be multiplied hundreds of thousands of times. Vera Kostrovitskaia was one of many Leningrad intellectuals who kept diaries to record the horrors. Of Polish origin, she had lost her husband a few years earlier in the Great Terror. Now she watched as her Russian neighbors starved. In April 1942 she recorded the fate of a stranger she saw every day: "With his back to the post, a man sits on the snow, tall, wrapped in rags, over his shoulders a knapsack. He is all huddled up against the post. Apparently he was on his way to the Finland Station, got tired, and sat down. For two weeks while I was going back and forth to the hospital, he 'sat':

1. without his knapsack
2. without his rags
3. in his underwear
4. naked
5. a skeleton with ripped-out entrails."[38]

The best-recalled Leningrad diary of a girl is that of eleven-year-old Tania Savicheva, which reads in its entirety as follows:

"Zhenia died on December 28th at 12:30 A.M. 1941
Grandma died on January 25th 3:00 P.M. 1942
Leka died on March 5th at 5:00 am. 1942

Uncle Vasya died on April 13th at 2:00 after midnight 1942
Uncle Lesha died on May 10th at 4:00 pm 1942
Mother died on May 13th 7:30 am 1942
Savichevs died
Everyone died
Only Tania is left"[39]

Tania Savicheva died in 1944.

The greater the control the Wehrmacht exercised over a population, the more likely that population was to starve. The one place where the Wehrmacht controlled the population completely, the prisoner-of-war camps, was the site of death on an unprecedented scale. It was in these camps where something very much like the original Hunger Plan was implemented.

Never in modern warfare had so many prisoners been taken so quickly. In one engagement, the Wehrmacht's Army Group Center took 348,000 prisoners near Smolensk; in another, Army Group South took 665,000 near Kiev. In those two September victories alone, more than a million men (and some women) were taken prisoner. By the end of 1941, the Germans had taken about three million Soviet soldiers prisoner. This was no surprise to the Germans. The three German Army Groups were expected to move even faster than they did, and thus even more prisoners could have been expected. Simulations had predicted what would happen. Yet the Germans did not prepare for prisoners of war, at least not in the conventional sense. In the customary law of war, prisoners of war are given food, shelter, and medical attention, if only to ensure that the enemy does the same.[40]

Hitler wished to reverse the traditional logic. By treating Soviet soldiers horribly, he wished to ensure that German soldiers would fear the same from the Soviets, and so fight desperately to prevent themselves from falling into the hands of the enemy. It seems that he could not bear the idea of soldiers of the master race surrendering to the subhumans of the Red Army. Stalin took much the same view: that Red Army soldiers should not allow themselves to be taken alive. He could not counsel the possibility that Soviet soldiers would retreat and surrender. They were supposed to advance and kill and die. Stalin announced in August 1941 that Soviet prisoners of war would be treated as deserters, and their families arrested. When Stalin's son was taken prisoner by the Germans, he had his own daughter-in-law arrested. This tyranny of the offensive in Soviet planning caused Soviet soldiers to be captured. Soviet commanders were fearful of ordering withdrawals, lest they be personally blamed (purged, and executed). Thus their soldiers held positions for too long, and were encircled and taken prisoner. The policies of Hitler and Stalin conspired to turn Soviet soldiers into prisoners of war and then prisoners of war into non-people.[41]

Once they had surrendered, Soviet prisoners were shocked by the savagery of their German captors. Captured Red Army soldiers were marched in long columns, beaten horribly along the way, from the field of battle to the camps. The soldiers captured at Kiev, for example, marched over four hundred kilometers in the open air. As one of them remembered, if an exhausted prisoner sat down by the side of the road, a German escort "would approach on his horse and lash with his whip. The person would continue to sit, with his head down. Then the escort would take a carbine from the saddle or a pistol from the holster." Prisoners who were wounded, sick, or tired were shot on the spot, their bodies left for Soviet citizens to find and clean and bury.[42]

When the Wehrmacht transported Soviet prisoners by train, it used open freight cars, with no protection from the weather. When the trains reached their destinations, hundreds or sometimes even thousands of frozen corpses would tumble from the opened doors. Death rates during transport were as high as seventy percent. Perhaps two hundred thousand prisoners died in these death marches and these death transports. All of the prisoners who arrived in the eighty or so prisoner-of-war camps established in the occupied Soviet Union were tired and hungry, and many were wounded or ill.[43]

Ordinarily, a prisoner-of-war camp is a simple facility, built by soldiers for other soldiers, but meant to preserve life. Such camps arise in difficult conditions and in unfamiliar places; but they are constructed by people who know that their own comrades are being held as prisoners by the opposing army. German prisoner-of-war camps in the Soviet Union, however, were something far out of the ordinary. They were designed to end life. In principle, they were divided into three types: the Dulag (transit camp), the Stalag (base camp for enlisted men and noncommissioned officers), and the smaller Oflags (for officers). In practice, all three types of camps were often nothing more than an open field surrounded by barbed wire. Prisoners were not registered by name, though they were counted. This was an astonishing break with law and custom. Even at the German concentration camps names were taken. There was only one other type of German facility where names were not taken, and it had not yet been invented. No advance provision was made for food, shelter, or medical care. There were no clinics and very often no toilets. Usually there was no shelter from the elements. The official calorie quotients for the prisoners were far below survival levels, and were often not met. In practice, only the stronger prisoners, and those who had been selected as guards, could be sure of getting any food at all.[44]

Soviet prisoners were at first confused by this treatment by the Wehrmacht. One of them guessed that "the Germans are teaching us to behave like comrades." Unable to imagine that hunger was a policy, he guessed that the Germans wanted the Soviet prisoners to show solidarity with one another by sharing whatever food they had among themselves. Perhaps this soldier simply could not believe that, like the Soviet Union, Nazi Germany was a state that starved by policy. Ironically, the entire essence of German policy toward the prisoners was that they were not actually equal human beings, and thus certainly not fellow soldiers, and under no circumstances comrades. The guidelines of May 1941 had instructed German soldiers to remember the supposedly "inhuman brutality" of Russians in battle. German camp guards were informed in September that they would be punished if they used their weapons too little.[45]

In autumn 1941, the prisoners of war in all of the Dulags and Stalags went hungry. Though even Göring recognized that the Hunger Plan as such was impossible, the priorities of German occupation ensured that Soviet prisoners would starve. Imitating and radicalizing the policies of the Soviet Gulag, German authorities gave less food to those who could not work than to those who could, thereby hastening the deaths of the weaker. On 21 October 1941, those who could not work saw their official rations cut by twenty-seven percent. This was for many prisoners a purely theoretical reduction, since in many prisoner-of-war camps no one was fed on a regular basis, and in most the weaker had no regular access to food anyway. A remark of the quartermaster general of the army, Eduard Wagner, made explicit the policy of selection: those prisoners who could not work, he said on 13 November, "are to be starved." Across the camps, prisoners ate whatever they could find: grass, bark, pine needles. They had no meat unless a dog was shot. A few prisoners got horsemeat on a few occasions. Prisoners fought to lick utensils, while their German guards laughed at their behavior. When the cannibalism began, the Germans presented it as the result of the low level of Soviet civilization.[46]

The drastic conditions of the war bound the Wehrmacht ever more closely to the ideology of National Socialism. To be sure, the Germany military had been progressively nazified since 1933. Hitler had dismissed the threat of Röhm and his SA in 1934, and announced German rearmament and conscription in 1935. He had directed German industry toward arms production and produced a series of very real victories in 1938 (Austria, Czechoslovakia), 1939 (Poland), and 1940 (Denmark, Norway, Luxembourg, Belgium, and above all France). He had had several years to choose his favorites among the higher officers, and to purge those whose outlook he found too traditional. The victory in France in 1940 had brought the German military command very close to Hitler, as officers began to believe in his talent.

Yet it was the *lack* of victory in the Soviet Union that made the Wehrmacht inseparable from the Nazi regime. In the starving Soviet Union in autumn 1941, the Wehrmacht was in a moral trap, from which National Socialism seemed to offer the only escape. Any remnants of traditional soldierly ideals had to be abandoned in favor of a destructive ethic that made sense of the army's predicament. To be sure, German soldiers had to be fed; but they were eating to gain strength to fight a war that had already been lost. To be sure, calories had to be extracted from the countryside to feed them; but this brought about essentially pointless starvation. As the army high command and the officers in the field implemented illegal and murderous policies, they found no justification except for the sort that Hitler provided: that human beings were containers of calories that should be emptied, and that Slavs, Jews, and Asians, the peoples of the Soviet Union, were less than human and thus more than expendable. Like Ukrainian communists in 1933, German officers in 1941 implemented a policy of starvation. In both cases, many individuals had objections or reservations at first, but the groups in the end implicated themselves in the crimes of the regime, and thus subordinated themselves to the moral claims of their leaders. They became the system as the system became catastrophe.

It was the Wehrmacht that established and ran the first network of camps, in Hitler's Europe, where people died in the thousands, the tens of thousands, the hundreds of thousands, and finally the millions.

Some of the most infamous prisoner-of-war camps were in occupied Soviet Belarus, where by late November 1941 death rates had reached two percent *per day*. At Stalag 352 near Minsk, which one survivor remembered as "pure hell," prisoners were packed together so tightly by barbed wire that they could scarcely move. They had to urinate and defecate where they stood. Some 109,500 people died there. At Dulag 185, Dulag 127, and Stalag 341, in the east Belarusian city Mahileu, witnesses saw mountains of unburied corpses outside the barbed wire. Some thirty to forty thousand prisoners died in these camps. At Dulag 131 at Bobruisk, the camp headquarters caught fire. Thousands of prisoners burned to death, and another 1,700 were gunned down as they tried to escape. All in all at least thirty thousand people died at Bobruisk. At Dulags 220 and 121 in Homel, as many as half of the prisoners had shelter in abandoned stables. The others had no shelter at all. In December 1941 death rates at these camps climbed from two hundred to four hundred to seven hundred a day. At Dulag 342 at Molodechno, conditions were so awful that prisoners submitted written petitions asking to be shot.[47]

The camps in occupied Soviet Ukraine were similar. At Stalag 306 at Kirovohrad, German guards reported that prisoners ate the bodies of comrades who had been shot, sometimes before the victims were dead. Rosalia Volkovskaia, a survivor of the women's camp at Volodymyr Volynskyi, had a view of what the men faced at the local Stalag 365: "we women could see from above that many of the prisoners ate the corpses." At Stalag 346 in Kremenchuk, where inmates got at most two hundred grams of bread per day, bodies were thrown into a pit every morning. As in Ukraine in 1933, sometimes the living were buried along with the dead. At least twenty thousand people died in that camp. At Dulag 162 in Stalino (today Donetsk), at least ten thousand prisoners at a time were crushed behind barbed wire in a small camp in the center of the city. People could only stand. Only the dying would lie down, because anyone who did would be trampled. Some twenty-five thousand perished, making room for more. Dulag 160 at Khorol, southwest of Kiev, was one of the larger camps.

Although the site was an abandoned brick factory, prisoners were forbidden to take shelter in its buildings. If they tried to escape there from the rain or snow, they were shot. The commandant of this camp liked to observe the spectacle of prisoners struggling for food. He would ride in on his horse amidst the crowds and crush people to death. In this and other camps near Kiev, perhaps thirty thousand prisoners died.[48]

Soviet prisoners of war were also held at dozens of facilities in occupied Poland, in the General Government (which had been extended to the southeast after the invasion of the Soviet Union). Here astonished members of the Polish resistance filed reports about the massive death of Soviet prisoners in the winter of 1941–1942. Some 45,690 people died in the camps in the General Government *in ten days*, between 21 and 30 October 1941. At Stalag 307 at Dęblin, some eighty thousand Soviet prisoners died over the course of the war. At Stalag 319 at Chełm some sixty thousand people perished; at Stalag 366 in Siedlce, fifty-five thousand; at Stalag 325 at Zamość, twenty-eight thousand; at Stalag 316 at Siedlce, twenty-three thousand. About half a million Soviet prisoners of war starved to death in the General Government. As of the end of 1941, the largest group of mortal victims of German rule in occupied Poland was neither the native Poles nor the native Jews, but Soviet prisoners of war who had been brought west to occupied Poland and left to freeze and starve. Despite the recent Soviet invasion of Poland, Polish peasants often tried to feed the starving Soviet prisoners they saw. In retaliation, the Germans shot the Polish women carrying the milk jugs, and destroyed whole Polish villages.[49]

Even had the Soviet prisoners all been healthy and well fed, death rates in winter 1941–1942 would have been high. Despite what many Germans thought, Slavs had no inborn resistance to cold. Unlike the Germans, Soviet soldiers had sometimes been equipped with winter gear; this the Germans stole. The prisoners of war were usually left without shelter and without warm clothing, enduring temperatures far below freezing. As the camps were often in fields, no trees or hills broke the ruthless winter winds. Prisoners would build for themselves, by hand in the hard earth, simple dugouts where they would sleep. At Homel three Soviet soldiers, comrades, tried to keep one another warm by sleeping in a tight group. Each would have a turn sleeping in the middle, in the best spot, taking the warmth of his friends. At least one of the three lived to tell the tale.[50]

For hundreds of thousands of prisoners of war, this was the second political famine in Ukraine in the space of eight years. Many thousands of soldiers from Soviet Ukraine saw their bellies swell for the second time, or witnessed cannibalism for the second time. No doubt very many survivors of the first mass starvation died in the second one. A few Ukrainians, such as Ivan Shulinskyi, managed to survive both. The son of a deported kulak, he recalled the starvation of 1933, and told people that he came from the "land of hunger." He would cheer himself in German captivity by singing a traditional Ukrainian song:[51]

> If I only had wings
> I would lift myself to the sky
> To the clouds
> Where there is no pain and no punishment

As during the Soviet starvation campaign of 1933, during the German starvation campaign of 1941 many local people in Ukraine did their best to help the dying. Women would identify men as relatives and thus arrange their release. Young women would marry prisoners who were on labor duty outside the camps. The Germans sometimes allowed this, since it meant that the men would be working in an area under German occupation to produce food for Germans. In the city of Kremenchuk, where the food situation seems not to have been dire, laborers from the camps would leave empty bags in the city when they went to work in the morning, and recover them full of food left by passersby in the evening. In 1941 conditions were favorable for such help, as the harvest was unusually good. Women (the reports are almost always of women) would try to feed the prisoners during the death marches or in the camps. Yet most prisoner-of-war camp commanders, most of the time, prevented civilians from approaching the camps with food. Usually such people were driven away by warning shots. Sometimes they were killed.[52]

The organization of the camps in the east revealed a contempt for life, the life of Slavs and Asians and Jews anyway, that made such mass starvation thinkable. In German prisoner-of-war camps for Red Army soldiers, the death rate over the course of the war was 57.5 percent. In the first eight months after Operation Barbarossa, it must have been far higher. In German prisoner-of-war camps for soldiers of the western Allies, the death rate was less than five percent.

As many Soviet prisoners of war died *on a single given day* in autumn 1941 as did British and American prisoners of war over the course of the entire Second World War.[53]

Just as the Soviet population could not be starved at will, the Soviet state could not be destroyed in one blow. But the Germans certainly tried. Part of the idea of the "lightning victory" was that the Wehrmacht would cover terrain so quickly that the soldiers, and the trailing Einsatzgruppen, would be able to kill Soviet political elites and Red Army political officers. The official "Guidelines for the Behavior of the Troops in Russia," issued on 19 May 1941, demanded a "crackdown" on four groups: agitators, partisans, saboteurs, and Jews. The "Guidelines for the Treatment of Political Commissars" of 6 June 1941 specified that captured political officers were to be killed.[54]

In fact, local Soviet elites fled to the east; and the more elite such people were, the more likely they were to have been evacuated or to have had the resources to arrange their own escape. The country was vast, and Hitler had no ally invading on another vector who might be able to capture such people. German policies of mass murder could affect the Soviet leadership only in the lands that were actually conquered: Ukraine, Belarus, the Baltic States, and a very thin wedge of Russia. This was not very much of the Soviet Union, and the people in question were not of critical importance to the Soviet system. People were shot, but with only minimal consequences for the Soviet state. Most Wehrmacht units seemed to have little difficulty in obeying the "commissar order"; eighty percent of them reported having executed commissars. The military archives preserve the records of 2,252 shootings of such people by the army; the actual number was probably greater.[55]

Shooting civilians was mainly the task of the Einsatzgruppen, one that they had already performed in Poland in 1939. As in Poland, the Einsatzgruppen were assigned to murder certain political groups so that the state would collapse. Four Einsatzgruppen followed the Wehrmacht into the Soviet Union: Einsatzgruppe A following Army Group North into the Baltics toward Leningrad, Einsatzgruppe B following Army Group Center through Belarus toward Moscow, Einsatzgruppe C following Army Group South into Ukraine, and Einsatzgruppe D following the 11th Army in the extreme south of Ukraine. As Heydrich clarified in a telegram of 2 July 1941, after having issued the relevant orders orally, the Einsatzgruppen were to kill communist functionaries, Jews in party and state positions, and other "dangerous elements." As with the Hunger Plan, so with the elimination of people defined as political threats: those in confinement were most vulnerable. By mid-July the orders had come through to carry out mass murder by shooting in the Stalags and Dulags. On 8 September 1941 Einsatzkommandos were ordered to make "selections" of the prisoners of war, executing state and party functionaries, political commissars, intellectuals, and Jews. In October the army high command gave the Einsatzkommandos and the Security Police unrestricted access to the camps.[56]

The Einsatzkommandos could not screen the Soviet prisoners of war very carefully. They would interrogate Soviet prisoners of war in their holding pens, immediately after they were taken. They would ask commissars, communists, and Jews to step forward. Then they would take them away, shoot them, and throw them into pits. They had few interpreters, and these tended to remember the selections as being somewhat random. The Germans had imprecise notions of the ranks and insignia of the Red Army, and initially mistook buglers for political officers. They knew that officers were allowed to wear their hair longer than enlisted men, but this was an uncertain indicator. It had been some time since most of these men had seen a barber. The only group that could easily be identified at this point were male Jews; German guards examined penises for circumcision. Very occasionally Jews survived by claiming to be circumcised Muslims; more often circumcised Muslims were shot as Jews. German doctors seem to have collaborated willingly in this procedure; medicine was a highly nazified profession. As a doctor at the camp at Khorol recalled: "For every officer and soldier it was, in those times, the most natural thing that every Jew was shot to death." At least fifty thousand Soviet Jews were shot after selection, and about fifty thousand non-Jews as well.[57]

The German prisoner-of-war camps in the East were far deadlier than the German concentration camps. Indeed, the existing concentration camps changed their character upon contact with prisoners of war. Dachau, Buchenwald, Sachsenhausen, Mauthausen, and Auschwitz became, as the SS used them to execute Soviet prisoners of war, killing facilities. Some eight thousand Soviet prisoners were executed at Auschwitz, ten thousand at Mauthausen, eighteen thousand at Sachsenhausen. At Buchenwald in November 1941, the SS arranged a method

of mass murder of Soviet prisoners that strikingly resembled Soviet methods in
the Great Terror, though exhibiting greater duplicity and sophistication. Prisoners were led into a room in the middle of a stable, where the surroundings
were rather loud. They found themselves in what seemed to be a clinical examination room, surrounded by men in white coats—SS-men, pretending to be
doctors. They would have the prisoner stand against the wall at a certain place,
supposedly to measure his height. Running through the wall was a vertical slit,
which the prisoner's neck would cover. In an adjoining room was another
SS-man with a pistol. When he saw the neck through the slit, he would fire. The
corpse would then be thrown into a third room, the "examination room," be
quickly cleaned, and the next prisoner invited inside. Batches of thirty-five to
forty corpses would be taken by truck to a crematorium: a technical advance
over Soviet practices.[58]

The Germans shot, on a conservative estimate, half a million Soviet prisoners
of war. By way of starvation or mistreatment during transit, they killed about
2.6 million more. All in all, perhaps 3.1 million Soviet prisoners of war were
killed. The brutality did not bring down the Soviet order; if anything, it strengthened Soviet morale. The screening of political officers, communists, and Jews
was pointless. Killing such people, already in captivity, did not much weaken
the Soviet state. In fact, the policies of starvation and screening stiffened the resistance of the Red Army. If soldiers knew that they would starve in agony as
German captives, they were certainly more likely to fight. If communists and
Jews and political officers knew that they would be shot, they too had little reason to give in. As knowledge of German policies spread, Soviet citizens began
to think that Soviet power was perhaps the preferable alternative.[59]

   As the war continued into November 1941, and more and more German soldiers died at the front and had to be replaced by conscripts from Germany,
Hitler and Göring realized that some prisoners of war would be needed as labor
inside the Reich. On 7 November Göring gave the order for positive selections
(for labor). By the end of the war more than a million Soviet prisoners of war
were working in Germany. Mistreatment and hunger were not easily overcome.
As a sympathetic German observer noted: "Of the millions of prisoners only a
few thousand are capable of work. Unbelievably many of them have died, many
have typhus, and the rest are so weak and wretched that they are in no condition
to work." Some four hundred thousand prisoners sent to Germany died.[60]

By the terms of the German plans, the invasion of the Soviet Union was an utter fiasco. Operation Barbarossa was supposed to bring a "lightning victory"; in late autumn 1941, no victory was in sight. The invasion of the Soviet Union was supposed to resolve all economic problems, which it did not. In the end, occupied Belgium (for example) was of greater economic value to Nazi Germany. The Soviet population was supposed to be cleared; in the event, the most important economic input from the Soviet Union was labor. The conquered Soviet Union was also supposed to provide the space for a "Final Solution" to what the Nazis regarded as the Jewish problem. Jews were supposed to be worked to death in the Soviet Union, or sent across the Ural Mountains, or exiled to the Gulag. The Soviet Union's self-defense in summer 1941 had made yet another iteration of the Final Solution impossible.[61]

By late 1941 the Nazi leadership had already considered, and been forced to abandon, four distinct versions of the Final Solution. The Lublin plan for a reservation in eastern Poland failed by November 1939 because the General Government was too close and too complicated; the consensual Soviet plan by February 1940 because Stalin was not interested in Jewish emigration; the Madagascar plan by August 1940 because first Poland and then Britain fought instead of cooperating; and now the coercive Soviet plan by November 1941 because the Germans had not destroyed the Soviet state. Though the invasion of the USSR provided no "solution," it certainly exacerbated the Jewish "problem." Germany's eastern zone of conquest was now essentially identical with the part of the world most densely inhabited by Jews. In occupying Poland, the Baltics, and the western Soviet Union, the Germans had taken control of the most important traditional homeland of European Jews. About five million Jews now lived under German rule. With the exception of the late Russian Empire, no polity in history had ever ruled so many Jews as Germany did in 1941.[62]

The fate of some of the Soviet prisoners who were released from camps in the east suggested what was to come for the Jews. At Auschwitz in early September 1941, hundreds of Soviet prisoners were gassed with hydrogen cyanide, a pesticide (trade name Zyklon B) that had been used previously to fumigate the barracks of the Polish prisoners in the camp. Later, about a million Jews would be asphyxiated by Zyklon B at Auschwitz. At about the same time, other Soviet prisoners of war were used to test a gas van at Sachsenhausen. It pumped its own exhaust into its hold, thereby asphyxiating by carbon monoxide the people locked inside. That same autumn, gas vans would be used to kill Jews in occupied Soviet Belarus and occupied Soviet Ukraine. As of December 1941, carbon monoxide would also be used, in a parked gas van at Chełmno, to kill Polish Jews in lands annexed to Germany.[63]

From among the terrorized and starving population of the prisoner-of-war camps, the Germans recruited no fewer than a million men for duties with the army and the police. At first, the idea was that they would help the Germans to control the territory of the Soviet Union after its government fell. When that did not happen, these Soviet citizens were assigned to assist in the mass crimes that Hitler and his associates pursued on occupied territory as the war continued. Many former prisoners were given shovels and ordered to dig trenches, over which the Germans would shoot Jews. Others were recruited for police formations, which were used to hunt down Jews. Some prisoners were sent to a training camp in Trawniki, where they learned to be guards. These Soviet citizens and war veterans, retrained to serve Nazi Germany, would spend 1942 in three death facilities in occupied Poland, Treblinka, Sobibór, and Bełżec, where more than a million Polish Jews would be gassed.[64]

Thus some of the survivors of one German killing policy became accomplices in another, as a war to destroy the Soviet Union became a war to murder the Jews.

CHAPTER 6

FINAL SOLUTION

Hitler's utopias crumbled upon contact with the Soviet Union, but they were refashioned rather than rejected. He was the Leader, and his henchmen owed their positions to their ability to divine and realize his will. When that will met resistance, as on the eastern front in the second half of 1941, the task of men such as Göring, Himmler, and Heydrich was to rearrange Hitler's ideas such that Hitler's genius was affirmed—along with their own positions in the Nazi regime. The utopias in summer 1941 had been four: a lightning victory that would destroy the Soviet Union in weeks; a Hunger Plan that would starve thirty million people in months; a Final Solution that would eliminate European Jews after the war; and a Generalplan Ost that would make of the western Soviet Union a German colony. Six months after Operation Barbarossa was launched, Hitler had reformulated the war aims such that the physical extermination of the Jews became the priority. By then, his closest associates had taken the ideological and administrative initiatives necessary to realize such a wish.[1]

No lightning victory came. Although millions of Soviet citizens were starved, the Hunger Plan proved impossible. Generalplan Ost, or any variant of postwar colonization plans, would have to wait. As these utopias waned, political futures depended upon the extraction of what was feasible from the fantasies. Göring, Himmler, and Heydrich scrambled amidst the moving ruins, claiming what they could. Göring, charged with economics and the Hunger Plan, fared worst. Regarded as "the second man in the Reich" and as Hitler's successor, Göring remained immensely prominent in Germany, but played an ever smaller role in the East. As economics became less a matter of grand planning for the postwar period and more a matter of improvising to continue the war, Göring lost his leading position to Albert Speer. Unlike Göring, Heydrich and Himmler were able to turn the unfavorable battlefield situation to their advantage, by reformulating the Final Solution so that it could be carried out during a war that was not going according to plan. They understood that the war was becoming, as Hitler began to say in August 1941, a "war against the Jews."[2]

Himmler and Heydrich saw the elimination of the Jews as their task. On 31 July 1941 Heydrich secured the formal authority from Göring to formulate the Final Solution. This still involved the coordination of prior deportation schemes with Heydrich's plan of working the Jews to death in the conquered Soviet East. By November 1941, when Heydrich tried to schedule a meeting at Wannsee to coordinate the Final Solution, he still had such a vision in mind. Jews who could not work would be made to disappear. Jews capable of physical labor would work somewhere in the conquered Soviet Union until they died. Heydrich represented a broad consensus in the German government, though his was not an especially timely plan. The Ministry for the East, which oversaw the civilian occupation authorities established in September, took for granted that the Jews would disappear. Its head, Alfred Rosenberg, spoke in November of the "biological eradication of Jewry in Europe." This would be achieved by sending the Jews across the Ural Mountains, Europe's eastern boundary. But by November 1941 a certain vagueness had descended upon Heydrich's vision of enslavement and deportation, since Germany had not destroyed the Soviet Union and Stalin still controlled the vast majority of its territory.[3]

While Heydrich made bureaucratic arrangements in Berlin, it was Himmler who most ably extracted the practical and the prestigious from Hitler's utopian thinking. From the Hunger Plan he took the categories of surplus populations and useless eaters, and would offer the Jews as the people from whom calories could be spared. From the lightning victory he extracted the four Einsatzgruppen. Their task had been to kill Soviet elites in order to hasten the Soviet collapse. Their first mission had not been to kill all Jews as such. The Einsatzgruppen had no such order when the invasion began, and their numbers were too small. But they had experience killing civilians, and they could find local help, and they could be reinforced. From Generalplan Ost, Himmler extracted the battalions of Order Police and thousands of local collaborators, whose preliminary assignment was to help control the conquered Soviet Union. Instead they provided the manpower that allowed the Germans to carry out truly massive shootings of Jews beginning in August 1941. These institutions, supported by the Wehrmacht and its Field Police, allowed the Germans to murder about a million Jews east of the Molotov-Ribbentrop line by the end of the year.[4]

Himmler succeeded because he grasped extremes of the Nazi utopias that operated within Hitler's mind, even as Hitler's will faced the most determined resistance from the world outside. Himmler made the Final Solution more radical, by bringing it forward from the postwar period to the war itself, and by showing (after the failure of four previous deportation schemes) how it could be achieved: by the mass shooting of Jewish civilians. His prestige suffered little from the failures of the lightning victory and the Hunger Plan, which were the responsibility of the Wehrmacht and the economic authorities. Even as he moved the Final Solution into the realm of the realizable, he still nurtured the dream of the Generalplan Ost, Hitler's "Garden of Eden." He continued to order revisions of the plan, and arranged an experimental deportation in the Lublin district of the General Government, and would, as opportunities presented themselves, urge Hitler to raze cities.[5]

In the summer and autumn of 1941, Himmler ignored what was impossible, pondered what was most glorious, and did what could be done: kill the Jews east of the Molotov-Ribbentrop line, in occupied eastern Poland, the Baltic States, and the Soviet Union. Aided by this realization of Nazi doctrine during the months when German power was challenged, Himmler and the SS would come to overshadow civilian and military authorities in the occupied Soviet Union, and in the German empire. As Himmler put it, "the East belongs to the SS."[6]

The East, until very recently, had belonged to the NKVD. One secret of Himmler's success was that he was able to exploit the legacy of Soviet power in the places where it had most recently been installed.

In the first lands that German soldiers reached in Operation Barbarossa, they were the war's second occupier. The first German gains in summer 1941 were the territories Germans had granted to the Soviets by the Treaty on Borders and Friendship of September 1939: what had been eastern Poland, Lithuania, Latvia, and Estonia, annexed in the meantime to the Soviet Union. In other words, in

Operation Barbarossa German troops first entered lands that had been independent states through 1939 or 1940, and only then entered the prewar Soviet
Union. Their Romanian ally meanwhile conquered the territories that it had
lost to the Soviet Union in 1940.[7]

The double occupation, first Soviet, then German, made the experience of
the inhabitants of these lands all the more complicated and dangerous. A single
occupation can fracture a society for generations; double occupation is even
more painful and divisive. It created risks and temptations that were unknown
in the West. The departure of one foreign ruler meant nothing more than the
arrival of another. When foreign troops left, people had to reckon not with peace
but with the policies of the next occupier. They had to deal with the consequences of their own previous commitments under one occupier when the next
one came; or make choices under one occupation while anticipating another.
For different groups, these alternations could have different meanings. Gentile
Lithuanians (for example) could experience the departure of the Soviets in 1941
as a liberation; Jews could not see the arrival of the Germans that way.

Lithuania had already undergone two major transformations by the time that
German troops arrived in late June 1941. Lithuania, while still an independent
state, had appeared to benefit from the Molotov-Ribbentrop Pact of August
1939. The Treaty on Borders and Friendship of September 1939 had granted
Lithuania to the Soviets, but Lithuanians had no way of knowing that. What the
Lithuanian leadership perceived that month was something else: Nazi Germany
and the Soviet Union destroyed Poland, which throughout the interwar period
had been Lithuania's adversary. The Lithuanian government had considered Vilnius, a city in interwar Poland, as its capital. Lithuania, without taking part in
any hostilities in September 1939, gained Polish lands for itself. In October 1939,
the Soviet Union granted Lithuania Vilnius and the surrounding regions (2,750
square miles, 457,500 people). The price of Vilnius and other formerly Polish
territories was basing rights for Soviet soldiers.[8]

Then, just half a year after Lithuania had been enlarged thanks to Stalin, it
was conquered by its seeming Soviet benefactor. In June 1940 Stalin seized control of Lithuania and the other Baltic States, Latvia and Estonia, and hastily incorporated them into the Soviet Union. After this annexation, the Soviet Union
deported about twenty-one thousand people from Lithuania, including many
Lithuanian elites. A Lithuanian prime minister and a Lithuanian foreign min-

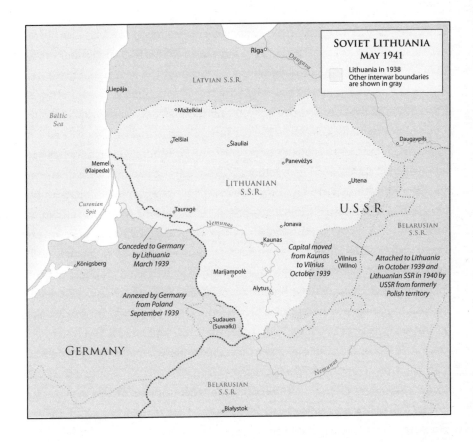

SOVIET LITHUANIA
MAY 1941

Lithuania in 1938
Other interwar boundaries
are shown in gray

Riga

Daugava

LATVIAN S.S.R.

Liepāja

Baltic
Sea

Mažeikiai

Telšiai   Šiauliai   Daugavpils

Panevėžys

Memel
(Klaipeda)

LITHUANIAN   Utena
S.S.R.

Curonian
Spit   Tauragė   U.S.S.R.

Nemunas   Jonava   BELARUSIAN
S.S.R.

Kaunas

Conceded to Germany   Capital moved
by Lithuania   from Kaunas   Vilnius   Attached to Lithuania
Königsberg   March 1939   to Vilnius   (Wilno)   in October 1939 and
Marijampolė   October 1939   Lithuanian SSR in 1940 by
USSR from formerly
Alytus   Polish territory

Annexed by Germany
from Poland
September 1939

Sudauen
(Suwałki)

GERMANY

Nemunas

BELARUSIAN
S.S.R.

Białystok

ister were among the exiled thousands. Some Lithuanian political and military leaders escaped the Gulag by fleeing to Germany. These were often people with some prior connections in Berlin, and always people embittered by their experience with Soviet aggression. The Germans favored the right-wing nationalists among the Lithuanian émigrés, and trained some of them to take part in the invasion of the Soviet Union.[9]

Thus when the Germans invaded the Soviet Union in June 1941, Lithuania occupied a unique position. It had profited from the Molotov-Ribbentrop Pact; then it had been conquered by the Soviets; now it would be occupied by the Germans. After the ruthless year of Soviet occupation, many Lithuanians welcomed this change; few Lithuanian Jews were among them. Two hundred thousand Jews lived in Lithuania in June 1941 (about the same number as in Germany). The Germans arrived in Lithuania with their handpicked nationalist Lithuanians and encountered local people who were willing to believe, or to act as if they believed, that Jews were responsible for Soviet repressions. The Soviet deportations had taken place that very month, and the NKVD had shot Lithuanians in prisons just a few days before the Germans arrived. The Lithuanian diplomat Kazys Škirpa, who returned with the Germans, used this suffering in his radio broadcasts to spur mobs to murder. Some 2,500 Jews were killed by Lithuanians in bloody pogroms in early July.[10]

As a result of trained collaboration and local assistance, German killers had all the help that they needed in Lithuania. The initial guidelines for killing Jews in certain positions were quickly exceeded by Einsatzgruppe A and the local collaborators it enlisted. Einsatzgruppe A had followed Army Group North into Lithuania. Einsatzkommando 3 of Einsatzgruppe A, responsible for the major Lithuanian city of Kaunas, had as many helpers as it needed. Einsatzkommando 3 numbered only 139 personnel, including secretaries and drivers, of which there were forty-four. In the weeks and months to come, Germans drove Lithuanians to killing sites around the city of Kaunas. By 4 July 1941 Lithuanian units were killing Jews under German supervision and orders. As early as 1 December Einsatzkommando 2 considered the Jewish problem in Lithuania resolved. It could report the killing of 133,346 persons, of whom some 114,856 were Jews. Despite Škirpa's wishes, none of this served any Lithuanian political purpose. After he tried to declare an independent Lithuanian state, he was placed under house arrest.[11]

The city of Vilnius had been the northeastern metropolitan center of independent Poland and briefly the capital of independent and Soviet Lithuania. But throughout all of these vicissitudes, and indeed for the previous half-millennium, Vilnius had been something else: a center of Jewish civilization, known as the Jerusalem of the North. Some seventy thousand Jews lived in the city when the war began. Whereas the rest of Lithuania and the other Baltic States were covered by Einsatzgruppe A, the Vilnius area (along with Soviet Belarus) fell to Einsatzgruppe B. The unit assigned to kill the Vilnius Jews was its Einsatzkommando 9. Here the shooting took place at the Ponary Forest, just beyond the city. By 23 July 1941 the Germans had assembled a Lithuanian auxiliary, which marched columns of Jews to Ponary. There, groups of twelve to twenty people at a time were taken to the edge of a pit, where they had to hand over valuables and clothes. Their gold teeth were removed by force. Some 72,000 Jews from Vilnius and elsewhere (and about eight thousand non-Jewish Poles and Lithuanians) were shot at Ponary.[12]

Ita Straż was one of the very few survivors among the Jews of Vilnius. She was pulled by Lithuanian policemen to a pit that was already full of corpses. Nineteen years old at the time, she thought: "This is the end. And what have I seen of life?" The shots missed her, but she fell from fear into the pit. She was then covered by the corpses of the people who came after. Someone marched over the pile and fired downward, to make sure that everyone was dead. A bullet hit her hand, but she made no sound. She crept away later: "I was barefoot. I walked and walked over corpses. There seemed to be no end to it."[13]

Neighboring Latvia, too, had been annexed by the Soviet Union just one year before the German invasion. Some twenty-one thousand Latvian citizens (many of them Latvian Jews) were deported by the Soviets, just weeks before the Germans arrived. The NKVD shot Latvian prisoners as the Wehrmacht approached Riga. The Germans' main collaborator here was Viktor Arajs, a Latvian nationalist (German on his mother's side) who happened to know the translator that German police forces brought to Riga. He was allowed to form the Arajs Commando, which in early July 1941 burned Jews alive in a Riga synagogue. As the Germans organized mass killings, they took care to choose Latvian shooters from among those whose families had suffered under Soviet rule. In July, under the supervision of Einsatzgruppe A commanders, the Arajs Commando marched Riga Jews to the nearby Bikernieki Forest and shot them. The Germans first carried out a "demonstration shooting," and then had the Arajs Commando do much of the rest. With the assistance of such Latvians, the Germans were able to kill at least 69,750 of the country's 80,000 Jews by the end of 1941.[14]

In the third Baltic State, Estonia, the sense of humiliation after the Soviet occupation was just as great as in Lithuania and Latvia, if not greater. Unlike Vilnius and Riga, Tallinn had not even partially mobilized its army before surrendering to the Soviets in 1940. It had yielded to Soviet demands before the other Baltic States, thus precluding any sort of Baltic diplomatic solidarity. The Soviets had deported some 11,200 Estonians, including most of the political leadership. In Estonia, too, Einsatzgruppe A found more than enough local collaborators. Estonians who had resisted the Soviets in the forests now joined a Self-Defense Commando under the guidance of the Germans. Estonians who had *collaborated* with the Soviets also joined, in an effort to restore their reputations.

Estonians greeted the Germans as liberators, and in return the Germans regarded Estonians as racially superior not only to the Jews but to the other Baltic peoples. Jews in Estonia were very few. Estonians from the Self-Defense Commando killed all 963 Estonian Jews who could be found, at German orders. In Estonia the murders and pogroms continued without the Jews. About five thousand non-Jewish Estonians were killed for their ostensible collaboration with the Soviet regime.[15]

East of the Molotov-Ribbentrop line, the Germans encountered the fresh traces of Soviet statebuilding as they began to build their own empire. The signs were even starker in what had been eastern Poland than in the Baltics. Whereas Estonia, Latvia, and Lithuania had been incorporated by the Soviet Union a year before the German invasion, in June 1940, eastern Poland had been annexed by the Soviets nine months before that, in September 1939. Here the Germans found evidence of a social transformation. Industry had been nationalized, some farms had been collectivized, and a native elite had been all but destroyed. The Soviets had deported more than three hundred thousand Polish citizens and shot tens of thousands more. The German invasion prompted the NKVD to shoot some 9,817 imprisoned Polish citizens rather than allow them to fall into German hands. The Germans arrived in the western Soviet Union in summer 1941 to find NKVD prisons full of fresh corpses. These had to be cleared out before the Germans could use them for their own purposes.[16]

Soviet mass murder provided the Germans with an occasion for propaganda. The Nazi line was that suffering under the Soviets was the fault of the Jews, and it found some resonance. With or without German agitation, many people in interwar Europe associated the Jews with communism. Interwar communist parties had in fact been heavily Jewish, especially in their leaderships, a fact upon which much of the press throughout Europe had commented for twenty years. Right-wing parties confused the issue by arguing that since many communists were Jews therefore many Jews were communists. These are very different propositions; the latter one was never true anywhere. Jews were blamed even before the war for the failings of national states; after the war began and national states collapsed during the Soviet or German invasion, the temptation for such scapegoating was all the greater. Estonians, Latvians, Lithuanians, and Poles had lost not only the independent states made for their nations but their status and local authority. They had surrendered all of this, in many cases, without putting up much of a fight. Nazi propaganda thus had a double appeal: it was no shame to lose to the Soviet communists, since they were backed by a powerful worldwide Jewish conspiracy; but since the Jews were ultimately to blame for communism, it was right to kill them now.[17]

In an arc that extended southward from the Baltic Sea to the Black Sea, the last week of June and the first weeks of July 1941 brought violence against Jews. In Lithuania and Latvia, where the Germans could bring local nationalists with them, and could pose at least for a moment as a liberator of whole states, the resonance of propaganda was greater and local participation more notable. In some important places in what had been eastern Poland, such as Białystok, the Germans carried out large-scale killings with their own forces, thereby setting a kind of example. Białystok, just east of the Molotov-Ribbentrop line, had been a city in northeastern Poland, then in Soviet Belarus. Immediately after it was taken by the Wehrmacht on 27 June, Order Police Battalion 309 began to plunder and kill civilians. German policemen killed about three hundred Jews and left the bodies lying around the city. Then they drove several hundred more Jews into the synagogue and set it on fire, shooting those who tried to escape. In the two weeks that followed, local Poles took part in some thirty pogroms in the Białystok region. Meanwhile, Himmler journeyed to Białystok, where he gave instructions that Jews were to be treated as partisans. The Order Police took a thousand Jewish men from Białystok to its outskirts and shot them between 8 and 11 July.[18]

Further south in what had been eastern Poland, in regions where Ukrainians were a majority, Germans appealed to Ukrainian nationalism. Here the Germans blamed the Jews for Soviet oppression of Ukrainians. In Kremenets, where more than a hundred prisoners were found murdered, some 130 Jews were killed in a pogrom. In Lutsk, where some 2,800 prisoners were found machine-gunned, the Germans killed two thousand Jews, and called this revenge for the wrongs done to Ukrainians by Jewish communists. In Lviv, where about 2,500 prisoners were found dead in the NKVD prison, Einsatzgruppe C and local militia organized a pogrom that lasted for days. The Germans presented these people as Ukrainian victims of Jewish secret policemen: in fact, some of the victims were Poles and Jews (and most of the secret policemen were probably Russians and Ukrainians). The diary of a man belonging to another of the Einsatzgruppen recorded the scene on 5 July 1941: "Hundreds of Jews are running down the street with faces covered with blood, holes in their heads, and eyes hanging out."

In the first few days of the war, local militias, with and without various kinds of German aid and encouragement, killed and instigated others to kill about 19,655 Jews in pogroms.[19]

Political calculation and local suffering do not entirely explain the participation in these pogroms. Violence against Jews served to bring the Germans and elements of the local non-Jewish population closer together. Anger was directed, as the Germans wished, toward the Jews, rather than against collaborators with the Soviet regime as such. People who reacted to the Germans' urging knew that they were pleasing their new masters, whether or not they believed that the Jews were responsible for their own woes. By their actions they were confirming the Nazi worldview. The act of killing Jews as revenge for NKVD executions confirmed the Nazi understanding of the Soviet Union as a Jewish state. Violence against Jews also allowed local Estonians, Latvians, Lithuanians, Ukrainians, Belarusians, and Poles who had themselves cooperated with the Soviet regime to escape any such taint. The idea that only Jews served communists was convenient not just for the occupiers but for some of the occupied as well.[20]

Yet this psychic nazification would have been much more difficult without the palpable evidence of Soviet atrocities. The pogroms took place where the Soviets had recently arrived and where Soviet power was recently installed, where for the previous months Soviet organs of coercion had organized arrests, executions, and deportations. They were a joint production, a Nazi edition of a Soviet text.[21]

The encounter with Soviet violence east of the Molotov-Ribbentrop line served the SS, and its leaders. Himmler and Heydrich had always maintained that life was a clash of ideologies, and that traditional European understandings of the rule of law had to give way to the ruthless violence needed to destroy the racial and ideological enemy in the East. The traditional enforcers of German law, the police, had to become "ideological soldiers." Thus before the war Himmler and Heydrich had purged the ranks of the police of men deemed unreliable, encouraged policemen to join the SS, and placed the SS and the Security Police (Order Police plus Gestapo) under a single structure of command. Their goal was to create a unified force dedicated to preemptive racial warfare. By the time of the invasion of the Soviet Union, about a third of German policemen with officer rank belonged to the SS, and about two thirds belonged to the National Socialist party.[22]

The German surprise attack had caught the NKVD off guard, and made the East appear to be a domain of lawlessness primed for a new German order. The NKVD, usually discreet, had been revealed as the murderer of prisoners. Germans broke through the levels of mystification, secrecy, and dissimulation that had covered the (far greater) Soviet crimes of 1937–1938 and 1930–1933. The Germans (along with their allies) were the only power ever to penetrate the territory of the Soviet Union in this way, and so the only people in a position to present such direct evidence of Stalinist murder. Because it was the Germans who discovered these crimes, the prison murders were politics before they were history. Fact used as propaganda is all but impossible to disentangle from the politics of its original transmission.

Because of the visible record of Soviet violence, German forces of order could present themselves as undoing Soviet crimes even as they engaged in crimes of their own. In light of their indoctrination, what Germans found in the doubly occupied lands made a certain kind of sense to them. It seemed to be a confirmation of what they had been trained and prepared to see: Soviet criminality, supposedly steered by and for the benefit of Jews. Soviet atrocities would help German SS-men, policemen, and soldiers justify to themselves the policies to which they were soon summoned: the murder of Jewish women and children. Yet the prison shootings, significant as they were to the local people who suffered Soviet criminality, were for Nazi leaders rather catalyst than cause.

In July 1941, Himmler was eager to show his master Hitler that he was attuned to the darker side of National Socialism, and ready to pursue policies of absolute ruthlessness. His SS and police were in competition for authority in the new eastern colonies with military and civilian occupation authorities. He was also in a personal contest for Hitler's favor with Göring, whose plans for economic expansion lost credibility as the war proceeded. Himmler would demonstrate that shooting was easier than starvation, deportation, and slavery. As Reich Commissar for the Strengthening of Germandom, Himmler's authority as chief of racial affairs extended only to conquered Poland, not to the conquered Soviet Union. But as German forces moved into the prewar Soviet Union, Himmler behaved as if it did, using his power as head of the police and the SS to begin a policy of racial transformation that depended upon mortal violence.[23]

In July 1941, Himmler traveled personally throughout the western Soviet Union to pass on the new line: Jewish women and children should be killed

along with Jewish men. The forces on the ground reacted immediately. Einsatzgruppe C, which had followed Army Group South into Ukraine, had been
slower than Einsatzgruppe A (the Baltic States) and Einsatzgruppe B (Vilnius
and Belarus) to undertake mass shootings of Jews as such. But then, at Himmler's instigation, Einsatzgruppe C killed some sixty thousand Jews in August and
September. These were organized shootings, not pogroms. Indeed, Einsatzkommando 5 of Einsatzgruppe C complained on 21 July that a pogrom by local
Ukrainians and German soldiers hindered them from shooting the Jews of
Uman. In the next two days, however, Einsatzkommando 5 did shoot about
1,400 Uman Jews (sparing a few Jewish women who were to take gravestones
from the Jewish cemetery and use them to build a road). Einsatzkommando 6
of Einsatzgruppe C seems not to have killed women and children until a personal inspection by Himmler.[24]

The killing of women and children was a psychological barrier, one that
Himmler made sure to break. Even as the Einsatzgruppen were generally killing
only Jewish men, Himmler sent units of his Waffen-SS, the combat troops of
the SS, to kill entire communities, including the women and children. On 17
July 1941, Hitler instructed Himmler to "pacify" the occupied territories. Two
days later Himmler dispatched the SS Cavalry Brigade to the marshy Polesie region between Ukraine and Belarus, with the direct order to shoot Jewish men
and to drive the Jewish women into the swamps. Himmler couched his instructions in the language of partisan warfare. But by 1 August the commander of
the Cavalry Brigade was clarifying that: "not one male Jew is to be left alive, not
one remnant family in the villages." Quickly the Waffen-SS understood Himmler's intentions, and helped to spread his message. By 13 August, 13,788 Jewish
men, women, and children had been murdered. Himmler also sent the 1st Infantry SS Brigade to aid the Einsatzgruppen and police forces in Ukraine. Over
the course of 1941, Waffen-SS formations killed more than fifty thousand Jews
east of the Molotov-Ribbentrop line.[25]

Himmler made sure that the Einsatzgruppen were sufficiently reinforced to
kill all the Jews that they found. From August 1941 forward, twelve battalions
of the Order Police would provide most of the German manpower for killing
actions. The Order Police were supposed to be deployed throughout the conquered Soviet Union; since the military campaign went more slowly than expected, they were available in larger-than-expected numbers in the occupied

rear areas. By August the manpower available for mass murder east of the Molotov-Ribbentrop line had reached about twenty thousand. By this time, Himmler seems to have authorized the practice, already widespread, of recruiting local policemen to assist in the shooting. Lithuanians, Latvians, and Estonians had taken part in the shooting almost from the beginning. By the end of 1941, tens of thousands of Ukrainians, Belarusians, Russians, and Tatars had also been recruited to local police forces. Ethnic Germans in the Soviet Union were most desired, and took a prominent part in the killings of Jews. With the Order Police and the local recruits, there was manpower enough for the extermination of the Jews of the occupied Soviet Union.[26]

Himmler took the initiative, directed the murders, and organized the coercive bureaucracy. Enjoying the confidence of Hitler, Himmler was able to arrange the institutions of the police to his liking. He extended the institution of Higher SS and Police Leaders to the occupied Soviet Union. In Germany itself, the Higher SS and Police Leaders had proven to be little more than another layer of administration; in the East, they became what Himmler had always wanted them to be: his personal representatives, a crucial stage in a simplified hierarchy of coercive police power. A Higher SS and Police Leader was assigned to Army Groups North, Center, and South, while a fourth was held ready for an advance into the Caucasus. These men were theoretically subordinate to the civilian occupation authorities (Reichskommissariat Ostland in the north, Reichskommissariat Ukraine in the south) established in September 1941. In fact, the Higher SS and Police Leaders reported to Himmler. They understood that to kill Jews was to fulfill his desires. At Bletchley Park, where the British were decoding German communications, it became clear that the Higher SS and Police Leaders "stand somewhat in competition with each other as to their 'scores.'"[27]

In late August 1941, the coordination of the German forces was on display at the mass shooting of Jews in the southwest Ukrainian city of Kamianets-Podilskyi. Here the war itself had created a problem of Jewish refugees.

Hungary, a German ally, had been allowed to annex subcarpathian Ruthenia, the far eastern district of Czechoslovakia. Rather than grant the native Jews of this region Hungarian citizenship, Hungary expelled "stateless" Jews to the east, to German-occupied Ukraine. The influx of Jews into a German-controlled territory strained limited resources. Friedrich Jeckeln, the Higher SS and Police

Leader for the area, took the initiative, likely so that he could report a success to Himmler at a meeting on 12 August. He flew in personally to make arrangements. The Germans chose a site outside Kamianets-Podilskyi, and forced Jewish refugees and some local Jews to march there. The Jews were shot in pits by Order Police Battalion 320 and Jeckeln's personal staff company. Some 23,600 Jews were killed in the course of four days, from 26 to 29 August. Jeckeln reported the number by radio to Himmler. This was by far the largest massacre yet carried out by the Germans, and it set a pattern for those to follow.[28]

The Wehrmacht aided and abetted such shooting operations, and sometimes requested them. By late August 1941, nine weeks into the war, the Wehrmacht had serious concerns about food supplies and the security of the rear. Murdering Jews would free up food and, according to Nazi logic, prevent partisan uprisings. After the mass shooting at Kamianets-Podilskyi, the Wehrmacht systematically cooperated with the Einsatzgruppen and the police forces in the destruction of

Jewish communities. When a town or a city was taken, the police (if present) would round up some of the Jewish men and shoot them. The army would register the surviving population, noting the Jews. Then the Wehrmacht and the police would negotiate over how many of the remaining Jews could be killed, and how many should be left alive as a labor force in a ghetto. After this selection, the police would proceed to a second mass shooting, with the army often providing trucks, ammunition, and guards. If the police were not present, the army would register Jews and organize forced labor itself. The police would arrange the killings later. As central directives became clearer and these protocols of cooperation were established, death tolls among Jews in occupied Soviet Ukraine roughly doubled from July to August 1941, and then again from August to September.[29]

In Kiev in September 1941, a further confrontation with the remnants of Soviet power provided the pretext for the next escalation: the first attempt to murder all of the native Jews present in a large city.

On 19 September 1941 the Wehrmacht's Army Group South took Kiev, several weeks behind schedule, and with the help of Army Group Center. On 24 September, a series of bombs and mines exploded, destroying the buildings in central Kiev where the Germans had established offices of their occupation regime. Some of these explosives were on timers set before Soviet forces withdrew from the city, but some seem to have been detonated by NKVD men who remained in Kiev. As the Germans pulled their dead and wounded from the rubble, the city suddenly seemed unsafe. As a local remembered, the Germans stopped smiling. They had to try to govern the metropolis with a very small number of people, dozens of whom had just been killed, even as they prepared a continued eastward march. The Germans had a clear ideological line to follow: if the NKVD was guilty, the Jews must be blamed. At a meeting on 26 September, military authorities agreed with representatives of the police and SS that the mass murder of Kiev Jews would be the appropriate reprisal for the bombing. Although most of the Jews of Kiev had fled before the Germans took the city, tens of thousands remained. They were all to be killed.[30]

Disinformation was the key to the entire operation. A Wehrmacht propaganda crew printed broadsheet notices that ordered the Jews of Kiev to appear, on pain of death, at a street corner in a westerly neighborhood of the city. In what would become the standard lie of such mass shooting actions, the Jews were told that they were being resettled. They should thus bring along their documents, money, and valuables. On 29 September 1941 most of the remaining Jewish community of Kiev did indeed appear at the appointed location. Some Jews told themselves that since Yom Kippur, the highest Jewish holiday, was the following day, they could not possibly be hurt. Many arrived before dawn, in the hopes of getting good seats on the resettlement train—which did not exist. People packed for a long journey, old women wearing strings of onions around their necks for food. Having been assembled, the more than thirty thousand people walked, as instructed, along Melnyk Street in the direction of the Jewish cemetery. Observers from nearby apartments recalled an "endless row" that was "overflowing the entire street and the sidewalks."[31]

The Germans had erected a roadblock near the gates of the Jewish cemetery, where documents were verified and non-Jews told to return home. From this point forward the Jews were escorted by Germans with automatic weapons and dogs. At the checkpoint, if no earlier, many of the Jews must have wondered what their true fate would be. Dina Pronicheva, a woman of thirty, walked ahead of her family to a point where she could hear gunshots. Immediately all was clear to her; but she chose not to tell her parents so as not to worry them. Instead she walked along with her mother and father until she reached the tables where the Germans demanded valuables and clothes. A German had already taken her mother's wedding ring when Pronicheva realized that her mother, no less than she, understood what was happening. Yet only when her mother whispered sharply to her—"you don't look like a Jew"—did she try to escape. Such plain communication is rare in such situations, when the human mind labors to deny what is actually happening, and the human spirit strives toward imitation, subordination, and thus extinction. Pronicheva, who had a Russian husband and thus a Russian surname, told a German at a nearby table that she was not Jewish. He told her to wait at one side until the work of the day was complete.[32]

Thus Dina Pronicheva saw what became of her parents, her sister, and the Jews of Kiev. Having surrendered their valuables and documents, people were forced to strip naked. Then they were driven by threats or by shots fired overhead, in groups of about ten, to the edge of a ravine known as Babi Yar. Many of them were beaten: Pronicheva remembered that people "were already bloody as they went to be shot." They had to lie down on their stomachs on the corpses already beneath them, and wait for the shots to come from above and behind. Then would come the next group. Jews came and died for thirty-six hours. People were perhaps alike in dying and in death, but each of them was different until that final moment, each had different preoccupations and presentiments until all was clear and then all was black. Some people died thinking about others rather than themselves, such as the mother of the beautiful fifteen-year-old girl Sara, who begged to be killed at the same time as her daughter. Here there was, even at the end, a thought and a care: that if she saw her daughter shot she would not see her raped. One naked mother spent what she must have known were her last few seconds of life breastfeeding her baby. When the baby was thrown alive into the ravine, she jumped in after it, and in that way found her death. Only there in the ditch were these people reduced to nothing, or to their number, which was 33,761. Since the bodies were later exhumed and burned on pyres, and the bones that did not burn crushed and mixed with sand, the count is what remains.[33]

At the end of the day, the Germans decided to kill Dina Pronicheva. Whether or not she was Jewish was moot; she had seen too much. In the darkness she was led to the edge of the ravine along with a few other people. She was not forced to undress. She survived in the only way possible in that situation: just as the shots began, she threw herself into the gorge, and then feigned death. She bore the weight of the German walking across her body, remaining motionless as the boots tread across her breast and her hand, "like a dead person." She was able to keep open a small air hole as the dirt fell down around her. She heard a small child calling for its mother, and thought of her own children. She began to talk to herself: "Dina, get up, run away, run to your children." Perhaps words made the difference, as they had earlier when her mother, now dead somewhere below, had whispered to her. She dug her way out, and crept away quietly.[34]

Dina Pronicheva joined the perilous world of the few Jewish survivors in Kiev. The law required that Jews be turned in to the authorities. The Germans offered material incentives: money, and sometimes the keys to the Jew's apartment. The local population, in Kiev as elsewhere in the Soviet Union, was of course accustomed to denouncing "enemies of the people." Not so very long before, in 1937 and 1938, the main local enemy, denounced at that time to the NKVD, had been "Polish spies." Now, as the Gestapo settled in to the former offices of the NKVD, the enemy was the Jew. Those who came to report Jews to the German police passed by a guard wearing a swastika armband—standing before friezes of the hammer and sickle. The office dealing with Jewish affairs was rather small, since the investigation of Jewish "crimes" was simple: a Soviet document with Jewish nationality recorded (or a penis without a foreskin) meant death. Iza Belozovskaia, a Kiev Jew in hiding, had a young son called Igor who was confused by all of this. He asked his mother: "What is a Jew?" In practice the answer was given by German policemen reading Soviet identity documents or by German doctors subjecting boys such as Igor to a "medical examination."[35]

Iza Belozovskaia felt death everywhere. "I felt a strong desire," she remembered, "to sprinkle my head, my whole self, with ashes, to hear nothing, to be changed into dust." But she kept going, and she lived. Those who gave up hope sometimes survived thanks to the devotion of their non-Jewish spouses or their families. The midwife Sofia Eizenshtayn, for example, was hidden by her husband in a pit he dug at the back of a courtyard. He led her there dressed as a beggar, and visited her every day as he walked their dog. He talked to her, pretending to talk to the dog. She pleaded with him to poison her. Instead he kept bringing her food and water. Those Jews who were caught by the police were killed. They were placed in cells of the Kiev prison that had held victims of the Great Terror three years before. When the prison was full, the Jews and other prisoners were driven away at dawn in a covered truck. Residents of Kiev learned to fear this truck, as they had feared the NKVD black ravens leaving these same gates. It took the Jews and other prisoners to Babi Yar, where they were forced to disrobe, kneel at the edge of the ravine, and wait for the shot.[36]

Babi Yar confirmed the precedent of Kamianets-Podilskyi for the destruction of Jews in central, eastern, and southern Ukrainian cities. Because Army Group South had captured Kiev late, and because news of German policies spread quickly, most Jews of these regions had fled east and therefore survived. Those who remained almost always did not. On 13 October 1941 about 12,000 Jews were killed at Dnipropetrovsk. The Germans were able to use the local administrations, established by themselves, to facilitate the work of gathering and then killing Jews. In Kharkiv, it appears that Sonderkommando 4a of Einsatzgruppe C had the city administration settle the remaining Jews in a single district. On 15 and 16 December more than 10,000 Kharkiv Jews were taken to a tractor factory at the edge of town. There they were shot in groups by Order Police Battalion 314 and Sonderkommando 4a in January 1942. Some of them were gassed in a truck that piped its own exhaust into its own cargo trailer, and thus into the lungs of Jews who were locked inside. Gas vans were also tried in Kiev, but rejected when the Security Police complained that they disliked removing mangled corpses covered with blood and excrement. In Kiev the German policemen preferred shooting over ravines and pits.[37]

The timing of the mass murder was slightly different in occupied Soviet Belarus, behind the lines of Army Group Center. In the first eight weeks of the war, through August 1941, Einsatzgruppe B under Artur Nebe killed more Jews, in Vilnius and in Belarus, than any of the other Einsatzgruppen. But the further mass murder of Jews in Belarus was then delayed somewhat by a military consideration. Hitler decided to send divisions from Army Group Center to aid Army Group South in the battle for Kiev of September 1941. This decision of Hitler's delayed the march of Army Group Center on Moscow, which was its main task.[38]

Once Kiev was taken and the march on Moscow could resume, so did the killing. On 2 October 1941, Army Group Center began a secondary offensive on Moscow, code-named Operation Typhoon. Police and security divisions began to clear Jews from its rear. Army Group Center advanced with a force of 1.9 million men in seventy-eight divisions. Then the policy of general mass murder of Jews, including women and children, was extended throughout occupied Soviet Belarus. Throughout September 1941 Sonderkommando 4a and Einsatzkommando 5 of Einsatzgruppe B were already exterminating all Jews of villages and small towns. In early October that policy was applied to cities.[39]

In October 1941, Mahileu became the first substantial city in occupied Soviet Belarus where almost all Jews were killed. A German (Austrian) policeman wrote to his wife of his feelings and experiences shooting the city's Jews in the first days of the month. "During the first try, my hand trembled a bit as I shot, but one gets used to it. By the tenth try I aimed calmly and shot surely at the many women, children, and infants. I kept in mind that I have two infants at home, whom these hordes would treat just the same, if not ten times worse. The death that we gave them was a beautiful quick death, compared to the hellish torments of thousands and thousands in the jails of the GPU. Infants flew in great arcs through the air, and we shot them to pieces in flight, before their bodies fell

into the pit and into the water." On the second and third of October 1941, the
Germans (with the help of auxiliary policemen from Ukraine) shot 2,273 men,
women, and children at Mahileu. On 19 October another 3,726 followed.[40]

Here in Belarus a direct order to kill women and children came from Erich
von dem Bach-Zelewski, the Higher SS and Police Leader for "Russia Center,"
the terrain behind Army Group Center. Bach, whom Hitler regarded as a "man
who could wade through a sea of blood," was the direct representative of Himmler, and was certainly acting in accordance with Himmler's wishes. In occupied
Soviet Belarus the accord between the SS and the army on the fate of the Jews
was especially evident. General Gustav von Bechtolsheim, commander of the
infantry division responsible for security in the Minsk area, fervently advocated
the mass murder of Jews as a preventive measure. Had the Soviets invaded Europe, he was fond of saying, the Jews would have exterminated the Germans.
Jews were "no longer humans in the European sense of the word," and thus
"must be destroyed."[41]

Himmler had endorsed the killing of women and children in July 1941, and
then the total extermination of Jewish communities in August 1941, as a small
taste of the paradise to come, the Garden of Eden that Hitler desired. It was a
post-apocalyptic vision of exaltation after war, of life after death, the resurgence
of one race after the extermination of others. Members of the SS shared the
racism and the dream. The Order Police sometimes shared in this vision, and
were of course corrupted by their own participation. The Wehrmacht officers
and soldiers often held essentially the same views as the SS, girded by a certain
interpretation of military practicality: that the elimination of the Jews could
help bring an increasingly difficult war to a victorious conclusion, or prevent
partisan resistance, or at least improve food supplies. Those who did not endorse
the mass killing of Jews believed that they had no choice, since Himmler was
closer to Hitler than they. Yet as time passed, even such military officers usually
came to be convinced that the killing of Jews was necessary, not because the war
was about to won, as Himmler and Hitler could still believe in summer 1941,
but because the war could easily be lost.[42]

Soviet power never collapsed. In September 1941, two months after the invasion, the NKVD was powerfully in evidence, directed against a most sensitive

target: the Germans of the Soviet Union. By an order of 28 August, Stalin had 438,700 Soviet Germans deported to Kazakhstan in the first half of September 1941, most of them from an autonomous region in the Volga River. In its speed, competence, and territorial range, this one act of Stalin made a mockery of the confused and contradictory deportation actions that the Germans had carried out in the previous two years. It was at this moment of Stalin's sharp defiance, in mid-September 1941, that Hitler took a strangely ambiguous decision: to send German Jews to the east. In October and November, the Germans began to deport German Jews to Minsk, Riga, Kaunas, and Łódź. Up to this point, German Jews had lost their rights and their property, but only rarely their lives. Now they were being sent, albeit without instructions to kill them, to places where Jews had been shot in large numbers. Perhaps Hitler wanted revenge. He could not have failed to notice that the Volga had not become Germany's Mississippi. Rather than settling the Volga basin as triumphant colonists, Germans were being deported from it as repressed and humbled Soviet citizens.[43]

Despair and euphoria were on intimate terms in Hitler's mind, and so an entirely different interpretation is also possible. It is perfectly conceivable that Hitler began to deport German Jews because he wished to believe, or wished others to believe, that Operation Typhoon, the secondary offensive on Moscow that began on 2 October 1941, would bring the war to an end. In a moment of exaltation Hitler even claimed as much in a speech of 3 October: "The enemy is broken and will never rise again!" If the war was truly over, then the Final Solution, as a program of deportations for the postwar period, could begin.[44]

Though Operation Typhoon brought no final victory, the Germans went ahead anyway with the deportations of German Jews to the east, which began a kind of chain reaction. The need to make room in these ghettos confirmed one mass killing method (in Riga, in occupied Latvia), and likely hastened the development of another (in Łódź, in occupied Poland).

In Riga, the police commander was now Friedrich Jeckeln, as Higher SS and Police Leader for Reichskommissariat Ostland. Jeckeln, a Riga native, had organized the first massive shooting of Jews at Kamianets-Podilskyi in August, in his former capacity as Higher SS and Police Leader for Reichskommissariat Ukraine. Now, after his transfer, he brought his industrial shooting methods to Latvia. First he had Soviet prisoners of war dig a series of pits in the Letbartskii woods, in the Rumbula Forest, near Riga. On a single day, 30 November 1941,

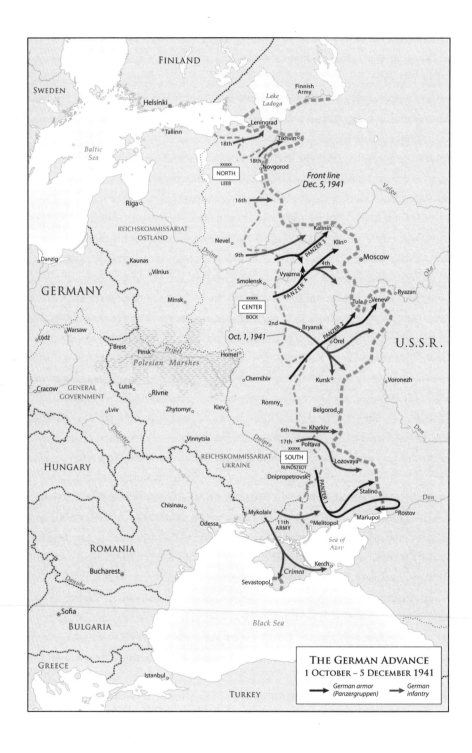

THE GERMAN ADVANCE
1 OCTOBER – 5 DECEMBER 1941

German armor
(Panzergruppen)

German
infantry

Germans and Latvians marched some fourteen thousand Jews in columns to the shooting sites, forced them to lie down next to each other in pits, and shot them from above.[45]

The city of Łódź fell within the domain of Arthur Greiser, who headed the Wartheland, the largest district of Polish territory added to the Reich. Łódź had been the second-most populous Jewish city in Poland, and was now the most populous Jewish city in the Reich. Its ghetto was overcrowded before the arrival of the German Jews. It could be that the need to remove Jews from Łódź inspired Greiser, or the SS and Security Police commanders of the Wartheland, to seek a more efficient method of murder. The Wartheland had always been at the center of the policy of "strengthening Germandom." Hundreds of thousands of Poles had been deported beginning in 1939, to be replaced by hundreds of thousands of Germans who arrived from the Soviet Union (before the German invasion of the USSR made shipping Germans westward utterly pointless). But the removal of the Jews, always a central element of the plan to make this new German zone racially German, had proven the hardest to implement. Greiser confronted a problem on the scale of his district that Hitler confronted on the scale of his empire: the Final Solution was officially deportation, but there was nowhere to send the Jews. By early December 1941 a gas van was parked at Chełmno.[46]

Hitler's deportation of German Jews in October 1941 smacked of improvisation at the top and uncertainty below. German Jews sent to Minsk and Łódź were not themselves killed but, rather, placed in the ghettos. The German Jews sent to Kaunas were however killed upon arrival, as were those of the first transport sent to Riga. Whatever Hitler's intentions, German Jews were now being shot. Perhaps Hitler had decided by this point to murder all of the Jews of Europe, including German Jews; if so, even Himmler had not yet grasped his intention. It was Jeckeln who killed the German Jews arriving in Riga, whom Himmler had *not* wished to murder.

Himmler did set in motion, also in October 1941, a search for a new and more effective way of killing Jews. He made contact with his client Odilo Globocnik, the SS and Police Leader for the Lublin district of the General Government, who immediately set to work on a new type of facility for the killing of Jews at a site known as Bełżec. By November 1941 the concept was not entirely clear and machinery was not yet in place, but certain outlines of Hitler's final version of the Final Solution were visible. In the occupied Soviet Union,

Jews were being killed by bullets on an industrial scale. In annexed and occupied Poland (in the Wartheland and in the General Government), gassing facilities were under construction (at Chełmno and Bełżec). In Germany, Jews were being sent to the east, where some of them had already been killed.[47]

The Final Solution as mass murder, initiated east of the Molotov-Ribbentrop line, was spreading to the west.

In November 1941 Army Group Center was pushing toward Moscow, to win the delayed, but no less glorious, final victory: the end of the Soviet system, the beginning of the apocalyptic transformation of blighted Soviet lands into a proud German frontier empire. In fact, German soldiers were heading into a much more conventional apocalypse. Their trucks and tanks were slowed by the autumn mud, their bodies by the lack of proper clothing and warm food. At one point German officers could see the spires of the Kremlin through their binoculars, but they would never reach the Soviet capital. Their men were at the very limits of their supplies and their endurance. The resistance of the Red Army was ever firmer, its tactics ever more intelligent.[48]

On 24 November 1941 Stalin ordered his strategic reserves from the Soviet East into battle against Army Group Center of the Wehrmacht. He was confident that he could take this risk. From a highly placed informer in Tokyo, and no doubt from other sources, Stalin had reports that there would be no Japanese attack on Soviet Siberia. He had refused to believe in a German attack in summer 1941 and was wrong; now he refused to believe in a Japanese attack in autumn 1941 and was right. He had kept his nerve. On 5 December the Red Army went on the offensive at Moscow. German soldiers tasted defeat. Their exhausted horses could not move their equipment back quickly enough. The troops would spend the winter outside, huddling in the cold, short on everything.[49]

Stalin's intelligence was correct. Japan was about to commit decisively to a war in the Pacific, which would all but exclude any Japanese offensive in Siberia. The southern course of Japanese imperialism had been set by 1937. It had been clear to all when Japan invaded French Indochina in September 1940. Hitler had discouraged his Japanese ally from joining in the invasion of the Soviet Union; now, as that invasion had failed, Japanese forces were moving further in the other direction.

Even as the Red Army marched west on 6 December 1941, a Japanese task force of aircraft carriers was sailing toward Pearl Harbor, the base of the United States Pacific Fleet. On 7 December, a German general, in a letter home, described the battles around Moscow. He and his men were "fighting for our own naked lives, daily and hourly, against an enemy who in all respects is superior." That same day, two waves of Japanese aircraft attacked the American fleet, destroying several battleships and killing two thousand servicemen. The following day the United States declared war on Japan. Three days later, on 11 December, Nazi Germany declared war on the United States. This made it very easy for President Franklin D. Roosevelt to declare war on Germany.[50]

Stalin's position in east Asia was now rather good. If the Japanese meant to fight the United States for control of the Pacific, it was all but inconceivable that they would confront the Soviets in Siberia. Stalin no longer had to fear a two-front war. What was more, the Japanese attack was bound to bring the United States into the war—as an ally of the Soviet Union. By early 1942 the Americans had already engaged the Japanese in the Pacific. Soon American supply ships would reach Soviet Pacific ports, unhindered by Japanese submarines—since the Japanese were neutral in the Soviet-German war. A Red Army taking American supplies from the east was an entirely different foe than a Red Army concerned about a Japanese attack from the east. Stalin just had to exploit American aid, and encourage the Americans to open a second front in Europe. Then the Germans would be encircled, and the Soviet victory certain.

Since 1933, Japan had been the great multiplier in the gambles that Hitler and Stalin took with and against each other. Both men, each for his own reasons, wished for Japan to fight its wars in the south, against China on land and the European empires and the United States at sea. Hitler welcomed the bombing of Pearl Harbor, believing that the United States would be slow to arm and would fight in the Pacific rather than in Europe. Even *after* the failure of Operations Barbarossa and Typhoon, Hitler wished for the Japanese to engage the United States rather than the Soviet Union. Hitler seemed to believe that he could conquer the USSR in early 1942 and then engage an America weakened by the Pacific War. Stalin, too, wished for the Japanese to move south, and had very carefully crafted foreign and military policy that had precisely this effect. His thought was in essence the same as Hitler's: the Japanese are to stay away, because the lands of the Soviet Union are mine. Berlin and Moscow both wanted

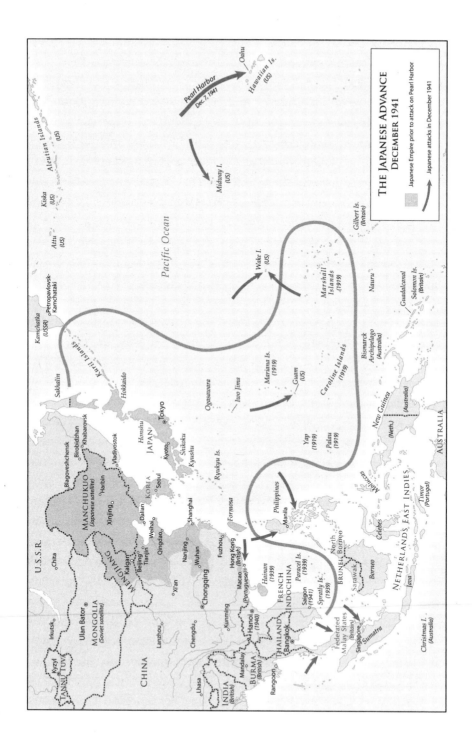

THE JAPANESE ADVANCE
DECEMBER 1941

Japanese Empire prior to attack on Pearl Harbor

Japanese attacks in December 1941

Pacific Ocean

Pearl Harbor
Dec. 7, 1941

Oahu
Hawaiian Is.
(US)

Aleutian Islands
(US)

Kiska
(US)

Attu
(US)

Midway I.
(US)

Gilbert Is.
(Britain)

Wake I.
(US)

Marshall
Islands
(1919)

Nauru

Petropavlovsk-
Kamchatski

Kamchatka
(USSR)

Kuril Islands

Sakhalin

Hokkaido

Honshu
Tokyo
JAPAN
Kyoto
Shikoku
Kyushu

Ryukyu Is.

Ogasawara

Iwo Jima

Mariana Is.
(1919)

Guam
(US)

Caroline Islands
(1919)

Bismarck
Archipelago
(Australia)

Guadalcanal
Solomon Is.
(Britain)

Yap
(1919)
Palau
(1919)

New Guinea
(Neth.)
(Australia)

AUSTRALIA

U.S.S.R.

Chita

Blagoveshchensk
Birobidzhan
Khabarovsk

MANCHUKUO
(Japanese satellite)

Harbin
Vladivostok

Xinjing
Dalian
KOREA
Seoul

Shanghai

Weihai
Qingdao

Formosa

Philippines

Manila

Irkutsk

Kyzyl
TANNU TUVA

Ulan Bator
MONGOLIA
(Soviet satellite)

MENGJIANG

Kalgan
Beijing
Tianjin

Nanjing
Wuhan

Xi'an

Chongqing

Lanzhou

Chengdu

Kunming

CHINA

Fuzhou

Hong Kong
(British)
Macao
(Portuguese)

Hainan
(1939)

FRENCH
INDOCHINA

Paracel Is.
(1939)

North
Borneo

Celebes

Moluccas

Timor
(Portugal)

Hanoi
(1940)

Saigon
(1941)

Spratly Is.
(1939)

BRUNEI
Sarawak

Borneo

NETHERLANDS EAST INDIES

Java

Lhasa

Mandalay

BURMA
(British)

THAILAND
Bangkok

Rangoon

INDIA
(British)

Federated
Malay States
(Britain)
Singapore

Sumatra

Christmas I.
(Australia)

to keep Japan in east Asia and in the Pacific, and Tokyo obliged them both. Whom this would serve depended upon the outcome of the German attack on the Soviet Union.[51]

Had the German invasion proceeded as envisioned, as a lightning victory that leveled the great Soviet cities and yielded Ukrainian food and Caucasian oil, the Japanese strike on Pearl Harbor might indeed have been good news for Berlin. In such a scenario, the attack on Pearl Harbor would have meant that the Japanese were diverting the United States as Germany consolidated a victorious position in its new colony. The Germans would have initiated Generalplan Ost or some variant, seeking to become a great land empire self-sufficient in food and oil and capable of defending themselves against a naval blockade by the United Kingdom and an amphibious assault by the United States. This had always been a fantasy scenario, but it had some light purchase upon reality so long as German troops were making for Moscow.

Since the Germans were turned back at Moscow at the very moment that the Japanese advanced, Pearl Harbor had exactly the opposite meaning. It meant that Germany was in the worst of all possible configurations: not a giant land empire intimidating Great Britain and preparing itself for a confrontation with the United States but rather a single European country at war against the Soviet Union, the United Kingdom, and the United States with allies either weak (Italy, Hungary, Romania, Slovakia) or uninvolved in the crucial east European theater (Japan, Bulgaria). The Japanese seemed to understand this better than the Germans. They wanted Hitler to make a separate peace with Stalin, and then fight the British and the Americans for control of Asia and North Africa. The Japanese wished to break Britain's naval power; the Germans tried to work within its bounds. This left Hitler with one world strategy, and he kept to it: the destruction of the Soviet Union and the creation of a land empire on its ruins.[52]

In December 1941, Hitler found a strange resolution to his drastic strategic predicament. He himself had told his generals that "all continental problems" had to be resolved by the end of 1941 so that Germany could prepare for a global conflict with the United Kingdom and the United States. Instead Germany found itself facing the timeless strategic nightmare, the two-front war, to be fought against three great powers. With characteristic audacity and political agility,

Hitler recast the situation in terms that were consistent with Nazi anti-Semitism, if not with the original planning for the war. What besides utopian planning, inept calculation, racist arrogance, and foolish brinksmanship could have brought Germany into a war with the United Kingdom, the United States, and the Soviet Union? Hitler had the answer: a worldwide Jewish conspiracy.[53]

In January 1939, Hitler had made a speech threatening the Jews with extinction if they succeeded in fomenting another world war. Since summer 1941, German propaganda had played unceasingly on the theme of a tentacular Jewish plot, uniting the British, the Soviets, and ever more the Americans. On 12 December 1941, a week after the Soviet counterattack at Moscow, four days after the Japanese attack on Pearl Harbor, and one day after the United States reciprocated the German declaration of war, Hitler returned to that speech. He referred to it as a prophecy that would have to be fulfilled. "The world war is here," he told some fifty trusted comrades on 12 December 1941; "the annihilation of Jewry must be the necessary consequence." From that point forward his most important subordinates understood their task: to kill all Jews wherever possible. Hans Frank, the head of the General Government, conveyed the policy in Warsaw a few days later: "Gentlemen, I must ask you to rid yourselves of all feeling of pity. We must annihilate the Jews wherever we find them, in order to maintain the structure of the Reich as a whole."[54]

Jews were now blamed for the looming disaster that could not be named. Nazis would have instantly grasped the connection between the Jewish enemy and the prospect of downfall. They all believed, if they accepted Hitler's view, that Germany had not been defeated on the battlefield in the last world war, but instead brought down by a "stab in the back," a conspiracy of Jews and other internal enemies. Now Jews would also take the blame for the American-British-Soviet alliance. Such a "common front" of capitalism and communism, went Hitler's reasoning, could only have been consecrated by the Jewish cabals in London, Moscow, and Washington. Jews were the aggressors, Germans the victims. If disaster were to be averted, Jews would have to be eliminated. Hitler's propaganda chief Joseph Goebbels recorded the moral reversal in his diary: "We are not here to have sympathy with the Jews, but only to have sympathy with our German nation."[55]

As the war turned Stalin's way, Hitler recast its purpose. The plan had been to destroy the Soviet Union and then eliminate the Jews. Now, as the destruction of the Soviet Union was indefinitely delayed, the utter extermination of the Jews became a wartime policy. The menace henceforth was less the Slavic masses and their supposed Jewish overlords, and more the Jews as such. In 1942, propaganda against Slavs would ease, as more of them came to work in the Reich. Hitler's decision to kill Jews (rather than exploit their labor) was presumably facilitated by his simultaneous decision to exploit the labor of Slavs (rather than kill them). These moves signified an abandonment of most of the initial assumptions about the course of the war, although of course Hitler would never have admitted that. But the mass killing of the Jews at least looked consistent with the initial vision of a frontier empire in the East.[56]

In fact, the decision to kill the Jews contradicted that vision, since it was an implicit acceptance that the Germans would never control the vast territories that they would have needed for a Final Solution by deportation. In logistical terms, mass murder is simpler than mass deportation. At this point, killing was Hitler's only option if he wished to fulfill his own prophecy. His was a land empire rather than a sea empire, but he controlled no wastelands into which Jews could disappear. Insofar as there had been progress in the Final Solution, it was in Himmler's demonstration of the method that did not require deportation: murder. The killing was less a sign of than a substitute for triumph. From late July 1941 Jews had been murdered as the envisaged lightning victory failed to materialize. From December 1941, Jews as such were to be killed as the alliance against Germany grew in strength. Hitler sought and found still deeper emotions and gave voice to more vicious goals, and a German leadership aware of its predicament accepted them.[57]

By defining the conflict as a "world war," Hitler drew attention away from the lack of a lightning victory and the unwelcome lessons of history that followed from this military failure. In December 1941, German soldiers were staring straight at the fate of Napoleon, whose Grande Armée had reached the outskirts of Moscow faster in 1812 than had the Wehrmacht in 1941. Yet in the end Napoleon had retreated from winter and Russian reinforcements. As German troops held their positions, they would inevitably confront a repetition of the kinds of battles that had been fought in 1914–1918: long days of sinking into trenches to escape machine guns and artillery, and long years of slow, meaningless movement and countless casualties. The kind of warfare that had supposedly been made obsolete by Hitler's genius was upon them. The German general staff had anticipated losses of about half a million and victory by September; losses were approaching a million as victory receded in December.[58]

All of the failed offensives and missed deadlines and depressing prospects would be less shameful if what the Wehrmacht was fighting was not an ill-planned colonial war of aggression but a glorious if tragic world war in defense of civilization. If German soldiers were fighting the powers of the whole world, organized by the Jewish cabals of Moscow and London and Washington, then their cause was great and just. If they had to fight a defensive war, as was indeed now in practice the case, then someone else could be handed the role of the aggressor. The Jews filled that place in the story, at least for Nazi believers and many German civilians waiting for fathers and husbands to return. German soldiers, whether or not they believed in Jewish responsibility for the war, likely needed ideological revisions less than the politicians and the civilians. They were desperate but they were still deadly; and they would fight well, and they would fight on, long enough, at least, for Hitler to fulfill his prophecy. The Wehrmacht was and would remain by far the most effective fighting force in the European theater, even though its chances for a traditional victory were now nil.

By the magic of racial thinking, killing the Jews itself was a German triumph, at a moment when any other victory receded beyond the horizon of the possible. The United States, Great Britain, and the Soviet Union were enemies of Germany, and the Jews were the enemy of Germany, and thus, went the spurious syllogism, they were under the influence of the Jews. If these were Jewish states, then Jews in Europe were their agents. Killing the Jews of Europe was thus an attack on Germany's enemies, directly and indirectly, and was justified not only by moral but by military logic. Himmler noted Hitler's desire that the Jews of Europe, as of December 1941, were to be destroyed "as partisans," as agents of Germany's foes behind the lines. By this time, the logic of killing Jews as "retribution" for partisan attacks had already been developed: in the Polesian swamps between Belarus and Ukraine, where Himmler had used it as the reason to kill Jewish men, women, and children beginning in July 1941; in Kiev, where the Germans had murdered more than thirty thousand Jews in retribution for the Soviet bombings in the city; and even further in Serbia, where the German armed forces had encountered serious resistance slightly earlier than in the Soviet Union.[59]

The Serbian example was, perhaps, especially pertinent. The German war in southeastern Europe had begun slightly earlier than the war in the Soviet Union, and had brought certain applicable lessons. Germany had invaded Yugoslavia and Greece in spring 1941, just before the beginning of Operation Barbarossa, mainly to rescue its bungling Italian ally from defeat in its own Balkan wars. Though Germany had quickly destroyed the Yugoslav army and created a Croatian puppet state, resistance in the Serbian occupation zone it shared with Italy was considerable. Some of it came from communists. The German commanding general in Serbia ordered that only Jews and Roma be killed as revenge for the deaths of Germans who fell in action against partisans—at a ratio of one hundred to one. In this way, almost all of the male Jews of Serbia had been shot by the time Himmler made his note about the destruction of Jews "as partisans." The logic of Serbia was universalized. Jews as such would be killed as retribution for the US-UK-USSR alliance. Neither Jews nor the Allies could be expected to understand this. It made sense only within the Nazi worldview, which Hitler had just adapted for future use.[60]

The fifth and final version of the Final Solution was mass death. In Nazi parlance, the word *resettlement* now shifted from description to euphemism. For years German leaders had imagined that they could "resolve" Europe's Jewish "problem" by resettling Jews to one place or another. Jews would be worked to death wherever they landed, and perhaps sterilized so that they could not reproduce, but they would not all be killed as such. Thus *resettlement* was incomplete though not entirely inaccurate as a description of Jewish policy in 1940 and into 1941. Henceforth *resettlement* or *resettlement to the East* would mean mass murder. Perhaps the *resettlement* euphemism, by suggesting an essential continuity of policy, helped Nazis to overlook the fact that German policy not only changed but had to change because the war was not going as expected. It might thus have allowed the Germans to shield from themselves the reality that military disaster conditioned their Jewish policy.[61]

The Germans had already shown, by December 1941, that they could do something far worse than deport Jews to Poland, Madagascar, or the Soviet Union. They could kill the Jews under their control, and blame the victims for their fate. The reality of *resettlement* from which the Germans now distanced themselves can be brought closer by simple quotation of German usage: "Resettlement site: on the resettlement site eight trenches are situated. One squad of ten officers and men are to work at each trench and are to be relieved every two hours."[62]

By the time Hitler conveyed his preferences in December 1941, Himmler's SS and police forces (aided by the Wehrmacht and local policemen) had already killed about a million Jews in the occupied Soviet Union. Retrospect conveys a sense of inevitability, and the new German policy of killing all European Jews may appear to be nothing more than the fulfillment of a goal that was, in some sense, already a given. While it is true that Hitler took for granted that the Jews would have no place in his future Europe, and that Himmler's escalating murder must have corresponded to Hitler's wishes, Hitler's decision to speak of the mass murder of all Jews must be seen as just that: a decision. Other responses to the same events, after all, were possible.[63]

Germany's ally Romania showed the possibility of such reversals. Bucharest had also been pursuing national purification. As of December 1941, Romanian Jews had suffered more than German Jews. Romania had joined in the invasion of the Soviet Union—like Germany, under propaganda associating communism with Jews. By invading the Soviet Union along with the Germans, Romania recovered the Bessarabian and Bukovinan territory that the Soviet Union had annexed in 1940. Romania then added a new region called "Transnistria," seized from the southern part of Soviet Ukraine. In this zone in 1941, Romanian policies toward Jews were every bit as brutal as their German equivalents. After taking Odessa, Romanian troops killed about twenty thousand local Jews in "reprisals" for an explosion that destroyed their headquarters in the city. In the Bohdanivka district the Romanians shot more than forty thousand Jews in a few days in late December 1941. The Romanians also created their own set of ghettos and labor camps in Transnistria, where tens of thousands of Jews from Bessarabia and Bukovina perished. All in all, Romania killed about three hundred thousand Jews.[64]

Yet Romania's leadership reacted to the changing course of the war differently than did Hitler. Its policies toward Jews remained brutal, but were gradually softened rather than hardened. By summer 1942 Romania was no longer deporting Jews to Transnistria. When the Germans built death facilities, Romania declined to send its Jews to them. By the end of 1942, Romanian policy had diverged significantly from the German. Romania would attempt to switch sides later in the war, and at that time the survival of remaining Jews would come to

ROMANIA
1940–1941
Romania in 1939

Ceded to Hungary
August 1940

Occupied in
August 1941

Bessarabia and Bukovina
annexed by the USSR in
August 1940, retaken
in July 1941

Ceded to Bulgaria
September 1940

seem an asset. The year 1942 was thus a crucial turning point, when German and Romanian policies turned in opposite directions. Germany would kill all Jews because the war was lost; Romania, late that year, would save some Jews for much the same reason. The Romanian dictator Ion Antonescu would leave open a crack in the door for negotiations with the Americans and the British; Hitler left the Germans no possibility to escape from their own guilt.[65]

Over the course of the year 1942, the Germans killed most of the remaining Jews who were under their occupation. West of the Molotov-Ribbentrop line, mass murder would be carried out at gassing facilities. East of the Molotov-Ribbentrop line, the Germans continued the mass shootings, and also used the gas vans that had been tested on the Soviet prisoners of war. In occupied Soviet Ukraine, the

REICHSKOMMISSARIAT
UKRAINE
1942

killing began again as soon as the earth had thawed enough for the digging of pits, and sometimes, where machines were available for digging, even sooner. In the eastern part of Soviet Ukraine, still under military occupation, the shooting simply continued without any pause from late 1941 through early 1942. In January, Einsatzgruppen, assisted by the Wehrmacht, killed smaller Jewish communities that had survived the first sweep, as well as groups of Jewish laborers. In spring 1942 the action shifted from the east to the west, from the military zone to the civilian occupation authority, the Reichskommissariat Ukraine. Here all of the actions were carried out by stationary police forces, battalions of German Order Police with the assistance of local militiamen. With the help of tens of thousands of local collaborators, the Germans had the necessary manpower.[66]

Killing became extermination last in the lands that the Germans took first. Though the Germans had overrun all of the former lands of eastern Poland in the first ten days of the war, in June 1941, many of the native Jews of Poland's southeast, now the west of the Reichskommissariat Ukraine, had survived until

1942. German forces had already passed through by the time Himmler began to order the destruction of whole Jewish communities. By the time German policy had shifted, most German forces had already departed. In 1942 the Germans undertook a second round of mass shootings in the western districts of the Reichskommissariat Ukraine, this time organized by the civilian authorities and implemented by the police, with a great deal of help from local auxiliary policemen.[67]

These west Ukrainian districts were typical of the many towns and small cities, in the lands that had been eastern Poland, where Jews numbered about half of the population, sometimes a bit less, sometimes a bit more. Jews usually inhabited the center of the cities, in stone houses around town squares, rather than the wood shanties of the outskirts. These were settlements where Jews had lived for more than half a millennium, under varying governments and with varying levels of prosperity, but with a success demonstrated by the simplest measures of architecture and demography. The majority of this Jewish population, in interwar Poland, had remained religiously observant and rather separated from the outside world. The languages remained Yiddish and (for religious purposes) Hebrew, and rates of intermarriage with Christians were low. Eastern Poland had remained the heartland of an Ashkenazic Jewish civilization, speaking Yiddish and dominated by rival clans of charismatic Hasidim. This Jewish tradition had outlived the Polish-Lithuanian Commonwealth where it had originated, it had outlived the Russian Empire, and it had outlived the interwar Polish Republic.[68]

After the Molotov-Ribbentrop Pact and the joint invasion of Poland, Soviet power and Soviet citizenship were extended to these Jews in 1939–1941, and thus they are usually counted as Soviet Jewish victims of the Nazis. These Jews did live for a time in the Soviet Union after Soviet borders were extended westward to include what had been eastern Poland, and they were subject to Soviet policies. Like the Poles and the Ukrainians and the Belarusians of these lands, they had been subject then to arrests, deportations, and shootings. Jews had lost their businesses and their religious schools. Yet this brief period of Soviet rule was hardly enough to make Soviet Jews of them. With the exception of the very youngest children, people in Rivne and similar settlements had been citizens of Poland, Lithuania, Latvia, or Romania for far longer than they were citizens of the Soviet Union. Of the 2.6 million or so Jews killed on the terrains of the Soviet

Union, some 1.6 million had been under Soviet jurisdiction for less than two
years. Their civilization had been seriously weakened by Soviet rule during
1939–1941; it would not survive the German Reich.[69]

Rivne, unusually for these cities, had already seen a mass killing action in 1941.
Although Kiev was the center of the German police state in Ukraine, Rivne was
in 1941 the provisional capital of the Reichskommissariat Ukraine. The Reichskommissar, Erich Koch, was a man known for his brutality. Hitler's advisors
called Koch a "second Stalin," and they meant it as a compliment. Koch had already in autumn 1941 ordered that most of the Jews of Rivne be killed. On 6
November 1941 the police had told all Jews without work permits to report for
resettlement. Some seventeen thousand people were then transported to nearby
woods, known as Sosenky. There they were shot over pits dug earlier by Soviet
prisoners of war. The remaining ten thousand or so Jews were then forced to
live in a ghetto in the worst part of the city.[70]

In early 1942, even after the majority of the Jews were dead, the Rivne Judenrat was trying to maintain for the survivors some means of subsistence. The
German authorities, however, had decided that Jews were not to exist at all. In
summer 1942 Koch, with an eye to food shortages, took the next step, asking
his subordinates for a "100% solution" to the Jewish problem. On the night of
13 July 1942 Rivne's Jews were herded by German police and Ukrainian auxiliaries from the ghetto. The Jews were forced to walk to the train station, where
they were enclosed in train cars. After two days without food and water, they
were transported to a quarry near woods outside the town of Kostopil. There
they were shot by German Security Police and the auxiliary policemen.[71]

In Lutsk, the Jews constituted about half the population, perhaps ten thousand people. In December 1941 the Jews were forced into a ghetto, where the
Germans appointed a Judenrat. Generally the Judenrat served to extract the
wealth of the community in exchange for various stays of execution, some true,
some false. The Germans also usually established a Jewish police force, which
was used to create the ghettos, and then later to clear them. On 20 August 1942
in Lutsk the local Jewish police set out to find Jews who might be in hiding. The
same day Jewish men were sent to woods near Hirka Polonka, seven kilometers
from Lutsk, to dig pits. The Germans guarding them made no effort to disguise
what was about to happen. They told the men to dig well, as their wives and
mothers would be resting in the pits the next day. On 21 August the women and

children of Lutsk were taken to Hirka Polonka. The Germans ate and drank and laughed, and forced the women to recite: "Because I am a Jew I have no right to live." Then the women were forced, five at a time, to undress and kneel naked over the pits. The next group then had to lie naked over the first layer of corpses, and were shot. That same day the Jewish men were taken to the courtyard of the Lutsk castle, and killed there.[72]

In Kovel, too, Jews were about half the local population, some fourteen thousand people. In May 1942 the Jews of the city were divided into two groups, workers and nonworkers, and placed in two separate ghettos, the first in the New Town and the second in the Old Town. One local Jew, having learned the Nazi terms, knew that the Germans saw the second ghetto as the one for "useless eaters." On 2 June German and local auxiliary police surrounded the ghetto in the Old Town. All six thousand of them were taken to a clearing near Kamin-Kashyrskyi and shot. On 19 August, the police repeated this action with the other ghetto, shooting eight thousand more Jews. Then began a hunt for Jews in hiding, who were rounded up and locked in the town's Great Synagogue with no food and water. Then they were shot, but not before a few of them left their final messages, in Yiddish or Polish, scraped with stones, knives, pens, or fingernails on the walls of the temple where some of them had observed the Sabbath.[73]

A wife left a note of love and devotion to her "dear husband" so that he might learn of her fate and that of their "beautiful" child. Two girls together wrote of their love of life: "one so wants to live, and they won't allow it. Revenge. Revenge." A young woman was more resigned: "I am strangely calm, though it is hard to die at twenty." A mother and father asked their children to say kaddish for them, and to observe the holidays. A daughter left a farewell note to her mother: "My beloved Mama! There was no escape. They brought us here from outside the ghetto, and now we must die a terrible death. We are so sorry that you are not with us. I cannot forgive myself this. We thank you, Mama, for all of your devotion. We kiss you over and over."

CHAPTER 7

HOLOCAUST AND REVENGE

Belarus was the center of the confrontation between Nazi Germany and the Soviet Union. After the German invasion of June 1941, its inhabitants observed, if they survived, the escalation of both German and Soviet violence. Their homeland was a German zone of occupation and a once and future Soviet republic. Its cities were battlefields of armies in advance and retreat, its towns centers of Jewish settlement destroyed by the Holocaust. Its fields became German prisoner-of-war camps, where Soviet soldiers starved in the tens and hundreds of thousands. In its forests Soviet partisans and German policemen and Waffen-SS conducted ferocious partisan warfare. The country as a whole was the site of a symbolic competition between Hitler and Stalin, represented not only by soldiers behind the lines, partisans in the forests, and policemen over pits but by propagandists in Berlin and Moscow and Minsk, the republic's capital city.

Minsk was a centerpiece of Nazi destructiveness. The German air force had bombed the city into submission on 24 June 1941; the Wehrmacht had to wait for the fires to die down before entering. By the end of July the Germans had shot thousands of educated people and confined the Jews to the northwest of the city. Minsk would have a ghetto, and concentration camps, and prisoner-of-war camps, and killing sites. Finally Minsk was transformed by the Germans into a kind of macabre theater, in which they could act out the ersatz victory of killing Jews.[1]

In Minsk in autumn 1941, the Germans were celebrating an imaginary triumph, even as Moscow held fast. On 7 November, the anniversary of the

Bolshevik Revolution, the Germans organized something more dramatic than mere mass shootings. On that morning, they rounded up thousands of Jews from the ghetto. The Germans forced the Jews to wear their best clothes, as though they were dressing up for the Soviet holiday. Then the Germans formed the captives into columns, gave them Soviet flags, and ordered them to sing revolutionary songs. People had to smile for the cameras that were filming the scene. Once beyond Minsk, these 6,624 Jews were taken in trucks to a former NKVD warehouse in the nearby village of Tuchinka. Jewish men returning that evening from forced labor assignments found their entire families gone. As one recalled: "Out of eight people—my wife, my three children, my elderly mother, and her two children—not a soul remained!"[2]

Terror itself was nothing new. People had been taken from Minsk to Tuchinka, in the black ravens of the NKVD, not so long before, in 1937 and 1938. Yet even at the height of Stalin's Great Terror of those years, the NKVD was always discreet, taking people by ones and twos in the dark of night. The Germans were carrying out a mass action in the middle of the day, made for public consumption, ripe with meaning, suitable for a propaganda film. The staged parade was supposed to prove the Nazi claim that communists were Jews and Jews were communists. It followed from this, to the Nazi way of thinking, that their removal not only secured the rear area of Army Group Center but was also a kind of victory in itself. Yet this hollow expression of triumph seemed designed to disguise a more obvious defeat. By 7 November 1941, Army Group Center was supposed to have taken Moscow, and had not.[3]

Stalin was still in the Soviet capital, and was organizing his own victory celebrations. He had never abandoned the city, not during the initial offensive of Operation Barbarossa of June 1941, not during the secondary offensive of Operation Typhoon of October. Lenin's embalmed corpse was sent away from the Kremlin for safekeeping, but Stalin remained and ruled. Leningrad was besieged, and Minsk and Kiev were taken, but Moscow defended itself under Stalin's obstinate command. On the 6th of November, Stalin spoke defiantly to Soviet citizens. Noting that the Germans called their campaign a "war of annihilation," he promised them the same. He referred, for the one and only time, to the Germans' murder of the Jews. In calling the Nazi regime an empire eager to organize "pogroms," however, he fell far short of a true description of the ongoing mass murder. The Minsk Jews taken to Tuchinka on 7 November (the Soviet holiday) were shot on

9 November (the National Socialist holiday). Five thousand more followed on 20 November. Traditional empires had never done anything like this to Jews. On any given day in the second half of 1941, the Germans shot more Jews than had been killed by pogroms in the entire history of the Russian Empire.[4]

The German murder of Jews was never going to play much of a role in the Soviet vision of the war. From a Stalinist perspective, it was not the killing of Jews that mattered but the possibilities for its political interpretation. The German identification of Jews with communism was not just a Nazi conviction and a pretext for mass murder; it was also a propaganda weapon against the Soviet Union. If the Soviet Union was nothing more than a Jewish empire, then surely (went the Nazi argument) the vast majority of Soviet citizens had no reason to defend it. In November 1941 Stalin was thus preparing an ideological as well as a military defense of the Soviet Union. The Soviet Union was not a state of the Jews, as the Nazis claimed; it was a state of the Soviet peoples, first among whom were the Russians. On 7 November, as the Jews marched through Minsk to their deaths, Stalin reviewed a military parade in Moscow. To raise the spirits of his Soviet peoples and to communicate his confidence to the Germans, he had actually recalled Red Army divisions from their defensive positions west of Moscow, and had them march through its boulevards. In his address that day he called upon the Soviet people to follow the example of their "great ancestors," mentioning six prerevolutionary martial heroes—all of them Russians. At a time of desperation, the Soviet leader appealed to Russian nationalism.[5]

Stalin was associating himself and his people with the earlier Russian Empire, which just one day before he had mentioned in connection with pogroms of Jews. As the General Secretary of the Communist Party of the Soviet Union summoned the heroes of prerevolutionary Russian history, he had to negotiate with their ghosts. By placing Russians at the center of history, he was implicitly reducing the role of other Soviet peoples, including those who suffered more than Russians from the German occupation. If this was a "Great Patriotic War," as Stalin's close associate Viacheslav Molotov had said on the day of the German invasion, what was the fatherland? Russia, or the Soviet Union? If the conflict was a war of Russian self-defense, what to make of the German mass murder of the Jews?

Hitler's public anti-Semitism had placed Stalin, like all the leaders of the Allies, in a profound dilemma. Hitler said that the Allies were fighting for the Jews, and so (fearing that their populations might agree) the Allies had to insist that they were fighting to liberate oppressed nations (but not Jews in particular). Stalin's answer to Hitler's propaganda shaped the history of the Soviet Union for as long as it existed: all of the victims of German killing policies were "Soviet citizens," but the greatest of the Soviet nations was the Russians. One of his chief propagandists, Aleksandr Shcherbakov, clarified the line in January 1942: "the Russian people—the first among equals in the USSR's family of peoples—are bearing the main burden of the struggle with the German occupiers." By the time Shcherbakov uttered those words, the Germans had killed a million Jews east of the Molotov-Ribbentrop line, including some 190,000 Jews in Belarus.[6]

As the freezing weather came to a Minsk ghetto without electricity and fuel, Jews called their home "a dead city." In winter 1941–1942, Minsk held the largest ghetto on the territory of the prewar Soviet Union, confining perhaps seventy thousand Jews. According to the last Soviet census (of 1939), some 71,000 Jews were among the 239,000 residents of the city. Some of the Jews native to Minsk had fled before the Germans took the city at the end of June 1941 and thousands more had been shot in the summer and fall; on the other hand, the Jewish population of the city had been swollen by Jews who had earlier arrived as refugees from Poland. These Polish Jews had fled the German invasion of Poland in 1939, but would flee no further after they were overtaken by German troops in 1941. The escape route east was now sealed. Once Soviet power disappeared from these lands, there could be no more Soviet deportations, which, deadly as they were, preserved Polish Jews from German bullets. There could be no more rescues of the kind organized by the Japanese spy Sugihara in Lithuania in 1940.[7]

Minsk was the provincial capital of General Commissariat White Ruthenia (as the Germans called Belarus). The General Commissariat comprised about one fourth of Soviet Belarus: the eastern part of the Soviet republic remained under military administration, the southern part was added to the Reichskommissariat Ukraine, and Białystok was annexed by the Reich. Along with the three occupied Baltic States, General Commissariat White Ruthenia constituted the Reichskommissariat Ostland. Belarusian Jews, whether in this civilian occupation authority or in the military occupation zone to its east, were behind the lines of Operation Typhoon. As the Wehrmacht advanced they were killed; as it stalled, some of them were kept alive, for a time. The inability of the Germans

REICHSKOMMISSARIAT
OSTLAND
1942

SWEDEN

Helsinki

Gulf of Finland

Leningrad

Narva

Tallinn

Lake Peipus

Estland

Novgorod

Pärnu

Tartu

Ösel

Gulf of Riga

Valmiera

Gulbene

U.S.S.R.

Riga   Lettland

Jelgava

Jēkabpils

Liepāja

Baltic Sea

Mažeikiai

Daugavpils

Dzvina

Memel

Litauen   Utena

Vitebsk

Tauragė

REICHSKOMMISSARIAT

Smolensk

Kaunas

OSTLAND

Königsberg

Mariampol

Vilnius

Molodechno

Mahileu

Danzig

Minsk

GERMANY

Weissruthenien

Bobruisk

Białystok

Baranavichy

Vistula

Homel

Posen

WARTHELAND

Warsaw

Brest

Pinsk

Polesian Marshes

Pripet

Chernihiv

Łódź

Radom

REICHSKOMMISSARIAT
UKRAINE

Breslau

Lublin

Oder

GENERAL
GOVERNMENT

Lutsk

Rivne

Kiev

Zhytomyr

to take Moscow in late 1941 saved the remainder of the Jews of Minsk, at least for the moment. As Red Army divisions reinforced from the Far East defended the Soviet capital, battalions of German Order Police were ordered to the front. These were the very policemen who otherwise would have been tasked with shooting Jews. As the German offensive stalled in late November, the army realized that the boots and coats taken from dead or captured Soviet soldiers would not suffice for the cold winter ahead. Jewish workers in Minsk would have to make more, and so they would have to be allowed to live through the winter.[8]

Because Moscow held, the Germans had to drop their initial plans for Minsk: it could not be starved; its hinterlands could not be emptied of peasants; some of its Jews would have to live for a time. Germans asserted their dominance in

Minsk by marching columns of prisoners of war through the ghetto and through the city. In late 1941, when prisoners of war were very likely to starve to death, some of them survived by fleeing—to the Minsk ghetto. The ghetto was still a safer place than the prisoner-of-war camps. In the last few months of 1941, more people died at nearby Dulags and Stalags than in the Minsk ghetto. The enormous Stalag 352, probably the deadliest prisoner-of-war camp of them all, was a complex of holding pens in and around Minsk. A camp on Shirokaia Street, in the middle of the city, held both prisoners of war and Jews. The former NKVD facility at Tuchinka now functioned as a German prison and execution site.[9]

German policy in occupied Minsk was one of savage and unpredictable terror. The carnivalesque death march of 7 November 1941 was only one of a series of murderous incidents that left Jews horrified and confused about their fate. Special humiliations were reserved for Jews who were known and respected before the war. A noted scientist was forced to crawl across Jubilee Square, the center of the ghetto, with a soccer ball on his back. Then he was shot. Germans took Jews as personal slaves to clean their houses and their clothes. The German (Austrian) medical doctor Irmfried Eberl, in Minsk after a tour of duty gassing the handicapped in Germany, wrote to his wife that he needed no money in this "paradise." When Himmler visited Minsk, he was treated to a show execution of Jews, which was recorded by movie cameras. He seems to have watched himself and the mass murder on film later.[10]

Jewish women suffered in particular ways. Despite regulations against "racial defilement," some Germans quickly developed a taste for rape as prelude to murder. At least once Germans carried out a "beauty contest" of Jewish women, taking them to the cemetery, forcing them to strip naked, and then killing them. In the ghetto, German soldiers would force Jewish girls to dance naked at night; in the morning only the girls' corpses remained. Perla Aginskaia recalled what she saw in a dark apartment in the Minsk ghetto one evening in autumn 1941: "a little room, a table, a bed. Blood was streaming down the girl's body from deep, blackish wounds in her chest. It was quite clear that the girl had been raped and killed. There were gunshot wounds around her genitals."[11]

Violence is not confidence, and terror is not mastery. For the first nine months of the occupation, from summer 1941 through early spring 1942, the bursts of murder and rape did not bring Minsk under complete German domination.

Minsk was an unusual city, a place whose social structure defied the Nazi mind as well as German experience in occupied Poland. Here, in a Soviet metropolis, the history of Jews had taken a different turn than in Poland. Twenty years of social opportunity and political coercion had done their work. The urbane Jews of the city were not organized in any sort of traditional community, since the Soviets had destroyed Jewish religious and communal institutions in the 1920s and 1930s. The younger generation of Jews was highly assimilated, to the point that many had "Belarusian" or "Russian" inscribed as their nationality on their Soviet documents. Although this probably meant little to them before 1941, it could save their lives under German rule. Some Minsk Jews had Belarusian or Russian friends and colleagues who were ignorant of or indifferent to religion and nationality. A striking example of the ignorance of Jewish origins was Isai Kaziniets, who organized the communist underground throughout the city of Minsk. Neither his friends nor his enemies knew that he was Jewish.[12]

Soviet rule had brought a certain sort of toleration and assimilation, at the price of habits of subordination and obedience to the commands of Moscow. Political initiative had not been rewarded in Stalin's Soviet Union. Anyone responding with too much avidity to a given situation, or even to a political line, was at risk when the situation or the line changed. Thus Soviet rule in general, and the Great Terror of 1937–1938 in particular, had taught people not to take spontaneous action. People who had distinguished themselves in the Minsk of the 1930s had been shot by the NKVD at Kuropaty. Even when it must have been clear in Moscow that Soviet citizens in Minsk had their own reasons to resist Germans, communists understood that this would not be enough to protect them from future persecution when the Soviets returned. Kaziniets and all local communists hesitated to create any sort of organization, knowing that Stalinism opposed any sort of spontaneous action from below. Left to themselves, they would have endured Hitler for fear of Stalin.[13]

An outsider, the Polish-Jewish communist Hersh Smolar, helped spur Minsk communists and Jews to action. His curious combination of Soviet and Polish experience provided him with the skills (and, perhaps, the naiveté) to push forward. He had spent the early 1920s in the Soviet Union, and spoke Russian—the main language of Minsk. After returning to a Poland where the communist party was illegal, he grew accustomed to operating underground and working against local authorities. Arrested by the Polish police and imprisoned, he had been spared the experiences of Stalinist mass shooting that weighed so heavily in Minsk. He was behind bars during the Great Terror of 1937–1938, when Polish communists were invited to the Soviet Union in order to be shot. Released from Polish prison when the Soviet Union invaded Poland in September 1939, Smolar served the new Soviet regime. He fled the Germans on foot in June 1941, and got as far as Minsk. After the German occupation of the city, he began to organize the ghetto underground, and persuaded Kaziniets that a general city underground was permissible as well. Kaziniets wanted to know whom Smolar was representing; Smolar told him truthfully that he stood for no one but himself. This denial seemed to have persuaded Kaziniets that Smolar was actually authorized by Moscow to work under deep cover. Both men found a large number of willing conspirators within and without the ghetto; by early autumn 1941 both the ghetto and the city were thoroughly penetrated by a dedicated communist underground movement.[14]

The underground subverted the organs of German control over Jewish life, the Judenrat and the Jewish police. In the occupied Soviet Union, as in occupied Poland, German rule forced Jews into ghettos, which were administered by a local Jewish council typically known by the German term *Judenrat*. In the cities of occupied Poland, the Judenrat was often composed of Jews of some standing in the prewar community, often the same people who had led the Jewish communal structures that had been legal in independent Poland. In Minsk, such continuity of Jewish leadership was impossible, since the Soviets had eliminated Jewish communal life. The Germans had no easy way to find people who represented Jewish elites, and who were accustomed to making compromises with the local authorities. It seems that they chose the initial Minsk Judenrat more or less at random—and chose badly. The entire Judenrat cooperated with the underground.[15]

In late 1941 and early 1942, Jews who wished to flee the ghetto could count on help from the Judenrat. Jewish policemen would be stationed away from places where escape attempts were planned. Because the Minsk ghetto was enclosed only by barbed wire, the momentary absence of police attention allowed people to flee to the forest—which was very close to the city limits. Very small children were passed through the barbed wire to gentiles who agreed to raise them or take them to orphanages. Older children learned the escape routes, and came to serve as guides from the city to the nearby forest. Sima Fiterson, one of these guides, carried a ball, which she would play with to signal danger to those following behind her. Children adapted quickly and well, but were in terrible danger all the same. To celebrate that first Christmas under German occupation, Erich von dem Bach-Zelewski, the Higher SS and Police Leader, sent thousands of pairs of children's gloves and socks to SS families in Germany.[16]

Unlike Jews elsewhere under German occupation, Jews in Minsk had somewhere to run. In the nearby forest, they could try to find Soviet partisans. They knew that the Germans had taken countless prisoners of war, and that some had escaped to the forests. These men had stayed in the woods because they knew that the Germans would shoot them or starve them. Stalin had called in July 1941 for loyal communists to organize partisan units behind the lines, in the hope of establishing some control over this spontaneous movement before it grew in importance. Centralization was not yet possible; the soldiers hid in the forest, and the communists, if they had not fled, did their best to hide their pasts from the Germans.[17]

The Minsk underground activists, however, did try to support their armed comrades. On at least one occasion, members of the ghetto underground liberated a Red Army officer from the camp on Shirokaia Street; he became an important partisan leader in the nearby forests, and saved Jews in his turn. Jewish laborers in German factories stole winter clothes and boots, meant for the German soldiers of Army Group Center, and diverted them to the partisans. Workers in arms factories, remarkably, did the same. The Judenrat, required to collect a regular "contribution" of money from the Jewish population of the ghetto, diverted some of these funds to the partisans. The Germans later concluded that the entire Soviet partisan movement was funded from the ghetto. This was an exaggeration arising from stereotypical ideas of Jewish wealth, but the aid from the Minsk ghetto was reality.[18]

Partisan warfare was a nightmare of German military planning, and German army officers had been trained to take a severe line. They had been taught to see Soviet soldiers as the servants of communist political officers, who taught them to fight as partisans in an illegal "Asiatic" fashion. Partisan warfare was (and is) illegal, since it undermines the convention of uniformed armies directing violence against each other rather than against surrounding populations. In theory partisans protect civilians from a hostile occupier; in practice they, like the occupier, must subsist on what they take from civilians. Since partisans hide among civilians, they bring down, and often intend to bring down, the occupier's retaliation against the local population. Reprisals then serve as recruitment propaganda for the partisans, or leave individual survivors with nowhere to go but the forest. Because German forces were always limited and always in demand at the front, military and civilian authorities were all the more fearful of the disruptions partisans could bring.[19]

Belarus, with its plentiful forests and swamps, was ideal territory for partisan warfare. The German army chief of staff later fantasized about using nuclear weapons to clear its wetlands of human population. This technology was not available, of course, but the fantasy gives a sense of both the ruthlessness of German planning and the fears aroused by difficult terrain. The policy of the army was to deter partisan warfare by striking "such terror into the population that it loses all will to resist." Bach, the Higher SS and Police Leader, later said that the ultimate explanation for the killing of civilians in anti-partisan actions was Himmler's desire to kill all the Jews and thirty million Slavs. There seemed to be little cost to the Germans in preemptive terror, since the people in question were meant to die anyway (in the Hunger Plan or Generalplan Ost). Hitler, who saw partisan warfare as a chance to destroy potential opposition, reacted energetically when Stalin urged local communists to resist the Germans in July. Even before the invasion of the Soviet Union, Hitler had already relieved his soldiers of legal responsibility for actions taken against civilians. Now he wanted soldiers and police to kill anyone who "even looks at us askance."[20]

The Germans had little trouble controlling the partisan movement in late 1941, and simply defined the ongoing mass murder of Jews as the appropriate reprisal. In September 1941 a clinic on anti-partisan warfare was held near Mahileu; its climax was the shooting of thirty-two Jews, of whom nineteen were women. The general line was that "Where there are partisans there are Jews; and where there are Jews there are partisans." Just why this was so was harder to establish. The anti-Semitic ideas of Jewish weakness and dissimulation conspired in a sort of explanation: military commanders were unlikely to believe that Jews would actually take up arms, but often saw the Jewish population as standing behind partisan actions. General Bechtolsheim, responsible for security in the Minsk area, believed that if "an act of sabotage is committed in a village, and one destroys all of the Jews of the village, one can be certain that one has destroyed the perpetrators, or at least those who stood behind them."[21]

In this atmosphere, where the partisans were weak and the German reprisals anti-Semitic, most Jews in the Minsk ghetto were in no hurry to escape to the forest. In Minsk, despite all of its horrors, they were at least at home. Despite the regular mass killings, no fewer than half of Minsk's Jews were still alive as 1942 began.

In 1942, the Soviet partisan movement took on new strength at the same moment as the fate of Belarusian Jews was sealed, and for much the same reason. In December 1941, confronted with a "world war," Hitler communicated his desire that all the Jews of Europe be killed. The Red Army's advance was one of the main sources of the weakening German position in Belarus, and of Hitler's newly explicit desire for the murder of all Jews. Advancing Soviet forces were even able to open a gap in the German lines in early 1942. The "Surazh Gates," as the space between Army Group North and Army Group Center was called, remained open for half a year. Until September 1942, the Soviets could send trusted men and arms to control and supply the partisans operating in Belarus. Soviet authorities thereby established more or less reliable channels of communication. In May 1942 a Central Staff of the Partisan Movement was established in Moscow.[22]

Hitler's express decision to kill all the Jews of Europe raised the association of Jews and partisans to a kind of abstraction: Jews were supporters of Germany's enemies, and so had to be preemptively eliminated. Himmler and Hitler associated the Jewish threat with the partisan threat. The logic of the connection between Jews and partisans was vague and troubled, but the significance for the Jews of Belarus, the heartland of partisan warfare, was absolutely clear. In the military occupation zone, the rear of Army Group Center, the killing of Jews began again in January 1942. An Einsatzkommando painted Stars of David on their trucks to broadcast their mission of finding Jews and killing them. The leaders of Einsatzgruppe B resolved to kill all the Jews in their zone of responsibility by 20 April 1942, which was Hitler's birthday.[23]

The civilian occupation authorities in Minsk also followed the new line. Wilhelm Kube, the General Commissar of White Ruthenia, met with his police leaders on 19 January 1942. All seemed to accept Kube's formulation: while Germany's great "colonial-political" task in the East demanded the murder of all Jews, some would have to be preserved for a time as forced labor. Killing actions in Minsk would begin in March, directed against the population that remained in the ghetto during the day while the labor brigades were outside the ghetto at work.[24]

On 1 March 1942 the Germans ordered the Judenrat to provide a quota of five thousand Jews the following day. The ghetto underground told the Judenrat not to bargain Jewish blood, which the Judenrat was probably not inclined to do anyway. Some of the Jewish policemen, rather than aiding the Germans to make their quota, warned their fellow Jews to hide. When the quota was not delivered on 2 March, the Germans shot children, and stabbed to death all the wards of the Jewish orphanage. They even killed some workers returning home. In all they murdered some 3,412 people that day. One Jewish child who escaped the bloodshed was Feliks Lipski. His father had been killed as a Polish spy in Stalin's Great Terror, disappearing as people did then, never to be seen again. Now the boy saw people he knew as corpses in ditches. He remembered shades of white: skin, undergarments, snow.[25]

After the failure of the action of early March 1942, the Germans broke the Minsk underground, and accelerated the mass murder of the Jews. In late March and early April 1942, the Germans arrested and executed some 251 underground activists, Jews and non-Jews, including the head of the Judenrat. (Kaziniets, the organizer of the underground, was executed that July.) At around the same time, Reinhard Heydrich visited Minsk, and apparently ordered the construction of a death facility. The SS set to work on a new complex at Maly Trastsianets, outside Minsk. Beginning in May 1942, some forty thousand people would be killed there. The wives of German officials remembered Maly Trastsianets as a nice place to ride horses and collect fur coats (taken from Jewish women before they were shot).[26]

Some ten thousand Minsk Jews were killed in the last few days of July 1942. On the last day of the month, Junita Vishniatskaia wrote a letter to her father to bid him farewell. "I am saying good-bye to you before I die. I am so afraid of this death because they throw small children into the mass graves alive. Farewell forever. I kiss you, I kiss you."[27]

It was true that Germans sometimes avoided shooting younger children, instead throwing them into the pits with the corpses, and allowing them to suffocate under the earth. They also had at their disposal another means of killing that allowed them to avoid seeing the end of young life. Gas vans roved the streets of Minsk, the drivers seeking stray Jewish children. The people called the gas vans by a name that had been used for the NKVD trucks during the Great Terror a few years earlier: "soul destroyers."[28]

The girls and boys knew what would happen to them if they were caught. They would ask for a tattered bit of dignity as they walked up the ramp to their death: "Please sirs," they would say to the Germans, "do not hit us. We can get to the trucks on our own."[29]

By spring 1942 the Jews of Minsk were coming to see the forest as less dangerous than the ghetto. Hersh Smolar himself was forced to leave the ghetto for the partisans. Of the ten thousand or so Minsk Jews who found Soviet partisan units, perhaps half survived the war. Smolar was among the survivors. Yet partisans did not necessarily welcome Jews. Partisan units were meant to defeat the German occupation, not to help civilians endure it. Jews who lacked arms were often turned away, as were women and children. Even armed Jewish men were sometimes rejected or even, in some cases, killed for their weapons. Partisan leaders feared that Jews from ghettos were German spies, an accusation that was not as absurd as it might appear. The Germans would indeed seize wives and children, and then tell Jewish husbands to go to the forest and return with information if they wished to see their families again.[30]

The situation of Jews in the forests slowly improved over the course of 1942, as some Jews formed their own partisan units, a development that the Central Staff of the Partisan Movement eventually sanctioned. Israel Lapidus formed a unit of some fifty men. Sholem Zorin's 106th Detachment counted ten times as many, and raided the Minsk ghetto to rescue Jews. In individual cases Soviet partisan units provided diversions that allowed Jews to escape from the ghetto. In one case, partisans attacked a German unit on its way to liquidate a ghetto. Oswald Rufeisen, a Jew who worked as a translator for the German police in the town of Mir, smuggled weapons into that ghetto, and warned its inhabitants when the liquidation was ordered.[31]

Tuvia Bielski, also a Jew, probably rescued more Jews than any other partisan leader. His special gift was to understand the perils of partisan warfare between Stalin and Hitler. Bielski hailed from western Belarus, which is to say from the part of northeastern Poland that the Soviets had annexed in 1939 and then lost to the Germans in 1941. He had served in the Polish Army, and thus had some military training. He and his family knew the woods well, probably because they were small-time smugglers. Yet his tactical sense was not reducible to any particular experience. On the one hand, he understood his goal as rescuing Jews rather than killing Germans. He and his men generally tried to avoid combat. "Don't rush to fight and die," he would say. "So few of us are left, we have to save lives. To save a Jew is much more important than to kill Germans." On the other hand, he was able to work with Soviet partisans, when they appeared, even though their task precisely was to kill Germans. Although his mobile camp was largely composed of women and children, he was able to secure recognition of his status as a partisan leader from the Soviets. By rescuing rather than resisting, Bielski saved more than one thousand people.[32]

Bielski was an anomaly within a Soviet partisan movement that was ever larger and ever more subordinate to Moscow. When 1942 began, there were (by Soviet reckonings) perhaps twenty-three thousand partisans in Belarus; the number probably doubled by the time that the Central Staff was established in May, and doubled again by the end of the year. Partisans in 1941 had scarcely been able to keep themselves alive; in 1942 they were able to attain specific objectives of military and political value. They laid mines and destroyed railroad tracks and locomotives. They were supposed to keep food from the Germans, and to destroy the German administration. In practice the safest way to attack the German occupation structure was to murder unarmed participants in the civilian administration: small-town mayors, schoolteachers, landowners, and their families. This was not an excess, this was the official policy of the Soviet partisan movement through November 1942. Partisans sought to gain full control of territories, which they called "partisan republics."[33]

Partisan operations, effective as they sometimes were, brought inevitable destruction to the Belarusian civilian population, Jewish and gentile alike. When the Soviet partisans prevented peasants from giving food to the Germans, they all but guaranteed that the Germans would kill the peasants. A Soviet gun threatened a peasant, and then a German gun killed him. Once the Germans believed that they had lost control of a given village to the partisans, they would simply torch houses and fields. If they could not reliably get grain, they could keep it from the Soviets by seeing that it was never harvested. When Soviet partisans sabotaged trains, they were in effect ensuring that the population near the site would be exterminated. When Soviet partisans laid mines, they knew that some would detonate under the bodies of Soviet citizens. The Germans swept mines by forcing locals, Belarusians and Jews, to walk hand in hand over minefields. In general, such loss of human life was of little concern to the Soviet leadership. The people who died had been under German occupation, and were therefore suspect and perhaps even more expendable than the average Soviet citizen. German reprisals also ensured that the ranks of the partisans swelled, as survivors often had no home, no livelihood, and no family to which to return.[34]

The Soviet leadership was not especially concerned with the plight of Jews. After November 1941 Stalin never singled out the Jews as victims of Hitler. Some partisan commanders did try to protect Jews. But the Soviets, like the Americans or the British, seem not to have seriously contemplated direct military action to rescue Jews. The logic of the Soviet system was always to resist independent initiatives and to value human life very cheaply. Jews in ghettos were aiding the German war effort as forced laborers, so their death over pits was of little concern to authorities in Moscow. Jews who were not aiding but hindering the Germans were showing signs of a dangerous capacity for initiative, and might later resist the reimposition of Soviet rule. By Stalinist logic, Jews were suspect either way: if they remained in the ghetto and worked for the Germans, or if they left the ghetto and showed a capacity for independent action. The previous hesitation of local Minsk communists turned out to be justified: their resistance organization was treated as a front of the Gestapo by the Central Staff of the Partisan Movement in Moscow. The people who rescued Minsk Jews and supplied Soviet partisans were labeled a tool of Hitler.[35]

Jewish men who did make it into the partisans "already felt liberated," as Lev Kravets recalled. Jewish women generally had a more difficult time. In partisan units the standard form of address to girls and women was "whore," and women usually had no choice but to seek a protector. This is perhaps what Rosa Gerassimova, who survived with the partisans, meant when she recalled that "life was actually unbearable, but the partisans did rescue me." Some partisan commanders, Jews and non-Jews, did try to protect "family camps" for women and children and the elderly. Children who had the good luck to be in family camps played a version of hide-and-seek, in which Germans hunted Jews who were protected by partisans. This was true in their case; yet while the partisans saved some thirty thousand Jews, it is unclear whether their actions on balance provoked or prevented the killing of Jews. Partisan warfare behind the lines drew

German police and military power away from the front and to the hinterland, where policemen and soldiers almost always found it easier to kill Jews than to hunt down and engage partisans.[36]

In the second half of 1942, German anti-partisan operations were all but indistinguishable from the mass murder of Jews. Hitler ordered on 18 August 1942 that partisans in Belarus be "exterminated" by the end of the year. It was already understood that the Jews were to be killed by the same deadline. The euphemism "special treatment," meaning shooting, appears in reports about both Jews and Belarusian civilians. The logic for the two undertakings was circular but nevertheless somehow compelling: Jews were initially to be killed "as partisans" in 1941, when there were not yet any truly threatening partisan formations; then once there were such partisan formations, in 1942, villagers associated with them were to be destroyed "like Jews." The equivalence between Jews and partisans was emphasized over and over again, in a downward cycle of rhetoric that could end only when both groups were simply gone.[37]

By the middle of 1942, the number of Jews was in rapid decline, but the number of partisans was in rapid ascent. This had no effect on Nazi reasoning, except to make the methods for dealing with Belarusian civilians ever more similar to the methods of dealing with Jews. As partisans became difficult to target because they were too powerful, and as Jews became difficult to target because they were too scarce, the Germans subjected the non-Jewish Belarusian population to ever more extraordinary waves of killing. From the perspective of the German police, the Final Solution and the anti-partisan campaigns blurred together.

To take a single example: on 22 and 23 September 1942, Order Police Battalion 310 was dispatched to destroy three villages for ostensible connections to the partisans. At the first village, Borki, the police apprehended the entire population, marched the men, women, and children seven hundred meters, and then handed out shovels so that people could dig their own graves. The policemen shot the Belarusian peasants without a break from 9:00 in the morning until 6:00 in the evening, killing 203 men, 372 women, and 130 children. The Order Police spared 104 people classified as "reliable," although it is hard to imagine how they could have remained so after this spectacle. The battalion reached the next village, Zabloitse, at 2:00 in the morning, and surrounded it at 5:30. They forced all of the inhabitants into the local school, and then shot 284 men, women, and children. At the third village, Borysovka, the battalion reported killing 169 men, women, and children. Four weeks later, the battalion was assigned to liquidate Jews at a work camp. When they killed 461 Jews on 21 October, they used very similar methods: the only difference was that there was no need to surprise the population, since it was already under guard in the camp.[38]

Despite new offensives, the "war" against the Jews was the only one that the Germans were winning in 1942. Army Group North continued the siege of Leningrad. Army Group Center made no progress toward Moscow. Army Group South was supposed to secure the Volga River and the oil supplies of the Caucasus. Some of its forces reached the Volga in August 1942, but were unable to take Stalingrad. German troops did race through southern Russia into the Caucasus, but were unable to control the crucial areas by winter. This would be the last major German offensive in the eastern front. By the end of 1942 the Germans had killed at least 208,089 Jews in Belarus. Killing Jewish civilians did nothing, however, to hinder the Red Army, or even to slow the partisans.[39]

Lacking personnel in the rear and needing to keep troops at the front, the Germans tried in autumn 1942 to make anti-partisan warfare more efficient. Himmler named Bach, the local Higher SS and Police Leader, chief of anti-partisan warfare in the areas under civilian authority. In practice the responsibility fell upon his deputy, Curt von Gottberg, a drunk whose SS career had been rescued by Himmler. Gottberg suffered no war injuries but had lost part of a leg (and his SS commission) by driving his automobile into a fruit tree. Himmler paid for the prosthetic leg and had Gottberg reinstated. The assignment to Belarus was a chance to prove his manhood, which he seized. After only one month of police training he formed his own Battle Group, which was active from November 1942 through November 1943. In their first five months of campaigning, the men of his Battle Group reported killing 9,432 "partisans," 12,946 "partisan suspects," and about 11,000 Jews. In other words, the Battle Group shot an average of two hundred people every day, almost all of them civilians.[40]

The unit responsible for more atrocities than any other was the SS Special Commando Dirlewanger, which had arrived in Belarus in February 1942. In Belarus and indeed in all the theaters of the Second World War, few could compete in cruelty with Oskar Dirlewanger. He was an alcoholic and drug addict, prone to violence. He had fought in the German right-wing militias after the First World War, and spent the early 1920s tormenting communists and writing a doctoral dissertation on planned economics. He joined the Nazi party in 1923, but jeopardized his political future by traffic accidents and sexual liaisons with an underage girl. In March 1940 Himmler placed him in charge of a special Poachers' Brigade, a unit made up of criminals imprisoned for hunting on the property of others. Some Nazi leaders romanticized these men, seeing them as pure primitive German types, resisting the tyranny of the law. The hunters were first assigned to Lublin, where the unit was strengthened by other criminals, including murderers and the clinically insane. In Belarus, Dirlewanger and his hunters did engage partisans. Yet more often they killed civilians whose villages were in the wrong place. Dirlewanger's preferred method was to herd the local population inside a barn, set the barn on fire, and then shoot with machine guns anyone who tried to escape. The SS Special Commando Dirlewanger killed at least thirty thousand civilians in its Belarusian tour of duty.[41]

Dirlewanger's unit was one of several Waffen-SS and Order Police formations assigned to Belarus to reinforce the battered regular army. By late 1942, German soldiers were horribly fatigued, conscious of defeat, relieved of normal legal obligations to civilians, and under orders to treat partisans with extreme brutality. When assigned to anti-partisan duty, soldiers faced the anxiety of fighting a foe who could appear and disappear at any time, and who knew the land as the soldiers did not. Wehrmacht troops were now cooperating with the police and the SS, whose main task for some time had been the mass murder of civilians, above all Jews. All knew that they were supposed to exterminate the partisans. In these circumstances, the death toll among civilians was bound to be terribly high, regardless of the particulars of German tactics.

The main German actions of mid-1942 and onward, known as "Large Operations," were actually *designed* to kill Belarusian civilians as well as Belarusian Jews. Unable to defeat the partisans as such, the Germans killed the people who might be aiding the struggle. Units were given a daily kill quota, which they generally met by encircling villages and shooting most or all of the inhabitants. They shot people over ditches or, in the case of Dirlewanger and those who followed his example, burned them in barns or blew them up by forcing them to clear mines. In autumn 1942 and early 1943, the Germans liquidated ghettos and whole villages associated with the partisans. In Operation Swamp Fever in

September 1942, the Dirlewanger Brigade killed the 8,350 Jews still alive in the ghetto in Baranovichi, and then proceeded to kill 389 "bandits" and 1,274 "bandit suspects." These attacks were led by Friedrich Jeckeln, the Higher SS and Police Chief for Reichskommissariat Ostland, the same man who had organized the mass shootings of Jews at Kamianets-Podilskyi in Ukraine and the liquidation of the Riga ghetto in Latvia. Operation Hornung of February 1943 began with the liquidation of the Slutsk ghetto, which is to say the shooting of some 3,300 Jews. In an area southwest of Slutsk the Germans killed about nine thousand more people.[42]

By early 1943, the people of Belarus, especially the young men, were caught in a deadly competition between German forces and Soviet partisans that made nonsense of the ideologies of both sides. The Germans, lacking personnel, had recruited local men to their police forces (and, in the second half of 1942, to a "self-defense" militia). Many of these people had been communists before the war. The partisans, for their part, began in 1943 to recruit Belarusian policemen in the German service, since these men had at least some arms and training.[43]

It was the battlefield failures of the Wehrmacht, rather than any local political or ideological commitment, that determined where Belarusians chose to fight, when they had a choice. The summer offensive of Army Group South failed, and the entire Sixth Army was destroyed in the Battle of Stalingrad. When news of the Wehrmacht's defeat reached Belarus in February 1943, as many as twelve thousand policemen and militiamen left the German service and joined the Soviet partisans. According to one report, eight hundred did so on 23 February alone. This meant that some Belarusians who had killed Jews in the service of Nazis in 1941 and 1942 joined the Soviet partisans in 1943. More than this: the people who recruited these Belarusian policemen, the political officers among the partisans, were sometimes Jews who had escaped death at the hands of Belarusian policemen by fleeing the ghettos. Jews trying to survive the Holocaust recruited its perpetrators.[44]

Only the Jews, or the few who remained in Belarus in 1943, had a clear reason to be on one side rather than the other. Since they were the Germans' obvious and declared enemy in this war, and German enmity meant murder, they had every incentive to join the Soviets, despite the dangers of partisan life. For Belarusians (and Russians and Poles) the risks were more balanced; but the possibility of uninvolvement kept receding. For the Belarusians who ended up fighting and dying on one side or the other, it was very often a matter of chance, a question of who was in the village when the Soviet partisans or the German police appeared on their recruiting missions, which often simply involved press-ganging the young men. Since both sides knew that their membership was largely accidental, they would subject new recruits to grotesque tests of loyalty, such as killing friends or family members who had been captured fighting on the other side. As more and more of the Belarusian population was swept into the partisans or the various police and paramilitaries that the Germans hastily organized, such events simply revealed the essence of the situation: Belarus was a society divided against itself by others.[45]

In Belarus, as elsewhere, local German policy was conditioned by general economic concerns. By 1943, the Germans were worried more about labor shortages than about food shortages, and so their policy in Belarus shifted. As the war against the Soviet Union continued and the Wehrmacht took horrible losses month upon month, German men had to be taken from German farms and factories and sent to the front. Such people then had to be replaced if the German economy was to function. Hermann Göring issued an extraordinary directive in October 1942: Belarusian men in suspicious villages were not to be shot but rather kept alive and sent as forced laborers to Germany. People who could work were to be "selected" for labor rather than killed—even if they had taken up arms against Germany. By now, Göring seemed to reason, their labor power was all that they could offer to the Reich, and it was more significant than their death. Since the Soviet partisans controlled ever more Belarusian territory, ever less food was reaching Germany in any case. If Belarusian peasants could not work for Germany in Belarus, best to force them to work in Germany. This was very grim reaping. Hitler made clear in December 1942 what Göring had implied: the women and children, regarded as less useful as labor, were to be shot.[46]

This was a particularly spectacular example of the German campaign to gather forced labor in the East, which had begun with the Poles of the General Government, and spread to Ukraine before reaching this bloody climax in Belarus. By the end of the war, some eight million foreigners from the East, most of them Slavs, were working in the Reich. It was a rather perverse result, even by the standards of Nazi racism: German men went abroad and killed millions

THE EASTERN FRONT
JULY 1943

Soviet advances in early 1943

of "subhumans," only to import millions of other "subhumans" to do the work in Germany that the German men would have been doing themselves—had they not been abroad killing "subhumans." The net effect, setting aside the mass killing abroad, was that Germany became more of a Slavic land than it had ever been in history. (The perversity would reach its extreme in the first months of 1945, when surviving Jews were sent to labor camps in Germany itself. Having killed 5.4 million Jews as racial enemies, the Germans then brought Jewish survivors home to do the work that the killers might have been doing themselves, had they not been abroad killing.)

Under this new policy, German policemen and soldiers were to kill Belarusian women and children so that their husbands and fathers and brothers could be used as slave laborers. The anti-partisan operations of spring and summer 1943 were thus slavery campaigns rather than warfare of any recognizable kind. Yet because the slave hunts and associated mass murder were sometimes resisted by the Soviet partisans, the Germans did take losses. In May and June 1943 in Operations Marksman and Gypsy Baron (named after an opera and an operetta), the Germans aimed to secure railways in the Minsk region as well as workers for Germany. They reported killing 3,152 "partisans" and deporting 15,801 laborers. Yet they took 294 dead of their own: an absurdly low ratio of 1:10, if one assumed (wrongly) that reported partisan dead were actual partisans rather than (generally) civilians, but still a significant number.[47]

In May 1943 in Operation Cottbus, the Germans sought to clear all partisans from an area about 140 kilometers north of Minsk. Their forces destroyed village after village by herding populations into barns and then burning the barns to the ground. On the following days, the local swine and dogs, now without masters, would be seen in villages with burned human limbs in their jaws. The official count was 6,087 dead; but the Dirlewanger Brigade alone reported fourteen thousand killed in this operation. The majority of the dead were women and children; about six thousand men were sent to Germany as laborers.[48]

Operation Hermann, named for Hermann Göring, reached the extreme of this economic logic in summer 1943. Between 13 July and 11 August, German battle groups were to choose a territory, kill all of the inhabitants except for promising male labor, take all property that could be moved, and then burn everything left standing. After the labor selections among the local Belarusian and Polish populations, the Belarusian and Polish women, children, and aged were shot. This operation took place in western Belarus—in lands that had been invaded by the Soviet Union and annexed from Poland in 1939 before the German invasion that followed in 1941.[49]

Polish partisans were also to be found in these forests, fighters who believed that these lands should be restored to Poland. Thus German anti-partisan actions here were directed against both the Soviet partisans (representing the power that had governed in 1939–1941) and the Polish underground (fighting for Polish independence and territorial integrity with the boundaries of 1918–1939). The Polish forces were part of the Polish Home Army, reporting to the Polish government in exile in London. Poland was one of the Allies, and so in principle Polish and Soviet forces were fighting together against the Germans. But because both the Soviet Union and Poland claimed these lands of western Soviet Belarus (from the Soviet perspective) or northeastern Poland (from the Polish), matters were not so simple in practice. Polish fighters found themselves trapped between lawless Soviet and German forces. Polish civilians were massacred by Soviet partisans when Polish forces did not subordinate themselves to Moscow. In Naliboki on 8 May 1943, for example, Soviet partisans shot 127 Poles.[50]

Red Army officers invited Home Army officers to negotiate in summer 1943, and then murdered them on the way to the rendezvous points. The commander of the Soviet partisan movement believed that the way to deal with the Home Army was to denounce its men to the Germans, who would then shoot the Poles. Meanwhile, Polish forces were also attacked by the Germans. Polish commanders were in contact with both the Soviets and the Germans at various points, but could make a true alliance with neither: the Polish goal, after all, was to restore an independent Poland within its prewar boundaries. Just how difficult that would be, as Hitler's power gave way to Stalin's, was becoming clear in the Belarusian swamps.[51]

The Germans called the areas cleared of populations in Operation Hermann and the succeeding operations of 1943 "dead zones." People found in a dead zone were "fair game." The Wehrmacht's 45th Security Regiment killed civilians in Operation Easter Bunny of April 1943. Remnants of Einsatzgruppe D, dispatched to Belarus in spring 1943, contributed to this undertaking. They came from southern Russia and southern Ukraine, where the remnants of Army Group South were falling back after the defeat at Stalingrad. The task of

Einstazgruppe D there had been to cover the German retreat by killing civilians wherever resistance had been reported. In Belarus, it was burning down villages where no resistance whatsoever was encountered, after taking whatever livestock it could. Einsatzgruppe D was no longer covering a withdrawal of the Wehrmacht, as it had been further south, but preparing for one.[52]

The resort to dead zones implied a recognition that Soviet power would soon return to Belarus. Army Group South (much reduced and fighting under other names) was in retreat. Army Group North still besieged Leningrad, pointlessly. Belarus itself was still behind the lines of Army Group Center, but not for long.

At various points during the German occupation of Belarus, it did dawn on some German military and civilian leaders that mass terror was failing, and that the Belarusian population had to be rallied by some means other than terror to support German rule if the Red Army was to be defeated. This was impossible. As everywhere in the occupied Soviet Union, the Germans had succeeded in making most people wish for a return of Soviet rule. A German propaganda specialist sent to Belarus reported that there was nothing that he could possibly tell the population.[53]

The German-backed Russian Popular Army of Liberation (RONA in a Russian abbreviation) was the most dramatic attempt to gain local support. It was led by Bronislav Kaminskii, a Soviet citizen of Russian nationality and Polish and perhaps German descent, who had apparently been sent to a Soviet special settlement in the 1930s. He presented himself as an opponent of collectivization. The Germans permitted him an experiment in local self-government in the town of Lokot, in northwestern Russia. There Kaminskii was placed in charge of anti-partisan operations, and locals were indeed allowed to keep more of the grain that they produced. As the war turned against the Germans, Kaminskii and his entire apparatus were dispatched from Russia to Belarus, where they were supposed to play a similar role. Kaminskii was ordered to fight the Soviet partisans in Belarus, but he and his group could barely protect themselves in their home base. Understandably, the Belarusian locals regarded RONA as foreigners who were taking land while speaking about property rights.[54]

In 1942 and 1943, Wilhelm Kube, the head of the General Commissariat White Ruthenia, tried to reverse some of the basic principles of German colonialism in the hope of rallying the population to resist the Red Army. He tried nationality concessions, sponsoring Belarusian schools and organizing various Belarusian advisory councils and militias. In June 1943 he went so far as to undo the collectivization of agriculture, decreeing that Belarusian peasants could own their own land. The policy was doubly absurd: much of the countryside was controlled by the partisans, who killed people who opposed collective farming; and the German army and police, in the meantime, were rejecting property rights in a comparably categorical way, by looting and burning farmsteads, killing farm families, and sending farmers to work as forced laborers in Germany. Since the Germans did not respect the Belarusian peasants' right to life, peasants found it hard to take seriously the new commitment to private property.[55]

Even if Kube had somehow succeeded, his policies revealed the impossibility of a German colonization of the East. The Slavs were meant to be starved and displaced; Kube wanted to govern and fight with their help. The collective farm was to be maintained to extract food; Kube proposed to dissolve it and allow Belarusians to farm as they wished. By undoing both Soviet and Nazi policies, Kube was revealing their basic similarity in the countryside. Both Soviet self-colonization and German racial colonization involved purposeful economic exploitation. But because the Germans were more murderous, and because German murders were fresher in the minds of the locals, Soviet power came to seem like the lesser evil, or even like a liberation. The Soviet partisans put an end to Kube's experiments. He was killed by a bomb that his maid placed under his bed in September 1943.[56]

In Belarus, more than anywhere else, the Nazi and Soviet systems overlapped and interacted. Its relatively small territory was the site of intensive warfare, partisan campaigning, and mass atrocity. It was the rear area of a German Army Group Center that would do anything to take Moscow, and the target of the Red Army divisions of the Belarusian Front who were planning to return. It was fully controlled by neither the German administration nor the partisans, each of which used terror in the absence of reliable material or moral inducements to loyalty. It was home to one of Europe's densest populations of Jews, doomed to destruction, but also unusually capable of resistance. It seems likely that more Jews resisted Hitler in Minsk and Belarus than anywhere else— although, with rare exceptions, they could not resist Nazi rule without aiding

Soviet power. Bielski's and Zorin's units were the largest Jewish partisan formations in Europe.[57]

There was no gray area, no liminal zone, no marginal space; none of the comforting clichés of the sociology of mass murder applied. It was black on black. Germans killed Jews as partisans, and many Jews became partisans. The Jews who became partisans were serving the Soviet regime, and were taking part in a Soviet policy to bring down retributions upon civilians. The partisan war in Belarus was a perversely interactive effort of Hitler and Stalin, who each ignored the laws of war and escalated the conflict behind the front lines. Once both Operation Barbarossa and Operation Typhoon had failed, the German position in the rear was doomed. Initial anti-partisan policy, like so much else in German planning, depended upon a quick and total victory. Personnel were sufficient to kill Jews but not to fight partisans. Lacking adequate personnel, the Germans murdered and intimidated. Terror served as a force multiplier, but the forces multiplied were ultimately Stalin's.

There was a Soviet partisan movement, and the Germans did try to suppress it. Yet German policies, in practice, were little more than mass murder. In one Wehrmacht report, 10,431 partisans were reported shot, but only ninety guns were reported taken. That means that almost all of those killed were in fact civilians. As it inflicted its first fifteen thousand mortal casualties, the Special Commando Dirlewanger lost only ninety-two men—many of them, no doubt, to friendly fire and alcoholic accidents. A ratio such as that was possible only when the victims were unarmed civilians. Under the cover of anti-partisan operations, the Germans murdered Belarusian (or Jewish, or Polish, or Russian) civilians in 5,295 different localities in occupied Soviet Belarus. Several hundred of these villages and towns were burned to the ground. All in all, the Germans killed about 350,000 people in their anti-partisan campaign, at the very least ninety percent of them unarmed. The Germans killed half a million Jews in Belarus, including thirty thousand during the anti-partisan operations. It was unclear just how these thirty thousand people were to be counted: as Jews killed in the Final Solution, or as Belarusian civilians killed in anti-partisan reprisals? The Germans themselves often failed to make the distinction, for very practical reasons. As one German commander confided to his diary, "The bandits and Jews burned in houses and bunkers were not counted."[58]

Of the nine million people who were on the territory of Soviet Belarus in 1941, some 1.6 million were killed by the Germans in actions away from battlefields, including about 700,000 prisoners of war, 500,000 Jews, and 320,000 people counted as partisans (the vast majority of whom were unarmed civilians). These three general campaigns constituted the three greatest German atrocities in eastern Europe, and together they struck Belarus with the greatest force and malice. Another several hundred thousand inhabitants of Soviet Belarus were killed in action as soldiers of the Red Army.[59]

The Soviet partisans also contributed to the total number of fatalities. They reported killing 17,431 people as traitors on the terrain of Soviet Belarus by 1 January 1944; this figure does not include civilians whom they killed for other reasons, or civilians whom they killed in the following months. In all, tens of thousands of people in Belarus were killed by the partisans in their own retribution actions (or, in the western regions taken from Poland, as class enemies). A few more tens of thousands of people native to the region certainly died after arrests during the Soviet occupation of 1939–1941 and especially during the Soviet deportations of 1940 and 1941, during the journey or in Kazakhstan.[60]

A rough estimate of two million total mortal losses on the territory of present-day Belarus during the Second World War seems reasonable and conservative. More than a million other people fled the Germans, and another two million were deported as forced labor or removed from their original residence for another reason. Beginning in 1944, the Soviets deported a quarter million more people to Poland and tens of thousands more to the Gulag. By the end of the war, half the population of Belarus had either been killed or moved. This cannot be said of any other European country.[61]

The Germans intended worse than they achieved. The starvation of prisoners of war at Stalag 352 in Minsk and other prisoner-of-war camps was only a fraction of the deaths foreseen by the Hunger Plan. The clearings of peasants were on a smaller scale than the massive depopulation of Belarus envisaged by Generalplan Ost. About a million Belarusians were exploited as forced labor, though not always worked to death as envisaged by Generalplan Ost. Mahileu, where the mass extermination of urban Jews began and where the anti-partisan clinic was held, was supposed to become a large killing facility. It did not; it seems that the crematoria ordered by the SS for Mahileu ended up in Auschwitz. Minsk, too, was to be the site of a killing facility, with its own crematoria. Once the work of killing was completed, Minsk itself was to be leveled. Wilhelm Kube imagined replacing the city with a German settlement named Asgard, after the mythical home of the Norse gods.[62]

Of the Nazi utopias, only the elimination of the Jews was realized, although again not exactly as the Germans had planned. In Belarus, as elsewhere, the Final Solution was the one atrocity that took on a more radical form in the realization than in the conception. Soviet Jews were supposed to work themselves to death building a German empire or be deported further east. This proved impossible; most Jews in the East were killed where they lived. In Minsk, there were a few exceptions: those Jews who escaped and survived, often at the price of partaking in the descent into mass violence; and those Jews kept for labor, who died a bit later than the others, and sometimes further from home. In September 1943, some of the last Jews of Minsk were deported west to occupied Poland, to a facility known as Sobibór.[63]

There they encountered a death factory of a kind unknown even in Belarus, where, one might have thought, all earthly horrors had already been revealed.

CHAPTER 8

THE NAZI DEATH FACTORIES

About 5.4 million Jews died under German occupation. Nearly half of them were murdered east of the Molotov-Ribbentrop line, usually by bullets, sometimes by gas. The rest perished west of the Molotov-Ribbentrop line, usually by gas, sometimes by bullets. East of the Molotov-Ribbentrop line, a million Jews were killed in the second half of 1941, in the first six months of the German occupation. Another million were killed in 1942. West of the Molotov-Ribbentrop line, Jews came under German control significantly earlier, but were killed later. In the east, the most economically productive Jews, the young men, were often shot right away, in the first days or weeks of the war. Then economic arguments were turned against the women, children, and elderly, who became "useless eaters." West of the Molotov-Ribbentrop line, ghettos were established pending a deportation (to Lublin, Madagascar, or Russia) that never came. Uncertainty about the final version of the Final Solution between 1939 and 1941 meant that Jews west of the Molotov-Ribbentrop line were put to work. This created a certain economic argument for their preservation.

The mass murder of Polish Jews in the General Government and in Polish lands annexed to Germany was initiated after more than two years of German occupation, and more than a year after Jews had been consigned to ghettos. These Polish Jews were gassed at six major facilities, four in the General Government and two in the lands annexed to the Reich, functioning in one combination or another from December 1941 through November 1944: Chełmno, Bełżec, Sobibór, Treblinka, Majdanek, Auschwitz. The core of the killing campaign west of the Molotov-Ribbentrop line was Operation Reinhard, the gassing of 1.3 million Polish Jews at Bełżec, Sobibór, and Treblinka in 1942. Its last chapter was Auschwitz, where about two hundred thousand Polish Jews and more than seven hundred thousand other European Jews were gassed, most of them in 1943 and 1944.[1]

The origins of Operation Reinhard lie in Himmler's interpretations of Hitler's desires. Aware of the successful gassing experiments performed on Soviet prisoners of war, Himmler entrusted the creation of a new gassing facility for Jews to his client Odilo Globocnik on about 13 October 1941. Globocnik was the SS and Police Leader of the Lublin district of the General Government, which was a crucial testing ground for Nazi racial utopias. Globocnik had expected that millions of Jews would be deported to his region, where he would put them to work in slave labor colonies. After the attack on the Soviet Union, Globocnik was charged with the implementation of Generalplan Ost. Though this grand design for exterminatory colonization was generally tabled after the Soviet Union failed to collapse, Globocnik actually implemented it in part in his Lublin district, driving a hundred thousand Poles from their homes. He wanted a general "cleansing of the General Government of Jews, and also of Poles."[2]

By late October 1941 Globocnik had chosen a site for the new gassing facility: Bełżec, just south and east of Lublin. The changing plans for the use of this place reveal the shift of Nazi utopias from exterminatory colonization to extermination as such. In 1940 Globocnik had established a slave labor site at Bełżec, where he imagined that two million Jews would dig anti-tank ditches by hand. He harbored such fantasies because an early version of the Final Solution had involved the deportation of European Jews to his Lublin district. In the event, Globocnik had to settle for a labor force at Bełżec of no more than thirty thousand Jews. He finally abandoned his defense project in October 1940. A year later, having spoken to Himmler, he imagined another way to exploit the site: for the extermination of the Jews.[3]

Globocnik would seek, and find, a way for Germans to kill Jews west of the Molotov-Ribbentrop line, where they lacked the personnel for mass shooting campaigns, and where they were unwilling to arm Poles as auxiliaries. The facility at Bełżec would require just a few German commanders to operate. The basic labor would be provided by Jewish slaves. The facility would be guarded

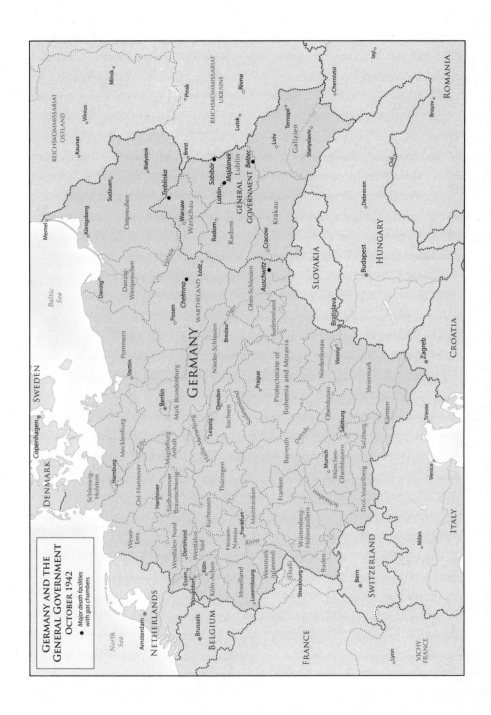

GERMANY AND THE
GENERAL GOVERNMENT
OCTOBER 1942

● Major death facilities
  with gas chambers

and operated chiefly with non-Germans chosen from the training camp at Trawniki, in the Lublin district. The first Trawniki men were captured Red Army soldiers taken from the prisoner-of-war camps. The Trawniki men were largely Soviet Ukrainians, but included representatives of other Soviet nationalities, including Russians and the occasional person of Jewish origin—chosen, of course, by accident. The Germans preferred Soviet Germans, when they could be found.[4]

The changing mission of the Trawniki men, like the changing use of Bełżec, revealed the transformation of Hitler's utopias. In Globocnik's initial scheme, these men were to serve as policemen, under German command, in the conquered Soviet Union. Since the Soviet Union was not in fact conquered, the Trawniki men could be prepared for another special task: operating the facilities where the Jews of Poland would be gassed. The Trawniki men knew nothing of this general design when they were recruited, and had no political or personal stake in this policy. For them, Poland was a foreign country, and its Jews were a foreign people. They presumably had a strong interest in keeping their jobs; their recruitment rescued them from a likely death by starvation. Even if they somehow had the courage to defy the Germans anyway, they knew that they could not safely return to the Soviet Union. In leaving the Dulags and Stalags they had stamped themselves as German collaborators.

In December 1941 the Trawniki men, wearing black uniforms, assisted in the construction of a ramp and a rail spur, which would allow communication by train to Bełżec. Soviet citizens were providing the labor for a German killing policy.[5]

Bełżec was not to be a camp. People spend the night at camps. Bełżec was to be a death factory, where Jews would be killed upon arrival.

There was a German precedent for such a facility, where people arrived under false pretenses, were told that they needed to be showered, and then were killed by carbon monoxide gas. Between 1939 and 1941 in Germany, six killing facilities had been used to murder the handicapped, the mentally ill, and others deemed "unworthy of life." After a test run of gassing the Polish handicapped in the Wartheland, Hitler's chancellery organized a secret program to kill German citizens. It was staffed by doctors, nurses, and police chiefs; one of its main organizers was Hitler's personal doctor. The medical science of the mass murder was simple: carbon monoxide (CO) binds much better than oxygen (O_2) to the hemoglobin in blood, and thereby prevents red blood cells from performing their normal function of bringing oxygen to tissues. The victims were brought in for ostensible medical examinations, and then led to "showers," where they were asphyxiated by carbon monoxide released from canisters. If the victims had gold teeth, they were marked beforehand with a chalk cross on their backs, so that these could be extracted after their death. Children were the first victims, the parents receiving mendacious letters from doctors about how they had died during treatment. Most of the victims of the "euthanasia" program were non-Jewish Germans, although German Jews with disabilities were simply killed without any screening whatsoever. At one killing facility, the personnel celebrated the ten-thousandth cremation by bedecking a corpse with flowers.[6]

The declared end of the "euthanasia" program coincided with Globocnik's mission to develop a new technique for the gassing of Polish Jews. By August 1941, when Hitler called the program to a halt for fear of domestic resistance, it had registered 70,273 deaths, and created a model of deceptive killing by lethal gas. The suspension of the "euthanasia" program left a group of policemen and doctors with certain skills but without employment. In October 1941, Globocnik summoned a group of them to the Lublin district to run his planned death facilities for Jews. Some 92 of the 450 or so men who would serve Globocnik in the task of gassing the Polish Jews had prior experience in the "euthanasia" program. The most important of them was Christian Wirth, who had overseen the "euthanasia" program. As the head of Hitler's chancellery put it, "a large part of my organization" was to be used "in a solution to the Jewish question that will extend to the ultimate possible consequences."[7]

Globocnik was not the only one to exploit the experience of the "euthanasia" crews. A gassing facility at Chełmno, in the Wartheland, also exploited the technical experience of the "euthanasia" program. Whereas Globocnik's Lublin district was the experimental site for the destructive side of Himmler's program for "strengthening Germandom," Arthur Greiser's Wartheland was the site of most actual deportation: hundreds of thousands of Poles were shipped to the General Government, and hundreds of thousands of Germans arrived from the Soviet Union. Greiser faced the same problem as Hitler, on a smaller scale: after all the movement, the Jews remained, and by late 1941 no plausible site for deportation was evident. Greiser did manage to deport a few thousand Jews to the

General Government, but these were replaced by Jews deported from the rest of Germany.[8]

The head of the Sicherheitsdienst (SD) in Greiser's regional capital Poznań had proposed a solution on 16 July 1941: "There is the danger this winter that the Jews can no longer all be fed. It is to be seriously considered whether the most humane solution might not be to finish off those Jews not capable of working by some sort of fast-working preparation. This would be in any event more pleasant than letting them starve." The "fast-working preparation" was carbon monoxide, as used in the "euthanasia" program. A gas van was tested on Soviet prisoners of war in September 1941; thereafter gas vans were used in occupied Belarus and Ukraine, especially to kill children. The killing machine at Chełmno was a parked gas van, operated under the supervision of Herbert Lange, who had gassed the handicapped in the "euthanasia" program. As of 5 December, Germans were using the Chełmno facility to kill Jews in the Wartheland. Some 145,301 Jews were killed at Chełmno in 1941 or 1942. Chełmno was operative until the Jewish population of the Wartheland was reduced, essentially, to a very functional labor camp inside the Łódź ghetto. But the killing paused, in early April: just as the killing in the Lublin district was beginning.[9]

Bełżec was to be a new model, more efficient and more durable than Chełmno. Most likely in consultation with Wirth, Globocnik decided to build a permanent facility where many people could be gassed at once behind walls (as with the "euthanasia" program), but one where carbon monoxide gas could be reliably generated from internal combustion engines (as with the gas vans). Rather than parking a vehicle, as at Chełmno, this meant removing the engine from a vehicle, linking it with pipes to a purpose-built gas chamber, surrounding that gas chamber with fences, and then connecting the death factory to population centers by rail. Such were the simple innovations of Bełżec, but they were enough.[10]

The Nazi leadership had always understood the Polish Jews to be at the heart of the Jewish "problem." The German occupation had divided Jews who had been Polish citizens into three different political zones. As of December 1941, some three hundred thousand Polish Jews were living in the Wartheland and other Polish lands annexed to Germany. They were now subject to gassing at Chełmno. The 1.3 million or so Polish Jews on the eastern side of the Molotov-

Ribbentrop line were subject to shooting from June 1941, and most of their number would be killed in 1942. The largest group of Polish Jews under German occupation were those in ghettos in the General Government. Until June 1941, the General Government held half of the prewar population of Polish Jews, about 1,613,000 people. (When a Galicia district was added after the German invasion of the Soviet Union, the number of Jews in the General Government reached about 2,143,000. Those half-million or so Jews in Galicia, east of the Molotov-Ribbentrop line, were subject to shooting.)[11]

When Himmler and Globocnik began, in March 1942, to kill the Polish Jews of the General Government, they were undertaking an unambiguous policy to destroy the major Jewish population of Europe. On 14 March 1942 Himmler spent the night in Lublin and spoke with Globocnik. Two days later the Germans began the deportation of Jews from the Lublin district to Bełżec. On the night of 16 March, about 1,600 Jews who lacked labor documents were rounded up in Lublin, shipped away, and gassed. In the second half of March 1942 the Germans began to clear the Lublin district of Jews, village by village, town by town. Hermann Höfle, Globocnik's lieutenant for "resettlement," led a staff that developed the necessary techniques. Jews from smaller ghettos were ordered to larger ones. Then Jews with dangerous associations, suspected communists, and Polish Army veterans, were shot. In the final preparatory step, the population was filtered and younger men and others deemed suitable for labor were given new papers.[12]

West of the Molotov-Ribbentrop line, the Germans arranged matters so that they did less of the actual killing themselves. The institutions of the ghetto, its Judenrat and Jewish police force, were turned toward its destruction. Globocnik's staff would begin an action in a given town or city by contacting the local Security Police, and then assemble a force of German policemen. If the Germans had at their disposal a Jewish police force, as they did in communities of any size, Jewish policemen were then required to do the bulk of the actual work of assembling their fellow Jews for transports. In cities, the Jewish police far outnumbered the Germans from whom they took orders. Since they had no firearms, they could only use force against fellow Jews. Sometimes Trawniki men were also available to help.[13]

The German police ordered the Jewish police to assemble the Jewish population at a given assembly point by a certain time. At first, Jews were often lured to the collection point with promises of food or more attractive labor assignments "in the east." Then, in roundups that took several days, the Germans and the Jewish police would blockade particular blocks or particular houses, and force their inhabitants to go to a collection point. Germans shot small children, pregnant women, and the handicapped or elderly on the spot. In larger towns and cities where more than one roundup was necessary, these measures were repeated with increasing violence. The Germans were aiming for daily quotas to fill trains, and would sometimes pass on quotas to the Jewish police who were responsible (at the risk of their own positions and thus lives) for filling them. The ghetto was sealed during and also after the action, so that the German police could plunder without hindrance from the local population.[14]

Once the Jews reached Bełżec, they were doomed. They arrived unarmed to a closed and guarded facility, with little chance of understanding their situation, let alone resisting the Germans and the armed Trawniki men. Much like the patients at the "euthanasia" centers, they were told that they had to enter a certain building in order to be disinfected. They were required to remove their clothes and discard their valuables, on the explanation that these too would be disinfected and returned. Then they were marched, naked, into chambers that were pumped full of carbon monoxide. Only two or three Jews who disembarked at Bełżec survived; about 434,508 did not. Wirth commanded the facility through the summer of 1942, and seems to have excelled in his duties. Thereafter he would serve as general inspector of Bełżec and the two other facilities that would be built on the same model.[15]

This system worked nearly to perfection in the Lublin district of the General Government. Deportations to Bełżec from the Cracow district began slightly later, with similar results. Jews from the Galicia district suffered from the overlap of two German killing methods: beginning in summer 1941 they were shot; and then from March 1942 they were gassed at Bełżec. Galicia was to the east of the Molotov-Ribbentrop line, and so Jews there were subject to shooting; but it had been added to the General Government, so its Jews were also subject to gassing. Thomas Hecht, a Galician Jew who survived, recounted some of the ways Jews might die in Galicia: two aunts, an uncle, and a cousin were gassed at Bełżec; his father, one of his brothers, an aunt, an uncle, and a cousin were shot; his other brother died at a labor camp.[16]

Meanwhile, Globocnik's staff and his Trawniki men built another death facility on the Bełżec model in the Lublin district: at Sobibór, just northeast of

Lublin. Functional from April 1942, it killed, in exactly the same way as Bełżec, some 180,000 Jews, with only about forty survivors. Globocnik and his men had mastered the necessary procedures for the core of the operation: roundups in the ghettos, carried out by Höfle's men, German police, and locals; order in the camps, as maintained by a crew of Trawniki men, a few Germans, and a large Jewish workforce; and the mass murder itself, carried out by suffocation through exposure to carbon monoxide from an internal combustion engine.[17]

Having achieved mortality rates of 99.99 percent at Bełżec and Sobibór, Himmler ordered on 17 April 1942 the construction of a third facility, this time in the Warsaw district of the General Government. A crew with "euthanasia" experience, accompanied by Trawniki men, was dispatched to a site near the village of Treblinka, where construction of the death factory began on 1 June 1942. The laborers were Jews from the region, who were killed when the project was complete. The man who oversaw the construction was, like the commanders of Bełżec and Sobibór, a veteran of the "euthanasia" program. Unlike Franz Stangl (at Sobibór) and Christian Wirth (at Bełżec), however, Irmfried Eberl was a medical doctor rather than a police chief. He had directed two of the "euthanasia" facilities.[18]

Eberl seemed delighted at his latest assignment. "It's going very well for me," he wrote to his wife during the construction of the death facility at Treblinka. "There's lots to do and that's fun." As the camp neared completion, he was "pleased and proud of this accomplishment." He was happy that Globocnik's Lublin model would be extended to Warsaw.[19]

Home to much of the Polish educated classes and to Europe's largest society of Jews, Warsaw was a metropolis that had no place in the Nazi worldview. As of spring 1942, more than 350,000 Jews were still alive in the Warsaw ghetto.

Warsaw was the largest city in the General Government, but not its administrative center. Hans Frank, the general governor, preferred to rule from Cracow, taking over the ancient Polish royal castle and presenting himself as latter-day racial royalty. In October 1939, he had stymied attempts to resolve the Jewish "problem" by transporting Jews into the Lublin district of the General Government. In December 1941, Frank told his subordinates that they "must get rid of the Jews." He had no idea, even then, how this could be achieved. But by spring 1942, Frank knew. Lublin had something to offer Frank: it was no longer the district that would attract more Jews to the General Government, but the place where Jews who already lived in the General Government could be murdered. This was welcome. Trawniki men arrived in Warsaw in February and April. In summer 1942 Frank ceded control of Jewish employment, and then the ghettos themselves, to the SS.[20]

The assassination of a very prominent SS commander provided the pretext for the next escalation. After Hitler and Himmler, Reinhard Heydrich was the most important architect of the policy to exterminate the Jews. He was also a typical example of the Nazi tendency to entrust several offices to one person: already the head of the Reich Security Main Office, he was placed in charge of the Protectorate of Bohemia and Moravia, the Czech lands annexed to Germany in 1939. On 27 May 1942, he was injured in an assassination attempt by a Czech and a Slovak employed by British intelligence, and died on 4 June. Hitler and Himmler were annoyed with him for travelling without a security detail, which Heydrich believed he did not need because of his popularity among Czechs. In the Czech lands the Germans pursued no repressive policies comparable to those in occupied Poland and the Soviet Union; Heydrich had made a special point of favoring the Czech working class.[21]

Heydrich's assassination meant the loss of a planner of the Final Solution, but the gain of a martyr. Hitler and Himmler met and spoke on June 3rd, 4th, and 5th 1942. Himmler gave the eulogy: "Ours is the holy duty to avenge his death, to take up his labor, and to destroy the enemies of our people without mercy or weakness." One Czech village, Lidice, would be totally destroyed as retribution for the assassination of Heydrich. Its men were shot on the spot, its women sent to the German concentration camp at Ravensbrück, and the children gassed at Chełmno.[22]

The Nazi policy of the complete elimination of Polish Jews in the General Government now took the name "Operation Reinhard," as a tribute to Heydrich. The reference to the assassination made victims of the Germans, and allowed the mass murder of Jews to be presented as retribution. Within the Nazi worldview, the assassination of Heydrich in May 1942 played a role similar to that of the American declaration of war in December 1941: it gave rise to a feeling of righteous solidarity among the ostensibly attacked Nazis, and it distracted attention from the true sources of German predicaments and policies. Heydrich became a prominent "victim" of the supposed international Jewish conspiracy that was responsible for the war.[23]

Jews were killed because Hitler had defined this as an aim of the war. But even after he made his desires known, the timing of their death was conditioned by German perceptions of the war's course and associated economic priorities. Jews were more likely to die when Germans were concerned with food shortages, and less likely to die when Germans were concerned with labor shortages.

Hitler announced his decision to kill all the Jews not long after he had announced his decision that Soviet prisoners of war should be used as labor rather than killed. In early 1942 surviving Soviet prisoners of war were integrated into the labor force in Germany proper, while Hans Frank succeeded in organizing a colonial Polish economy in his General Government. With labor supplies momentarily assured, food became the primary concern, both in the Reich and in occupied Poland. Göring had to announce cuts in food rations for Germans in the Reich in April 1942, and the average consumption of calories in the Reich did indeed decline considerably that year. Frank, for his part, was concerned with the improvement of food supplies to his Polish working class.[24]

Thus in summer 1942 economic concerns, as understood by the Germans, hastened rather than hindered the plan to murder all of the Polish Jews. When food rather than labor was the primary anxiety, Jews became "useless eaters," and even those working for the benefit of the German economy and the Wehrmacht were in danger. By the end of 1942, Hans Frank again wanted labor more than he wanted food, and thus wanted remaining Jews to be kept alive. By then, most Polish Jews were already dead. The German economy was like a razor tightrope that Jews were forced to walk, barefoot, blindfolded, and without a net. It was all that was between them and death, it was bloody and treacherous, it was certain to fail them.[25]

The death facility at Treblinka was completed on 11 July 1942. Eight days later, on 19 July 1942, Himmler ordered the complete "resettlement of the entire Jewish population of the General Government by 31 December 1942." This meant, before all, Warsaw.[26]

In Warsaw on 22 July 1942, Globocnik's "resettlement" specialist Hermann Höfle and his group of SS ghetto clearers briefed the local Security Police in

Warsaw, and then paid a visit to Adam Czerniaków, head of the Judenrat. Höfle told Czerniaków that he would have to present five thousand Jews at a transfer point, or Umschlagplatz, the following day. Czerniaków, who knew of the earlier ghetto clearings in the Lublin district, seemed to grasp what was afoot. Rather than accept responsibility for a part in the coordination of the murder of his people, he killed himself. With Czerniaków dead, the Germans then turned to deception, ordering the Jewish police to hang signs promising bread and marmalade to those who would appear at the Umschlagplatz. The first transport of about five thousand Jews departed Warsaw for Treblinka on 23 July. As Bluma Bergman recalled, people who were starving would do anything for a bit of food, "even if you know that you're going to be killed."[27]

Thus began the operation in the Warsaw ghetto that the Germans called the "Large Action." Höfle and his crew installed themselves in the ghetto, at Żelazna 103. As they had done in other cities and towns in the Lublin, Cracow, and Galicia districts of the General Government, they and the local Security Police now turned to coercion. With the help of a few hundred Trawniki men and about two thousand Jewish policemen, the Germans organized roundups in the Warsaw ghetto almost every single day for the next two months. After the very hungry were gone, the Jewish police next took groups who seemed helpless: the orphans, the poor, the homeless, prisoners. The old and the young had no chance whatsoever. Children under the age of fifteen disappeared entirely from the ghetto. The Germans shot very young children, the sick, the handicapped, and the aged on the spot.[28]

At first, the Jewish police were able to carry out the task with little German supervision. After a few days of deporting the hungry and the helpless, the Germans applied the same technique in Warsaw as elsewhere: the surprise blockade of an apartment building or part of a street, the verification of papers, and the deportation of all Jews not deemed necessary for labor. The Jewish police, supervised by the German police, carried out the first blockade on 29 July 1942. The Germans decided which areas were to be cleared at what times; the Jewish policemen would open at dawn a sealed envelope with instructions about which areas were to be cleared on that day. In general the Germans carried out two actions each day, aiming to fill a quota.[29]

Selections for labor kept some individuals alive, but undermined any collective spirit of resistance. Although the Germans were far from precise in their observation of the difference between documented laborers and others, selection created a crucial social division between those Jews who had papers and those who did not, and brought a general preoccupation with personal security. People tended to believe that they and their families could remain in the ghetto with the right jobs and the right papers. This privatization of hope was doom for the collectivity. Available energy was spent in the hunt for documents, rather than in the coordination of resistance. No one tried (as yet) to wrest the monopoly of force within the ghetto from the Germans and the Jewish police. So long as there was no Jewish group willing to resist the Jewish police, the roundups and deportations could continue, with German oversight but quite limited German personnel.[30]

By August 1942 the Germans required that Jewish policemen each produce five Jews a day for deportation, or else see members of their own families deported. This had the effect of removing those who could not defend themselves. The major orphanages were emptied on 5 August. The famous educator Janusz Korczak led his children to the Umschlagplatz. He held two of them by the hand and walked with his head high. Among the 6,623 people deported that day with him were the educators and caretakers of the ghetto's orphans: his colleague Stefania Wilczyńska and many others. Policemen took the old and the young to Umschlagplatz on carts. Jewish policemen took a small girl from her home when her mother was away running an errand. Her last words before deportation to Treblinka were recorded: "I know that you are a good man, sir. Be so kind as to not take me away. My mama left for just a moment. She'll be back in just a moment, and I won't be there, be so kind as to not take me away."[31]

In the first two months of the Large Action, some 265,040 Jews were taken to the Umschlagplatz, and another 10,380 or so killed in the ghetto itself. Perhaps sixty thousand Jews remained. They were predominantly fit younger males.[32]

Each stage of the mass murder of the Warsaw Jews was so dreadful that it gave rise to hopes that the near future might at least be better than the immediate past. Some Jews really did believe that labor in the east would be better than life in the ghetto. Once assembled at Umschlagplatz, Jews could be forgiven for believing that embarking on trains would be better than indefinite waiting under the hot sun without food, water, and sanitary facilities. The supervision of Umschlagplatz was assigned to the Jewish police, who occasionally freed people they knew, or people who could afford to bribe them. As the historian Emanuel Ringelblum recorded, the Jewish police sometimes demanded, in addition to cash, payment "in kind," which is to say sex with the women whom they saved.[33]

In the trains, illusions faded. Although assured that their destination was a labor camp "in the east," some Jews must have suspected that this was false: after all, people with labor certificates were precisely the ones who remained in Warsaw. If work was the goal, then why were the very old and the very young sent first? The trains were accorded the lowest priority in the railway system, and often took days to reach a destination that was in fact rather close to Warsaw— Treblinka was only about a hundred kilometers to the northeast. The Jews were given no food or water, and died in large numbers on many of the transports. Children licked each other's sweat. Mothers sometimes threw small children from trains, guessing that they would be more likely to survive in the wild than wherever the train was going. Some parents explained to their very small children, born in the ghetto, what could be seen through windows or cracks in doors. The very youngest had never seen fields or forests before. Nor would they again.[34]

Poles would yell at the trains going by. The gesture of a finger across the throat, remembered with loathing by a few Jewish survivors, was meant to communicate to the Jews that they were going to die—though not necessarily that the Poles wished this upon them. Some Poles called for money; others, perhaps more merciful, perhaps with other needs, asked for children. Yankiel Wiernik remembered his own transport, an early one from Warsaw: "My view took in everyone and everything, yet I could not take in the enormity of the misfortune." No one could.[35]

Each transport was assembled from fifty-seven to sixty train cars, or about five to six thousand people. Upon arrival at the rail station nearest Treblinka, the train stopped. Then, sometimes after a wait of hours or even days, another engine pulled up, and moved nineteen or twenty of the cars—1,700 to 2,000 people—to a rail spur inside the Treblinka death factory. The second engine pushed rather than pulled these cars, so that the engineer was going backward, and never himself faced or entered the facility.[36]

The Jews who were still alive were then forced from each car by Trawniki men brandishing guns and cracking whips. The Jews deported to Treblinka died, almost all of them, in these first few weeks, but not as smoothly as at Bełżec and

Sobibór, and not as the Germans intended. The regular and massive transports of Jews had overwhelmed the small gas chambers at Treblinka very quickly, and so the Germans and the Trawniki men had to resort to shooting. This was not the task for which the Trawniki men had been trained. They did it badly, but they did it. By August the rail spur inside the Treblinka death factory was surrounded by piles of corpses.

Oskar Berger, who arrived on a transport of August 22nd, remembered "hundreds of bodies lying around." Yankiel Wiernik recalled his arrival on 24 August: "The camp yard was littered with corpses, some still in their clothes and some naked, their faces distorted with fright and awe, black and swollen, the eyes wide open, with protruding tongues, skulls crushed, bodies mangled." A Jew who had arrived the day before, 23 August, had just avoided joining that pile. He was chosen for labor, which chiefly meant the disposal of human remains. He recalled how the killing was done in those early weeks of Treblinka: "After we left the wagon the Germans and Ukrainians, whips in their hands, drove us into a courtyard, where they ordered us to lie down with our faces to the ground. Then they walked through and shot us in the back of the neck." Adam Krzepicki, who arrived on 25 August, recorded a similar impression: "Corpses of people of different ages, in different positions, with different expressions on their faces the moment they breathed their last. All around, just earth, sky, and corpses!" The next day, 26 August, was remembered by Edward Weinstein: "And I looked out, and I saw Hell. Bodies, as high as the windows on the cattle car, on the ramp." Franz Stangl, the German (Austrian) police officer who commanded the death factory at Sobibór, was called in to investigate the chaos of Treblinka. He was, presumably, not a man who was easily overwhelmed by death, and unlike the arriving Jews he had some idea of what to expect. Nevertheless he was shocked by what he found: "The smell was indescribable; the hundreds, no, the thousands of bodies everywhere, decomposing, putrefying."[37]

Irmfried Eberl, the German (Austrian) medical doctor who commanded Treblinka, had hoped to prove his worth. He wanted his kill rates to exceed those of the other death facility commanders, the police chiefs at Bełżec and Sobibór. He continued to accept transports in August 1942 even as the number of people to be killed far exceeded the facility's capacity to asphyxiate them. Death then radiated outward: from the gas chambers to the waiting area in the courtyard, and from the courtyard to the trains waiting at the station, or on the tracks, or somewhere far away in occupied Poland. The Jews died all the same, almost all of them; but now a few escaped from the trains, which had very rarely happened during earlier transports to Sobibór and Bełżec.[38]

Escapees from the trains made their way back to the Warsaw ghetto, often with an idea of what they had been spared. The disorganization also drew the attention of onlookers. Because of all the delays, trains conveying German soldiers to the eastern front were more likely to pass or to be caught behind one of the death trains; a few onlookers took photographs, others vomited from the stench. Some of these soldiers were on their way to southwestern Soviet Russia to take part in the offensive at Stalingrad. Those German soldiers who saw the Treblinka transports knew, if they wanted to know, just what they were fighting for.[39]

Eberl was removed from his post for incompetence, and in August 1942 Stangl took command at Treblinka. Stangl, who later said that he regarded the mass gassing of Jews as his "profession" and that he "enjoyed it," quickly put Treblinka in order. He called a temporary halt to transports, and had the bodies buried by Jewish laborers. When the death facility was opened again in early September 1942, it functioned much more like the machine that it was designed to be.[40]

Stangl commanded with the help of a particularly vicious assistant, Kurt Franz, whom the Jewish laborers called "the Doll" (for his vanity and good looks). Franz liked to watch Jews box, he liked to watch his dog attack Jews, and he liked to watch animals in general: at one point he had the Jewish laborers construct a zoo. The Germans were assisted by a few dozen Trawniki men, who served as guards, and performed a few essential functions within the facility, such as herding Jews into the gas chambers and releasing the carbon monoxide gas. The rest of the labor was performed by a few hundred Jews, spared from death only in order to carry out tasks associated with mass killing and plunder, and doomed themselves to a quick death if they showed any sign of weakness. Like Bełżec and Sobibór, Treblinka was designed to function on Jewish labor, such that the Trawniki men had to do little and the Germans next to nothing.[41]

As rumors of Treblinka spread, the Germans engaged in propaganda. The Polish government, in exile in London, had been passing on to its British and American allies reports of the gassings, along with other German killings of Polish citizens. Throughout the summer it urged the British and the Americans to take retributive actions upon German civilians, to no effect. Officers of the Polish resistance, the Home Army, considered an attack on Treblinka, but did not carry one out. The Germans denied the gassings. The chief of the Jewish police in

Warsaw and the official "resettlement commissioner," Józef Szerzyński, claimed that he had received postcards from Treblinka. There was indeed a postal service inside the Warsaw ghetto, which functioned even during these weeks. The postmen wore caps with bright orange bills so that they would not be seized in the roundups. But they brought, of course, no news from Treblinka.[42]

The transports from Warsaw to Treblinka began again on 3 September 1942. The last transport of the Large Action, on 22 September 1942, included the Jewish police and their families. As the Jewish policemen neared the station, they threw from the windows their hats and any other markers of their former mission or social status (Jewish policemen often came from prosperous families). This was prudent behavior, since Jewish policemen could meet a hard reception from fellow Jews in a concentration camp. Yet Treblinka was no camp. It was a death facility, so their actions made no difference. The policemen were gassed like everyone else.

Within a few months, Stangl had changed the appearance of Treblinka, and thereby increased its lethal functionality. Jews who arrived at Treblinka in late 1942 disembarked not to a simple ramp surrounded by dead bodies but inside a mock train station, painted by a Jewish laborer to resemble a real one. It had a clock, a timetable, and ticket counters. As Jews stepped from the "station," they could hear the sound of music, played by an orchestra led by the Warsaw musician Artur Gold. Those Jews who limped or hobbled or otherwise revealed themselves to be weak at this point were taken to a "clinic." Jewish workers with red armbands helped them to a building marked with a red cross. Behind this building the sick Jews were shot in the back of the neck over a ditch, by Germans dressed as doctors. The chief executioner was August Miete, whom the Jewish laborers called the Angel of Death, *Malakh Ha-Mavet*. Those Jews who could move themselves took a few steps forward into a kind of courtyard, where the men and the women were separated: men to the right, women to the left, as they were told in German and Yiddish.[43]

In the courtyard, the Jews were forced to strip naked, on the pretext that they were to be disinfected before a further transport "to the east." Jews had to bundle their clothes neatly and tie their shoes together by the laces. They had to surrender any valuables; women were subjected to cavity searches. At this point a few women, in some of the transports, were selected for rape; and a few men, in some of the transports, were selected for labor. The women then shared the fate of the rest, whereas the men would live for a few more days, weeks, or even months as slave laborers.[44]

All the women went to the gas chambers without their clothes, and without their hair. Each woman had to sit before a Jewish "barber." Religiously observant women who wore wigs had to surrender them. Even at this very last moment before death, people reacted differently, individually. For some women, the hair-cutting was confirmation of the "disinfection" story; for others it was the proof that they were about to be killed. The women's hair was to be used to make stockings for German railway workers and to line the slippers worn by German submarine crews.[45]

Both groups, first the women and then the men, naked, humiliated, and help-less, were forced to run through a tunnel. It was a few meters wide and about a hundred meters long; the Germans called it "the road to Heaven." At its end Jews might see a large Star of David in the gable over the entrance to a dark room. A ceremonial curtain hung with a Hebrew inscription: "This is the gate-way to G-d. The righteous shall pass through." Probably few enough of them noticed these details, as they were forced roughly inside by the two guards posted at the entrance, both of them Trawniki men. One of the Trawniki men held a piece of pipe, the other a sword, and both yelled and beat the Jews. Then one of them closed and locked the door, and called for "Water!"—the very last element of the deception, no longer necessary for this doomed group, now sealed in a gas chamber, but for whoever else might be waiting. A third Trawniki man threw a lever, and a tank engine pumped carbon monoxide into the chamber.[46]

After twenty minutes or so the Trawniki men opened a rear door of the gas chamber, and Jewish laborers removed the bodies. As a result of feverish strug-gles and death agonies, the bodies were twisted together, limb through limb, and sometimes very fragile. As the Treblinka laborer Chil Rajchman recalled, they underwent "an atrocious metamorphosis." Their corpses were covered, as was the chamber itself, with blood, feces, and urine. The Jewish laborers had to clean the chamber, so that the next group would not disbelieve the disinfection lie and panic upon entering. Then they had to separate the bodies and lay them face up on the earth so that a crew of Jewish "dentists" could do their work: re-moving gold teeth. Sometimes the faces were entirely black, as if burned, and the jaws clenched so tightly that the "dentists" could barely open them. Once the gold teeth were removed, the Jewish laborers dragged the bodies to pits to be buried. The entire process, from disembarkation of live Jews to the disposal of their bodies, took no more than two hours.[47]

In the winter of 1942–1943, the Germans began to separate the Jews not into two but into three groups: the men, the older women, and the young women. They sent the young women into the gas last, because they liked to look at their naked bodies in the cold. By then the corpses were burned rather than buried. The pyres were huge grills made from railway rails laid upon concrete pillars, some thirty meters across. By spring 1943, fires burned at Treblinka day and night, sometimes consuming the corpses of decomposed bodies exhumed from the earth by Jewish laborers, sometimes the bodies of those who had just been asphyxiated. Women, with more fatty tissue, burned better than men; so the laborers learned to put them on the bottom of the pile. The bellies of pregnant women would tend to burst, such that the fetus could be seen inside. In the cold nights of spring 1943, the Germans would stand by the flame, and drink, and warm themselves. Once again, human beings were reduced to calories, units of warmth. The burning was to remove any evidence of the crime, but the Jewish laborers made sure that this was not achieved. They left whole skeletons intact, and buried messages in bottles for others to find.[48]

It was very difficult for the victims to leave any other sort of trace. Chil Rajchman had come to Treblinka with his sister. As soon as he saw the facility, he put their suitcases down. His sister did not understand why. "It's no use" were his last words to her. He was chosen to be a laborer. Sorting through clothing, he "came upon the dress that my sister was wearing. I paused, I took the dress, I held it in my hands, contemplated it." Then it had to go and he had to go on. Tamara and Itta Willenberg left their bundles of clothes next to each other. Their brother Samuel, a Jewish laborer, chanced to find the clothes clinging together "as if in a sister's embrace." Because the women had their hair cut, they had a last few moments in which they could speak to fellow Jews, who might, just possibly, survive them and remember their words. Ruth Dorfmann was able to accept from her barber the consolation that her death would be quick, and to cry with him. Hanna Levinson told her barber to escape and to tell the world what was happening at Treblinka.[49]

Only with much forethought could Jews control their possessions, even in such small ways. In general, their instinct was to keep their portable wealth (if they had any) on their persons, in the hopes of later bartering or bribing.

Sometimes Jews, when they grasped what awaited them, threw their money and valuables from the train, so that they would not enrich their persecutors. Usually this was near Treblinka. Within the death factory, it was the job of Jewish laborers to seek valuables, and of course they pocketed some. They gave these to the Trawniki men, who had the right to come and go, in exchange for food from nearby villages. The Trawniki men gave the valuables to local women and to prostitutes, who apparently came from as far away as Warsaw. Having thereby contracted venereal diseases, the Trawniki men consulted Jewish doctors among the laborers. Thus the special closed circle of the local economy, which one witness recalled as a bejeweled and degraded "Europe."[50]

Through such connections, Jewish laborers alive in 1943 knew something of the outside world and the course of the war. Trawniki men could usually read Russian, and managed to get their hands on Soviet propaganda and the Soviet press. They were among the millions of Soviet citizens laboring for the Germans in one capacity or another, and so heard gossip. They knew, and so Jewish laborers learned, about the German defeat at Stalingrad in February 1943. The laborers could see for themselves that the transports slowed in 1943, and feared, quite rightly, that their own reason for being was coming to an end. By then the tremendous majority of Polish Jews were already dead. Guessing that their facility was soon to be closed, some of the Jewish workers rebelled on 2 August 1943, seizing weapons and setting parts of the facility on fire. A few hundred laborers ran through a hole in the fence; a few dozen survived the war. Chil Rajchman and the other laborers who wrote memoirs of Treblinka were among them.[51]

The facility was indeed closed on 17 November 1943. Its last victims were thirty remaining Jewish laborers who did the work of dismantling it. At the very end, they were shot in groups of five, with the remaining Jews cremating each group. Trawniki men cremated the final group of five. At about the same time, the Germans undertook a mass shooting action against other Jewish laborers, those still at work in concentration camps in the General Government. Some forty-two thousand Jews were killed in this operation, known as "Harvest Festival."[52]

One of the fifty or so Treblinka survivors, Saul Kuperhand, understood that at Treblinka "numbers ruled." The 265,040 Warsaw Jews deported in the Large Action were carefully counted. In some fourteen weeks, between 4 August and mid-November, at least 310,000 Jews of the Radom district of the General Government were gassed at Treblinka. In sum, about 780,863 people were killed at Treblinka, the vast majority of them Polish Jews from the General Government. Most of the Jews of the General Government who were not gassed at Bełżec or Sobibór were gassed at Treblinka. In all, Operation Reinhard claimed the lives of some 1.3 million Polish Jews.[53]

The purpose of Treblinka was ever clearer as the war continued: to rid a shrinking racial empire of its Jewish population, and so to claim a thin victory and its grisly fruits. A body can be burned for warmth, or it can feed the microorganisms that make soil fertile. Even human ash fertilizes. After Treblinka had been dismantled, the Germans used the bricks of the gas chambers to make a farmhouse, and turned the killing fields into a farm. A couple of the Trawniki men agreed to stay on as farmers. In this lay a darkly literal rendering of the Nazi fantasy of redeeming the land by destroying the Jew. The corpses and ashes of Jews were to fertilize the soil for crops to be eaten by Germans. Yet no harvest ever came.[54]

Once Treblinka was no longer functioning, the center of the Holocaust shifted west, to a very special facility in the annexed territories of Poland added to the Reich, at Auschwitz. This was a camp established in 1940 in a territory that Germany had annexed from Poland. Auschwitz was in operation as a concentration camp almost a year before Germany invaded the Soviet Union, and more than a year before Hitler had clarified just what the Final Solution would mean. Unlike the death factories at Treblinka, Sobibór, and Bełżec, which were established for the single purpose of killing the Jews of Poland, the complex at Auschwitz evolved as German policies toward Jews and others changed. The development of the Auschwitz facility illustrates the transformation of a dream of eastern colonization into a program of Jewish extermination.

The German camp established at Auschwitz in 1940 was meant to intimidate the Polish population. After the attack on the Soviet Union in summer 1941, Soviet prisoners of war joined Poles, and the camp was used as an execution site for both. Himmler wished for Auschwitz to become an example of the SS colonial economy, in which the captured lands of an enemy nation could be given to a German firm, which would exploit slave labor to manufacture goods needed for the German war economy. Because Auschwitz was well supplied with water and well connected by rail, Himmler saw it, as did the upper management of IG Farben, as an ideal site for the production of artificial rubber. Himmler sought Jewish laborers in Slovakia, whose leaders were happy to be rid of them. Himmler made the case in October 1941; within a year Slovakia had deported 57,628 of its Jewish citizens. Almost all of them would die.[55]

In 1942 a second major facility was added, and Auschwitz became a death factory as well as a concentration camp and execution site. Rudolf Höss, its commander, was a veteran of the concentration camps at Dachau and Buchenwald, not of the killing facilities of the "euthanasia" program. Under his command Auschwitz became a special sort of hybrid, a labor facility with a death factory attached. Non-Jewish laborers continued to arrive, and to work in awful conditions. Jews were now selected for labor when they arrived at Auschwitz, with those deemed unusable (the substantial majority) immediately gassed. In 1942, the approximately 140,146 Jews not selected for labor were gassed in chambers known as Bunker 1 and Bunker 2 in Auschwitz. After February 1943 most of the murdered Jews were killed in new gas chambers constructed in nearby Birkenau, and their bodies burned in attached crematoria. In the Auschwitz-Birkenau gas chambers, pellets of Zyklon B would sublimate on contact with air, producing a gas that would kill at a ratio of one milligram per kilogram of body weight. Cyanide kills at the cellular level, interfering with the ability of the mitochondria in cells to produce the energy that sustains life.[56]

Like the other five death factories, Auschwitz was located in occupied Poland. It served, however, as the main extermination site for Jewish populations from *beyond* Poland. Though some Jews from beyond Poland were killed in the five other death factories, the vast majority of their victims were Polish Jews. Auschwitz was the only death factory of the six where Polish Jews were not the majority of the victims. It became a killing facility at about the same time that German exterminatory policies moved beyond occupied Poland and the occupied Soviet Union, to embrace other populations of European Jews. Within the Reich Security Main Office, Adolf Eichmann and the men in his Jewish section organized deportations from France, Belgium, and the Netherlands in 1942. In 1943 Eichmann organized the transport of Jews from Greece and from occupied Italy. Fascist Italy had not sent its Jews to Hitler so long as Mussolini was in power and Germany and Italy were allies. But after the Americans, British,

Canadians, and Poles landed in southern Italy and the Italians capitulated, the Germans occupied the northern part of the country, and deported Jews themselves. In 1943, some 220,000 Jews were gassed at Auschwitz.[57]

In 1944, shooting Soviet Jews was no longer possible because the Germans had been driven from the Soviet Union, and the Reinhard facilities were closed due to the approach of the Red Army; that year, Auschwitz became the site of the Final Solution. Almost all of the six hundred thousand or so Jews killed by the Germans in 1944 died at Auschwitz. Most of them were Hungarian Jews. Hungary, like Italy, had not sent its Jews to the death facilities so long as it was a sovereign country and a German ally. (As a rule, Jews fared less badly in countries allied with Germany than in countries occupied by Germany.) After the Hungarian leadership attempted to switch sides in the war in March 1944, the Germans installed their own government. A new Hungarian fascist regime began in May to deport its Jews. About 437,000 Hungarian Jews arrived at Auschwitz in eight weeks. About 110,000 of them were selected for labor, many of whom survived; at the very least, 327,000 of them were gassed. Over the course of the war, about 300,000 Polish Jews were shipped to Auschwitz, of whom some 200,000 were killed. Taken together, Hungarian and Polish Jews account for the majority of the Jewish victims of Auschwitz.[58]

Auschwitz was the climax of the Holocaust, reached at a moment when most Soviet and Polish Jews under German rule were already dead. Of the million or so Soviet Jews killed in the Holocaust, fewer than one percent died at Auschwitz. Of the three million or so Polish Jews killed in the Holocaust, only about seven percent perished at Auschwitz. Nearly 1.3 million Polish Jews were killed, usually shot, east of the Molotov-Ribbentrop line. Another 1.3 million or so Polish Jews were gassed in Operation Reinhard in the General Government (more than 700,000 at Treblinka, roughly 400,000 at Bełżec, 150,000 at Sobibór, and 50,000 at Majdanek). Another 350,000 more were gassed in the lands annexed to the Reich (besides the 200,000 at Auschwitz, about 150,000 at Chełmno). Most of the remaining Polish-Jewish victims were shot during the ghetto clearings (about 100,000) or in Operation Harvest Festival (42,000), or during the many smaller actions and in individual executions. Many more died of hunger or disease in the ghettos or as laborers in concentration camps.[59]

A considerable number of the mortal victims of Auschwitz, more than 200,000, were not Jews. Some 74,000 non-Jewish Poles and some 15,000 Soviet prisoners of war also died at Auschwitz: either executed or worked to death. With the exception of the Soviet prisoners of war who were experimentally gassed, these people were not sent to the gas chambers. But Roma and Sinti were.

Though never pursued with the same energy as the Jews, the Roma and Sinti ("gypsies") were subjected to a killing policy wherever German power extended. They were shot by Einsatzgruppen in the occupied Soviet Union (about 8,000 documented cases); included in the killing orders for reprisal actions in Belarus; shot by police in occupied Poland; shot in reprisal actions along with Jews in Serbia; killed in a concentration camp of Germany's puppet ally Croatia (about 15,000); ethnically cleansed from territories conquered by Germany's ally Romania; and gassed at Chełmno in January 1942 (about 4,400) and then at Auschwitz in May 1943 (about 1,700) and August 1944 (about 2,900, after many more had died of hunger, disease, or mistreatment). At least a hundred thousand Roma and Sinti, and more likely two or three times that number, were killed by the Germans.[60]

———————

Although no one survived the gas chambers of Auschwitz, more than a hundred thousand people survived the concentration camp known by the same name. That name would be remembered after the war, a dark shadow behind an iron curtain, a hint of the greater darkness to the east. Fewer than one hundred Jewish laborers saw the inside of a Reinhard death factory and survived. Yet even Treblinka left a few traces in the air.

Prisoners sang at Treblinka, at German orders, but also for themselves. "El male rachamim" was chanted for the Jews killed each day. SS men would stand outside and listen. Trawniki men brought with them from the east, as one of the Jewish laborers recognized, a "strange gift" for "wonderful song." It was less elevated music, popular Polish songs, that reminded Treblinka laborers of life outside the camp, and helped give them the courage to prepare their escape. Those songs recalled love and foolishness, and so life and freedom. A few weddings were celebrated at Treblinka, between laborers and the women who handled domestic chores for the Germans.[61]

The Jewish barbers, who cut the hair of thousands of women, remembered the beautiful ones.

CHAPTER 9

RESISTANCE AND INCINERATION

The night of 21 June 1944 belonged to the Soviet partisans of Belarus. Three years earlier the Wehrmacht had quickly overrun Belarus on its way to Moscow—which it never quite reached. The Soviets were now advancing toward the Molotov-Ribbentrop line, and onward toward Warsaw and Berlin. Army Group Center of the Wehrmacht was back in Belarus, but in retreat. Red Army commanders had planned a massive summer offensive, beginning on the third anniversary of Operation Barbarossa, timed to remind the Germans of their own disastrous ambitions. The Soviet partisans had laid thousands of explosive charges on rail lines in Belarus. When Soviet soldiers attacked, German troops could not be reinforced, nor could they quickly retreat. So the day of 22 June 1944 belonged to the soldiers of the First, Second, and Third Belarusian Fronts of the Red Army. They and two other army groups assembled well over a million troops, more than twice as many as the Wehrmacht's Army Group Center could muster. The offensive, Operation Bagration, delivered one of the most important Soviet victories in the war.[1]

Two weeks earlier, the Americans had joined the battle for Europe. Having gained mastery over the Japanese fleet in the Pacific, the United States opened a major European front in the war on 6 June 1944. The US Army landed (along with the British and other western Allies) 160,000 men on the beaches of Normandy. Yet American power was also on display in the depths of Belarus, where motorized Soviet units, equipped with American trucks and jeeps, encircled hapless German forces. German encirclement tactics had been mastered, accelerated, and turned against the Germans themselves. The Soviet breakthrough in Belarus was more dramatic than the American advance through France. German soldiers were outnumbered and its officers outsmarted. German commanders had expected the Soviet offensive to pass through Ukraine rather than Belarus. The Germans lost some four hundred thousand missing, wounded, or killed. Army Group Center was smashed. The way to Poland was open.[2]

Quickly the Red Army crossed the Molotov-Ribbentrop line and entered the region that had been the Lublin district of the General Government. Vasily Grossman, a Soviet writer following the Red Army as a journalist, contemplated what the Germans had left behind. The Red Army discovered the camp at Majdanek on 24 July 1944. In early August, Grossman found a still greater horror, one that might have defied a poorer imagination. Coming upon Treblinka, he realized quickly just what had happened: the Jews of Poland had been murdered in gas chambers, their bodies burned, their ashes and bones buried in fields. He walked upon "earth that is as unsteady as the sea," and found the remnants: photographs of children in Warsaw and Vienna; a bit of Ukrainian embroidery; a sack of hair, blonde and black.[3]

By this time, Polish lands had been under German occupation for nearly four years. For the Jews of Warsaw, or almost all of them, Operation Bagration was the liberation that never came. The remains of more than a quarter-million Warsaw Jews were among the ashes and bones that Grossman found at Treblinka.

In 1939, the occupiers of Poland had been two, German and Soviet. For the non-Jewish Poles in Warsaw who were conspiring to resist German rule, Operation Bagration portended the arrival of a very questionable ally. It meant the second incursion of the Red Army into Polish territory during the Second World War.

This was the difference between Polish and Polish-Jewish experiences of the war. Non-Jewish Poles suffered horribly from both German and Soviet occupations, but comparably from each. Non-Jewish Poles who wished to resist could sometimes make choices: about which occupier to resist, and in what circumstances.

Surviving Polish Jews had every reason to prefer the Soviets to the Germans, and to see the Red Army as liberators. Many of those sixty thousand or so Jews

SWEDEN

FINLAND

Helsinki

Baltic
Sea

*Lake
Ladoga*

Tallinn

Leningrad
Jan 1944

LENINGRAD

Tikhvin

Novgorod
Jan 1944

3rd BALTIC

XXXXX
NORTH

Pskov

Demyansk

Volga

Riga

Kholm

2nd BALTIC

Kalinin

U.S.S.R.

Velikiye Luki

Nevel

Rzhev

1st BALTIC

Danzig

REICHSKOMMISSARIAT
OSTLAND

Kaunas

Vitebsk
June 1944

Moscow

Oka

Smolensk

3rd BELARUS

Ryazan

GERMANY

Vilnius
July 1944

XXXXX
CENTER

*Front line
Aug. 19, 1944*

Bialystok
July 1944

Minsk
July 1944

2nd BELARUS

Warsaw

Bobruisk

Bryansk

Orel

Łódź

Brest
July 1944

Pinsk

Pripet

Homel

1st BELARUS

Lublin
July 1944

Polesian Marshes

Chernihiv

Kursk

Voronezh

Cracow

Lutsk

Rivne
Feb 1944

'GENERAL
GOVERNMENT'

Lviv
July 1944

Zhytomyr

Kiev
Dec 1943

Belgorod

1st UKRAINIAN

4th UKRAINIAN

Kharkiv
Aug 1943

*Front line
July 17, 1943*

Don

HUNGARY

XXXXX
NORTH
UKRAINE

Vinnytsia

Chernivtsi

Dnipro

REICHSKOMMISSARIAT
UKRAINE

Dnipropetrovsk

2nd UKRAINIAN

Stalino

Don

Chisinau

Dniestr

Mariupol

Taganrog

Rostov

XXXXX
SOUTH
UKRAINE

Mykolaiv

Melitopol

Odessa

*Sea of
Azov*

3rd UKRAINIAN

ROMANIA

Bucharest

Crimea

Kerch

Sevastopol
May 1944

Novorossiysk

Danube

Sofia

BULGARIA

Black Sea

GREECE

Istanbul

TURKEY

**SOVIET FORCES
1943–1944**

Summer 1944 *Spring 1944* *Autumn 1943*

who were still alive in the Warsaw ghetto after the Large Action of summer 1942 did choose to resist. But they could not choose the time and the place of their resistance. All they could do was fight.

———————

Warsaw was the center of urban resistance to Nazi rule in occupied Europe. In the two years between September 1942, by which time Treblinka had taken the lives of most of the Jews of Warsaw, and September 1944, when its workings were described by Grossman in his article "Treblinka Hell," both Poles and Jews led uprisings against the German occupation, separately but also together, in uprisings of April 1943 and August 1944.

The consequences of Jewish and Polish resistance in Warsaw were much the same: destruction. By the time the Red Army (and Grossman) arrived in the city in January 1945, it was rubble and ash. Half of the population was dead, and the survivors were gone. Grossman reached for a literary reference that his readers would have known: the last remaining people, Jews and Poles he found living together in the remains of one building, were Warsaw "Robinsons": like Robinson Crusoe, the hero of the novel by Daniel Defoe, left on an island by himself for years, lost to civilization. The Polish poet Czesław Miłosz, who lived during the war in Warsaw, spent some of his time writing literary criticism of the same novel. For him, *Robinson Crusoe* was the "legend of the island," the idea that moral flaws come from experience, that if we were left alone we might be good. In this essay, and in his poetry about Poles and Jews in Warsaw, he suggested the contrary, that the only hope for ethics was that each remember the solitude of the other.[4]

In Warsaw during the Second World War, Poles and Jews were alone in some of the same ways, beyond help from the outside world, even from those whom they regarded as friends and allies. They were also alone in different ways, confronting different fates in the same war. They shared a city that had been the center of both Polish and Jewish civilizations. That city is now gone; what remains of it is legend, or rather two legends, one Polish, one Jewish, between solidarity and solitude, each aware of the other but alone in the postwar world.

———————

Polish and Jewish conspiracies against German rule, distinct but connected, had begun much earlier, with the German invasion of Poland in September 1939.

On 7 September 1939, in the basement of a bank, eight men and women, most of them Free Masons, began the conspiracy that would become the Polish underground army. Known at first as the Servants of the Victory of Poland, it was led by a general with orders to organize a national underground. By 1940, when the Polish government had established itself in exile in France, the armed underground at home was given the name Union of Armed Struggle. In 1940 and 1941, its main task was to unify the hundreds of smaller resistance groups that had formed in Poland, and to collect intelligence for the Polish government and its allies. The Union of Armed Struggle was active in the German zone of occupation; attempts to create a network under Soviet occupation were thwarted by the NKVD. After the Germans invaded the Soviet Union in June 1941, the Polish resistance was able to operate in all of the territories of occupied Poland.[5]

In early 1942 the Union of Armed Struggle was transformed into a Home Army. The Home Army was meant to be the counterpart of the Polish Army fighting abroad with allies on the western front. Like the Polish government, by now in exile in London, the Home Army was to represent all political and social forces in the country. It was to fight for the restoration of Poland within its prewar boundaries, as a democratic republic with equal rights for all citizens. Most Poles who chose resistance did find their way to the Home Army, although the extreme communist left and the extreme nationalist right founded their own partisan forces. The communists organized a People's Guard, later known as the People's Army, which was closely connected to the Soviet Union and the NKVD. The nationalists, who regarded the communists and the Soviets as a greater enemy than the Germans, fought within the ranks of the National Armed Forces.[6]

Jewish resistance in Warsaw followed a different path, even though this was not clear at first. In the early months of the German occupation of Poland, in 1939, Jewish resistance as such seemed to make little sense. It was not evident, at first, that the fate of Polish Jews was to be much different from that of non-Jews. Many of the Warsaw Jews who felt most threatened by the German invasion fled to the Soviet occupation zone of Poland, whence many of them were deported to Kazakhstan. The establishment of the ghettos in 1940 did not necessarily convey to Polish Jews that their fate was worse than that of non-Jewish Poles, who were at the time being shot and sent to concentration camps in large numbers. In 1940 Poles from beyond the ghetto were sent to Auschwitz, whereas Jews were generally not. But the ghettos did mean that any Jewish resistance would have to be a response to particularly Jewish predicaments. When the Germans forcibly separated Jews from non-Jewish Poles in Warsaw in October 1940, they were creating a new social reality, creating categories that would define different fates.[7]

The ghetto did not, however, bring agreement to Jews about how and whether to take action against the Germans. Polish Jews in the Warsaw ghetto had prior political commitments, arising from the vibrant intra-Jewish political life of interwar Poland. Jews had taken part in local and national elections in Poland, as well as in their own communal elections. Parties were legion and party loyalties ran deep. At the far right of the spectrum were the Revisionist Zionists, who had been preparing themselves before the war for armed resistance against the British in Palestine. They were among the first to believe that armed struggle against the Germans was necessary and possible in the conditions of the ghetto. Revisionists and members of their youth organization Betar learned from party comrades as early as summer 1941 of the killings of Jews in Vilnius. They also heard, more or less as it happened, about the liquidation of the ghetto in Lublin in spring 1942. They had some sense of the spread of the Final Solution, from east of the Molotov-Ribbentrop line to west of the Molotov-Ribbentrop line, from bullets to gas.[8]

It took the Large Action in Warsaw of July–September 1942 to prompt the Revisionists to form a Jewish Military Union. Its military commander was Paweł Frenkel; the members of its political committee were Michał Strykowski, Leon Rodal, and Dawid Wdowiński. It was anchored in prewar traditions of cooperation with the Polish state, which might explain why it was well armed. In the late 1930s, the Polish regime had hoped to export much of its Jewish population to the Near East. Polish leaders thus developed close relationships with the Revisionist Zionists, who hoped to lead much of the Polish-Jewish population to Palestine. The Revisionists were willing to use violence to create a Jewish state, an approach with which Polish authorities sympathized. Before the war, the Revisionist Zionist youths of Betar had been preparing themselves in prewar Poland to fight for Palestine. Like the young men of Irgun, the resistance organization in Palestine that some of them joined, they were sometimes trained by the Polish Army. Inside the ghetto in 1942, the Revisionists also collected money, and robbed rich Jews, to purchase arms from outside the ghetto.[9]

Whereas the history of the Jewish Military Union is one of a militarist right-wing political party adapting itself to conditions even harsher than those it had ever anticipated, the history of the other resistance group in the Warsaw ghetto, the Jewish Combat Organization, is one of multiple centrist and left-wing political parties deciding that only military action could serve Jews.

Like the right-wing Jewish Military Union, the Jewish Combat Organization arose as a result of the Large Action. The very old and the very young were almost all deported and dead. It seems likely that the deportations, although they touched all groups, eliminated what had been the conservative center of Jewish politics: the religiously Orthodox and politically accommodationist Agudas Israel. Its platform before the war had been cooperation with the Polish government in exchange for communal and religious autonomy. This compromising approach had been tested by anti-Semitic violence and anti-Semitic legislation in Poland in the late 1930s, but it had remained popular among the older generations of Warsaw Jewish believers—who by now were almost all dead at Treblinka. Nothing in Poland had prepared Agudas for the Nazis, who repaid compromises with murder.[10]

After September 1942, the Warsaw ghetto was essentially a Jewish labor camp inhabited predominantly by young men. Fathers who might earlier have feared to endanger their families no longer had that reason for restraint. Left-wing politics came to the fore. The Jewish Left in prewar Poland had been divided over a number of fundamental issues: whether to leave for Palestine or stay in Poland, whether to trust or distrust the Soviet Union, whether to agitate in Yiddish or Polish or Hebrew, and so on. The most radical form of left-wing politics, communism, reappeared among Warsaw Jews at this time. Stalin, who had dissolved the Communist Party of Poland in 1938, permitted its reconstitution as the Polish Workers' Party in January 1942. Some of its Polish-Jewish activists then smuggled themselves *into* the Warsaw ghetto, where they urged armed resistance. The largest Jewish socialist party, the Bund, was much less inclined to use violence. In general, these organizations continued their work as distinct entities. In the three months after the Large Action, general accord about the need for armed resistance was reached. The Jewish Combat Organization was established in December 1942. As a group of politicians with little or no military background and no weapons to speak of, its first need was arms. Its first action was to ask for them, from the Home Army.[11]

Beyond the ghetto, the Large Action forced the Home Army to undertake a Jewish policy. The Polish resistance had already taken some clear stands in 1941, condemning for instance guard duty at concentration camps as "national treason." But the Home Army, before summer 1942, tended to treat the plight of Poland and that of Poles as one and the same. Prompted by the mass shootings of Polish Jews in the east, the Home Army created a Jewish section in February 1942. It collected evidence of the killings that was transmitted to the Allies and the BBC in April 1942. The deportations of summer 1942 prompted Catholic Poles to organize a rescue organization, which by December was sponsored by the Polish government under the cryptonym Żegota. (Poles were subject to the death penalty for assisting Jews.) Some Home Army officers took part. Home Army intelligence officers supplied identification documents for Jews in hiding beyond ghetto walls. When the Jewish Combat Organization requested weapons in December 1942, the Home Army offered to help Jews escape from the ghetto, perhaps to fight later on. This offer was declined by the Jewish Combat Organization. Its leaders wanted to fight, and so denied themselves an exit strategy.[12]

Warsaw Home Army commanders had strategic concerns that militated against giving the Jews any weapons at all. Although the Home Army was moving in the direction of partisan action, it feared that a rebellion in the ghetto would provoke a general uprising in the city, which the Germans would crush. The Home Army was not ready for such a fight in late 1942. Home Army commanders saw a premature uprising as a communist temptation to be avoided. They knew that the Soviets, and thus the Polish communists, were urging the local population to take up arms immediately against the Germans. The Soviets wanted to provoke partisan warfare in Poland in order to weaken the Germans— but also to hinder any future Polish resistance to their own rule when it came. The Red Army's task would be easier if German troops were killed by partisan warfare, as would the NKVD's if Polish elites were killed for resisting Germans. The Jewish Combat Organization included the communists, who were following the Soviet line, and believed that Poland should be subordinated to the Soviet Union. As the Home Army command could not forget, the Second World War had begun when *both* the Germans *and* the Soviets had invaded Poland. Half of Poland had spent half of the war inside the Soviet Union. The Soviets wanted eastern Poland back, and perhaps even more. From the perspective of the Home Army, rule by the Soviets was little better than rule by the Nazis. Its goal was independence. There were hardly any circumstances that would seem to justify a Polish independence organization arming communists inside Poland.[13]

Despite these reservations, the Home Army did give the Jewish Combat Organization a few pistols in December 1942. The Jewish Combat Organization used these to win authority and power in the ghetto. To resist the Judenrat and a Jewish police force armed only with clubs, pistols and audacity were enough. By killing (or trying to kill) Jewish policemen and Gestapo informers in late 1942 and early 1943, the Jewish Combat Organization created the sense that a new moral order was arising in the ghetto. Józef Szerzyński, the Jewish police chief, was shot in the neck, although he failed to die. The Jewish Combat Organization did assassinate Jakub Lejkin, who led the police during the major deportation action, and later Mieczysław Brzeziński, who had driven his fellow Jews onto the trains at Umschlagplatz. The Jewish Combat Organization printed leaflets, explaining that collaboration with the enemy was a crime punishable by death. The Jewish Combat Organization thus supplanted the Judenrat, whose head was forced to admit that he no longer had "authority in the ghetto, here there is another authority." Without an effective Jewish administrative and coercive apparatus, the Germans could no longer do as they pleased in the ghetto.[14]

German decisions about the fate of the ghetto and its remaining inhabitants were influenced by considerations that Jews could not possibly have understood. For the Germans, the Warsaw ghetto had first been a transit point for envisioned deportations to the Lublin district, Madagascar, or the Soviet Union; then a temporary labor camp; and then a transit point for deportations to Treblinka. In late 1942 and early 1943 it was again a labor camp, provisional and reduced in size, whose workers were those who had been selected for labor during the Large Action. Though Himmler never wavered in his determination to kill the Jews under German rule, other authorities wished, at this point at least, to keep some Jewish laborers alive. Hans Frank was worried about labor shortages in his General Government. Many Poles were working in Germany, so Jewish labor had become more important in occupied Poland. The Jews were working for the German war economy, so the Wehrmacht, too, had an interest in their remaining alive.[15]

Himmler was capable of making compromises. In early 1943 he meant to allow most of the surviving Jews of the Warsaw ghetto to live a bit longer, but also to eliminate the ghetto itself, which he saw as a center of political resistance, disorder, and disease. Himmler intended to kill the Jews who were living illegally in the ghetto without labor documents. Then he wanted to deport the remaining Jews as laborers to other concentration camps, where they would continue to work. Visiting Warsaw, Himmler ordered on 9 January 1943 that the ghetto be dissolved. The eight thousand or so Jews who were there illegally were to be shipped to Treblinka and gassed, and the rest, about fifty thousand, were to be sent to concentration camps. But when the Germans entered the ghetto nine days later to carry out Himmler's orders, Jews hid or resisted. A few Jews fired on the first Germans to enter the ghetto, surprising them and leading to panic. The Germans killed some 1,170 Jews on the streets and deported perhaps five thousand. After four days the Germans had to withdraw and reconsider. Home Army commanders in Warsaw were impressed. The arms that they had given the Jewish Combat Organization had been put to good use.[16]

This was not the first instance of Jews resisting Germans in Poland. There were a large number of people of Jewish origin within the Home Army itself. Although this was a fact known to Home Army commanders, it was almost never discussed. Many of the people of Jewish origin in the Home Army regarded themselves as Poles rather than as Jews. Others kept their Jewish identities secret, on the grounds that it was best in wartime Warsaw not to spread the news of one's Jewishness. Although anti-Semites in the Home Army were a minority, just one betrayal could mean death. What was new in January 1943 was that Jews had used arms against the Germans as Jews, in an open act of *Jewish* resistance. This worked powerfully against the anti-Semitic stereotype, present in the Home Army and in Polish society, that Jews would not fight. Now the Warsaw command of the Home Army gave the Jewish Combat Organization a substantial proportion of its own modest arms cache: guns, ammunition, explosives.[17]

In Berlin, Himmler was furious. On 16 February 1943 he decided that the ghetto must be destroyed not only as a society but as a physical place. That neighborhood of Warsaw was of no value to the racial masters, since houses that had been (as Himmler put it) "used by subhumans" could never be suitable for Germans. The Germans planned an assault on the ghetto for 19 April. Again, its immediate purpose was not to kill all the Jews but, rather, to redirect their labor power to concentration camps, and then to destroy the ghetto. Himmler had no doubt that this would work. He was thinking ahead to the uses of the site: in the long term it would become a park, in the meantime a concentration camp until the war was won. Jewish laborers from Warsaw would be worked to death at other sites.[18]

Right before the planned assault on the Warsaw ghetto, German propaganda chief Joseph Goebbels made his own special contribution. In April 1943, the

Germans had discovered Katyn, one of the sites where the NKVD had murdered Polish prisoners of war in 1940. "Katyn," declared Goebbels, "is my victory." He chose 18 April 1943 to announce the discovery of the corpses of Polish officers. Katyn could be used to create problems between Soviets and Poles, and between Poles and Jews. Goebbels expected, and quite rightly, that the evidence that the Soviet secret police had shot thousands of Polish officers would make cooperation between the Soviet Union and the Polish government-in-exile more problematic. The two were uneasy allies at best, and the Polish government had never gotten a satisfactory reply from the Soviets about those missing officers. Goebbels also wished to use Katyn to display the anti-Polish policies of the supposedly Jewish leadership of the Soviet Union, and thus to alienate Poles from Jews. So went the propaganda on the eve of the German attack on the Warsaw ghetto.[19]

The Jewish Combat Organization had made its plans as well. The Germans' abortive January 1943 ghetto clearing had confirmed Jewish leaders' expectation that a final reckoning was coming. The sight of dead Germans on the streets had broken the barrier of fear, and the second transfer of arms from the Home Army had also increased confidence. The Jews in the ghetto assumed that any further deportation would be straight to the gas chambers. This was not quite true; if they had not fought they would have been sent, most of them, to concentration camps as laborers. But only for the next few months. The surviving Warsaw Jews were fundamentally correct in their judgments. The "last stage of resettlement," as one of their number had written, "is death." Few of them would die in Treblinka, but almost all of them would die before the end of 1943. They were right to think that resistance could scarcely reduce their chances of survival. If the Germans won the war, they would kill remaining Jews within their empire. If they continued to lose the war, the Germans would kill Jewish laborers as a security risk as the Soviets advanced. A distant but approaching Red Army meant a moment more of life, as the Germans extracted labor. But a Red Army at the doorstep would mean the gas chamber or a gunshot.[20]

It was Jewish certainty of common death that enabled cooperative Jewish resistance. So long as German policy had allowed Jews to believe that some would survive, individuals could hope that they would be the exceptions, and social divisions were inevitable. Now that German policy had convinced all remaining Jews in the Warsaw ghetto that they would die, Jewish society in the ghetto evinced an impressive unity. Between January and April 1943, Jews built

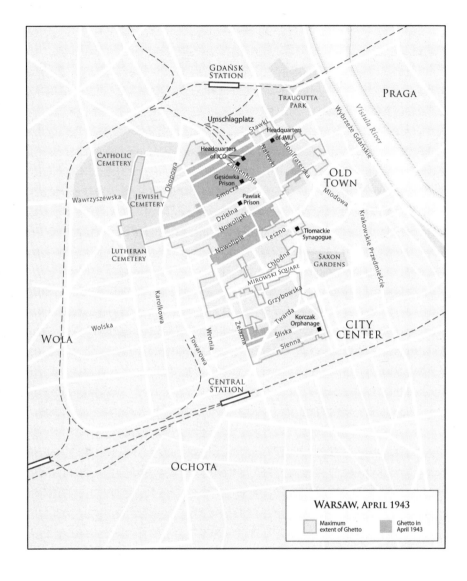

themselves countless bunkers in cellars, sometimes linked by secret passages. The Jewish Combat Organization established its command structure. The overall commander was Mordechai Anielewicz; the three leaders in three defined sectors of the ghetto were Marek Edelman, Izrael Kanał, and Icchak Cukierman (who was replaced at the last moment by Eliezer Geller). It bought more arms and trained its members in their use. Some Jews, working in German armaments factories, managed to steal materials for improvised explosives. The Jewish Combat Organization learned of German plans to attack the ghetto a day in advance, and so when the Germans came, all were ready.[21]

Some members of the Home Army, in surprise and in admiration, called it the "Jewish-German War."[22]

When the SS, Order Police, and Trawniki men entered the ghetto on 19 April 1943, they were repulsed by sniper fire and Molotov cocktails. They actually had to retreat from the ghetto. German commanders reported twelve men lost in battle. Mordechai Anielewicz wrote a letter to his Jewish Combat Organization comrade Icchak Cukierman, who at the time was beyond the ghetto walls: the Jewish counterattack "had surpassed our wildest dreams: the Germans ran away from the ghetto twice." The Home Army press wrote of "immeasurably strong and determined armed resistance."[23]

The right-wing Jewish Military Union seized the heights of the tallest building in the ghetto and raised two flags: the Polish and the Zionist, white eagle and yellow star. Its units would fight with great determination near their headquarters, at Muranowska Square. On 20 April, the SS and Police Leader for Warsaw district, Ferdinand von Sammern-Frankenegg, was relieved of duty. His replacement, Jürgen Stroop, took a telephone call from an enraged Himmler: "You must take down those flags at any cost!" The Germans did take them down, on 20 April (Hitler's birthday), although they took losses of their own in doing so. On that day the Germans managed to enter the ghetto and remain, although their prospects for clearing its population seemed dim. Most Jews were in hiding, and many were armed. The Germans would have to develop new tactics.[24]

From the first day of the Warsaw Ghetto Uprising, Jews were killed in battle. Jews who were unable to work, when discovered by the Germans, were also killed. The Germans knew that they had no use for the people whom they found at the hospital on Gęsia Street, the last Jewish hospital in Warsaw. Marek Edelman found there dozens of corpses in hospital gowns. In the gynecology and obstetrics sections, the Germans murdered pregnant women, women who had just given birth, and their babies. At the corner of Gęsia and Zamenhof Streets, someone had placed a live infant at the naked breast of a dead woman. Although Jewish resistance looked like a war from the outside, the Germans were not following any of the laws and customs of war inside the ghetto walls. The simple existence of Jewish subhumans was essentially criminal to the SS, and their resistance was an infuriating act that justified any response.[25]

Stroop decided that the only way to clear the bunkers and houses was to burn them. Since Himmler had already ordered the physical destruction of the ghetto, burning down its residences was no loss. Indeed, since Himmler had not known just how the demolition was to be accomplished, the fires solved two Nazi problems at once. On 23 April 1943, Stroop's men began to burn down the buildings of the ghetto, block by block. The Wehrmacht played little role in the combat, but its engineers and flamethrowers were used in the destruction of the residences and bunkers. Edelman recalled "enormous firestorms that closed whole streets." Suffocating Jews had no choice but to flee their bunkers. As one survivor remembered: "we wanted to get killed by shooting rather than by burning." Jews trapped on the upper floors of buildings had to jump. The Germans took many prisoners with broken legs. These people were interrogated and then shot. The only way that Jews could escape the arson was to flee from one bunker to another during the day, or from one house to another during the night. For several days the SS would not feel safe moving through the streets of the ghetto in darkness, so Jewish fighters and civilians could use the dark hours to move and regroup. But so long as they could not stop the burning, their days were numbered.[26]

The Germans had attacked the ghetto on 19 April 1943, the eve of Passover. Easter fell on the following Sunday, the 25th. The Polish poet Czesław Miłosz recorded the Christian holiday from the other side of the ghetto walls, recalling in his poem "Campo di Fiori" that people rode the carousel at Krasiński Square, just beyond the ghetto wall, as the Jews fought and died. "I thought then," wrote Miłosz, "of the loneliness of the dying." The merry-go-round ran every day, throughout the uprising. It became the symbol of Jewish isolation: Jews died in their own city, as Poles beyond the walls of the ghetto lived and laughed. Many Poles did not care what happened to the Jews in the ghetto. Yet others were concerned, and some tried to help, and a few died trying.[27]

A full year before the Warsaw Ghetto Uprising began, the Home Army had alerted the British and the Americans to the gassing of Polish Jews. The Home Army had passed on reports of the death facility at Chełmno, and Polish authorities had seen to it that they reached the British press. The western Allies took no action of any consequence. In 1942 the Home Army had informed London and Washington of the deportations from the Warsaw ghetto and the mass murder of Warsaw Jews at Treblinka. To be sure, these events were always presented by the Polish government as an element in the larger tragedy of the citizens of Poland. The key information, however, was communicated. Poles and Jews alike had believed, wrongly, that publicizing the deportations would bring them to a halt. The Polish government had also urged the Allies to respond to the mass killing of Polish citizens (including Jews) by killing German civilians. Again, Britain and the United States did not act. The Polish president and the Polish ambassador to the Vatican urged the pope to speak out about the mass murder of Jews, to no effect.[28]

Among the western Allies, only Polish authorities took direct action to halt the killing of Jews. By spring 1943 Żegota was assisting about four thousand Jews in hiding. The Home Army announced that it would shoot Poles who blackmailed Jews. On 4 May, as the Jews of the Warsaw ghetto fought on, Prime Minister Władysław Sikorski issued an appeal: "I call on my countrymen to give all help and shelter to those being murdered, and at the same time, before all humanity, which has for too long been silent, I condemn these crimes." As Jews and Poles alike understood, the Warsaw command of the Home Army could not have saved the ghetto, even if it had devoted all of its troops and weapons to that purpose. It had, at that point, almost no combat experience itself. Nevertheless, seven of the first eight armed operations carried out by the Home Army in Warsaw were in support of the ghetto fighters. Two Poles died at the very beginning of the Warsaw Ghetto Uprising, trying to breach the ghetto walls. Several further attempts to breach the walls of the ghetto failed. All in all, the Home Army made some eleven attempts to help the Jews. Soviet propagandists, seeing an opportunity, claimed that the Home Army denied aid to the fighting ghetto.[29]

Aryeh Wilner, whom the Poles of the Home Army knew as Jurek, was an important liaison between the Jewish Combat Organization and the Home Army. He was killed during the Warsaw Ghetto Uprising, but not before passing on an important message, almost a legend in itself, to his Polish contacts. It was he who spread the description of Jewish resistance that the Home Army would approve and itself publish: that the Ghetto Uprising was not about preserving Jewish life but about rescuing human dignity. This was understood in Polish

Romantic terms: that deeds should be judged by their intentions rather than their outcomes, that sacrifice ennobles and sacrifice of life ennobles eternally. Often overlooked or forgotten was the essence of Wilner's point: Jewish resistance in Warsaw was not only about the dignity of the Jews but about the dignity of humanity as such, including those of the Poles, the British, the Americans, the Soviets: of everyone who could have done more, and instead did less.[30]

Shmuel Zygielbojm, the representative of the Bund to the Polish government-in-exile in London, knew that the ghetto was going up in flames. He had a clear idea of the general course of the Holocaust from Jan Karski, a Home Army courier who had brought news of the mass murder to Allied leaders in 1942. Zygielbojm would not have known the details, but he grasped the general course of events, and made an effort to define it for the rest of the world. In a careful suicide note of 12 May 1943, addressed to the Polish president and prime minister but intended to be shared with other Allied leaders, he wrote: "Though the responsibility for the crime of the murder of the entire Jewish nation rests above all upon the perpetrators, indirect blame must be borne by humanity itself." The next day he burned himself alive in front of the British parliament, joining in, as he wrote, the fate of his fellow Jews in Warsaw.[31]

The Jews of Warsaw fought on, without hope. By May 1943 Stroop's reports to his superiors had become calm and methodical, a matter of numbers. An unknown number of Jews had burned to death or committed suicide in bunkers; about 56,065 had been captured, of whom about 7,000 were shot on the spot; 6,929 more were sent to Treblinka, and the rest, the large majority, assigned to labor duty at camps such as Majdanek. On 15 May Stroop declared victory in the Warsaw ghetto by dynamiting the Tłomackie Synagogue. Now the Germans began to destroy what was left of the ghetto, as Himmler had ordered. All the remaining buildings were brought down, the cellars and sewers filled. On 1 June 1943, Himmler gave the order to build a new concentration camp, on the ghetto's smoldering ruins.[32]

———————

Some Jews did survive the ghetto uprising, but found a hard welcome beyond the ghetto. In 1943 the Home Army was even more concerned about communism than it had been in 1942. As a result of an arrest and a plane crash in summer 1943, a more sympathetic Polish commander and prime minister were replaced by less sympathetic ones. Despite its promises to do so, the Home Army never organized a Jewish unit from veterans of the Warsaw Ghetto Uprising. Over the course of 1943, units of the Home Army sometimes shot armed Jews in the countryside as bandits. In a few cases, Home Army soldiers killed Jews in order to steal their property. On the other hand, the Home Army did execute Poles who turned in Jews or tried to blackmail them.[33]

The same German labor campaign that provoked the Warsaw Ghetto Uprising also reoriented the Polish resistance. During the same January 1943 visit to Warsaw when he had first demanded the liquidation of the ghetto, Himmler had also ordered massive roundups of Poles for labor. The random hunts for workers that followed were massively disruptive to Polish society, as women and children suddenly found themselves without husbands and fathers. In the first three months of 1943, about three thousand Poles from Warsaw were sent to Majdanek. They were joined there that May by thousands of Warsaw Jews, transported from the Warsaw ghetto after the defeat of the uprising. Warsaw Poles and Jews, separated by ghetto walls in 1941 and 1942, found themselves enclosed within the same barbed wire in 1943. Majdanek was by then a labor camp with a gassing facility attached, like Auschwitz although on a far smaller scale. About fifty thousand Polish Jews died there, along with perhaps ten thousand non-Jewish Poles.[34]

Knowledge of deportations to places like Majdanek inclined men and women to join the Home Army. Since they could be seized as laborers and sent to a concentration camp at any moment, life underground could seem safer than open life in Warsaw. The underground also offered camaraderie as an antidote to fear, and revenge as a salve to helplessness. The Germans had tried to prevent organized resistance to their labor roundups by killing the Polish educated classes, in the tens of thousands at the time of the 1939 invasion, and then in the thousands in the AB Aktion of 1940. The planners of those actions had in mind precisely the problem that they experienced now: treating Poland as a pool of mindless labor would bring resistance if anyone was alive who could lead Poles against Germans. Yet the Polish educated classes were far larger than the Germans had assumed, and in conditions of oppression there was no shortage of people willing to take command.

Home Army commanders preferred to remain underground, organize, gather men and arms, and await the best moment for a general uprising. Such patience and calculation were increasingly difficult in 1943. The Soviets in their radio and printed propaganda were urging Poles to begin an uprising as soon as possible. Poles, aware of the fate of the Jews in their country, were afraid that they too could be exterminated should German rule continue. A particular shock was the implementation of Generalplan Ost in part of the Lublin district of the General Government. Though that massive German colonization plan had generally been deferred, Odilo Globocnik carried it out. Beginning in November 1942 and continuing through the first half of 1943, the Germans emptied three hundred Polish villages around Zamość in order to re-create the area as a racially German colony. About one hundred thousand Poles were deported in this Zamość Action, many to Majdanek and Auschwitz. Because the Zamość Action began just as Operation Reinhard was concluding, and in the same district where Operation Reinhard had begun, many Poles saw it as the beginning of a Final Solution to the Polish problem. This was not quite correct, since Generalplan Ost envisioned the destruction of most but not all Poles; but it was a logical conclusion in the circumstances.[35]

So as German labor policies shifted, and Warsaw Jews rebelled, many Poles in Warsaw and elsewhere also shifted toward a more decisive form of resistance. Whereas Jews in the ghetto saw no choice but to throw themselves into an all-or-nothing struggle, non-Jewish Poles had some ability to modulate their resistance along a certain scale between underground conspiracy and open battle. In March 1943 the Home Army emerged from the shadows, and turned to assassinations and partisan warfare. Its attempts to aid the ghetto fighters were among its earliest, and still quite amateurish, public acts of armed resistance. With time the operations became more effective. German policemen were shot, as were Polish citizens who collaborated with the Gestapo. During the month of August 1943 the Germans recorded 942 instances of partisan resistance in the Warsaw district of the General Government, and 6,214 such incidents in the General Government as a whole.[36]

The Home Army's shift to armed resistance was bound to provoke a German response. A cycle of terror and counterterror continued for the next year. On 13 October 1943 the Germans began to apply the technique of blockades, perfected in the Warsaw ghetto during the Large Action of summer 1942, to neighborhoods in the rest of Warsaw. Men were seized at random for public reprisal shootings, designed to cow the population and quell the growing resistance. At a time and place announced in advance, those arrested were taken in groups of five or ten, blindfolded, and executed by firing squad. The men tended to call out "Long live Poland!" before they were shot; and so then the Germans gagged them, or put sacks over their heads, or plastered their mouths shut. Poles did indeed gather to watch the shootings, but it was not at all clear that they were learning the lessons that the Germans wished for them to learn. After the shootings, women would gather earth soaked with blood, place it in jars, and take it with them to church.[37]

The Germans accepted the propaganda failure, but continued to kill Poles in Warsaw in large numbers: sometimes people who were involved with resistance, sometimes random hostages. They moved their execution site to the terrain of the former ghetto, where the shootings would not be seen. The major prison where Poles were held was also within the walls of the former ghetto. A large number of Poles would be shot on most days of autumn 1943 in the former ghetto along with a few Jews discovered in the ruins. On 9 December 1943, for example, 139 Poles were shot along with sixteen Jewish women and a Jewish child. On 13 January 1944, more than three hundred Poles were shot. These shootings in the ghetto were still technically "public," although no one was actually allowed to watch them. The families were informed of the fate of their loved ones. After 15 February 1944 Poles simply disappeared from their homes or their streets, and were shot in the ghetto, with no public record of the event. Some 9,500 people were shot in the ghetto ruins from October 1943 through July 1944, some of them Jewish survivors, the majority non-Jewish Poles.[38]

Blindfolded and bound, these Poles could not have known that they had been delivered for death to Himmler's newest concentration camp. Opened on 19 July 1943 within the ruins of the Warsaw ghetto, Concentration Camp Warsaw was one of the ghastliest creations of Nazi rule.[39]

First the Germans had forced Jews to live in a defined area of Warsaw and called it a ghetto. Then they had ordered deportations from neighboring regions to the overcrowded ghetto, ensuring tens of thousands of deaths by starvation and disease. Then they had deported more than a quarter of a million Jews from the ghetto to the gas chambers of Treblinka, shooting some seventeen thousand more during these deportations. Then they had liquidated the ghetto, their own creation. They suppressed the resistance that this brought, shooting some fourteen thousand more Jews. Then they had burned down the buildings of the Warsaw ghetto. Finally they built a new camp within this nonplace.

This was Concentration Camp Warsaw. It was an island of very conditional life located within an urban zone of death. All around were blocks and blocks of burned buildings, with human remains rotting within. Encircled broadly by the walls of the former ghetto, Concentration Camp Warsaw was encircled narrowly by barbed wire and watchtowers. The inmates were a few hundred Poles and a few hundred Jews. These were not, for the most part, Polish Jews but, rather, Jews from other parts of Europe. They had been deported from their home countries to Auschwitz, selected for labor there rather than gassed, and then sent to Concentration Camp Warsaw. They came from Greece, France, Germany, Austria, Belgium, and the Netherlands, and in 1944 from Hungary. The conditions that they found in Concentration Camp Warsaw were so appalling that some of them asked to be sent back to Auschwitz and gassed.[40]

The Jewish laborers of Concentration Camp Warsaw were to perform three major tasks in the ruins: destroy the buildings in the former ghetto that still stood after the arson of April and May 1943; search for valuables that Jews might have left behind; and bait Jews still in hiding to come and surrender themselves. Some of the Jewish laborers were also sent, in their striped uniforms and wooden shoes, to labor beyond the walls of the former ghetto. Friendships grew up between these foreign Jews and Poles in Warsaw, despite barriers of language. One of these laborers remembered a scene beyond the ghetto walls: "A Polish boy, maybe fourteen years old, badly dressed, was standing just next to us with a little basket, in which there were a few small apples. He looked at us, thought for a moment, and then grabbed his little basket and threw it to us. Then he ran to the other boys selling food, and suddenly bread and fruit rained down on us from all sides. At first the SS-men guarding us didn't know what to do, they were so surprised by this unexpected expression of solidarity. Then they began to scream at the boys and point their machine guns at them, and to beat us for accepting the food. But that didn't hurt us, we paid no attention. We waved our thanks to those boys."[41]

After October 1943, the Jews of Concentration Camp Warsaw were forced to perform yet another task: the disposal of the bodies of Poles taken from Warsaw and executed in the ruins of the ghetto. Poles were brought in trucks in groups of fifty or sixty to the terrain of the former ghetto, where they were executed in or near Concentration Camp Warsaw by machine gunners of the local SS and another police unit. Jewish prisoners then had to form a Death Commando that would eliminate the traces of the execution. They would build a pyre from wood taken from the ruins of the ghetto, and then stack bodies and wood in layers. Then the Jews poured gasoline on the pyres and lit them. Yet this was a Death Commando in more than the usual sense. Once the bodies of the Poles were burning, the SS-men shot the Jewish laborers who had built the pyre, and tossed their bodies into the flames.[42]

Miłosz's poem "A Poor Christian Looks at the Ghetto," written in 1943, speaks of an unearthly power able to undo the grey of rubble and soot and distinguish "the ash of each man." No earthly agent could sort the Jewish ashes from the Polish ones.

In summer 1944 in such a city, resistance was all but inevitable. Its form and its direction were not. The commanders of the Home Army, and the Polish government in London, had a very difficult decision to make. Their people suffered more than those of any Allied capital, but they faced an unforgiving strategic position. Poles had to consider the present German occupation in light of the threat of a future Soviet occupation. After the success of the Red Army's Operation Bagration in late June, German soldiers could be seen streaming through Warsaw in July. It seemed as if the Germans were about to be defeated, which was good news; it also seemed that the Soviets would soon replace them in Warsaw, which was not. If the Home Army fought the Germans openly, and succeeded, they might greet the arriving Red Army as masters of their own house. If they fought the Germans openly, and failed, they would be prone and powerless when the Soviets arrived. If they did nothing, they would have no bargaining position with the Soviets—or with their western Allies.[43]

Although their British and American allies could afford to have illusions about Stalin, Polish officers and politicians could not. They had not forgotten that the Soviet Union had been an ally of Nazi Germany in 1939–1941, and that its occupation of eastern Poland had been ruthless and oppressive. Poles knew about the deportations to Kazakhstan and Siberia; they knew about the shootings at Katyn. Stalin broke off diplomatic relations with the Polish government over the Katyn discovery, which was one more reason not to trust the Soviet

Union. If Stalin would use his own massacre as a reason to end relations with the Polish government, how could he be expected to negotiate in good faith about anything? And if the Soviet Union would not recognize the legitimate Polish government during a common war against Nazi Germany, what were the chances that it would support Polish independence when the war was over and the Soviet position much stronger?

The British and the Americans had larger concerns. The Red Army was winning the war against the Wehrmacht on the eastern front, and Stalin was a more important ally than any Polish government. It was more comfortable for the British and the Americans to accept the mendacious Soviet version of the Katyn massacre and blame the Germans. It was much easier for them to encourage their Polish ally to compromise than it was to try to prevail upon Stalin. They wanted the Poles to accept that the Germans rather than the Soviets had killed the Polish officers, which was false; and would have preferred that Poland grant the eastern half of its territory to the Soviet Union, which was an unlikely action for any sovereign government.

For that matter, London and Washington had already agreed, in late 1943, that the Soviet Union would reclaim the eastern half of prewar Poland after the war. The western Soviet border accorded Stalin by Hitler was confirmed by Churchill and Roosevelt. London and Washington endorsed the Molotov-Ribbentrop line (with minor changes) as the future Soviet-Polish frontier. In that sense Poland was betrayed not only by the Soviet Union but also by its western Allies, who urged Poles to make compromises at a time when less was to be gained by them than Poles might have thought. Half of their country had already been conceded, without their participation.[44]

Left alone by its allies, the Polish government in London ceded the initiative to the Polish fighters in Warsaw. Seeing little other hope to establish Polish sovereignty, the Home Army chose an uprising in the capital, to commence on 1 August 1944.

The Warsaw Uprising of August 1944 took place within the framework of Operation Tempest, a long-planned national uprising that was meant to give Polish forces a prominent role in the liberation of prewar Polish territory. By late July, however, Operation Tempest had already failed. The Home Army had planned to engage German units as they retreated from the Red Army in what had been eastern Poland. It had been impossible to make prior political arrangements with the Soviet Union about the terms of this cooperation, since Stalin had broken diplomatic relations. Polish commanders did make local agreements with Soviet counterparts in summer 1944, but at a heavy price. Negotiation meant leaving hiding places and revealing identities, and the Soviets exploited Polish vulnerability to the maximum. Poles who revealed themselves to join the common fight against Germans were treated as people who might resist future Soviet rule. The Soviet Union never had any intention of supporting any institution that claimed to represent an independent Poland. The Soviet leadership and the NKVD treated every Polish political organization (except the communists) as part of an anti-Soviet plot.[45]

In July 1944, Polish units were allowed to assist the Red Army in attacks on Vilnius and Lviv, the major cities of prewar eastern Poland, but were then disarmed by their ostensible Soviet allies. The Polish soldiers were given the choice of Soviet command or prison. After the disarmaments, the NKVD arrested everyone with a political past. Soviet partisans were allowed to take part in the victorious campaign against the Germans; Polish partisans were not. Indeed, in some cases Soviet partisans were turned against the Polish fighters. The partisan unit of Tuvia Bielski, for example, took part in the disarming of the Home Army. The tragedy of Operation Tempest was triple: the Home Army lost men and its arms; Poland's government saw its military strategy fail; and Poles lost their lives or their freedom fighting for lands that Poland could not regain in any event, since Churchill and Roosevelt had already ceded them to Stalin.[46]

Still, news from Germany gave some hope to Polish commanders in Warsaw. On 20 July 1944, German military officers tried (and failed) to assassinate Adolf Hitler. The news led some Home Army commanders to believe that Germany had lost the will to fight, and thus that a bold blow might drive them from Warsaw. On 22 July the Soviets gave another prod to the Polish resistance by unveiling, in Lublin, their own provisional government for Poland. The laboratory of Nazi exterminatory policies now became the center of a future communist puppet government. Stalin was claiming the authority to determine who would form the Polish government. If the Home Army did nothing, his clients would be installed in Warsaw, and Poland would shift directly from Nazi to Soviet occupation. As in 1939, so in 1944, the fact that the Poles had Western allies meant little or nothing. It was clear by July 1944, with the Red Army already occupying more than half of prewar Poland, that the country would be liberated by Soviet force of arms. In late July the Americans were a month away from Paris (where they would support a French uprising); there was no chance that US forces would liberate any of Poland. Any political resistance to Soviet plans would have to come from the Poles themselves.[47]

On 25 July 1944, the Polish government granted the Home Army in Warsaw the authority to begin an uprising in the capital at a time of its choosing. Warsaw itself had originally been excluded from the planning for Operation Tempest; the Warsaw district of the Home Army had sent many of its arms to the east of the country, where they were now lost to the Soviets. The logic of an immediate uprising in Warsaw was not easy for everyone to follow. The command structure of the Polish Army fighting on the western front, under General Władysław Anders, was excluded from the discussions. Given German anti-partisan tactics, an uprising looked like suicide to many. The Germans had been killing Poles in massive reprisals throughout the war; if an uprising failed, reasoned some commanders in Warsaw, the entire civilian population would suffer. The argument in favor of the uprising was that the rebellion could not fail: whether or not the Poles defeated the Germans, the Red Army was moving fast and would arrive in Warsaw in a few days. On this logic, which prevailed, the only question seemed to be whether Poles would first make an effort to liberate their own capital.[48]

The Poles were caught between an approaching Red Army and occupying German forces. They could not defeat the Germans on their own, so they had to hope that the Soviet advance would prompt a German retreat and that there would be some interval between the Wehrmacht's withdrawal and the Red Army's arrival. Their hope was that the interval would not be too brief, so that they could establish themselves as the Polish government before the Soviets arrived.

In fact, the interval was too long.

Polish soldiers in uniforms and armbands began their assault on German positions in the afternoon of 1 August 1944. The vast majority were from the Home Army; smaller units of the far-right National Armed Forces and the communist People's Army also joined the fight. On this first day of the Warsaw Uprising, the Home Army secured a great deal of the downtown and Old Town of the city,

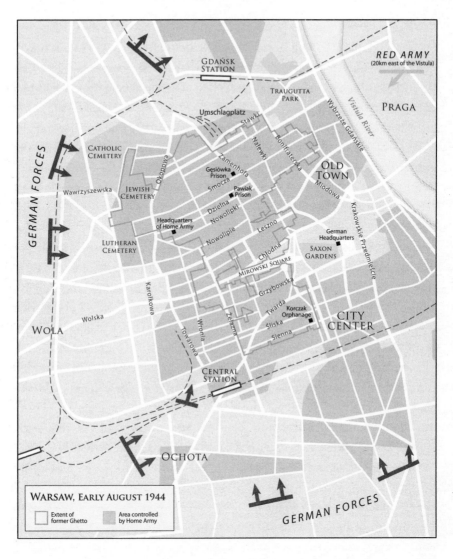

WARSAW, EARLY AUGUST 1944

☐ Extent of former Ghetto ▨ Area controlled by Home Army

but failed to capture most of the essential military targets. The Germans had made few preparations, but were not caught completely by surprise. It had been hard to disguise the mobilization going on within the city itself. German forces had gone on alert at 4:30, half an hour before the uprising began. The Poles chose to attack in daylight on a long summer afternoon, and for that reason took many casualties. The inexperienced and lightly armed troops had an especially difficult time with guarded and fortified objectives. Nevertheless, the mood among the fighters and in the city itself was euphoric.[49]

When and where Polish power replaced German power in those early days of August 1944, surviving Jews emerged from their places of shelter among Poles. Many asked to be allowed to fight. As Michał Zylberberg recalled: "A Jewish perspective ruled out passivity. Poles had taken up arms against the mortal enemy. Our obligation as victims and as fellow citizens was to help them." Other combatants in the Warsaw Uprising were veterans of the ghetto uprising of 1943. Most of these Jews joined the Home Army; others found the People's Army, or even the anti-Semitic National Armed Forces. Some Jews (or Poles of Jewish origin) were already enlisted in the Home Army and the People's Army. Almost certainly, more Jews fought in the Warsaw Uprising of August 1944 than in the Warsaw Ghetto Uprising of April 1943.[50]

In early August, as the Home Army failed to take the important German positions in Warsaw, its soldiers did register one victory. Officers gathered volunteers for a dangerous attack upon a heavily guarded position. On 5 August, Home Army soldiers entered the ruins of the ghetto, attacked Concentration Camp Warsaw, defeated the ninety SS-men who guarded it, and liberated its remaining 348 prisoners, most of them foreign Jews. One of the Home Army soldiers in this operation was Stanisław Aronson, who had himself been deported from the ghetto to Treblinka. Another recalled a Jew who greeted them with tears on his cheeks; yet another, the plea of a Jew for a weapon and a uniform, so that he could fight. Many of the liberated Jewish slave laborers did join the Home Army, fighting in their striped camp uniforms and wooden shoes, with "complete indifference to life or death," as one Home Army soldier recalled.[51]

Now Himmler again saw an opportunity, as he had during the Warsaw Ghetto Uprising, to demonstrate his strength and to win a symbolic victory. Despite Polish expectations, the Red Army had ceased its rapid advance. With the Wehrmacht stubbornly holding its positions at the Vistula River, just east of downtown Warsaw, the uprising would be a matter for the SS and the German police. These were Himmler's institutions, and Himmler wished to make this his uprising, to show Hitler one more time that he was the ruthless master of the situation.[52]

Unlike the Ghetto Uprising, however, this campaign would require reinforcements. Following the German withdrawal from Belarus, experienced anti-partisan units were available. Erich von dem Bach-Zelewski, the chief of German anti-partisan formations and a veteran of the partisan warfare in Belarus, was given overall command in Warsaw. Other veterans of the anti-partisan warfare in Belarus were also summoned. The SS Commando Dirlewanger was dispatched from northeastern Poland, the Kaminskii unit from southwestern Poland. They were reinforced by a police unit sent from Poznań and a few hundred foreign fighters, mostly Azerbaijanis who had defected from the Red Army. About half of the people who fought in Warsaw in German uniforms did not speak German. This probably made the action that followed no more bloody, but it did make it more confusing, even for the Germans themselves.[53]

Kaminskii and his Russians were given personal permission from Himmler to loot, and they accepted this part of their assignment with gusto. They entered Ochota, a southwesterly neighborhood of Warsaw, on 9 August 1944. Over the course of the next ten days, they concentrated on theft, but also killed several thousand Polish civilians. As one of Kaminskii's officers recalled, "Mass executions of civilians without investigation were the order of the day." The soldiers also became known for systematic rape. They burned down the hospital of the Marie Curie Institute, killing everyone inside, but scrupulously raped the nurses ahead of time. As one of Kaminskii's men characterized the Ochota campaign, "they raped nuns and plundered and stole anything they could get their hands on." German commanders complained that Kaminskii and his men were concerned only with "robbing, drinking, and raping women." Bach had Kaminskii apprehended and executed: not for the killing or the sexual violence but for his habit of stealing for himself rather than for the coffers of the Reich.[54]

The comportment of the SS Special Commando Dirlewanger was even worse. Its men were now a motley group of criminals, foreigners, and SS-men released from punishment camps. Dirlewanger was indiscipline itself; even Himmler had to order him twice to go to Warsaw. The unit was fresh from its Belarusian campaigns, where it had killed tens of thousands of civilians in the countryside and the towns. Now it would kill more civilians in a large city. The most infamous Waffen-SS unit in Belarus now became the most infamous Waffen-SS unit in Poland. The Dirlewanger unit was the bulk of a combat group under the command of Heinz Reinefarth, the SS and Police Chief for the Warthegau, the largest district of occupied Poland annexed to Germany.[55]

Reinefarth received an extraordinary three-part order from Himmler: all Polish combatants were to be shot; all Polish noncombatants, including women and children, were also to be shot; and the city itself was to be razed to the ground. The police formations and the SS Special Commando Dirlewanger carried out these orders to the letter on 5 and 6 August 1944, shooting some forty thousand civilians in the course of those two days alone. They had a military objective: they were to march through the west-central Wola neighborhood and relieve German headquarters in the Saxon Gardens. They lifted the Home Army's barricades on Wola Street by marching Poles in front of them and forcing them to do the work, using women and children as human shields in the meantime, and raping some of the women. As they moved west they destroyed each and every building, one by one, using gasoline and hand grenades. Wola Street ran just south of the terrain that had been the ghetto, and indeed through some of its most southerly extremes, so their work of destruction brought an adjoining neighborhood to ruins.[56]

The men of the Dirlewanger Brigade burned down three hospitals with patients inside. At one hospital, wounded Germans who were being treated by Polish doctors and nurses asked that no harm come to the Poles. This was not to be. The men of the Dirlewanger Brigade killed the Polish wounded. They brought the nurses back to camp that evening, as was the custom: each night selected women would be whipped by officers and then gang-raped before being murdered. This evening was unusual even by those standards. To the accompaniment of flute music, the men raised a gallows, and then hanged the doctors and the naked nurses.[57]

As houses burned in Wola, people sought refuge in factories, which then became convenient killing grounds for the German SS and police units. At one factory, two thousand people were shot; at another, five thousand more. Wanda Lurie, one of the few survivors of the mass shootings at the Ursus factory, was expecting a child. "I went in last and kept back, always lagging behind in the hope that they would not kill a pregnant woman. However, I was taken in the last group. I saw a heap of bodies about a meter high." She lost her children. "The first salvo hit my elder son, the second me and the third my younger children." She fell wounded, but was able later to dig herself from the pile of bodies. She later gave birth to a healthy baby. The mass killing slowed on 6 August, possibly because bullets were short and were needed elsewhere.[58]

The massacres in Wola had nothing in common with combat. The Germans lost six dead and killed about twenty Home Army soldiers while murdering at least thirty thousand people. The ratio of civilian to military dead was more than a thousand to one, even if military casualties on both sides are counted. On 13 August Bach countermanded Himmler's killing orders, and the organized shooting of civilians in large numbers came to a halt. Many more Poles would be killed, however, in more or less unplanned ways. When the Germans took the Old Town, they killed seven thousand wounded in field hospitals by gunfire and flamethrowers. Some thirty thousand civilians would be killed in the Old Town before the uprising was over.[59]

In the Wola neighborhood, where the worst of the killing took place, the bodies had to be found and removed. The Germans assembled a group of Polish slave laborers, whom they called the Cremation Commando. Between 8 and 23 August 1944, these people were ordered to pick through the ruins of the Wola neighborhood, extract the rotting bodies, and burn them on pyres. In Wola, the remnants of the ghetto were all around them. The laborers marched along Wola, Elektoralna, and Chłodna Streets, now from east to west, following in reverse the route the German police and the Dirlewanger Brigade had taken. Their first five pyres were just to the east of the ghetto, their next thirteen just to the west. The Polish slave laborers (one of whom was Jewish) burned the bodies while their SS guards played cards and laughed.[60]

The Warsaw Uprising did not defeat the Germans, and it was little more than a passing annoyance to the Soviets. The Red Army had been halted, by unexpectedly strong German resistance, just beyond Warsaw. The Germans were making a last stand in Poland, the Wehrmacht at the Vistula, the SS and the police in Warsaw. Despite what some Poles had hoped, the Nazi regime had not collapsed after the assassination attempt on Hitler. Instead, the Germans had consolidated the eastern front. Operation Bagration had broken Army Group Center, but not the Wehrmacht itself. It had brought Vasily Grossman to the site where Warsaw's Jews were killed, but not to Warsaw itself. Meanwhile, the Red Army's Ukrainian Front was engaged in major operations elsewhere, to the southeast. Stalin had no pressing need to take Warsaw just then, in August 1944.

It made perfect Stalinist sense to *encourage* an uprising, and then not to assist one. Right to the last moment, Soviet propaganda had called for an uprising in Warsaw, promising Soviet assistance. The uprising came, but the help did not.

Though there is no reason to believe that Stalin deliberately halted military operations at Warsaw, the delay at the Vistula suited Stalin's political purposes.
From the Soviet perspective, an uprising in Warsaw was desirable because it
would kill Germans—and Poles who were willing to risk their lives for independence. The Germans would do the necessary work of destroying the remnants of the Polish intelligentsia and the soldiers of the Home Army, groups that
overlapped. As soon as the Home Army soldiers took up arms, Stalin called
them adventurers and criminals. Later on, when the Soviet Union gained control
of Poland, resistance to Hitler would be prosecuted as a crime, on the logic that
armed action not controlled by the communists undermined the communists,
and that communism was the only legitimate regime for Poland.

The British and the Americans were all but unable to provide meaningful
help to the Poles in Warsaw. Winston Churchill, whose own personal obstinacy
was a crucial element of the war, could do little but urge Britain's Polish allies to
compromise with the Soviets. In summer 1944 Churchill had been advising the
Polish prime minister, Stanisław Mikołajczyk, to visit Moscow and seek some
arrangement that would allow the restoration of Soviet-Polish diplomatic relations. When Mikołajczyk arrived in Moscow in late July 1944, he was told by
the British ambassador to concede everything: to give up the eastern half of the
country, and to accept the Soviet version of the Katyn massacre (that the Germans, not the Soviets, were guilty). As Mikołajczyk knew, Roosevelt also preferred not to question the Soviet account of Katyn. The beginning of the Warsaw
Uprising found Mikołajczyk in Moscow. In this unexpected position, Mikołajczyk was forced to ask Stalin for help, which Stalin refused to give. Churchill
did then ask Stalin to aid the Poles. On 16 August Stalin brushed him off, saying
that he had no intention of helping a "foolish adventure."[61]

Great Britain had gone to war five years earlier on the question of Polish independence, which it was now unable to protect from its Soviet ally. The British
press often echoed the Stalinist line, presenting the Poles as adventurous and
wayward, rather than as British allies seeking to take back their own capital.
Both George Orwell and Arthur Koestler protested: Orwell speaking of the "dis-
honesty and cowardice" of Britons who denied the responsibility of the Allies
to help the uprising, and Koestler calling Stalin's inaction "one of the great in-
famies of the war."[62]

The Americans had no better luck. If American planes could be refueled on Soviet territory, then they could fly missions from Italy to Poland, bombing German positions and supplying the Poles. On the same day that Stalin rebuffed Churchill, 16 August 1944, American diplomats added Polish targets to Operation Frantic, the bombing campaign in eastern and southeastern Europe. Stalin denied his American ally permission to refuel for such missions. An American junior diplomat, George Kennan, saw where the logic led: the refusal was "a gauntlet thrown down with malicious glee." Stalin had in effect told the Americans that he would be taking control of Poland, and preferred that the Polish fighters die and the uprising fail. A month later, when the uprising was effectively defeated, Stalin showed his strength and intelligence, and muddied the historical record. In mid-September, when it could make absolutely no difference to the outcome in Warsaw, he finally allowed American bombing runs and carried out a few of his own.[63]

By then, the Home Army controlled so little of Warsaw that supplies fell to the Germans. Polish troops had fallen back to a few pockets of resistance. Then, like Jewish fighters before them, they tried to escape through the sewers. The Germans, prepared for this by their own experiences of 1943, burned or gassed them out.

In early October 1944, Himmler told Paul Geibel, the SS and Police Chief for Warsaw, that Hitler had no fonder wish than to destroy the city. Stone should not be left upon stone. The wish was also Himmler's own. The war as such was clearly lost: the British had liberated Antwerp, the Americans were approaching the Rhine, and the Soviets would soon besiege Budapest. But Himmler saw an opportunity to fulfill one of his own war aims, the destruction of Slavic and Jewish cities integral to Generalplan Ost.

Himmler issued orders, apparently on 9 and 12 October, that the entire city of Warsaw be destroyed, building by building, block by block. At this point huge swaths of the city were already in ruins: the ghetto, the adjoining Wola neighborhood, and buildings hit by German bombs in September 1939—or for that matter in August 1944, when German planes bombed Warsaw from its own airport. But most of the city was still standing, and many of its inhabitants were still present. Now the Germans evacuated the survivors to a temporary camp at

Pruszków, whence some sixty thousand people would be sent to concentration camps, and some ninety thousand more to forced-labor assignments in the Reich. German engineers equipped with dynamite and flamethrowers, and aware of the experience of the destruction of the ghetto, would burn down their businesses and schools and homes.[64]

Himmler's decision to destroy Warsaw served a certain vision of the Nazi East, but it did not serve the German military cause in the Second World War. Erich von dem Bach-Zelewski did show signs of wanting to recruit the Home Army as a future ally in a final struggle against the Soviets; he reversed Himmler's killing orders in mid-August without (it seems) having the proper authority to do so, and then agreed to negotiate with the Home Army command as with a defeated adversary in late September. By the terms of the surrender of 2 October 1944, Home Army officers and soldiers, men and women alike, were to receive the rights accorded to prisoners of war by international law. For the same reasons, Bach opposed Himmler's preferred conclusion of the uprising, the total destruction of the city.

It is very unlikely that Bach could have found many allies in Warsaw, for the same reason that he found few in Belarus: the actions of Dirlewanger's men and other German anti-partisan formations had been too unforgettably bloody. The German reaction was so unbelievably destructive that Polish fighters had no alternative but to await Soviet liberation. As one Home Army soldier put it in his poetry: "We await you, red plague / To deliver us from the black death." Like Bach, the Wehrmacht opposed Himmler's policy. German troops were holding the Red Army at the Vistula River, and hoped to use Warsaw as a fortress, or at least its buildings as shelters. None of this mattered. Bach was transferred; the army was ignored; Himmler had his way; and a European capital was destroyed. On the day before the Soviets arrived, the Germans torched the last library.[65]

No other European capital suffered such a fate: destroyed physically, and bereft of about half of its population. Perhaps 150,000 Polish noncombatants were killed by the Germans in August and September 1944 alone, during the Warsaw Uprising. A similar number of non-Jewish Poles from Warsaw had already been killed in concentration camps, at execution sites in the ghetto, by German bombing, or in combat. Warsaw Jews died in higher absolute numbers and in much higher proportions. The percentage of Jews from Warsaw who died, more than ninety percent, exceeds that of non-Jews, which was about thirty percent. Only the fate of cities further east, such as Minsk or Leningrad, bore comparison to that of Warsaw. All in all, about half of the inhabitants of the city perished in a city whose prewar population was about 1.3 million.[66]

The distinction between Poles and Jews was for some victims artificial. Ludwik Landau, for example, might have been killed by the Germans because he was a Home Army officer and an effective propagandist for an independent Poland. As it happens, he was killed as a Jew. Some fates were permanently entangled. The Jewish historian Emanuel Ringelblum secretly created archives in the ghetto, on the basis of which a future history of Jews in wartime Warsaw would be possible. He was taken to a concentration camp after the defeat of the Ghetto Uprising, but was then rescued with the help of a Home Army officer. He was sheltered in Warsaw by Poles, until a Pole gave him away to the Germans. Then he and the Poles who had given him refuge were shot in the ruins of the Warsaw ghetto. The Home Army hunted down and killed the Pole who had betrayed them.[67]

Nevertheless, when the uprising was over and German power replaced Polish, the plight of the Jews was again distinct. After the destruction of the city, they had, quite literally, no place to hide. They did their best to disappear within the columns of exiled civilians or, in some cases, to find and join Soviet forces. Before the Warsaw Uprising, there were probably still some sixteen thousand Jews hiding with Poles beyond the walls of the former ghetto. Afterward, perhaps twelve thousand were still alive.[68]

————

The Germans had won the second battle for Warsaw, but the political victory fell to the Soviets. The Germans had applied the same tactics they had used in Belarus, ordered by much the same chain of command: Himmler-Bach-Dirlewanger. This time, anti-partisan warfare worked: not because the patriots of the Home Army were less determined than the Belarusian partisans but because they were more isolated. The Soviet Union supported communist partisans whom it could control, and opposed noncommunist fighters whom it could not. Polish troops were fighting against the Germans, but also for their own liberty. This was their doom. Stalin was happy to support the much smaller People's Army, a communist force that also fought in the uprising. Had it been the People's Army rather than the Home Army that had led the uprising, his attitude might have been entirely different.

Yet that would have been an entirely different Poland. The People's Army did have some popular support, but far less than that enjoyed by the Home Army. Polish politics had shifted to the left during the war, as was the case throughout occupied Europe. Yet communism was not popular. Poles had experienced Soviet communism during the war itself, in the eastern half of the country. No sovereign Poland would become communist. The Warsaw Uprising, destroying as it did many of the brightest and the bravest of a generation, did indeed make further resistance much more difficult. But the Warsaw Uprising also, as some of its more clearsighted (and coldblooded) commanders expected, brought Stalin's ruthlessness to the attention of the Americans and British. The American diplomat George Kennan was right: Stalin's cynical treatment of the Home Army was a slap in the face to his British and American allies. In this sense the Warsaw Uprising was the beginning of the confrontation that was to come when the Second World War was over.

While the Red Army hesitated just east of the Vistula River from early August 1944 through mid-January 1945, the Germans were killing the Jews to its west. During those five months, the Red Army was less than a hundred kilometers from Łódź, by this point the largest concentration of Jews left in occupied Poland, and less than a hundred kilometers from Auschwitz, where Polish and European Jews were still being gassed. The Red Army's halt at the Vistula doomed not only the Polish fighters and the civilians of Warsaw but also the Jews of Łódź. Their numbers had been much reduced by a series of deportations to Chełmno between December 1941 and September 1942. But in 1943 and 1944 the number of Jews had been relatively stable: some ninety thousand Jewish laborers and their families. The German civilian authorities, who sometimes preferred death through labor, had a longer hold here than elsewhere. Łódź Jews were building weapons, so the Wehrmacht also preferred that they survive.

Most of the remaining Łódź Jews died in the interval between the beginning of Operation Bagration and the final Soviet advance over the Vistula. The day after Operation Bagration, on 23 June 1944, the civilian authorities in Łódź yielded to Himmler and the SS, and allowed the liquidation of the Łódź ghetto. For a brief period the gassing facility at Chełmno was reopened, and some 7,196 Jews from Łódź were asphyxiated there between 23 June and 14 July. Then the facility at Chełmno was finally closed. The Jews of Łódź, meanwhile, knew that the Red Army was close by. They believed that if they could just remain in the ghetto for a few more days or weeks, they would survive. On 1 August, the day that the Warsaw Uprising began, the Łódź Judenrat was informed that all Jews would be "evacuated." The German mayor of the city even tried to persuade Jews that they should hasten to board the trains before the Red Army arrived, because the Soviet soldiers would take revenge on people who had spent the war making weapons for the Germans. As the Warsaw Uprising raged, and the Red Army waited, some sixty-seven thousand Jews of Łódź were deported to Auschwitz in August 1944. Most of them were gassed upon arrival.[69]

When Soviet soldiers finally crossed the Vistula and advanced into the ruins of Warsaw on 17 January 1945, they found very few buildings still standing. The site of Concentration Camp Warsaw, however, was still available. The Soviet NKVD took over its facilities, and used them for familiar purposes. Home Army soldiers were interrogated and shot there by the Soviets in 1945, as they had been by the Germans in 1944.[70]

On 19 January 1945, two days after reaching Warsaw, Soviet soldiers were already in Łódź. On 27 January they reached Auschwitz. From there it would take them a little more than three months for them to reach Berlin. As the Red Army moved forward, SS camp guards were driving Jews from Auschwitz to labor camps in Germany. In these hurried and brutal marches, thousands more Jews lost their lives. These marches, which left surviving Jews in Germany itself, were the last of the Nazi atrocities. The Belarusian Front of the Red Army began to shell Berlin on 20 April 1945, Hitler's birthday; by early May it had met the Ukrainian Front in the German capital. Berlin fell, and the war was over. Hitler had ordered subordinates to apply a scorched earth policy to Germany itself, but he was not obeyed. Although much young German life was wasted in the defense of Berlin, Hitler could effect no further policies of mass killing.[71]

In these last few months of war, from January to May 1945, the inmates of the German concentration camps died in very large numbers. Perhaps three hundred thousand people died in German camps during this period, from hunger and neglect. The American and British soldiers who liberated the dying inmates from camps in Germany believed that they had discovered the horrors of Nazism. The images their photographers and cameramen captured of the corpses and the living skeletons at Bergen-Belsen and Buchenwald seemed to convey the worst crimes of Hitler. As the Jews and Poles of Warsaw knew, and as Vasily Grossman and the Red Army soldiers knew, this was far from the truth. The worst was in the ruins of Warsaw, or the fields of Treblinka, or the marshes of Belarus, or the pits of Babi Yar.

The Red Army liberated all of these places, and all of the bloodlands. All of the death sites and dead cities fell behind an iron curtain, in a Europe Stalin made his own even while liberating it from Hitler.

Grossman wrote his article about Treblinka while Soviet troops were paused at the Vistula, watching the Germans defeat the Home Army in the Warsaw Uprising. The ashes of Warsaw were still warm when the Cold War began.

CHAPTER 10

ETHNIC CLEANSINGS

By the time the Red Army reached the remains of Warsaw in January 1945, Stalin knew what sort of Poland he wished to build. He knew where its borders would run, who would be forced to live within them, who would be forced to go. Poland would be a communist state, and an ethnically homogeneous country. Although Stalin would undertake no policies of mass killing in the east European empire he foresaw, Poland was to be the center of a zone of ethnic purity. Germany would be for Germans, Poland for Poles, and the western part of Soviet Ukraine for Ukrainians. He expected Polish communists, including those who personally represented a national minority, to cleanse their country of national minorities. Stalin had revived a Polish communist party, and chosen its leaders, and sent them to Poland. He knew that he would have support not only from Poles but from the Americans and the British for the removal of a large number of Germans. Hitler's own policies of moving Germans during the war suggested how Germans might be treated thereafter. German wartime colonization made a certain amount of forced population transfers seem inevitable. The only questions were how many Germans, and from which territories. Stalin had precise answers, even if his American and British allies did not.[1]

At the conference with his British and American allies at Yalta in February 1945 Stalin made himself understood, and had no reason to expect opposition. Roosevelt and Churchill would not object as Stalin took again the lands that he had received from Hitler: half of Poland, as well as the Baltic States and northeastern Romania. Stalin would compensate Poland, his communist Poland, by punishing Germany. Poland would be shifted to the west, absorbing German territory to a line defined by the Oder and the Lusatian Neiße Rivers. In the lands that Stalin foresaw as Polish lived no fewer than ten million Germans. Moving them out, or keeping them out, would be the task of a government dominated by Polish communists. They would profit from the desire of many Poles to remove the Germans, and take credit for the achievement of a goal, ethnic purity, that seemed self-evident to most leading Polish politicians by the end of the war. Communists would gain support among Poles by distributing the lands left by Germans, and keep it by reminding Poles that only the Red Army could prevent the Germans from coming back and claiming their lost property.[2]

Poland's communists had accepted these borders, and knew that they were to remove the Germans. "We have to throw them out," said Władysław Gomułka, general secretary of the Polish party in May 1945, "since all countries are built on national, not multinational, principles." Moving Poland to the west would not in itself make Poland a "national" state in this sense: the shift in borders simply replaced large Ukrainian and Belarusian minorities with a very large German minority. Poland would require a massive displacement of millions of Germans to be "national" in the way that Gomułka had in mind. Perhaps 1.5 million of them were German administrators and colonists, who would never have come to Poland without Hitler's war. They lived in houses or apartments that they had taken from Poles expelled (or killed) during the war or from Jews who had been killed. More than half a million more were Germans who were native to Poland, and had lived within Poland's prewar borders. The remaining eight million or so were to lose their homes in lands that had been in Germany even before Hitler's expansion, and had been predominantly German in population for centuries.[3]

In creating his Poland, Stalin turned Hitler's Generalplan Ost on its head. Germany, rather than expanding eastward to create a huge land empire, would be confined in the west. The Soviets, Americans, and British occupied Germany together, and its immediate political future was not entirely clear. What was obvious was that it would be a Germany for the Germans—but not in Hitler's sense. It would be a compact area in the middle of Europe, separated from Austria, separated from the Sudetenland taken from Czechoslovakia, collecting Germans from the East rather than sending them there as colonists. Rather than a master race commanding slaves along a brave new eastern frontier, Germans would be one more homogeneous nation. Yet unlike Hitler, Stalin did not understand "resettlement" as a euphemism for mass killing. He knew that people would die in the course of mass population transfers, but the destruction of the German nation was not his goal.

Communist and noncommunist, all leading Polish politicians agreed with Stalin that Poland should move as far as possible to the west, and that the Germans should go. When the Home Army had initiated the Warsaw Uprising on 1 August 1944, the Polish government in London had deprived Germans of citizenship and obliged them to leave the country. Stanisław Mikołajczyk, the prime minister of the London government, was no less categorical than his communist foes about what the postwar settlement should mean for Germans: "The experience with the fifth column and with German occupation methods make impossible the cohabitation of Polish and German populations on the territory of one state." This position represented a consensus not only of Polish society but also among the allied leaders. Roosevelt had said that the Germans "deserved" to be expelled by terror (while his predecessor, Herbert Hoover, called population transfers a "heroic remedy"). Churchill had promised the Poles "a clean sweep."[4]

At Yalta in February 1945, the Americans and the British agreed in principle that Poland should be shifted west, but were not convinced that Poland should be moved all the way to the Oder-Neiße line. Nevertheless, as Stalin anticipated, they came around to his way of thinking by the next summit at Potsdam in July. By that time, much of his policy had already been achieved on the ground. By March the Red Army had already conquered all of the German lands that Stalin intended to concede to Poland. By May the Red Army was in Berlin, and the war in Europe was over. Soviet troops had moved through eastern Germany with such extraordinary haste and violence that suddenly anything seemed possible. Six million or so Germans had been evacuated by German authorities or had fled before the Red Army, creating the basic preconditions for Stalin's ethnic and geographic version of Poland. Many of them would try to come back after Germany's surrender, but precious few would succeed.[5]

In Britain, George Orwell raised his voice one last time, in February 1945, calling the planned expulsion of the Germans an "enormous crime" that could not be "carried through." He was wrong. For once, his political imagination had failed him.[6]

During the march on Berlin, the Red Army followed a dreadfully simple procedure in the eastern lands of the Reich, the territories meant for Poland: its
men raped German women and seized German men (and some women) for
labor. The behavior continued as the soldiers reached the German lands that
would remain in Germany, and finally Berlin. Red Army soldiers had also raped
women in Poland, and in Hungary, and even in Yugoslavia, where a communist
revolution would make the country a Soviet ally. Yugoslav communists complained to Stalin about the behavior of Soviet soldiers, who gave them a little
lecture about soldiers and "fun."[7]

The scale of the rape increased once Soviet soldiers reached Germany itself.
It is hard to be sure just why. The Soviet Union, though egalitarian in principle,
did not instill respect for the female body in this most elemental sense. Aside
and apart from their experience with Germans, Red Army soldiers were prod-

ucts of the Soviet system, and often of its most vicious institutions. About a million Gulag prisoners were released early so that they could fight on the front. All Soviet soldiers seemed frustrated by the utter senselessness of the German attack on their poor country. Every German worker's house was finer than their own homes. Soldiers sometimes said that they attacked only "capitalists," but from their perspective a simple German farmer was unthinkably rich. And yet despite their obviously higher standard of living the Germans had come to the Soviet Union, to rob and to kill. Soviet soldiers may have understood the rape of German women as a way to humiliate and dishonor German men.[8]

As the Red Army took enormous losses as it moved west, its ranks were filled by conscripts from the Belarusian and Ukrainian Soviet republics whose families had suffered at the hands of Germans and whose young lives had been shaped by German occupation. Many Soviet soldiers thus had personal reasons to endorse the propaganda that they read and heard, which sometimes blamed the entire German nation for the Soviet tragedy. The vast majority of Red Army soldiers were not avenging the Holocaust as such, but they were reading the propaganda of people who had been deeply wounded by the mass murder of Jews. Ilya Ehrenburg, the Soviet-Jewish writer now working as a journalist for the army newspaper *The Red Star*, was at this point a specialist in hate propaganda. "From now on," he had written in 1942, "we have understood that the Germans are not humans."[9]

Whatever the motivations, the outburst of violence against German women was extraordinary. Men who tried to defend daughters or wives were beaten and sometimes killed. The women had few men to protect them. Theirs were dead in battle (some five million German men had been killed in action by this point), drafted into the Wehrmacht, summoned to the emergency civil defense, or seized by the Soviets as labor. Most of the men present were aged or disabled. In some villages, every single female was raped, whatever her age. As the German novelist Günter Grass learned later in life, his mother had offered herself so that his sister might be spared. Neither was. Gang rapes were very common. Many women died as a result of wounds sustained during successive rapes.[10]

German women often committed suicide, or tried to kill themselves, to prevent rape or to evade the shame of having been raped. As one recalled her flight, "With the darkness came an indescribable fright. Many women and girls were right there and raped by the Russians." Hearing their screams, she and her sister slit their wrists, but survived: likely because they were too cold to bleed to death, and because they were treated by a Soviet doctor the following day. They were spared during the night, probably because they had passed out and seemed to be dead. Indeed, death was one of the few defenses against rape. Martha Kurzmann and her sister were spared only because they were burying their mother. "Just as we had washed our dead mother and wished to dress her body, a Russian came and wanted to rape us." He spat and turned away. That was the exception.[11]

Women who were raped were sometimes then taken as forced labor; but most of those seized for labor were men. The Soviets seized about 520,000 Germans—so about a tenth as many people as the Germans had taken from the Soviet Union for forced labor. The Soviets also took some 287,000 people as laborers from east European countries, and deported at least 40,000 Poles thought to represent a threat to Soviet power or future communist rule. They seized Hungarian civilians in Budapest, treated them as prisoners of war, and forced them to work in camps. Germans were sent to do dark and dangerous work in the mines of Polish Silesia, or eastern Ukraine, or Kazakhstan, or Siberia. Death rates among Germans were far higher than among Soviet citizens. At Camp 517 in Karelia, Germans died at five times the usual Gulag rates.[12]

About 600,000 Germans taken as prisoners of war or laborers at the end of the war would die. Perhaps 185,000 German civilians died in Soviet captivity during and after the war, and perhaps 30,000 more in Polish camps. About 363,000 German prisoners of war also perished in the Soviet camps (an 11.8 percent fatality rate, as compared to 57.5 percent for Soviet soldiers in German camps). Many more prisoners died on the way to the camps, or were shot after surrendering without being registered as prisoners of war.[13]

As so often, Stalin's crimes were enabled by Hitler's policies. In large measure, the German men were there to be seized, and the German women to be raped, because the Nazis failed to organize systematic evacuations. In the last few weeks of the war, Germans troops were racing west to surrender to the British or the Americans rather than to the Soviets; civilians often lacked such an option.

Hitler had presented the war as a matter of will, and thereby accentuated the tendency, always present in war, to deny defeat and therefore to worsen its consequences. He saw armed conflict as a test of the German race: "Germany will either be a world power, or there will be no Germany." His nationalism was always of a particular kind: he believed that the German nation was potentially great, but that it required the challenges of empire to purge itself of degeneracy. Thus Germans could be favored so long as a war was going on, and going well. If Germans disappointed Hitler by failing to cleanse themselves in the blood of their defeated enemies, then that was their fault. Hitler had showed them the way, but Germans had failed to follow. If Germans lost their war of salvation, there was no longer any reason why they should survive. For Hitler, any suffering that Germans might endure was a consequence of their own weakness: "If the German people are not prepared to stand up for their own preservation, fine. Let them perish."[14]

Hitler himself chose suicide. His were not the sort of pragmatic attitudes necessary to preserve the lives of civilians. The civilian authorities in eastern Germany, the Gauleiters, were dedicated Nazi party men, and among Hitler's most loyal followers. In three crucial provinces, the Gauleiters failed to organize evacuations. In East Prussia, the Gauleiter was Erich Koch, the same man who had been Reichskommissar for Ukraine. He had once said that he would have to shoot any Ukrainian who was worthy of eating at his table. Now, in January 1945, an army composed quite significantly of Ukrainians was bearing down on his German province, and he could not seem quite to believe it. In Pomerania, Franz Schwede-Coburg actually tried to halt the flow of German refugees. In Lower Silesia, Karl Hanke was concerned that flight would undermine his campaign to make of Breslau (today Wrocław) a fortress that could stop the Red Army. In fact, the Red Army surrounded Breslau so quickly that people were trapped. Because German civilians left too late, they died in far higher numbers than they might have. The Soviet navy sank 206 of the 790 ships used to evacuate Germans from the Baltic coast. One of these, the *Wilhelm Gustloff*, was recalled later by Günter Grass in his novel *Crabwalk*.[15]

Germans fleeing by land were often caught, quite literally, in the crossfire of the Red Army and the Wehrmacht. Over and over again, Soviet tank units crashed into columns of German civilians and their horse carts. Eva Jahntz recalled what happened then: "The few men were shot, the women raped, and the children beaten and separated from their mothers." Grass, who saw such a scene as a Waffen-SS soldier, "saw a women scream, but could not hear her scream."[16]

The new Poland was founded at the moment when flight became deportation. The end of hostilities brought organized ethnic cleansing to the new western lands of Poland, officially known as the "recovered territories." On 26 May 1945 the central committee of the Polish party resolved that all Germans on Polish territory were to be removed. By then, Germans were already coming back. They had fled the Red Army, but had no wish to lose all of their property and belongings, or to abandon their homeland. They also had no way of knowing that their return was pointless, that their homeland was to become Polish, and their homes to be given to Poles. By June 1945 perhaps a million of the six million or so German refugees had returned. The Polish communists decided to send the newly constituted army, now under their command, to "cleanse" these Germans from what they understood to be Polish territory.[17]

In summer 1945, the Polish communists were looking ahead nervously to the final peace settlement. If they could not keep the Germans west of the Oder-Neiße line, perhaps they would not be awarded these territories. They were also following the example set by democratic Czechoslovakia, just to the south. Its president, Edvard Beneš, had been wartime Europe's most articulate advocate of deporting Germans. He had told his citizens on 12 May that the German nation "had ceased to be human." The day before, the leader of the Czechoslovak communist party had spoken of postwar Czechoslovakia as "a republic of Czechs and Slovaks." The Czechoslovaks, whose German minority numbered about three million (a quarter of the population), had been marching their German citizens across the border since May. As many as thirty thousand Germans would be killed in these expulsions; some 5,558 Germans committed suicide in Czechoslovakia in 1945. Günter Grass, by then a prisoner of war in an American camp in Czechoslovakia, wondered if the GIs were there to guard him or to protect the Germans from the Czechs.[18]

The officers of the new Polish army told their troops to treat the German peasants as the enemy. The entire German nation was guilty, and not to be pitied. The commanding general issued instructions to "treat them as they treated us." It never came to that, but the conditions of the military deportations of 20 June–20 July 1945 reflected haste, indifference, and the primacy of high politics. The army deported people who lived closest to the Oder-Neiße line, to create the impression that these territories were ready for transfer to Poland. The army surrounded villages, gave people a few hours to pack, formed them into columns, and then marched them across the border. The army reported moving some 1.2 million people in this way, although that is likely a very considerable exaggeration; some people, in any event, were deported twice, since slipping back after the soldiers had gone was none too difficult.[19]

In all likelihood, these Polish efforts of summer 1945 made no difference to the final outcome. Although the British and the Americans had agreed between themselves that they should resist Stalin's plans for the Polish western frontier, they conceded the point at Potsdam in late July 1945. They accepted Stalin's proposed border for Poland, the Oder-Neiße line; the only condition, which Stalin probably understood as window dressing for Polish-American voters, was that the next Polish government be chosen in free elections. The three powers agreed that population transfers from Poland and Czechoslovakia (and Hungary) should be continued, but only after a pause necessary to ensure more humane conditions for the people resettled. Germans lands were under joint occupation, the Soviets in the northeast, the British in the west, and the Americans in the south. The Americans and British were concerned that further chaotic population movements would bring chaos to their occupation zones in Germany.[20]

After Potsdam, the Polish government sought precisely to create inhumane conditions for Germans in Poland, so that Germans would decide to leave. Stalin had told Gomułka that he "should create such conditions for the Germans that they will want to escape themselves." From July 1945, Polish authorities did just this, under the euphemistic guise of "voluntary repatriations." The policy of indirect expulsion was perhaps most flagrant in Silesia, where the regional governor forbade the use of German in public places, banned German schools, seized German property, and ordered German men to work in the mines. The approach was perhaps most guileless (or cynical) in the city of Olsztyn, formerly in East Prussia, where Germans were summoned "voluntarily" to go to Germany by the end of October 1945—and at the same time informed that "those who resist shall be directed to the camps."[21]

Polish prisons and temporary penal and labor camps were at this time full of Germans, who, along with all other prisoners, were treated very badly. The prisons and camps were placed under the jurisdiction of the communist-led Ministry of Public Security, rather than under the ministry of justice or internal affairs. At this time the Polish government was still a coalition; but it was dominated by the communists, who always made sure to control such offices as Public Security. The camp commanders, generally free of discipline from above, presided over general chaos and frequent murder. In the village of Nieszawa in north-central Poland, thirty-eight men, women, and children were thrown into the Vistula River; the men and women were shot first, the children were not. At the camp at Lubraniec, the commander danced on a German woman who was so badly beaten that she could not move. In this way, he exclaimed, "we lay the foundation for a new Poland."[22]

In some places the revenge was quite literal. At the camp at Łambinowice, Czesław Gęborski consciously modeled the regulations on those of the Germans (despite orders to the contrary) and openly proclaimed his desire for vengeance. On 4 October 1945 forty prisoners in Łambinowice were murdered; all in all, some 6,488 Germans died there in 1945 and 1946. Gęborski had been in prison under the Germans; other commanders of Polish camps had other reasons for revenge. Izydor Cedrowski, the commander at the camp at Potulice, was a Jewish Auschwitz survivor whose family had been shot by the Germans. Germans and others died of exposure, disease, and mistreatment in these camps by the hundreds each day. All in all, some two hundred thousand Germans labored in Polish camps, of whom a very high number, perhaps thirty thousand, died in 1945 or 1946.[23]

By the second half of 1945, Germans had good reason to depart Poland "voluntarily," though leaving proved to be just as dangerous as staying. Trains were now allocated for the transports, although these were freight trains, often with open cars. When the cars were not open, the Germans sometimes feared that they would be gassed. This, of course, never happened—though it does demonstrate that Germans knew that other people had very recently been led into enclosed spaces and asphyxiated. Indeed, in one of the places from which Germans were now expelled, at Stutthof, the Germans had used a railcar as a gas chamber.[24]

The trains moved very slowly, turning journeys that should have lasted hours into horrible odysseys. The Germans who boarded the trains were very often hungry or sick. They were allowed to take with them only what they could

carry on their backs. This was promptly stolen from them by bandits—or by
the Polish militia who were supposed to protect them. One reason why the
trains stopped so frequently was to allow bandits to rob people of what they
had left. In these situations, mortality on the trains was considerable, although
it should have been negligible. Germans had to bury their dead along the way,
at these anonymous stops, in the middle of nowhere, without markers or any
way of knowing just where to return. They had no one to look after their interests in Poland, and very often no one to greet them on the other side. About
six hundred thousand Germans reached Germany in this fashion in the second
half of 1945.[25]

The Allies agreed to a plan for the further deportations in November 1945,
and the British and the Soviets prepared themselves to greet and care for the
Germans who were to arrive in 1946. Because much of the death and disorder
was a result of the conditions of boarding and embarkation, the Soviets and the
British now sent representatives to monitor the deportations on the Polish side.
The expectation, largely fulfilled, was that more orderly transports would mean
less chaos in Germany. Over the course of 1946 about two million more Germans were dispatched by train to the British and the Soviet occupation zones
of Germany; another six hundred thousand or so followed in 1947. Although
conditions were far from humane, fatalities during these transports were much
lower, no more than a few thousand or, at most, a few tens of thousands.[26]

By the end of 1947 some 7.6 million Germans had left Poland, roughly half
of them as refugees fleeing the Red Army, roughly half as deportees. These proportions and these numbers can never be rendered with precision, as many
people fled, returned, and were deported; others were deported more than once.
Many people who had presented themselves as Germans during (or even before)
the war now claimed to be Poles, and so eluded the transports. (By this time,
the Polish government, more interested in labor than in ethnic purity, looked
favorably upon requests in ambiguous cases that people be regarded as Poles.
And by this time, many people who had earlier called themselves Poles were
presenting themselves as Germans, believing that Germany's economic future
was brighter than Poland's.) But the general balance is clear: the vast majority
of people who regarded themselves as Germans had left Poland by the end of
1947. In all of this flight and transport, from early 1945 to late 1947, perhaps
four hundred thousand Germans native to lands that were annexed by Poland

died: most of them in Soviet and Polish camps, and a second large group caught between armies or drowned at sea.[27]

The last weeks of the war itself, and the belated evacuations, were far more dangerous than the expulsions that followed the end of the war. In the final four months of the war, Germans suffered in one of the ways that other civilians had during the previous four years of war on the eastern front, during the advance and the retreat of the Wehrmacht. Millions of people had fled the German attack in 1941; millions more had been taken for labor between 1941 and 1944; still more were forced to evacuate by the retreating Wehrmacht in 1944. Far more Soviet and Polish citizens died after fleeing Germans than did Germans as a result of flight from Soviets. Although such displacements were not policies of deliberate murder (and have therefore received almost no attention in this study), flight, evacuation, and forced labor led, directly or indirectly, to the death of a few million Soviet and Polish citizens. (German policies of deliberate mass murder killed an *additional* ten million people.)[28]

The war had been fought in the name of the German race, but ended with unconcern for actual German civilians. Much responsibility for the deaths associated with flight and expulsion thus rested with the Nazi regime. German civilians knew enough about German policy during the war to know that they should flee, but their flight was not well organized by the German state. The behavior of many Soviet soldiers was certainly tolerated by the high command and expected by Stalin; the Red Army would not have been in Germany, however, had the Wehrmacht not invaded the Soviet Union. Stalin favored ethnic homogeneity, but this was an idea that Hitler's own policies made seem inevitable, and not only in Moscow. The expulsions themselves were a result of an international consensus of victors and victims.

———————

In the end, the expulsions were one more way that Stalin won Hitler's war. By taking so much of Germany on Poland's behalf, Stalin guaranteed that Poles would be beholden, whether they liked it or not, to Soviet military power. Who but the Red Army could be counted upon to defend such a westerly Polish border from a resurgent Germany at some later point?[29]

In these years, Poland was a nation in movement. Even as the Germans had to move west to a more westerly Germany, Poles had to move west to a more westerly Poland. As Germans were cleansed from communist Poland, Poles were cleansed from the Soviet Union. Despite the preferences of all Polish political parties, including the communists, the Soviet Union once again annexed the lands that had been eastern Poland. The people who were then "repatriated" (as the Stalinist euphemism had it) to Poland had no reason to love communism or Stalin. Yet they were indeed bound to the communist system. Communists could take land but also grant it, expel people but also give them refuge. People who had both lost old homes and gained new ones were utterly dependent upon whomever could defend them. This could only be the Polish communists, who could promise that the Red Army would protect Poland's gains. Communism had little to offer Poland as an ideology, and was never very popular. But Stalin's ethnic geopolitics took the place of the class struggle, creating a durable basis of support, if not legitimacy, for the new regime.[30]

The Americans and the British had supported expulsions at Potsdam, in the expectation of democratic elections in Poland. These never took place. Instead the first postwar government, dominated by communists, intimidated and arrested opponents. The Americans then began to see the Oder-Neiße line as an issue that could be used against the Soviet Union. When the American secretary of state questioned its permanence in September 1946, he was increasing American and weakening Soviet influence in Germany, among Germans unreconciled to the loss of territory and the expulsions. But he was also helping to consolidate the Soviet position in Poland. The Polish regime held parliamentary elections in January 1947, but falsified the results. The Americans and the British then watched their own chances for influence in Poland disappear. Stanisław Mikołajczyk, the prime minister of Poland's government in exile, had returned to contest the elections as the head of a peasant party. Now he had to escape.[31]

The Polish regime could make the powerful claim that only its Soviet ally could protect the new western frontier from the Germans, whom the Americans were only encouraging. By 1947, Poles themselves, regardless of what they thought about the communists, could hardly contemplate losing the "the recovered territories." As Gomułka had correctly anticipated, the expulsion of the Germans would "bind the nation to the system." The gifted communist ideologist Jakub Berman believed that communists should make the most of their ethnic cleansing. The "recovered territories" gave many Poles who had suffered during the war a better house or a bigger farm. It allowed for land reform, the first step in any communist takeover. Perhaps most of all, it gave a million Polish migrants from eastern Poland (annexed by the USSR) a place to go. Precisely because Poland had lost so much in the east, the west was all the more precious.[32]

The ethnic cleansing of Germans from newly Polish lands came at the end of the war. It was, however, the second half of a Soviet policy that had actually begun much earlier, during the war itself, in the prewar lands of eastern Poland, east of the Molotov-Ribbentrop line. Just as Germans had to leave lands that were no longer German, Poles had to leave lands that were no longer Polish. Although Poland was technically a victor in the war, it lost almost half (forty-seven percent) of its prewar territory to the Soviet Union. After the war, Poles (and Polish Jews) were no longer welcome in what became the western parts of the Soviet Belarusian and Soviet Ukrainian republics and the Vilnius region of the Soviet Lithuanian republic.[33]

The alteration of the population structure of eastern Poland to the detriment of Poles and Jews began earlier, during the war itself. The Soviets had deported hundreds of thousands of people during their first occupation, in 1940 and in 1941. A disproportionate number of these had been Poles. Many made their way from the Gulag through Iran and Palestine to fight with the Allies on the western front, and sometimes they reached Poland at war's end; but they almost never made it back to their homes. The Germans had killed about 1.3 million Jews in the former eastern Poland in 1941 and 1942, with the help of local policemen. Some of these Ukrainian policemen helped to form a Ukrainian partisan army in 1943, which under the leadership of Ukrainian nationalists cleansed the former southwest Poland—which it saw as western Ukraine—of remaining Poles. The OUN-Bandera, the nationalist organization that led the partisan army, had long pledged to rid Ukraine of its national minorities. Its capacity to kill Poles depended upon German training, and its determination to kill Poles had much to do with its desire to clear the terrain of purported enemies before a final confrontation with the Red Army. The UPA, as the partisan army was known, murdered tens of thousands of Poles, and provoked reprisals from Poles upon Ukrainian civilians.[34]

Although the UPA was a determined (perhaps the most determined) opponent of communism, the ethnic conflict that it started only strengthened Stalin's

empire. What Ukrainian nationalists had started, Stalin would conclude. He continued the removal of Poles, attaching the contested territories to his Soviet Ukraine. Polish communists signed agreements in September 1944 providing for population exchanges between Poland and Soviet Ukraine (as well as Soviet Belarus and Soviet Lithuania). In Soviet Ukraine, Poles remembered Soviet rule from the very recent past, and faced now a continuing threat from Ukrainian nationalists. They thus had every reason to take part in these "repatriations." Some 780,000 Poles were shipped to communist Poland, within its new frontiers, along with a comparable number from Soviet Belarus and Soviet Lithuania. Some 1,517,983 people had left the Soviet Union as Poles by the middle of 1946, along with a few hundred thousand who did not register for the official transports. About a hundred thousand of these people were Jewish: Soviet policy was to remove both ethnic Poles and ethnic Jews from the former eastern Poland, but to keep Belarusians, Ukrainians, and Lithuanians. About a million Polish citizens were resettled in what had been eastern Germany, now the "recovered territories" of western Poland. Meanwhile, about 483,099 Ukrainians were dispatched from communist Poland to Soviet Ukraine in 1944–1946, most of them by force.[35]

Even as the Soviet regime was dispatching people across borders, it was also sending its own citizens to camps and special settlements. Most of the new Gulag prisoners were people from the lands that Stalin had taken in 1939 with German consent and then took again in 1945. Between 1944 and 1946, for example, 182,543 Ukrainians were deported from Soviet Ukraine to the Gulag: not for committing a particular crime, not even for being Ukrainian nationalists, but for being related to or acquainted with Ukrainian nationalists. At about the same time, in 1946 and 1947, the Soviets sentenced 148,079 Red Army veterans to the Gulag for collaboration with the Germans. There were never more Soviet citizens in the Gulag than in the years after the war; indeed, the number of Soviet citizens in the camps and special settlements increased every year from 1945 until Stalin's death.[36]

Communist Poland had no Gulag, but in 1947 its rulers did propose a "final solution" to their "Ukrainian problem": by the dispersion of remaining Ukrainians far from home but within the boundaries of Poland. Between April and July 1947, the Polish regime itself carried out one more operation against Ukrainians on its territory, under the cryptonym "Vistula." Some 140,660 Ukrainians, or people identified as such, were resettled by force from the south and southeast of the country to the west and north, to the "recovered territories" that until recently had been German. Operation Vistula was supposed to force Ukrainians in Poland, or at least their children, to assimilate into Polish culture. At the same time, Polish forces defeated the units of the Ukrainian partisan army, the UPA, on Polish soil. Ukrainian nationalist fighters in Poland had been given a new lease on life as defenders of people who did not wish to be deported. But once almost all Ukrainians had in fact been deported, the UPA's position in Poland was untenable. Some UPA fighters fled to the West, others to the Soviet Union to continue the fight.[37]

Operation Vistula, originally codenamed Operation East, was undertaken entirely by Polish forces, with little Soviet assistance inside Poland. But the crucial people involved in planning the operation were Soviet clients, and it was certainly coordinated with Moscow. It took place at the same time as a number of Soviet operations, on adjacent Soviet territories, which bore similar cryptonyms. The most obviously related was Operation West, which took place on adjoining territories of Soviet Ukraine. As Operation Vistula was brought to a close, the Soviets ordered the deportation of Ukrainians from western Ukraine to Siberia and central Asia. In a few days in October 1947, some 76,192 Ukrainians were transported to the Gulag. In western Ukraine, Soviet special forces were engaged with the UPA in a fantastically bloody conflict. Both sides committed atrocities, including the public display of the mutilated corpses of the enemy or his supposed collaborators. But in the end the technology of deportation gave the Soviets a decided advantage. The Gulag kept growing.[38]

After this success at the Ukrainian-Polish border, the Soviets turned to other European borderlands, and applied similar means in similar operations. In Operation Spring in May 1948, some 49,331 Lithuanians were deported. The following March, Operation Priboi saw the removal of 31,917 more people from Lithuania, as well as 42,149 from Latvia and 20,173 from Estonia. All in all, between 1941 and 1949, Stalin deported some two hundred thousand people from the three small Baltic States. Like all of the thrice-occupied (Soviet, then German, then Soviet) lands east of the Molotov-Ribbentrop line, the Baltic States entered the USSR in 1945 having lost much of their elite, and indeed a significant share of the total population.[39]

Under Stalin, the Soviet Union had evolved, slowly and haltingly, from a revolutionary Marxist state into a large, multinational empire with a Marxist covering ideology and traditional security concerns about borders and minorities. Because Stalin inherited, maintained, and mastered the security apparatus of the revolutionary years, these anxieties could be released in bursts of national killing in 1937–1938 and 1940, and in bouts of national deportation that began in 1930 and continued throughout Stalin's lifetime. The deportations of the war continued a certain evolution in Soviet deportation policy: away from the traditional resettlements of individuals thought to represent enemy classes, and toward an ethnic cleansing that matched populations to borders.

In the prewar period, the deportations to the Gulag were always meant to serve two purposes: the growth of the Soviet economy and the correction of the Soviet population. In the 1930s, as the Soviets began to deport large numbers of people on ethnic grounds, the goal was to move national minorities away from sensitive border regions toward the interior. These national deportations could hardly be seen as a specific punishment of individuals, but they were still premised on the assumption that those deported could be better assimilated into Soviet society when they were separated from their homes and homelands. The national actions of the Great Terror killed a quarter of a million people in 1937 and 1938, but also dispatched hundreds of thousands of people to Siberia and Kazakhstan, where they were expected to work for the state and reform themselves. Even the deportations of 1940–1941, from annexed Polish, Baltic, and Romanian territories, can be seen in Soviet terms as a class war. Men of elite families were killed at Katyn and other sites, and their wives, children, and parents left to the mercy of the Kazakh steppe. There they would integrate with Soviet society, or they would die.

During the war, Stalin undertook punitive actions that targeted national minorities for their association with Nazi Germany. Some nine hundred thousand Soviet Germans and about eighty-nine thousand Finns were deported in 1941 and 1942. As the Red Army moved forward after the victory at Stalingrad in early 1943, Stalin's security chief Lavrenty Beria recommended the deportation of whole peoples accused of collaborating with the Germans. For the most part, these were the Muslim nations of the Caucasus and Crimea.[40]

As Soviet troops retook the Caucasus, Stalin and Beria put the machine into action. On a single day, 19 November 1943, the Soviets deported the entire Karachai population, some 69,267 people, to Soviet Kazakhstan and Kyrgyzstan. Over the course of two days, 28–29 December 1943, the Soviets dispatched 91,919 Kalmyks to Siberia. Beria went to Grozny personally to supervise the deportations of the Chechen and Ingush peoples on 20 February 1944. Leading about 120,000 special forces, he rounded up and expelled 478,479 people in just over a week. He had at his disposal American Studebaker trucks, supplied during the war. Because no Chechens or Ingush were to be left behind, people who could not be moved were shot. Villages were burned to the ground everywhere; in some places, barns full of people were burned as well. Over the course of two days, 8–9 March 1944, the Soviets removed the Balkar population, 37,107 people, to Kazakhstan. In April 1944, right after the Red Army reached the Crimea, Beria proposed and Stalin agreed that the entire Crimean Tatar population be resettled. Over the course of three days, 18–20 March 1944, 180,014 people were deported, most of them to Uzbekistan. Later in 1944, Beria had the Meshketian Turks, some 91,095 people, deported from Soviet Georgia.[41]

Against this backdrop of essentially continuous national purges, Stalin's decision to cleanse the Soviet-Polish border seems like an unsurprising development of a general policy. From a Soviet perspective, Ukrainian, Baltic, or Polish partisans were simply more bandits causing trouble along the periphery, to be dealt with by overwhelming force and deportations. There was, however, an important difference. All of the kulaks and members of national minorities deported in the 1930s found themselves far from home, but still within the USSR. The same was true of the Crimean and Caucasian and Baltic populations deported during and shortly after the war. Yet in September 1944, Stalin opted to move Poles (and Polish Jews), Ukrainians, and Belarusians back and forth across a *state* border in order to create ethnic homogeneity. The same logic was applied, on a far greater scale, to the Germans in Poland.

Working in parallel, and sometimes together, the Soviet and communist Polish regimes achieved a curious feat between 1944 and 1947: they removed the ethnic minorities, on both sides of the Soviet-Polish border, that had made the border regions mixed; and at the very same time, they removed the ethnic nationalists who had fought the hardest for precisely that kind of purity. Communists had taken up the program of their enemies. Soviet rule had become ethnic cleansing—cleansed of the ethnic cleansers.

The territory of postwar Poland was the geographical center of Stalin's campaign of postwar ethnic cleansing. In that campaign, more Germans lost their homes than any other group. Some 7.6 million Germans had left Poland by the end of 1947, and another three million or so were deported from democratic Czechoslovakia. About nine hundred thousand Volga Germans were deported within the Soviet Union during the war. The number of Germans who lost their homes during and after the war exceeded twelve million.

Enormous as this figure was, it did not constitute a majority of the forced displacements during and after the war. Two million or so non-Germans were deported by Soviet (or communist Polish) authorities in the same postwar period. Another eight million people, most of them forced laborers taken by the Germans, were returned to the Soviet Union at the same time. (Since many if not most of them would have preferred not to return, they could be counted twice.) In the Soviet Union and Poland, more than twelve million Ukrainians, Poles, Belarusians, and others fled or were moved during the war or in its aftermath. This does not include the ten million or so people who were deliberately killed by the Germans, most of whom were displaced in one way or another before they were murdered.[42]

The flight and deportation of the Germans, though not a policy of deliberate mass killing, constituted the major incident of postwar ethnic cleansing. In all of the civil conflict, flight, deportation, and resettlement provoked or caused by the return of the Red Army between 1943 and 1947, some 700,000 Germans died, as did at least 150,000 Poles and perhaps 250,000 Ukrainians. At a minimum, another 300,000 Soviet citizens died during or shortly after the Soviet deportations from the Caucasus, Crimea, Moldova, and the Baltic States. If the struggles of Lithuanian, Latvian, and Estonian nationalists against the reimposition of Soviet power are regarded as resistance to deportations, which in some measure they were, another hundred thousand or so people would have to be added to the total dead associated with ethnic cleansing.[43]

In relative terms, the percentage of Germans moved as a part of the total population of Germans was much inferior to that of the Caucasian and Crimean peoples, who were deported down to the last person. The percentage of Germans who moved or were moved at the end of the war was greater than that of Poles, Belarusians, Ukrainians, and Balts. But if the population movements caused by the Germans during the war are added to those caused by the Soviet occupation at war's end, this difference disappears. Over the period 1939–1947, Poles, Ukrainians, Belarusians, and Balts were about as likely (some a bit more, some a bit less) to have been forcibly moved as Germans. Whereas all of the other peoples in question faced hostile German and Soviet policies, the Germans (with some exceptions) experienced oppression only from the Soviet side.

In the postwar period, Germans were about as likely to lose their lives as Poles, the other group that was mainly sent west to a national homeland. Germans and Poles were much less likely to die than Ukrainians, Romanians, Balts, and the Caucasian and Crimean peoples. Fewer than one in ten Germans and Poles died during or as a direct result of flight, exile, or deportation; among Balts and Soviet citizens, the rate was more like one in five. As a general rule, the further east the deportation, and the more directly Soviet power was involved, the more deadly the outcome. This is evident in the case of the Germans themselves: the tremendous majority of Germans who fled Poland and Czechoslovakia survived, whereas a large proportion of those transported east within or to the Soviet Union died.

It was better to be sent west than east, and better to be sent to an awaiting homeland than to a distant and alien Soviet republic. It was also better to land in developed (even if bombed and war-torn) Germany than in Soviet wastelands that deportees were supposed to develop themselves. It was better to be received by British and American authorities in occupation zones than by the local NKVD in Kazakhstan or Siberia.

Rather quickly, within about two years after the end of the war, Stalin had made his new Poland and his new frontiers, and moved peoples to match them. By 1947, it might have seemed that the war was finally over, and that the Soviet Union had well and truly won a military victory over the Germans and their allies and a political victory over opponents of communism in eastern Europe.

Poles, always a troublesome group, had been dispatched from the Soviet Union to a new communist Poland, bound now to the Soviet Union as the anchor of a new communist empire. Poland, it might have seemed, had been subdued: twice invaded, twice subject to deportations and killings, altered in its borders and demography, ruled by a party dependent on Moscow. Germany had been utterly defeated and humiliated. Its territories as of 1938 were divided into multiple occupation zones, and would find their way into five different sovereign states: the Federal Republic of Germany (West Germany), the German Democratic Republic (East Germany), Austria, Poland, and the USSR (at Kaliningrad). Japan had been utterly defeated by the Americans, its cities firebombed or, at the very end, destroyed by nuclear weapons. It was no longer a power in continental Asia. Stalin's traditional threats had been removed. The prewar nightmare of a Japanese-Polish-German encirclement was passé.

More Soviet citizens had died in the Second World War than any people in any war in recorded history. At home, Soviet ideologists had taken advantage of the suffering to justify Stalinist rule: as the necessary price of victory in what was called "the Great Patriotic War." The patria in question was Russia as well as the Soviet Union; Stalin himself famously raised a toast to "the great Russian

**WESTERN SOVIET UNION
AND EASTERN EUROPE**
c. 1945

nation" just after the war's end, in May 1945. Russians, he maintained, had won the war. To be sure, about half the population of the Soviet Union was Russian, and so in a numerical sense Russians had played a greater part in the victory than any other people. Yet Stalin's idea contained a purposeful confusion: the war on Soviet territory was fought and won chiefly in Soviet Belarus and in Soviet Ukraine, rather than in Soviet Russia. More Jewish, Belarusian, and Ukrainian civilians had been killed than Russians. Because the Red Army took such horrible losses, its ranks were filled by local Belarusian and Ukrainian conscripts at both the beginning and the end of the war. The deported Caucasian and Crimean peoples, for that matter, had seen a higher percentage of their young people die in the Red Army than had the Russians. Jewish soldiers had been more likely to be decorated for valor than Russian soldiers.

The Jewish tragedy, in particular, could not be enclosed within the Soviet experience, and was thus a threat to postwar Soviet mythmaking. About 5.7 million Jewish civilians had been murdered by the Germans and Romanians, of whom some 2.6 million were Soviet citizens in 1941. This meant not only that more Jewish civilians were murdered in absolute terms than members of any other Soviet nationality. It also meant that more than half of the cataclysm took place beyond the postwar boundaries of the Soviet Union. From a Stalinist perspective, even the experience of the mass murder of one's peoples was a worrying example of exposure to the outside world. In 1939–1941, when the Soviet Union had annexed Poland and the Germans had not yet invaded the USSR, Soviet Jews mingled with Polish Jews, who reminded them of religious and linguistic traditions, of the world of their grandparents. Soviet and Polish Jews, during that brief but important moment, lived together. Then, after the German invasion, they died together. Precisely because extermination was a fate common to Jews across borders, its recollection could not be reduced to that of an element in the Great Patriotic War.

It was precisely exposure to the West that concerned Stalin, even as his system was replicated in several states of eastern and central Europe. In the interwar period, Soviet citizens really had believed that they were better off than the masses suffering under capitalist exploitation in the West. Now America had emerged from the Second World War as an unrivalled economic power. In 1947 it offered economic aid, in the form of the Marshall Plan, to European countries willing to cooperate with one another on elementary matters of trade and financial policy. Stalin could reject Marshall aid and force his clients to reject it as well, but he could not banish the knowledge that Soviet citizens had gained during the war. Every returning Soviet soldier and forced laborer knew that standards of living in the rest of Europe, even in relatively poor countries such as Romania and Poland, were far higher than in the Soviet Union. Ukrainians returned to a country where famine was raging again. Perhaps a million people starved to death in the two years after the war. It was western Ukraine, with a private agricultural sector that the Soviets had not yet had time to collectivize, that saved the rest of Soviet Ukraine from even greater suffering.[44]

Russians were a safer basis for a Stalinist legend of the war. The battles for Moscow and Stalingrad were victories. Russians were the largest nation, theirs was the dominant language and culture, and their republic was further away from the West, both in its Nazi and in its emerging American incarnations. Russia is vast: the Germans never even aimed to colonize more than its western fifth, and never conquered more than its western tenth. Soviet Russia had not suffered total occupation for months and years, as had the Baltics, Belarus, or Ukraine. Everyone who remained in Soviet Belarus and Soviet Ukraine experienced German occupation; the vast majority of the inhabitants of Soviet Russia did not. Soviet Russia was much less marked by the Holocaust than Soviet Ukraine or Soviet Belarus, simply because the Germans arrived later and were able to kill fewer Jews (about sixty thousand, or about one percent of the Holocaust). In this way, too, Soviet Russia was more distant from the experience of the war.

Once the war was over, the task was to insulate the Russian nation, and of course all of the other nations, from cultural infection. One of the most dangerous intellectual plagues would be interpretations of the war that differed from Stalin's own.

The victory of Soviet-style communism in eastern Europe gave rise to as much anxiety as triumphalism. The political victories were certainly impressive: communists in Albania, Bulgaria, Hungary, Poland, Romania, and Yugoslavia dominated their countries by 1947, thanks to Soviet help but also thanks to their own training, ruthlessness, and ingenuity. Communists proved rather good at mobilizing human resources for the immediate problems of postwar reconstruction, as for example in Warsaw.

But how long could the Soviet-economic model of rapid industrialization produce growth in countries that were more industrial than the Soviet Union had been at the time of the first Five-Year Plan, and whose citizens expected higher standards of living? How long could east European societies accept that communism was national liberation, when their communist leaders were obviously beholden to a foreign power, the Soviet Union? How could Moscow sustain the image of the West as a constant enemy, when the United States seemed to represent both prosperity and freedom? Stalin needed his appointed east European leaders to follow his wishes, exploit nationalism, and isolate their peoples from the West, which was a very difficult combination to achieve.

It was the task of Andrei Zhdanov, Stalin's new propaganda chief and favorite, to square all of these circles. Zhdanov was to theorize the inevitable victory of the Soviet Union in the postwar world, and protect Russian purity in the meantime. In August 1946 the Soviet communist party had passed a resolution condemning Western influence on Soviet culture. The pollution might flow from western Europe, or America, but also through cultures that crossed boundaries, such as the Jewish or the Ukrainian or the Polish. Zhdanov also had to account for the new rivalry between the Soviet Union and the United States, in a way that the east European leaders could understand and apply in their own countries.

In September 1947, the leaders of Europe's communist parties gathered in Poland to hear Zhdanov's new line. Meeting in Szklarska Poręba, a formerly German resort town until very recently known as Schreiberhau, they were told that their parties would be taking part in a "Communist Informational Bureau," or "Cominform." It would be the means by which Moscow would communicate the line and coordinate their policies. The assembled communist leaders learned that the world was divided into "two camps," progressive and reactionary, with the Soviet Union destined to lead the new "people's democracies" of eastern Europe, and the United States doomed to inherit all the flaws of degenerate capitalism, on display so recently in Nazi Germany. The unalterable laws of history guaranteed the final victory of the forces of progress.[45]

Communists needed only to play their allotted role in the progressive camp, led of course by the Soviet Union, and avoid the temptation to take any separate national road to socialism. So all was well.

Then Zhdanov suffered a heart attack, the first of several. Somehow all was not well.

CHAPTER 11

STALINIST ANTI-SEMITISM

In January 1948, Stalin was killing a Jew. Solomon Mikhoels, the chairman of the Jewish Anti-Fascist Committee and the director of the Moscow Yiddish Theater, had been sent to Minsk to judge a play for the Stalin Prize. Once arrived, he was invited to the country house of the head of the Soviet Belarusian state police, Lavrenty Tsanava, who had him murdered, along with an inconvenient witness. Mikhoels's body, crushed by a truck, was left on a quiet street.

Minsk had seen the ruthless German mass murder of Jews only a few years before. The irony of the Soviets killing one more Soviet Jew in Minsk would not have been lost on Tsanava, a policeman-cum-historian. He was finishing a history of the Belarusian partisan movement, which ignored the special plight and struggle of the Jews under German occupation. A Soviet history of Jewish partisans had been written, but would be suppressed. The Jews had suffered more than anyone else in Minsk during the war; it seemed that liberation by the Soviets had not brought the suffering of Soviet Jews to an end. It also seemed that the history of the Holocaust in the USSR would remain unwritten.[1]

Mikhoels had stood for issues that Stalin wanted to avoid. He was personally acquainted with people of Jewish origin in Stalin's immediate milieu, such as the politburo member Lazar Kaganovich and the wives of politburo members Viacheslav Molotov and Kliment Voroshilov. What was worse, Mikhoels had sought to reach Stalin in order to communicate with him about the fate of the Jews during the war. Like Vasily Grossman, Mikhoels had been a member of the Soviet Union's official Jewish Anti-Fascist Committee during the war.

Mikhoels had worked, at Stalin's instructions, to bring the plight of Soviet Jews to the attention of the world—in order to raise money for the Soviet war effort. After the war, Mikhoels found himself unable to let the mass murder of the Jews pass into historical oblivion, and unwilling to submerge the special suffering of the Jews into that of Soviet peoples generally. In September 1945 he had brought ashes from Babi Yar in a crystal vase to a lecture in Kiev, and had continued in the years after the war to speak openly of the death pits. Mikhoels also petitioned Stalin's propaganda chief Andrei Zhdanov in 1947 to allow the publication of the *Black Book of Soviet Jewry*, a collection of documents and testimonies about the mass killing edited by Grossman, Ilya Ehrenburg, and others. This was in vain. The Zhdanov era in Soviet culture could not endorse a Jewish history of the war. In the postwar Soviet Union, memorial obelisks could not have Stars of David, only five-pointed red stars. In the western Soviet Union, in the lands the Soviets annexed during and again after the war, in the lands where some 1.6 million Jews were killed, monuments to Lenin were raised on pedestals built from Jewish tombstones. The synagogue where the Kovel Jews had left their final messages was being used to store grain.[2]

Svetlana Allilueva, Stalin's daughter, overheard her father arranging the cover story for the murder with Tsanava: "car accident." Mikhoels was a person of some stature in Soviet culture, and his political campaigning was unwelcome. Yet Stalin's hostility toward Mikhoels as a Jew probably had as much to do with patrimony as it did with politics. Stalin's son Iakov, who died in German captivity, had married a Jew. Svetlana's first love had been a Jewish actor, whom Stalin called a British spy and sent to the Gulag. Svetlana's first husband was also Jewish; Stalin called him stingy and cowardly, and forced her to divorce him so that she could marry the son of Zhdanov, Stalin's purifier of Soviet culture. The match smacked of the founding of a royal family, one that was less Jewish than Svetlana's own affections. Stalin had always had close collaborators who were Jewish, most notably Kaganovich. Yet now, as he neared seventy years of age, and as concerns about succession must have been growing in his mind, his own attitude about Jews seemed to be shifting.[3]

After Mikhoels was dead, the Soviet political police, now under the name Ministry of State Security, retroactively provided the reason why the killing was in the Soviet interest: Jewish nationalism. Viktor Abakumov, head of the Ministry (or MGB), concluded in March 1948 that Mikhoels was a Jewish nationalist who had fallen in with dangerous Americans. By Soviet standards, this was an easy enough case to make. Mikhoels had been instructed by the Soviet leadership, as a member of the Jewish Anti-Fascist Committee during the war, to appeal to the national sentiments of Jews. He had traveled in 1943 to the United States to raise money, and there he had made sympathetic remarks about Zionism. By sheer accident, his airplane rested for a few hours on a runway in Palestine, where by his own account he kissed the air of the Holy Land. In February 1944, Mikhoels had joined a campaign to make of the Crimean Peninsula, cleared by the Soviets of supposed Muslim enemies after 1943, a "Jewish socialist republic." Crimea, on the Black Sea, was a maritime border region of the Soviet Union. The idea that it might serve as a Soviet Jewish homeland had been raised several times, and was supported by some prominent American Jews. Stalin preferred the Soviet solution, Birobidzhan, the Jewish autonomous region deep in the Soviet Far East.[4]

Given the centrality of the Second World War to the experience of all east Europeans, in the USSR and in the new satellite states, everyone in the new communist Europe would have to understand that the Russian nation had struggled and suffered like no other. Russians would have to be the greatest victors and the greatest victims, now and forever. The Russian heartland, perhaps, could be protected from the dangerous West: by the other Soviet republics, and by the new satellite states of eastern Europe. The contradiction here was obvious: those peoples who were forming the buffer had the least reason to accept the Stalinist claim about Russian martyrdom and purity. The case would be a particularly hard one to make in places such as Estonia, Latvia, and Lithuania, where the Second World War had begun and ended with a Soviet occupation. It would be none too simple in western Ukraine, where nationalist partisans fought the Soviets for years after the war. Poles were unlikely to forget that the Second World War had begun with allied German and Soviet armies invading Poland.

The logical difficulties would be all the greater among Jews. Since the Germans had killed Soviet Jews, then Polish Jews, and then other European Jews, the Holocaust could hardly be contained in any Soviet history of the war—least of all one that moved the center of gravity of suffering east to Russia where relatively few Jews died. It was one thing for Jews to regard the return of Soviet power as liberation, which most did, but quite another for them to recognize that other Soviet citizens had suffered more than they. Jews understood the Red Army as a liberating force *precisely because* Nazi policy had been to exterminate them. Yet this sense of gratitude, because of its special sources, did not convert automatically into a political legend about a Great Fatherland War and Russia. Jews, after all, had also fought in the Red Army, and had been more likely to have been decorated for bravery than Soviet citizens generally.[5]

The number of Jews killed by the Germans in the Soviet Union was a state secret. The Germans killed about a million native Soviet Jews, plus about 1.6 million more Polish, Lithuanian, and Latvian Jews brought into the USSR by the Soviet annexations of 1939 and 1940. The Romanians also killed Jews chiefly on territories that after the war were within the boundaries of the Soviet Union. These numbers were of an obvious sensitivity, since they revealed that, even by comparison with the dreadful suffering of other Soviet peoples, the Jews had suffered a very special fate. Jews were less than two percent of the population and Russians more than half; the Germans had murdered more Jewish civilians than Russian civilians in the occupied Soviet Union. Jews were in a category of their own, even by comparison with the Slavic peoples who had suffered more than the Russians, such as Ukrainians and Belarusians and Poles. The Soviet leadership knew this, and so did Soviet citizens who lived in the lands that the Germans had occupied. But the Holocaust could never become part of the Soviet history of the war.[6]

These high figures of murdered Jews also raised the troubling question of just how the Germans had managed to kill so many civilians in such a short time in the occupied Soviet Union. They had help from Soviet citizens. As everyone with experience of the war knew, the German armies were enormous, but the German occupying forces in the rear were sparse. German civilian authorities and police lacked the numbers to govern the western Soviet Union in any recognizable fashion, let alone to carry out a thorough policy of mass murder. Local officials continued to do their jobs under their new masters, local young men volunteered for the police, and in the ghettos some Jews took on the task of policing the rest. The shootings east of the Molotov-Ribbentrop line had implicated, in one way or another, hundreds of thousands of Soviet citizens. (For that matter, much of the crucial work at the death facilities west of the Molotov-Ribbentrop line in occupied Poland had been performed by Soviet citizens. It was unmentionable that Soviet citizens had staffed Treblinka, Sobibór, and Bełżec.) That the Germans needed collaborators, and found them, is not surprising. But collaboration undermined the myth of a united Soviet population defending the honor of the fatherland by resisting the hated fascist invader. Its prevalence was one more reason that the mass murder of the Jews was to be forgotten.

During the war, the Soviets and their allies had been in general agreement that the war was not to be understood as a war of the liberation of Jews. From different perspectives, the Soviet, Polish, American, and British leaderships all believed that Jewish suffering was best understood as one aspect of a generally wicked German occupation. Though Allied leaders were quite aware of the course of the Holocaust, none treated it as a reason to make war on Nazi Germany, or to turn much special attention to the suffering of Jews. The Jewish issue was generally avoided in propaganda. When Stalin, Churchill, and Roosevelt issued a "Declaration Concerning Atrocities" in Moscow in October 1943, they mentioned, among the Nazi crimes, "the wholesale shooting of Polish officers," which was a reference to Katyn, actually a Soviet crime; and "the execution of French, Dutch, Belgian or Norwegian hostages" and "Cretan peasants"—but not Jews. The "peoples" of Poland and the Soviet Union were mentioned, but the Jewish minority in each country was not named. By the time that summary of atrocities was published, over five million Jews had been shot or gassed because they were Jews.[7]

In its more enlightened form, this reticence about racial murder reflected a principled hesitation to endorse Hitler's racist understanding of the world. The Jews were not citizens of any one country, went the reasoning, and thus to group them together, went the fear, was to acknowledge their unity as a race, and to accept Hitler's racial view of the world. In its less enlightened form, this view was a concession to popular anti-Semitism—very much present in the Soviet Union, Poland, Britain, and the United States. For London and Washington, this tension was resolved with victory in the war in 1945. The Americans and the British liberated no part of Europe that had a very significant Jewish population before the war, and saw none of the German death facilities. The politics of postwar economic, political, and military cooperation in western Europe had relatively little to do with the Jewish question.

The territory of Stalin's enlarged state included most of the German killing fields, and that of his postwar empire (including communist Poland) the sites of all of the German death factories. Stalin and his politburo had to confront, after the war, continued resistance to the reimposition of Soviet power, in ways that made the wartime fate of the Jews unavoidable as a matter of ideology and politics. Postwar resistance in the western Soviet Union was a continuation of the war in two senses: these were the lands that the Soviets had won by conquest in the first place, and the lands where people had taken up arms in large numbers to fight them. In the Baltics and Ukraine and Poland, some partisans were openly anti-Semitic, and continued to use the Nazi tactic of associating Soviet power with Jewry.

In this situation, the Soviets had every political incentive to continue to distance themselves and their state from Jewish suffering, and indeed to make special efforts to ensure that anti-Semites did not associate the return of Soviet power with the return of Jews. In Lithuania, once again incorporated into the Soviet Union, the general secretary of the local branch of the Soviet communist party counted the Jews killed in the Holocaust as "sons of the nation," Lithuanians who died as martyrs for communism. Nikita Khrushchev, politburo member and general secretary of the party in Ukraine, went even further. He was in charge of the struggle to defeat Ukrainian nationalists in what had been southeastern Poland, a place that before the war had been densely settled with Jews and Poles. The Germans had killed the Jews, and the Soviets had deported the Poles. Khrushchev wanted Ukrainians to thank the Soviet Union for the "unification" of their country at the expense of Poland and for the "cleansing" of Polish landlords. Knowing that the nationalists wanted ethnic purity, he did not want Soviet power to stand for anything else.[8]

Sensitive as he was to the mood of the population, Stalin sought a way to present the war that would flatter the Russians while marginalizing the Jews (and, for that matter, every other people of the Soviet Union). The whole Soviet idea of the Great Patriotic War was premised on the view that the war began in 1941, when Germany invaded the USSR, not in 1939, when Germany and the Soviet Union together invaded Poland. In other words, in the official story, the territories absorbed as a result of Soviet aggression in 1939 had to be considered as somehow always having been Soviet, rather than as the booty of a war that Stalin had helped Hitler to begin. Otherwise the Soviet Union would figure as one of the two powers that started the war, as one of the aggressors, which was obviously unacceptable.

No Soviet account of the war could note one of its central facts: German and Soviet occupation together was worse than German occupation alone. The populations east of the Molotov-Ribbentrop line, subject to one German and two Soviet occupations, suffered more than those of any other region of Europe.

From a Soviet perspective, all of the deaths in that zone could simply be lumped together with Soviet losses, even though the people in question had been Soviet citizens for only a matter of months when they died, and even though many of them were killed by the NKVD rather than the SS. In this way, Polish, Romanian, Lithuanian, Belarusian, and Ukrainian deaths, sometimes caused by the Soviet rather than the German forces, served to make the tragedy of the Soviet Union (or even, to the inattentive, of Russia) seem all the greater.

The vast losses suffered by Soviet Jews were mostly the deaths of Jews in lands just invaded by the Soviet Union. These Jews were citizens of Poland, Romania, and the Baltic States, brought under Soviet control by force only twenty-one months before the German invasion in the case of Poland, and only twelve months before in the case of northeastern Romania and the Baltics. The Soviet citizens who suffered most in the war had been brought by force under Soviet rule right before the Germans came—as a result of a Soviet alliance with Nazi Germany. This was awkward. The history of the war had to begin in 1941, and these people had to be "peaceful Soviet citizens."

Jews in the lands east of the Molotov-Ribbentrop line, so recently conquered by the Soviet Union, were the first to be reached by the Einsatzgruppen when Hitler betrayed Stalin and Germany invaded the Soviet Union in 1941. They had been shielded by the Soviet press from knowledge of German policies toward Jews of 1939 and 1940. They had virtually no time to evacuate since Stalin had refused to believe in a German invasion. They had been subject to terror and deportation in the enlarged Soviet Union in 1939–1941 during the period when Stalin and Hitler were allied, and then terribly exposed to German forces by the breaking of that alliance. These Jews in this small zone made up more than a quarter of the total victims of the Holocaust.

If the Stalinist notion of the war was to prevail, the fact that the Jews were its main victims had to be forgotten. Also to be forgotten was that the Soviet Union had been allied to Nazi Germany when the war began in 1939, and that the Soviet Union had been unprepared for the German attack in 1941. The murder of the Jews was not only an undesirable memory in and of itself; it called forth other undesirable memories. It had to be forgotten.

———

After the Second World War, it was much harder for the Soviet leadership to control the mental world of Soviet citizens. Although the apparatus of censorship remained in force, too many people had experienced life beyond the Soviet Union for Soviet norms to seem like the only norms, or Soviet lives necessarily the best sort of lives. The war itself could not be contained within a Fatherland, be it Russian or Soviet; it had touched too many other peoples and its aftermath shaped not just a country but a world. In particular, the establishment of the State of Israel made Soviet political amnesia about the fate of the Jews impossible. Even after the Holocaust, more Jews lived in the Soviet Union than in Palestine, but the latter was to become the national homeland of the Jews. If Jews were to have a national state, would this be a blow to British imperialism in the Middle East, to be supported, or a challenge to the loyalty of Soviet Jews, to be feared?[9]

At first, the Soviet leadership seemed to expect that Israel would be a socialist state friendly to the Soviet Union, and the communist bloc supported Israel in ways that no one else could. In the second half of 1947, about seventy thousand Jews were permitted to leave Poland for Israel; many of them had just been expelled from the Soviet Union to Poland. After the United Nations recognized the State of Israel in May 1948 (with the Soviets voting in favor), the new state was invaded by its neighbors. Its nascent armies defended itself and, in dozens of cases, cleared territories of Arabs. The Poles trained Jewish soldiers on their own territory, then dispatched them to Palestine. The Czechoslovaks sent arms. As Arthur Koestler noted, the weapons shipments "aroused a feeling of gratitude among the Jews towards the Soviet Union."[10]

Yet by the end of 1948 Stalin had decided that Jews were influencing the Soviet state more than the Soviets were influencing the Jewish state. Spontaneous signs of affection for Israel were apparent in Moscow, and in Stalin's own court. Muscovites seemed to adore the new Israeli ambassador, Golda Meir (born in Kiev and raised in the United States). The high holidays were observed with enormous fanfare. Rosh Hashanah saw the largest public gathering in Moscow in twenty years. Some ten thousand Jews crowded in and around the Choral Synagogue. When the shofar blew and people promised each other to meet "next year in Jerusalem," the mood was euphoric. The anniversary of the Bolshevik Revolution, 7 November 1948, fell during the Days of Awe, between Rosh Hashanah and Yom Kippur. Polina Zhemchuzhina, the wife of the commissar for foreign affairs Viacheslav Molotov, saw Golda Meir that day, and encouraged her to continue to go to synagogue. What was worse, Zhemchuzhina said this

EASTERN EUROPE
AND ISRAEL c. 1949

Soviet satellites

Other communist states

in Yiddish, the language of her parents and of Meir's—in that paranoid setting, a suggestion of national unity among Jews across borders. Ekaterina Gorbman, the wife of another politburo member, Kliment Voroshilov, was heard to exclaim: "Now we too have our own homeland!"[11]

In late 1948 and early 1949, public life in the Soviet Union veered toward anti-Semitism. The new line was set, indirectly but discernibly, by *Pravda* on 28 January 1949. An article on "unpatriotic theater critics," who were "bearers of stateless cosmopolitanism," began a campaign of denunciation of Jews in every sphere of professional life. *Pravda* purged itself of Jews in early March. Jewish officers were cashiered from the Red Army and Jewish activists removed from leadership positions in the communist party. A few dozen Jewish poets and novelists who used Russian literary pseudonyms found their real or prior names published in parentheses. Jewish writers who had taken an interest in Yiddish culture or in the German murder of Jews found themselves under arrest. As Grossman recalled, "Throughout the whole of the USSR it seemed that only Jews thieved and took bribes, only Jews were criminally indifferent towards the sufferings of the sick, and only Jews published vicious or badly written books."[12]

The Jewish Anti-Fascist Committee was formally dissolved in November 1948, and more than a hundred Jewish writers and activists were arrested. The writer Der Nister, for example, was arrested in 1949, and died in police custody the following year. His novel *The Family Mashber* contained a vision that now seemed prophetic, as Soviet practices seemed to converge with Nazi models: "a heavily laden freight train with a long row of uniformly red cars, its black wheels rolling along, all turning at the same speed while seeming to be standing still." Jews across the Soviet Union were in a state of distress. The MGB reported the anxieties of the Jews in Soviet Ukraine, who understood that the policy must come from the top, and worried that "no one can say what form this is going to take." Only five years had passed since the end of the German occupation. For that matter, only eleven years had passed since the end of the Great Terror.[13]

Soviet Jews now risked two epithets: that they were "Jewish nationalists" and "rootless cosmopolitans." Although these two charges might have seemed mutually contradictory, since a nationalist is someone who emphasizes his roots, within a Stalinist logic they could function together. Jews were "cosmopolitans" in that their attachment to Soviet culture and the Russian language was supposedly insincere. They could not be counted upon to defend the Soviet Union or the Russian nation from penetration by various currents coming from the west. In this guise, the Jew was inherently attracted to the United States, where Jews (as Stalin believed Jews thought) could go and become rich. American industrial power was obvious to the Soviets, who used Studebaker automobiles to deport their own populations. Technological superiority (and simple ruthlessness) had also been on display at the end of the war in Japan, in the atomic bombing of Hiroshima and Nagasaki.

America's power was visible as well during the blockade of Berlin in the second half of 1948. Germany was still occupied by the four victorious powers: the Soviets, Americans, British, and French. Berlin, which lay within the Soviet zone, was under joint occupation. The western Allies had announced that they would introduce a new German currency, the Deutschmark, in the zones they controlled. The Soviets blockaded west Berlin, with the evident goal of forcing west Berliners to accept supplies from the Soviets, and thus accept Soviet control of their society. The Americans then undertook to supply the isolated city by air, which Moscow claimed could never work. In May 1949, the Soviets had to give up the blockade. The Americans, along with the British, proved capable of supplying thousands of tons of supplies by air every day. In this one action, goodwill, prosperity, and power were all on display. As the Cold War began, America and Americans seemed able to do what none of Moscow's previous rivals had: to present a universal and attractive vision of life. It was all well and good to lump the Americans with the Nazis as members of the same reactionary "camp," but Jews (and others, of course) would find such an association implausible.

Soviet Jews were also called "Zionists," in that they might prefer Israel, the Jewish national state, to the Soviet Union, their homeland. Israel after the war, like Poland or Latvia or Finland before the war, was a national state that might attract the loyalty of a diaspora nationality within the Soviet Union. In the interwar period, Soviet policy had first sought to support all nationalities in their cultural development, but then turned sharply against certain national minorities, such as the Poles, Latvians, and Finns. The Soviet Union could offer education and assimilation to Jews (as to all other groups), but what if those educated Soviet Jews, after the establishment of Israel and the triumph of the United States, sensed a better alternative elsewhere?

A Soviet Jew could appear to be both a "rootless cosmopolitan" and a "Zionist," insofar as Israel, in the emerging Soviet view, was seen as an American satellite.

A Jew attracted to America might support America's new client; a Jew attracted to Israel was supporting Israel's new patron. Either way, or both ways, Soviet Jews were no longer dependable citizens of the Soviet Union. So, perhaps, it appeared to Stalin.

Now that Jewishness and Jewish connections with the United States were suspect, Viktor Abakumov, head of the MGB, tried to find a way to make the former activists of the dissolved Anti-Fascist Committee into agents of American espionage. In some sense, the job was easy. The Committee had been created to allow Soviet Jews to speak to world Jewry, so its members could easily be called both Jewish nationalists and cosmopolitans. Yet this logic did not immediately seem to justify a mass terror action, or the model of the national operations of 1937–1938. Abakumov found himself frustrated from above. Without Stalin's express approval, he could not drag any truly important Jews into the plot, let alone begin anything like a mass operation.

During the national operations of 1937–1938, no member of the politburo had belonged to any of the targeted nationalities. Matters would be different for any prospective Jewish operation. In 1949, Lazar Kaganovich was no longer Stalin's closest associate and no longer his presumed successor, but he was still a member of the Soviet politburo. Any claim of Jewish nationalist penetration of top Soviet organs (on the analogy of Polish nationalist penetration of 1937–1938) would have to begin with Kaganovich. Stalin refused to allow Kaganovich, the only Jewish politburo member, to be investigated. At this time, five of the 210 full and candidate members of the central committee of the Soviet communist party were men of Jewish origin; none of them was investigated.

Abakumov's search for Jewish spies did reach the families of politburo members. Polina Zhemchuzhina, Molotov's wife, was arrested in January 1949. She denied the charges of treason. In his one act of rebellion, Molotov abstained from the vote to condemn his wife. Later, though, he apologized: "I acknowledge my heavy sense of remorse for not having prevented Zhemchuzhina, a person very dear to me, from making her mistakes and from forming ties with anti-Soviet Jewish nationalists such as Mikhoels." The next day she was arrested. Zhemchuzhina was sentenced to forced labor, and Molotov divorced her. She spent five years in exile in Kazakhstan, among kulaks, the kind of people her husband had helped to deport in the 1930s. It seems that they helped her to survive. Molotov, for his part, lost his position as commissar for foreign affairs. He had been appointed to the job in 1939, in part because he (unlike his predecessor Litvinov) was not Jewish, and Stalin had then needed someone with whom Hitler would negotiate. He lost the same job in 1949, at least in part because his wife *was* Jewish.[14]

Those people who were investigated were not very cooperative. When fourteen more or less unknown Soviet Jews were finally chosen to be tried in May 1952, the result was an unusual sort of judiciary chaos. Only two of the accused confessed to all of the charges during the investigations; the rest admitted only some of the charges or denied them all. Then, during the trial itself, every single one of them claimed to be innocent. Even Itzik Fefer, a police informant all along, and during the trial a witness for the prosecution, refused in the end to cooperate. Thirteen of the fourteen defenders were sentenced to death in August 1952 and executed. Although the trial created a precedent for executing Jews for spying for the Americans, it was of little political value. The people in question were too little known to arouse much interest, and their comportment was inappropriate for a show trial.[15]

If Stalin indeed wanted a spectacular Jewish affair, he would have to look elsewhere.

———

Communist Poland looked like a promising place for an anti-Semitic show trial, though in the end one never took place. The Jewish question was even more sensitive in Warsaw than in Moscow. Poland had been the home to more than three million Jews before the war; by 1948 it had been remade as a nationally homogeneous ethnic Polish state ruled by communists—some of whom were of Jewish origin. Poles were co-opted by formerly German property in the west and formerly Jewish property in the cities—the Polish language developed words meaning "formerly German" and "formerly Jewish," applied to property. Yet while Ukrainians and Germans were deported *from* communist Poland, Jews were actually deported *to* Poland: about one hundred thousand from the Soviet Union. Poles could hardly fail to notice that the highest ranks of the communist party and its security apparatus remained multinational even as the country was ethnically cleansed: party and secret police leaders were disproportionately of Jewish origin. Jews who chose to stay in Poland after the war were often communists with a sense of mission, who believed in the transformation of the country for the good of all.[16]

Poland had been the center of Jewish life in Europe for five hundred years; now that history seemed to be over. Some ninety percent of Poland's prewar Jewish population had been killed during the war. Most of the Polish-Jewish survivors of the war left their homeland in the years following the war. Many of them could not return to their homes in any event, since these now lay in the Soviet Union, which had annexed eastern Poland. In Soviet ethnic cleansing policies, Ukrainians and Belarusians and Lithuanians were to remain in the Soviet republics that bore their names, whereas Jews, like Poles, were to go to Poland. Jews who tried to return home were often greeted with distrust and violence. Some Poles were perhaps also afraid that Jews would claim property that they had lost during the war, because Poles had, in one way or another, stolen it from them (often after their own homes had been destroyed). Yet Jews were often resettled in formerly German Silesia, a "recovered territory" taken from Germany, where this issue could not have arisen. Even so, here as elsewhere in postwar Poland, Jews were beaten and killed and threatened to such an extent that most survivors decided to leave. It mattered, of course, that they had places to go: the United States or Israel. To get to these places, Polish Jews first went to Germany to displaced persons camps.

The voluntary movement of Holocaust survivors to Germany was not only a melancholy irony. It was also the latest stage in a journey that revealed many of the dreadful policies to which Jews and others had been subjected. Jews in displaced persons camps in Germany were very often Jews from western and central Poland who had fled from the Germans in 1939, or been deported by the Soviets to the Gulag in 1940, only to return to a postwar Poland where people wanted to keep their property and blamed them personally for Soviet rule. It was very dangerous to be a Jew in postwar Poland—though no more so than to be a Ukrainian or a German or a Pole in the anti-communist underground. These other groups generally wished to stay in their homeland. Jews, however, had a special reason to be unsure of themselves in their own country: three million of their fellows had just been killed in occupied Poland.

The departure of Polish Jews to Israel and the United States made the role of Jewish communists in Polish politics even more visible than it would otherwise have been. The Polish communist regime faced a double political handicap: it was not national in a geopolitical sense, since it was dependent upon the support of Moscow; and it was not national in an ethnic sense, since some of its prominent representatives were Jewish (and these people had spent the war in the Soviet Union).[17]

Polish communists of Jewish origin could be in power in 1949 because of the international politics of the early Cold War in 1948. For reasons that had nothing to do with Poland, and everything to do with a larger rupture within the communist bloc, Stalin paid more attention to the risk of majority nationalism than to the risk of Jewish "cosmopolitanism" or "Zionism" in summer 1948.

Since Stalin was trying to coordinate and control his new group of communist allies, Moscow's ideological line reacted to perceived disloyalty in eastern Europe. As Stalin must have observed, it was much harder for the leaders of communist regimes to follow the Soviet line than it had been for leaders of communist parties before the war: these comrades actually had to govern. Stalin also had to adjust his ideological line to the realities of American power. These anxieties came to the fore in summer 1948; the concern with Jews dropped momentarily into the background. This was crucial for Poland, since it allowed communists of Jewish origin to secure power, and then to make sure that no anti-Semitic show trial took place.

In summer 1948, Stalin's major worry in eastern Europe was communist Yugoslavia. In this important Balkan country, communism involved admiration for the Soviet Union but not dependence upon Soviet power. Tito (Josip Broz), the leader of the Yugoslav communists and Yugoslav partisans, had succeeded in taking power without Soviet help. After the war, Tito showed signs of independence from Stalin in foreign policy. He spoke of a Balkan federation after Stalin had abandoned the idea. He was supporting communist revolutionaries in neighboring Greece, a country that Stalin regarded as falling within the American and British sphere of influence. President Harry Truman had made clear, in his "doctrine" announced in March 1947, that the Americans would take action to prevent the spread of communism to Greece. Stalin cared more about stabilizing his gains in Europe than about further revolutionary adventures. He clearly believed that he could bring down Tito and have him replaced with more solicitous Yugoslav leadership.[18]

The Tito-Stalin split shaped international communism. Tito's independent stand, and the expulsion of Yugoslavia from the Cominform that followed, made him a negative model of "national communism." Between April and September

1948, Moscow's satellite regimes were encouraged to concern themselves with the supposed nationalist danger (the "right-wing deviation" from the party line) rather than the (Jewish) cosmopolitan one (the "left-wing deviation"). When Polish general secretary Władysław Gomułka objected to the new line, he opened himself to charges that he too exemplified a national "deviation." In June 1948, Andrei Zhdanov instructed rival Polish communists to bring down Gomułka. The Polish politburo member Jakub Berman agreed that the Polish party suffered from a national deviation. That August, Gomułka was removed from his position as general secretary. At the end of the month he had to issue a self-criticism to the assembled central committee of the Polish party.[19]

Gomułka was in fact a national communist, and Polish comrades of Jewish origins were perhaps right to fear him. He was not Jewish (though he did have a Jewish wife), and was seen as more attentive to the interests of non-Jewish Poles than his comrades. Unlike Jakub Berman and several other leading communists, he had remained in Poland during the war, and so was less well known to the Soviet leadership in Moscow than were comrades who had fled to the Soviet Union. He had certainly profited from national questions: he had presided over the dual ethnic cleansings of Germans and Ukrainians, and had taken personal responsibility for the settlement of Poles in the western "recovered territories." He had gone so far as to make a speech to the central committee in which he criticized certain traditions of the Polish Left for their disproportionate attention to Jews.

After his fall, Gomułka was replaced by a triumvirate of Bolesław Bierut, Jakub Berman, and Hilary Minc (the latter two of whom were of Jewish origin). The new Polish troika came to power just in time to avoid an anti-Semitic action in Poland. Disconcertingly for them, the line from Moscow altered during the very weeks when they were trying to consolidate their position. While the right-wing national deviation was still possible, Stalin's most explicit signals in autumn 1948 concerned the role of Jews in east European communist parties. He made clear that Zionists and cosmopolitans were no longer welcome. Perhaps sensing the new mood, Gomułka appealed to Stalin that December: there were too many "Jewish comrades" in the Polish party leadership who "do not feel connected to the Polish nation." This, according to Gomułka, led to the alienation of the party from Polish society and risked "national nihilism."[20]

The year 1949 thus brought a particular sort of Stalinism to Poland. Jewish Stalinists exercised a great deal of power, but were caught between Stalinist anti-Semitism in Moscow and popular anti-Semitism in their own country. Neither of these was important enough to make their rule impossible, but they had to make sure that the two did not meet. Jewish communists had to stress that their political identification with the Polish nation was so strong that it erased their Jewish origins and removed any possibility of distinct Jewish policies.

One striking example of this tendency was the reimagining of the Warsaw Ghetto Uprising of 1943, the major instance of Jewish resistance to the Holocaust, as a Polish national revolt led by communists. Hersh Smolar, the Polish-Jewish communist who had been the hero of the Minsk ghetto, now drained the Jewishness from Jewish resistance to Nazis. He described the Warsaw Ghetto Uprising in the obligatory ideological terms of Zhdanov: there had been "two camps" within the ghetto, one progressive and one reactionary. Those who spoke of Israel were in the reactionary camp now, as they had been then. The progressives were the communists, and the communists had fought. This was an extraordinary distortion: while the communists had indeed urged armed resistance in the ghetto, the left-wing Zionists and the Bund had more popular support, and the right-wing Zionists more guns. Smolar promised purges to Jewish political activists who failed to accept Polish national communism: "And if there turn out to be people among us who are going to buzz on like flies about some sort of supposedly higher and more essential Jewish national goals, then we will eliminate those people from our society, just like the fighters of the ghetto pushed aside the cowards and those of weak will."[21]

All resistance to fascism was by definition led by communists; if it was not led by communists, then it was not resistance. The history of the Warsaw Ghetto Uprising of 1943 had to be rewritten such that communists could be seen as leading Polish Jews—just as they were supposedly leading the Polish anti-Nazi resistance generally. In the politically acceptable history of the Second World War, the resistance in the ghetto had little to do with the mass murder of Jews, and much to do with the courage of communists. This fundamental shift of emphasis obscured the Jewish experience of the war, as the Holocaust became nothing more than an instance of fascism. It was precisely Jewish communists who had to develop and communicate these misrepresentations, so that they could not be charged with attending to Jewish rather than Polish goals. In order to seem like plausible Polish communist leaders, Jewish communists had to delete from history the single most important example of Jews resisting Nazis from Jewish motivations. The bait in Stalin's political trap was left by Hitler.[22]

This was Polish-Jewish Stalinist self-defense from Stalin's own anti-Semitism. If Jewish resistance heroes were willing, in effect, to deny the significance of Hitler's anti-Semitism to Jewish life and politics, and in some cases to their own desire to resist the German occupation, then surely they had proven their devotion. Stalinism involved denying the most obvious historical facts, and their most pressing personal significance: in the case of the Warsaw Ghetto Uprising of 1943, Polish-Jewish communists managed both. By comparison, the associated slander of the Home Army and the Warsaw Uprising of 1944 was an easy labor. Since it had not been led by communists, it could not have been an uprising. Since the Home Army soldiers were not communists, they were reactionaries, acting against the interests of the toiling masses. The Polish patriots who died seeking to liberate their capital were fascists, little better than Hitler. The Home Army, which had fought the Germans with much greater determination than the Polish communists, was a "bespittled dwarf of reaction."[23]

Jakub Berman was the politburo member responsible for both ideology and security in 1949. He repeated a key Stalinist argument for terror: as the revolution nears completion, its enemies fight ever more desperately, and so committed revolutionaries must resort to ever more extreme measures. With feigned deafness to the Soviet line, he framed the struggle as one against the right-wing, or national, deviation. No one could fault Berman for lack of attention to nationalism after the Tito-Stalin split. Meanwhile, no one could have done more than Berman to discolor the Jewish memory of German mass killing in occupied Poland. Berman, who had lost much of his immediate family to Treblinka in 1942, presided over a Polish national communism in which, only a few years later, the gas chambers fell deep into the historical background.[24]

The Holocaust had drawn many Jews toward communism, the ideology of the Soviet liberator; and yet now, in order to rule Poland and to appease Stalin, leading Jewish communists had to deny the Holocaust's importance. Berman had already made a first important move in this direction in December 1946, when he directed that the official estimate of non-Jewish Polish dead be significantly increased and that of Jewish dead somewhat decreased so that the two numbers were equal: three million each. The Holocaust was already politics, and of a dangerous and difficult sort. It, like every other historical event, had to be understood "dialectically," in terms that corresponded to Stalin's ideological line and the political desiderata of the present moment. Perhaps more Jews than non-Jewish Poles had died. But perhaps that was politically inconvenient. Perhaps it would be better if the number were even. To allow one's personal sense of factuality or fairness to interfere with such dialectical adjustments was to fail as a communist. To recall one's own family's deaths in the gas chamber was pure bourgeois sentimentality. A successful communist had to look ahead, as Berman did, to see just what the moment demanded from the truth, and act accordingly and decisively. The Second World War, like the Cold War, was a struggle of progressive against reactionary forces, and that was that.[25]

Berman, a very intelligent man, understood all of this as well as anyone could, and he brought these premises to their logical conclusions. He presided over a security apparatus that arrested members of the Home Army who had accepted the special assignment of saving Jews. They and their actions had no historical resonance within a Stalinist worldview: the Jews had suffered no more than anyone else, and the soldiers of the Home Army were no better than fascists.

Berman's most glaring fault, from the perspective of Stalin himself, was that he was himself of Jewish origin (though his documents showed Polish nationality). This was not exactly a secret: he had married under a khuppah. In July 1949, the Soviet ambassador complained in a note to Moscow that the Polish leadership was dominated by Jews such as Berman, and that the security apparatus was run by Jews—an exaggerated assessment, although not without some basis. In the period 1944–1954, 167 of 450 high-ranking Ministry of Public Security officers were Jewish by self-declaration or origin, so about thirty-seven percent in a country where Jews were fewer than one percent of the population. Most though far from all people of Jewish origin in the upper reaches of the security service defined themselves as Poles in their identity documents. This may or may not have reflected how they regarded themselves; these matters were rarely simple. But passport identity, even when it did (as it often did) reflect a sincere identification with the Polish state or nation, did not prevent people of Jewish background from being seen as Jews by much of the Polish population or by the Soviet leadership.[26]

Berman, the most important communist of Jewish origin in Poland, was the obvious target of any potential anti-Semitic show trial. He understood this perfectly well. To make matters worse, he could be connected with the leading actors of the main drama of the early Cold War, the Field brothers. The Americans Noel and Hermann Field were by then under arrest in Czechoslovakia and Poland as

American spies. Noel Field had been an American diplomat, but also an agent of Soviet intelligence; he was friendly with Allen Dulles, the American intelligence chief who had directed the OSS office in Bern, Switzerland; he also ran a relief organization that aided communists after the war. Field came to Prague in 1949, probably believing that the Soviets again wished for his services; he was arrested. His brother Hermann came to look for him, and was himself arrested in Warsaw. The two of them, under torture, confessed to having organized a vast espionage organization in eastern Europe.[27]

Though they were never tried themselves, the Field brothers' alleged activities provided the plot line for a number of the show trials that were then being held throughout communist eastern Europe. In Hungary in September 1949, for example, Lászlo Rájk was show-tried and executed as an agent of Noel Field. The Hungarian investigation had supposedly discovered cells of the Fields' organization in fraternal communist countries as well. As it happened, Hermann Field knew Berman's secretary and had once given her a letter for him. The Fields were dangerous precisely because they did in fact know many communists, could in fact be associated with American intelligence, and now under torture could be expected to say anything. At a certain point, Stalin himself asked Berman about Field.[28]

Jakub Berman could also be linked to Jewish politics of a kind that were no longer permitted. He knew the members of the Jewish Anti-Fascist Committee, since he had met with Mikhoels and Fefer before their 1943 visit to the United States. He came from a family that represented some of the range of Jewish politics in Poland. A brother (killed at Treblinka) had been a member of Poalei-Zion Right, one branch of socialist Zionism. Another brother, Adolf, who had survived the Warsaw ghetto, was a member of Poalei-Zion Left, another branch of left-wing Zionism. Adolf Berman had organized social services for children in the Warsaw ghetto, and after the war directed the Central Committee of Polish Jews. As Poland became communist, he remained a left-wing Zionist, in the conviction that these political positions could somehow be reconciled.[29]

In 1949, it was becoming clear that people such as Adolf Berman had no place in postwar Poland. Indeed, it was to him personally that Smolar had directed the harsh words about the reactionary character of Zionism and the need to eliminate cowardly Jews from Polish society. In so doing Smolar was creating a kind of Stalinist defense against Stalin himself: if Jewish communists in Poland were ostentatiously anti-Zionist and pro-Polish, they could elude accusations of Zionism and cosmopolitanism. But it was less than clear that even this categorical approach could defend Jakub Berman from the association with his brother. Stalinist anti-Semitism could not be so easily resisted by individual loyalty and commitment.

Jakub Berman survived because he was defended by his friend and ally Bolesław Bierut, the general secretary of the Polish party and the gentile face of its ruling triumvirate. Stalin once asked Bierut whom he needed more, Berman or Minc: Bierut was too wise to fall into that trap. Bierut placed himself between Stalin and Berman, which was to take a risk. In general, Polish communists never permitted themselves the brutality to one another that was evident in Czechoslovakia, Romania, or Hungary. Even the disgraced Gomułka was never forced to sign a humiliating confession or face trial. Polish communists who were in power in the late 1940s usually knew, from personal experience, just what had happened to their comrades in the 1930s. Back then, Stalin had sent a signal; Polish communists had duly denounced each other, which led to mass murder, and the end of the party itself. Although all foreign communists suffered in the Great Terror, this Polish experience was unique, and perhaps created a certain sense of concern for the lives of one's own closest comrades.[30]

As the pressure from the Soviet Union built, Berman finally allowed the security services to follow the anti-Jewish line in 1950. Polish Jews fell under special suspicion as American or Israeli spies. This was not without a certain awkwardness, as those building the cases against Polish Jews were sometimes themselves Polish Jews. The Polish security apparatus itself was purged of some of its Jewish officers. Because this often involved Jews purging other Jews, the relevant department of the security apparatus was informally called the bureau of "self-extermination." It was directed by Józef Światło, whose own sister had left for Israel in 1947.[31]

Yet Berman, Minc, and Bierut held on, maintaining that they were the proper Poles, the proper communists, the proper patriots, both to an incredulous society and to a doubting Stalin. Although Jews, communists and otherwise, were forced to stifle the memory of the Holocaust, there was no public campaign in Poland in those years against Zionists and cosmopolitans. Making concessions and relying on the loyalty of his friend Bierut, Berman was able to maintain that in Poland the main danger came from the Polish, not the Jewish, national deviation.

When in July 1951 Gomułka was finally arrested, the two security officers who came for him, as he likely remembered, were men of Jewish origin.

––––––––––––

In the years 1950–1952, as the Poles dragged their feet, the Cold War became a military confrontation. The Korean War sharpened Stalin's concerns about American power.

In the early 1950s, the Soviet Union seemed to be in a much stronger position than it had been before the war. The three powers then presented as encircling the Soviet Union—Germany, Poland, and Japan—had all been substantially weakened. Poland was now a Soviet satellite whose minister of defense was a Soviet officer. Soviet troops had reached Berlin, and remained. In October 1949 the Soviet occupation zone of Germany had been transformed into the German Democratic Republic, a Soviet satellite ruled by German communists. East Prussia, the formerly German district on the Baltic Sea, had been divided between communist Poland and the USSR itself. Japan, the great threat of the 1930s, had been defeated and disarmed. Yet here the Soviet Union had not contributed to the victory, and so took little part in the occupation. The Americans were building military bases in Japan and teaching the Japanese to play baseball.[32]

Even in defeat, Japan had changed the politics of east Asia. The Japanese incursion in China in 1937 had, in the end, only aided the Chinese communists. In 1944 the Japanese had mounted a successful ground offensive against the Chinese nationalist government. This made no difference to the outcome of the war, but it did fatally weaken the nationalist regime. Once the Japanese surrendered, their forces were withdrawn from the Chinese mainland. Then the Chinese communists had their moment, much as Russia's communists had thirty years before. Japan in the Second World War played the role that Germany had played in the First World War: having failed to win a great empire for itself, it served as the handmaiden to a communist revolution in a neighbor. The People's Republic of China was declared in October 1949.[33]

Although in Washington Chinese communism looked like the continuation of a world communist revolution, it was ambivalent news for Stalin. Mao Zedong, the leader of the Chinese communists, was not a personal client of Stalin, as were many of the east European communists. Although Chinese communists accepted the Stalinist version of Marxism, Stalin had never exercised personal

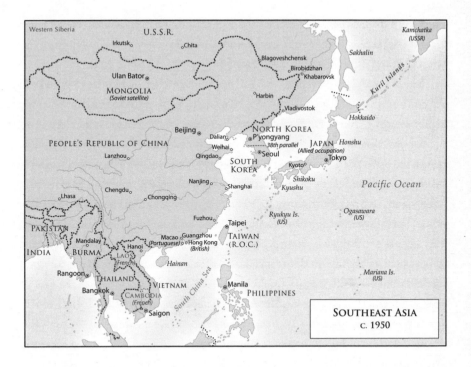

SOUTHEAST ASIA
c. 1950

control of their party. Stalin knew that Mao would be an ambitious and unpredictable rival. "The battle of China," he said, "isn't over yet." In making policy in east Asia, Stalin had now to ensure that the Soviet Union maintained its position of leader of the communist world. This concern arose first with respect to Korea, where a communist state had also just been established. Japan, which had ruled Korea since 1905, withdrew after the war. The Korean peninsula was then occupied by the Soviet Union in the north and the United States in the south. North Korean communists established a people's republic in North Korea in 1948.[34]

In spring 1950 Stalin had to decide what to say to Kim Il-Sung, the North Korean communist leader, who wished to invade the southern part of the peninsula. Stalin knew that the Americans considered Korea beyond the "defensive perimeter" they were constructing in Japan and the Pacific, because the secretary of state had said as much in January. The US Army had withdrawn from the peninsula in 1949. Kim Il-Sung told Stalin that his forces would quickly overcome the South Korean army. Stalin gave Kim Il-Sung his blessing for war, and sent Soviet arms to the North Koreans, who invaded the South on 25 June 1950.

Stalin even dispatched several hundred Soviet Koreans from Soviet central Asia to fight on the North Korean side—the same people who had been deported by order of Stalin only thirteen years earlier.[35]

The Korean War looked very much like an armed confrontation between the communist and capitalist worlds. The Americans responded quickly and firmly, sending troops from Japan and elsewhere in the Pacific, and were able to push the North Koreans across the original border. In September, Truman approved NSC-68, a secret and formal confirmation of the American grand strategy of containment of communism throughout the world—an idea formulated by George Kennan. In October, the Chinese intervened on the side of the North Koreans. Until 1952 the United States and its allies were making war against communist North Korea and communist China, with American tanks battling Soviet-made tanks, and American aircraft engaging Soviet-made fighters.

Stalin seemed to fear a broader war, perhaps a war on two fronts. In January 1951, Stalin called together the leaders of his east European satellites, and ordered them to build up their armies in preparation for a war in Europe. In 1951 and 1952, the troop strength of the Red Army doubled.[36]

During precisely these years, in 1951 and 1952, the idea that Soviet Jews were undercover agents of the United States seems to have gained resonance in Stalin's mind. Defied in Berlin, frustrated in Poland, and embattled in Korea, Stalin faced again, at least in his own increasingly troubled imagination, encirclement by enemies. As in the 1930s, so in the 1950s, it was possible to see the Soviet Union as the object of an international plot, masterminded no longer from Berlin, Warsaw, and Tokyo (with London in the background) but from Washington (with London in the background). Stalin apparently believed that a Third World War was inevitable, and reacted to what he saw as the coming threat much as he had in the late 1930s.

In some respects, the international situation could seem more threatening now than then. The Great Depression had at least brought poverty to the capitalist world. But by the early 1950s it seemed that the countries liberated by the Western powers would undergo a quick economic recovery. In the 1930s, the capitalist powers were divided against one another. As of April 1949, the most important of them were united in a new military alliance, the North Atlantic Treaty Organization, or NATO.[37]

Stalin found a way in July 1951 to turn his own security services against an imagined Jewish plot inside the Soviet Union. The narrative of the plot, as it emerged in the second half of that year, had two parts: Russians who might have been seen as anti-Jewish had been murdered, and their murders had been covered up by the Soviet security apparatus.

One of the supposed victims was Aleksandr Shcherbakov, the wartime propagandist who had claimed that Russian people were "bearing the main burden" of the war. He had overseen the Jewish Anti-Fascist Committee, and had purged newspapers of Jewish journalists at Stalin's orders. The other was Andrei Zhdanov, Stalin's purifier of Soviet culture, who had blocked the publication of the *Black Book of Soviet Jewry*. Their deaths were supposedly the beginning of a wave of Jewish medical terrorism, sponsored by American paymasters, which was to end only with the slaughter of the Soviet leadership.

One of the ostensible murderers was the Jewish doctor Yakov Etinger, who had died in police custody in March 1951. Viktor Abakumov, director of the MGB, had supposedly failed to report on this plot, because he was himself involved in it. In order to prevent his own role from being known, he had deliberately killed Etinger. Because Abakumov had killed Etinger, Etinger had been unable to confess to the full range of his crimes.[38]

A first outline of these extraordinary claims was presented in a denunciation of Abakumov sent to Stalin by Abakumov's MGB subordinate Mikhail Riumin. The choice of Etinger played to Stalin's worries. Etinger had been arrested not as part of any medical plot but as a Jewish nationalist. By his clever initiative, Riumin had linked Jewish nationalism, Stalin's recent anxiety, with medical murder, one of his traditional preoccupations. None of Riumin's particular claims, of course, made very much sense. Shcherbakov had died the day after he had insisted, against doctors' orders, on taking part in a Victory Day parade. Zhdanov, too, had ignored doctors' orders to rest. As for Etinger, the Jewish doctor in question, he had been killed not by Abakumov *but by Riumin himself*, in March 1951. Riumin had exhausted Etinger by the unceasing interrogations known as the "conveyer method," after doctors had told him that this would endanger the man's life.[39]

Yet Riumin had hit upon a connection that he believed would appeal to Stalin: terrorist Jewish doctors killing prominent (Russian) communists. Henceforth the direction of the investigation would be clear: purge the MGB of Jews and their lackeys, and find more Jewish killer doctors. Abakumov was duly arrested on 4 July 1951 and replaced by Riumin, who began an anti-Jewish purge of the MGB. The central committee then ordered further investigation of the "terrorist activities of Etinger" on 11 July. Five days later the MGB arrested the electrocardiogram specialist Sofia Karpai. She was extremely important to the entire investigation: she was the only Jewish doctor still alive who could be linked in any way to the death of a Soviet leader. She had indeed taken and interpreted two readings of Zhdanov's heart. Yet under arrest she declined to endorse the story of medical murder, and refused to implicate anyone else.[40]

The case was weak. But further evidence of Jewish plots could be generated elsewhere.

———————

Another Soviet satellite, communist Czechoslovakia, would provide the anti-Semitic show trial that Poland did not. A week after Sofia Karpai's arrest, on 23 July 1951, Stalin signaled to Klement Gottwald, the communist president of Czechoslovakia, that he should rid himself of his close associate Rudolf Slánský, who ostensibly represented "Jewish bourgeois nationalism." On 6 September, Slánský was removed from his position as general secretary.[41]

Moscow's evident disfavor provoked a real espionage plot, or at least a botched attempt at one. Czechs working for American intelligence noticed that Moscow had sent no congratulations to Slánský on the occasion of his fiftieth birthday (on 31 July 1951). They moved ahead to encourage Slánský to defect from Czechoslovakia. In early November they sent him a letter in which they offered refuge in the West. The courier who was to deliver the message was in fact a double agent, working for the communist Czechoslovak security services. He gave the letter to his superiors, who showed it to the Soviets. On 11 November 1951 Stalin sent a personal envoy to Gottwald to demand Slánský's immediate arrest. Although neither Slánský nor Gottwald had seen the letter at this point, Gottwald now seemed to believe that he had no choice. Slánský was arrested on 24 November and interrogated for a year.[42]

The final result of the Slánský case was spectacular: a Czechoslovak Stalinist show trial on the Soviet model of 1936, with an overlay of unabashed anti-Semitism. Although some of the most prominent victims of the Moscow show trials of 1936 had been Jewish, they were not tried for their Jewishness. In Prague eleven out of the fourteen defendants were of Jewish origin, and were identified as such in the trial record. The word *cosmopolitan* was used as if it were a term of legal art whose meaning was known to all. On 20 November 1952, Slánský set the tone of the political séance, summoning forth the spirits of communists who had gone before him to their deaths: "I acknowledge fully my guilt and wish honestly and truthfully to describe everything that I have done and the crimes that I have committed." He was obviously following a rehearsed script. At one point in the trial, he answered a question that the prosecutor had forgotten to ask.[43]

Slánský confessed to a conspiracy that ran the gamut of the obligatory obsessions of the day: with Titoists, Zionists, Free Masons, and American intelligence officers who recruited only Jews. Among his supposed crimes was the medical murder of Gottwald. Rudolf Margolius, another of the defendants, had to denounce his parents, both of whom had died at Auschwitz. As during the Great Terror, the various plots turned out to be coordinated by a "center," in this case an "Anti-State Conspiratorial Center." All fourteen defendants asked for the death penalty, and eleven of them got it. As the noose was placed around Slánský's neck on 3 December 1952, he thanked the hangman and said: "I am getting what I deserve." The bodies of the eleven executed defendants were cremated; their ashes were later used to fill the ruts of a road.[44]

At such a moment, it could hardly have seemed unlikely that a public trial of Soviet Jews would follow. Thirteen Soviet citizens had been executed in Moscow in August 1952 on charges of espionage for the United States, on the basis of allegations of cosmopolitanism and Zionism rather than reliable information. These had been people incriminated as Jewish nationalists and American spies by evidence generated from torture, and then tried in secret. Eleven Czechoslovak citizens had been executed in Prague in December 1952, on much the same basis, but after a public trial that recalled the Great Terror. Now even the Polish regime began to arrest people as Israeli spies.[45]

In autumn 1952 several more Soviet doctors were under investigation. None of them had anything to do with Zhdanov or Shcherbakov, but they had treated other Soviet and foreign communist dignitaries before their deaths. One of them was Stalin's personal doctor, who had advised him to retire in early 1952. At Stalin's express and repeated orders, these people were beaten terribly, and some of them then produced the right kind of scripted confessions. Miron Vovsi, who happened to be a cousin of Solomon Mikhoels, confessed in the robotic language of Stalinism: "Thinking it all over, I came to the conclusion that despite the rottenness of my crimes, I must disclose the terrible truth to the investigation of my villainous work conducted with the aim of destroying the health and shortening the life of specific, leading state workers of the Soviet Union."[46]

Once these confessions were in hand, the time must have seemed right to an aging man. Stalin usually planned well before he struck his blow, but he now seemed to be in a hurry. On 4 December 1952, the day after the execution of Slánský, the Soviet central committee took cognizance of a "doctors' plot," in which a leading role was played by "Jewish nationals." One of the plotters was supposedly Stalin's doctor, who was Russian; those who were of Jewish origin were listed as such. Stalin had now contrived to condemn his physician, the man who had advised him to end his political career. Stalin showed other signs that his political worries were linked to his personal fears. He clung, literally, to his daughter Svetlana, dancing with her at his seventy-third birthday party on 21 December 1952.[47]

It was as if, that December, Stalin wanted to purge his own death. A communist cannot believe in the immortal soul, but he must believe in History: as revealed in changes in the modes of production, as reflected by the rise of the proletariat, as represented by the communist party, as distilled by Stalin, and thus in fact as made by Stalin's will. If life was nothing but a social construction, then perhaps death was too, and all could be reversed by the exercise of courageous and willful dialectics. Doctors caused it rather than delayed it; the man who warned of forthcoming death was a murderer rather than a counselor. What was needed was the right performance. Solomon Mikhoels was at his best in the role of King Lear, a ruler who foolishly conceded power too soon, and to the wrong successors. Now Mikhoels had been banished, like a specter of impotence. No doubt his Jewish people, and all they stood for, the risk of the defilement of the Soviet Union, the risk of another history of the Second World War, the risk of the wrong future, could be banished as well.[48]

Stalin, a sick man of seventy-three, listening to no counsel but his own, pushed forward. In December 1952 he said that "every Jew is a nationalist and an agent of American intelligence," a paranoid formulation even by his standards. The Jews, he said that same month, "believed that their nation had been saved by the United States." Here was a legend that had not yet even arisen; but Stalin was not entirely wrong. With characteristic perspicacity, Stalin correctly forecast one of the major myths of the Cold War, and even of the decades that followed its end. None of the Allies did very much to rescue Jews; the Americans never even saw the major killing sites.[49]

On 13 January 1953, the party newspaper *Pravda* revealed an American plot to murder the Soviet leadership by medical means. The doctors, it was understood, were Jews. The news agency TASS characterized the "terrorist group of doctors" as "monsters in human form." Yet despite the vitriolic language, so redolent of the Great Terror, all was not quite ready. The people named in the article had not yet all admitted to their supposed crimes, which was a precondition to any show trial. Those accused must confess in private before they can be expected to do so in public: this was the minimum condition of the scenography of Stalinism. The accused could not be expected to follow a show trial in a public courtroom if they had not already agreed to it in the confines of an interrogation chamber.[50]

Sofia Karpai, the cardiologist who was the key defendant, had not confessed to anything at all. She was Jewish and a woman; perhaps the interrogators assumed that she would be the first to break. In the end, she was the only one of all of the accused with the strength to stand by her story and defend her innocence. At what turned out to be her last interrogation, on 18 February 1953, she held firm, explicitly denying the charges against her. Like Stalin, she was ill and dying; unlike him, she must have understood this to be the case. She seemed to believe that it mattered to speak the truth. By doing so, she slowed the investigation. She outlived Stalin, if only by a matter of days; she perhaps ensured that other people outlived Stalin as well.[51]

In February 1953, the Soviet leadership was drafting and redrafting a collective Jewish self-denunciation, including phrases that might have come straight from Nazi propaganda. It was to be signed by prominent Soviet Jews and published in *Pravda*. Vasily Grossman was among those intimidated into signing the letter. In vicious press attacks, it suddenly emerged that his recently published novel of the war, *For a Just Cause*, was not patriotic enough. *For a Just Cause* was a vast novel of the Battle of Stalingrad, mostly within Stalinist conventions. (Now Grossman's perspective changed. In its sequel, his masterpiece *Life and Fate*, Grossman would have a Nazi interrogator contemplate the future:

"Today you're appalled by our hatred of the Jews. Tomorrow you may make use of our experience yourselves.") In the latest known draft of the letter, of 20 February 1953, the signatories were to affirm that there were "two camps," progressive and reactionary, among Jews. Israel was in the reactionary camp: its leaders were "Jewish millionaires connected with American monopolists." Soviet Jews were also to acknowledge that "the nations of the Soviet Union and above all the great Russian nation" had saved humanity and the Jews.[52]

The letter condemned imperialism generally and the Jews of the doctors' plot by name. In Stalinist terms, it could be read as a justification, or even an invitation, to a large-scale purge of Soviet Jews who were not sufficiently anti-imperialist. The Soviet citizens who were to sign the letter would have had to identify themselves as Jews (not all of them were seen as such, or saw themselves as such), and as leaders of a community that was clearly in danger. Ilya Ehrenburg, like Grossman a Soviet writer of Jewish origin, had allowed Stalin to sign his name over polemical articles about Israel. Now, however, he hesitated to endorse such a document. He wrote a disingenuous letter to Stalin, asking him what to do. He mounted the same sort of defense as had Berman and the Polish-Jewish communists a few years earlier: since Jews are not a nation, and we personally are loyal communists, how can we take part in a campaign against ourselves as representatives of some collective national entity known as Jewry?[53]

Stalin never replied. He was found in a coma on 1 March 1953 and died four days later. What Stalin had wanted can only be guessed; he might not have been entirely sure himself; he might have been awaiting the response of Soviet society to the first probes. Plagued by mortality and doubts about the succession, worried by the influence of Jews in the Soviet system, and fighting a Cold War against a powerful enemy that he understood only dimly, he turned to the traditional means of self-defense: trials and purges. Judging by the rumors circulating at the time, Soviet citizens had no trouble imagining the possible outcomes: doctors would have been show-tried with Soviet leaders who were their supposed allies; remaining Jews would have been purged from the state police and the armed forces; the thirty-five thousand Soviet Jewish doctors (and perhaps scientists as well) might have been deported to camps; and perhaps even the Jewish people as such would have been subject to forced removal or even mass shootings.[54]

Such an action, had it taken place, would have been one more in a series of national operations and ethnic deportations, which had begun in 1930 with the

Poles and then continued through the Great Terror and during and after the Second World War. All of this would have been in line with Stalin's previous practice, and would have fit a traditional logic. The national minorities to be feared and punished were those with apparent connections to the non-Soviet world. Though it had brought death to 5.7 million Jews, the war had also contributed to the establishment of a Jewish national homeland, beyond the reach of Stalin. Like the enemy nations of the 1930s, the Jews now had reasons for grievance inside the Soviet Union (four years of purges and official anti-Semitism), an external protector outside the Soviet Union (Israel), and a role to play in an international struggle (led by the United States). The precedents were clear and the logic was known. But Stalinism was coming to an end.

───────────

Taking into account all the trials in the Soviet Union and eastern Europe, and all the people who died in police custody, Stalin killed no more than a few dozen Jews in these last years of his life. If he did indeed want one final national terror operation, which is far from clear, he was unable to see it to completion. It is tempting to imagine that only his death prevented this outcome, that the Soviet Union was hurtling toward another national purge on the scale of the 1930s, but the evidence is very mixed. Stalin's own actions were surprisingly hesitant, and the reactions of his organs of power slow.

Stalin was not the master of his country in the 1950s as he was in the 1930s, and it was no longer the same country. He had become more a cult than a personality. He visited no factories, farms, or government offices after the Second World War, and made only three public speeches between 1946 and 1953. By 1950 Stalin no longer led the Soviet Union as a lone tyrant, as he had for most of the previous fifteen years. In the 1950s the key members of the politburo met regularly during his long absences from Moscow, and had their own networks of clients in the Soviet bureaucracies. Like the Great Terror of 1937–1938, a mass death purge of Jews would have created possibilities for upward mobility in Soviet society generally. But it was not at all clear that Soviet citizens, anti-Semitic though many of them certainly were, would have wanted such an opportunity at such a price.[55]

What was most striking was the fussiness of it all. During the Great Terror, Stalin's suggestions were transformed into orders, the orders into quotas, the quotas into corpses, the corpses into numbers. Nothing of the kind happened in the Jewish case. Though Stalin spent much of the last five years of his life preoccupied with Soviet Jews, he was unable to find the security chief who could make the right kind of case. In the old days, Stalin rid himself of security chiefs after they had completed some sort of mass action, and then blamed them for its excesses. Now officers of the MGB, perhaps understandably, seemed hesitant to commit the excesses in the first place. First Stalin had Abakumov work the case, although Lavrenty Beria was in overall charge of state security. Then he let Abakumov be denounced by Riumin, who in his turn fell in November 1952. Riumin's successor had a heart attack on his first day on the job. Finally the investigation was taken up by S. A. Goglidze, a client of Beria.[56]

Stalin had lost his once total power to draw people into his fictitious world. He found himself threatening security chiefs, rather than instructing them. His subordinates understood that Stalin wanted confessions and coincidences that could be presented as proof. But they were constantly hindered by a certain attention to bureaucratic propriety and even, in some measure, to law. The judge who sentenced the members of the Jewish Anti-Fascist Committee advised the defendants of their right to appeal. In the persecutions of Soviet Jews, security chiefs sometimes had trouble making their subordinates—and, perhaps most important, the defendants—understand what was expected of them. Interrogations, though brutal, did not always produce the kind of evidence that was needed. Torture, though it took place, was a last resort, and one upon which Stalin had personally to insist.[57]

Stalin was right to be concerned about the influence of the war and of the West, and about the continuation of the Soviet system as he had formed it. In the years after the Second World War, far from all Soviet citizens were eager to accept that the 1940s had justified the 1930s, that the victory over Germany had retrospectively justified the repressions of Soviet citizens. That, of course, had been the logic of the Great Terror at the time: that a war was coming, and so dangerous elements had to be removed. In Stalin's mind, a coming war with the Americans likely justified another round of preemptive repressions in the 1950s. It is not at all clear that Soviet citizens were willing to take that step. Although many went along with the anti-Semitic hysteria of the early 1950s, refusing for example to see Jewish doctors or to take medicine from Jewish pharmacists, this was not an endorsement of a return to mass terror.

The Soviet Union lasted almost four decades after Stalin's death, but its security organs never again organized a famine or a mass shooting. Stalin's successors, brutal though they were, abandoned the practice of mass terror in the Stalinist sense. Nikita Khrushchev, who eventually triumphed in the struggle for Stalin's succession, released most of the Ukrainian prisoners he had sent to the Gulag a decade before. It was not that Khrushchev was personally incapable of mass killing: he had been bloodthirsty during the Terror of 1937–1938 and the reconquest of western Ukraine after the Second World War. It was rather that he believed that the Soviet Union could no longer be run in the same fashion. He even revealed some of Stalin's crimes in a speech to a party congress in February 1956, although he emphasized the suffering of communist party elites rather than the groups who had suffered in far larger numbers: peasants, workers, and the members of the national minorities.

East European states remained satellites of the Soviet Union, but none of them moved beyond show trials (the prelude to the Great Terror of the late 1930s) to mass killing. Most of them (Poland was an exception) collectivized agriculture, but never denied peasants the right to private plots. There was no starvation in the satellite states, as there had been in the Soviet Union. Under Khrushchev, the Soviet Union would invade its communist satellite Hungary in 1956. Although the civil war that followed killed thousands of people and the intervention forced a change of leadership, no mass blood purges followed. Relatively few people were purposefully killed in communist eastern Europe after 1953. The numbers were orders of magnitude less than during the eras of mass killing (1933–1945) and ethnic cleansing (1945–1947).

Stalinist anti-Semitism haunted eastern Europe long after the death of Stalin. It was rarely a major tool of governance, but it was always available in moments of political stress. Anti-Semitism allowed leaders to revise the history of wartime suffering (recalled as the suffering only of Slavs) and also the history of Stalinism itself (which was portrayed as the deformed, Jewish version of communism).

In Poland in 1968, fifteen years after Stalin's death, the Holocaust was revisited for the purposes of communist nationalism. By this time Władysław Gomulka had returned to power. In February 1956, when Khrushchev criticized some aspects of Stalin's rule; he undermined the position of east European communist leaders associated with Stalinism, and strengthened the hand of those who could call themselves reformers. This was the end for the triumvirate of Berman, Bierut, and Minc. Gomułka was released from prison, rehabilitated, and allowed to take power that October. He represented the hope of some Poles for a reform communism, of others for a more national communism. Poland had already gained what it could from postwar reconstruction and rapid industrialization; attempts to improve the economic system proved either counterproductive or politically risky. After all attempts to improve the economic system failed, nationalism remained.[58]

In Poland in 1968, Gomułka's regime enacted an anti-Zionist purge that recalled the rhetoric of Stalin's last years. Twenty years after his own fall from grace in 1948, Gomułka took revenge on Polish-Jewish communists, or rather upon some of their children. As in the Soviet Union in 1952 and 1953, so in Poland in 1967 and 1968 the question of succession loomed. Gomułka had been in power for a long time. Like Stalin, he was willing to discredit rivals by way of their association with the Jewish question, and in particular by their softness on the supposed Zionist threat.

"Zionism" returned to the communist Polish press with the Israeli victory in the Six-Day War of June 1967. In the Soviet Union, the war confirmed the status of Israel as an American satellite, a line that was to be followed in the east European communist states. Yet Poles sometimes supported Israel ("our little Jews," as people said) against the Arabs, who were backed by the Soviet Union. Some Poles saw Israel at that point much as they saw themselves: as the persecuted underdog, opposed by the Soviet Union, representing Western civilization. For such people, Israel's victory over Arab states was a fantasy of Poland defeating the Soviet Union.[59]

The official Polish communist position was rather different. The Polish communist leadership identified Israel with Nazi Germany, and Zionism with National Socialism. These claims were often made by people who had lived through, and indeed sometimes fought in, the Second World War. Yet these grotesque comparisons followed from a certain political logic, now common to communist leaders in Poland and the Soviet Union. In the communist worldview, it was not the Jews but the Slavs (Russians in the USSR, Poles in Poland) who were the central figures (as victors and victims) of the Second World War. The Jews, always an immense problem for this story of suffering, had been assimilated to it in the postwar years, counted when necessary as "Soviet citizens" in the USSR and as "Poles" in Poland. In Poland, Jewish communists had done the most to eliminate Jews from the history of the German occupation in Poland. Having performed this task by 1956, the Jewish communists lost power. It was the non-Jewish communist Gomułka who exploited the legend of ethnic Polish innocence.

This recitation of the Second World War was also a propaganda stance in the Cold War. Poles and Russians, Slavic victims of the last German war, were accordingly still threatened by Germany, which now meant West Germany and its patron the United States. In the world of the Cold War, this was not entirely unconvincing. The chancellor of West Germany at the time was a former Nazi. Maps of Germany in German schoolbooks included the lands lost to Poland in 1945 (marked as "under Polish administration"). West Germany had never extended diplomatic recognition to postwar Poland. In the western democracies, as in West Germany, there was then little public discussion of German war crimes. In admitting West Germany to NATO in 1955, the United States in effect overlooked the atrocities of its recent German enemy.

As in the 1950s, Stalinist anti-Semitism assigned Israel a perfidious place in the Cold War. Picking up a theme from the Soviet press of January 1953, the Polish press in 1967 explained that West Germany had conveyed Nazi ideology to Israel. Political cartoons portrayed the Israeli army as the Wehrmacht. Thus Israel's claim that its existence was morally sanctioned by the Second World War and the Holocaust was supposed to be reversed: on the Polish communist account, capitalism had led to imperialism, of which National Socialism was an example. At the moment, the leader of the imperialist camp was the United States, of which Israel and West Germany alike were the cat's paws. Israel was just one more instance of imperialism, sustaining a world order that generated crimes against humanity, rather than a small state with a special historical claim to victimhood. The communists wished to monopolize claims of victimhood for themselves.[60]

These Nazi-Zionist comparisons began in communist Poland with the Six-Day War in June 1967, but came home when the Polish regime repressed opponents the following spring. Polish university students, protesting the ban on the performance of a play, called a peaceful rally against the regime for 8 March 1968. The regime then castigated their leaders as "Zionists." The previous year Jews in Poland had been called a "fifth column," supporting Poland's enemies abroad. Now the problems of Poland as a whole were blamed upon the Jews, categorized once again, as in the USSR fifteen years before, as both "Zionists" and "cosmopolitans." As in the Soviet Union, this was only an apparent contradiction: the "Zionists" supposedly favored Israel, and the "cosmopolitans" were supposedly drawn to the United States, but both were allies of imperialism and thus enemies of the Polish state. They were outsiders and traitors, indifferent to Poland and Polishness.[61]

In an agile maneuver, Polish communists were now claiming an old European anti-Semitic argument for their own. The Nazi stereotype of "Judeobolshevism," Hitler's own idea that communism was a Jewish plot, had been quite widespread in prewar Poland. The prominence of Polish Jews in the early communist regime, though a product of very special historical circumstances, had done little to dispel the popular association between Jews and communists. Now, in spring 1968, Polish communists played to this stereotype by claiming that the problem with Stalinism was its Jewishness. If anything had gone wrong in communist Poland in the 1940s and 1950s, it was the fault of the Jews who exerted too much control over the party and thereby deformed the whole system. Some communists might have done harm to Poles, was the implication, but these communists had been Jews. But Polish communism, it followed, could be cleansed of such people, or at least of their sons and daughters. Gomułka's regime, in this way, tried to make communism ethnically Polish.

The solution could only be a purge of Jews from public life and positions of political influence. But who was a Jew? In 1968, students with Jewish names or Stalinist parents received disproportionate attention in the press. Polish authorities used anti-Semitism to separate the rest of the population from the students, organizing huge rallies of workers and soldiers. The Polish working class became, in the pronouncements of the country's leaders, the ethnically Polish working class. But matters were not so simple. The Gomułka regime was happy to use the Jewish label to rid itself of criticism in general. A Jew, by the party definition, was not always someone whose parents were Jewish. Characteristic of the campaign was a certain vagueness about Jews: often a "Zionist" was simply an intellectual or someone unfavorable to the regime.[62]

The campaign was calculatedly unjust, deliberately provocative, and absurd in its historical vacuity. It was not, however, lethal. The anti-Semitic tropes of Polish communism recalled late Stalinism, and thus stereotypes familiar in Nazi

Germany. There was never any plan, however, to murder Jews. Although at least one suicide can be connected to the "anti-Zionist campaign," and many people were beaten by the police, no one was actually killed. The regime made about 2,591 arrests, drafted a few hundred more students to garrisons distant from Warsaw, and sentenced some of the student leaders to prison. About seventeen thousand Polish citizens (most but not all of Jewish origin) accepted the regime's offer of one-way travel documents and left the country.[63]

Residents of Warsaw could not help but notice that they left from a railway station not far from the Umschlagplatz, whence the Jews of Warsaw had been deported by train to Treblinka only twenty-six years earlier. Three million Jews at least had lived in Poland before the Second World War. After this episode of communist anti-Semitism, perhaps thirty thousand remained. For Polish communists and those who believed them, the Jews were not victims in 1968 or at any earlier point: they were people who conspired to deprive Poles of their righteous claim to innocence and heroism.

The Stalinist anti-Semitism of Poland in 1968 changed the lives of tens of thousands of people, and ended the faith in Marxism of many intelligent young men and women in eastern Europe. Marxism, of course, had other problems. By this time the economic potential of the Stalinist model was exhausted in communist Poland, as it was throughout the communist bloc. Collectivization was no boon to agrarian economies. Only so much fast growth could be generated by forced industrialization. After a generation, it was clear more or less everywhere that western Europe was more prosperous than the communist world, and that the gap was growing. Polish communist leaders, in embracing anti-Semitism, were implicitly admitting that their system could not be improved. They alienated many of the people who might earlier have believed in a reform of communism, and had no idea how they might improve the system themselves. In 1970 Gomułka would fall from power after trying to increase prices, and be replaced by an entirely unideological successor who would try to borrow his way to Poland's prosperity. The failure of that scheme led to the emergence of the Solidarity movement in 1980.[64]

Even as the Polish students were falling under police batons in March 1968, Czechoslovak communists were trying to reform Marxism in eastern Europe. During the Prague Spring, the communist regime allowed a great deal of free public expression, in the hope of generating support for economic reform. Predictably, discussions had led in other directions than the regime had expected. Despite Soviet pressure, Aleksandr Dubček, the general secretary of the Czechoslovak party, allowed gatherings and debates to continue. That August, Soviet (and Polish and East German and Bulgarian and Hungarian) troops invaded Czechoslovakia and crushed the Prague Spring.

Soviet propaganda confirmed that the Polish leadership's experiment with anti-Semitism was no deviation. In the Soviet press, much attention was devoted to the real or imagined Jewish origins of Czechoslovak communist reformers. In Poland in the 1970s and 1980s, the secret police made a point of emphasizing the Jewish origins of some members of the opposition. When Mikhail Gorbachev came to power in 1985 as a reformer in the Soviet Union, opponents of his reforms tried to exploit Russian anti-Semitism in defense of the old system.[65]

Stalinism had displaced east European Jews from their historical position as victims of the Germans, and embedded them instead in an account of an imperialist conspiracy against communism. From there, it was but a small step to present them as part of a conspiracy of their own. And thus the communists' hesitation to distinguish and define Hitler's major crime tended, as the decades passed, to confirm an aspect of Hitler's worldview.

Stalinist anti-Semitism in Moscow, Prague, and Warsaw killed only a handful of people, but it confused the European past. The Holocaust complicated the Stalinist story of the suffering of Soviet citizens as such, and displaced Russians and Slavs as the most victimized of groups. It was the communists and their loyal Slavic (and other) followers who were to be understood as both the victors and the victims of the Second World War. The scheme of Slavic innocence and Western aggression was to be applied to the Cold War as well, even if this meant that Jews, associated with Israel and America in the imperialist Western camp, were to be regarded as the aggressors of history.

So long as communists governed most of Europe, the Holocaust could never be seen for what it was. Precisely because so many millions of non-Jewish east Europeans had indeed been killed on the battlefields, in the Dulags and Stalags, in besieged cities, and in reprisals in the villages and the countryside, the communist emphasis upon non-Jewish suffering always had a historical foundation. Communist leaders, beginning with Stalin and continuing to the end, could rightly say that few people in the West appreciated the role of the Red Army in the defeat of the Wehrmacht, and the suffering that the peoples of eastern Europe endured under German occupation. It took just one modification, the submersion of the Holocaust into a generic account of suffering, to externalize that which had once been so central to eastern Europe, Jewish civilization. During the Cold War, the natural response in the West was to emphasize the enormous suffering that Stalinism had brought to the citizens of the Soviet Union. This, too, was true; but like the Soviet accounts it was not the only truth, or the whole truth. In this competition for memory, the Holocaust, the other German mass killing policies, and the Stalinist mass murders became three different histories, even though in historical fact they shared a place and time.

Like the vast majority of the mass killing of civilians by both the Nazi and the Soviet regimes, the Holocaust took place in the bloodlands. After the war, the traditional homelands of European Jewry lay in the communist world, as did the death factories and the killing fields. By introducing a new kind of anti-Semitism into the world, Stalin made of the Holocaust something less than it was. When an international collective memory of the Holocaust emerged in the 1970s and 1980s, it rested on the experiences of German and west European Jews, minor groups of victims, and on Auschwitz, where only about one in six of the total number of murdered Jews died. Historians and commemorators in western Europe and the United States tended to correct that Stalinist distortion by erring in the other direction, by passing quickly over the nearly five million Jews killed east of Auschwitz, and the nearly five million non-Jews killed by the Nazis. Deprived of its Jewish distinctiveness in the East, and stripped of its geography in the West, the Holocaust never quite became part of European history, even as Europeans and many others came to agree that all should remember the Holocaust.

Stalin's empire covered Hitler's. The iron curtain fell between West and East, and between the survivors and the dead. Now that it has lifted, we may see, if we so wish, the history of Europe between Hitler and Stalin.

HUMANITY

Each of the living bore a name. The toddler who imagined he saw wheat in the fields was Józef Sobolewski. He starved to death, along with his mother and five of his brothers and sisters, in 1933 in a famished Ukraine. The one brother who survived was shot in 1937, in Stalin's Great Terror. Only his sister Hanna remained to recall him and his hope. Stanisław Wyganowski was the young man who foresaw that he would meet his arrested wife, Maria, "under the ground." They were both shot by the NKVD in Leningrad in 1937. The Polish officer who wrote of his wedding ring was Adam Solski. The diary was found on his body when his remains were disinterred at Katyn, where he was shot in 1940. The wedding ring he probably hid; his executioners probably found it. The eleven-year-old Russian girl who kept a simple diary in besieged and starving Leningrad in 1941 was Tania Savicheva. One of her sisters escaped across the frozen surface of Lake Ladoga; Tania and the rest of her family died. The twelve-year-old Jewish girl who wrote to her father in Belarus in 1942 of the death pits was Junita Vishniatskaia. Her mother, who wrote alongside her, was named Zlata. They were both killed. "Farewell forever" was the last line of Junita's letter. "I kiss you, I kiss you."

Each of the dead became a number. Between them, the Nazi and Stalinist regimes murdered more than fourteen million people in the bloodlands. The killing began with a political famine that Stalin directed at Soviet Ukraine, which claimed more than three million lives. It continued with Stalin's Great Terror of 1937 and 1938, in which some seven hundred thousand people were shot, most of them peasants or members of national minorities. The Soviets and the Germans then cooperated in the destruction of Poland and of its educated classes, killing some two hundred thousand people between 1939 and 1941. After Hitler betrayed Stalin and ordered the invasion of the Soviet Union, the Germans starved the Soviet prisoners of war and the inhabitants of besieged Leningrad, taking the lives of more than four million people. In the occupied Soviet Union, occupied Poland, and the occupied Baltic States, the Germans shot and gassed some 5.4 million Jews. The Germans and the Soviets provoked one another to ever greater crimes, as in the partisan wars for Belarus and Warsaw, where the Germans killed about half a million civilians.

These atrocities shared a place, and they shared a time: the bloodlands between 1933 and 1945. To describe their course has been to introduce to European history its central event. Without an account of all of the major killing policies in their common European historical setting, comparisons between Nazi Germany and the Soviet Union must be inadequate. Now that this history of the bloodlands is complete, the comparison remains.

The Nazi and the Stalinist systems must be compared, not so much to understand the one or the other but to understand our times and ourselves. Hannah Arendt made this case in 1951, uniting the two regimes under the rubric of "totalitarianism." Russian literature of the nineteenth century offered her the idea of the "superfluous man." The pioneering Holocaust historian Raul Hilberg later showed her how the bureaucratic state could eradicate such people in the twentieth century. Arendt provided the enduring portrait of the modern superfluous man, made to feel so by the crush of mass society, then made so by totalitarian regimes capable of placing death within a story of progress and joy. It is Arendt's portrayal of the killing epoch that has endured: of people (victims and perpetrators alike) slowly losing their humanity, first in the anonymity of mass society, then in a concentration camp. This is a powerful image, and it must be corrected before a historical comparison of Nazi and Soviet killing can begin.[1]

The killing sites that most closely fit such a framework were the German prisoner-of-war camps. They were the only type of facility (German or Soviet) where the purpose of concentrating human beings was to kill them. Soviet prisoners of war, crushed together in the tens of thousands and denied food and medical care, died quickly and in great numbers: some three million perished, most of them in a few months. Yet this major example of killing by concentration had little to do with Arendt's concept of modern society. Her analysis directs our attention to Berlin and Moscow, as the capitals of distinct states that exemplify the totalitarian system, each of them acting upon their own citizens. Yet the Soviet prisoners of war died as a result of the *interaction* of the two systems. Arendt's account of totalitarianism centers on the dehumanization *within* modern mass industrial society, not on the historical overlap *between* German and Soviet aspirations and power. The crucial moment for these soldiers was their capture, when they passed from the control of their Soviet superior officers and the NKVD to that of the Wehrmacht and the SS. Their fate cannot be understood as progressive alienation within one modern society; it was a consequence of the belligerent encounter of two, of the criminal policies of Germany on the territory of the Soviet Union.

Elsewhere, concentration was not usually a step in a killing process but rather a method for correcting minds and extracting labor from bodies. With the important exception of the German prisoner-of-war camps, neither the Germans nor the Soviets intentionally killed by concentration. Camps were more often the alternative than the prelude to execution. During the Great Terror in the Soviet Union, two verdicts were possible: death or the Gulag. The first meant a bullet in the nape of the neck. The second meant hard labor in a faraway place, in a dark mine or a freezing forest or on the open steppe; but it also usually meant life. Under German rule, the concentration camps and the death factories operated under different principles. A sentence to the concentration camp Belsen was one thing, a transport to the death factory Bełżec something else. The first meant hunger and labor, but also the likelihood of survival; the second meant immediate and certain death by asphyxiation. This, ironically, is why people remember Belsen and forget Bełżec.

Nor did extermination policies arise from concentration policies. The Soviet concentration camp system was an integral part of a political economy that was meant to endure. The Gulag existed before, during, and after the famines of the early 1930s, and before, during, and after the shooting operations of the late 1930s. It reached its largest size in the early 1950s, after the Soviets had ceased to kill their own citizens in large numbers—in part for that very reason. The Germans began the mass killing of Jews in summer 1941 in the occupied Soviet Union, by gunfire over pits, far from a concentration camp system that had already been in operation for eight years. In a matter of a given few days in the second half of 1941, the Germans shot more Jews in the east than they had inmates in all of their concentration camps. The gas chambers were not developed for concentration camps, but for the medical killing facilities of the "euthanasia" program. Then came the mobile gas vans used to kill Jews in the Soviet east, then the parked gas van at Chełmno used to kill Polish Jews in lands annexed to Germany, then the permanent gassing facilities at Bełżec, Sobibór, and Treblinka in the General Government. The gas chambers allowed the policy pursued in the occupied Soviet Union, the mass killing of Jews, to be continued west of the Molotov-Ribbentrop line. The vast majority of Jews killed in the Holocaust never saw a concentration camp.[2]

The image of the German concentration camps as the worst element of National Socialism is an illusion, a dark mirage over an unknown desert. In the early months of 1945, as the German state collapsed, the chiefly non-Jewish prisoners in the SS concentration camp system were dying in large numbers. Their fate was much like that of Gulag prisoners in the Soviet Union between 1941 and 1943, when the Soviet system was stressed by the German invasion and occupation. Some of the starving victims were captured on film by the British and the Americans. These images led west Europeans and Americans toward erroneous conclusions about the German system. The concentration camps did kill hundreds of thousands of people at the end of the war, but they were not (in contrast to the death facilities) designed for mass killing. Although some Jews were sentenced to concentration camps as political prisoners and others were dispatched to them as laborers, the concentration camps were not chiefly for Jews. Jews who were sent to concentration camps were among the Jews who survived. This is another reason the concentration camps are familiar: they were described by survivors, people who would have been worked to death eventually, but who were liberated at war's end. The German policy to kill all the Jews of Europe was implemented not in the concentration camps but over pits, in gas vans, and at the death facilities at Chełmno, Bełżec, Sobibór, Treblinka, Majdanek, and Auschwitz.[3]

As Arendt recognized, Auschwitz was an unusual combination of an industrial camp complex and a killing facility. It stands as a symbol of both concentration and extermination, which creates a certain confusion. The camp first held Poles, and then Soviet prisoners of war, and then Jews and Roma. Once the death factory was added, some arriving Jews were selected for labor, worked until exhaustion, and then gassed. Thus chiefly at Auschwitz can an example be found of Arendt's image of progressive alienation ending with death. It is a rendering that harmonizes with the literature of Auschwitz written by its survivors: Tadeusz Borowski, or Primo Levi, or Elie Wiesel. But this sequence is exceptional. It does not capture the usual course of the Holocaust, even at Auschwitz. Most of the Jews who died at Auschwitz were gassed upon arrival, never having spent time inside a camp. The journey of Jews from the camp to the gas chambers was a minor part of the history of the Auschwitz complex, and is misleading as a guide to the Holocaust or to mass killing generally.

Auschwitz was indeed a major site of the Holocaust: about one in six murdered Jews perished there. But though the death factory at Auschwitz was the last killing facility to function, it was not the height of the technology of death: the most efficient shooting squads killed faster, the starvation sites killed faster, and Treblinka killed faster. Auschwitz was also not the main place where the two largest Jewish communities in Europe, the Polish and the Soviet, were exterminated. Most Soviet and Polish Jews under German occupation had already been murdered by the time Auschwitz became the major death factory. By the time the gas chamber and crematoria complexes at Birkenau came on line in spring 1943, more than three quarters of the Jews who would be killed in the Holocaust were already dead. For that matter, the tremendous majority of all of the people who would be deliberately killed by the Soviet and the Nazi regimes, well over ninety percent, had already been killed by the time those gas chambers at Birkenau began their deadly work. Auschwitz is the coda to the death fugue.

Perhaps, as Arendt argued, Nazi and Soviet mass murder was a sign of some deeper dysfunctionality of modern society. But before we draw such theoretical conclusions, about modernity or anything else, we must understand what actually happened, in the Holocaust and in the bloodlands generally. For the time being, Europe's epoch of mass killing is overtheorized and misunderstood.

Unlike Arendt, who was extraordinarily knowledgeable within the limits of the available documentation, we have little excuse for this disproportion of theory to knowledge. The numbers of the dead are now available to us, sometimes more precisely, sometimes less, but firmly enough to convey a sense of the destructiveness of each regime. In policies that were meant to kill civilians or prisoners of war, Nazi Germany murdered about ten million people in the bloodlands (and perhaps eleven million people total), the Soviet Union under Stalin over four million in the bloodlands (and about six million total). If fore-seeable deaths resulting from famine, ethnic cleansing, and long stays in camps are added, the Stalinist total rises to perhaps nine million and the Nazi to per-haps twelve. These larger numbers can never be precise, not least because mil-lions of civilians who died as an indirect result of the Second World War were victims, in one way or another, of *both* systems.

The region most touched by both the Nazi and Stalinist regimes was the bloodlands: in today's terms, St. Petersburg and the western rim of the Russian Federation, most of Poland, the Baltic States, Belarus, and Ukraine. This is where the power and the malice of the Nazi and Soviet regimes overlapped and interacted. The bloodlands are important not only because most of the victims were its inhabitants but also because it was the center of the major policies that killed people from elsewhere. For example, the Germans killed about 5.4 mil-lion Jews. Of those, more than four million were natives of the bloodlands: Pol-ish, Soviet, Lithuanian, and Latvian Jews. Most of the remainder were Jews from other east European countries. The largest group of Jewish victims from beyond the region, the Hungarian Jews, were killed in the bloodlands, at Auschwitz. If Romania and Czechoslovakia are also considered, then east Eu-ropean Jews account for nearly ninety percent of the victims of the Holocaust. The smaller Jewish populations of western and southern Europe were deported to the bloodlands to die.

Like the Jewish victims, the non-Jewish victims either were native to the bloodlands or were brought there to die. In their prisoner-of-war camps and in Leningrad and other cities, the Germans starved more than four million people to death. Most but not all of the victims of these deliberate starvation policies were natives of the bloodlands; perhaps a million were Soviet citizens from be-yond the region. The victims of Stalin's policies of mass murder lived across the length and breadth of the Soviet Union, the largest state in the history of the world. Even so, Stalin's blow fell hardest in the western Soviet borderlands, in the bloodlands. The Soviets starved more than five million people to death dur-ing collectivization, most of them in Soviet Ukraine. The Soviets recorded the killing of 681,691 people in the Great Terror of 1937–1938, of whom a dispro-portionate number were Soviet Poles and Soviet Ukrainian peasants, two groups

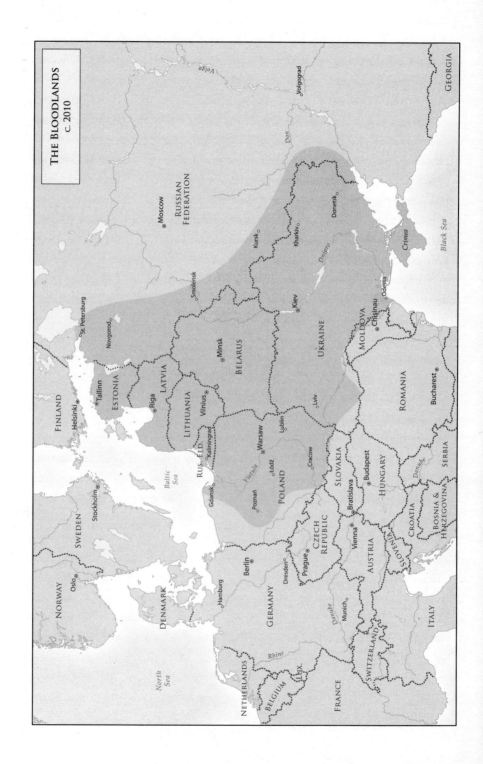

THE BLOODLANDS
c. 2010

that inhabited the western Soviet Union, and thus the bloodlands. These numbers do not themselves constitute a comparison of the systems, but they are a point of departure, perhaps an obligatory one.[4]

In May 1941 Arendt escaped to the United States, where she applied her formidable German philosophical training to the question of the origins of the National Socialist and Soviet regimes. A few weeks after her departure, Germany invaded the Soviet Union. In her Europe, Nazi Germany and the Soviet Union had arisen separately, and then sealed an alliance.

The Europe of Vasily Grossman, the founder of a second tradition of comparison, was one in which the Soviet Union and Nazi Germany were at war. Grossman, a fiction writer who became a Soviet war correspondent, saw many of the important battles on the eastern front, and evidence of all of the major German (and Soviet) crimes. Like Arendt, he tried to understand the German mass murder of the Jews in the east in universal terms. For him this meant, at first, not a critique of modernity as such but a condemnation of fascism and Germany. Just as Arendt published her *Origins of Totalitarianism*, Grossman was liberated from this political framework by the personal experience of anti-Semitism in the Soviet Union. He then broke the taboos of a century, placing the crimes of the Nazi and Soviet regimes on the same pages, in the same scenes, in two novels whose reputations only grow with time. Grossman meant not to unify the two systems analytically within a single sociological scheme (such as Arendt's totalitarianism) but rather to relieve them of their own ideological accounts of themselves, and thereby lift the veil on their common inhumanity.

In *Life and Fate* (completed in 1959, published abroad in 1980), Grossman has one of the heroes, a sort of holy fool, recall the German shootings of Jews in Belarus and the cannibalism in Soviet Ukraine in the same breath. In *Everything Flows* (incomplete at Grossman's death in 1964, published abroad in 1970), he uses familiarity with scenes of German concentration camps to introduce the famine in Ukraine: "As for the children—did you see the newspaper photographs of children from the German camps? They looked just the same: heads heavy as cannonballs; thin little necks, like the necks of storks; and on their arms and legs you could see every little bone. Every single little bone moving under their skin, and the joints between them." Grossman returns to this Nazi-Soviet comparison, over and over, not to arouse controversy but to create a convention.[5]

As one of Grossman's characters exclaims, the key to both National Socialism and Stalinism was their ability to deprive groups of human beings of their right to be regarded as human. Thus the only answer was to proclaim, again and again, that this was simply not true. The Jews and the kulaks "are people. They are human beings. I can see now that we are all human beings." This is literature working against what Arendt called the fictitious world of totalitarianism. People can be killed in large numbers, she maintained, because leaders such as Stalin and Hitler can imagine a world without kulaks, or without Jews, and then make the real world conform, if only imperfectly, to their visions. The dying loses its moral weight, not so much because it is hidden but because it is permeated with the story that brought it about. The dead, too, lose their human character; they are helplessly reincarnated as actors in a drama of progress, even when, or perhaps especially when, that story is resisted by an ideological foe. Grossman extracted the victims from the cacophony of a century and made their voices audible within the unending polemic.

From Arendt and Grossman together, then, come two simple ideas. First, a legitimate comparison of Nazi Germany and the Stalinist Soviet Union must not only explain the crimes but also embrace the humanity of all concerned by them, including the victims, perpetrators, bystanders, and leaders. Second, a legitimate comparison must begin with life rather than death. Death is not a solution, but only a subject. It must be a source of disquiet, never of satisfaction. It must not, above all, supply the rounding rhetorical flourish that brings a story to a defined end. Since life gives meaning to death, rather than the other way around, the important question is not: what political, intellectual, literary, or psychological closure can be drawn from the fact of mass killing? Closure is a false harmony, a siren song masquerading as a swan song.

The important question is: how could (how can) so many human lives be brought to a violent end?

———————

In both the Soviet Union and Nazi Germany, utopias were advanced, compromised by reality, and then implemented as mass murder: in autumn 1932 by Stalin, and autumn 1941 by Hitler. Stalin's utopia was to collectivize the Soviet Union in nine to twelve weeks; Hitler's was to conquer the Soviet Union in the same span of time. Each of these seems, in retrospect, to be horrendously impractical. Yet each of them was implemented, under the cover of a big lie, even after failure was obvious. Dead human beings provided retrospective arguments for the rectitude of policy. Hitler and Stalin thus shared a certain politics of tyranny: they brought about catastrophes, blamed the enemy of their choice, and then used the death of millions to make the case that their policies were necessary or desirable. Each of them had a transformative utopia, a group to be blamed when its realization proved impossible, and then a policy of mass murder that could be proclaimed as a kind of ersatz victory.

In both collectivization and the Final Solution, mass sacrifice was needed to protect a leader from the unthinkability of error. After collectivization brought resistance and hunger to Soviet Ukraine, Stalin blamed kulaks and Ukrainians and Poles. After the Wehrmacht was halted at Moscow and the Americans entered the Second World War, Hitler blamed Jews. Just as kulaks and Ukrainians and Poles had taken the blame for slowing the construction of the Soviet system, Jews took the blame for preventing its destruction. Stalin had chosen collectivization, Hitler had chosen war: but it was more convenient, for them and their comrades, to shift the responsibility for the associated catastrophe elsewhere. Stalin's interpretation was used to justify the starvation of Ukraine and then the mass shootings of kulaks and members of national minorities; Hitler's interpretation was used to justify the shooting and gassing of all Jews. After collectivization starved millions to death, this was adduced by Stalin to be evidence of a victorious class struggle. As the Jews were shot and then gassed, Hitler presented this, in ever clearer terms, as a war aim in and of itself. When the war was lost, Hitler called the mass murder of the Jews his victory.

Stalin had the capacity to reformulate utopias. Stalinism itself was a retreat: from the impulse toward European revolution that had inspired the Bolsheviks in 1917, to the defense of the Soviet Union after that revolution did not take place. When the Red Army failed to spread communism to Europe in 1920, Stalin had a fallback plan: socialism would be made in one country, the Soviet Union. When his Five-Year Plan to build socialism brought disaster, he presided over the starvation of millions. But he explained the events as part of the policy, and reaped the benefits as the fearsome father of the nation and the dominant figure in the politburo. After turning the NKVD against the kulaks and the national minorities in 1937–1938, he explained that this was necessary for the security of the homeland of socialism. After the retreat of the Red Army in 1941, and indeed after its victory in 1945, he appealed to Russian nationalism. When the Cold War began, he blamed Jews (and others, of course) for the vulnerabilities of the Soviet Union.

Hitler, too, could revise utopia. The tens of millions of dead envisioned by the Hunger Plan and Generalplan Ost became the millions of dead of the starvation policies and of deportations. Insofar as the war forced a major change in his thinking, it was in the nature of what the Nazis called the Final Solution. Rather than wait until the war was won to "resolve" the Jewish "problem," Hitler endorsed a policy of extermination during the war itself. The killing of Jews was escalated in the Soviet Union in July 1941 after a month of war without decisive results, and then escalated again when Moscow did not fall in December 1941. The policy of killing certain Jews was initially grounded in the rhetoric of military necessity, and had some connection to political and economic planning. But its escalation after the military situation changed, and after those plans were discarded or suspended, reveals that the elimination of Jews was for Hitler an end in itself.

The final version of the Final Solution was not designed, as were Stalin's improvisations, to protect the leader or his system. It was not a step in a logical plan so much as an element in an aesthetic vision. The original justifications for the killing of Jews gave way to the anti-Semitic incantation, always present, of a cosmic Jewish plot, the struggle against which was the very definition of German virtue. For Stalin, the political struggle always had political meaning. His achievement in that respect was nearly the opposite of Hitler's: whereas Hitler transformed a republic into a revolutionary colonial empire, Stalin translated the poetics of revolutionary Marxism into durable workaday politics. Stalin's class conflict could always be expressed in public as the Soviet line; the chain that bound Soviet citizens and foreign communists to his person was a logical one. For Hitler struggle itself was the good, and a struggle that destroyed the Jews was to be welcomed. If the Germans were defeated, then that was their fault.

Stalin was able to realize his fictitious world, but to restrain himself when necessary. With the help of able associates such as Heinrich Himmler and Reinhard Heydrich, Hitler moved from one fictitious world to another, and brought much of the German people with him.

Only an unabashed acceptance of the similarities between the Nazi and Soviet systems permits an understanding of their differences. Both ideologies opposed liberalism and democracy. In both political systems, the significance of the word *party* was inverted: rather than being a group among others competing for power according to accepted rules, it became the group that determined the rules. Nazi Germany and the Soviet Union were both one-party states. In both the Nazi and Soviet polities the party played a leading role in matters of ideology and social discipline. Its political logic demanded exclusion of outsiders, and its economic elite believed that certain groups were superfluous or harmful. In both administrations, economic planners assumed that more people existed in the countryside than was really necessary. Stalinist collectivization would remove superfluous peasants from the countryside and send them to the cities or the Gulag to work. If they starved, that was of little consequence. Hitlerian colonization projected the starvation and deportation of tens of millions of people.[6]

Both the Soviet and the Nazi political economies relied upon collectives that controlled social groups and extracted their resources. The collective farm, the instrument of Stalin's great transformation of the Soviet countryside from 1930, was used by German occupation authorities from 1941. In the occupied Polish, Lithuanian, Latvian, and Soviet cities the Germans added a new collective: the ghetto. The urban Jewish ghettos, although originally meant as resettlement points, became zones for the extraction of Jewish property and Jewish labor. Their nominal Jewish authorities of the Judenrat could usually be relied upon to raise "contributions" and organize labor brigades. Both the ghettos and the collective farms were administered by local people. Both the Nazi and the Soviet systems built large systems of concentration camps. Hitler would have used the Soviet camps for Jews and other ostensible enemies if he could have, but Germany never conquered enough of the Soviet Union to make that possible.

Although the instruments of local exploitation looked the same, and sometimes were the same, they served different visions of the future. In the National Socialist vision, inequality between groups was inherent and desirable. The inequalities found in the world, between a richer Germany and a poorer Soviet Union for example, were to be multiplied. The Soviet system, when it was expanded, brought to others the Soviet version of equality. There was no more dramatic plan than that, and that was dramatic enough. If the Soviet system encountered nomads, it forced them to settle. If it encountered peasants, it forced them to supply the state with food. If it encountered nations, it eliminated their upper classes: by co-optation, deportation, or murder. If it encountered contented societies, it required them to embrace the Soviet system as the best of all possible worlds. It was, in this special sense, inclusive. Whereas the Germans excluded the majority of the inhabitants of their empire from equal membership in the state, the Soviets included almost everyone in their version of equality.

Stalin, no less than Hitler, spoke of liquidations and cleansings. Yet the Stalinist rationale for elimination always had to do with a defense of the Soviet state or the advance of socialism. In Stalinism mass murder could never be anything more than a successful defense of socialism, or an element in a story of progress toward socialism; it was never the political victory itself. Stalinism was a project of self-colonization, expanded when circumstances permitted. Nazi colonization, by contrast, was totally dependent upon the immediate and total conquest of a vast new eastern empire, which would have dwarfed prewar Germany in size. It assumed the destruction of tens of millions of civilians as a precondition of the enterprise. In practice, the Germans generally killed people who were not Germans, whereas the Soviets usually killed people who were Soviet citizens.

The Soviet system was most lethal when the Soviet Union was not at war. The Nazis, on the other hand, killed no more than a few thousand people before the war began. During the war of conquest, Germany killed millions of people faster than any state in history (to that point).[7]

At a great distance in time, we can choose to compare the Nazi and Soviet systems, or not. The hundreds of millions of Europeans who were touched by both regimes did not have this luxury.

The comparisons between leaders and systems began the moment that Hitler came to power. From 1933 through 1945 hundreds of millions of Europeans had to weigh what they knew about National Socialism and Stalinism as they made the decisions that would, all too often, determine their fate. This was true of unemployed German workers in early 1933, who had to decide whether they would vote for social democrats, communists, or Nazis. It was true, at the same moment, of starving Ukrainian peasants, some of whom hoped for a German invasion that might rescue them from their plight. It held for European politicians of the second half of the 1930s, who had to decide whether or not to enter Stalin's Popular Fronts. The dilemma was felt sharply in Warsaw in these years, as Polish diplomats sought to keep an equal distance between their powerful German and Soviet neighbors in the hope of avoiding war.

When both the Germans and the Soviets invaded Poland in 1939, Polish officers had to decide to whom they would surrender, and Polish Jews (and other Polish citizens besides) whether to flee to the other occupation zone. After

Germany invaded the Soviet Union in 1941, some Soviet prisoners of war weighed the risks of collaboration with the Germans against the likelihood of starving to death in prisoner-of-war camps. Belarusian youth had to decide whether to join the Soviet partisans or the German police—before they were press-ganged into one or the other. Jews in Minsk in 1942 had to choose between remaining in the ghetto or fleeing to the forest to seek Soviet partisans. Polish Home Army commanders in 1944 had to decide whether or not to try to liberate Warsaw from the Germans themselves, or to wait for the Soviets. Most survivors of the Ukrainian famine of 1933 later experienced German occupation; most survivors of the German starvation camps of 1941 returned to Stalin's Soviet Union; most survivors of the Holocaust who remained in Europe also experienced communism.

These Europeans, who inhabited the crucial part of Europe at the crucial time, were condemned to compare. We have the possibility, if we wish, to consider the two systems in isolation; people who lived under them experienced overlap and interaction. The Nazi and Soviet regimes were sometimes allies, as in the joint occupation of Poland. They sometimes held compatible goals as foes: as when Stalin chose not to aid the rebels in Warsaw in 1944, thereby allowing the Germans to kill people who would later have resisted communist rule. This is what François Furet called their "belligerent complicity." Often the Germans and the Soviets goaded each other into escalations that cost more lives than the policies of either state by itself would have. Partisan warfare was the supreme occasion for each leader to tempt the other into further brutality. From 1942, Stalin encouraged guerrilla actions in occupied Soviet Belarus, knowing that it would bring down massive reprisals against his own citizens. Hitler welcomed the opportunity to kill "anyone who even looks at us askance."[8]

During the Second World War, the bloodlands were subjected not to one invasion but to two or three, not to one occupation regime but to two or three. The mass murder of Jews began as the Germans crossed into lands that the Soviets had just annexed for themselves a matter of months before, from which they had deported tens of thousands of people just weeks before, and in which they had shot thousands of prisoners just days before. The German Einsatzgruppen were able to mobilize local anger over the murder of prisoners by the Soviet NKVD. The twenty thousand or so Jews who were killed in these orchestrated pogroms were only a very small part, fewer than one half of one percent, of the victims of the Holocaust. But precisely the overlap between Soviet and German power allowed the Nazis to propagate their own description of Bolshevism as a Jewish plot.

Other episodes of mass murder were a result of this same accumulation of Nazi and Soviet rule. In occupied Belarus, Belarusians killed other Belarusians, some of them as policemen in the German service, some of them as Soviet partisans. In occupied Ukraine, policemen fled the German service to join nationalist partisan units. These people then killed tens of thousands of Poles and fellow Ukrainians in the name of a social and national revolution. This sort of accumulation could also affect, and indeed end, the lives of millions of people who were thousands of miles away from the bloodlands. Masses of Soviet citizens fled the bloodlands to the east, to the heartland of a Soviet state that was poorly equipped to support them. Death rates in the Gulag increased drastically during the war, as a result of food shortages and logistical problems associated with the German invasion. More than half a million people died as a result, victims of the war and of both regimes.

Even so, the impact of multiple continuous occupation was most dramatic in the lands that Hitler conceded to Stalin in the secret protocol to the nonaggression pact of 1939, then took from him in the first days of the invasion of 1941, then lost to him again in 1944. Before the Second World War, these lands were: independent Estonia, Latvia, Lithuania, and eastern Poland. Though these states were governed by authoritarian nationalist regimes, and popular nationalism was certainly on the rise, the number of people killed either by the state or in civil strife in the 1930s was no more than a few thousand in all of these countries taken together. Under Soviet rule between 1939 and 1941, hundreds of thousands of people from this zone were deported to Kazakhstan and Siberia and tens of thousands more shot. The region was the heartland of Jewish settlement in Europe, and its Jews were trapped when the Germans invaded the newly extended Soviet Union in 1941. Almost all of the Jews native to the region were killed. It was here that Ukrainian partisans ethnically cleansed Poles in 1943 before Soviet forces ethnically cleansed both Ukrainians and Poles from 1944 onward.

This zone, east of the Molotov-Ribbentrop line, was where the Holocaust began, *and* where the Soviets twice extended their boundaries to the west. In this special strip of territory within the bloodlands, most of the NKVD persecutions of the 1940s took place, as did more than a quarter of the German killings of Jews, as did massive ethnic cleansing. Molotov-Ribbentrop Europe was a joint production of the Soviets and the Nazis.

The transformations envisioned by both Hitler and Stalin were economic, and the consequences of their economic policies were felt most painfully in the bloodlands. Though National Socialist and Stalinist ideologies were essentially different, Nazi and Soviet planners were preoccupied with certain basic economic problems, and Nazi and Soviet leaders inhabited and sought to alter the same world political economy. Ideology cannot function without economics, and economics in the time and place was very much a matter of the control of territory. Animal and human labor still moved ploughs and armies. Capital was less mobile then, and scarcer. Food was a natural resource, as were oil and minerals and precious metals. Globalization had been halted by the First World War, and free trade further hindered by the Great Depression.

From the Marxist point of view, peasant societies had no right to exist in the modern world. From the Nazi perspective, Slavic peasants (though not German farmers) were superfluous. German farmers would reclaim the fertile soil with their own sweat and the blood of others. These were ideological perspectives, of course: but like all ideologies they arose from, and spoke to, a certain understanding of economic interests. As theory became practice, Nazi colonization and Soviet self-colonization could function only when economic interests and ideological presuppositions seemed to confirm each other. Leaders, planners, and killers needed the sight of gold as well as the smell of ink. The mass killing policies of Hitler and Stalin exhibited three economic dimensions: (1) as elements of grand plans of political economic transformation; (2) as causes of the (upward and downward) modulation of mass killing policies; (3) and as plunder from below, during and after mass murder.

In Stalin's grand plan, the collectivization of agriculture was to transform the Soviet Union into an industrial power, more or less within its present boundaries. Collectivization brought famine, which Stalin consciously directed toward Ukrainians. It also contributed to the Great Terror, which was aimed first at alienated peasants who might side with an invading foreign power. Hitler's grand plan was more or less the reverse. He would begin with a terror abroad, destroying the people he saw as the leadership of the Soviet Union, and thus bringing down the regime. Then he would exploit collective farms to divert a grain surplus to Germany. In the long run, he would create a vast frontier empire ruled by Germans, bereft of Jews, and scantly peopled by Slavs reduced to slavery. Hitler always wanted to rid Europe of Jews. But he would never have ruled, and could never have killed, the millions of Jews of Poland, the Soviet Union, and the Baltics had he not pursued this eastern colonial vision with military force.

When Hitler and Stalin had to decide who was to bear the consequences of shortages, planned or unplanned, they also revealed ideological priorities. For Stalin, profits from grain exports in 1933 were more important than the lives of millions of peasants. He decided that peasants would die, and he decided which peasants would die in the largest numbers: the inhabitants of Soviet Ukraine. The grain that could have saved their lives was shipped south by the trainload, before their eyes, to the ports of the Black Sea. The Wehrmacht found itself holding huge numbers of Soviet soldiers as prisoners in autumn 1941. Most of them would die of starvation or related diseases. Yet even in the Dulags and the Stalags, where general killing was the rule, certain priorities were visible: Jews were shot right away, Russians and Belarusians were more likely to be left to starve, and ethnic Germans (and then Ukrainians) were more likely to be recruited for labor.

A certain amount of adaptation to circumstances is even visible in German policy toward Jews. Eliminating the Jews of Europe was Hitler's intention all along, and killing them all was an explicit policy as of late 1941. Nevertheless, even a policy of total destruction could be adapted to the economic demands of the moment. In winter 1941, for example, the Jews of Minsk survived in order to sew winter coats and boots for the beleaguered Wehrmacht. This was obviously no humane gesture: Hitler had sent his army to war with no winter gear, and the need to keep them from freezing to death momentarily outweighed the imperative to kill Jews. Most of these Jewish laborers were later killed. In summer 1942 food supply seemed more pressing than labor supply, which became an argument for the acceleration of the policy of gassing the Jews of occupied Poland. From 1943 onward, labor seemed more important than food, and some of the surviving Jews were kept alive longer, worked to death rather than shot or gassed.

Mass killing allowed plunder and social advancement. This bound the people who profited to the regime, and sometimes to its ideology. The deportation of richer peasants in the Soviet Union in 1930 allowed for the theft of their belongings, as did the deportation of Polish elites ten years later. The Great Terror allowed younger cadres in the party to make careers after their superiors were shot or deported. The Holocaust allowed non-Jews to take Jewish apartments and houses. Of course, the regimes themselves stole. Poles and other east Europeans who took from Jews had very often lost their own property to Germans. The Polish officers at Katyn had to surrender their watches and wedding rings before they were shot. German children wore the socks of Jewish children shot in Minsk, German men the watches of Jewish men shot at Babi Yar, German women the fur coats of Jewish women shot at Maly Trastsianets.

Tsvetan Todorov has claimed that "given the goals that they set for themselves, the choices of Stalin and Hitler were, alas, rational." This was not always true, but it was often true. Rationality in the sense he meant, which is also the narrow sense used in economics, concerns only whether one chooses the correct means to achieve an end. It has nothing to do with the end itself, with what leaders desired. Political goals must be judged separately by some ethical criterion. Discussions of rationality and irrationality cannot substitute for discussions of right and wrong. The Nazi (and Soviet) attention to economics does not morally attenuate the crimes of the regimes. If anything, it reveals the common indifference to individual human life that is as horrible as any other aspect of their rule. The modulation and the plunder are, if anything, even greater reasons for moral condemnation. Economic considerations do not displace an ideology of murderous racism. Rather, they confirm and illustrate its power.[9]

In colonization, ideology interacts with economics; in administration, it interacts with opportunism and fear. In both the Nazi and the Soviet cases, periods of mass murder were also periods of enthusiastic, or at least uniform, administrative performance. The closest thing to resistance from within a bureaucratic apparatus took place at the beginning of the era of mass killing, in Soviet Ukraine, among Ukrainian party activists who tried to report on the famine. They were quickly silenced by the threat of expulsion from the party, arrest, and deportation. Some of those who dared to raise doubts then became fervent campaigners for starvation. During the Great Terror of 1937–1938 and the first wave of the murder of Jews in 1941, signals from above led to killing below, and often to requests for higher quotas. The NKVD was subject to purges at the very same time. In 1941 in the western Soviet Union, SS officers, like NKVD officers a few years earlier, competed among themselves to kill more people and thus to demonstrate their competence and loyalty. Human lives were reduced to the moment of pleasure of a subordinate reporting to a superior.

Of course, the SS and the NKVD were elites of a certain kind, specially selected and ideologically trained. When other sorts of cadres (policemen, soldiers, local collaborators) were used, something more than a simple signal from above was sometimes needed. Both Hitler and Stalin excelled at placing organizations within moral dilemmas in which mass killing seemed like the lesser evil. Ukrainian party members hesitated in 1932 to requisition grain, but realized that their own careers, and lives, depended upon targets being met. Not all Wehrmacht officers were inclined to starve out Soviet cities: but when they believed that the choice was between Soviet civilians and their own men, they made the decision that seemed self-evident. Among populations, the rhetoric of war, or more precisely of preemptive self-defense, was convincing, or at least convincing enough to forestall resistance.[10]

In the decades since Europe's era of mass killing came to an end, much of the responsibility has been placed at the feet of "collaborators." The classic example of collaboration is that of the Soviet citizens who served the Germans as policemen or guards during the Second World War, among whose duties was the killing of Jews. Almost none of these people collaborated for ideological reasons, and only a small minority had political motives of any discernible sort. To be sure, some collaborators were motivated by a political affiliation with an occupying regime: the nationalist Lithuanian refugees from Soviet occupation whom the Germans brought with them to Lithuania in 1941, for example. In eastern Europe, it is hard to find political collaboration with the Germans that is not related to a previous experience of Soviet rule. But even where politics or ideas did matter, ideological alignment was impossible: Nazis could not regard non-Germans as equals, and no self-respecting non-German nationalist accepted the Nazi claim to German racial superiority. There was often an overlap of ideology and interests between Nazis and local nationalists in destroying the Soviet Union and (less often) in killing Jews. Far more collaborators simply said the right things, or said nothing and did what they were told.

Local policemen serving the Germans in occupied Soviet Ukraine or Soviet Belarus had little or no power within the regimes themselves. They were not quite at the very bottom: the Jews were below them, of course, as were people who were not policemen. But they were low enough that their behavior requires less (not more) explanation than that of SS-men, party members, soldiers, and policemen. This sort of local cooperation is just as predictable as obedience to authority, if not more so. Germans who declined to shoot Jews suffered no serious consequences. Locals who decided not to join the police or who elected to resign from its ranks, on the other hand, faced risks that the Germans themselves did not: starvation, deportation, and forced labor. A Soviet prisoner of war who accepted a German offer of collaboration might avoid starvation. A Soviet peasant who worked for the police knew that he would be able to stay at home to bring in his crops, and that his family would not go hungry. This was negative opportunism, the hope to avoid a still worse personal fate. Jewish policemen in the ghetto exemplified an extreme version of negative opportunism—even if, in the end, their choices saved no one, including themselves.

Within the Soviet system, the category of "collaborator" is harder to define. Unlike the Germans, the Soviets killed greater numbers of civilians during peacetime than during war, and did not usually occupy territory for long without either annexing it into the Soviet Union or granting it formal sovereignty. That said, within the Soviet Union certain policies were presented as "campaigns" and "wars." In this atmosphere, for example, Ukrainian communist party activists were induced to starve their fellow citizens. Whether or not the requisition of food from the starving is called "collaboration," it is a spectacular example of a regime generating cooperation in a policy of neighbors killing neighbors. Starvation is nasty, brutal, and long, and party activists and local officials had to watch and bring about the death of people they knew. Arendt regarded the collectivization famines as the inauguration of moral isolation, as people found themselves helpless before the powerful modern state. As Leszek Kołakowski understood, that was only half of the truth. The involvement of practically everyone in the famine, as collectors or as consumers of food, created a "new species of moral unity."[11]

If people had served regimes only by following their own prior ideological preferences, there would have been little collaboration. The majority of Nazi collaborators in the bloodlands had been educated in the Soviet Union. In the zone east of the Molotov-Ribbentrop line, where national independence yielded first to Soviet and only then to German rule, some people collaborated with the Germans because they had already collaborated with the Soviets. When Soviet occupation gave way to German occupation, people who had been Soviet militiamen became policemen in the service of the Germans. Local people who had collaborated with the Soviets in 1939–1941 knew that they could cleanse themselves in the eyes of the Nazis by killing Jews. Some Ukrainian nationalist partisans had earlier served both the Germans and the Soviets. In Belarus, simple chance often determined which young men joined the Soviet partisans or the German police. Former Soviet soldiers, indoctrinated in communism, staffed the German death facilities. Holocaust perpetrators, indoctrinated in racism, joined the Soviet partisans.

Ideologies also tempt those who reject them. Ideology, when stripped by time or partisanship of its political and economic connections, becomes a moralizing form of explanation for mass killing, one that comfortably separates the people who explain from the people who kill. It is convenient to see the perpetrator just as someone who holds the wrong idea and is therefore different for that reason. It is reassuring to ignore the importance of economics and the complications of politics, factors that might in fact be common to historical perpetrators and those who later contemplate their actions. It is far more inviting, at least today in the West, to identify with the victims than to understand the historical setting that they shared with perpetrators and bystanders in the bloodlands. The identification with the victim affirms a radical separation from the perpetrator. The Treblinka guard who starts the engine or the NKVD officer who pulls the trigger is not me, he is the person who kills someone like myself. Yet it is unclear whether this identification with victims brings much knowledge, or whether this kind of alienation from the murderer is an ethical stance. It is not at all obvious that reducing history to morality plays makes anyone moral.

Unfortunately, claiming victim status does not itself bring sound ethical choices. Stalin and Hitler both claimed throughout their political careers to be victims. They persuaded millions of other people that they, too, were victims: of an international capitalist or Jewish conspiracy. During the German invasion of Poland, a German soldier believed that the death grimace of a Pole proved that Poles irrationally hated Germans. During the famine, a Ukrainian communist found himself beleaguered by the corpses of the starved at his doorstep. They both portrayed themselves as victims. No major war or act of mass killing in the twentieth century began without the aggressors or perpetrators first claiming innocence and victimhood. In the twenty-first century, we see a second wave of aggressive wars with victim claims, in which leaders not only present their peoples as victims but make explicit reference to the mass murders of the twentieth century. The human capacity for subjective victimhood is apparently limitless, and people who believe that they are victims can be motivated to perform acts of great violence. The Austrian policeman shooting babies at Mahileu imagined what the Soviets would do to his children.

The victims were people; a true identification with them would involve grasping their lives rather than grasping at their deaths. By definition the victims are dead, and unable to defend themselves from the use that others make of their deaths. It is easy to sanctify policies or identities by the deaths of the victims. It is less appealing, but morally more urgent, to understand the actions of the perpetrators. The moral danger, after all, is never that one might become a victim but that one might be a perpetrator or a bystander. It is tempting to say that a Nazi murderer is beyond the pale of understanding. Outstanding politicians and intellectuals—for example, Edvard Beneš and Ilya Ehrenburg—yielded to this temptation during the war. The Czechoslovak president and the Soviet-Jewish writer were justifying revenge upon the Germans as such. People who called others subhuman were themselves subhuman. Yet to deny a human being his human character is to render ethics impossible.[12]

To yield to this temptation, to find other people to be inhuman, is to take a step toward, not away from, the Nazi position. To find other people incomprehensible is to abandon the search for understanding, and thus to abandon history.

To dismiss the Nazis or the Soviets as beyond human concern or historical understanding is to fall into their moral trap. The safer route is to realize that their motives for mass killing, however revolting to us, made sense to them. Heinrich Himmler said that it was good to see a hundred, or five hundred, or a thousand corpses lying side by side. What he meant was that to kill another person is a sacrifice of the purity of one's own soul, and that making this sacrifice elevated the killer to a higher moral level. This was an expression of a certain kind of devotion. It was an instance, albeit an extreme one, of a Nazi value that is not entirely alien to us: the sacrifice of the individual in the name of the community. Hermann Göring said that his conscience was named Adolf Hitler. For Germans who accepted Hitler as their Leader, faith was very important. The object of their faith could hardly have been more poorly chosen, but their capacity for faith is undeniable. It was Gandhi who noted that evil depends upon good, in the sense that those who come together to commit evil deeds must be devoted one to the other and believe in their cause. Devotion and faith did not make the Germans good, but they do make them human. Like everyone else, they had access to ethical thinking, even if their own was dreadfully misguided.[13]

Stalinism, too, was a moral as well as a political system, in which innocent and guilty were psychic as well as legal categories, and moral thinking was ubiquitous. A young Ukrainian communist party activist who took food from the starving was sure that he was contributing to the triumph of socialism: "I believed because I wanted to believe." His was a moral sensibility, if a mistaken one. When Margarete Buber-Neumann was in the Gulag, at Karaganda, a fellow prisoner told her that "you can't make an omelet without breaking a few eggs." Many Stalinists and their sympathizers explained the losses of the famines and the Great Terror as necessary to the construction of a just and secure Soviet state. The very scale of the death seemed to make the appeal of such a hope all the stronger.

Yet the romantic justification for mass murder, that present evil when properly described is future good, is simply wrong. Perhaps doing nothing at all would have been far better. Or perhaps a milder policy would better have achieved the desired ends. To believe that vast suffering must be associated with great progress is to accept a kind of hermetic masochism: the presence of pain is a sign of some immanent or emergent good. To advance this sort of reasoning oneself is hermetic sadism: if I caused pain, it was because there was a higher purpose, known to me. Because Stalin represented the politburo which represented the central committee which represented the party which represented the working class which represented history, he had a special claim to speak for what was historically necessary. Such a status allowed him to absolve himself of all responsibility, and to place the blame for his failings upon others.[14]

It cannot be denied that mass starvation brings political stability of a certain kind. The question must be: is that the sort of peace that is desired, or that should be desired? Mass murder does bind perpetrators to those who give them orders. Is that the right sort of political allegiance? Terror does consolidate a certain kind of regime. Is that kind of regime preferable? Killing civilians is in the interest of certain kinds of leaders. The question is not whether all this is historically true; the question is what is desirable. Are these leaders good leaders, and these regimes good regimes? If not, the question is: how can such policies be prevented?

Our contemporary culture of commemoration takes for granted that memory prevents murder. If people died in such large numbers, it is tempting to think, they must have died for something of transcendent value, which can be revealed, developed, and preserved in the right sort of political remembrance. The transcendent then turns out to be the national. The millions of victims must have died so that the Soviet Union could win a Great Patriotic War, or America a good war. Europe had to learn its pacifist lesson, Poland had to have its legend of freedom, Ukraine had to have its heroes, Belarus had to prove its virtue, Jews had to fulfill a Zionist destiny. Yet all of these later rationalizations, though they convey important truths about national politics and national psychologies, have little to do with memory as such. The dead are remembered, but the dead do not remember. Someone else had the power, and someone else decided how they died. Later on, someone else still decides why. When meaning is drawn from killing, the risk is that more killing would bring more meaning.

Here, perhaps, is a purpose for history, somewhere between the record of death and its constant reinterpretation. Only a history of mass killing can unite the numbers and the memories. Without history, the memories become private, which today means national; and the numbers become public, which is to say an instrument in the international competition for martyrdom. Memory is mine and I have the right to do with it as I please; numbers are objective and you must accept my counts whether you like them or not. Such reasoning allows a nationalist to hug himself with one arm and strike his neighbor with the other. After the end of the Second World War, and then again after the end of communism, nationalists throughout the bloodlands (and beyond) have indulged in the quantitative exaggeration of victimhood, thereby claiming for themselves the mantle of innocence.

In the twenty-first century, Russian leaders associate their country with the more or less official numbers of Soviet victims of the Second World War: nine million military deaths, and fourteen to seventeen million civilian deaths. These figures are highly contested. Unlike most of the numbers presented in this book, they are demographic projections, rather than counts. But whether they are right or wrong, they are *Soviet* numbers, not Russian ones. Whatever the correct Soviet figures, *Russian* figures must be much, much lower. The high Soviet numbers include Ukraine, Belarus, and the Baltics. Particularly important are the lands that the Soviet Union occupied in 1939: eastern Poland, the Baltic States, northeastern Romania. People died there in horribly high proportions—and many of the victims were killed not by the German but by the Soviet invader. Most important of all for the high numbers are the Jews: not the Jews of Russia, of whom only about sixty thousand died, but the Jews of Soviet Ukraine and Soviet Belarus (nearly a million) and those whose homeland was occupied by the Soviet Union before they were killed by the Germans (a further 1.6 million).

The Germans deliberately killed perhaps 3.2 million civilians and prisoners of war who were native to Soviet Russia: fewer *in absolute terms* than in Soviet Ukraine or in Poland, much smaller countries, each with about a fifth of Russia's population. Higher figures for Russian civilian losses, sometimes offered, would (if accurate) permit two plausible interpretations. First, more Soviet soldiers died than Soviet statistics indicate, and these people (presented as civilians in the higher numbers) were in fact soldiers. Alternatively, these people (presented as war losses in the higher numbers) were not killed directly by the Germans but died from famine, deprivation, and *Soviet* repression during the war. The second alternative suggests the possibility that more Russians died prematurely during the war in the lands controlled by Stalin than in the lands controlled by Hitler. This is very possibly true, although the blame for many of the deaths is shared.[15]

Consider the Gulag. Most of the Soviet concentration camps were located in Soviet Russia, far beyond the zone occupied by the Germans. Some four million Soviet citizens were in the Gulag when Germany invaded the Soviet Union in June 1941. Soviet authorities sentenced more than 2.5 million of their citizens to the Gulag during the war. The NKVD was at work everywhere that the Germans did not reach, including besieged and starving Leningrad. Between 1941 and 1943, the deaths of some 516,841 Gulag inmates were registered, and the figure might have been higher. These hundreds of thousands of additional deaths would presumably not have happened had the Germans not invaded the Soviet Union: but those people would not have been so vulnerable had they not been in the Gulag. People who died in Soviet concentration camps cannot simply be counted as victims of Germany, even if Hitler's war hastened their deaths.[16]

Other people, such as the inhabitants of Soviet Ukraine, suffered more under both Stalin and Hitler than did inhabitants of Soviet Russia. In the prewar Soviet Union, Russians were far less likely to be touched by Stalin's Great Terror (though many of them were) than the small national minorities, and far less likely to be threatened by famine (though many were) than Ukrainians or Kazakhs. In Soviet Ukraine, the whole population was under German occupation for much of the war, and death rates were far higher than in Soviet Russia. The lands of today's Ukraine were at the center of both Stalinist and Nazi killing policies throughout the era of mass killing. Some 3.5 million people fell victim to Stalinist killing policies between 1933 and 1938, and then another 3.5 million to German killing policies between 1941 and 1944. Perhaps three million more inhabitants of Soviet Ukraine died in combat or as an indirect consequence of the war.

Even so, the independent Ukrainian state has sometimes displayed the politics of exaggeration. In Ukraine, which was a major site of both Stalin's famine of 1932–1933 and the Holocaust in 1941–1944, the number of Ukrainians killed in the former has been exaggerated to exceed the total number of Jews killed in the latter. Between 2005 and 2009, Ukrainian historians connected to state institutions repeated the figure of ten million deaths in the famine, without any attempt at demonstration. In early 2010, the official estimation of starvation deaths fell discretely, to 3.94 million deaths. This laudable (and unusual) downward adjustment brought the official position close to the truth. (In a divided country, the succeeding president denied the specificity of the Ukrainian famine.)[17]

Belarus was the center of the Soviet-Nazi confrontation, and no country endured more hardship under German occupation. Proportionate wartime losses were greater than in Ukraine. Belarus, even more than Poland, suffered social decapitation: first the Soviet NKVD killed the intelligentsia as spies in 1937–1938, then Soviet partisans killed the schoolteachers as German collaborators in 1942–1943. The capital Minsk was all but depopulated by German bombing, the flight of refugees and the hungry, and the Holocaust; and then rebuilt after the war as an eminently Soviet metropolis. Yet even Belarus follows the general trend. Twenty percent of the prewar population of Belarusian territories was killed during the Second World War. Yet young people are taught, and seem to believe, that the figure was not one in five but one in three. A government that celebrates the Soviet legacy denies the lethality of Stalinism, placing all of the blame on Germans or more generally on the West.[18]

Exaggeration is not just a post-Soviet or post-communist phenomenon, as the case of Germany reveals. To be sure, the German reckoning with the Holocaust is exceptional and paradigmatic. That is not the problem. German commemoration of German mass murder of Jews is a singular example of unambiguous political, intellectual, and pedagogical responsibility for mass murder, and the main source of hope that other societies might follow a similar course. German journalists and (some) historians, however, have exaggerated the number of Germans killed during wartime and postwar evacuation, flight, or deportation since the end of the Second World War. Figures of one and even two million deaths are still cited, with no demonstration.

As long ago as 1974, a report of West German archives placed the number of deaths of Germans who fled or were deported from Poland at about four hundred thousand; it was suppressed because the numbers were too low to serve the political purpose of documenting victimhood. This report also estimated deaths of Germans from Czechoslovakia at two hundred thousand. According to a joint report of Czech and German historians, this second figure is exaggerated by a factor of about ten. So the figure of four hundred thousand Germans killed leaving Poland (cited in an earlier chapter) is perhaps better regarded as a maximum than a minimum.

The fate of Germans who fled or were evacuated during the war was similar to that of the higher numbers of Soviet and Polish citizens who fled or were evacuated during the German advance and the German retreat. The experience of those Germans deported at war's end was comparable to that of the higher number of Soviet and Polish citizens who were deported during and after the war. The experience of the fleeing, evacuated, and deported Germans was not, however, comparable to that of the ten million Polish, Soviet, Lithuanian, and Latvian citizens, Jews and others, who were subject to deliberate German policies of mass murder. Ethnic cleansing and mass killing, though related in a number of ways, are not the same thing. Even at their worst, the horrors visited on Germans in flight or during deportation were not mass killing policies in the sense of the planned starvations, the Terror, or the Holocaust.[19]

Beyond Poland, the extent of Polish suffering is underappreciated. Even Polish historians rarely recall the Soviet Poles who were starved in Soviet Kazakhstan and Soviet Ukraine in the early 1930s, or the Soviet Poles shot in Stalin's Great Terror in the late 1930s. No one ever notes that Soviet Poles suffered more than any other European national minority in the 1930s. The striking fact that the Soviet NKVD made more arrests in occupied eastern Poland in 1940 than in the rest of the USSR is rarely recalled. About as many Poles were killed in the bombing of Warsaw in 1939 as Germans were killed in the bombing of Dresden in 1945. For Poles, that bombing was just the beginning of one of the bloodiest occupations of the war, in which Germans killed millions of Polish citizens. More Poles were killed during the Warsaw Uprising alone than Japanese died in the atomic bombing of Hiroshima and Nagasaki. A *non-Jewish* Pole in Warsaw alive in 1933 had about the same chances of living until 1945 as a Jew in Germany alive in 1933. Nearly as many *non-Jewish* Poles were murdered during the war as European Jews were gassed at Auschwitz. For that matter, more *non-Jewish* Poles died at Auschwitz than did Jews of any European country, with only two exceptions: Hungary and Poland itself.

The Polish literary critic Maria Janion said of Poland's accession to the European Union: "to Europe, yes, but with our dead." It is important to know as much as we can about those dead, including how many of them there were. Despite its tremendous losses, Poland, too, exemplifies the politics of inflated victimhood. Poles are taught that six million Poles and Jews were killed during the war. This number seems to have been generated in December 1946 by a leading Stalinist, Jakub Berman, for the domestic political purpose of creating an apparent balance between the Polish and Jewish dead. The estimate that he "corrected," 4.8 million, is probably closer to the truth. This is still of course a titanic figure. Poland probably lost about a million non-Jewish civilians to the Germans and about a hundred thousand more to the Soviets. Perhaps another million Poles died as a result of mistreatment and as casualties of war. These numbers are appallingly high. The fate of non-Jewish Poles was unimaginably difficult compared to that of people under German occupation in western Europe. Even so, a Jew in Poland was about fifteen times more likely to be deliberately killed during the war than a non-Jewish Pole.[20]

Fourteen million people were deliberately murdered by two regimes over twelve years. This is a moment that we have scarcely begun to understand, let alone master. By repeating exaggerated numbers, Europeans release into their culture millions of ghosts of people who never lived. Unfortunately, such specters have power. What begins as competitive martyrology can end with martyrological imperialism. The wars for Yugoslavia of the 1990s began, in part, because Serbs believed that far larger numbers of their fellows had been killed in the Second World War than was the case. When history is removed, numbers go upward and memories go inward, to all of our peril.

Can the dead really belong to anyone? Of the more than four million Polish citizens murdered by the Germans, about three million were Jews. All of these three million Jews are counted as Polish citizens, which they were. Many of them identified strongly with Poland; certain people who died as Jews did not even consider themselves as such. More than a million of these Jews are also counted as Soviet citizens, because they lived in the half of Poland annexed by the USSR at the beginning of the war. Most of these million lived on lands that now belong to independent Ukraine.

Does the Jewish girl who scratched a note to her mother on the wall of the Kovel synagogue belong to Polish, or Soviet, or Israeli, or Ukrainian history? She wrote in Polish; other Jews in that synagogue on that day wrote in Yiddish. What about Dina Pronicheva's Jewish mother, who urged her daughter in Russian to flee from Babi Yar, which is in Kiev, which is now the capital of independent Ukraine? Most Jews in Kovel and Kiev, as in much of eastern Europe, were neither Zionists nor Poles nor Ukrainians nor communists. Can they really be said to have died for Israel, Poland, Ukraine, or the Soviet Union? They were Jews, they were Polish or Soviet citizens, their neighbors were Ukrainians or Poles or Russians. They belong, in some measure, to the histories of four countries— insofar as the histories of these four countries are really distinct.

Victims left behind mourners. Killers left behind numbers. To join in a large number after death is to be dissolved into a stream of anonymity. To be enlisted posthumously into competing national memories, bolstered by the numbers of which your life has become a part, is to sacrifice individuality. It is to be abandoned by history, which begins from the assumption that each person is irreducible. With all of its complexity, history is what we all have, and can all share. So even when we have the numbers right, we have to take care. The right number is not enough.

Each record of death suggests, but cannot supply, a unique life. We must be able not only to reckon the number of deaths but to reckon with each victim as an individual. The one very large number that withstands scrutiny is that of the Holocaust, with its 5.7 million Jewish dead, 5.4 million of whom were killed by the Germans. But this number, like all of the others, must be seen not as 5.7 million, which is an abstraction few of us can grasp, but as 5.7 million *times one*. This does not mean some generic image of a Jew passing through some abstract notion of death 5.7 million times. It means countless individuals who nevertheless have to be counted, in the middle of life: Dobcia Kagan, the girl in the synagogue at Kovel, and everyone with her there, and all the individual human beings who were killed as Jews in Kovel, in Ukraine, in the East, in Europe.

Cultures of memory are organized by round numbers, intervals of ten; but somehow the remembrance of the dead is easier when the numbers are not round, when the final digit is not a zero. So within the Holocaust, it is perhaps easier to think of 780,863 different people at Treblinka: where the three at the end might be Tamara and Itta Willenberg, whose clothes clung together after they were gassed, and Ruth Dorfmann, who was able to cry with the man who cut her hair before she entered the gas chamber. Or it might be easier to imagine the one person at the end of the 33,761 Jews shot at Babi Yar: Dina Pronicheva's mother, let us say, although in fact every single Jew killed there could be that one, must be that one, is that one.

Within the history of mass killing in the bloodlands, recollection must include the one million (times one) Leningraders starved during the siege, 3.1 million (times one) distinct Soviet prisoners of war killed by the Germans in 1941–1944, or the 3.3 million (times one) distinct Ukrainian peasants starved by the Soviet regime in 1932–1933. These numbers will never be known with precision, but they hold individuals, too: peasant families making fearful choices, prisoners keeping each other warm in dugouts, children such as Tania Savicheva watching their families perish in Leningrad.

Each of the 681,692 people shot in Stalin's Great Terror of 1937–1938 had a different life story: the two at the end might be Maria Juriewicz and Stanisław Wyganowski, the wife and husband reunited "under the ground." Each of the 21,892 Polish prisoners of war shot by the NKVD in 1940 was in the midst of life. The two at the end might be Dobiesław Jakubowicz, the father who dreamed about his daughter, and Adam Solski, the husband who wrote of his wedding ring on the day that the bullet entered his brain.

The Nazi and Soviet regimes turned people into numbers, some of which we can only estimate, some of which we can reconstruct with fair precision. It is for us as scholars to seek these numbers and to put them into perspective. It is for us as humanists to turn the numbers back into people. If we cannot do that, then Hitler and Stalin have shaped not only our world, but our humanity.

NUMBERS AND TERMS

Fourteen million is the approximate number of people killed by purposeful policies of mass murder implemented by Nazi Germany and the Soviet Union in the bloodlands. I define the bloodlands as territories subject to *both* German and Soviet police power and associated mass killing polices at some point between 1933 and 1945. They correspond closely to the places were the Germans killed Jews between 1941 and 1945. In the east, more or less of Soviet Russia might have been included; but the existing line allows the consideration of the main German killing sites of the war as well as the western Soviet lands disproportionately struck by earlier Soviet terror. Though I discuss the western lands of today's Poland, which belonged until 1945 to Germany, I do not include them in the bloodlands. This is to respect the difference between mass killing and ethnic cleansing. Hungary might arguably have been included, since it was occupied briefly by the Germans late in the war, after years as a German ally, and then occupied by the Soviets. After Polish and Soviet Jews, Hungarian Jews were the third-largest group of victims of the Holocaust. Romania, too, would have a kind of claim to belong to the bloodlands, since many of its Jews were killed and the country was occupied at the end of the war by the Soviet Union. Romania, however, was also a German ally rather than a victim of German aggression, and the murder of Romanian Jews was a Romanian rather than a German policy; this is a related but different history. Yugoslav citizens suffered many of the fates described here, including the Holocaust and mass reprisals; but the Jewish population of Yugoslavia was very small, and Yugoslavia was not occupied by the Soviet Union.

These matters of political geography are debatable on the margin; what is not is the existence of a zone in Europe where Soviet and German power overlapped and where the tremendous majority of the deliberate killing of both regimes took place. It is indisputable, to state the point differently, that the contiguous area from central Poland to western Russia where Germans killed Jews covers the regions where all of the other major German and Soviet policies of mass killing had already taken place or were concurrently taking place—if not completely, then in very significant part. The purposeful starvation of Ukraine took place within the zone of the Holocaust. The purposeful starvation of Soviet prisoners of war took place within the zone of the

Holocaust. Most Soviet and German shootings of Polish elites took place within the zone of the Holocaust. Most German "reprisal actions" took place within the zone of the Holocaust. A disproportionate amount of the shooting of the Stalinist Great Terror took place within the zone of the Holocaust.

I use the term *Molotov-Ribbentrop line* to signify an important boundary running north to south through the bloodlands. This line (which appears on some of the maps) is the German-Soviet border as agreed in September 1939 after the joint invasion of Poland. It was significant for Polish citizens, since it marked the division between German and Soviet occupation policies. This line took on another meaning after the Germans betrayed their allies and invaded the Soviet Union in 1941. To its west, Germans were holding Jews in ghettos; to its east, Germans began to shoot Jews in very large numbers. The Holocaust began east of the Molotov-Ribbentrop line with shooting actions, and then shifted west of the Molotov-Ribbentrop line, where most victims were gassed.

In the historical literature on the Holocaust, people east of the Molotov-Ribbentrop line are often referred to as "Soviet Jews," and people to the west as "Polish Jews." This is an inaccurate description of the people in question: more of the people killed *east* of the Molotov-Ribbentrop line had Polish than Soviet citizenship in 1939, when the war began. Referring to these people as "Soviet Jews" also tends to confirm an account of the war in which the Soviet invasion and occupation of its western neighbors are marginalized or overlooked entirely. If these people were "Soviet Jews," then their homeland must have been the Soviet Union, and the war must have begun with the German invasion of the Soviet Union. In fact, the war began with the German-Soviet alliance that destroyed Poland and left such Jews in an expanded Soviet Union. The use of the term *Molotov-Ribbentrop line*, though it may seem awkward at first, allows us to see a very special zone of Europe, whose peoples suffered three rounds of occupation during the Second World War: first Soviet, then German, then Soviet again.

On the wall of a Gestapo prison in Warsaw, a Polish prisoner wrote: "It's easy to talk about Poland. It's harder to work for her. Even harder to die. And hardest of all to suffer." With a few exceptions, this is a study of the dying rather than the suffering. Its subject is policies that were meant to kill, and the people who were their victims. In a deliberate mass killing operation, mass death is the desired goal of policy. It is an end in itself or a means to some other end. The count of fourteen million is not a complete reckoning of all of the death that German and Soviet power brought to the region. It is an estimate of the number of people killed in deliberate policies of mass murder.

I therefore generally exclude from the count the people who died of exertion or disease or malnutrition in concentration camps or during deportations, evacuations, or flight from armies. I also exclude the people who died as forced laborers. I am not counting people who died of hunger as a result of wartime shortfalls, or civilians who died in bombings or as a result of other acts of war. I am not counting soldiers who died on the fields of battle of the Second World War. In the course of the book I do discuss camps and deportations and battles, and provide figures of those killed. These are not, however, included in the final figure of fourteen million. I also exclude acts of violence carried out by third parties that were clearly a result of German or Soviet occupation, but not German or Soviet policy. Sometimes these brought very significant numbers of deaths, as with the Romanian murder of Jews (some three hundred thousand) or the Ukrainian nationalist ethnic cleansing of Poles (at least fifty thousand).

This is a book about deliberate mass murder more than a book about abuse. It is a book about civilians (and prisoners of war) rather than a book about soldiers on active duty. By all of these distinctions and exclusions I do not mean to suggest that such people were not victims, direct or indirect, of the Nazi and Soviet systems. I do not wish to minimize the horror of German and Soviet concentration camps, or the murderous character of ethnic cleansing, or the repressive nature of forced labor, or the awful total of war death. I wish to test the proposition that deliberate and direct mass murder by these two regimes in the bloodlands is a distinct phenomenon worthy of separate treatment, by writing a history whose subject is the purposeful murder of fourteen million people by two regimes over a short time and in certain parts of Europe.

Fourteen million, after all, is a very large number. It exceeds by more than ten million the number of people who died in all of the Soviet and German concentration camps (as opposed to the death facilities) taken together over the entire history of both the Soviet Union and Nazi Germany. If current standard estimates of military losses are correct, it exceeds by more than two million the number of German and Soviet soldiers, taken together, killed on the battlefield in the Second World War (counting starved and executed prisoners of war as victims of a policy of mass murder rather than as military casualties). It exceeds by more than thirteen million the number of American and British casualties, taken together, of the Second World War. It also exceeds by more than thirteen million all of the American battlefield losses in all of the foreign wars that the United States has ever fought.

The count of fourteen million mortal victims of deliberate killing policies in the bloodlands is the sum of the following approximate figures, defended in the text and notes: 3.3 million Soviet citizens (mostly Ukrainians) deliberately starved by their own government in Soviet Ukraine in 1932–1933; three hundred thousand Soviet citizens (mostly Poles and Ukrainians) shot by their own government in the western USSR among the roughly seven hundred thousand victims of the Great Terror of 1937–1938; two hundred thousand Polish citizens (mostly Poles) shot by German and Soviet forces in occupied Poland in 1939–1941; 4.2 million Soviet citizens (largely Russians, Belarusians, and Ukrainians) starved by the German occupiers in 1941–1944; 5.4 million Jews (most of them Polish or Soviet citizens) gassed or shot by the Germans in 1941–1944; and seven hundred thousand civilians (mostly Belarusians and Poles) shot by the Germans in "reprisals" chiefly in Belarus and Warsaw in 1941–1944.

In general, these numbers are sums of counts made by the Germans or the Soviets themselves, complemented by other sources, rather than statistical estimates of losses based upon censuses. Accordingly, my counts are often lower (even if stupefyingly high) than others in the literature. The major case where I do rely upon estimates is the famine in Soviet Ukraine, where data are simply insufficient for a count, and where I present a total figure on the basis of a number of demographic calculations and contemporary estimates. Again, my reckoning is on the conservative side.

With such a subject, care must be taken with the use of terms, and with their definitions. There is a notable difference, usually not noted, between *Final Solution* and *Holocaust*. The first was the general term that the Nazis used for their intention to eliminate the Jews from Europe. For much of the time that it was used, it indicated one of four deportation plans, all of which were eventually discarded. At some point in the second half of 1941, Hitler endorsed mass killing as the method by which Jews were to be eliminated from Europe, and made this widely known that December. At that point the *Final Solution* was understood to mean the murder of all Jews. The term *Holocaust* was introduced after the war and, by the 1990s, was generally (although by no means always) understood to mean the mass murder of the Jews by the Germans.

In this book the term *Holocaust* signifies the final version of the Final Solution, the German policy to eliminate the Jews of Europe by murdering them. Although Hitler certainly wished to remove the Jews from Europe in a Final Solution earlier, the Holocaust on this definition begins in summer 1941, with the shooting of Jewish women and children in the occupied Soviet Union. The term *Holocaust* is sometimes used in two other ways: to mean all German killing policies during the war, or to mean all oppression of Jews by the Nazi regime. In this book, *Holocaust* means the murder of the Jews in Europe, as carried out by the Germans by guns and gas between 1941 and 1945.

I refrain from using the term *Holodomor* for Stalin's deliberate starvation of Soviet Ukraine, not because the term is less precise than *Holocaust* but simply because it is unfamiliar to almost all readers of English. I use *Great Terror* to mean the Soviet mass shooting and deportation actions of 1937 and 1938, of which the most important were the kulak and national operations.

I prefer *mass killing* to *genocide* for a number of reasons. The term *genocide* was coined by the Polish-Jewish international lawyer Rafał Lemkin in 1943. Through a miracle of energy and persistence, he managed to encode it in international law. By the terms of the Convention on the Prevention and Punishment of the Crime of Genocide, adopted by the United Nations General Assembly in 1948, genocide involves "acts committed with intent to destroy, in whole or in part, a national, ethnical, racial or religious group, as such." It lists five ways in which genocide is committed: by "killing members of the group"; "causing serious bodily or mental harm to members of the group"; "deliberately inflicting on the group conditions of life calculated to bring about its physical destruction in whole or in part"; "imposing measures intended to prevent births within the group"; and "forcibly transferring children of this group to another group." This legal instrument has allowed for prosecutions, if only recently. As a guide to historical and moral interpretation, however, the term *genocide* has limitations.

The term *genocide* gives rise to inevitable and intractable controversies. It relies upon the intention of the perpetrator in two places: "intent to destroy" a certain group "as such." It can be argued that policies of mass killing were not genocide, because rulers had some other "intent," or because they intended to kill someone, but not a specified group "as such."

Though the term *genocide* in fact has wide application, it is often thought to refer only to the Holocaust. People who associate themselves with victims will wish to define past crimes as *genocide*, thinking that this will lead to recognition of the kind awarded to the Holocaust. Meanwhile, people associated with states that perpetrated a genocide resist the term with great energy, because they believe that its acceptance would be tantamount to acceptance of a role in the Holocaust. Thus, for example, Turkish governments resist the classification as genocide of the mass killing of a million or more Armenians during the First World War.

A final problem arises from a known political modification of the definition. The Soviets made sure that the term *genocide*, contrary to Lemkin's intentions, excluded political and economic groups. Thus the famine in Soviet Ukraine can be presented as somehow less genocidal, because it targeted a class, kulaks, as well as a nation, Ukrainians. Lemkin himself regarded the Ukrainian famine as genocide. But since the authors of the policy of starvation edited his definition, this has been controversial. It is remarkable that we have the legal instrument of genocide; nevertheless, one must not forget that this particular murder statute was co-drafted by some of the murderers. Or, to put the matter less moralistically: all laws arise within and reflect a certain political setting. It is not always desirable to export the politics of that moment into a history of another.

In the end, historians who discuss genocide find themselves answering the question as to whether a given event qualifies, and so classifying rather than explaining. The discussions take on a semantic or legalistic or political form. In each of the cases discussed in this book, the question "Was it genocide?" can be answered: yes, it was. But this does not get us far.

The peoples of the bloodlands functioned in a world of daunting linguistic complexity. Most of the victims described here knew or had regular contact with two or more languages, and many of them were bilingual or trilingual. Broader histories of Europe involve problems of transliteration, since words from languages written in non-Roman characters must be rendered in Roman characters in English. The problem arises not with languages such as French, German, Polish, or Czech, which are written in Roman characters with more or less familiar diacritical marks. But Yiddish and Hebrew are written in Hebrew characters, and Belarusian, Russian, and Ukrainian are written in Cyrillic alphabets.

For each of these languages there are competing systems of transliteration, each with its advantages and disadvantages. To make matters worse, many of the people and places discussed in this book were known by different names in different languages written with different characters. So there might be a dozen legitimate ways, for example, to spell the name of a Jew from Ukraine in English. For many readers, the people and places discussed in this book will be unfamiliar enough without the burden of the more elaborate solutions to the transliteration problem. The risk with too much precision is that people and places become more rather than less exotic.

I have generally given names in simpler and more familiar forms rather than those that correspond perfectly to transliteration. I spell Russian surnames ending with a double *ii* just that way, partly so that readers can tell the difference between Russian surnames (ending with *ii*), Ukrainian surnames (ending with *yi*), and Polish surnames (ending with *i*). I usually give city names in an English form if one is familiar, so Warsaw rather than Warszawa and Kiev rather than Kyïv. All of the cities were spelled differently by different inhabitants at any given time—and at different times fell under different rulers with different official topographies. I tend to favor current English spellings, although I make exceptions when it would seem absurd not to do so. Cities in the Soviet Union had a tendency to change names; I use the names under which they were known at the time. Thus famine and terror strike Stalino (not Donetsk) in the 1930s and the German Sixth Army is destroyed at Stalingrad (not Volgograd) in 1942. I try to refer to cities by the same name throughout the book, although in certain cases where boundaries moved and populations were transferred (Lwów/Lviv, Wilno/Vilnius) this would have been too distorting. In citations I give the name of the author as it appears in the cited work, even though this means that some authors' names will be spelled different ways in different citations. In the notes and bibliography I transliterate more precisely than in the main text, following simplified versions of the Library of Congress guidelines. These are all matters of judgment; readers with experience in these problems will understand the impossibility of avoiding certain compromises. Translations, except where otherwise noted, are my own.

ABSTRACT

The killing in the bloodlands took five forms. First, Stalin undertook *modernization* by way of the self-colonization of his Soviet Union. The Soviets created a vast system of labor camps known as the Gulag, collectivized agriculture, and built factories, mines, and canals. When collectivized agriculture led to hunger, this was blamed on particular groups, primarily the Ukrainians. More than five million people starved to death in the Soviet Union in the early 1930s, most of them in Soviet Ukraine. The hunger was caused by collective agriculture, but the starvation was caused by politics.

Then the Soviets effected a *retreat* into terror. In the Great Terror of 1937 and 1938, the Soviet leadership identified peasants, the victims of collectivization, as the primary threat to Soviet power. People who had survived hunger and the Gulag were shot. At the same time, the Soviet leadership defined certain national minorities as enemies. Nearly seven hundred thousand people were recorded as executed in the Terror, although the true number may be somewhat higher. These people were disproportionately agricultural laborers and Soviet Poles.

In 1939, the Soviets and the Germans invaded Poland together, and carried out a policy of *de-Enlightenment*. Reasoning from different ideologies, but drawing similar conclusions, the Germans and Soviets killed some two hundred thousand Polish citizens between 1939 and 1941, disproportionately the educated people who represented European culture and who might have led resistance. When the Soviets executed the 21,892 Polish officers and others at Katyn and four other sites in spring 1940, they were mirroring a German killing campaign that was going on at the same time. The Soviets and Germans also deported about a million Polish citizens at this time, swelling the Soviet and the German camp systems. The Germans put Polish Jews in ghettos, in the anticipation that they would all be deported. Tens of thousands of Jews died of hunger and disease as the ghettos become improvised labor camps.

After the Germans broke the alliance and invaded the Soviet Union in June 1941, the two enemies killed civilians in a pattern of *belligerent complicity*. In German-occupied Soviet Belarus the Soviets encouraged partisan activity, and the Germans executed more than three hundred thousand people in return. These mass killings had little to do with reprisals in any conventional sense. By the end the Germans were shooting Belarusian women and children as an encumbrance, and taking the men as slave laborers. In Warsaw, Soviet forces first encouraged a Polish uprising and then watched, without involving themselves, as the Germans killed more than one hundred thousand Poles and then destroyed the city itself.

Hitler imagined a *colonial demodernization* of the Soviet Union and Poland that would take tens of millions of lives. The Nazi leadership envisioned an eastern frontier to be depopulated and deindustrialized, and then remade as the agrarian domain of German masters. This vision had four parts. First, the Soviet state was to collapse after a *lightning victory* in summer 1941, just as the Polish state had in summer 1939, leaving the Germans with complete control over Poland, Belarus, Ukraine, western Russia, and the Caucasus. Second, a *Hunger Plan* would starve to death some thirty million inhabitants of these lands in winter 1941–1942, as food was diverted to Germany and western Europe. Third, the Jews of the Soviet Union who survived the starvation, along with Polish Jews and other Jews under German control, were to be eliminated from Europe in a *Final Solution*. Fourth, a *Generalplan Ost* foresaw the deportation, murder, enslavement, or assimilation of remaining populations, and the resettlement of eastern Europe by German colonists in the years after the victory. Living space for Germans was to be dying space for others.

When the Soviet Union defended itself and no lightning victory could be won, Hitler and the German leadership adapted the three remaining plans to the new situation, killing about ten million people, which was fewer than originally planned. The *Hunger Plan* was abandoned in its original conception, and applied only to areas under total German control. Thus a million people were purposefully starved in besieged Leningrad and more than three million Soviet prisoners of war died of starvation and neglect. As the war continued, the Germans began to use prisoners as forced laborers, rather than allowing most of them to starve. The grand colonial scheme of *Generalplan Ost* could not be implemented without a total victory, which was not forthcoming. It was tried in areas of occupied Poland, where Poles were deported to create space for German racial colonies. Its essential concept was also visible in the German decision to destroy the city of Warsaw physically in response to the uprising of summer 1944. In the cases of both the *Hunger Plan* and *Generalplan Ost*, plans for mass killing had to be scaled back and delayed. The general goal of colonization was never abandoned.

The *Final Solution*, by contrast, was implemented as fully as possible. It was originally to take place after the war. As it became clear in the second half of 1941 that the war was not going according to plan, Hitler made clear that he wanted a Final Solution to be effected immediately. By then, four versions of a Final Solution by deportation had been proposed and found to be impracticable. The invasion of the Soviet Union, and its failure, demonstrated how the Jews could be removed from Europe: by mass murder. Einsatzgruppen originally tasked with eliminating political enemies were used to shoot Jews. Battalions of German Order Police originally tasked with patrolling the conquered Soviet Union were used in massive killing actions. By December 1941, when Hitler made clear that he expected all of the Jews under German control to be exterminated, a new technique of mass murder was available. Asphyxiation by carbon monoxide, used first in a "euthanasia" program, was adapted for use in gas vans in the occupied Soviet Union, and then in permanent gassing facilities in occupied Poland. To the labor camp at Auschwitz was added a death factory, where hydrogen cyanide rather than carbon monoxide was used as the agent of killing. The Jews of occupied Poland, already gathered into ghettos for deportation, were instead sent to Bełżec, Sobibór, Chełmno, Treblinka, Auschwitz, and Majdanek, and gassed.

ACKNOWLEDGMENTS

Writing is punctuated solitude; the pleasure of finishing a book is acknowledging those who helped it take form.

Krzysztof Michalski and Klaus Nellen of the Institut für die Wissenschaften vom Menschen in Vienna forced me to specify the original thought. Thanks to the workshops organized by the Institute within the project "United Europe/Divided Memory," I enjoyed the company of several dozen outstanding historians in meetings in Vienna and at Yale University. I drafted the manuscript at Yale, my scholarly home, in the company of colleagues who set very high standards; and then rewrote the book during a stay at the IWM, made productive by the efforts of its staff, especially Susanne Froeschl, Mary Nicklas, and Marie-Therese Porzer. I am appreciative of my sabbatical year from Yale, and especially of the consideration shown by Laura Engelstein as chair of the Department of History. Ian Shapiro and the Macmillan Center at Yale supported my research. The competence and cheer of Marcy Kaufman and Marianne Lyden allowed me to balance administrative duties at Yale with research and teaching.

During the conception and drafting of this book, I had the good fortune to be surrounded by generous and talented graduate students at Yale. Some of them took part in demanding seminars on the subjects of the book, and all of them read draft chapters or discussed the book with me. I appreciate their work, their frankness, their good humor, and their intellectual company. Particular thanks go to Jadwiga Biskupska, Sarah Cameron, Yedida Kanfer, Kathleen Minahan, Claire Morelon, and David Petrucelli. The students and I could not have held our seminars, and I could not have researched this book, without the marvelous collections of the Sterling Memorial Library at Yale and the assistance of Tatjana Lorkovic and William Larsh of its Slavic Reading Room. Two outstanding Yale then-undergraduates, Beth Reisfeld and Andrew Koss, also helped me with aspects of the research. I cannot imagine Yale, let alone taking up a project of this sort in New Haven, without Daniel Markovits, Sarah Bilston, Stefanie Markovits, and Ben Polak.

A number of friends and colleagues put down their own work in order to read chapters of mine, to my great benefit. They include Bradley Abrams, Pertti Ahonen, Pavel Barša, Tina Bennett, David Brandenberger, Archie Brown, Christopher Browning, Jeff

Dolven, Ben Frommer, Olivia Judson, Alex Kay, Ben Kiernan, Hiroaki Kuromiya, Mark Mazower, Wolfgang Mueller, Stuart Rachels, Thomas W. Simons, Jr., Will Sulkin, Adam Tooze, Jeffrey Veidlinger, Lynne Viola, and Iryna Vushko. Dieter Pohl and Wendy Lower read considerable portions of the manuscript. Nancy Wingfield kindly read and commented upon an entire draft. So did Marci Shore, who sets an example of humane scholarship that I wish I could match. It goes without saying that readers did not always agree with my interpretations. Critique helped the manuscript enormously; the responsibility for its flaws is mine.

From the beginning of the project to the end, Ray Brandon regularly contributed his superior bibliographic knowledge and vigorous critical spirit. Timothy Garton Ash helped me, at important points, to clarify my purposes. As I was drafting this book, I was speaking weekly with Tony Judt, in connection with another one. This altered my thinking on subjects such as the Popular Front and the Spanish Civil War. A decade of agreeing and disagreeing with Omer Bartov, Jan Gross, and Norman Naimark in various settings has sharpened my thinking on a host of questions. I have learned much over the years from conversations with Piotr Wandycz, my predecessor at Yale. Teaching a course in east European history at Yale with Ivo Banac broadened my knowledge. I found myself returning to basic problems of Marxism that I first perceived while studying under Mary Gluck (and Chris Mauriello) at Brown and then pursued at Oxford with the late Leszek Kołakowski. I did not continue the study of economics as John Williamson long ago counseled me to do, but I do owe a good deal of whatever economic intuition and knowledge remain to his support. My grandmother Marianna Snyder talked to me about the Great Depression, and my parents Estel Eugene Snyder and Christine Hadley Snyder helped me to think about agricultural economics. My brothers Philip Snyder and Michael Snyder helped me to frame the introduction.

This book draws from research carried out in a number of archives over the course of many years. A good deal of the thinking also took place in archives. The archivists of the institutions mentioned in the bibliography are owed my thanks. The talk of archives in eastern Europe is often of what is closed; historians know that very much is open, and that we owe our productive work to those who keep it so. This study involved reading in German, Polish, Russian, Ukrainian, Belarusian, Yiddish, Czech, Slovak, and French as well as English. It required cognizance of debates within the major historiographies, above all the German. I am sure that it would have benefited from literatures that I could not read. The friends who helped me with the languages I do read know who they are, and what I owe them. Special thanks are due to two excellent language teachers, Volodymyr Dibrova and Kurt Krottendorfer. Early on, Mark Garrison and the late Charles William Maynes impressed upon me the importance of learning languages and taking risks. In eastern Europe, Milada Anna Vachudová taught me about some of the overlaps. Stephen Peter Rosen and the late Samuel Huntington encouraged me to keep learning languages and deepening connections with eastern Europe, and provided the necessary support. It was at Harvard that I became a historian of this region, as opposed to a historian of some of its countries; this book is a pendant to the one that I wrote there.

Sources and inspiration for this book came from many other directions. Karel Berkhoff, Robert Chandler, Martin Dean, and Grzegorz Motyka graciously allowed me to read unpublished work, Dariusz Gawin directed me to forgotten works on the Warsaw Uprising, and Gerald Krieghofer found important press articles. Rafał Wnuk very kindly discussed with me the history of his family. The late Jerzy Giedroyc, Ola Hnatiuk, Jerzy Jedlicki, Kasia Jesień, Ivan Krastev, the late Tomasz Merta, Andrzej Paczkowski, Oxana Shevel, Roman Szporluk, and Andrzej Waśkiewicz helped me to ask some of the right questions. It was very instructive, as always, to think through the maps with Jonathan Wyss and Kelly Sandefer of Beehive Mapping. Steve Wasserman of Kneerim and Williams helped me with the title and the book project, and offered me an opportunity in a book review to consider some of the issues. I appreciated the work of Chris Arden, Ross Curley, Adam Eaglin, Alex Littlefield, Kay Mariea, Cassie Nelson, and Brandon Proia of Perseus Books. I learned much that was necessary to conceive and write this book from Lara Heimert of Basic Books.

Carl Henrik Fredriksson invited me to give a lecture at the Eurozine conference in Vilnius on the imbalance between the memory and the history of mass killing. Robert Silvers helped me to temper the argument of that lecture in an essay that arose from that lecture, which states the problem that this book attempts to resolve. He and his colleagues at the *New York Review of Books* also published, in 1995, an essay by Norman Davies that drew my attention to some of the shortcomings of previous approaches to the problems treated in this book.

Lectures and seminars at the Museum of Jewish Heritage in New York, the Stiftung Genshagen, the Universidade Católica Portuguesa in Lisbon, the Central European Forum in Bratislava, the Deutsches Historisches Institut in Warsaw, the Instytut Batorego in Warsaw, the Einstein Forum in Berlin, the Forum för Levande Historia in Stockholm, the Kreisky Forum in Vienna, Harvard University, Columbia University, Princeton University, Birkbeck College London, and the University of Cambridge were welcome opportunities to test conclusions. Presentations generate exchanges: I think in particular of Eric Weitz's remark about implicit and explicit comparisons, or Nicholas Stargardt's notion of the economics of catastrophe, or Eric Hobsbawm's willingness to counsel comparison in London and Berlin.

I recall all of these and many other moments of contact with gratitude.

BIBLIOGRAPHY

ARCHIVES (AND ABBREVIATIONS USED IN THE NOTES)

AAN   Archiwum Akt Nowych
      Archive of New Files, Warsaw

AMP   Archiwum Muzeum Polskiego
      Archive of the Polish Museum, London

AVPRF   Arkhiv Vneshnei Politiki Rossiiskoi Federatsii
      Archive of the Foreign Policy of the Russian Federation, Moscow

AW   Archiwum Wschodnie, Ośrodek Karta
      Eastern Archive, Karta Institute, Warsaw

BA-MA   Bundesarchiv-Militärarchiv
      Bundesarchiv, Military Archive, Freiburg, Germany

CAW   Centralne Archiwum Wojskowe
      Central Military Archive, Rembertów, Poland

DAR   Derzhavnyi Arkhiv Rivnens'koï Oblasti
      State Archive of Rivne Oblast, Ukraine

FVA   Fortunoff Video Archive of Holocaust Testimonies
      Yale University, New Haven, Connecticut

GARF   Gosudarstvennyi Arkhiv Rossiiskoi Federatsii
      State Archive of the Russian Federation, Moscow

HI   Hoover Institution Archive, Stanford University, California

IfZ(M)   Institut für Zeitgeschichte, München
      Institute for Contemporary History, Munich

IPN   Instytut Pamięci Narodowej
      Institute of National Remembrance, Warsaw

OKAW   Ośrodek Karta, Archiwum Wschodnie
      Karta Institute, Eastern Archive, Warsaw

SPP   Studium Polski Podziemnej
      Polish Underground Movement Study Trust, London

TsDAVO   Tsentral'nyi Derzhavnyi Arkhiv Vyshchykh Orhaniv Vlady ta
          Upravlinnia
          Central State Archive of Higher Organs of Government and
          Administration, Kiev
USHMM   United States Holocaust Memorial Museum, Washington, D.C.
ŻIH   Żydowski Instytut Historyczny
          Jewish Historical Institute, Warsaw

PRESS ARTICLES (CHRONOLOGICAL ORDER)

Gareth Jones, "Will there be soup?" *Western Mail*, 17 October 1932.

"France: Herriot a Mother," *Time*, 31 October 1932.

"The Five-Year Plan," *New York Times*, 1 January 1933.

"The Stalin Record," *New York Times*, 11 January 1933.

"Die Weltgefahr des Bolschewismus. Rede des Reichskanzlers Adolf Hitler im
    Berliner Sportpalast," *Deutschösterreichische Tageszeitung*, 3 March 1933, 2.

Gareth Jones, "Famine grips Russia," *New York Evening Post*, 30 March 1933.

Walter Duranty, "Russians Hungry, but not Starving," *New York Times*, 31 March
    1933, 13.

"Kardinal Innitzer ruft die Welt gegen den Hungertod auf," *Reichspost*, 20 August
    1933, 1.

"Foreign News: Karakhan Out?" *Time*, 11 September 1933.

"Die Hilfsaktion für die Hungernden in Rußland," *Reichspost*, 12 October 1933, 1.

"Helft den Christen in Sowjetrußland," *Die Neue Zeitung*, 14 October 1933, 1.

"Russia: Starvation and Surplus," *Time*, 22 January 1934.

Mirosław Czech, "Wielki Głód," *Gazeta Wyborcza*, 22–23 March 2003, 22.

Michael Naumann, "Die Mörder von Danzig," *Die Zeit*, 10 September 2009, 54–55.

"Vyrok ostatochnyi: vynni!" *Dzerkalo Tyzhnia*, 15–22 January 2010, 1.

BOOKS (INCLUDING DOCUMENT COLLECTIONS) AND ARTICLES

Natal'ja Ablažej, "Die ROVS-Operation in der Westsibirischen Region," in Rolf
    Binner, Bernd Bonwetsch, and Marc Junge, eds., *Stalinismus in der sowjetischen
    Provinz 1937–1938*, Berlin: Akademie Verlag, 2010, 287–308.

Vladimir Abramov, *The Murderers of Katyn*, New York: Hippocrene Books, 1993.

Bradley Abrams, "The Second World War and the East European Revolution," *East
    European Politics and Societies*, Vol. 16, No. 3, 2003, 623–664.

Henry Abramson, *A Prayer for the Government: Ukrainians and Jews in
    Revolutionary Times*, Cambridge, Mass.: Harvard University Press, 1997.

Ya'acov Adini, *Dubno: sefer zikaron*, Tel Aviv: Irgun yots'e Dubno be-Yisra'el, 1966.

Pertti Ahonen, *After the Expulsion: West Germany and Eastern Europe, 1945–1990*,
    Oxford: Oxford University Press, 2003.

Pertti Ahonen, Gustavo Corni, Jerzy Kochanowski, Rainer Schulze, Tamás Stark, and Barbara Stelzl-Marx, *People on the Move: Forced Population Movements in the Second World War and Its Aftermath*, Oxford: Berg, 2008.

Götz Aly and Susanne Heim, *Architects of Annihilation: Auschwitz and the Logic of Destruction*, Princeton: Princeton University Press, 2002.

Truman Anderson, "Incident at Baranivka: German Reprisals and the Soviet Partisan Movement in Ukraine, October-December 1941," *Journal of Modern History*, Vol. 71, No. 3, 1999, 585–623.

Christopher Andrew and Oleg Gordievsky, *KGB: The Inside Story of Foreign Operations from Lenin to Gorbachev*, London: Hodder & Stoughton, 1990.

Andrej Angrick, *Besatzungspolitik und Massenmord: Die Einsatzgruppe D in der südlichen Sowjetunion 1941–1943*, Hamburg: Hamburger Edition, 2003.

Andrej Angrick and Peter Klein, *The "Final Solution" in Riga: Exploitation and Annihilation, 1941–1944*, New York: Berghahn Books, 2009.

Anonyma, *Eine Frau in Berlin: Tagebuchaufzeichnungen vom 20. April bis 22. Juni 1945*, Munich: btb Verlag, 2006.

Anne Applebaum, *Gulag: A History*, New York: Doubleday, 2003.

Yitzhak Arad, *Belzec, Sobibor, Treblinka: The Operation Reinhard Death Camps*, Bloomington: Indiana University Press, 1987.

Yitzhak Arad, *The Holocaust in the Soviet Union*, Lincoln: University of Nebraska Press and Jerusalem: Yad Vashem, 2009.

Yitzhak Arad, Shmuel Krakowski, and Shmuel Spector, eds., *The Einsatzgruppen Reports*, New York: Holocaust Library, 1989.

Hannah Arendt, *Eichmann in Jerusalem: A Report on the Banality of Evil*, London: Faber and Faber, 1963.

Hannah Arendt, *In der Gegenwart*, Munich: Piper, 2000.

Hannah Arendt, *The Origins of Totalitarianism*, New York: Harcourt, Brace, 1951.

Moshe Arens, "The Jewish Military Organization (ŻZW) in the Warsaw Ghetto," *Holocaust and Genocide Studies*, Vol. 19, No. 2, 2005, 201–225.

John Armstrong, *Ukrainian Nationalism*, New York: Columbia University Press, 1963.

Klaus Jochen Arnold, "Die Eroberung und Behandlung der Stadt Kiew durch die Wehrmacht im September 1941: Zur Radikalisierung der Besatzungspolitik," *Militärgeschichtliche Mitteilungen*, Vol. 58, No. 1, 1999, 23–64.

Jerzy Autuchiewicz, "Stan i perspektywa nad deportacjami Polaków w głąb ZSRS oraz związane z nimi problemy terminologiczne," in Marcin Zwolski, ed., *Exodus: Deportacje i migracje (wątek wschodni)*, Warsaw: IPN, 2008, 13–30.

T. B., "Waldemar Schön—Organizator Getta Warszawskiego," *Biuletyn Żydowskiego Instytutu Historycznego*, No. 49, 1964, 85–90.

Jörg Baberowski, *"Der Feind ist überall": Stalinismus im Kaukasus*, Munich: Deutsche Verlags-Anstalt, 2003.

Jörg Baberowski, *Der rote Terror: Die Geschichte des Stalinismus*, Munich: Deutsche Verlags-Anstalt, 2003.

Jörg Baberowski and Anselm Doering-Manteuffel, "The Quest for Order and the Pursuit of Terror," in Michael Geyer and Sheila Fitzpatrick, eds., *Beyond Totalitarianism: Stalinism and Nazism Compared*, Cambridge: Cambridge University Press, 2009, 180–227.

Gershon C. Bacon, *The Politics of Tradition: Agudat Yisrael in Poland, 1916–1939*, Jerusalem: Magnes Press, 1996.

Peter Baldwin, ed., *Reworking the Past: Hitler, the Holocaust, and the Historians' Debate*, Boston: Beacon Press, 1990.

Alan Ball, *Russia's Last Capitalists: The Nepmen, 1921–1929*, Berkeley: University of California Press, 1987.

Ivo Banac, *With Stalin Against Tito: Cominformist Splits in Yugoslav Communism*, Ithaca: Cornell University Press, 1988.

Władysław Bartoszewski, *Warszawski pierścień śmierci*, Warsaw: Świat Książki, 2008.

Władysław Bartoszewski and Zofia Lewinówna, *Ten jest z ojczyzny mojej: Polacy z pomocą Żydom 1939–1945*, Warsaw: Świat Książki, 2007.

Omer Bartov, "Eastern Europe as the Site of Genocide," *Journal of Modern History*, No. 80, 2008, 557–593.

Omer Bartov, *The Eastern Front 1941–1945: German Troops and the Barbarisation of Warfare*, Basingstoke: Palgrave Macmillan, 2001.

Omer Bartov, *Hitler's Army: Soldiers, Nazis, and War in the Third Reich*, New York: Oxford University Press, 1991.

Piotr Bauer, *Generał Józef Dowbor-Muśnicki 1867–1937*, Poznań: Wydawnictwo Poznańskie, 1988.

Yehuda Bauer, *Rethinking the Holocaust*, New Haven: Yale University Press, 2001.

Bernhard H. Bayerlein, "Abschied von einem Mythos: Die UdSSR, die Komintern, und der Antifaschismus 1930–1941," *Osteuropa*, Vol. 59, Nos. 7–8, 2009, 125–148.

Daniel Beauvois, *La bataille de la terre en Ukraine, 1863–1914: Les polonais et les conflits socio-ethniques*, Lille: Presses Universitaires de Lille, 1993.

Antony Beevor, *The Battle for Spain: The Spanish Civil War 1936–1939*, London: Penguin, 2006.

Werner Beinecke, *Die Ostgebiete der Zweiten Polnischen Republik*, Köln: Böhlau Verlag, 1999.

Z. I. Beluga, ed., *Prestupleniya nemetsko-fashistskikh okkupantov v Belorussii 1941–1944*, Minsk: Belarus, 1965.

Sara Bender, "The Jews of Białystok During the Second World War, 1939–1943," doctoral dissertation, Hebrew University, 1994.

Wolfgang Benz, Konrad Kwiet, and Jürgen Matthäus, eds., *Einsatz im "Reichskommissariat Ostland": Dokumente zum Völkermord im Baltikum und in Weißrußland 1941–1944*, Berlin: Metropol, 1998.

Tatiana Berenstein, "Praca przymusowa Żydów w Warszawie w czasie okupacji hitlerowskiej," *Biuletyn Żydowskiego Instytutu Historycznego*, Nos. 45–46, 1963, 43–93.

Karel C. Berkhoff, "Dina Pronicheva's Story of Surviving the Babi Yar Massacre: German, Jewish, Soviet, Russian, and Ukrainian Records," in Ray Brandon and Wendy Lower, eds., *The Shoah in Ukraine: History, Testimony, Memorialization*, Bloomington: Indiana University Press, 2008, 291–317.

Karel C. Berkhoff, "The Great Famine in Light of the German Invasion and Occupation," *Harvard Ukrainian Studies*, forthcoming.

Karel C. Berkhoff, *Harvest of Despair: Life and Death in Ukraine Under Nazi Rule*, Cambridge, Mass.: Harvard University Press, 2004.

Isaiah Berlin, *Personal Impressions*, Princeton: Princeton University Press, 2001.

Zygmunt Berling, *Wspomnienia: Z łagrów do Andersa*, Warsaw: PDW, 1990.

Miron Białoszewski, *Pamiętnik z Powstania Warszawskiego*, Warsaw: Państwowy Instytut Wydawniczy, 1970.

Frank Biess, "Vom Opfer zum Überlebenden des Totalitarismus: Westdeutsche Reaktionen auf die Rückkehr der Kriegsgefangenen aus der Sowjetunion, 1945–1953," in Günter Bischof and Rüdiger Overmans, eds., *Kriegsgefangenschaft im Zweiten Weltkrieg: Eine vergleichende Perspektive*, Ternitz-Pottschach: Gerhard Höller, 1999, 365–389.

Anna Bikont, *My z Jedwabnego*, Warsaw: Prószyński i S-ka, 2004.

Ivan Bilas, *Represyvno-karal'na systema v Ukraïni, 1917–1953*, Kiev: Lybid', 1994.

Rolf Binner and Marc Junge, "'S etoj publikoj ceremonit'sja ne sleduet': Die Zielgruppen des Befehls Nr. 00447 und der Große Terror aus der Sicht des Befehls Nr. 00447," *Cahiers du Monde russe*, Vol. 43, No. 1, 2002, 181–228.

Rolf Binner and Marc Junge, "Wie der Terror 'Gross' wurde: Massenmord und Lagerhaft nach Befehl 00447," 11 *Cahiers du Monde russe*, Vol. 42, Nos. 2–3/4, 2001, 557–614.

Ruth Bettina Birn, "Two Kinds of Reality? Case Studies on Anti-Partisan Warfare During the Eastern Campaign," in Bernd Wegner, ed., *From Peace to War: Germany, Soviet Russia, and the World, 1939–1941*, Providence: Berghahn Books, 1997, 277–324.

Peter Black, "Handlanger der Endlösung: Die Trawniki-Männer und die Aktion Reinhard 1941–1943," in Bogdan Musial, ed., *Aktion Reinhardt, Der Völkermord an den Juden im Generalgouvernement 1941–1944*, Osnabrück: Fibre, 2004, 309–352.

Peter Black, "Prosty żołnierz 'akcji Reinhard'. Oddziały z Trawnik i eksterminacja polskich Żydów," in Dariusz Libionka, ed., *Akcja Reinhardt: Zagłaga Żydów w Generalnym Gubernatorstwie*, Warsaw: IPN, 2004, 103–131.

David Blackbourn, *The Long Nineteenth Century: A History of Germany, 1780–1918*, New York: Oxford University Press, 1986.

Jochen Böhler, *"Größte Härte": Verbrechen der Wehrmacht in Polen September/Oktober 1939*, Osnabrück: Deutsches Historisches Institut, 2005.

Jochen Böhler, *Der Überfall: Deutschlands Krieg gegen Polen*, Frankfurt am Main: Eichborn, 2009.

Włodzimierz Borodziej, *The Warsaw Uprising of 1944*, trans. Barbara Harshav, Madison: University of Wisconsin Press, 2001.

Włodzimierz Borodziej, Hans Lemberg, and Claudia Kraft, eds., *Niemcy w Polsce: Wybór dokumentów*, Vol. 1, Warsaw: Neriton: 2000.

Jerzy Borzęcki, *The Soviet-Polish Peace of 1921 and the Creation of Interwar Europe*, New Haven: Yale University Press, 2008.

Karl Dietrich Bracher, *Zeit der Ideologien: Eine Geschichte politischen Denkens im 20. Jahrhundert*, Stuttgart: Deutsche Verlags-Anstalt, 1984.

Rodric Braithwaite, *Moscow 1941: A City and Its People at War*, New York: Knopf, 2006.

Aleksander Brakel, "'Das allergefährlichste ist die Wut der Bauern': Die Versorgung der Partisanen und ihr Verhältnis zur Zivilbevölkerung. Eine Fallstudie zum Gebiet Baranowicze 1941–1944," *Vierteljahrshefte für Zeitgeschichte*, No. 3, 2007, 393–424.

Alexander Brakel, *Unter Rotem Stern und Hakenkreuz: Baranowicze 1939 bis 1944*, Paderborn: Schöningh, 2009.

David Brandenberger, *National Bolshevism: Stalinist Mass Culture and the Formation of Modern Russian National Identity, 1931–1956*, Cambridge, Mass.: Harvard University Press, 2002.

David Brandenberger, "Stalin's Last Crime? Recent Scholarship on Postwar Soviet Antisemitism and the Doctor's Plot," *Kritika*, Vol. 6, No. 1, 2005, 187–204.

Detlef Brandes, *Der Weg zur Vertreibung: Pläne und Entscheidungen zum "Transfer" aus der Tschechoslowakei und aus Polen*, Munich: Oldenbourg, 2005.

Ray Brandon, "The First Wave," unpublished manuscript, 2009.

Ray Brandon, "The Holocaust in 1942," unpublished manuscript, 2009.

Ray Brandon and Wendy Lower, "Introduction," in idem, eds., *The Shoah in Ukraine: History, Testimony, Memorialization*, Bloomington: Indiana University Press, 2008, 1–12.

Jonathan Brent and Vladimir Naumov, *Stalin's Last Crime: The Plot Against the Jewish Doctors 1948–1953*, New York: HarperCollins, 2003.

Archie Brown, *The Rise and Fall of Communism*, New York: HarperCollins, 2009.

Kate Brown, *A Biography of No Place*, Cambridge, Mass.: Harvard University Press, 2004.

Christopher R. Browning, "The Nazi Decision to Commit Mass Murder: Three Interpretations. The Euphoria of Victory and the Final Solution: Summer–Fall 1941," *German Studies Review*, Vol. 17, No. 3, 1994, 473–481.

Christopher R. Browning, *The Origins of the Final Solution: The Evolution of Nazi Jewish Policy, September 1939–March 1942*, Lincoln: University of Nebraska Press, 2004.

Jan Jacek Bruski, *Hołodomor 1932–1933: Wielki głód na Ukrainie w dokumentach polskiej dyplomacji i wywiadu*, Warsaw: PISM, 2008.

Margarete Buber-Neumann, *Under Two Dictators: Prisoner of Hitler and Stalin*, London: Pimlico, 2008 [1949].

Celina Budzyńska, *Strzępy rodzinnej sagi*, Warsaw: Żydowski Instytut Historyczny, 1997.

Alan Bullock, *Hitler and Stalin: Parallel Lives*, London: HarperCollins, 1991.

Jeffrey Burds, "Agentura: Soviet Informants Networks and the Ukrainian Underground in Galicia," *East European Politics and Societies*, Vol. 11, No. 1, 1997, 89–130.

Michael Burleigh, *Germany Turns Eastwards: A Study of Ostforschung in the Third Reich*, Cambridge: Cambridge University Press, 1988.

Michael Burleigh, *The Third Reich: A New History*, New York: Hill and Wang, 2000.

Philippe Burrin, *Fascisme, nazisme, autoritarisme*, Paris: Seuil, 2000.

Sarah Cameron, "The Hungry Steppe: Soviet Kazakhstan and the Kazakh Famine, 1921–1934," doctoral dissertation, Yale University, 2010.

Tatiana Cariewskaja, Andrzej Chmielarz, Andrzej Paczkowski, Ewa Rosowska, and Szymon Rudnicki, eds., *Teczka specjalna J. W. Stalina*, Warsaw: Rytm, 1995.

Holly Case, *Between States: The Transylvanian Question and the European Idea During World War II*, Stanford: Stanford University Press, 2009.

David Cesarini, *Eichmann: His Life and Crimes*, London: William Heinemann, 2004.

William Chase, *Enemies Within the Gates? The Comintern and the Stalinist Repression, 1934–1939*, New Haven: Yale University Press, 2001.

Bernhard Chiari, *Alltag hinter der Front: Besatzung, Kollaboration und Widerstand in Weißrußland 1941–1944*, Düsseldorf: Droste Verlag, 1998.

Shalom Cholawsky, "The Judenrat in Minsk," in Yisrael Gutman and Cynthia J. Haft, eds., *Patterns of Jewish Leadership in Nazi Europe*, Jerusalem: Yad Vashem, 1979, 113–132.

Bohdan Chyrko, "Natsmen? Znachyt' voroh. Problemy natsional'nykh menshyn v dokumentakh partiinykh i radians'kykh orhaniv Ukraïny v 20–30-x rr.," *Z arkhiviv V.U.Ch.K H.P.U N.K.V.D K.H.B*, Vol. 1, No. 2, 1995, 90–115.

Jan M. Ciechanowski, *Powstanie Warszawskie*, Warsaw: Państwowy Instytut Wydawniczy, 1989.

Anna M. Cienciala, Natalia S. Lebedeva, and Wojciech Materski, eds., *Katyn: A Crime Without Punishment*, New Haven: Yale University Press, 2007.

Margeret Siriol Colley, *Gareth Jones: A Manchukuo Incident*, Newark: self-published, 2001.

Margaret Siriol Colley, *More Than a Grain of Truth: The Biography of Gareth Richard Vaughan Jones*, Newark: self-published, 2006.

Robert Conquest, *The Harvest of Sorrow: Soviet Collectivization and the Terror-Famine*, New York: Oxford University Press, 1986.

Lorenzo Cotula, Sonja Vermeulen, Rebeca Leonard, and James Keeley, *Land Grab or Development Opportunity? Agricultural investment and international land deals in Africa*, London: IIED/FAO/IFAD, 2009.

Stéphane Courtois, Nicolas Werth, Jean-Louis Panné, Andrzej Paczkowski, Karel Bartosek, and Jean-Louis Margolin, *Le livre noir du communisme: Crimes, terreur, repression*, Paris: Robert Laffont, 1997.

The Crime of Katyń: Facts and Documents, London: Polish Cultural Foundation, 1965.

Martin Cüppers, *Wegbereiter der Shoah. Die Waffen-SS, der Kommandostab Reichsführer-SS und die Judenvernichtung 1939–1945*, Darmstadt: Wissenschaftliche Buchgesellschaft, 2005.

T. David Curp, *A Clean Sweep? The Politics of Ethnic Cleansing in Western Poland, 1945–1960*, Rochester: University of Rochester Press, 2006.

Józef Czapski, *Na nieludzkiej ziemi*, Paris: Editions Spotkania, 1984.

Józef Czapski, *Wspomnienia starobielskie*, Nakład Oddziału Kultury i Prasy II Korpusu (published in the field), 1945.

Czech-German Joint Commission of Historians, *A Conflictual Community, Catastrophe, Detente*, trans. Ruth Tusková, Prague: Ústav Mezinarodních Vztahů, 1996.

Alexander Dallin, *The Kaminsky Brigade: 1941–1944*, Cambridge, Mass.: Russian Research Center, 1956.

Alexander Dallin and F. I. Firsov, eds., *Dimitrov and Stalin: Letters from the Soviet Archives*, New Haven: Yale University Press, 2000.

Dana G. Dalrymple, "The Soviet Famine of 1932–1934," *Soviet Studies*, Vol. 15, No. 3, 1964, 250–284.

Dana G. Dalrymple, "The Soviet Famine of 1932–1934: Some Further References," *Soviet Studies*, Vol. 16, No. 4, 1965, 471–474.

V. Danilov et al., eds., *Tragediia sovetskoi derevni: Kollektivizatsiia i raskulachivanie*, Vols. 1–2, Moscow: Rosspen, 1999–2000.

The Dark Side of the Moon, London: Faber and Faber, 1946.

Szymon Datner, *55 Dni Wehrmachtu w Polsce*, Warsaw: MON, 1967.

Szymon Datner, *Zbrodnie Wehrmachtu na jeńcach wojennych w II Wojniej Światowej*, Warsaw: MON, 1964.

Norman Davies, "The Misunderstood Victory in Europe," *New York Review of Books*, Vol. 42, No. 9, 25 May 1995.

Norman Davies, *Rising '44: "The Battle for Warsaw,"* London: Macmillan, 2003.

R. W. Davies, Oleg V. Khlevniuk, E. A. Rhees, Liudmila P. Kosheleva, and Larisa A. Rogovaya, eds., *The Stalin-Kaganovich Correspondence 1931–36*, New Haven: Yale University Press, 2003.

R. W. Davies, M. B. Tauger, and S. G. Wheatcroft, "Stalin, Grain Stocks and the Famine of 1932–33," *Soviet Studies*, Vol. 54, No. 3, 1995, 642–657.

R. W. Davies and Stephen G. Wheatcroft, *The Years of Hunger: Soviet Agriculture, 1931–1933*, London: Palgrave, 2004.

Martin Dean, *Collaboration in the Holocaust: Crimes of the Local Police in Belorussia and Ukraine*, London: Macmillan, 2000.

Martin Dean, "Jewish Property Seized in the Occupied Soviet Union in 1941 and 1942: The Records of the Reichshauptkasse Beutestelle," *Holocaust and Genocide Studies*, Vol. 14, No. 1, 2000, 83–101.

Martin Dean, *Robbing the Jews: The Confiscation of Jewish Property in the Holocaust, 1933–1945*, Cambridge: Cambridge University Press, 2008.

Sławomir Dębski. *Między Berlinem a Moskwą. Stosunki niemiecko-sowieckie 1939–1941*, Warsaw: PISM, 2003.

Dennis Deletant, "Transnistria and the Romanian Solution to the 'Jewish Problem,'" in Ray Brandon and Wendy Lower, eds., *The Shoah in Ukraine: History, Testimony, Memorialization*, Bloomington: Indiana University Press, 2008, 156–189.

Deportacje obywateli polskich z Zachodniej Ukrainy i Zachodniej Białorusi w 1940/Deportatsii pol'skikh grazhdan iz Zapadnoi Ukrainy i Zapadnoi Belorussii v 1940 godu, Warsaw: IPN, 2003.

Der Nister, *The Family Mashber*, trans. Leonard Wolf, New York: NYRB, 2008.

Jared Diamond, *Collapse: How Societies Choose to Fail or Succeed*, New York: Penguin, 2005.

Wacław Długoborski, "Żydzi z ziem polskich wcielonych do Rzeszy w KL Auschwitz-Birkenau," in Aleksandra Namysło, ed., *Zagłada Żydów na polskich terenach wcielonych do Rzeszy*, Warsaw: IPN, 2008, 127–149.

Nikolai M. Dronin and Edward G. Bellinger, *Climate Dependence and Food Problems in Russia 1900–1990*, Budapest: Central European Press, 2005.

Marian Marek Drozdowski, "The History of the Warsaw Ghetto in the Light of the Reports of Ludwig Fischer," *Polin*, Vol. 3, 1988, 189–199.

I. A. Dugas and F. Ia. Cheron, *Sovetskie Voennoplennye v nemetskikh kontslageriakh (1941–1945)*, Moscow: Avuar konsalting, 2003.

I. A. Dugas and F. Ia. Cheron, *Vycherknutye iz pamiati: Sovetskie Voennoplennye mezhdu Gitlerom i Stalinym*, Paris: YMCA Press, 1994.

Krzysztof Dunin-Wąsowicz, "Akcja AB w Warszawie," in Zygmunt Mańkowski, ed., *Ausserordentliche Befriedungsaktion 1940 Akcja AB na ziemiach polskich*, Warsaw: GKBZpNP-IPN, 1992, 19–27.

Debórah Dwork and Robert Jan van Pelt, *Auschwitz*, New York: Norton, 1996.

John Dziak, *Chekisty: A History of the KGB*, Lexington: Lexington Books, 1988.

Roman Dzwonkowski, ed., *Głód i represje wobec ludności polskiej na Ukrainie 1932–1947*, Lublin: Towarzystwo Naukowe KUL, 2004.

Mark Edele and Michael Geyer, "States of Exception," in Michael Geyer and Sheila Fitzpatrick, eds., *Beyond Totalitarianism: Stalinism and Nazism Compared*, Cambridge: Cambridge University Press, 2009, 345–395.

Robert Edelman, *Proletarian Peasants: The Revolution of 1905 in Russia's Southwest*, Ithaca: Cornell University Press, 1987.

Ilya Ehrenburg and Vasily Grossman, *The Black Book: The Ruthless Murder of Jews by German-Fascist Invaders Throughout the Temporarily-Occupied Regions of the Soviet Union and in the Death Camps of Poland During the War of 1941–1945*, New York: Holocaust Publications, 1981.

Ludwig Eiber, "Gewalt in KZ Dachau. Vom Anfang eines Terrorsystems," in Andreas Wirsching, ed., *Das Jahr 1933: Die nationalsozialistische Machteroberung und die deutsche Gsellschaft*, Göttingen: Wallstein Verlag, 2009, 169–184.

Dietrich Eichholtz, *Krieg um Öl: Ein Erdölimperium als deutsches Kriegsziel (1938–1943)*, Leipzig: Leipziger Universitätsverlag, 2006.

S. N. Eisenstadt, *Die Vielfalt der Moderne*, Weilerswist: Velbrück Wissenschaft, 2000.

Jerzy Eisler, "1968: Jews, Antisemitism, Emigration," *Polin*, Vol. 21, 2008, 37–62.

Michael Ellman, "A Note on the Number of 1933 Famine Victims," *Soviet Studies*, Vol. 43, No. 2, 1991, 375–379.

Michael Ellman, "The Role of Leadership Perceptions and of Intent in the Soviet Famine of 1931–1934," *Europe-Asia Studies*, Vol. 57, No. 6, 2005, 823–841.

Michael Ellman and S. Maksudov, "Soviet Deaths in the Great Patriotic War: A Note," *Europe-Asia Studies*, Vol. 46, No. 4, 1994, 671–680.

Barbara Engelking and Jacek Leociak, *Getto warszawskie: Przewodnik po nieistniejącym mieście*, Warsaw: OFiS PAN, 2003.

Barbara Engelking and Jacek Leociak, *The Warsaw Ghetto: A Guide to the Perished City*, New Haven: Yale University Press, 2009.

Barbara Engelking and Dariusz Libionka, *Żydzi w powstańczej Warszawie*, Warsaw: Polish Center for Holocaust Research, 2009.

David Engerman, *Modernization from the Other Shore: American Intellectuals and the Romance of Russian Development*, Cambridge, Mass.: Harvard University Press, 2003.

Barbara Epstein, *The Minsk Ghetto: Jewish Resistance and Soviet Internationalism*, Berkeley: University of California Press, 2008.

Richard J. Evans, *The Coming of the Third Reich*, New York: Penguin, 2003.

Richard J. Evans, *The Third Reich in Power*, London: Penguin, 2005.

Richard J. Evans, *The Third Reich at War*, New York: Penguin, 2009.

Barbara Falk, *Sowjetische Städte in der Hungersnot 1932/33*, Cologne: Böhlau Verlag, 2005.

Niall Ferguson, *The War of the World: History's Age of Hatred*, London: Allan Lane, 2006.

Joachim C. Fest, *Das Gesicht des Dritten Reiches*, Munich: Piper, 2006.

Orlando Figes, *A People's Tragedy: The Russian Revolution, 1891–1924*, London: Penguin, 1998.

Barbara Fijałkowska, *Borejsza i Różański: Przyczynek do historii stalinizmu w Polsce*, Olsztyn: Wyższa Szkoła Pedagogiczna, 1995.

M. V. Filimoshin, "Ob itogakh ischisleniya poter' sredi mirnogo naseleniya na okkupirovannoi territorii SSSR i RSFSR v gody Velikoi Otechestvennoi Voiny," in R. B. Evdokimov, ed., *Liudskie poteri SSSR v period vtoroi mirovoi voiny*, St. Petersburg: RAN, 1995, 124–132.

Sheila Fitzpatrick, *Education and Social Mobility in the Soviet Union, 1921–1934*, Cambridge: Cambridge University Press, 1979.

Jürgen Förster, "The German Army and the Ideological War against the Soviet Union," in Gerhard Hirschfeld, ed., *The Policies of Genocide: Jews and Soviet Prisoners of War in Nazi Germany*, London: Allen & Unwin, 1986, 15–29.

Matthew Frank, *Expelling the Germans: British Opinion and Post-1945 Population Transfers in Context*, Oxford: Oxford University Press, 2007.

Henry Friedlander, *The Origins of Nazi Genocide: From Euthanasia to the Final Solution*, Chapel Hill: University of North Carolina Press, 1995.

Saul Friedländer, *The Years of Extermination: Nazi Germany and the Jews, 1939–1945*, New York: HarperCollins, 2007.

François Furet, *Le passé d'une illusion: Essai sur l'idée communiste au XXe siècle*, Paris: Robert Laffont, 1995.

François Furet and Ernst Nolte, *Fascism and Communism*, Lincoln: University of Nebraska Press, 2001.

John Lewis Gaddis, *The Long Peace: Inquiries into the History of the Cold War*, Oxford: Oxford University Press, 1987.

John Lewis Gaddis, *The United States and the Coming of the Cold War*, New York: Columbia University Press, 1972.

W. Horsley Gantt, *Russian Medicine*, New York: Paul B. Hoeber, 1937.

Michael Gelb, "An Early Soviet Ethnic Deportation: The Far-Eastern Koreans," *Russian Review*, Vol. 54, No. 3, 1995, 389–412.

Robert Gellately, *Lenin, Stalin, and Hitler: The Age of Social Catastrophe*, New York: Knopf, 2007.

John Gordon Gerard, *The Bones of Berdichev: The Life and Fate of Vassily Grossman*, New York: Free Press, 1996.

Christian Gerlach, "Failure of Plans for an SS Extermination Camp in Mogilëv, Belorussia," *Holocaust and Genocide Studies*, Vol. 11, No. 1, 1997, 60–78.

Christian Gerlach, *Kalkulierte Morde: Die deutsche Wirtschafts-und Vernichtungspolitik in Weißrußland 1941 bis 1944*, Hamburg: Hamburger Edition, 1999.

Christian Gerlach, *Krieg, Ernährung, Völkermord: Forschungen zur deutschen Vernichtungspolitik im Zweiten Weltkrieg*, Hamburg: Hamburger Edition, 1998.

Christian Gerlach, "The Wannsee Conference, the Fate of German Jews, and Hitler's Decision in Principle to Exterminate All European Jews," *Journal of Modern History*, Vol. 70, 1998, 759–812.

Christian Gerlach and Nicolas Werth, "State Violence—Violent Societies," in Michael Geyer and Sheila Fitzpatrick, eds., *Beyond Totalitarianism: Stalinism and Nazism Compared*, Cambridge: Cambridge University Press, 2009, 133–179.

J. Arch Getty and Oleg V. Naumov, *Road to Terror: Stalin and the Self-Destruction of the Bolsheviks, 1932–1939*, New Haven: Yale University Press, 1999.

J. Arch Getty and Oleg V. Naumov, *Yezhov: The Rise of Stalin's "Iron Fist,"* New Haven: Yale University Press, 2008.

Glenda Gilmore, *Defying Dixie: The Radical Roots of Civil Rights, 1919–1950*, New York: Norton, 2008.

Eagle Glassheim, "The Mechanics of Ethnic Cleansing: The Expulsion of Germans from Czechoslovakia, 1945–1947," in Philipp Ther and Ana Siljak, eds., *Redrawing Nations: Ethnic Cleansing in East-Central Europe, 1944–1948*, Lanham: Rowman and Littlefield, 2001, 197–200.

Richard Glazar, *Die Falle mit dem grünen Zaun: Überleben in Treblinka*, Frankfurt am Main: Fischer Verlag, 1992.

Henryk Głębocki, ed., "Pierwszy naród ukarany: świadectwa Polaków z Leningradu," *Arcana*, Nos. 64–65, 2005, 155–192.

Albin Głowacki, *Sowieci wobec Polaków na ziemiach wschodnich II Rzeczypospolitej 1939–1941*, Łódź: Wydawnictwo Uniwersytetu Łódzkiego, 1998.

Mateusz Gniazdowski, "'Ustalić liczbę zabitych na 6 milionów ludzi': dyrektywy Jakuba Bermana dla Biura Odszkodowań Wojennych przy Prezydium Rady Ministrów," *Polski Przegląd Diplomatyczny*, No. 1 (41), 2008, 99–113.

C. Goeschel and N. Wachsmann, "Introduction," in idem, eds., *The Nazi Concentration Camps, 1933–39: A Documentary History*, Lincoln: Nebraska University Press, 2010.

Aleksandr Gogun, *Stalinskie kommandos: Ukrainskie partizanskie formirovaniia, 1941–1944*, Moscow: Tsentrpoligraf, 2008.

Daniel J. Goldhagen, *Hitler's Willing Executioners: Ordinary Germans and the Holocaust*, New York: Knopf, 1996.

Golod v SSSR, 1930–1934 gg., Moscow: Federal'noe arkhivnoe agentstvo, 2009.

Jan Góral, "Eksterminacja inteligencji i tak zwanych warstw przywódczych w zachodnich powiatach Dystryktu Radomskiego (1939–1940)," in Zygmunt Mańkowski, ed., *Ausserordentliche Befriedungsaktion 1940 Akcja AB na ziemiach polskich*, Warsaw: GKBZpNP-IPN, 1992, 71–82.

Yoram Gorlizki and Oleg Khlevniuk, *Cold Peace: Stalin and the Soviet Ruling Circle, 1945–1953*, Oxford: Oxford University Press, 2004.

Sergei Gorlov, *Sovershenno sekretno, Moskva-Berlin, 1920–1933: Voenno-politicheskie otnosheniia mezhdu SSSR i Germaniei*, Moscow: RAN, 1999.

Alexandra Goujon, "Kurapaty (1937–1941): NKVD Mass Killings in Soviet Belarus," unpublished paper, 2008.

Alexandra Goujon, "Memorial Narratives of WWII Partisans and Genocide in Belarus," *East European Politics and Societies*, Vol. 24, No. 1, 2010, 6–25.

Alvin Gouldner, "Stalinism: A Study of Internal Colonialism," *Telos*, No. 34, 1978, 5–48.

Catherine Goussef, "Les déplacements forcés des populations aux frontières russes occidentales (1914–1950)," in S. Audoin-Rouzeau, A. Becker, Chr. Ingrao, and H. Rousso, eds., *La violence de guerre 1914–1945*, Paris: Éditions Complexes, 2002, 177–190.

Michael Grabher, *Irmfried Eberl: "Euthanasie"-Arzt und Kommandant von Treblinka*, Frankfurt am Main: Peter Lang, 2006.

Günter Grass, *Beim Häuten der Zwiebel*, Munich: Deutscher Taschenbuch Verlag, 2008.

Günter Grass, *Im Krebsgang*, Munich: Deutscher Taschenbuch Verlag, 2004.

Andrea Graziosi, "Collectivisation, révoltes paysannes et politiques gouvernementales a travers les rapports du GPU d'Ukraine de février-mars 1930," *Cahiers du Monde russe*, Vol. 34, No. 3, 1994, 437–632.

Andrea Graziosi, *The Great Soviet Peasant War*, Cambridge, Mass.: Harvard University Press, 1996.

Andrea Graziosi, "Italian Archival Documents on the Ukrainian Famine 1932–1933," in Wsevolod Isajiw, ed., *Famine-Genocide in Ukraine, 1932–1933*, Toronto: Ukrainian Canadian Research and Documentation Centre, 2003, 27–48.

Andrea Graziosi, "The Soviet 1931–1933 Famines and the Ukrainian Holodomor: Is a New Interpretation Possible, and What Would Its Consequences Be?" *Harvard Ukrainian Studies*, Vol. 37, Nos. 1–4, 2004–2005.

Paul R. Gregory, *Terror by Quota: State Security from Lenin to Stalin*, New Haven: Yale University Press, 2009.

Jan T. Gross, *Neighbors: The Destruction of the Jewish Community in Jedwabne, Poland*, Princeton: Princeton University Press, 2001.

Jan T. Gross, "Polish POW Camps in Soviet-Occupied Western Ukraine," in Keith Sword, ed., *The Soviet Takeover of the Polish Eastern Provinces, 1939–1941*, London: Macmillan, 1991.

Jan T. Gross, *Polish Society Under German Occupation: The Generalgouvernement, 1939–1944*, Princeton: Princeton University Press, 1979.

Jan T. Gross, *Revolution from Abroad: The Soviet Conquest of Poland's Western Ukraine and Western Belorussia*, Princeton: Princeton University Press, 2002.

Jan T. Gross, "The Social Consequences of War: Preliminaries for the Study of the Imposition of Communist Regimes in Eastern Europe," *East European Politics and Societies*, 3, 1989, 198–214.

Jan T. Gross, *Upiorna dekada: trzy eseje o sterotypach na temat Żydów, Polaków, Niemców, i komunistów, 1939–1948*, Cracow: Universitas, 1948.

Vasily Grossman, *Everything Flows*, trans. Robert Chandler, New York: NYRB Classics, 2010.

Vasily Grossman, *Life and Fate*, trans. Robert Chandler, New York: Harper and Row, 1985.

Vasily Grossman, *The Road*, trans. Robert Chandler, New York: NYRB Classics, 2010.

Irena Grudzińska Gross and Jan Tomasz Gross, *War Through Children's Eyes: The Soviet Occupation and the Deportations, 1939–1941*, Stanford: Hoover Institution Press, 1981.

Michał Grynberg and Maria Kotowska, eds., *Życie i zagłada Żydów polskich 1939–1945: Relacje świadków*, Warsaw: Oficyna Naukowa, 2003.

A. Ie. Gurianov, "Obzor sovetskikh repressivnykh kampanii protiv poliakov i pols's'kikh grazhdan," in A. V. Lipatov and I. O. Shaitanov, eds., *Poliaki i russkie: Vzaimoponimanie i vzaimoneponimanie*, Moscow: Indrik, 2000, 199–207.

A. Ie. Gurianov, "Pol'skie spetspereselentsy v SSSR v 1940–1941 gg.," in idem, ed., *Repressii protiv poliakov i pol'skikh grazhdan*, Moscow: Zven'ia, 1997.

Israel Gutman, *Resistance: The Warsaw Ghetto Uprising*, Boston: Houghton Mifflin, 1994.

Ingo Haar, "Die deutschen 'Vertreibungsverluste'—Zur Entstehungsgeschichte der 'Dokumentation der Vertreibung,'" *Tel Aviver Jahrbuch für deutsche Geschichte*, Vol. 35, 2007, 251–271.

Eva and H. H. Hahn, "Die Deutschen und 'ihre' Vertreibung," *Transit*, No. 23, 2002, 103–116.

Joanna K. M. Hanson, *The Civilian Population and the Warsaw Uprising of 1944*, Cambridge: Cambridge University Press, 1982.

Stephen Hanson, *Time and Revolution: Marxism and the Design of Soviet Economic Institutions*, Chapel Hill: University of North Carolina Press, 1997.

Mark Harrison, *Soviet Planning in Peace and War*, Cambridge: Cambridge University Press, 1985.

Christian Hartmann, "Massensterben oder Massenvernichtung? Sowjetische Kriegsgefangene im 'Unternehmen Barbarossa.' Aus dem Tagebuch eines deutschen Lagerkommandanten," *Vierteljahrshefte für Zeitgeschichte*, Vol. 49, No. 1, 2001, 97–158.

Tsuyoshi Hasegawa, *Racing the Enemy: Stalin, Truman, and the Surrender of Japan*, Cambridge, Mass.: Harvard University Press, 2005.

Jonathan Haslam, *The Soviet Union and the Struggle for Collective Security in Europe, 1933–39*, Houndsmills: Macmillan, 1984.

Jonathan Haslam, *The Soviet Union and the Threat from the East*, Houndsmills: Macmillan, 1992.

Milan Hauner, *India in Axis Strategy: Germany, Japan, and Indian Nationalists in the Second World War*, Stuttgart: Klett-Cotta, 1981.

Thomas T. Hecht, *Life Death Memories*, Charlottesville: Leopolis Press, 2002.

Susanne Heim, "Kalorien-Agrarforschung, Ernährungswirtschaft und Krieg: Herbert Backe als Wissenschaftspolitiker," in idem, ed., *Kalorien, Kautschuk, Karrieren: Pflanzenzüchtung und landwirtschaftliche Forschung in Kaiser-Wilhelm-Instituten, 1933–1945*, Wallstein: Göttingen, 2003, 23–63.

James W. Heinzen, *Inventing a Soviet Countryside: State Power and the Transformation of Rural Russia, 1917–1929*, Pittsburgh: University of Pittsburgh Press, 2003.

Ulrich Herbert, *Best: Biographische Studien über Radikalismus, Weltanschauung und Vernunft, 1903–1989*, Bonn: J.H.W. Dietz, 1996.

Jeffrey Herf, *The Jewish Enemy: Nazi Propaganda During World War II and the Holocaust*, Cambridge, Mass.: Harvard University Press, 2006.

Dagmar Herzog, *Sex After Fascism: Memory and Morality in Twentieth-Century Germany*, Princeton: Princeton University Press, 2005.

Raul Hilberg, *The Destruction of the European Jews*, New Haven: Yale University Press, 2003, 3 vols..

Raul Hilberg, "The Ghetto as a Form of Government," *Annals of the American Academy of Political and Social Science*, Vol. 450, 1980, 98–112.

Raul Hilberg, "The Judenrat: Conscious or Unconscious 'Tool,'" in Yisrael Gutman and Cynthia J. Haft, eds., *Patterns of Jewish Leadership in Nazi Europe*, Jerusalem: Yad Vashem, 1979, 31–44.

Raul Hilberg, *Perpetrators, Victims, Bystanders: The Jewish Catastrophe*, New York: HarperPerennial, 1993.

Klaus Hildebrand, *Vom Reich zum Weltreich: Hitler, NSDAP und koloniale Frage 1919–1945*, Munich: Wilhelm Fink Verlag, 1969.

Manfred Hildermeier, *Sozialrevolutionäre Partei Russlands: Agrarsozialismus und Modernisierung im Zarenreich*, Cologne: Böhlau, 1978.

Andreas Hillgruber, *Germany and the Two World Wars*, Cambridge, Mass.: Harvard University Press, 1981.

John-Paul Himka, "Ethnicity and Reporting of Mass Murder: *Krakivski visti*, the NKVD Murders of 1941, and the Vinnytsia Exhumation," unpublished paper, 2009.

Francine Hirsch, *Empire of Nations: Ethnographic Knowledge and the Making of the Soviet Union*, Ithaca: Cornell University Press, 2005.

Eric Hobsbawm, *The Age of Extremes: A History of the World, 1914–1991*, London: Vintage, 1996.

Peter Holquist, *Making War, Forging Revolution: Russia's Continuum of Crisis*, Cambridge, Mass.: Harvard University Press, 2002.

Gordon J. Horwitz, *Ghettostadt: Łódź and the Making of a Nazi City*, Cambridge, Mass.: Harvard University Press, 2008.

Grzegorze Hryciuk, "Victims 1939–1941: The Soviet Repressions in Eastern Poland," in Elazar Barkan, Elisabeth A. Cole, and Kai Struve, eds., *Shared History—Divided Memory: Jews and Others in Soviet-Occupied Poland*, Leipzig: Leipzig University-Verlag, 2007, 173–200.

Isabel Hull, *Absolute Destruction: Military Culture and the Practices of War in Imperial Germany*, Ithaca: Cornell University Press, 2005.

Taras Hunczak and Roman Serbyn, eds., *Famine in Ukraine 1932–1933: Genocide by Other Means*, New York: Shevchenko Scientific Society, 2007.

Hungersnot: Authentische Dokumente über das Massensterben in der Sowjetunion, Vienna, 1933.

Ich werde es nie vergessen: Briefe sowjetischer Kriegsgefangener 2004–2006, Berlin: Ch. Links Verlag, 2007.

Hennadii Iefimenko, "Natsional'na polityka Kremlia v Ukraïni pislia Holodomoru 1932–33 rr.," *Harvard Ukrainian Studies*, forthcoming.

Melanie Ilic, "The Great Terror in Leningrad: a Quantitative Analysis," *Europe-Asia Studies*, Vol. 52, No. 8, 2000, 1515–1534.

I. I. Il'iushyn, *OUN-UPA i ukraïns'ke pytannia v roky druhoï svitovoï viiny v svitli pol's'kykh dokumentiv*, Kiev: NAN Ukraïny, 2000.

Christian Ingrao, *Les chasseurs noirs: La brigade Dirlewanger*, Paris: Perrin, 2006.

Christian Ingrao, "Violence de guerre, violence génocide: Les Einsatzgruppen," in S. Audoin-Rouzeau, A. Becker, Chr. Ingrao, and H. Rousso, eds., *La violence de guerre 1914–1945*, Paris: Éditions Complexes, 2002, 219–240.

Mikołaj Iwanow, *Pierwszy naród ukarany: Stalinizm wobec polskiej ludności kresowej 1921–1938*, Warsaw: Omnipress, 1991.

George D. Jackson, Jr., *Comintern and Peasant in East Europe, 1919–1930*, New York: Columbia University Press, 1966.

Egbert Jahn, "Der Holodomor im Vergleich: Zur Phänomenologie der Massenvernichtung," *Osteuropa*, Vol. 54, No. 12, 2004, 13–32.

Harold James, *Europe Reborn: A History, 1914–2000*, Harlow: Pearson, 2003.

Maria Janion, *Do Europy: tak, ale razem z naszymi umarłymi*, Warsaw: Sic!, 2000.

Stanisław Jankowiak, "'Cleansing' Poland of Germans: The Province of Pomerania, 1945–1949," in Philip Ther and Ana Siljak, eds., *Redrawing Nations: Ethnic Cleansing in East-Central Europe, 1944–1948*, Lanham: Rowman and Littlefield, 2001, 87–106.

Stanisław Jankowiak, *Wysiedlenie i emigracja ludności niemieckiej w polityce władz polskich w latach 1945–1970*, Warsaw: IPN, 2005.

Andrzej Jankowski, "Akcja AB na Kielecczyźnie," in Zygmunt Mańkowski, ed., *Ausserordentliche Befriedungsaktion 1940 Akcja AB na ziemiach polskich*, Warsaw: GKBZpNP-IPN, 1992, 65–82.

Marc Jansen and Nikolai Petrov, *Stalin's Loyal Executioner: Nikolai Ezhov, 1895–1940*, Stanford: Hoover University Press, 2002.

Krzysztof Jasiewicz, *Zagłada polskich Kresów. Ziemiaństwo polskie na Kresach Północno-Wschodnich Rzeczypospolitej pod okupacją sowiecką 1939–1941*, Warsaw: Volumen, 1998.

Katherine R. Jolluck, *Exile and Identity: Polish Women in the Soviet Union During World War II*, Pittsburgh: University of Pittsburgh Press, 2002.

Die Judenausrottung in Polen. Die Vernichtungslager, Geneva, 1944.

Tony Judt, *The Burden of Responsibility: Blum, Camus, Aron, and the French Twentieth Century*, Chicago: University of Chicago Press, 1998.

Tony Judt, *Postwar: A History of Europe Since 1945*, New York: Penguin, 2005.

Marc Junge, Gennadii Bordiugov, and Rolf Binner, *Vertikal' bol'shogo terrora*, Moscow: Novyi Khronograf, 2008.

Sławomir Kalbarczyk, "Przedmioty odnalezione w Bykowni a Kuropatach świadczą o polskości ofiar," *Biuletyn Instytutu Pamięci Narodowej*, Nos. 10–11, 2007, 47–54.

Ivan Kamenec, "The Deportation of Jewish Citizens from Slovakia," in *The Tragedy of the Jews of Slovakia*, Oświęcim: Auschwitz-Birkenau State Museum and Museum of the Slovak National Uprising, 2002, 111–140.

Ivan Kamenec, "The Holocaust in Slovakia," in Dušan Kováč, ed., *Slovak Contributions to 19th International Congress of Historical Sciences*, Bratislava: Veda, 2000, 195–206.

Samuel D. Kassow, *Who Will Write Our History? Rediscovering a Hidden Archive from the Warsaw Ghetto*, New York: Vintage, 2009.

Nikolaus Katzer, "Brot und Herrschaft: Die Hungersnot in der RSFSR," *Osteuropa*, Vol. 54, No. 12, 2004, 90–110.

Alex J. Kay, *Exploitation, Resettlement, Mass Murder: Political and Economic Planning for German Occupation Policy in the Soviet Union, 1940–1941*, New York: Berghahn Books, 2006.

Alex J. Kay, "'Hierbei werden zweifellos zig Millionen Menschen verhungern': Die deutsche Wirtschaftsplanung für die besetzte Sowjetunion und ihre Umsetzung, 1941 bis 1944," *Transit*, No. 58, 2009, 57–77.

John Keegan, *The Face of Battle*, New York: Viking, 1976.

Oleg Ken, *Collective Security or Isolation: Soviet Foreign Policy and Poland, 1930–1935*, St. Petersburg: Evropeiskii Dom, 1996.

O. N. Ken and A. I. Rupasov, eds., *Politbiuro Ts.K. VKP(b) i otnosheniia SSSR s zapadnymi sosednimi gosudarstvami*, St. Petersburg: Evropeiskii Dom, 2001.

Paul M. Kennedy, *Aufstieg und Verfall der britischen Seemacht*, Herford: E. S. Mittler & Sohn, 1978.

Ian Kershaw, *Fateful Choices: Ten Decisions That Changed the World, 1940–1941*, London: Penguin Books, 2007.

Ian Kershaw, *Hitler: A Biography*, New York: W. W. Norton, 2008.

Ian Kershaw, *Hitler, the Germans, and the Final Solution*, New Haven: Yale University Press, 2008.

Krystyna Kersten, *The Establishment of Communist Rule in Poland*, Berkeley: University of California Press, 1991.

Krystyna Kersten, "Forced Migration and the Transformation of Polish Society in the Postwar Period," in Philip Ther and Ana Siljak, eds., *Redrawing Nations: Ethnic Cleansing in East-Central Europe, 1944–1948*, Lanham: Rowman and Littlefield, 2001, 75–86.

Vladimir Khaustov, "Deiatel'nost' organov gosudarstvennoi bezopasnosti NKVD SSSR (1934–1941 gg.)," doctoral dissertation, Akademia Federal'noi Sluzhby Bezopasnosti Rossiiskoi Federatsii, 1997.

Oleg Khlevniouk, *Le cercle du Kremlin: Staline et le Bureau politique dans les années 30: les jeux du pouvoir*, Paris: Éditions du Seuil, 1996.

Oleg V. Khlevniuk, *The History of the Gulag: From Collectivization to the Great Terror*, New Haven: Yale University Press, 2004.

Oleg Khlevnyuk, "The Objectives of the Great Terror, 1937–1938," in Julian Cooper, Maureen Perrie, and E. A. Rhees, eds., *Soviet History 1917–1953: Essays in Honour of R. W. Davies*, Houndmills: Macmillan, 1995, 158–176.

Oleg Khlevniuk, "Party and NKVD: Power Relationships in the Years of the Great Terror," in Barry McLoughlin and Kevin McDermott, eds., *Stalin's Terror: High Politics and Mass Repression in the Soviet Union*, New York: Palgrave Macmillan, 2003.

Oleg Khlevniuk, "Stalin as dictator: the personalisation of power," in Sarah Davies and James Harris, eds., *Stalin: A New History*, Cambridge: Cambridge University Press, 2005, 109–120.

Ben Kiernan, *Blood and Soil: A World History of Genocide and Extermination from Sparta to Darfur*, New Haven: Yale University Press, 2007.

Lucjan Kieszczyński, "Represje wobec kadry kierowniczej KPP," in Jarema Maciszewski, ed., *Tragedia Komunistycznej Partii Polski*, Warsaw: Książka i Wiedza, 1989, 198–216.

Charles King, *The Moldovans: Russia, Romania, and the Politics of Culture*, Stanford: Hoover Institution, 2000.

Gary King, Ori Rosen, Martin Tanner, and Alexander F. Wagner, "Ordinary Voting Behavior in the Extraordinary Election of Adolf Hitler," *Journal of Economic History*, Vol. 68, No. 4, 2008, 951–996.

Esther Kingston-Mann, *Lenin and the Problem of Marxist Peasant Revolution*, New York: Oxford University Press, 1983.

Lisa A. Kirschenbaum, *The Legacy of the Siege of Leningrad, 1941–1995: Myth, Memories, and Monuments*, Cambridge: Cambridge University Press, 2006.

Ernst Klee and Willi Dreßen, eds., *Gott mit uns: Der deutsche Vernichtungskrieg im Osten 1939–1945*, Frankfurt: S. Fischer, 1989.

Peter Klein, "Curt von Gottberg—Siedlungsfunktionär und Massenmörder," in Klaus-Michael Mallmann, ed., *Karrieren der Gewalt: Nationalsozialistische Täterbiographien*, Darmstadt: Wissenschaftliche Buchgesellschaft, 2004, 95–103.

Peter Klein, "Zwischen den Fronten. Die Zivilbevölkerung Weißrusslands und der Krieg der Wehrmacht gegen die Partisanen," in Babette Quinkert, ed., *Wir sind die Herren dieses Landes. Ursachen Verlauf und Folgen des deutschen Überfalls auf die Sowjetunion*, Hamburg: VSA Verlag, 2002, 82–103.

Tadeusz Klimaszewski, *Verbrennungskommando Warschau*, Warsaw: Czytelnik, 1959.

Gerd Koenen, *Der Russland-Komplex: Die Deutschen und der Osten, 1900–1945*, Munich: Beck, 2005.

Arthur Koestler, untitled, in Richard Crossman, ed., *The God That Failed*, London: Hamilton, 1950, 25–82.

Arthur Koestler, *Darkness at Noon*, New York: Macmillan, 1941.

Arthur Koestler, "Vorwort," to Alexander Weißberg-Cybulski, *Im Verhör*, Vienna: Europaverlag, 1993, 9–18 [1951].

Arthur Koestler, *The Yogi and the Commissar*, New York: Macmillan, 1946.

Leszek Kołakowski, *Main Currents of Marxism, Vol. 3: The Breakdown*, Oxford: Oxford University Press, 1978.

Piotr Kołakowski, *NKWD i GRU na ziemiach polskich 1939–1945*, Warsaw: Bellona, 2002.

Bogusław Kopka, *Konzentrationslager Warschau: Historia i następstwa*, Warsaw: IPN, 2007.

Edward Kopówka, *Stalag 366 Siedlce*, Siedlce: SKUNKS, 2004.

Edward Kopówka, *Treblinka. Nigdy więcej*, Siedlce: Muzeum Rejonowe, 2002.

Marek Kornat, *Polityka równowagi: Polska między Wschodem a Zachodem*, Cracow: Arcana, 2007.

Marek Kornat, *Polska 1939 roku wobec paktu Ribbentrop-Mołotow*, Warsaw: Polski Instytut Spraw Międzynarodowych, 2002.

Reinhart Koselleck, *Futures Past: On the Semantics of Historical Time*, trans. Keith Tribe, Cambridge, Mass.: MIT Press, 1985.

I. I. Kostiushko, ed., *Materialy "Osoboi papki": Politbiuro Ts.K. RKP(b)-VKP(b) po voprosu sovetsko-pol'skikh otnoshenii 1923–1944 gg.*, Moscow: RAN, 1997.

G. V. Kostyrchenko, *Gosudarstvennyi antisemitizm v SSSR ot nachala do kul'minatsii 1938–1953*, Moscow: Materik, 2005.

Gennadi Kostyrchenko, *Out of the Red Shadows: Anti-Semitism in Stalin's Russia*, Amherst, NY: Prometheus Books, 1995.

G. V. Kostyrchenko, *Tainaia politika Stalina: Vlast' i antisemitizm*, Moscow: Mezhdunarodnye otnosheniia, 2001.

Stephen Kotkin, *Magnetic Mountain: Stalinism as a Civilization*, Berkeley: University of California Press, 1995.

Stephen Kotkin, "Peopling Magnitostroi: The Politics of Demography," in William G. Rosenberg and Lewis H. Siegelbaum, eds., *Social Dimensions of Soviet Industrialization*, Bloomington: Indiana University Press, 1993, 63–104.

Lidia Kovalenko and Volodymyr Maniak, eds., *33'i: Holod: Narodna knyha-memorial*, Kiev: Radians'kyi pys'mennyk, 1991.

Heda Margolius Kovály, *Under a Cruel Star: A Life in Prague 1941–1968*, trans. Franci Epstein and Helen Epstein, New York: Holmes and Maier, 1997.

Tadeusz Kowalski, "Z badań nad eksterminacją inteligencji w Rzeszowskim w okresie II wojny światowej," in Zygmunt Mańkowski, ed., *Ausserordentliche Befriedungsaktion 1940 Akcja AB na ziemiach polskich*, Warsaw: GKBZpNP-IPN, 1992, 83–89.

Beata Kozaczyńska, "Wysiedlenie mieszkańców Zamojszczyzny do dystryktu warszawskiego w latach 1942–1943 i los deportowanych," in Marcin Zwolski, ed., *Exodus: Deportacje i migracje (wątek wschodni)*, Warsaw: IPN, 2008, 70–92.

Denis Kozlov, "The Historical Turn in Late Soviet Culture: Retrospectivism, Factography, Doubt, 1953–1991," *Kritika*, Vol. 2, No. 3, 2001, 577–600.

Denis Kozlov, "'I Have Not Read, But I Will Say': Soviet Literary Audiences and Changing Ideas of Social Membership, 1958–1966," *Kritika*, Vol. 7, No. 3, 2006, 557–597.

Mark Kramer, "Die Konsolidierung des kommunistischen Blocks in Osteuropa 1944–1953," *Transit*, No. 39, 2009, 78–95.

Hans von Krannhals, *Der Warschauer Aufstand 1944*, Frankfurt am Main: Bernard & Graefe Verlag für Wehrwesen, 1964.

Victor Kravchenko, *I Chose Freedom: The Personal and Political Life of a Soviet Official*, New York: Charles Scribner's Sons, 1946.

Gerhard Krebs, "Japan and the German-Soviet War, 1941," in Bernd Wegner, ed., *From Peace to War: Germany, Soviet Russia, and the World, 1939–1941*, Providence: Berghahn Books, 1997, 541–560.

G. Krivosheev, ed., *Grif sekretnosti sniat: Poteri vooruzhennykh sil SSSR v voinakh*, Moscow: Voenizdat, 1993.

Bernhard R. Kroener, "The 'Frozen Blitzkrieg': German Strategic Planning against the Soviet Union and the Causes of its Failure," in Bernd Wegner, ed., *From Peace to War: Germany, Soviet Russia, and the World, 1939–1941*, Providence: Berghahn Books, 1997, 135–150.

Jerzy Królikowski, "Budowałem most kolejowy w pobliżu Treblinki," *Biuletyn Żydowskiego Instytutu Historycznego*, No. 49, 1964, 46–57.

Peter Krüger, *Die Außenpolitik der Republik von Weimar*, Darmstadt: Wissenschaftliche Buchgesellschaft, 1985.

A. I. Kruglov, *Entsiklopediia Kholokosta*, Kiev: Evreiskii sovet Ukrainy, 2000.

Alexander Kruglov, "Jewish Losses in Ukraine," in Ray Brandon and Wendy Lower, eds., *The Shoah in Ukraine: History, Testimony, Memorialization*, Bloomington: Indiana University Press, 2008, 272–290.

Abraham Krzepicki, "Treblinka," *Biuletyn Żydowskiego Instytutu Historycznego*, Nos. 43–44, 1962, 84–109.

Stanisław Kulczycki, *Hołodomor: Wielki głód na Ukrainie w latach 1932–1933 jako ludobójstwo*, Wrocław: Kolegium Europy Wschodniej, 2008.

S. V. Kul'chyts'kyi, ed., *Kolektyvizatsiia i holod na Ukraïni 1929–1933*, Kiev: Naukova Dumka, 1993.

S. V. Kul'chyts'kyi, "Trahichna statystyka holodu," in F. M. Rudych, I. F. Kuras, M. I. Panchuk, P. Ia. Pyrih, and V. F Soldatenko, eds., *Holod 1932–1933 rokiv na Ukraïni: Ochyma istorykiv, movoiu dokumentiv*, Kiev: Vydavnytstvo Politychnoi Literatury Ukrainy, 1990, 66–85.

Janusz Kupczak, *Polacy na Ukrainie w latach 1921–1939*, Wrocław: Wydawnictwo Uniwersytetu Wrocławskiego, 1994.

Hiroaki Kuromiya, "Accounting for the Great Terror," *Jahrbücher für Geschichte Osteuropas*, Vol. 53, No. 1, 2003, 86–101.

Hiroaki Kuromiya, "The Great Terror and 'Ethnic Cleansing': The Asian Nexus," unpublished paper, October 2009.

Hiroaki Kuromiya, *Stalin*, Harlow: Pearson Longman, 2005.

Hiroaki Kuromiya, *Freedom and Terror in the Donbas: A Ukrainian-Russian Borderland, 1870s-1990s*, Cambridge: Cambridge University Press, 1998.

Hiroaki Kuromiya, *The Voices of the Dead: Stalin's Great Terror in the 1930s*, London: Yale University Press, 2007.

Hiroaki Kuromiya, "World War II, Jews, and Post-War Soviet Society," *Kritika*, Vol. 3, No. 3, 2002, 521–531.

Hiroaki Kuromiya and Paweł Libera, "Notatka Włodzimierza Bączkowskiego na temat współpracy polsko-japońskiej wobec ruchu prometejskiego (1938)," *Zeszyty Historyczne*, 2009, 114–135.

Hiroaki Kuromiya and Georges Mamoulia, "Anti-Russian and Anti-Soviet Subversion: The Caucasian-Japanese Nexus, 1904–1945," *Europe-Asia Studies*, Vol. 61, No. 8, 2009, 1415–1440.

Hiroaki Kuromiya and Andrzej Pepłoński, *Między Warszawą a Tokio: Polsko-japońska współpraca wywiadowcza 1904–1944*, Toruń: Wydawnictwo Adam Marszałek, 2009.

Hiroaki Kuromiya and Andrzej Pepłonski, "Stalin und die Spionage," *Transit*, No. 38, 20–33.

Robert Kuśnierz, *Ukraina w latach kolektywizacji i wielkiego głodu*, Toruń: Grado, 2005.

Ihar Kuz'niatsou, ed., *Kanveer s'mertsi*, Minsk: Nasha Niva, 1997.

Pieter Lagrou, "La 'Guerre Honorable' et une certaine idée de l'Occident. Mémoires de guerre, racisme et réconciliation après 1945," in François Marcot and Didier Musiedlak, eds., *Les Résistances, miroir des régimes d'oppression. Allemagne, France, Italie*, Besançon: Presses Universitaires de Franche-Comté, 2006, 395–412.

Stephen J. Lee, *European Dictatorships 1918–1945*, London: Routledge, 2000.

Leningradskii martirolog 1937–1938, St. Petersburg: Rossiiskaia natsional'naia biblioteka, 1996, Vol. 4.

S. V. Leonov, *Rozhdenie Sovetskoi imperii: Gosudarstvo i ideologiia, 1917–1922 gg.*, Moscow: Dialog MGU, 1997.

Zofia Lesczyńska, "Z badań nad stratami inteligencji na Lubelszczyźnie w latach 1939–1944," in Zygmunt Mańkowski, ed., *Ausserordentliche Befriedungsaktion 1940 Akcja AB na ziemiach polskich*, Warsaw: GKBZpNP-IPN, 1992, 58–70.

Hillel Levine, *In Search of Sugihara*, New York: The Free Press, 1996.

Dariusz Libionka, "Apokryfy z dziejów Żydowskiego Związku Wojskowego i ich autorzy," *Zagłada Żydów. Studia i materiały*, No. 1, 2005, 165–198.

Dariusz Libionka, "Głową w mur. Interwencje Kazimierza Papée, polskiego ambasadora przy Stolicy Apostolskiej, w sprawie zbrodni niemieckich w Polsce, listopad 1942-styczeń 1943," *Zagłada Żydów. Studia i materiały*, No. 2, 2006, 292–314.

Dariusz Libionka, "Polska konspiracja wobec eksterminacji Żydów w dystrykcie warszawskim," in Barbara Engelking, Jacek Leociak, and Dariusz Libionka, eds., *Prowincja noc. Życie i zagłada Żydów w dystrykcie warszawskim*, Warsaw: IFiS PAN, 2007, 443–504.

Dariusz Libionka, "ZWZ-AK i Delegatura Rządu RP wobec eksterminacji Żydów polskich," in Andrzej Żbikowski, ed., *Polacy i Żydzi pod okupacją niemiecką 1939–1945, Studia i materiały*, Warsaw: IPN, 2006, 15–208.

Dariusz Libionka and Laurence Weinbaum, "Deconstructing Memory and History: The Jewish Military Union (ZZW) and the Warsaw Ghetto Uprising," *Jewish Political Studies Review*, Vol. 18, Nos. 1–2, 2006, 1–14.

Dariusz Libionka and Laurence Weinbaum, "Pomnik Apfelbauma, czyli klątwa 'majora' Iwańskiego," *Więź*, No. 4, 2007, 100–111.

Benjamin Lieberman, *Terrible Fate: Ethnic Cleansing in the Making of Modern Europe*, Chicago: Ivan R. Dee, 2006.

Lars T. Lih, *Bread and Authority in Russia, 1914–1921*, Berkeley: University of California Press, 1990.

Lars T. Lih, Oleg. V. Naumov, and Oleg Khlevniuk, eds., *Stalin's Letters to Molotov*, New Haven: Yale University Press, 1995.

Peter Longerich, *Heinrich Himmler: Biographie*, Berlin: Siedler, 2008.

Peter Longerich, *Politik der Vernichtung: Eine Gesamtdarstellung der nationalsozialistischen Judenverfolgung*, Munich: Piper, 1998.

Peter Longerich, *The Unwritten Order: Hitler's Role in the Final Solution*, Stroud: Tempus, 2001.

Andrea Löw, *Juden im Getto Litzmannstadt: Lebensbedingungen, Selbstwahrnehmung, Verhalten*, Göttingen: Wallstein Verlag, 2006.

Wendy Lower, *Nazi Empire-Building and the Holocaust in Ukraine*, Chapel Hill: University of North Carolina Press, 2005.

Wendy Lower, "'On Him Rests the Weight of the Administration': Nazi Civilian Rulers and the Holocaust in Zhytomyr," in Ray Brandon and Wendy Lower, eds., *The Shoah in Ukraine: History, Testimony, and Memorialization*, Bloomington: Indiana University Press, 2008, 224–227.

Moritz Felix Lück, "Partisanenbekämpfung durch SS und Polizei in Weißruthenien 1942. Die Kampfgruppe von Gottberg," in Alfons Kenkmann and Christoph Spieker, eds., *Im Auftrag: Polizei, Verwaltung und Verantwortung*, Essen: Klartext Verlag, 2001, 225–247.

John Lukacs, *Five Days in London, May 1940*, New Haven: Yale University Press, 1999.

John Lukacs, *June 1941: Hitler and Stalin*, New Haven: Yale University Press, 2007.

John Lukacs, *The Last European War*, New Haven: Yale University Press, 1976.

Igor Lukes, "The Rudolf Slansky Affair: New Evidence," *Slavic Review*, Vol. 58, No. 1, 1999, 160–187.

Leonid Luks, "Zum Stalinschen Antisemitismus: Brüche und Widersprüche," *Jahrbuch für Historische Kommunismus-Forschung*, 1997, 9–50.

Arno Lustiger, *Stalin and the Jews: The Red Book*, New York: Enigma Books, 2003.

Paweł Machcewicz and Krzysztof Persak, eds., *Wokół Jedwabnego*, Warsaw: Instytut Pamięci Narodowej, 2002, 2 vols.

French MacLean, *The Cruel Hunters: SS-Sonderkommando Dirlewanger: Hitler's Most Notorious Anti-Partisan Unit*, Atglen: Schiffer Military History, 1998.

French MacLean, *The Field Men: The SS Officers Who Led the Einsatzkommandos*, Atglen: Schiffer, 1999.

Michael MacQueen, "Nazi Policy Toward the Jews in the Reichskommissariat Ostland, June-December 1941: From White Terror to Holocaust in Lithuania," in Zvi Gitelman, ed., *Bitter Legacy: Confronting the Holocaust in the USSR*, Bloomington: Indiana University Press, 1997, 91–103.

Czesław Madajczyk, "Vom 'Generalplan Ost' zum 'Generalsiedlungsplan,'" in Mechtild Rössler and Sabine Schleiermacher, eds., *Der "Generalplan Ost": Hauptlinien der nationalsozialistischen Planungs-und Vernichtungspolitik*, Berlin: Akademie Verlag, 1993, 12–19.

Czesław Madajczyk, Marek Getter and Andrzej Janowski, eds., *Ludność cywilna w Powstaniu Warszawskim*, Vol. 2, Warsaw: Państwowy Instytut Wydawniczy, 1974.

Krzysztof Madeja, Jan Żaryn, and Jacek Żurek, eds., *Księga świadectw. Skazani na karę śmierci w czasach stalinowskich i ich losy*, Warsaw: IPN, 2003.

Sergei Maksudov, "Victory over the Peasantry," *Harvard Ukrainian Studies*, Vol. 25, Nos. 3/4, 2001, 187–236.

Sergui Maksudov, "Raschelovechivanie," *Harvard Ukrainian Studies*, forthcoming.

Martin Malia, *Alexander Herzen and the Birth of Russian Socialism, 1812–1855*, Cambridge, Mass.: Harvard University Press, 1961.

Klaus-Michael Mallmann, "'Rozwiązać przez jakikolwiek szybko działający środek: Policja Bezpieczeństwa w Łodzi a Shoah w Kraju Warty," in Aleksandra Namysło, ed., *Zagłada Żydów na polskich terenach wcielonych do Rzeszy*, Warsaw: IPN, 2008, 85–115.

Klaus-Michael Mallmann, Jochen Böhler, and Jürgen Matthäus, *Einsatzgruppen in Polen: Darstellung und Dokumentation*, Darmstadt: WGB, 2008.

Zygmunt Mańkowski, "Ausserordentliche Befriedungsaktion," in Zygmunt Mańkowski, ed., *Ausserordentliche Befriedungsaktion 1940 Akcja AB na ziemiach polskich*, Warsaw: GKBZpNP-IPN, 1992, 6–18.

Walter Manoschek, *"Serbien ist judenfrei": Militärische Besatzungspolitik und Judenvernichtung in Serbien 1941/1942*, Munich: R. Oldenbourg Verlag, 1993.

Vasyl' Marochko and Ol'ha Movchan, *Holodomor v Ukraïni 1932–1933 rokiv: Khronika*, Kiev: Kyievo-Mohylians'ka Akademiia, 2008.

David Marples, "Kuropaty: The Investigation of a Stalinist Historical Controversy," *Slavic Review*, Vol. 53, No. 2, 1994, 513–523.

Michael R. Marrus, "Jewish Resistance to the Holocaust," *Journal of Contemporary History*, Vol. 30, No. 1, 1995, 83–110.

Józef Marszałek, "Akcja AB w dystrykcie lubelskim," in Zygmunt Mańkowski, ed., *Ausserordentliche Befriedungsaktion 1940 Akcja AB na ziemiach polskich*, Warsaw: GKBZpNP-IPN, 1992, 48–57.

Terry Martin, *Affirmative Action Empire*, Ithaca: Cornell University Press, 2001.

Terry Martin, "The 1932–1933 Ukrainian Terror: New Documentation on Surveillance and the Thought Process of Stalin," in Wsevolod Isajiw, ed., *Famine-Genocide in Ukraine, 1932–1933*, Toronto: Ukrainian Canadian Research and Documentation Centre, 2003, 97–114.

Terry Martin, "The Origins of Soviet Ethnic Cleansing," *Journal of Modern History*, Vol. 70, No. 4, 1998, 813–861.

Vojtech Mastny, *The Cold War and Soviet Insecurity: The Stalin Years*, Oxford: Oxford University Press, 1996.

Vojtech Mastny. *The Czechs Under Nazi Rule: The Failure of National Resistance, 1939–1942*, New York: Columbia University Press, 1971.

Wojciech Materski, *Tarcza Europy. Stosunki polsko-sowieckie 1918–1939*, Warsaw: Książka i Wiedza, 1994.

Jürgen Matthäus, "Controlled Escalation: Himmler's Men in the Summer of 1941 and the Holocaust in the Occupied Soviet Territories," *Holocaust and Genocide Studies*, Vol. 21, No. 2, Fall 2007, 218–242.

Jürgen Matthäus, "Reibungslos und planmäßig: Die Zweite Welle der Judenvernichtung im Generalkommissariat Weißruthenien (1942–1944)," *Jahrbuch für Antisemitismusforschung*, Vol. 4, No. 4, 1995, 254–274.

Ralph Mavrogordato and Earl Ziemke, "The Polotsk Lowland," in John Armstrong, ed., *Soviet Partisans in World War II*, Madison: University of Wisconsin Press, 1964.

Mark Mazower, *Dark Continent: Europe's Twentieth Century*, New York, Vintage, 2000.

Mark Mazower, *Hitler's Empire: Nazi Rule in Occupied Europe*, London: Allen Lane, 2008.

Mark Mazower, "Violence and the State in the Twentieth Century," *American Historical Review*, Vol. 107, No. 4, 2002, 1147–1167.

Barry McLoughlin, "Mass Operations of the NKVD, 1937–8: A Survey," in Barry McLoughlin and Kevin McDermott, eds., *Stalin's Terror: High Politics and Mass Repression in the Soviet Union*, Houndsmill: Palgrave, 2003, 118–152.

Geoffrey Megargee, *War of Annihilation: Combat and Genocide on the Eastern Front, 1941*, Lanham: Rowman & Littlefield, 2007.

Ezra Mendelsohn, *The Jews of East Central Europe Between the World Wars*, Bloomington: Indiana University Press, 1983.

Catherine Merridale, *Ivan's War: Life and Death in the Red Army, 1939–1945*, New York: Henry Holt, 2006.

Catherine Merridale, *Night of Stone: Death and Memory in Twentieth-Century Russia*, New York: Viking, 2000.

Włodzimierz Michniuk, "Z historii represji politycznych przeciwko Polakom na Białorusi w latach trzydziestych," in Wiesław Balcerak, ed., *Polska-Białoruś 1918–1945: Zbiór studiów i materiałów*, Warsaw: IH PAN, 1993, 112–120.

Piotr Mierecki i Wasilij Christoforow et al., eds., *Varshavskoe vosstanie 1944/Powstanie Warszawskie 1944*, Moscow-Warsaw, IHRAN-IPN, 2007.

Anna Mieszkowska, *Matka dzieci Holocaustu: Historia Ireny Sendlerowej*, Warsaw: Muza SA, 2008.

Stanley Milgram, "Behavior Study of Obedience," *Journal of Abnormal and Social Psychology*, Vol. 67, No. 2, 1963, 371–378.

James A. Millward, *Eurasian Crossroads: A History of Xinjiang*, London: Hurst & Company, 2007.

Czesław Miłosz, *Legends of Modernity: Essays and Letters from Occupied Poland, 1942–43*, New York: Farrar, Strauss, and Giroux, 2005.

Sybil Milton, ed., *The Stroop Report*, New York: Random House, 1979.

Alan S. Milward, *The German Economy at War*, London: Athlone Press, 1965.

Eugeniusz Mironowicz, *Białoruś*, Warsaw: Trio, 1999.

Jacek Andrzej Młynarczyk, "Akcja Reinhardt w gettach prowincjonalnych dystryktu warszawskiego 1942–1943," in Barbara Engelking, Jacek Leociak, and Dariusz Libionka, eds., *Prowincja noc. Życie i zagłada Żydów w dystrykcie warszawskim*, Warsaw: IFiS PAN, 2007, 39–74.

Jacek Andrzej Młynarczyk, *Judenmord in Zentralpolen: Der Distrikt Radom im Generalgouvernement 1939–1945*, Darmstadt: WGB, 2007.

Jacek Andrzej Młynarczyk, "Treblinka–ein Todeslager der 'Aktion Reinhard,'" in
    Bogdan Musial, ed., *Aktion Reinhardt, Der Völkermord an den Juden im
    Generalgouvernement 1941–1944*, Osnabrück: Fibre, 2004, 257–281.

Bronisław Młynarski, *W niewoli sowieckiej*, London: Gryf Printers, 1974.

Kazimierz Moczarski, *Rozmowy z katem*, Cracow: Znak, 2009.

Simon Sebag Montefiore, *Stalin: The Court of the Red Tsar*, London: Weidenfeld &
    Nicolson, 2003.

James Morris, "The Polish Terror: Spy Mania and Ethnic Cleansing in the Great
    Terror," *Europe-Asia Studies*, Vol. 56, No. 5, July 2004, 751–766.

Grzegorz Motyka, "Tragedia jeńców sowieckich na ziemiach polskich podczas II
    wojny światowej," unpublished manuscript, 2009.

Grzegorz Motyka, *Ukraińska partyzantka 1942–1960*, Warsaw: Rytm, 2006.

Samuel Moyn, "In the Aftermath of Camps," in Frank Biess and Robert Mueller,
    eds., *Histories of the Aftermath: The Legacies of the Second World War*, New York:
    Berghahn Books, 2010.

Timothy Patrick Mulligan, *The Politics of Illusion and Empire: German Occupation
    Policy in the Soviet Union, 1942–1943*, New York: Praeger, 1988.

Bogdan Musiał, *Na zachód po trupie Polski*, Warsaw: Prószyński, 2009.

Bogdan Musiał, "'Przypadek modelowy dotyczący eksterminacji Żydów': Początki
    'akcji Reinhardt'—planowanie masowego mordu Żydów w Generalnym
    Gubernatorstwîe," Dariusz Libionka, ed., *Akcja Reinhardt. Zagłada Żydów w
    Generalnym Gubernatorstwie*, Warsaw: IPN, 2004, 15–38.

Bogdan Musial, *Sowjetische Partisanen 1941–1944: Mythos und Wirklichkeit*,
    Paderborn: Ferdinand Schöningh, 2009.

Bogdan Musial, ed., *Sowjetische Partisanen in Weißrussland: Innenansichten aus
    dem Gebiet Baranoviči*, Munich: R. Oldenbourg Verlag, 2004.

Norman Naimark, *Fires of Hatred: Ethnic Cleansing in Twentieth-Century Europe*,
    Cambridge, Mass.: Harvard University Press, 2001.

Norman Naimark, "Gomułka and Stalin: The Antisemitic Factor in Postwar Polish
    Politics," in Murray Baumgarten, Peter Kenez, and Bruce Thompson, eds.,
    Varieties of Antisemitism: History, Ideology, Discourse, Newark: University of
    Delaware Press, 2009, 237–250.

Norman Naimark, *The Russians in Germany: A History of the Soviet Zone of
    Occupation, 1945–1949*, Cambridge, Mass.: Harvard University Press, 1995.

Leonid Naumov, *Bor'ba v rukovodstve NKVD v 1936–1938 gg.*, Moscow: Modern-A,
    2006.

Leonid Naumov, *Stalin i NKVD*, Moscow: Iauza, 2007.

Vladimir Nikol'skij, "Die 'Kulakenoperation' im ukrainischen Donbass," in Rolf
    Binner, Bernd Bonwetsch, and Marc Junge, eds., *Stalinismus in der sowjetischen
    Provinz 1937–1938*, Berlin: Akademie Verlag, 2010, 613–640.

V. M. Nikol's'kyi, *Represyvna diial'nist' orhaniv derzhavnoï bezpeky SRSR v Ukraïni*, Donetsk: Vydavnytstvo Donets'koho Natsional'noho Universytetu, 2003.

Bernadetta Nitschke, *Wysiedlenie ludności niemieckiej z Polski w latach 1945–1949*, Zielona Góra: Wyższa Szkoła Pedagogiczna im. Tadeusza Kotarbińskiego, 1999.

Hans-Heinrich Nolte, "Partisan War in Belorussia, 1941–1944," in Roger Chickering, Stig Förster, and Bernd Greiner, eds., *A World at Total War: Global Conflict and the Politics of Destruction, 1937–1945*, Cambridge: Cambridge University Press, 2005, 261–276.

Andrzej Nowak, *Polska a trzy Rosje*, Cracow: Arcana, 2001.

"Obóz zagłady Treblinka," *Biuletyn Glownej Komisji Badania Zbrodni Niemieckich w Polsce*, No. 1, 1946, 133–144.

Viorica Olaru-Cemirtan, "Wo die Züge Trauer trugen: Deportationen in Bessarabien, 1940–1941," *Osteuropa*, Vol. 59, Nos. 7–8, 2009, 219–226.

Operatsia "Seim" 1944–1946/Operacja "Sejm" 1944–1946, Warsaw-Kiev: IPN, 2007.

Karin Orth, *Das System der nationalsozialistischen Konzentrationslager. Eine politische Organisationsgeschichte*, Hamburg: Hamburger Edition, 1999.

George Orwell, *Homage to Catalonia*, San Diego: Harcourt Brace Jovanovich, 1980.

George Orwell, *Orwell and Politics*, London: Penguin, 2001.

Rüdiger Overmans, *Deutsche militärische Verluste im Zweiten Weltkrieg*, Munich: Oldenbourg, 1999.

Rüdiger Overmans, "Die Kriegsgefangenenpolitik des Deutschen Reiches 1939 bis 1945," in Jörg Echternkamp, ed., *Das Deutsche Reich und der Zweite Weltkrieg*, Vol. 9/2, Munich: Deutsche Verlags-Anstalt, 2005.

Rüdiger Overmans, "Personelle Verluste der deutschen Bevölkerung durch Flucht und Vertreibung," *Dzieje Najnowsze*, Vol. 26, No. 2, 1994, 50–65.

Andrzej Paczkowski, "Pologne, la 'nation ennemie,'" in Stéphane Courtois, Nicolas Werth, Jean-Louis Panné, Andrzej Paczkowski, Karel Bartosek, and Jean-Louis Margolin, eds., *Le livre noir du communisme: Crimes, terreur, repression*, Paris: Robert Laffont, 1997.

Andrzej Paczkowski, *Pół wieku dziejów Polski*, Warsaw: PWN, 2005.

Andrzej Paczkowski, *Trzy twarze Józefa Światła. Przyczynek do historii komunizmu w Polsce*, Warsaw: Prószyński i S-ka, 2009.

Pamiętniki znalezione w Katyniu, Paris: Editions Spotkania, 1989.

Andrzej Pankowicz, "Akcja AB w Krakowie," in Zygmunt Mańkowski, ed., *Ausserordentliche Befriedungsaktion 1940 Akcja AB na ziemiach polskich*, Warsaw: GKBZpNP-IPN, 1992, 43–47.

Yaroslav Papuha, *Zakhidna Ukraïna i holodomor 1932–1933 rokiv*, Lviv: Astroliabiia, 2008.

Michael Parris, *The Lesser Terror: Soviet State Security, 1939–1953*, Santa Barbara: Praeger, 1996.

Gunnar S. Paulsson, *Secret City: The Hidden Jews of Warsaw 1940–1945*, New Haven: Yale University Press, 2002.

Stevan L. Pawlowitch, *Hitler's New Disorder: The Second World War in Yugoslavia*, New York: Columbia University Press, 2008.

Nikita Petrov and K. V. Skorkin, *Kto rukovodil NKVD, 1934–1941*, Moscow, Zven'ia, 1999.

N. V. Petrov and A. B. Roginsksii, "'Pol'skaia operatsiia' NKVD 1937–1938 gg.," in A. Ie. Gurianov, ed., *Repressii protiv poliakov i pol'skikh grazhdan*, Moscow: Zven'ia, 1997, 22–43.

Niccolo Pianciola, "The Collectivization Famine in Kazakhstan," in Halyna Hryn, ed., *Hunger by Design: The Great Ukrainian Famine in Its Soviet Context*, Cambridge, Mass.: Harvard University Press, 2008, 103–116.

Jan Pietrzykowski, "Akcja AB na ziemi częstochowskiej i radomszczańskiej," in Zygmunt Mańkowski, ed., *Ausserordentliche Befriedungsaktion 1940 Akcja AB na ziemiach polskich*, Warsaw: GKBZpNP-IPN, 1992, 107–123.

Jan Pietrzykowski, *Akcja AB w Częstochowie*, Katowice: Wydawnictwo Śląsk, 1971.

Benjamin Pinkus, "The Deportation of the German Minority in the Soviet Union, 1941–1945," in Bernd Wegner, ed., *From Peace to War: Germany, Soviet Russia, and the World, 1939–1941*, Providence: Berghahn Books, 1997, 449–462.

Richard Pipes, *The Formation of the Soviet Union*, Cambridge, Mass.: Harvard University Press, 1997.

Richard Pipes, *Struve*, Cambridge, Mass.: Harvard University Press, 1970–1980, 2 vols.

Dieter Pohl, *Nationalsozialistische Judenverfolgung in Ostgalizien: Organisation und Durchführung eines staatlichen Massenverbrechens*, Munich: Oldenbourg, 1996.

Dieter Pohl, "Schauplatz Ukraine: Der Massenmord an den Juden im Militärverwaltungsgebiet und im Reichskommissariat 1941–1943," in Norbert Frei, Sybille Steinbacher, and Bernd C. Wagner, eds., *Ausbeutung, Vernichtung, Öffentlichkeit: Neue Studien zur nationalsozialistischen Lagerpolitik*, Munich: K. G. Saur, 2000, 135–179.

Dieter Pohl, "Ukrainische Hilfskräfte beim Mord an den Juden," in Gerhard Paul, ed., *Die Täter der Shoah*, Göttingen: Wallstein Verlag, 2002.

Dieter Pohl, *Verfolgung und Massenmord in der NS-Zeit 1933–1945*, Darmstadt: Wissenschaftliche Buchgesellschaft, 2008.

Dieter Pohl, "Znaczenie dystrykyu lubelskiego w 'ostatecznym rozwiązaniu kwestii żydowskiej'," in Dariusz Libionka, ed., *Akcja Reinhardt: Zagłada Żydów w Generalnym Gubernatorstwie*, Warsaw: IPN, 2004, 39–53.

Pavel Polian, *Against Their Will: The History and Geography of Forced Migrations in the USSR*, Budapest: CEU Press, 2004.

Pavel Polian, "Hätte der Holocaust beinahe nicht stattgefunden? Überlegungen zu einem Schriftwechsel im Wert von zwei Millionen Menschenleben," in Johannes

Hurter and Jürgen Zarusky, eds., *Besatzung, Kollaboration, Holocaust*, Munich: R. Oldenbourg Verlag, 2008, 1–20.

Pavel Polian, "La violence contre les prisonniers de guerre soviétiques dans le IIIe Reich et un URSS," in S. Audoin-Rouzeau, A. Becker, Chr. Ingrao, and H. Rousso, eds., *La violence de guerre 1914–1945*, Paris: Éditions Complexes, 2002, 117–131.

Antony Polonsky, *Politics in Independent Poland 1921–1939: The Crisis of Constitutional Government*, Oxford: Clarendon Press, 1972.

Joseph Poprzeczny, *Odilo Globocnik, Hitler's Man in the East*, Jefferson: McFarland & Company, 2004.

Peter J. Potichnij, "The 1946–1947 Famine in Ukraine: A Comment on the Archives of the Underground," Wsevolod Isajiw, ed., *Famine-Genocide in Ukraine, 1932–1933*, Toronto: Ukrainian Canadian Research and Documentation Centre, 2003, 185–189.

Robert Potocki, *Polityka państwa polskiego wobec zagadnienia ukraińskiego w latach 1930–1939*, Lublin: IEŚW, 2003.

Samantha Power, *"A Problem from Hell": America and the Age of Genocide*, New York: Basic Books, 2002.

Volodymyr Prystaiko and Iurii Shapoval, eds., *Sprava "Spilky Vyzvolennia Ukraïny,"* Kiev: Intel, 1995.

Proces z vedením protistátního spikleneckého centra v čele s Rodolfem Slánským, Prague: Ministerstvo Spravedlnosti, 1953.

Projektgruppe Belarus, ed., *"Existiert das Ghetto noch?" Weißrussland: Jüdisches Überleben gegen nationalsozialistische Herrschaft*, Berlin: Assoziation A, 2003.

T. S. Prot'ko, *Stanovlenie sovetskoi totalitarnoi sistemy v Belarusi: 1917–1941 gg: (1917–1941)*, Minsk: Tesei, 2002.

Alexander V. Prusin, "A Community of Violence: The SiPo/SD and its Role in the Nazi Terror System in Generalbezirk Kiew," *Holocaust and Genocide Studies*, Vol. 21, No. 1, 2007, 1–30.

Adam Puławski, *W obliczu Zagłady. Rząd RP na Uchodźstwie, Delegatura Rządu RP na Kraj, ZWZ-AK wobec deportacji Żydów do obozów zagłady (1941–1942)*, Lublin: IPN, 2009.

E. A. Radice, "Economic Developments in Eastern Europe Under German Hegemony" in Martin McCauley, ed., *Communist Power in Europe 1944–1949*, New York: Harper and Row, 1977, 3–21.

E. A. Radice, "General Characteristics of the Region Between the Wars," in Michael Kaser, ed., *An Economic History of Eastern Europe*, Vol. 1, New York: Oxford University Press, 1984.

Chil Rajchman, *Je suis le dernier Juif*, trans. Gilles Rozier, Paris: Éditions des Arenes, 2009.

J. Rajgrodzki, "Jedenaście miesięcy w obozie zagłady w Treblince," *Biuletyn Żydowskiego Instytutu Historycznego*, No. 25, 1958, 101–118.

Donald J. Raleigh, "The Russian Civil War, 1917–1922," in Ronald Grigor Suny, ed., *Cambridge History of Russia*, Vol. 3, Cambridge: Cambridge University Press, 2006, 140–167.

Shimon Redlich, *Propaganda and Nationalism in Wartime Russia: The Jewish Anti-Fascist Committee in the USSR, 1941–1948*, Boulder: East European Monographs, 1982.

Shimon Redlich, *War, Holocaust, and Stalinism: A Documented History of the Jewish Anti-Fascist Committee in the USSR*, Luxembourg: Harwood, 1995.

Jan Alfred Reguła [Józef Mitzenmacher or Mieczysław Mützenmacher], *Historia Komunistycznej Partji Polski*, Toruń: Portal, 1994 [1934].

Leonid Rein, "Local Collaboration in the Execution of the 'Final Solution' in Nazi-Occupied Belarussia," *Holocaust and Genocide Studies*, Vol. 20, No. 3, 2006, 381–409.

"Relacje dwóch zbiegów z Treblinki II," *Biuletyn Żydowskiego Instytutu Historycznego*, No. 40, 1961, 78–88.

Alfred J. Rieber, "Civil Wars in the Soviet Union," *Kritika*, Vol. 4, No. 1, 2003, 129–162.

Berndt Rieger, *Creator of the Nazi Death Camps: The Life of Odilo Globocnik*, London: Vallentine Mitchell, 2007.

Volker Rieß, "Christian Wirth—Inspekteur der Vernichtungslager," in Klaus-Michael Mallmann and Gerhard Paul, eds. *Karrieren der Gewalt: Nationalsozialistische Täterbiographien*, Darmstadt: Wissenschaftliche Buchgesellschaft, 2004, 239–251.

Gabor Rittersporn, *Stalinist Simplifications and Soviet Complications: Social Tensions and Political Conflict in the USSR, 1933–1953*, Chur: Harwood, 1991.

Henry L. Roberts, *Rumania: Political Problems of an Agrarian State*, New Haven: Yale University Press, 1951.

Daniel Romanowsky, "Nazi Occupation in Northeastern Belarus and Western Russia," in Zvi Gitelman, ed., *Bitter Legacy: Confronting the Holocaust in the USSR*, Bloomington: Indiana University Press, 1997, 230–252.

Felix Römer, *Der Kommissarbefehl: Wehrmacht und NS-Verbrechen an der Ostfront 1941/42*, Paderborn: Ferdinand Schöningh, 2008.

Hans Roos, *Polen und Europa: Studien zur polnischen Außenpolitik*, Tübingen: J.C.B. Mohr, 1957.

Mark Roseman, *The Villa, the Lake, the Meeting: Wannsee and the Final Solution*, New York: Penguin, 2003.

Alexander B. Rossino, *Hitler Strikes Poland: Blitzkrieg, Ideology, and Atrocity*, Lawrence: University Press of Kansas, 2003.

Joseph Rothschild, *Piłsudski's Coup d'Etat*, New York: Columbia University Press, 1966.

David Rousset, *L'univers concentrationnaire*, Paris: Éditions du Pavois, 1946.

Włodzimierz Rozenbaum, "The March Events: Targeting the Jews," *Polin*, Vol. 21, 2008, 62–93.

Joshua Rubenstein and Ilya Altman, eds., *The Unknown Black Book: The Holocaust in the German-Occupied Soviet Territories*, Bloomington: Indiana University Press, 2008.

Oleksandr Rubľov and Vladimir Reprintsev, "Represii proty poliakiv v Ukraïni u 30-ti roky," *Z arkhiviv V.U.Ch.K H.P.U N.K.V.D K.H.B*, Vol. 1, No. 2, 1995, 119–146.

F. M. Rudych, I. F. Kuras, M. I. Panchuk, P. Ia. Pyrih, and V. F Soldatenko, eds., *Holod 1932–1933 rokiv na Ukraïni: Ochyma istorykiv, movoiu dokumentiv*, Kiev: Vydavnytstvo Politychnoï Literatury Ukrainy, 1990.

Martyna Rusiniak, *Obóz zagłady Treblinka II w pamięci społecznej (1943–1989)*, Warsaw: Neriton, 2008.

Hartmut Ruß, "Wer war verantwortlich für das Massaker von Babij Jar?" *Militärgeschichtliche Mitteilungen*, Vol. 57, No. 2, 1999, 483–508.

Philip T. Rutherford, *Prelude to the Final Solution: The Nazi Program for Deporting Ethnic Poles, 1939–1941*, Lawrence: University Press of Kansas, 2007.

Pamela Rotner Sakamoto, *Japanese Diplomats and Jewish Refugees: A World War II Dilemma*, Westport: Praeger, 1998.

A. N. Sakharov et al., eds., *"Sovershenno sekretno": Lubianka-Stalinu o polozhenii v strane (1922–1934 gg.)*, Vol. 6, Moscow: RAN 2002.

Ruta Sakowska, ed., *Archiwum Ringelbluma. Tom 2: Dzieci—tajne nauczanie w getcie warszawskim*, Warsaw: ŻIH, 2000.

Ruta Sakowska, *Ludzie z dzielnicy zamkniętej. Żydzi w Warszawie w okresie hitlerowskiej okupacji*, Warsaw: PAN, 1975.

Harrison E. Salisbury, *The 900 Days: The Siege of Leningrad*, New York: Harper & Row, 1969.

Antonella Salomini, *L'Union soviétique et la Shoah*, trans. Marc Saint-Upéry, Paris: La Découverte, 2007.

Thomas Sandkühler, *"Endlösung" in Galizien: Der Judenmord in Ostpolen und die Rettungsinitiativen von Berthold Beitz, 1941–1944*, Bonn: Dietz, 1996.

[Jerzy Sawicki], *Zburzenie Warszawy*, Katowice: Awir, 1946.

Wolfgang Scheffler, "Probleme der Holocaustforschung," in Stefi Jersch-Wenzel, ed. *Deutsche—Polen—Juden. Ihre Beziehungen von den Anfängen bis ins 20. Jahrhundert*, Berlin: Colloquium Verlag, 1987, 259–281.

Cornelia Schenke, *Nationalstaat und nationale Frage: Polen und die Ukraine 1921–1939*, Hamburg: Dölling und Galitz Verlag, 2004.

Thomas Schlemmer, *Die Italiener an der Ostfront*, Munich: R. Oldenbourg Verlag, 2005.

Karl Schlögel, *Terror und Traum: Moskau 1937*, Munich: Carl Hanser Verlag, 2008.

Simon Sebag Montefiore, *Stalin: The Court of the Red Tsar*, New York: Knopf, 2004.

Sefer Lutsk, Tel Aviv: Irgun Yots'e Lutsk be-Yisrael, 1961.

Robert Seidel, *Deutsche Besatzungspolitik in Polen: Der Distrikt Radom 1939–1945*, Paderborn: Ferdinand Schöningh, 2006.

Amartya Sen, *Poverty and Famines: An Essay on Entitlement and Deprivation*, Oxford: Oxford University Press, 1982.

Roman Serbyn, "Lemkin on Genocide of Nations," *Journal of International Criminal Justice*, Vol. 7, No. 1, 2009, 123–130.

Gitta Sereny, *Into That Darkness: From Mercy Killing to Mass Murder*, New York: McGraw Hill, 1974.

Robert Service, *Stalin: A Biography*, Cambridge, Mass.: Harvard University Press, 2004.

Edward Serwański, *Życie w powstańczej Warszawie*, Warsaw: Instytut Wydawniczy PAX, 1965.

G. N. Sevostianov et al., eds., *"Sovershenno sekretno": Lubianka-Stalinu o polozhenii v strane (1922–1934 gg.)*, Vol. 4, Moscow: RAN, 2001.

Jurij Šapoval, "Die Behandlung der 'ukrainischen Nationalisten' im Gebiet Kiev," in Rolf Binner, Bernd Bonwetsch, and Marc Junge, eds., *Stalinismus in der sowjetischen Provinz 1937–1938*, Berlin: Akademie Verlag, 2010, 334–351.

Iurii Shapoval, "Holodomor i ioho zv'iazok iz represiiamy v Ukraïni u 1932–1934 rokakh," *Harvard Ukrainian Studies*, forthcoming.

Iurii Shapoval, *Liudyna i systema: Shtrykhy do portretu totalitarnoï doby v Ukraïni*, Kiev: Natsional'na Akademiia Nauk Ukraïny, 1994.

Jurij Šapoval, "Lügen und Schweigen: Die unterdrückte Erinnerung an den Holodomor," *Osteuropa*, Vol. 54, No. 12, 2009, 131–145.

Iurii Shapoval, "III konferentsiia KP(b)U: proloh trahedii holodu," in Valerii Vasiliev and Iurii Shapoval, eds., *Komandyry velykoho holodu*, Kiev: Heneza, 2001, 152–165.

Iurii Shapoval, "Vsevolod Balickij, bourreau et victime," *Cahiers du Monde russe*, Vol. 44, Nos. 2–3, 2003, 371–384.

Iurii Shapoval, Volodymyr Prystaiko, and Vadym Zolotar'ov, eds., *ChK-HPU-NKVD v Ukraïni: Osoby, fakty, dokumenty*, Kiev: Abrys, 1997.

Iurii Shapoval, Volodymyr Prystaiko, and Vadym Zolotar'ov, "Vsevolod Balyts'kyi," in *ChK-HPU-NKVD v Ukraini: Osoby, fakty, dokumenty*, Kyiv: Abrys, 1997.

David R. Shearer, "Social Disorder, Mass Repression, and the NKVD During the 1930s," *Cahiers du Monde russe*, Vol. 42, Nos. 2–3/4, 2001, 506–534.

Ben Shepherd, *War in the Wild East: The German Army and Soviet Partisans*, Cambridge, Mass.: Harvard University Press, 2004.

Marci Shore, *Caviar and Ashes: A Warsaw Generation's Life and Death in Marxism*, New Haven: Yale University Press, 2006.

Marci Shore, "Children of the Revolution: Communism, Zionism, and the Berman Brothers," *Jewish Social Studies*, Vol. 10, No. 3, 2004, 23–86.

Marci Shore, "Język, pamięć i rewolucyjna awangarda. Kształtowanie historii powstania w getcie warszawskim w latach 1944–1950," *Biuletyn Żydowskiego Instytutu Historycznego*, No. 3 (188), 1998, 43–60.

Zachary Shore, *What Hitler Knew: The Battle for Information in Nazi Foreign Policy*, Oxford: Oxford University Press, 2003.

M. F. Shumejko, "Die NS-Kriegsgefangenenlager in Weißrussland in den Augen des Militärarztes der Roten Armee, L. Atanasyan," in V. Selemenev et al., eds., *Sowjetische und deutsche Kriegsgefangene in den Jahren des Zweiten Weltkriegs*, Dresden-Minsk, 2004.

Danylo Shumuk, *Perezhyte i peredumane*, Kiev: Vydavnyts'tvo imeni Oleny Telihy, 1998.

Lewis Siegelbaum, *Soviet State and Society Between Revolutions*, Cambridge: Cambridge University Press, 1992.

Lewis Siegelbaum and Andrei Sokolov, *Stalinism as a Way of Life*, New Haven: Yale University Press, 2004.

Cynthia Simmons and Nina Perlina, eds., *Writing the Siege of Leningrad*, Pittsburgh: University of Pittsburgh Press, 2002.

Gerhard Simon, "Holodomor als Waffe: Stalinismus, Hunger und der ukrainische Nationalismus," *Osteuropa*, Vol. 54, No. 12, 2004, 37–56.

Thomas W. Simons, Jr., *Eastern Europe in the Postwar World*, New York: St. Martin's, 1993.

Kenneth Slepyan, *Stalin's Guerillas: Soviet Partisans in World War II*, Lawrence: University of Kansas Press, 2006.

Kenneth Slepyan, "The Soviet Partisan Movement and the Holocaust," *Holocaust and Genocide Studies*, Vol. 14, No. 1, 2000, 1–27.

Ivan Slivka, ed., *Deportatsiï*, Lviv: Natsional'na Akademiia Nauk Ukraïny, 1996.

Leonid Smilovitsky, "Antisemitism in the Soviet Partisan Movement, 1941–1944: The Case of Belorussia," *Holocaust and Genocide Studies*, Vol. 20, No. 2, 2006, 207–234.

Jeremy Smith, *The Bolsheviks and the National Question*, New York: St. Martin's, 1999.

Hersh Smolar, *The Minsk Ghetto: Soviet-Jewish Partisans Against the Nazis*, New York: Holocaust Library, 1989.

Timothy Snyder, "Caught Between Hitler and Stalin," *New York Review of Books*, Vol. 56, No. 7, 30 April 2009.

Timothy Snyder, "The Causes of Ukrainian-Polish Ethnic Cleansing, 1943," *Past and Present*, No. 179, 2003, 197–234.

Timothy Snyder, "The Life and Death of West Volhynian Jews, 1921–1945," in Ray Brandon and Wendy Lower, eds., *The Shoah in Ukraine: History, Testimony, and Memorialization*, Bloomington: Indiana University Press, 2008, 77–113.

Timothy Snyder, "Nazis, Soviets, Poles, Jews," *New York Review of Books*, Vol. 56, No. 19, 3 December 2009.

Timothy Snyder, *The Reconstruction of Nations: Poland, Ukraine, Lithuania, Belarus, 1569–1999*, New Haven: Yale University Press, 2003.

Timothy Snyder, "'To Resolve the Ukrainian Problem Once and for All': The Ethnic Cleansing of Ukrainians in Poland, 1943–1947," *Journal of Cold War Studies*, Vol. 1, No. 2, 1999, 86–120.

Timothy Snyder, *Sketches from a Secret War: A Polish Artist's Mission to Liberate Soviet Ukraine*, New Haven: Yale University Press, 2005.

Timothy Snyder, "Wartime Lies," *The Nation*, 6 January 2006.

Anna Sobór-Świderska, *Jakub Berman: biografia komunisty*, Warsaw: IPN, 2009.

Alfred Sohn-Rethel, *Industrie und Nationalsozialismus: Aufzeichnungen aus dem "Mitteleuropäischen Wirtschaftstag,"* ed. Carl Freytag, Wagenbach: Berlin, 1992.

A. K. Sokolov, "Metodologicheskie osnovy ischisleniia poter' naseleniia SSSR v gody Velikoi Otechestvennoi Voiny," in R. B. Evdokimov, ed., *Liudskie poteri SSSR v period vtoroi mirovoi voiny*, St. Petersburg: RAN, 1995, 18–24.

Boris Sokolov, "How to Calculate Human Losses During the Second World War," *Journal of Slavic Military Studies*, Vol. 22, No. 3, 2009, 437–458.

Peter J. Solomon, *Soviet Criminal Justice Under Stalin*, Cambridge: Cambridge University Press, 1996.

Shmuel Spector, *The Holocaust of Volhynian Jews 1941–1944*, Jerusalem: Yad Vashem, 1990.

Szmuel Spektor, "Żydzi wołyńscy w Polsce międzywojennej i w okresie II wojny światowej (1920–1944)," in Krzysztof Jasiewicz, ed., *Europa Nieprowincjonalna*, Warsaw: Instytut Studiów Politycznych PAN, 1999, 566–578.

"Sprawozdania świetliczanek z getta warszawskiego," *Biuletyn Żydowskiego Instytutu Historycznego*, No. 94, 1975, 57–70.

Knut Stang, "Dr. Oskar Dirlewanger—Protagonist der Terrorkriegsführung," in Klaus-Michael Mallmann, ed., *Karrieren der Gewalt: Nationalsozialistische Täterbiographien*, Darmstadt: Wissenschaftliche Buchgesellschaft, 2004, 66–75.

Witold Stankowski, *Obozy i inne miejsca odosobnienia dla niemieckiej ludności cywilnej w Polsce w latach 1945–1950*, Bydgoszcz: Akademia Bydgoska, 2002.

Tomáš Staněk, *Odsun Němců z Československa 1945–1947*, Prague: Akademia Naše Vojsko, 1991.

Tamás Stark, *Hungarian Jews During the Holocaust and After the Second World War: A Statistical Review*, Boulder: East European Monographs, 2000.

Tamás Stark, *Hungary's Human Losses in World War II*, Uppsala: Centre for Multiethnic Research, 1995.

Jonathan Steinberg, "The Third Reich Reflected: German Civil Administration in the Occupied Soviet Union," *English Historical Review*, Vol. 110, No. 437, 1995, 620–651.

Stanisław Stępień, ed., *Polacy na Ukrainie: Zbiór dokumentów 1917–1939*, Przemyśl: Południowo-Wschodni Instytut Naukowy, 1998.

Dariusz Stola, "The Hate Campaign of March 1968: How Did It Become Anti-Jewish?" *Polin*, Vol. 21, 2008, 16–36.

Dariusz Stola, *Kampania antysyjonistyczna w Polsce 1967–1968*, Warsaw: IH PAN, 2000.

Norman Stone, *The Eastern Front, 1914–1917*, New York: Penguin, 1998.

Alfred Streim, *Die Behandlung sowjetischer Kriegsgefangener im "Fall Barbarossa*," Heidelberg: C. F. Müller Juristischer Verlag, 1981.

Christian Streit, "The German Army and the Policies of Genocide," in Gerhard Hirschfeld, ed., *The Polices of Genocide: Jews and Soviet Prisoners of War in Nazi Germany*, London: Allen & Unwin, 1986.

Christian Streit, *Keine Kameraden: Die Wehrmacht und die sowjetischen Kriegsgefangenen 1941–1945*, Stuttgart: Deutsche Verlags-Anstalt, 1978.

Henryk Stroński, "Deportacja—masowe wywózki ludności polskiej z Ukrainy do Kazachstanu w 1936 roku," *Przegląd Polonijny*, Vol. 23, No. 3, 1997, 108–121.

Henryk Stroński, *Represje stalinizmu wobec ludności polskiej na Ukrainie w latach 1929–1939*, Warsaw: Wspólnota Polska, 1998.

Andrzej Strzelecki, *Deportacja Żydów z getta łódzkiego do KL Auschwitz i ich zagłada*, Oświęcim: Państwowe Muzeum Auschwitz Birkenau, 2004.

Orest Subtelny, "German Diplomatic Reports on the Famine of 1933," in Wsevolod Isajiw, ed., *Famine-Genocide in Ukraine, 1932–1933*, Toronto: Ukrainian Canadian Research and Documentation Centre, 2003, 13–26.

Gordon R. Sullivan et al., *National Security and the Threat of Climate Change*, Alexandra: CNA Corporation, 2007.

Ronald Grigor Suny, "Reading Russia and the Soviet Union in the Twentieth Century: How 'the West' Wrote Its History of the USSR," in idem, ed., *Cambridge History of Russia*, Vol. 3, Cambridge: Cambridge University Press, 2006, 5–64.

Stanisław Swianiewicz, *In the Shadow of Katyń*, Calgary: Borealis, 2002.

Paweł Szapiro, ed., *Wojna żydowsko-niemiecka*, London: Aneks, 1992.

Bożena Szaynok, *Z historią i Moskwą w tle: Polska a Izrael 1944–1968*, Warsaw: IPN, 2007.

Roman Szporluk, *Russia, Ukraine, and the Breakup of the Soviet Union*, Stanford: Hoover Press, 2000.

Zachar Szybieka, *Historia Białorusi, 1795–2000*, Lublin: IESW, 2002.

Sally J. Taylor, "A Blanket of Silence: The Response of the Western Press Corps in Moscow to the Ukraine Famine of 1932–1933," in Wsevolod Isajiw, ed.,

Famine-Genocide in Ukraine, 1932–1933, Toronto: Ukrainian Canadian Research and Documentation Centre, 2003, 77–95.

Nechama Tec, *Defiance: The Bielski Partisans*, New York: Oxford University Press, 1993.

Philipp Ther, *Deutsche und polnische Vertriebene: Gesellschaft und Vertriebenenpolitik in SBZ/DDR und in Polen 1945–1956*, Göttingen: Vandenhoeck & Ruprecht, 1998.

Tzvetan Todorov, *Les Aventuriers de l'Absolu*, Paris: Robert Laffont, 2006.

Tzvetan Todorov, *Face à l'extrême*, Paris: Editions de Seiul, 1991.

Tsvetan Todorov, *Mémoire du mal, Tentacion du Bien: Enquête sur le siècle*, Paris: Robert Laffont, 2000.

Michał Tokarzewski-Karaszewicz, "U podstaw tworzenia Armii Krajowej," *Zeszyty Historyczne*, No. 56, 1981, 124–157.

Jerzy Tomaszewski, *Preludium Zagłady. Wygnanie Żydów polskich z Niemiec w 1938 r.*, Łódź: PWN SA, 1998.

Monika Tomkiewicz, *Zbrodnia w Ponarach 1941–1944*, Warsaw: IPN, 2008.

Adam Tooze, *The Wages of Destruction: The Making and Breaking of the Nazi Economy*, New York: Viking, 2007.

Teresa Torańska, *Oni*, London: Aneks, 1985.

Ryszard Torzecki, *Kwestia ukraińska w Polsce w latach 1923–1939*, Cracow: Wydawnictwo Literackie, 1989.

"Treblinka," in M. Blumental, ed., *Dokumenty i materiały. Obozy*, Łódź: Wydawnictwa Centralnej Żydowskiej Komisji Historycznej, 1946, 173–195.

Isaiah Trunk, *Judenrat: The Jewish Councils in Eastern Europe Under Nazi Occupation*, New York: Macmillan, 1972.

Henry Ashby Turner, *Stresemann and the Politics of the Weimar Republic*, Princeton: Princeton University Press, 1963.

Krisztián Ungvary, *Die Schlacht um Budapest: Stalingrad an der Donau, 1944/45*, Munich: Herbig, 1998.

Thomas Urban, *Der Verlust: Die Vertreibung der Deutschen und Polen im 20. Jahrhundert*, Munich: C. H. Beck, 2004.

Krzysztof Urbański, *Zagłada Żydów w dystrykcie radomskim*, Cracow: Wydawnictwo Naukowe Akademii Pedagogicznej, 2004.

Marcin Urynowicz, "Gross Aktion—Zagłada Warszawskiego Getta," *Biuletyn Instytutu Pamięci Narodowej*, No. 7, 2007, 105–115.

Benjamin Valentino, *Final Solutions: Mass Killing and Genocide in the Twentieth Century*, Ithaca: Cornell University Press, 2004.

Jacques Vallin, France Meslé, Serguei Adamets, and Serhii Pyrozhkov, "A New Estimate of Ukrainian Population Losses During the Crises of the 1930s and 1940s," *Population Studies*, Vol. 56, No. 3, 2002, 249–264.

A. Iu. Vashlin, *Terror raionnogo masshtaba: "Massovye operatsii" NKVD v Kuntsevskom raione Moskovskoi oblasti 1937–1938 gg.*, Moscow: Rosspen, 2004.

Valerii Vasiliev, "Tsina holodnoho khliba. Polityka kerivnytstva SRSR i USRR v 1932–1933 rr.," in Valerii Vasiliev and Iurii Shapoval, eds., *Komandyry velykoho holodu: Poizdky V. Molotova i L. Kahanovycha v Ukraïnu ta na Pivnichnyi Kavkaz 1932–1933 rr.*, Kiev: Heneza, 2001, 12–81.

Jeffrey Veidlinger, *The Moscow State Yiddish Theater: Jewish Culture on the Soviet Stage*, Bloomington: Indiana University Press, 2000.

Jeffrey Veidlinger, "Soviet Jewry as a Diaspora Nationality: The 'Black Years' Reconsidered," *East European Jewish Affairs*, Vol. 33, No. 1, 2003, 4–29.

Verbrechen der Wehrmacht: Dimensionen des Vernichtungskrieges 1941–1944, Hamburg: Institut für Sozialforschung, 2002.

Vertreibung und Vertreibungsverbrechen 1945–1948: Bericht des Bundesarchivs vom 28. Mai 1974, Bonn: Kulturstiftung der Deutschen Vertriebenen, 1989.

Lynne Viola, *The Best Sons of the Fatherland: Workers in the Vanguard of Soviet Collectivization*, Oxford: Oxford University Press, 1987.

Lynne Viola, *Peasant Rebels Under Stalin: Collectivization and the Culture of Popular Resistance*, New York: Oxford University Press, 1996.

Lynne Viola, "Selbstkolonisierung der Sowjetunion," *Transit*, No. 38, 34–56.

Lynne Viola, *The Unknown Gulag: The Lost World of Stalin's Special Settlements*, New York: Oxford University Press, 2007.

Lynn Viola, V. P. Danilov, N. A., Ivnitskii, and Denis Kozlov, eds., *The War Against the Peasantry, 1927–1930: The Tragedy of the Soviet Countryside*, New Haven: Yale University Press, 2005.

T. V. Volokitina et al., eds., *Sovetskii faktor v Vostochnoi Evrope 1944–1953*, Moscow: Sibirskii khronograf, 1997.

Ricarda Vulpius, "Ukrainische Nation und zwei Konfessionen. Der Klerus und die ukrainische Frage 1861–1921," *Jahrbücher für Geschichte Osteuropas*, Vol. 49, No. 2, 2001, 240–256.

Andrzej Walicki, *The Controversy over Capitalism: Studies in the Social Philosophy of the Russian Populists*, Oxford: Clarendon Press, 1969.

Martin Walsdorff, *Westorientierung und Ostpolitik: Stresemanns Rußlandpolitik in der Locarno-Ära*, Bremen: Schünemann Universitätsverlag, 1971.

Piotr Wandycz, *Soviet-Polish Relations, 1917–1921*, Cambridge, Mass.: Harvard University Press, 1969.

Piotr Wandycz, *Z Piłsudskim i Sikorskim: August Zaleski, minister spraw zagranicznych w latach 1926–1932 i 1939–1941*, Warsaw: Wydawnictwo Sejmowe, 1999.

Bruno Wasser, *Himmlers Raumplannung im Osten*, Basel: Birkhäuser Verlag, 1993.

Eugen Weber, *The Hollow Years: France in the 1930s*, New York: Norton, 1994.

David Wdowinski, *And Are We Not Saved*, New York: Philosophical Library, 1985.

Gerhard L. Weinberg, *The Foreign Policy of Hitler's Germany*, Chicago: University of Chicago Press, 1980.

Gerhard L. Weinberg, *A World at Arms: A Global History of World War II*,
    Cambridge: Cambridge University Press, 1994.
Amir Weiner, *Making Sense of War: The Second World War and the Fate of the
    Bolshevik Revolution*, Princeton: Princeton University Press, 2001.
Amir Weiner, "Nature, Nurture, and Memory in a Socialist Utopia: Delineating the
    Soviet Socio-Ethnic Body in the Age of Socialism," *American Historical Review*,
    Vol. 104, No. 4, 1999, 1114–1155.
Anton Weiss-Wendt, *Murder Without Hatred: Estonians and the Holocaust*,
    Syracuse: Syracuse University Press, 2009.
Aleksander Weissberg-Cybulski, *Wielka czystka*, trans. Adam Ciołkosz, Paris:
    Institut Litteraire, 1967.
Eric D. Weitz, "From the Vienna to the Paris System: International Politics and the
    Entangled Histories of Human Rights, Forced Deportations, and Civilizing
    Missions," American Historical Review, Vol. 113, No. 5, 2008, 1313–1343.
Bernd-Jürgen Wendt, *Großdeutschland: Außenpolitik und Kriegsvorbereiterung des
    Hitler-Regimes*, Munich: Deutscher Taschenbuch Verlag, 1987.
Nicolas Werth, "Un État contre son peuple," in Stéphane Courtois, Nicolas Werth,
    Jean-Louis Panné, Andrzej Paczkowski, Karel Bartosek, and Jean-Louis
    Margolin, eds., *Le livre noir du communisme: Crimes, terreur, repression*, Paris:
    Robert Laffont, 1997.
Nicolas Werth, *La terreur et le désarroi: Staline et son système*, Paris: Perrin, 2007.
Edward B. Westermann, "'Ordinary Men' or 'Ideological Soldiers'? Police Battalion
    310 in Russia, 1942," *German Studies Review*, Vol. 21, No. 1, 1998, 41–68.
Stephen G. Wheatcroft, "Agency and Terror: Evdokimov and Mass Killing in Stalin's
    Great Terror," *Australian Journal of Politics and History*, Vol. 53, No. 1, 2007,
    20–43.
Stephen G. Wheatcroft, "The Scale and Nature of German and Soviet Repression
    and Mass Killings, 1930–45," *Europe-Asia Studies*, Vol. 48, No. 8, 1996,
    1319–1353.
Stephen G. Wheatcroft, "Towards Explaining the Changing Levels of Stalinist
    Repression in the 1930s: Mass Killings," in idem, ed., *Challenging Traditional
    Views of Russian History*, Houndmills: Palgrave, 2002, 112–138.
John W. Wheeler-Bennett, *Brest-Litovsk: The Forgotten Peace*, London: Macmillan,
    1938.
Paweł Piotr Wieczorkiewicz, *Łańcuch śmierci. Czystka w Armii Czerwonej
    1937–1939*, Warsaw: Rytm, 2001.
Mieczysław Wieliczko, "Akcja AB w Dystrykcie Krakowskim," in Zygmunt
    Mańkowski, ed., *Ausserordentliche Befriedungsaktion 1940 Akcja AB na ziemiach
    polskich*, Warsaw: GKBZpNP-IPN, 1992, 28–40.
Yankiel Wiernik, *A Year in Treblinka*, New York: General Jewish Workers' Union of
    Poland, 1944.

Hans-Heinrich Wilhelm, *Die Einsatzgruppe A der Sicherheitspolizei und des SD 1941/1942*, Frankfurt am Main: Peter Lang, 1996.

Samuel Willenberg, *Revolt in Treblinka*, Warsaw: Jewish Historical Institute, 1992.

Kieran Williams, *The Prague Spring And Its Aftermath: Czechoslovak Politics, 1968–1970*, New York: Cambridge University Press, 1997.

Andreas Wirsching, *Die Weimarer Republik in ihrer inneren Entwicklung: Politik und Gesellschaft*, Munich: Oldenbourg, 2000.

Peter Witte, Michael Wildt, Martina Voigt, Dieter Pohl, Peter Klein, Christian Gerlach, Christoph Dieckmann, and Andrej Angrick, eds., *Der Dienstkalender Heinrich Himmlers 1941/42*, Hamburg: Hans Christians Verlag, 1999.

Peter Witte and Stephen Tyas, "A New Document on the Deportation and Murder of Jews During 'Einsatz Reinhardt' 1942," *Holocaust and Genocide Studies*, Vol. 15, No. 3, 2001, 468–486.

Rafał Wnuk, *"Za pierwszego Sowieta." Polska konspiracja na Kresach Wschodnich II Rzeczypospolitej*, Warsaw: IPN, 2007.

Janusz Wróbel and Joanna Żelazko, eds., *Polskie dzieci na tułaczych szlakach 1939–1950*, Warsaw: IPN, 2008.

Józef Wroniszewski, *Ochota 1939–1946*, Warsaw: MON, 1976.

Dali L. Yang, *Calamity and Reform in China: State, Rural Society, and Institutional Change Since the Great Leap Famine*, Stanford: Stanford University Press, 1996.

Serhy Yekelchyk, *Stalin's Empire of Memory: Russian-Ukrainian Relations in the Soviet Historical Imagination*, Toronto: University of Toronto Press, 2004.

Zagłada polskich elit. Akcja AB–Katyń, Warsaw: Instytut Pamięci Narodowej, 2006.

Steven J. Zaloga, *Bagration 1944: The Destruction of Army Group Center*, Westport: Praeger, 2004.

Jürgen Zarusky, "'Hitler bedeutet Krieg': Der deutsche Weg zum Hitler-Stalin-Pakt," *Osteuropa*, Vol. 59, Nos. 7–8, 2009, 97–114.

Andrzej Żbikowski, "Lokalne pogromy Żydów w czerwcu i lipcu 1941 r. na wschodnich rubieżach II Rzeczypospolitej," *Biuletyn Żydowskiego Instytutu Historycznego*, Nos. 162–163, 1992, 3–18.

Andrzej Żbikowski, "Żydowscy przesiedleńcy z dystryktu warszawskiego w getcie warszawskim, 1939–1942," in Barbara Engelking, Jacek Leociak, and Dariusz Libionka, eds., *Prowincja noc. Życie i zagłada Żydów w dystrykcie warszawskim*, Warsaw: IFiS PAN, 2007, 223–279.

I. Zelenin et al., eds., *Tragediia sovetskoi derevni: Kollektivizatsiia i raskulachivanie*, Vol. 3, Moscow: Rosspen, 2001.

V. N. Zemskov, "Smertnost' zakliuchennykh v 1941–1945 gg.," in R. B. Evdokimov, ed., *Liudskiie poteri SSSR v period vtoroi mirovoi voiny*, St. Petersburg: RAN, 1995, 174–177.

V. N. Zemskov, *Spetsposelentsy v SSSR, 1930–1960*, Moscow: Nauka, 2003.

Joshua D. Zimmerman, "The Attitude of the Polish Home Army (AK) to the Jewish Question During the Holocaust: The Case of the Warsaw Ghetto Uprising," in Murray Baumgarten, Peter Kenez, and Bruce Thompson, eds., *Varieties of Antisemitism: History, Ideology, Discourse*, Newark: University of Delaware Press, 2009, 105–126.

Ewa Ziółkowska, "Kurapaty," *Biuletyn Instytutu Pamięci Narodowej*, Nos. 96–97, 2009, 44–53.

D. Zlepko, ed., *Der ukrainische Hunger-Holocaust*, Sonnenbühl: Helmut Wild, 1988.

Vadim Zolotar'ov, "Nachal'nyts'kyi sklad NKVS USRR u seredyni 30-h rr.," *Z arkhiviv VUChK-HPU-NKVD-KGB*, No. 2, 2001, 326–331.

Vladislav M. Zubok, *A Failed Empire: The Soviet Union in the Cold War from Stalin to Gorbachev*, Chapel Hill: University of North Carolina Press, 2007.

Marcin Zwolski, "Deportacje internowanych Polaków w głąb ZSRS w latach 1944–1945," in Marcin Zwolski, ed., *Exodus: Deportacje i migracje (wątek wschodni)*, Warsaw: IPN, 2008, 40–49.

Yitzhak Zuckerman, *A Surplus of Memory: Chronicle of the Warsaw Ghetto Uprising*, Berkeley: University of California Press, 1993.

NOTES

CHAPTER 1: THE SOVIET FAMINES

1. Quotation: Siriol Colley, *More Than a Grain*, 161.

2. On the journalist Gareth Jones, see Siriol Colley, *More Than a Grain*, 224–238; Jones, "Will there be soup?"; Conquest, *Harvest*, 309; and Dalrymple, "Further References," 473. On Kharkiv, see Falk, *Sowjetische Städte*, 140, 172–175, 288; Kovalenko, *Holod*, 557; and Werth, *Terreur*, 130. The image is Vasily Grossman's.

3. Falk, *Sowjetische Städte*, 284–285, 288, 298–300.

4. Quotations: Falk, *Sowjetische Städte*, 299, see also 297–301; Kuśnierz, *Ukraina*, 157, 160. On the schoolgirl and the hospitals, see Davies, *Years*, 160, 220. See also Kuromiya, *Freedom and Terror*, 171, 184. On the use of survivor testimony, see Graziosi, *War*, 4.

5. Quotation: Siriol Colley, *More Than a Grain*, 233. On Dnipropetrovsk: Kravchenko, *I Chose Freedom*, 111. On Stalino, see Maksudov, "Victory," 211.

6. On fainting from weakness, see Kovalenko, *Holod*, 61; see also Siriol Colley, *More Than a Grain*, 235. On Khartsyzsk, see Kuromiya, *Freedom and Terror*, 170. On Grossman, see Todorov, *Mémoire du mal*, 61. See also Koestler, *Yogi*, 137.

7. Quotation: Serbyn, "Ukrainian Famine," 131; see also Falk, *Sowjetische Städte*, 289.

8. For a sophisticated guide to the meanings of the Plan, see Harrison, *Soviet Planning*, 1–5.

9. Quotations: Kuromiya, *Stalin*, 85; Kuśnierz, *Ukraina*, 37.

10. Quotation and poster: Viola, *War*, 177; Viola, *Unknown Gulag*, 32.

11. Quotations: Viola, *War*, 238; Conquest, *Harvest*, 121. For details on the shootings and deportations, see Davies, *Years*, 20, 46; Werth, *Terreur*, 463; Viola, *Unknown Gulag*, 6, 32; Kuśnierz, *Ukraina*, 51, 56; Khlevniuk, *Gulag*, 11; Graziosi, *War*, 48; and Davies, *Years*, 46.

12. On the 113,637 people forcibly transported, see Viola, *War*, 289; see also Kulczycki, *Hołodomor*, 158. For details on some of the arrivals, see Kotkin, "Peopling," 70–72.

13. For the lament, see Kovalenko, *Holod*, 259. On Solovki, see Applebaum, *Gulag*, 18–20, 49. On the special settlements, see Viola, *Unknown Gulag* (the numbers of Ukrainian peasants deported are given at 195 and 32).

14. Quotation: Applebaum, *Gulag*, 48. For the death estimates, see Viola, *Unknown Gulag*, 3; and Applebaum, *Gulag*, 583. For the characterization of the Gulag, see Khlevniuk, *Gulag*, 1–10; Applebaum, *Gulag*, xvi–xvii; and Viola, *Unknown Gulag*, 2–7.

15. Quotations: Siegelbaum, *Stalinism*, 45 (first two); Viola, *Unknown Gulag*, 53. On Belomor, see Khlevniuk, *Gulag*, 24–35; and Applebaum, *Gulag*, 62–65.

16. Applebaum, *Gulag*, 64–65.

17. Quotation: Viola, *Unknown Gulag*, 35. See also, generally, Viola, *Best Sons*. On the pace of collectivization, see Kuśnierz, *Ukraina*, 39.

18. On the percentage of arable land, see Kuśnierz, *Ukraina*, 40.

19. Quotation: Snyder, *Sketches*, 93. For background on the struggle of peasants in Ukraine for land, see Beauvois, *Bataille*; Edelman, *Proletarian Peasants*; Hildermeier, *Sozialrevolutionäre Partei*; Kingston-Mann, *Lenin*; and Lih, *Bread and Authority*.

20. Quotation: Dzwońkowski, *Głód*, 84. For the Stalinist "First Commandment," see Kulczycki, *Hołodomor*, 170. See also Kuśnierz, *Ukraina*, 70.

21. On livestock and on feminine rebellions, see Kuśnierz, *Ukraina*, 66, 72; and Conquest, *Harvest*, 158.

22. Graziosi, *War*, 53–57; Viola, *War*, 320; Kulczycki, *Hołodomor*, 131; Snyder, *Sketches*, 92–94.

23. Quotation: Morris, "The Polish Terror," 753. On the Soviet concern about Poland's new policy to Ukrainian minorities, see Report of 13 July 1926, AVPRF, 122/10/34. See also, generally, Snyder, *Sketches*, 83–114.

24. Kuromiya, "Spionage," 20–32.

25. Cameron, "Hungry Steppe," chap. 6. On Xinjiang, see Millward, *Eurasian Crossroads*, 191–210.

26. Snyder, *Sketches*, 101–102.

27. Kuśnierz, *Ukraina*, 74; Snyder, *Sketches*, 103–104.

28. Davies, *Years*, 8–11, 24–37; Kuśnierz, *Ukraina*, 86–90.

29. Quotations: Viola, *Unknown Gulag*, 75; Kravchenko, *I Chose Freedom*, 106. On the 32,127 households deported from Soviet Ukraine, see Kulczycki, *Hołodomor*, 158. On the percentage of collectivized farmland, see Kuśnierz, *Ukraine*, 86.

30. Davies, *Years*, 48–56.

31. On the harvest, see Davies, *Years*, 57–69, 110–111; Graziosi, "New Interpretation," 1–5; and Dronin, *Climate Dependence*, 118. On Kosior and Kaganovich, see Davies, *Years*, 72, 82, 89, 95.

32. Kuśnierz, *Ukraina*, 102–103; Davies, *Years*, 112–114.

33. On the Red Cross, see Davies, *Years*, 112–113. Quotations: Kul'chyts'kyi, *Kolektyvizatsiia*, 434; Kul'chyts'kyi, "Trahichna," 151.

34. On the reports of death by starvation, see Kuśnierz, 104–105. On Stalin, see Davies, *Kaganovich Correspondence*, 138. On the request for food aid, see Lih, *Letters to Molotov*, 230. On Kaganovich (23 June 1932), see Hunchak, *Famine*, 121.

35. Cameron, "Hungry Steppe," chap. 2; Pianciola, "Collectivization Famine," 103–112; Mark, "Hungersnot," 119.

36. Quotation: Davies, *Kaganovich Correspondence*, 138. On Stalin's predisposition to personalized politics, see Kulczycki, *Hołodomor*, 180; and Kuśnierz, *Ukraina*, 152.

37. On Stalin, see Marochko, *Holodomor*, 21. On the objective problems recounted by local party officials, see Davies, *Years*, 105–111, 117–122.

38. Cited in Kovalenko, *Holod*, 110.

39. Quotation: Davies, *Years*, 146. See also Kuśnierz, *Ukraina*, 107; and Werth, *Terreur*, 119.

40. On "our father," see Sebag Montefiore, *Court*, 69. On talk of starvation as an excuse for laziness, see Šapoval, "Lügen," 136. For a sense of the relationships among Molotov, Kaganovich, and Stalin, consult Lih, *Letters to Molotov*; and Davies, *Kaganovich Correspondence*.

41. Quotations: Davies, *Kaganovich Correspondence*, 175, 183.

42. Snyder, *Sketches*, 83–95; Kuromiya, "Great Terror," 2–4.

43. Snyder, *Sketches*, 102–104; Haslam, *East*, 31.

44. Quotation: Report of 6 June 1933, CAW I/303/4/1928. On the Polish consulate, see Marochko, *Holodomor*, 36. On Poland's caution, see Snyder, *Sketches*, 102–108; and Papuha, *Zakhidna Ukraïna*, 80.

45. Kuśnierz, *Ukraina*, 108; Maksudov, "Victory," 204.

46. On the Soviet judges, see Solomon, *Soviet Criminal Justice*, 115–116. Quotation: Kuśnierz, *Ukraina*, 116.

47. Quotations: Kuśnierz, *Ukraina*, 139; Kovalenko, *Holod*, 168. On the watchtowers and their number, see Kuśnierz, *Ukraina*, 115; see also Maksudov, "Victory," 213; and Conquest, *Harvest*, 223–225.

48. On the limited gains from such methods of requisition, see Maksudov, "Victory," 192. On the party activists' abuses, see Kuśnierz, *Ukraina*, 144–145, 118–119; and Kuromiya, *Freedom and Terror*, 170–171.

49. As against fifty-seven percent for the USSR as a whole; see Davies, *Years*, 183. On Molotov, see Davies, *Years*, 171–172.

50. On Stalin, see Sebag Montefiore, *Court*, 21, 107.

51. Quotation: Kovalenko, *Holod*, 44. On the two politburo telegrams, see Marochko, *Holodomor*, 152; and Davies, *Years*, 174. On the 1,623 arrested kolkhoz officials, see Davies, *Years*, 174. On the 30,400 resumed deportations, see Kuśnierz, *Ukraina*, 59.

52. For the "fairy tale" reference, see Šapoval, "Lügen," 159; and Davies, *Years*, 199.

53. Quotations: Kuśnierz, *Ukraina*, 124. See also Vasiliev, "Tsina," 60; and Kuromiya, *Stalin*, 110.

54. Quotation: Kuromiya, *Freedom and Terror*, 174. On the family interpretation (Stanisław Kosior), see Davies, *Years*, 206.

55. For similar judgments, see, for example, Jahn, *Holodomor*, 25; Davies, Tauger, and Wheatcroft, "Grain Stocks," 657; Kulczycki, *Hołodomor*, 237; and Graziosi, "New Interpretation," 11.

56. Sen, *Poverty and Famines*, quotation at 7; see also 154–155. A convincing national interpretation of the famine is Martin, "Ukrainian Terror," at 109 and passim. See also Simon, "Waffe," 45–47; and Conquest, *Harvest*, 219. On Kaganovich in November 1932, see Kulczyski, *Hołodomor*, 236.

57. Graziosi, "New Interpretation," 8; Kuśnierz, *Ukraina*, 143; Maksudov, "Victory," 188, 190; Davies, *Years*, 175 and, on seed grain, 151.

58. On the meat penalty, see Shapoval, "Proloh trahedii holodu," 162; and Maksudov, "Victory," 188. Quotation: Dzwonkowski, *Głód*, 71. For the example described, Dzwonkowski, *Głód*, 160; see also 219. On the general decline of livestock, see Hunczak, *Famine*, 59.

59. Shapoval, "Proloh trahedii holodu," 162; Maksudov, "Victory," 188; Marochko, *Holodomor*, 171; Werth, *Terreur*, 123.

60. Shapoval, "Holodomor."

61. Davies, *Years*, 190; Marochko, *Holodomor*, 171.

62. Snyder, *Sketches*, 107–114.

63. Quotation: Davies, *Years*, 187. Regarding 20 December, see Vasiliev, "Tsina," 55; Graziosi, "New Interpretation," 9; and Kuśnierz, *Ukraina*, 135.

64. Davies, *Years*, 190–192.

65. On the interpretation of starving people as spies, see Shapoval, "Holodomor." On the 190,000 peasants caught and sent back, see Graziosi, "New Interpretation," 7. On the events of 22 January, see Marochko, *Holodomor*, 189; and Graziosi, "New Interpretation," 9.

66. On the 37,392 people arrested, see Marochko, *Holodomor*, 192. See also Davies, *Years*, 161–163.

67. For the recollections of the activist, see Conquest, *Harvest*, 233. For quotation and details on the importance of purges, see Šapoval, "Lügen," 133. On purges of the heights, see Davies, *Years*, 138.

68. On the deathly quiet of Soviet Ukraine, see Kovalenko, *Holod*, 31; and Dzwonkowski, *Głód*, 104. See also Arendt, *Totalitarianism*, 320–322.

69. Quotation: Dalrymple, "Soviet Famine," 261. On Vel'dii, see Kovalenko, *Holod*, 132.

70. Quotations: *New York Evening Post*, 30 March 1933.

71. On Łowińska, see Dzwonkowski, *Głód*, 104. On Panasenko, see Kuśnierz, *Ukraina*, 105. Kravchenko recounted this experience in *I Chose Freedom*, 104–106.

72. On the fifteen thousand people deported, see Davies, *Years*, 210. On the sixty thousand people deported from Kuban, see Martin, "Ethnic Cleansing," 846.

73. On the 67,297 people who died in the camps, see Khlevniuk, *Gulag*, 62, 77. On the 241,355 people who died in the special settlements, see Viola, *Unknown Gulag*, 241.

74. Quotation: Khlevniuk, *Gulag*, 79.

75. Quotations: Dzwonkowski, *Głód*, 215–219; Kul'chyts'kyi, *Kolektyvizatsiia*, 365. On life expectancy in Soviet Ukraine, see Vallin, "New Estimate," 256.

76. On the schoolgirl and the severed head, see Kovalenko, *Holod*, 471, 46.

77. On prostitution for flour, see Kuromiya, *Famine and Terror*, 173. On Vynnitsia, see Kovalenko, *Holod*, 95. On fear of cannibals, see Kovalenko, *Holod*, 284. On the peasants in train stations, see Kuśnierz, *Ukraina*, 155. On the city police, see Falk, *Sowjetische Städte*. On Savhira, see Kovalenko, *Holod*, 290.

78. Quotation: Czech, "Wielki Głód," 23. On the cannibalized son, see Kovalenko, *Holod*, 132. For the knife-sharpening incident, see Kuśnierz, *Ukraina*, 168. On pigs, see Kuromiya, *Freedom and Terror*, 172.

79. On the half a million boys and girls in the watchtowers, see Maksudov, "Victory," 213. Quotation: Kuśnierz, *Ukraina*, 119.

80. On the woman doctor, see Dalrymple, "Soviet Famine," 262. On the orphans, see Kuśnierz, *Ukraina*, 157; and Dzwonkowski, *Głód*, 142. See also Graziosi, "Italian Archival Documents," 41.

81. Kuśnierz, *Ukraina*, 157.

82. On the 2,505 people sentenced for cannibalism, see Davies, *Years*, 173. For details of the chimney example, see Kovalenko, *Holod*, 31. On the meat quota, see Conquest, *Harvest*, 227.

83. On the anti-cannibalism ethic, see Kuromiya, *Freedom and Terror*, 173. On Kolya Graniewicz, see Dzwonkowski, *Głód*, 76. For the mother's request, see Conquest, *Harvest*, 258.

84. Quotation: Bruski, *Holodomor*, 179. On the agronomist, see Dalrymple, "Soviet Famine," 261. On the crews and burials, see Kovalenko, *Holod*, 31, 306, 345.

85. Quotation: Graziosi, "Italian Archival Documents." See also Davies, *Years*, 316.

86. On the 493,644 hungry people in Kiev oblast, see Marochko, *Holodomor*, 233.

87. On the Soviet census, see Schlögel, *Terror*. For discussion of 5.5 million as a typical estimate, see Dalrymple, "Soviet Famine," 259.

88. The demographic retrojection is Vallin, "New Estimate," which finds 2.6 million "extraordinary deaths" at 252 in Soviet Ukraine for 1928–1937, from which one would have to subtract other mass murders to find a famine total. For a summary of the January 2010 government study, see *Dzerkalo Tyzhnia*, 15–22 January 2010. The estimate of c. 2.5 million *on the basis of recorded deaths only* is in Kul'chyts'kyi, "Trahichna," 73–74. Ellman estimates 9.0–12.3 million total famine deaths in the Soviet Union for 1933 and 1934 ("Note on the Number," 376). Maksudov estimates losses of 3.9 million Ukrainians between 1926 and 1937 ("Victory," 229). Graziosi estimates 3.5–3.8 million in Soviet Ukraine ("New Interpretation," 6).

89. Quotation: Serbyn, "Lemkin." See also, generally, Martin, *Affirmative Action Empire*; and Snyder, *Sketches*.

90. Quotations: Koestler, *God That Failed*, 68; Weissberg-Cybulski, *Wielka Czystka*, 266; Koestler, *God That Failed*, 77.

91. On the arch, see Kuśnierz, *Ukraina*, 178. On the wealth transfers, see Falk, *Sowjetische Städte*, 288; Davies, *Years*, 158; and Conquest, *Harvest*, 237. On the "sausage makers," see Kuromiya, *Freedom and Terror*, 172.

92. Quotation: Conquest, *Harvest*, 256. See also, generally, Slezkine, *Jewish Century*; and Fitzpatrick, *Education*.

93. Quotations: Subtelny, "German Diplomatic Reports," 17; Polish Consul-General, 4 February 1933, CAW I/303/4/1867; Border Defense Corps, 15 November 1933, CAW I/303/4/6906. On the hopes for war, see Snyder, *Sketches*, 110. For letters of Soviet Germans to Germany, see *Hungersnot*. See also Berkhoff, "Great Famine."

94. A relevant speech from Hitler can be found in *Deutschösterreichische Tageszeitung*, 3 March 1933. On the cardinals, see Dalrymple, "Soviet Famine," 254. for Innitzer's interventions, see *Reichspost*, 20 August 1933 and 12 October 1933; and *Die Neue Zeitung*, 14 October 1933.

95. For Duranty, see *New York Times*, 31 March 1933. On Muggeridge, see Taylor, "Blanket of Silence," 82. For Orwell, see *Orwell and Politics*, 33–34. See also Engerman, *Modernization*, 211. In fairness to the *New York Times*: two anonymous articles of 1 and 11 January 1933 used the concepts of "man-made" hunger and "war with the peasantry."

96. Papuha, *Zakhidna Ukraïna*, 33, 46, 57.

97. On Soviet counterpropaganda, see Papuha, *Zakhidna Ukraïna*, 56. On Herriot's weight, see *Time*, 31 October 1932. See also Zlepko, *Hunger-Holocaust*, 177; and Conquest, *Harvest*, 314.

98. Quotations: Kovalenko, *Holod*, 353; Zlepko, *Hunger-Holocaust*, 180; see also 175–179. See also Mark, *Hungersnot*, 26–27; Subtelny, "German Diplomatic Reports," 21; Marochko, *Holodomor*, 256–257, 283; *Time*, 22 January 1934.

99. Marochko, *Holodomor*, 257; Zlepko, *Hunger-Holocaust*, 176–177; *Time*, 11 September 1933. Final paragraph: Werth, "Un État"; Marochko, *Holodomor*, 283. In fairness to Herriot: he abstained in the June 1940 parliamentary vote to grant Petain full powers in France and was arrested and sent to Germany at the end of the German occupation.

CHAPTER 2: CLASS TERROR

1. Quotations: Siriol Colley, *More Than a Grain*, 212, 216.

2. Jones is cited in Siriol Colley, *More Than a Grain*, 218.

3. Quotation: Evans, *Coming*, 330.

4. On German voters, see King, "Ordinary," 987–988 and passim. On Dachau, see Goeschel, *Concentration Camps*, 14. For quotation and analysis of Himmler, see Eiber, "Gewalt in KZ Dachau," 172.

5. Evans, *Power*, 23.

6. Quotation: *Deutschösterreichische Tageszeitung*, 3 March 1933.

7. On "class against class," see Brown, *Rise and Fall*, 85. On voting behavior, see King, "Ordinary," 987–988. See also, generally, Bayerlein, "Abschied."

8. Longerich, *Politik der Vernichtung*, 26–32, quotation at 38; Tooze, *Wages of Destruction*, 73.

9. On the 37,000 German Jews, see Evans, *Power*, 15. See also Longerich, *Politik der Vernichtung*, 126.

10. Longerich, *Politik der Vernichtung*, 35.

11. Goeschel, *Concentration Camps*, 7.

12. See, generally, Krüger, *Die Außenpolitik*; Turner, *Stresemann*; Snyder, *Sketches*.

13. Roos, *Polen*, 130–154; Ken, *Collective Security*, 94, 157; Kornat, *Polityka*, 32–33; Rossino, *Hitler*, 2.

14. Quotation: Davies, *Kaganovich Correspondence*, 33.

15. The surest guide is Kołakowski, *Main Currents*. The most famous anecdotal definition is that provided by the veteran communist to Jorgé Semprun at Buchenwald: "C'est l'art et la manière de toujours retomber sur ces pattes, mon vieux!"

16. Graziosi, "New Interpretation."

17. See, generally, Haslam, *Collective Security*; Furet, *Passé*; and Brown, *Rise and Fall*.

18. These numbers will be elucidated in this and the following chapter.

19. On the dialectics involved, see Burrin, *Fascisme, nazisme, autoritarisme*, 202, 209. See also, generally, Weber, *Hollow Years*. On Blum, see Judt, *Burden of Responsibility*.

20. Haslam, *Collective Security*, 120–121. On the Soviet press, see Schlögel, *Terror*, 136–137. See also, generally, Beevor, *Battle for Spain*. On the essential point, I am following Furet, *Passé*.

21. Orwell, *Homage*, 53–64. Quotation: Schlögel, *Terror*, 148. See also Brown, *Rise and Fall*, 89.

22. On 11 May, see Kuromiya, "Anti-Russian," 1427.

23. Quotation: Kuromiya, "Notatka," 133, also 119.

24. Levine, *In Search of Sugihara*, 13–89; Kuromiya, *Między Warszawą a Tokio*, 160–175; Siriol Colley, *Incident*.

25. Haslam analyzes China within the Popular Front framework; see *East*, 64–70. On Xinjiang, see Millward, *Eurasian Crossroads*, 206–207. On the "Long March," see Brown, *Rise and Fall*, 100.

26. See Kuromiya, *Stalin*, 136.

27. Quotation: McLoughlin, "Mass Operations," 121.

28. Khlevniuk, "Objectives"; Kuromiya, *Stalin*, 118–119.

29. Quotation: Kuromiya, *Stalin*, 134, also 101.

30. On the history of the troika, see Wheatcroft, "Mass Killings," 126–139. For general introductions to the state police, see Andrew, *KGB*; and Dziak, *Chekisty*.

31. Getty, *Yezhov*, 140; Kuromiya, *Stalin*, 116.

32. On Yezhov's associates and their methods, see Wheatcroft, "Agency," 38–40. For Stalin's solicitude about Yezhov's health, see Getty, *Yezhov*, 216.

33. Quotation: Haslam, *Collective Security*, 129. For Bukharin's threat, see Kuromiya, *Stalin*, 83.

34. Quotation: Brown, *Rise and Fall*, 122. There were of course exceptions, such as Antoni Słonimski; see Shore, *Caviar and Ashes*, 150. On fascism and anti-fascism, see Furet, *Passé*.

35. Werth, *Terreur*, 282. See also Kuromiya, *Stalin*, 121. The theme of strength in weakness was developed by Furet, *Passé*.

36. Orwell, *Homage*, 145–149, at 149. See also Furet, *Passé*, 296, 301, 306; and Haslam, *Collective Security*, 133.

37. 56,209 is the number of executions remaining after the subtraction: of those in the national actions (see next chapter) and the kulak action from the total 681,692 executions carried out in the Great Terror of 1937–1938. I provide a general figure because slightly different totals for the kulak action circulate; see Jansen, *Executioner*, 75. On the Red Army generals, see Wieczorkiewicz, *Łańcuch*, 296. This is a fundamental work on the military purges.

38. Evans, *Power*, 21–22.

39. Ibid., 34, 39; Shore, *Information*, 31, 37.

40. On Himmler's rise, see Longerich, *Himmler*. On the police structures, see Westermann, "Ideological Soldiers," 45. I am simplifying the situation considerably by not discussing the federal structure of the German state. This, too, was seen by Himmler as a problem to be overcome. The police institutions noted here will be discussed further in Chapters 5, 6, and 7.

41. Evans, *Power*, 627; Lee, *Dictatorships*, 172.

42. These killing actions by German police are the subjects of Chapters 6 and 7.

43. Compare Wheatcroft, "Mass Killing," 139.

44. Quotations: Baberowski, *Feind*, 758–759.

45. Werth, *Terreur*, 280; Viola, *Forgotten Gulag*, 195.

46. On religious faith, see McLoughlin, "Mass Operations," 124; and Binner, "S etoj," 181–183.

47. Shearer, "Social Disorder," 527–531, quotation at 531.

48. On the Siberian Terror, see Ablažej, "Die ROVS-Operation," 287–298; Baberowski, *Terror*, 189–190; and Kuromiya, "Accounting," 93.

49. Binner, "Massenmord," 561–562; Werth, *Terreur*, 283. On "an extra thousand," Jansen, *Executioner*, 82, 87.

50. For "once and for all," see Binner, "Massenmord," 565, also 567. For the cited numbers, see Nikol's'kyi, "Represyvna," 93.

51. Vashlin, *Terror*, 38. For "better too far . . . ," see Baberowski, *Terror*, 192.

52. Binner, "Massenmord," 565–568.

53. Ibid., 567.

54. Ibid., 568. On the latrine incident, see Michniuk, "Przeciwko Polakom," 118. See also Weissberg, *Wielka czystka*, 293. For the signing of blank pages, see McLoughlin, "Mass Operations," 127.

55. Binner, "Massenmord," 571–577. Sometimes Stalin's orders were very local and precise; for examples, see Kuz'niatsou, *Kanveer*, 72–73. Some 1,825 prisoners of Solovki would eventually be shot.

56. On Omsk, see Binner, "Massenmord," 657–580. On the sentencing of 1,301 people in a single night, see McLoughlin, "Mass Operations," 129. See also Khlevniuk, *Gulag*, 150.

57. For quotation and details on the execution techniques, see McLoughlin, "Mass Operations," 130, 131; and Schlögel, *Terror*, 602, 618. On the explosives, see Gregory, *Terror*, 71.

58. On the shooting of 35,454 people, see Junge, *Vertikal'*, 201. On the remaining numbers, see Binner, "S etoj," 207. On the camps, see Werth, *Terreur*, 285; and Khlevniuk, *Gulag*, 332. On the elderly, see Nikol's'kyi, "Represyvna," 99. On the shooting of thirty-five deaf and dumb people," see Schlögel, *Terror*, 624; McLoughlin, "Mass Operations," 136; and Binner, "Massenmord," 590.

59. On the events of December and February, see Nikol'skij, "Kulakenoperation," 623; and Nikol's'kyi, "Represyvna," 100. On Leplevskii's interpretations of the categories of Order 00447, see Šapoval, "Behandlung," 339, 341. On the arrests of 40,530 people, see Nikol's'kyi, "Represyvna," 153. On the 23,650 people added to the death quota, see Šapoval, "Behandlung," 343. For the figures 70,868 and 35,563 and 830, see Junge, *Vertikal'*, 533. For the figures 1,102 and 1,226, see Nikol'skij, "Kulakenoperation," 634–635.

60. Stroński, *Represje*, 243. For discussion, see Weiner, *Making Sense*.

61. Pasternak made this general point in *Dr. Zhivago*.

62. Gurianov, "Obzor," 202.

63. Goeschel, *Concentration Camps*, 26–27. Perhaps 5,000–15,000 people were sent to concentration camps for homosexuality, of whom perhaps half died by the end of the Second World War; see Evans, *Third Reich at War*, 535.

64. Goeschel, *Concentration Camps*, 4, 20, 21, 27; Evans, *Power*, 87. The argument about the swinging pendulum of nationality policy is powerfully formulated by Martin in *Affirmative Action Empire*.

65. On the 267 sentences in Nazi Germany, see Evans, *Power*, 69–70.

CHAPTER 3: NATIONAL TERROR

1. Martin, "Origins," brings analytical rigor to the national operations. Quotation: Jansen, *Executioner*, 96; see also Baberowski, *Terror*, 198.

2. For greater detail on the Polish line, see Snyder, *Sketches*, 115–132.

3. Snyder, *Sketches*, 115–116. The "Polish Military Organization" idea seems to have originated in 1929, when a Soviet agent was placed in charge of the security commission of the Communist Party of Poland; see Stroński, *Represje*, 210.

4. Stroński, *Represje*, 211–213. On Sochacki, see Kieszczyński, "Represje," 202. For further details on Wandurski, see Shore, *Caviar and Ashes*. At least one important Polish communist did return from the Soviet Union and work for the Poles: his book is Reguła, *Historia*.

5. On January 1934, see Stroński, *Represje*, 226–227. For the motives and numbers of later deportations, see Kupczak, *Polacy*, 324.

6. On the first cue, see Kuromiya, *Voices*, 221. For "know everything," see Stroński, *Represje*, 2336–227. See also Morris, "Polish Terror," 756–757.

7. Stroński, *Represje*, 227; Snyder, *Sketches*, 119–120.

8. Nikol's'kyi, *Represyvna*, 337; Stroński, *Represje*, 227. For details on Balyts'kyi, see Shapoval, "Balyts'kyi," 69–74. A similar fate awaited Stanisław Kosior, the former head of the Ukrainian section of the party, who was Polish. He too had played a major role in the starvation campaign of 1933, and he too was executed as a Polish spy.

9. For further discussion of the origins of the Polish operation, see Rubl'ov "Represii proty poliakiv," 126; Paczkowski, "Pologne," 400; and Stroński, *Represje*, 220.

10. For the text of Order 00485 see *Leningradskii martirolog*, 454–456.

11. For some further examples, see Gilmore, *Defying Dixie*.

12. Petrov, "Polish Operation," 154; Nikol's'kyi, *Represyvna*, 105. Figures on representatives of national minorities are given later in the chapter.

13. On the "suppliers," see Kuromiya, *Stalin*, 118. On the Polish diplomats, see Snyder, *Sketches*, 121–127. For the date on the central committee, see Kieszczyński, "Represje," 198. On the experiences of Polish communists in the USSR, Budzyńska's *Strzępy* is invaluable.

14. Quotation: Petrov, "Pol'skaia operatsiia," 23. The phone book anecdote is in Brown, *No Place*, 158.

15. Stroński, *Represje*, 240.

16. Petrov, "Pol'skaia operatsiia," 28; Werth, *Terreur*, 294.

17. Quotation and number: Naumov, *NKVD*, 299–300. For examples, see Stroński, *Represje*, 223, 246.

18. On the Juriewicz family, see Głębocki, "Pierwszy," 158–166, at 164.

19. On the Makowski family, see Głębowski, "Pierwszy," 166–172. For the figure 6,597, see Petrov, "Polish Operation," 168.

20. Ilic, "Leningrad," 1522.

21. Awakened: Dzwonkowski, *Głód*, 236. *Black raven* appears in Polish and Russian, *black maria* in Russian. For attestation to *soul destroyer*, which was later used in reference to German gas vans, see Schlögel, *Terror*, 615. On Kuntsevo, see Vashlin, *Terror*, 40, 44.

22. On the sources of Polish borderland identity, see Snyder, *Reconstruction of Nations*. The redefinitions of Soviet Poles is the central subject of Brown, *No Place*.

23. On the national purge, see Naumov, *NKVD*, 262–266; flower quotation at 266. Berman quotation: Michniuk, "Przeciwko Polakow," 115. On the 218 writers, see Mironowicz, *Białoruś*, 88–89. See also Junge, *Vertikal'*, 624.

24. For further discussion of this method of killing, see Goujon, "Kurapaty"; and Marples, "Kurapaty," 513–517. See also Ziółkowska, "Kurapaty," 47–49.

25. For the figure of 17,772 sentences, see Petrov, "Pol'skaia operatsiia," 168. On the total number of deaths (61,501), see Morris, "Polish Terror," 759.

26. Jansen, *Yezhov*, 258. On Uspenskii, compare Parrish, *Lesser Terror*, 6, 11; and Kuromiya, *Freedom and Terror*, 240.

27. Werth, *Terreur*, 292.

28. On Moszyńska and Angielczyk, see Kuromiya, *Voices*, 49–51, 221–223.

29. Quotation: Dzwonkowski, *Głód*, 94. On Zhmerynka, see Stroński, *Represje*, 225.

30. Quotation: Dzwonkowski, *Głód*, 244. See also Stroński, *Represje*, 235; and Iwanow, *Stalinizm*, 153.

31. On Koszewicz, the undergarments, and the message, see Dzwonkowski, *Głód*, 90, 101, 147.

32. On autumn 1937 and the orphanages, see Petrov, "Pol'skaia operatsiia," 26; Kupczak, *Polacy*, 327, 329; and Jansen, *Executioner*, 97. On Piwiński and Paszkiewicz, see Dzwonkowski, *Głód*, 151, 168.

33. On Sobolewska, see Dzwonkowski, *Głód*, 215–219, at 219.

34. Petrov, "Pol'skaia operatsiia," 30; Binner, "Massenmord," 591; Werth, *Terreur*, 294, 470.

35. On the sentencing of 100 and 138 people, see Stroński, *Represje*, 228.

36. For the figure 111,091, see Petrov, "Pol'skaia operatsiia," 32. For the estimate of eighty-five thousand executions of Soviet Poles, see Petrov, "Polish Operation," 171. Jansen, *Executioner*, 99, draws a similar conclusion. Naumov estimates the Polish dead at 95,000; see *NKVD*, 299. See also Schlögel, *Terror*, 636.

37. Compare Morris, "Polish Terror," 762, whose calculations are almost identical.

38. For comparative arrest numbers, see Khaustov, "Deiatel'nost," 316. Here and elsewhere, remarks about the weakness of the Polish intelligence presence in 1937 and 1938 are based upon weeks of review of the pertinent files of the Second Department of the Polish General Staff in the Polish military archives (the Centralne Archiwum Wojskowe, or CAW). See Snyder, *Sketches*, 83–112, for a more detailed discussion and a range of archival citations. I also discuss there the question of the harm the Terror did to the Soviet security position.

39. In the Caucasus, smaller numbers of people were also forcibly transferred; see Baberowski, *Feind*, 771–772. On the killing of 20,474 people, see Kuromiya, "Asian Nexus," 13. See also Gelb, "Koreans."

40. Quotation: Evans, *Power*, 357. On the German action, see Order 00439 (55,005 sentences, 41,989 death sentences). See also Schlögel, *Terror*, 628.

41. Khlevniuk, *Gulag*, 147. I am citing the figures in Binner, "S etoj," 207. Martin gives 386,798 deaths under Order 00447; see "Origins," 855.

42. Soviet Ukraine represented twenty-two percent of the population and saw twenty-seven percent of the convictions; see Gregory, *Terror*, 265. For the 123,421

death sentences, see Nikol's'kyi, *Represyvna*, 402; at 340 are the national proportions of those arrested during 1937–1938 in Soviet Ukraine: Ukrainians 53.2 percent (78.2 percent of population), Russians 7.7 percent (11.3 percent of population), Jews 2.6 percent (5.2 percent of population), Poles 18.9 percent (1.5 percent of population), and Germans 10.2 percent (1.4 percent of population).

43. Khlevniuk, "Party and NKVD," 23, 28; Binner, "Massenmord," 591–593.

44. On the proportions of ranking officers, see Petrov, *Kto rukovodil*, 475; and Gregory, *Terror*, 63. The representation of Jews in summer 1936 was still higher at the rank of general (fifty-four percent) and in the central apparatus of the NKVD in Moscow (sixty-four percent) and among ranking officers in Soviet Ukraine (sixty-seven percent). See Naumov, *Bor'ba*, 119, for the first two; Zolotar'ov, "Nachalnyts'kyi," 326–331, for the third. Latvians, Germans, and Poles disappeared entirely from the top ranks of the NKVD during the Great Terror. The Pole Stanisław Redens, for example, was the head of the Moscow NKVD and, as such, had signed the orders to execute 20,761 people in the Terror. He himself was arrested and later executed as a Polish nationalist.

45. On the state pensions, see Kotkin, *Magnetic Mountain*, 122.

46. Haslam, *Collective Security*, 194.

47. Hirsch, *Empire*, 293–294.

48. On Austria, see Dean, *Robbing*, 86, 94, 105.

49. On the expulsion, see Tomaszewski, *Preludium*, 5, 139, passim. See also Longerich, *Politik der Vernichtung*, 193–204; and Kershaw, *Hitler*, 459, 472.

50. Goeschel, *Concentration Camps*, 24.

51. On 12 November 1938, see Polian, "Schriftwechsel," 4.

52. On Madagascar, see Polian, "Schriftwechsel," 4, 8. On the Revisionists, see Arens, "Jewish Military," 205; and Spektor, "Żydzi wołyńscy," 539.

53. On Polish-German relations, see Roos, *Polen*, 253, 396; Kershaw, *Hitler*, 475; and Weinberg, *Foreign Policy*, 20, 404, 484.

54. Quotation: Evans, *Power*, 604.

55. Kershaw, *Hitler*, 482; Zarusky, "Hitler bedeutet Krieg," 106–107.

56. See Haslam, *Collective Security*, 90, 153. On Litvinov, see Herf, *Jewish Enemy*, 104; and Orwell, *Orwell and Politics*, 78.

57. Quotation: Wieczorkiewicz, *Łańcuch*, 323.

58. Haslam, *Collective Security*, 227. Quotation: Weinberg, *World at Arms*, 25. I have not discussed Koestler's experiences in Spain, which coincided with the imprisonment of his friend Weissberg in the USSR; see *God That Failed*, 75–80.

59. Quotations: Lukacs, *Last European War*, 58–59.

60. Krebs, "Japan," 543; Haslam, *East*, 132.

61. Levine, *In Search of Sugihara*, 121; Sakamoto, *Japanese Diplomats*, 102; Kuromiya, *Między Warszawą a Tokio*, 470–485; Hasegawa, *Racing*, 13.

CHAPTER 4: MOLOTOV-RIBBENTROP EUROPE

1. Böhler, *Verbrechen*, 16, 69, 72, 74, Böhler, *Überfall*, 100. Datner counts 158; see *55 Dni*, 94.

2. On Warsaw, see Böhler, *Überfall*, 171–172. On the strafing, see Datner, *55 Dni*, 96; and Mazower, *Hitler's Empire*, 67.

3. Naumann, "Die Mörder," 54–55; Grass, *Beim Häuten*, 15–16.

4. On the death of German soldiers as "murder," see Datner, *Zbrodnie*, 73. For "insolence," see Lukacs, *Last European War*, 58. On the barn and cavalry, see Datner, *Zbrodnie*, 72, 69; Rossino, *Hitler*, 166, 169; and Böhler, *Verbrechen*, 23.

5. Here is the instruction in somewhat greater detail: "Close your hearts to pity. Brutal action. Eighty million must get their due. Their existence must be secured. The stronger has the right. The greatest of severity." See Mallman, *Einsatzgruppen*, 54. On Ciepielów, see Böhler, *Verbrechen*, 131. On the red cross, see Rossino, *Hitler*, 181; see also 184. For other tank incidents, see Datner, *Zbrodnia*, 62.

6. For "Poles are the slaves" and the death grimace, see Rossino, *Hitler*, 141, 204. On "the intention of the Leader to destroy and exterminate the Polish people," see Mallmann, *Einsatzgruppen*, 57.

7. Rossino, *Hitler*, 138, 141; Böhler, *Verbrechen*, 100.

8. Bartoszewski, *Warszawski pierścień*, 52–53.

9. Böhler, *Verbrechen*, 19.

10. On Solec, see Böhler, *Verbrechen*, 116. On the Jewish boy who asked for water, see Rossino, *Hitler*, 172. On Dynów, see Böhler, *Überfall*, 200. Rossino estimates that Jews were seven thousand of the fifty thousand Polish civilians killed by the Germans by the end of 1939; see *Hitler*, 234. Mallman, Böhler, and Mathäus also give these figures in *Einsatzgruppen*, at 88. Böhler estimates about thirty thousand by the end of October (*Verbrechen*, 140) and forty-five thousand, of whom seven thousand were Jews, by the end of the year (*Überfall*, 138).

11. On the possibility of such hope, see Młynarski, *W niewoli*, 54–59.

12. Quotation: Weinberg, *World at Arms*, 57.

13. On the Lwów betrayal, see Cienciala, *Crime*, 20; Czapski, *Wspomnienia*, 9–10; and Wnuk, *Za pierwszego Sowieta*, 35.

14. On the Ukrainian steppe, see Czapski, *Wspomnienia*, 15. On the Polish farmers' distress, see Młynarski, *W niewoli*, 98–99.

15. Hrycak estimates 125,000 prisoners of war ("Victims," 179); Cienciala, 230,000–240,000 (*Crime*, 26). The Soviets also kept about fifteen thousand people for hard labor in the mines and in road-building, of whom some two thousand died in 1941 during evacuations; see Hryciuk, "Victims," 180.

16. For examples of people moving from prison to power, taken from multiple regions, see HI 209/1/10420, HI 209/6/5157, HI 209/11/4217, HI 210/14/10544, HI 210/14/4527, HI 210/14/2526, HI 209/13/2935, and HI 210/12/1467. The instances

of violence given here are in Gross, *Revolution*, 37, 44. For details on similar incidents, see HI 209/13/2935, HI 209/13/3124, HI 210/1/4372, HI 210/5/4040, HI 210/14/4908, and HI 209/7/799.

17. On the typical sentence, see Jasiewicz, *Zagłada*, 172. On the 109,400 people arrested and the 8,513 people sentenced to death, see Hryciuk, 182. On the disproportion between arrest and imprisonment numbers, see Khlevniuk, *Gulag*, 236; and Głowacki, *Sowieci*, 292.

18. On the sixty-one thousand Polish citizens, see Rossino, *Hitler*, 15, also 30; "destroy Poland" is at 77. See also, generally, Ingrao, "Violence," 219–220. On Heydrich and Hitler, see Mallman, *Einsatzgruppen*, 57; and Mańkowski, "Ausserordentliche," 7. On the doctorates, see Browning, *Origins*, 16.

19. On Katowice, see Rossino, *Hitler*, 78. On the absence of good records, see Mallman, *Einsatzgruppen*, 80.

20. The Einsatzgruppe z. b. V had the assignment of expelling Jews. See Rossino, *Hitler*, 90, 94, 98; the figure of twenty-two thousand is at 101. On Przemyśl, see Böhler, *Überfall*, 202–203. See also Pohl, *Herrschaft*, 52.

21. On Hitler, see Rutherford, *Prelude*, 53. On Frank, see Seidel, *Besatzungspolitik*, 184 (including quotation). On Frank as Hitler's former lawyer, see Mazower, *Hitler's Empire*, 74.

22. Wnuk, *Za pierwszego Sowieta*, 13–23. The locus classicus is Gross, *Revolution*.

23. Wnuk, *Za pierwszego Sowieta*, 23; Hryciuk, "Victims," 199.

24. On the 139,794 people taken from their homes, see Hryciuk, "Victims," 184. Głowacki records temperatures of minus 42 Celsius, which is minus 43 Fahrenheit; see *Sowieci*, 328. See also Jolluck, *Exile*, 16.

25. On "hell" and the adult dead, see Wróbel, *Polskie dzieci*, 156, 178. See also Gross, *Revolution*, 214–218. For "their dreams and their wishes," see Gross, *Children's Eyes*, 78.

26. Jolluck, *Exile*, 41.

27. There were 10,864 dead among deportees in special settlements by 1 July 1941; see Khlevniuk, *Gulag*, 279. On "the natives," see *Dark Side*, 143. On the boots and swelling, see Gross, *Children's Eyes*, 63, 88.

28. On the skeletons, "what was in his heart," and the white eagle emblem, see Gross, *Children's Eyes*, 191, 202, 78 (also 71, 194).

29. Pankowicz, "Akcja," 43; Burleigh, *Germany Turns Eastwards*, 275.

30. Quotation: Shore, *Information*, 15. See also Rutherford, *Prelude*, 56.

31. Rutherford, *Prelude*, 59, 75.

32. On the numbers cited, see Rutherfold, *Prelude*, 59; Grynberg, *Relacje*, xii; and Hilberg, *Destruction* (vol. I), 156, 189.

33. For the deportation numbers, see Rutherford, *Prelude*, 1, also 75, 88. On Owińska, see Kershaw, *Hitler*, 535; and Evans, *Third Reich at War*, 75–76. On the murder of 7,700 Polish citizens found in mental institutions, see Browning, *Origins*, 189. See also Mazower, *Hitler's Empire*, 85.

34. Quotation: Urbański, *Zagłada*, 32. On Łowicz, see Grynberg, *Relacje*, 239–240.

35. Rutherford, *Prelude*, 9, quotations at 88 and 102.

36. For general descriptions of the three camps, see Cienciala, *Crime*, 29–33; also Abramov, *Murder*, 46, 83, 101; and Młynarski, *W niewoli*, 113–114. On the Christmas Day observances, see Młynarski, *W niewoli*, 156–157.

37. Cienciala, *Crime*, 33. On the outlines and skeletons, see Czapski, *Wspomnienia*, 16, 31; and Młynarski, *W niewoli*, 115–117. For the ravens, see Berling, *Wspomnienia*, 34.

38. Czapski, *Wspomnienia*, 18; Swianiewicz, *Shadow*, 58; Młynarski, *W niewoli*, 205–209; Cienciala, *Crime*, 33–35, 84–99, and for her estimate of the total number of informers (about one hundred), 159.

39. Jakubowicz: *Pamiętniki znalezione*, 30, 38, 43, 53. On the return addresses, see Swianiewicz, *Shadow*, 65.

40. On the dogs befriended by prisoners, see Młynarski, *W niewoli*, 256–257; Abramov, *Murderers*, 86, 102; and Czapski, *Wspomnienia*, 43. On the veterinarian who looked after them, see Młynarski, *W niewoli*, 84, 256.

41. On the Polish underground, see Wnuk, *Za pierwszego Sowieta*, 368–371. On the decision to execute the prisoners, see Cienciala, *Crime*, 116–120, quotations at 118. See also Jasiewicz, *Zagłada*, 129.

42. Jasiewicz, *Zagłada*, 131, 144–145, 159. These 7,305 people were apparently shot at Bykivnia and Kuropaty, major killing sites of the Great Terror; see Kalbarczyk, "Przedmioty," 47–53.

43. Swianiewicz, *Shadow*, 75; Cienciala, *Crime*, 122, 129–130, 175, quotation at 130. For additional passages from Adam Solski's diary, see *Zagłada polskich elit*, 37.

44. Cienciala, *Crime*, 124; *Zagłada polskich elit*, 43.

45. Cienciala, *Crime*, 124; *Zagłada polskich elit*, 43. On Blokhin, see Braithwaite, *Moscow*, 45.

46. Cienciala, *Crime*, 126–128; *Zagłada polskich elit*, 39.

47. Cienciala, *Crime*, 122–123; Czapski, *Wspomnienia*, 7, 8, 15, 17, 18, 45.

48. Abramov, *Murderers*, 46; Swianiewicz, *Shadow*, 63, 66.

49. Cienciala, *Crime*, 34; Czapski, *Wspomnienia*, 18; Swianiewicz, *Shadow*, 64; Młynarski, *W niewoli*, 225. For an informer on the system, see Berling, *Wspomnienia*, 32.

50. Quotation: Swianiewicz, *Shadow*, 69.

51. This is the sum of the execution figures given in Cienciala, *Crime*, passim.

52. Cienciala, *Crime*, 118, 173–174, 198–199, quotation about fathers at 198. On the 60,667 people sent to special settlements in Kazakhstan, see Hryciuk, "Victims," 187. On the "former people," see Khlevniuk, *Gulag*, 282. See also Goussef, "Les déplacements," 188. For wives being told they would be joining their husbands, see Jolluck, *Exile*, 16. For the "eternal mud and snow," see Gross, *Children's Eyes*, 79.

53. On the dung and the NKVD office, see Jolluck, *Exile*, 40, 122–123. On the economist, see Czapski, *Wspomnienia*, 27.

54. Of the 78,339 people deported, about eighty-four percent were Jewish; see Hryciuk, "Victims," 189.

55. Gross, *Children's Eyes*, 221.

56. See Snyder, *Reconstruction*.

57. Krebs, "Japan," 545, 548; Levine, *Sugihara*, 132, 218, 262, 273; Sakamoto, *Japanese Diplomats*, 102, 107, 113–114.

58. For the numbers cited, see Polian, *Against Their Will*, 123. See also Weinberg, *World at Arms*, 167–169; and Kuromiya, *Między Warszawą a Tokio*, 470–485.

59. This figure—408, 525 deportations—is the sum of the major actions. Rutherford estimates 500,000 total; see *Prelude*, 7.

60. On Eichmann and the January 1940 proposal, see Polian, "Schriftwechsel," 3, 7, 19.

61. On the origins of Łódź's ghetto, see Grynberg, *Życie*, 430. Unrivalled in its description of the Warsaw ghetto is Engelking, *Getto warszawskie*, in English translation as *The Warsaw Ghetto: A Guide to the Perished City*. On Schön, see T. B., "Organizator," 85–90. On German intentions and on population movements, see Browning, *Origins*, 100–124.

62. Drozdowski, "Fischer," 189–190. See also Engelking, *Getto warszawskie*, chap. 2. Ringelblum is cited in Friedländer, *Extermination*, 160; on tourists, see also Mazower, *Hitler's Empire*, 95.

63. Quotation: *Zagłada polskich elit*, 23. See also Longerich, *Unwritten Order*, 55; Kershaw, *Fateful Choices*, 447. Some 11,437 people died in the Łódź ghetto in 1941; see Grynberg, *Życie*, 430.

64. See, above all, Żbikowski, "Żydowscy przesiedleńcy," 224–228; also Grynberg, *Relacje*, 244; Browning, *Origins*, 124; and Kassow, *Archive*, 107, 273. These movements were senseless, even from a German perspective: Jews were cleared from the Warsaw district from January to March 1941 to make room for Poles who were to be expelled from the Warthegau, who were removed to make room for Germans, who were coming west from the Soviet Union: but Germany would invade the Soviet Union in June 1941, so that Germans could move east and colonize its lands.

65. On Sborow and Lederman, see Sakowska, *Dzieci*, 51, 50. Quotation: Żbikowski, "Żydowscy przesiedleńcy," 260.

66. "Sprawozdania Świetliczanek," 65, quotations at 70, 69.

67. On the two different approaches to elites, see Friedländer, *Extermination*, 40. See also Tooze, *Wages of Destruction*, 364–365; and Mańkowski, "Ausserordentliche," 9–11, quotation at 11. Compare Cienciala, *Crime*, 114–115; and Jolluck, *Exile*, 15.

68. Wieliczko, "Akcja," 34–35; Pankowicz, "Akcja," 43–45; *Zagłada polskich elit*, 62, 67.

69. Bartoszewski, *Warszawski pierścień*, 64–65; Dunin-Wąsowicz, "Akcja," 24.

70. Pietrzykowski, "Akcja," 113–115; Jankowski, "Akcja," 65–66. On the brothel for Germans, see Pietrzykowski, *Akcja AB*, 77–78.

71. Pietrzykowski, "Akcja," 114–115.

72. See, for example, Pankowicz, "Akcja," 44. On "We can't tell . . . ," see Cienciala, *Crime*, 182.

73. On all three men, see Pietrzykowski, "Akcja," 117–118.

74. Dunin-Wąsowicz, "Akcja," 22–25; Bauer, *Dowbor*, 217, 241; *Crime of Katyń*, 33; *Zagłada polskich elit*, 73.

75. *Zagłada polskich elit*, 77.

76. On Himmler and the transports, see Bartoszewski, *Warszawski pierścień*, 59, 60, 123–125. For further details on the transports, see *Zagłada polskich elit*, 69; Seidel, *Besatzungspolitik in Polen*. On Bach-Zelewski and the execution site, see Dwork, *Auschwitz*, 166, 177. On IG Farben, see Tooze, *Wages of Destruction*, 443.

77. On collectivization, see Report of 25 November 1941, SPP 3/1/1/1/1; also Shumuk, *Perezhyte*, 17.

78. On the Ukrainians targeted, see HI 210/14/7912. These operations were part of a series of June 1941 deportation actions that were then organized throughout the newly annexed regions of the Soviet Union, from the Baltics to Romania. On the 11,328 and 22,353 Polish citizens, see Hryciuk, "Victims," 191, 193. See also Olaru-Cemirtan, "Züge."

79. On the bombing, see Jolluck, *Exile*, 16. Quotation: Gross, *Children's Eyes*, 52.

80. Some 292,513 Polish citizens were deported in four waves, along with thousands more individually or in smaller actions. See *Deportacje obywateli*, 29; and Hryciuk, "Victims," 175. Of the deportees, some 57.5 percent were counted by the Soviets as Poles, 21.9 percent as Jews, 10.4 percent as Ukrainians, and 7.6 percent as Belarusians; see Hryciuk, "Victims," 195. For overall counts I rely on Hryciuk, "Victims," 175; and Autuchiewicz, "Stan," 23. See also Gurianov, "Obzor," 205.

81. Czapski, *Na nieludzkiej ziemi*, 68.

82. King James Bible, Matthew 5:37; Koestler, *Darkness at Noon*, 249. Czapski's meeting with Reikhman took place on 3 February 1942; see *Crimes of Katyń*, 90.

83. Czapski, *Na nieludzkiej ziemi*, 120, 141–143, 148.

84. Czapski, *Na nieludzkiej ziemi*, 149.

85. On Frank, see Longerich, *Unwritten Order*, 47. On the NKVD, see Kołakowski, *NKWD*, 74. On Hitler, see Mańkowski, "Ausserordentliche," 7. Compare Aly, *Architects*, 151.

CHAPTER 5: THE ECONOMICS OF APOCALYPSE

1. This is not an intellectual history, and I can permit myself only the briefest of remarks about these complex issues. As individuals, Hitler and Stalin embodied different forms of the early-nineteenth-century German response to the Enlightenment: Hitler the tragic romantic hero who must bear the burden of leading a flawed nation, Stalin the Hegelian world spirit that reveals reason in history and dictates it to others. A more complete comparison, as Christopher Clark has suggested, would account for

different views of time. The Nazi and Soviet regimes both rejected the basic Enlightened assumption that time was moving forward on its own, bringing knowledge and thus progress. Each was instead racing ahead to a point that was supposed to be in the past. Marxism was indeed a scheme of progress, but Lenin had leapt ahead of Marx's predictions to make a revolution in a backward country, while the more industrial countries defied Marx's predictions by not having socialist revolutions at all. The Soviets under Stalin were thus hastening, in the 1930s, so that the homeland of socialism could defend itself from the imperialist world. The Nazis were in an even greater hurry toward an even more fantastic vision. They imagined a cataclysm that would destroy the Soviet Union, remake eastern Europe, and restore German greatness and purity. Hitler was anxious to make the Germany of his dreams in his own lifetime, one that he feared would be short. An introduction to attempts to bind discussions of Nazi Germany and the Soviet Union within intellectual history is Bracher, *Zeit der Ideologien*.

2. This is a recasting of the argument developed in Chapters 1–3. For "Garden of Eden" (16 July 1941), see Mulligan, *Illusion*, 8.

3. Compare Goulder, "Internal Colonialism"; and Viola, "Selbstkolonisierung."

4. Britain is more an external factor in this study than a subject of inquiry; but there is a case to be made for the importance of individuals in history here as well. See Lukacs, *Hitler and Stalin*; and Lukacs, *Five Days in London*. See also Isaiah Berlin's essay "Winston Churchill in 1940" in *Personal Impressions*, 1–23.

5. See the Preface; also Streit, *Keine Kameraden*, 26–27. Oil was necessary for both industry and agriculture. Here, too, Germany was dependent upon imports, and true autarky seemed to require the conquest of the Soviet Caucasus and its oil fields.

6. Consult Tooze, *Wages of Destruction*, 409, 424, 429, 452. For the "most autarkic state in the world," see Kennedy, *Aufstieg*, 341. On the oil reserves, see Eichholtz, *Krieg um Öl*, 8, 15, passim. Compare Hildebrand, *Weltreich*, 657–658. The German military was convinced that Soviet resources were needed to fight the war; see Kay, *Exploitation*, 27, 37, 40, and "immense riches" at 212.

7. On Germany's naval capacity, see Weinberg, *World at Arms*, 118; also Tooze, *Wages of Destruction*, 397–399; and Evans, *Third Reich at War*, 143–146. Quotation: Mazower, *Hitler's Empire*, 133. Alan Milward long ago drew attention to the significance of the assumption of a rapid victory; see *German Economy*, 40–41.

8. On Generalplan Ost, see Madajczyk, "Generalplan," 12–13, also 64–66; Aly, *Architects*, 258; Kay, *Exploitation*, 100–101, 216; Wasser, *Himmlers Raumplannung*, 51–52; Aly, *Architects*, 258; Tooze, *Wages of Destruction*, 466–467; Rutherford, *Prelude*, 217; Mazower, *Hitler's Empire*, 206, 210; and Longerich, *Himmler*, 597–599.

9. On Himmler, see Longerich, *Himmler*, 599. On Hitler, see Kershaw, *Hitler*, 651. See also Tooze, *Wages of Destruction*, 469.

10. Hitler's proclamation of 31 January 1941 is cited after Tooze, *Wages of Destruction*, 465. The final form of the Final Solution is the subject of the next chapter. Evans argues that Hitler needed to begin the war against the Soviet Union before the war

against Britain was over because German citizens would have opposed a new war; see *Third Reich at War*, 162.

11. *Deutschösterreichische Tageszeitung*, 3 March 1933; Kershaw, *Fateful Choices*, 267. On the percentage cited, see Kay, *Exploitation*, 56, 143.

12. Quotations: Kay, *Exploitation*, 211, 50, 40. See also Tooze, *Wages of Destruction*, 469; and Kershaw, *Hitler*, 650.

13. Quotation: Gerlach, *Kalkulierte Morde*, 342. The institutional apparati are clarified in Kay, *Exploitation*, 17–18, 148.

14. Kay, *Exploitation*, 138, 162–163.

15. On the "extinction of . . . a great part of the population," see *Verbrechen der Wehrmacht*, 65. The long quotation is in Kay, *Exploitation*, 133; see also Gerlach, *Kalkulierte Morde*, 52–56. Given the settlement patterns of Soviet Jews, these "superfluous people" included not only Russians, Belarusians, Ukrainians, and Balts but at least three quarters of the Soviet Jewish population as well.

16. Kay, *Exploitation*, 164. In June, Hitler confirmed Göring's overall responsibility for economic planning.

17. Hauner, *Axis Strategy*, 378–383.

18. Hitler's capacity for improvisation makes it difficult to speak of strategy in the conventional sense. In my view the dispute between those who argue for a continental and a world strategy is most easily resolved thus: Hitler and his commanders agreed that a conquered Soviet Union was needed to pursue the war, whatever form it took. Hitler had in mind a war of continents and believed that it would come. Winning that world war required an earlier victory in the continental war.

19. On the neutrality pact, see Weinberg, *World at Arms*, 167–169; and Hasegawa, *Racing*, 13–14.

20. Burleigh, *Third Reich*, 484, 487.

21. On the Japanese wavering, see Weinberg, *World at Arms*, 253. On "for the time being," see Hasegawa, *Racing*, 13. On the reaffirmation, see Krebs, "Japan," 554. On the oft-forgotten Italian role, see Schlemmer, *Italianer*.

22. Quotations: Römer, *Kommissarbefehl*, 204. Regarding Hitler's quotation, see Kershaw, *Hitler*, 566. See also Pohl, *Herrschaft*, 64; and Bartov, *Hitler's Army*, 16.

23. On the use of civilians as human shields, see the order of 13 May 1941, text in *Verbrechen der Wehrmacht*, 46. See also Bartov, *Hitler's Army*, 71; Pohl, *Herrschaft*, 71, and discussion of women in uniform at 205; Römer, *Kommissarbefehl*, 228, also 551; and Gerlach, *Kalkulierte Morde*, 774.

24. Gerlach, *Kalkulierte Morde*, 244, 266; Bartov, *Eastern Front*, 132.

25. *Verbrechen der Wehrmacht*, 344; Pohl, *Herrschaft*, 185; Gerlach, *Kalkulierte Morde*, 266.

26. Quotation: Arnold, "Eroberung," 46.

27. Compare Edele, "States," 171. The problem of feeding German soldiers without reducing food rations is examined in Tooze, *Wages of Destruction*.

28. Gerlach, *Kalkulierte Morde*, 798. As Tooze has pointed out, Germans were indeed willing to make economic sacrifices for the war effort; see *Wages of Destruction*.

29. Streit, *Keine Kameraden*, 143, 153. On Walther von Reichenau (28 September), see Arnold, "Eroberung," 35.

30. Streit, *Keine Kameraden*, 143, 153. Compare Kay, *Exploitation*, 2.

31. See Keegan, *Face of Battle*, 73; Gerlach, *Kalkulierte Morde*, 51; Förster, "German Army," 22; and *Verbrechen der Wehrmacht*, 288.

32. Arnold, "Eroberung," 27–33.

33. On Kiev, see Berkhoff, *Harvest*, 170–186, maximum death total (56,400) at 184; also Arnold, "Eroberung," 34. On Kharkiv, see Pohl, *Herrschaft*, 192; *Verbrechen der Wehrmacht*, at 328, gives a minimum of 11,918.

34. Kay, *Exploitation*, 181, 186.

35. Wagner was in 1944 one of the plotters against Hitler. See *Verbrechen der Wehrmacht*, at 193 and 311, for quotations. One million is the estimate usually given in the Western literature; see, for example, Kirschenbaum, *Siege*; and Salisbury, *900 Days*. The Soviet estimate is 632,000; see *Verbrechen der Wehrmacht*, 308. On food and fuel, see Simmons, *Leningrad*, 23.

36. Gerlach, *Krieg*, 36; Salisbury, *900 Days*, 508–509; Simmons, *Leningrad*, xxi; Kirschenbaum, *Siege*, 1.

37. Głębocki, "Pierwszy," 179–189.

38. Simmons, *Leningrad*, 51.

39. The diary is on display at the State Museum of the History of St. Petersburg in the exhibition "Leningrad in the Years of the Great Patriotic War."

40. On the numbers cited, see *Verbrechen der Wehrmacht*, 209. On the projected number of prisoners, see Gerlach, *Kalkulierte Morde*, 783.

41. Bartov, *Hitler's Army*, 87; Polian, "Violence," 123; Overmans, "Kriegsgefangenpolitik," 800–801. See also Merridale, *Ivan's War*, 28; and Braithwaite, *Moscow*, 165.

42. Berkhoff, *Harvest*, 94–96; Gerlach, *Kalkulierte Morde*, 845–857. For a general perspective on the treatment of prisoners of war, see the superb Keegan, *Face of Battle*, 49–51.

43. Polian, "Violence," 121. Datner estimates 200,000–250,000; see *Zbrodnie*, 379.

44. Overmans, "Kriegsgefangenpolitik," 805; Gerlach, *Krieg*, 24.

45. On "comrades," see Dugas, *Vycherknutye*, 30.

46. On the chain of authority, see Streim, *Behandlung*, 7. Quotation: Pohl, *Herrschaft*, 219; also Gerlach, *Kalkulierte Morde*, 801. See also Overmans, "Kriegsgefangenpolitik," 808. On cannibalism, see Shumejko, "Atanasyan," 174; and Hartmann, "Massenvernichtung," 124.

47. On ration cuts, see Megargee, *Annihilation*, 119. For "pure hell," see *Ich werde es nie vergessen*, 178. On Minsk, see *Verbrechen der Wehrmacht*, 227–229; Gerlach, *Kalkulierte Morde*, 768, 856; Gerlach, *Krieg*, 51; Polian, "Violence," 121; Overmans, "Kriegsgefangenpolitik," 807; and Beluga, *Prestupleniya*, 199. On Bobruisk, see Pohl,

Herrschaft, 224. On Homel, see Pohl, *Herrschaft*, 224; and Dugas, *Sovetskie Voennoplen-nye*, 125. On Mahileu, see Pohl, *Herrschaft*, 224–225. On Molodechno, see Gerlach, *Krieg*, 34; and Magargee, *Annihilation*, 90; also Bartov, *Hitler's Army*, 79.

48. On Kirovohrad, see *Verbrechen der Wehrmacht*, 239–244. On Khorol, see Pohl, *Herrschaft*, 226. On Stalino, see Pohl, *Herrschaft*, 227; and Datner, *Zbrodnie*, 404.

49. Motyka, "Tragedia jeńców," 2–6; Kopówka, *Stalag 366*, 47. On the 45,690 people who died in the General Government camps, see Dugas, *Sovetskie Voennoplennye*, 131. Compare Młynarczyk, *Judenmord*, 245 (250,000–570,000).

50. On the lack of warm clothing, see Bartov, *Eastern Front*, 112. On the three Soviet soldiers, see Dugas, *Sovetskie Voennoplennye*, 125.

51. *Ich werde es nie vergessen*, 113.

52. On the civilians who tried to bring food to camps, see Berkhoff, *Harvest*, 95, 101; and Overmans, "Kriegsgefangenpolitik," 808. On Kremenchuk, see Pohl, *Herrschaft*, 226.

53. Compare *Verbrechen der Wehrmacht*, 188.

54. On the intention to kill Soviet elites, see Kay, *Exploitation*, 104. On Hitler in March 1941, Streim, *Behandlung*, 36. For the text of the guidelines, see *Verbrechen der Wehrmacht*, 53–55.

55. On the 2,252 shootings, see Römer, *Kommissarbefehl*, 581.

56. On 2 July 1941, see *Verbrechen der Wehrmacht*, 63; Kay, *Exploitation*, 105; and Kershaw, *Fateful Choices*, 453. On the instructions given to the Einsatzgruppen and their fulfillment, see Datner, *Zbrodnie*, 153; Streim, *Behandlung*, 69, 99; and Berkhoff, *Harvest*, 94. On October 1941, see Streit, "German Army," 7.

57. Pohl, *Herrschaft*, 204 (and 153 and 235 for the estimates of fifty and one hundred thousand). Overmans estimates one hundred thousand shootings in "Kriegsge-fangenpolitik," 815. Arad estimates eighty thousand total Jewish POW deaths; see *Soviet Union*, 281. Quotation (doctor): Datner, *Zbrodnie*, 234. On medicine as a naz-ified profession, see Hilberg, *Perpetrators*, 66.

58. Streim, *Behandlung*, 102–106.

59. For an estimate at the low end, see Streim, *Behandlung*, 244: minimum 2.4 million. For estimates of 3–3.3 million, see Pohl, *Herrschaft*, 210; Overmans, "Kriegsge-fangenpolitik," 811, 825; Dugas, *Sovetskie Voennoplennye*, 185; and Hartmann, "Massenvernichtung," 97. For an estimate at the high end, see Sokolov, "How to Cal-culate," 452: 3.9 million. On morale, see *Verbrechen der Wehrmacht*, 204.

60. On 7 November 1941, see Gerlach, *Kalkulierte Morde*, 817. Compare Gerlach and Werth, "State Violence," 164. See also Streim, *Behandlung*, 99–102, 234. On the four hundred thousand total deaths among those released, see Pohl, *Herrschaft*, 215. Quotation (Johannes Gutschmidt): Hartmann, "Massenvernichtung," 158; a similar estimation by Rosenberg is in Klee, "Gott mit uns," 142.

61. Belgium: Kay, *Exploitation*, 121.

62. On Goebbels, see Evans, *Third Reich at War*, 248. Compare Kay, *Exploitation*, 109; Longerich, *Unwritten Order*, 55, 60; Browning, *Origins*; Gerlach, *Kalkulierte Morde*, 747; Gerlach, *Krieg*, 178; Arad, *Reinhard*, 14; and Aly, *Architects*, 160.

63. On the asphyxiation experiments, see Overmans, "Kriegsgefangenpolitik," 814; Longerich, *Unwritten Order*, 82; Longerich, *Himmler*, 567; Datner, *Zbrodnie*, 208, 428; *Verbrechen*, 281; Mazower, *Hitler's Empire*, 383; Browning, *Origins*, 357; and Klee, "Gott mit uns," 136.

64. On the number of prisoners recruited, see Pohl, *Herrschaft*, 181. See also Black, "Handlanger," 313–317; and Gerlach, *Kalkulierte Morde*, 207–208.

CHAPTER 6: FINAL SOLUTION

1. Browning and Gerlach have debated whether Hitler's decision came in summer/autumn or in December 1941. In this chapter I am arguing that shooting Jews was the fifth version of the Final Solution, and the first one to show promise. The idea that the Jews could be removed from Europe by killing them must have been in the minds of Himmler and Hitler no later than August. It is quite possible that the two of them discussed this explicitly, although they need not have done so. Reinhard Koselleck (*Futures Past*, 222) cites Hitler, who is himself citing (unknowingly, I assume) Dostoevsky in *Crime and Punishment*: one need not admit to having plans, even to oneself, in order to have them. For my purposes, December 1941 is the more important date, since that was the time when other associates of Hitler grasped that the Final Solution meant the total mass murder of Jews rather than the murder of some and the deportation of others.

2. See however the important revisions of Speer's role in Tooze, *Wages of Destruction*. The problem was posed in its classical form by Milward, *German Economy*, 6–7 and passim. Quotation: Longerich, *Himmler*, 561. The massive debate over "institutionalism" and "functionalism" cannot be presented here. This discussion began before the centrality of the eastern front to the Holocaust was understood. Like several other scholars, I am arguing that the thinkability and the possibility of a Final Solution by mass murder emerged from a combination of signals from above (for example, Hitler to Himmler, Himmler to Bach) and from below (for example, Einsatzgruppe A to Himmler, Himmler to Hitler) or indeed in both directions (the relationship between Jeckeln and Himmler). The place where murder emerged as the method of the Final Solution was the eastern front, where the main technique was shooting.

3. Quotation: Mazower, *Hitler's Empire*, 368. On Wannsee, see Gerlach, "Wannsee"; and Longerich, *Unwritten Order*, 95. See also, generally, Roseman, *Villa*. The connection between Hitler and Rosenberg's civilian administration is made in Lower, "Nazi Civilian Rulers," 222–223.

4. Einsatzgruppe A, B, C, D respectively: 990 men, 655 men, 700 men, 600 men. See MacLean, *Field Men*, 13. On "numbers . . . too small," see Browning, "Nazi Decision," 473. On the importance of the Order Police, see Pohl, "Schauplatz," 152. The

death count is from Brandon, "First Wave." At least 457,436 Jews were killed by the Einsatzgruppen by the end of 1941.

5. This is not explicitly argued in these terms in Longerich, *Himmler*, but I believe that the interpretation squares with the arguments presented there. Compare Gerlach, *Kalkulierte Morde*, 115; and Lück, "Partisanbekämpfung," 229.

6. Quotation: Wasser, "Raumplannung," 51. See also Mazower, *Hitler's Empire*, 378 and passim; and Steinberg, "Civil Administration," 647.

7. The Romanian lands taken by Stalin were invaded by the Romanian army, not the German. They were followed by Einsatzgruppe D; see Angrick, *Besatzungspolitik*.

8. See Snyder, *Reconstruction*.

9. The deportation figures are in Angrick, *Riga*, 46. If conscription is included, the total rises to 34,000.

10. MacQueen, "White Terror," 97; Angrick, *Riga*, 59. Among the two hundred thousand I include Jews in Vilnius and surrounding areas annexed to Lithuania.

11. Arad, *Soviet Union*, 144, 147; MacQueen, "White Terror," 99–100; Angrick, *Riga*, 60.

12. Tomkiewicz, *Ponary*, 191–197.

13. Ibid., 203.

14. Angrick, *Riga*, 66–76. See also Arad, *Soviet Union*, 148.

15. Weiss-Wendt, *Estonians*, 39, 40, 45, 90, 94–105.

16. The 9,817 count in *Verbrechen* is at 93. See also Wnuk, *Za pierwszego Sowieta*, 371 (11,000–12,000); and Hryciuk, "Victims," 183 (9,400).

17. On interwar anti-Jewish politics, see, generally, Polonsky, *Politics*; and Mendelsohn, *Jews*.

18. On Białystok, see Matthäus, "Controlled Escalation," 223; and *Verbrechen der Wehrmacht*, 593. Spektor (in "Żydzi wołyńscy," 575) counts thirty-eight pogroms in Volhynia; and the authors and editors of *Wokół Jedwabnego*, about thirty in the Białystok region.

19. On the total number of Jews killed (19,655), see Brandon, "First Wave." For the "Hundreds of Jews . . . running down the street," see *Verbrechen der Wehrmacht*, 99. On the nationality of the prisoners, see Himka, "Ethnicity," 8.

20. The idea of double collaboration as biographical self-cleansing is advanced in Gross, *Neighbors*. For examples from Estonia, Ukraine, and Belarus of double collaboration, see Weiss-Wendt, *Estonians*, 115–119; *Dubno: sefer zikaron*, 698–701; Rein, "Local Collaborators," 394; Brakel, *Unter Rotem Stern*, 304; Musial, *Mythos*, 266; and Mironowicz, *Białoruś*, 160. See also Snyder, "West Volhynian Jews." A systematic study of double collaboration would be worthwhile.

21. This is the closest that I would come to an Arendtian argument about alienation. Arendt's follower Jan Gross makes a similar argument about the privatization of violence in his study of the first Soviet occupation, *Revolution from Abroad*. But then in his studies of the consequences of two occupations, *Neighbors* and *Fear*, he

shifts away from sociology and toward ethics, as if Poles should have remembered themselves when German occupation was added to Soviet, or Soviet to German. In my view the logical move would have been to press forward with the Arendtian argument, but claiming that the overlap of both "totalitarian" powers plays the historical role that Arendt assigned to modernity. This is not quite what Gross claims (although he makes gestures in this direction in *Upiorna dekada* and in a few passages in both *Neighbors* and *Fear*). But I do think it follows from his occupation studies as a whole, if they are read as studies of human behavior (rather than of Polish ethics). This line of argument is pursued in the Conclusion.

22. Westermann, "Ideological Soldiers," 46 (30% and 66%).

23. Compare Gerlach, "Nazi Decision," 476.

24. Longerich, *Himmler*, 551; Kay, *Exploitation*, 106. On Uman, see USHMM-SBU 4/1747/19–20.

25. Matthäus, "Controlled Escalation," 225; Gerlach, *Kalkulierte Morde*, 555; Kershaw, *Fateful Choices*, 456, 458. Cüppers, in *Wegbereiter*, develops the argument about the crucial early role of the Waffen-SS.

26. Kay, *Exploitation*, 107; Browning, "Nazi Decision," 474. Pohl notes that the reinforcements came first to Ukraine; see *Herrschaft*, 152. He specifies early August as the time when Einsatzgruppe C understood that women and children were to be killed; see "Schauplatz," 140.

27. Mallmann, *Einsatzgruppen*, 97.

28. Pohl, "Schauplatz," 142; Kruglov, "Jewish Losses," 274–275; *Verbrechen der Wehrmacht*, 135.

29. Kruglov, "Jewish Losses," 275.

30. Ruß, "Massaker," 494, 503, 505; Berkhoff, "Records," 294; Pohl, "Schauplatz," 147.

31. Berkhoff, *Harvest*, 65–67, at 65; FVA 3267.

32. Darmstadt testimony, 29 April 1968, IfZ(M), Gd 01.54/78/1762.

33. Ruß, "Massaker," 486; Berkhoff, *Harvest*, 68. On Sara, see Ehrenburg, *Black Book*, Borodyansky-Knysh testimony. On the valuables, see Dean, "Jewish Property," 86. On the people "already bloody," see "Stenogramma," 24 April 1946, TsDAVO, 166/3/245/118. On the bones and ash and sand, see Klee, *Gott mit uns*, 136.

34. Darmstadt testimony, 29 April 1968, IfZ(M), Gd 01.54/78/1764–1765; Berkhoff, "Records," 304.

35. Prusin, "SiPo/SD," 7–9; Rubenstein, *Unknown*, 57. Romanowsky makes the point about the rotation of official enemies in "Nazi Occupation," 240.

36. Rubenstein, *Unknown*, 54, 57, 61; Prusin, "SiPo/SD," 7–9.

37. On Kharkiv, see Pohl, "Schauplatz," 148; and *Verbrechen der Wehrmacht*, 179. On Kiev, see Prusin, "SiPo/SD," 10.

38. Gerlach, *Kalkulierte Morde*, 544, 567. Nebe was a member of the resistance to Hitler in 1944.

39. Megargee, *Annihilation*, 99.

40. Quotation and figures are from Gerlach, *Kalkulierte Morde*, 588, 585; see also Ingrao, "Violence," 231.

41. For the "sea of blood," see Gerlach, *Kalkulierte Morde*, 182. For "thus must be destroyed," see *Verbrechen*, 138.

42. This was an argument of the previous chapter.

43. The Soviet rationale was a classic one. First, the NKVD "established" that Germany had hundreds of spies among the Volga Germans. Then, the NKVD argued that the entire population was guilty, since none of the Volga Germans had reported all of this espionage to the proper authorities. In a particularly refined move, the NKVD used the presence of swastikas in German households as evidence of Nazi collaboration. In fact, the Soviets had themselves distributed those swastikas, in 1939, when Moscow and Berlin were allies, and a friendly visit from Hitler was expected. By the end of 1942, the Soviets had resettled some nine hundred thousand Germans, the vast majority of the German population in the Soviet Union. The Soviets deported some eighty-nine thousand Finns, most of them to Siberia. On Stalin, see Polian, *Against Their Will*, 134. On Hitler, see Longerich, *Unwritten Order*, 75; Gerlach, *Krieg*, 96; Gerlach, "Wannsee," 763; Pinkus, "Deportation," 456–458; Mazower, *Hitler's Empire*, 370; and Friedlander, *Extermination*, 239, 263–264.

44. Quotation: Lukacs, *Last European War*, 154; see also Friedlander, *Extermination*, 268.

45. Angrick, *Riga*, 133–150.

46. Chełmno is discussed in Chapter 8. The connection is made by Kershaw, *Fateful Choices*, 462; see also Kershaw, *Hitler*, 66. Mazower emphasizes the centrality of the Wartheland in *Hitler's Empire*, for example at 191. I am excluding in this judgment Jews killed in the "euthanasia" program.

47. Himmler and Globocnik will be discussed at greater length in Chapter 8.

48. Megargee, *Annihilation*, 115.

49. Arguing from the periphery, from Belarus and Ukraine to Berlin, Gerlach and Pohl each make a case for the importance of food supplies in the extermination of the Jews. Aly and Heim, arguing forward from the logic of prewar planning, present a kind of negative explanation for the Holocaust: the Jews were already regarded as harmful in future designs and as useless consumers of present necessities. Hitler certainly undertook the war against the Soviet Union on the understanding that food supplies could thereby be secured during the war and for future wars. It is certainly true that the Hunger Plan, real supply difficulties for the Wehrmacht, and the perceived need to satisfy German civilians mattered a great deal on the eastern front generally. The concern for food made it easier for officers to endorse killing Jews. As the war continued, the economic argument about Jewish labor would be countered by the economic argument about the food Jews would eat. I agree that food played a much greater role in the process than it might appear from English-language literature on the Holocaust. But I do not believe that food (or any other economic consideration) can explain the timing or the precise content of Hitler's policy as conveyed in December 1941. It was

an ideological expression and political resolution of pressing problems arising from a failed colonial war. It was also a choice.

50. Quotation: Edele, "States," 374.

51. On the 3 January meeting of Hitler with the Japanese ambassador, see Hauner, *Axis Strategy*, 384. See also Lukacs, *Last European War*, 143.

52. Krebs, "Japan," 547–554.

53. German propaganda was making the case explicitly; see Herf, *Jewish Enemy*, 100, 128. Compare Gerlach, "Wannsee." The recent scholarly emphasis upon Himmler and December has much to do with Gerlach's work and with the publication of Witte, *Dienstkalendar*, and Longerich, *Himmler*. Himmler was the crucial executor of a policy for which Hitler was responsible.

54. Quoted and discussed, for example, in Longerich, *Unwritten Order*, 95; Gerlach, *Krieg*, 123; Gerlach, "Wannsee," 783, 790; Kershaw, *Fateful Choices*, 466; Tooze, *Wages of Destruction*, 504; and Mazower, *Hitler's Empire*, 376 (for the Frank quotation as well). As Friedländer points out in a persuasive passage, this was one of a cluster of such statements; see *Extermination*, 281.

55. On Hitler ("common front"), see Herf, *Jewish Enemy*, 132. On Goebbels, see Pohl, *Verfolgung*, 82.

56. Madajczyk, "Generalplan Ost," 17; Mazower, *Hitler's Empire*, 198.

57. Compare Browning, "Nazi Decision"; and Gerlach, "Wannsee." See also Kershaw, *Fateful Choices*, 433.

58. See Kroener, "Frozen Blitzkrieg," 140, 148.

59. See Gerlach, *Kalkulierte Morde*, 582, for quotation and interpretation.

60. On Serbia, see Manoschek, *Serbien*, 79, 107, 186–197; and Evans, *Third Reich at War*, 237, 259. The blame for the death of the Jews, in this conception, did not rest on the Germans. If the United States was a Jewish state, went the Nazi reasoning, its leaders must have understood that Hitler was keeping alive the Jews of Europe as hostages. If the United States entered the war, it followed, Washington was responsible for the death of these hostages. Of course, no one in the United States actually reasoned in this way, and the American entry into the war had little if anything to do with European or American Jews. See Longerich, *Unwritten Order*, 55; Friedländer, *Extermination*, 265, 281; Arad, *Soviet Union*, 139; and Gerlach, "Wannsee."

61. That such camouflage was felt to be necessary is a telling sign, since it reveals the Nazis' supposition that someone else might read their documents, which would happen only if they lost the war. Stalinists and Stalin himself had no such difficulties writing, signing, and filing direct orders to kill large numbers of people.

62. Birn, "Anti-Partisan Warfare," 289.

63. For the count, see Brandon, "The First Wave."

64. Deletant, "Transnistria," 157–165; Pohl, *Verfolgung*, 78–79; Hilberg, *Destruction* (vol. I), 810.

65. Deletant, "Transnistria," 172; Pohl, *Verfolgung*, 79. See also Case, *Between States*.

66. Pohl, "Schauplatz," 153, 162. The gas chambers are the subject of Chapter 8.

67. Pohl counts thirty-seven thousand auxiliary policemen active in July 1942 in the Reichskommissariat Ukraine; see "Hilfskräfte," 210.

68. These Volhynian communities are treated in greater detail in Spector, *Volhynian Jews*, and Snyder, "West Volhynian Jews," 77–84. The fate of Galician Jews, discussed in Chapter 8, was different; see Pohl, *Ostgalizien*, and Sandkühler, *Galizien*.

69. Arad, in *Soviet Union* at 521 and 524, counts 1,561,000–1,628,000 murdered Jews in the lands annexed by the USSR, as well as 946,000–996,000 Jews of the prewar Soviet Union. See also Snyder, "West Volhynian Jews," 85–89.

70. Grynberg, *Życie*, 602; Spektor, "Żydzi wołyńscy," 477; Snyder, "West Volhynian Jews," 91–96; Pohl, "Schauplatz," 158–162.

71. For the Judenrat negotiations, see letters of 8 and 10 May 1942, DAR 22/1/10=USHMM RG-31.017M-2. See also Grynberg, *Życie*, 588; Spektor, "Żydzi wołyńscy," 477; and Snyder, "West Volhynian Jews," 91–96.

72. ŻIH 301/1982; ŻIH 301/5657; *Sefer Lutsk*, "Calendar of Pain, Resistance and Destruction"; Grynberg, *Życie*, 584–586, quotation at 586.

73. Spektor, "Żydzi wołyńscy," 477; Snyder, "West Volhynian Jews," 91–96. For "useless eaters," see Grynberg, *Życie*, 577. Regarding the Great Synagogue in Kovel and for the quotations in the next paragraph, see ŻIH/1644. The inscriptions were noted by Hanoch Hammer. The Soviets used the synagogue to store grain.

CHAPTER 7: HOLOCAUST AND REVENGE

1. Gerlach, *Kalkulierte Morde*, 374; Szybieka, *Historia*, 337. Compare Edele, "States," 348, 361. On the 19 July ghetto order, see *Verbrechen*, 80.

2. On the first killing actions, see Gerlach, *Kalkulierte Morde*, 506, 549, 639; Matthäus, "Reibungslos," 260; Longerich, *Vernichtung*, 370 (women); Epstein, *Minsk*, 81; and Ehrenburg, *Black Book*, 116. On the 7–9 November killings, see Gerlach, *Kalkulierte Morde*, 506, 509, 624; Smolar, *Ghetto*, 41; Ehrenburg, *Black Book*, 118; and Rubenstein, *Unknown*, 237–238, 245, 251. Other symbolic murders: the Germans carried out an action on 23 February 1942 (Red Army Day) and shot Jewish women on 8 March 1942 (International Women's Day).

3. On the promised parade, see Braithwaite, *Moscow*, 252.

4. Smilovitsky, "Antisemitism," 207–208; Braithwaite, *Moscow*, 262.

5. See Brandenberger, *National Bolshevism*, 118–119.

6. Quotation: Brandenberger, *National Bolshevism*, 119.

7. Quotation: Projektgruppe, "Existiert," 90.

8. On the boots taken from dead or captured soldiers, see *Ich werde es nie vergessen*, 66, 188; and Merridale, *Ivan's War*, 138.

9. Gerlach, *Kalkulierte Morde*, 768; Epstein, *Minsk*, 22; Smolar, *Ghetto*, 15; Projektgruppe, "Existiert," 221.

10. On the humiliations reserved for Jews, see Rubenstein, *Unknown*, 256; also Ehrenburg, *Black Book*, 125. On Eberl, see Grabher, *Eberl*, 66. On the film, see Longerich, *Himmler*, 552.

11. On the "beauty contest," see Ehrenburg, *Black Book*, 132; and Smolar, *Ghetto*, 22. On the evening in autumn 1941, see Smolar, *Ghetto*, 46. Quotation: Rubenstein, *Unknown*, 244. At the nearby Koldychevo concentration camp, guards serially raped and murdered women; see Chiari, *Alltag*, 192.

12. Epstein, *Minsk*, 42 and passim. On the Soviet documents, see *Chiari*, Alltag, 249.

13. Epstein, *Minsk*, 130.

14. Projektgruppe, "Existiert," 228. For biographical details on Smolar, see "Ankieta," 10 August 1949, AAN, teczka osobowa 5344.

15. Cholawsky, "Judenrat," 117–120; Chiari, *Alltag*, 240; Smolar, *Ghetto*, 19.

16. On the signaling of danger, see Smolar, *Ghetto*, 62. On the Jewish policemen, see Epstein, *Minsk*, 125. On the gloves and socks, see Gerlach, *Kalkulierte Morde*, 680. On the guides, see Smolar, *Ghetto*, 95; and Projektgruppe, "Existiert," 164. For the ball, see Epstein, *Minsk*, 215.

17. Brakel, "Versorgung," 400–401.

18. On the funding, see Epstein, *Minsk*, 96, 194.

19. Klein, "Zwischen," 89. See also Hull, *Absolute Destruction*; Anderson, "Incident"; and Lagrou, "Guerre Honorable."

20. On Franz Halder and his nuclear-weapon fantasy, see Gerlach, *Kalkulierte Morde*, 558. On Himmler and the thirty million Slavs, see Sawicki, *Zburzenie*, 284. Quotation: Lück, "Partisanbekämpfung," 228.

21. Quotations: Birn, "Anti-Partisan Warfare," 286; *Verbrechen*, 469. See also Gerlach, *Kalkulierte Morde*, 566.

22. Szybieka, *Historia*, 348; Mironowicz, *Białoruś*, 158; Lück, "Partisanbekämpfung," 232; Klein, "Zwischen," 90.

23. Gerlach, *Kalkulierte Morde*, 680, 686.

24. Quotation: Matthäus, "Reibungslos," 261.

25. Smolar, *Ghetto*, 72; Cholawsky, "Judenrat," 125. For the figure 3,412, see Matthäus, "Reibungslos," 262. On Lipski, see Projektgruppe, "Existiert," 158.

26. Cholawsky, "Judenrat," 123; Epstein, *Minsk*, 133. On Heydrich, see Gerlach, *Kalkulierte Morde*, 694. On the fur coats, see Browning, *Origins*, 300.

27. On the figure cited, see Smolar, *Ghetto*, 98. Quotation: Ehrenburg, *Black Book*, 189. See also Cholawsky, "Judenrat," 126; and Gerlach, *Kalkulierte Morde*, 704.

28. On the gas vans, see Gerlach, *Kalkulierte Morde*, 1075; and Rubenstein, *Unknown*, 245, 248, 266–267. For "soul destroyers," see Projektgruppe, "Existiert," 162.

29. Rubenstein, *Unknown*, 246; see also Ehrenburg, *Black Book*, 132.

30. Smolar, *Ghetto*, 158; Projektgruppe, "Existiert," 231; Brakel, "Versorgung," 400–401. On the women and children, see Smilovitsky, "Antisemitism," 218.

31. On Zorin, see Slepyan, *Guerillas*, 209; and Epstein, *Minsk*, 24. On the raid, see Ehrenburg, *Black Book*, 135. On Rufeisen, see Matthäus, "Reibungslos," 254.

32. Tec, *Defiance*, 80, 82, 145, 185, quotation at 80; Slepyan, *Guerillas*, 210; Musial, "Sowjetische," 185, 201–202.

33. On the 23,000 partisans and the "partisan republics," see Lück, "Partisan-bekämpfung," 231. On the civilians, see Brakel, *Unter Rotem Stern*, 290, 304; Szybieka, *Historia*, 349; Slepyan, *Guerillas*, 81; and Mironowicz, *Białoruś*, 160. On the locomotives, see Gerlach, *Kalkulierte Morde*, 868.

34. Musial, *Mythos*, 189, 202; Lück, "Partisanbekämpfung," 238; Ingrao, *Chasseurs*, 131; *Verbrechen*, 495.

35. Slepyan, *Guerillas*, 17, 42.

36. Kravets and Gerassimova are quoted in Projektgruppe, "Existiert," 47, 126. For the use of "whore" as the standard mode of address, see Chiari, *Alltag*, 256. On the game of hide-and-seek, see Projektgruppe, "Existiert," 164.

37. On 18 August, see Lück, "Partisanbekämpfung," 232; and Westermann, "Ideological Soldiers," 57. On "special treatment," see Musial, *Mythos*, 145. On the villagers to be destroyed "like Jews," see Lück, "Partisanbekämpfung," 239.

38. Westermann, "Ideological Soldiers," 53, 54, 60; Gerlach, *Kalkulierte Morde*, 705, 919.

39. For the reckoning of 208,089 Jews killed in Belarus in 1942, see Brandon, "The Holocaust in 1942." This does not include the Białystok region, which was part of the BSSR in 1939–1941 but not after the war.

40. On Gottberg, see Klein, "Massenmörder," 95–99. On Bach and for the numbers cited, see Lück, "Partisanbekämpfung," 233, 239.

41. Stang, "Dirlewanger," 66–70; Ingrao, *Chasseurs*, 20–21, figure ("at least thirty thousand civilians") at 26, 132; Gerlach, *Kalkulierte Morde*, 958; MacLean, *Hunters*, 28, 133.

42. On the kill quotas, see Gerlach, *Kalkulierte Morde*, 890. On Operation Swamp Fever, see Gerlach, *Kalkulierte Morde*, 911–913, 930; Benz, *Einsatz*, 239; Matthäus, "Reibungslos," 267; and Ingrao, *Chasseurs*, 34. On Jeckeln, see Brakel, *Unter Rotem Stern*, 295. On Hornung, see Gerlach, *Kalkulierte Morde*, 946; and Klein, "Massen-mörder," 100.

43. Brakel, *Unter Rotem Stern*, 304; Smilovitsky, "Antisemitism," 220. On the prewar communists, see Rein, "Local Collaborators," 394.

44. On the eight hundred policemen and militiamen, see Musial, *Mythos*, 266. On the twelve thousand, see Mironowicz, *Białoruś*, 160. See also Slepyan, *Guerillas*, 209.

45. Szybieka, *Historia*, 345, 352; Mironowicz, *Białoruś*, 159.

46. On October 1942, see Nolte, "Partisan War," 274.

47. Klein, "Zwischen," 100.

48. On Operation Cottbus, see Gerlach, *Kalkulierte Morde*, 948; Pohl, *Herrschaft*, 293; Musial, *Mythos*, 195; and *Verbrechen*, 492. On the swine, see Lück, "Partisan-bekämpfung," 241.

49. On Operation Hermann, see Musial, *Mythos*, 212; and Gerlach, *Kalkulierte Morde*, 907.

50. On the shooting of 127 Poles, see Musial, *Mythos*, 210. See also Jasiewicz, *Zagłada*, 264–265.

51. Brakel, *Unter Rotem Stern*, 317; Gogun, *Stalinskie komandos*, 144.

52. Shephard, "Wild East," 174; Angrick, *Einsatzgruppe D*, 680–689. Quotation: Lück, "Partisanbekämpfung," 242.

53. Birn, "Anti-Partisan Warfare," 291; see also, generally, Klein, "Zwischen," 96.

54. Dallin, *Brigade*, 8–58.

55. Chiari, *Alltag*, 138; Szybieka, *Historia*, 346; Mironowicz, *Białoruś*, 148, 155.

56. Szybieka, *Historia*, 346.

57. Musial, "Sowjetische," 183.

58. On the figures cited ("fifteen thousand" and "ninety-two"), see Ingrao, *Chasseurs*, 36. For the figure of 5,295 localities, see Gerlach, *Kalkulierte Morde*, 943. On the 10,431 partisans reported shot, see Klee, *Gott mit uns*, 55. On the diary, see Lück, "Partisanbekämpfung," 239. See also Matthäus, "Reibungslos," 268.

59. Gerlach, *Kalkulierte Morde*, 1158.

60. On the killing of 17,431 people as traitors, see *Musial*, Mythos, 261. On class enemies, see Jasiewicz, *Zagłada*, 264–265.

61. Gerlach, *Kalkulierte Morde*, 1160. Chiari estimates that 276,000 Poles had been killed or moved by the end of the war; see *Alltag*, 306.

62. On the crematoria, see Gerlach, "Mogilev," 68. On Asgard, see Gerlach, *Kalkulierte Morde*, 425.

63. Arad, *Reinhard*, 136–137.

CHAPTER 8: THE NAZI DEATH FACTORIES

1. Compare two fundamental works by one historian: Arad, *Reinhard*, and Arad, *Soviet Union*.

2. Quotation: Wasser, *Raumplannung*, 61, also 77. On the special status of Lublin, see Arad, *Reinhard*, 14; Musiał, "Przypadek," 24; and Dwork, *Auschwitz*, 290. On the implementation of Generalplan Ost known as the "Zamość Action," see Autuchiewicz, "Stan," 71; Aly, *Architects*, 275; and Tooze, *Wages of Destruction*, 468. On the date cited (13 October 1941), see Pohl, "Znaczenie," 45.

3. Browning, *Origins*, 419; Rieger, *Globocnik*, 60.

4. On the lack of personnel, see Musiał, "Przypadek," 31. On German preferences, see Black, "Handlanger," 315.

5. Browning, *Origins*, 419; Black, "Handlanger," 320.

6. Evans, *Third Reich at War*, 84–90.

7. Quotation: Gerlach, "Wannsee," 782. See also Rieß, "Wirth," 244; Pohl, "Znaczenie," 45; and Poprzeczny, *Globocnik*, 163. On Wirth's role, see Black, "Prosty," 105; and Scheffler, "Probleme," 270, 276. The "euthanasia" program continued, with greater

stealth, now with the use of lethal injections and drug overdoses. Tens of thousands more Germans were killed in the years to come.

8. Kershaw, *Final Solution*, 71; Mazower, *Hitler's Empire*, 191 and passim.

9. Quotation: Kershaw, *Final Solution*, 66. See also, generally, Mallmann, "Rozwiązać," 85–95, date at 95; Horwitz, *Ghettostadt*, 154; and Friedländer, *Origins*, 314–318. On Lange, see Friedlander, *Origins*, 286; and Kershaw, *Final Solution*, 71.

10. According to Arad, Wirth was responsible for the design; see *Reinhard*, 24.

11. See Pohl, *Ostgalizien*; and Sandkühler, *Galizien*.

12. Arad, *Reinhard*, 44, 56; Młynarczyk, *Judenmord*, 252, 257. On 14 March, see Rieger, *Globocnik*, 108. On the 1,600 Jews who lacked labor documents, see Poprzeczny, *Globocnik*, 226.

13. Młynarczyk, *Judenmord*, 260.

14. On the daily quotas and more generally, see Młynarczyk, *Judenmord*, 260; and Pohl, *Verfolgung*, 94.

15. For the figure 434,508, see Witte, "New Document," 472. Pohl counts three survivors; see *Verfolgung*, 95. On Wirth, see Black, "Prosty," 104. The commander of Bełżec as of August 1942 was Gottlieb Hering.

16. On Cracow, see Grynberg, *Życie*, 3; Pohl, *Verfolgung*, 89; and Hecht, *Memories*, 66.

17. Pohl, *Verfolgung*, 95.

18. On 17 April, see Pohl, "Znaczenie," 49. On 1 June, see "Obóz zagłady," 134.

19. Grabher, *Eberl*, 70, 74.

20. On Frank, see Arad, *Reinhard*, 46; Berenstein, "Praca," 87; and Kershaw, *Final Solution*, 106. On the Trawniki men, see Młynarczyk, "Akcja," 55.

21. Quotation: Longerich, *Himmler*, 588.

22. Friedländer, *Extermination*, 349.

23. Gerlach, "Wannsee," 791. See also Pohl, "Znaczenie," 49.

24. Tooze, *Wages of Destruction*, 365, 549.

25. Gutman, *Resistance*, 198. Compare Aly, *Architects*, 211.

26. Quotation: Witte, "New Document," 477.

27. Arad, *Reinhard*, 61; Młynarczyk, "Akcja," 55; Urynowicz, "Zagłada," 108; Friedländer, *Extermination*, 428; Hilburg, "Ghetto," 108. On the promised bread and marmalade, see Berenstein, "Praca," 142. Quotation: FVA 2327.

28. Engelking, *Getto*, 661–665; Gutman, *Resistance*, 142.

29. Urynowicz, "Zagłada," 108–109; Trunk, *Judenrat*, 507.

30. Urynowicz, "Zagłada," 109–111. See also Gutman, *Resistance*, 142.

31. On Korczak, see Kassow, *History*, 268; and Friedländer, *Extermination*, 429. Quotation: Engelking, *Getto*, 676.

32. For the cited figures, see Friedländer, *Extermination*, 230. Higher estimates are in Drozdowski, "History," 192 (315,000), and Bartoszewski, *Warszawski pierścień*, 195 (310,322).

33. "Treblinka," 174. On the payment "in kind," see Trunk, *Judenrat*, 512.

34. On the sweat, see Arad, *Reinhard*, 64. On the fields and forests, see Wdowinski, *Saved*, 69.

35. On Wiernik, see Kopówka, *Treblinka*, 28.

36. Arad, *Reinhard*, 81; Mlynarczyk, "Treblinka," 266; "Obóz zagłady," 141; Królikowski, "Budowałem," 49.

37. On 22 August, see Evans, *Third Reich at War*, 290. On 23 August, see Mlynarczyk, "Treblinka," 262. On 24 August, see Wiernik, *Year*, 8. On 25 August, see Krzepicki, "Treblinka," 98. On 26 August, see Shoah 02694, in FVA. Stangl quotation (21 August): Sereny, *Darkness*, 157.

38. Arad, *Reinhard*, 87.

39. Wdowinski, *Saved*, 78; Arad, *Reinhard*, 65.

40. Stangl quotation: Arad, *Reinhard*, 186.

41. On Franz, see Arad, *Reinhard*, 189; Kopówka, *Treblinka*, 32; Glazar, *Falle*, 118; and "Treblinka," 194.

42. On the Polish government, see Libionka, "ZWZ-AK," 36–53. On the contemplated attack, see Libionka, "Polska konspiracja," 482. On the postcards, see Hilberg, "Judenrat," 34. On the postal service, see Sakowska, *Ludzie*, 312.

43. On the "clinic," see "Obóz zagłady," 137; Glazar, *Falle*, 51; Arad, *Reinhard*, 122; and Mlynarczyk, "Treblinka," 267. On the "station," see "Obóz zagłady," 137; Arad, *Reinhard*, 123; and Willenberg, *Revolt*, 96. On the orchestra, see "Tremblinki," 40; and "Treblinka," 193. On the Yiddish, see Krzepicki, "Treblinka," 89.

44. "Treblinka," 178; Arad, *Reinhard*, 37; Mlynarczyk, "Treblinka," 269. On the rapes, see Willenberg, *Revolt*, 105.

45. Arad, *Reinhard*, 108; Młynarczyk, "Treblinka," 267; Willenberg, *Revolt*, 65.

46. Arad, *Reinhard*, 119; Mlynarczyk, "Treblinka," 259, 269.

47. Kopówka, *Treblinka*, 34; Mlynarczyk, "Treblinka," 263, 269. On the "metamorphosis," see Rajchman, *Le dernier Juif*, 88.

48. Rajgrodzki, "W obozie zagłady," 107. Arad, *Reinhard*, 174. On the Germans warming themselves, see Wiernik, *Year*, 29. On the women naked in the cold, see Rajchman, *Le dernier Juif*, 96.

49. For "It's no use," see Rajchman, *Le dernier Juif*, 33. On the embrace and Ruth Dorfmann, see Willenberg, *Revolt*, 56, 65.

50. On the local economy, see Willenberg, *Revolt*, 30; and Rusiniak, *Obóz*, 26. On "Europe," see Rusiniak, *Obóz*, 27.

51. Friedländer, *Extermination*, 598. On Stalingrad, see Rajgrodzki, "W obozie zagłady," 109.

52. On the dismantling, see Arad, *Reinhard*, 373. On Operation Harvest Festival (Erntefest), see Arad, *Reinhard*, 366. Some 15,000 Białystok Jews were also shot; see Bender, "Białystok," 25.

53. The sources of the Treblinka count are Witte, "New Document," 472, which provides the Germans' count for 1942 of 713,555 (intercepted by the British); and

Młynarczyk, "Treblinka," 281, which supplies a 1943 reckoning of 67,308. For the Radom estimate, see Młynarczyk, *Judenmord*, 275. Wiernik claims that there were two transports of (uncircumcised) Poles; see *Year*, 35. "Obóz zagłady," a report published in Warsaw in early 1946, gives the estimate 731,600, and provides much basic information.

54. Rusiniak, *Obóz*, 20.

55. Kamenec, "Holocaust," 200–201; Kamenec, "Deportation," 116, 123, figure at 130.

56. Hilberg, *Destruction* (vol. III), 939, 951; Browning, *Origins*, 421.

57. Compare Brandon, "Holocaust in 1942"; Dwork, *Auschwitz*, 326.

58. Pohl, *Verfolgung*, 107; Hilberg, *Destruction* (vol. III), 959; Stark, *Hungarian Jews*, 30; Długoborski, "Żydzi," 147.

59. Although we know the number of dead in these facilities with some precision, the precise number of Polish Jews is difficult to extract from the larger figure. Although Treblinka, Sobibór, and Bełżec were primarily killing centers for the Polish Jews of the General Government, other people also died in these three places, especially in 1943: Czechoslovak Jews, German Jews, Dutch Jews, French Jews, as well as Poles and Roma.

60. On the Roma, see Pohl, *Verfolgung*, 113–116; Evans, *Third Reich at War*, 72–73, 531–535; and Klein, "Gottberg," 99.

61. For the "wonderful song," see Glazar, 57. On music as "revolutionary," see Rajgrodzki, "W obozie zagłady," 109. On "el male rachamim," see Arad, *Reinhard*, 216.

CHAPTER 9: RESISTANCE AND INCINERATION

1. Lück, "Partisanbekämpfung," 246; Zaloga, *Bagration*, 27, 28, 43, 56.

2. Zaloga, *Bagration*, 7, 69, 71. The Americans had been in Italy since 1943.

3. Grossman, *Road*, 27. See also Furet, *Passé*, 536; and Gerard, *Bones*, 187–189. Grossman may not have understood that the signs of the mass murder were visible because the local Polish population had been looking for valuables. It would have been impossible for him to write that the guards at Treblinka were Soviet citizens.

4. Engelking, *Żydzi*, 260. See also Miłosz, *Legends*; and Snyder, "Wartime Lies."

5. Tokarzewski-Karaszewicz, "U podstaw tworzenia Armii Krajowej," 124–157.

6. On fighting for the restoration of Poland as a democratic republic, see Libionka, "ZWZ-AK," 19, 23, 34. On the NKVD, see Engelking, *Żydzi*, 147.

7. Libionka, "ZWZ-AK," 24.

8. Wdowinski, *Saved*, 78; Arens, "Jewish Military," 205.

9. Wdowinski, *Saved*, 79, 82; Libionka, "Pomnik," 110; Libionka, "Deconstructing," 4; Libionka, "Apokryfy," 166.

10. On Agudas Israel, see Bacon, *Politics of Tradition*.

11. The story of the formation of the Jewish Combat Organization is complex. See Sakowska, *Ludzie*, 322–325; and Zuckerman, *Surplus*.

12. On the rescue organization, see Bartoszewski, *Warszawski pierścień*, 16; and Libionka, "ZWZ-AK," 27, 33, 36, 39, 56.

13. Libionka, "ZWZ-AK," 60, 71.

14. Bartoszewski, *Ten jest*, 32; Sakowska, *Ludzie*, 321, quotation (Marek Lichtenbaum) at 326.

15. Gutman, *Resistance*, 198.

16. Engelking, *Warsaw Ghetto*, 763; Kopka, *Warschau*, 33–34.

17. On the arms cache, see Libionka, "ZWZ-AK," 69; and Moczarski, *Rozmowy*, 232. On the anti-Semitic minority, see Engelking, *Żydzi*, 193, and passim.

18. Quotation (Himmler): Kopka, *Warschau*, 36.

19. Szapiro, *Wojna*, 9; Milton, *Stroop*, passim; Libionka, "Polska konspiracja," 472.

20. Quotation (Gustawa Jarecka): Kassow, *History*, 183.

21. Engelking, *Warsaw Ghetto*, 774; Engelking, *Getto warszawskie*, 733; Gutman, *Resistance*, 201.

22. Szapiro, *Wojna*, passim; also Libionka, "ZWZ-AK," 82.

23. Quotations: Zuckerman, *Surplus*, 357; Szapiro, *Wojna*, 35.

24. On the flags, see Milton, *Stroop.* Quotation: Moczarski, *Rozmowy*, 200.

25. The Edelman testimony is in "Proces Stroopa Tom 1," SWMW-874, IVk 222/51, now at IPN.

26. Moczarski, *Rozmowy*, 252, quotation at 253.

27. Engelking, *Warsaw Ghetto*, 794.

28. Puławski, *W obliczu*, 412, 420–421, 446. On the pope, see Libionka, "Głową w mur."

29. Quotation: Engelking, *Warsaw Ghetto*, 795. On the eleven attempts to help Jews, see Engelking, *Getto warszawskie*, 745; and Libionka, "ZWZ-AK," 79. On the Soviet propaganda, see Redlich, *Propaganda*, 49.

30. On Wilner, see Sakowska, Ludzie, 326.

31. Quotation: Engelking, *Getto warszawskie*, 750; Gutman, *Resistance*, 247; Marrus, "Jewish Resistance," 98; Friedländer, *Extermination*, 598.

32. For the numbers cited, see Bartoszewski, *Warszawski pierścień*, 256. On 1 June 1943, see Kopka, *Warschau*, 39.

33. See Zimmerman, "Attitude," 120; and Libionka, "ZWZ-AK," 119–123.

34. Bartoszewski, *Warszawski pierścień*, 242.

35. Madajczyk, "Generalplan," 15; Rutherford, *Prelude*, 218; Aly, *Architects*, 275; Ahonen, *People*, 39.

36. On March 1943, see Borodziej, *Uprising*, 41. On the extermination of Jews as a motive, see Puławski, *W obliczu*, 442. For the 6,214 instances of partisan resistance, see BA-MA, RH 53–23 (WiG), 66.

37. On 13 October 1943, see Bartoszewski, *Warszawski pierścień*, 286. On the plaster and earth, see Kopka, *Warschau*, 58–59.

38. Bartoszewski, *Warszawski pierścień*, 331, 348, 376, 378, 385, figure at 427.

39. Kopka, *Warschau*, 40.

40. Ibid., 46, 53, 75.

41. Quotation: Kopka, *Warschau*, 69.

42. Kopka, *Warschau*, 60.

43. On the Bagration connection, see Zaloga, *Bagration*, 82.

44. The Allies discussed the future Polish border at the Tehran summit of 28 November–1 December 1943; see Ciechanowski, *Powstanie*, 121.

45. *Operatsia "Seim,"* 5 and passim.

46. On Bielski's partisan unit, see Libionka, "ZWZ-AK," 112. For multiple perspectives on Bielski, see Snyder, "Caught Between."

47. On 22 July 1944, see Borodziej, *Uprising*, 64.

48. On the exclusion and the arms, see Borodziej, *Uprising*, 61.

49. The atmosphere is conveyed and the battles described in Davies, *Rising '44*. On the fact that no major targets were captured, see Borodziej, *Uprising*, 75.

50. Engelking, *Żydzi*, 91 for Zylberberg, and passim; National Armed Forces at 62, 86, 143.

51. On Aronson, see Engelking, *Żydzi*, 61, National Armed Forces at 62, 86, 143; and Kopka, *Warschau*, 42, 106, 110, "indifference" quotation at 101.

52. Krannhals, *Warschauer Aufstand*, 124.

53. Ibid., 124–127.

54. Wroniszewski, *Ochota*, 567, 568, 627, 628, 632, 654, 694; Dallin, *Kaminsky*, 79–82. On the Marie Curie Institute, see Hanson, *Civilian Population*, 90. Quotations: Mierecki, *Varshavskoe*, 642 ("Mass executions"); Dallin, *Kaminsky*, 81 ("they raped . . . "); Mierecki, *Varshavskoe*, 803 ("robbing . . . ").

55. Madaczyk, *Ludność*, 61.

56. On Himmler's orders, see Sawicki, *Zburzenie*, 32, 35; and Krannhals, *Warschauer Aufstand*, 420. On the human shields (and other atrocities), see Stang, "Dirlewanger," 71; Serwański, *Życie*, 64; Mierecki, *Varshavskoe*, 547, 751; and MacLean, *Hunters*, 182. See also Ingrao, *Chasseurs*, 180. For estimates of forty thousand civilians murdered, see Hanson, *Civilian Population*, 90; and Borodziej, *Uprising*, 81. Ingrao gives the figure of 12,500 shot in one day by the Dirlewanger unit alone; see *Chasseurs*, 53.

57. On the three hospitals, see Hanson, *Civilian Population*, 88; and MacLean, *Hunters*, 182. On the gang rapes and murder, see Ingrao, *Chasseurs*, 134, 150.

58. On the factory where two thousand people were shot, see Mierecki, *Varshavskoe*, 547. Quotation: Hanson, *Civilian Population*, 88.

59. Borodziej, *Uprising*, 81.

60. Klimaszewski, *Verbrennungskommando*, 25–26, 53, 69, 70. On the Jewish laborer, see Engelking, *Żydzi*, 210. See also Białoszewski, *Pamiętnik*, 28.

61. Quotation: Borodziej, *Uprising*, 91. See also Ciechanowski, *Powstanie*, 138, 145, 175, 196, 205.

62. Quotations: Borodziej, *Uprising*, 94.

63. Quotation: Borodziej, *Uprising*, 94. See also Davies, *Rising '44*.

64. On Himmler, see Borodziej, *Uprising*, 79, 141; Mierecki, *Varshavskoe*, 807; Krannhals, *Warschauer Aufstand*, 329 (and ghetto experience); and Ingrao, *Chasseurs*, 182.

65. On Bach and the Wehrmacht, see Sawicki, *Zburzenie*, 284; and Krannhals, *Warschauer Aufstand*, 330–331. On the last library, see Borodziej, *Uprising*, 141.

66. Estimates: Ingrao, *Les chasseurs* (200,000); Borodziej, *Uprising*, 130 (185,000); Pohl, *Verfolgung*, 121 (170,000); Krannhals, *Warschauer Aufstand*, 124 (166,000).

67. On Landau and Ringelblum, see Bartoszewski, *Warszawski pierścień*, 385. On Ringelblum specifically, see Engelking, *Warsaw Ghetto*, 671; see also, generally, Kassow, *History*.

68. Estimates of the numbers of people in hiding are in Paulson, *Secret City*, 198.

69. Strzelecki, *Deportacja*, 25, 35–37; Długoborski, "Żydzi," 147; Löw, *Juden*, 455, 466, 471, Bradfisch and trains at 472, 476.

70. Kopka, *Warschau*, 51, 116.

71. Strzelecki, *Deportacja*, 111.

CHAPTER 10: ETHNIC CLEANSINGS

1. On the importance of German precedents, see Brandes, *Weg*, 58, 105, 199, and passim; also Ahonen, *After the Expulsion*, 15–25.

2. On Polish and Czech wartime planning for deportations, generally less radical than what would actually be achieved, see Brandes, *Weg*, 57, 61, 117, 134, 141, 160, 222, 376, and passim.

3. Quotation: Borodziej, *Niemcy*, 61. In Polish the distinction is between *narodowy* and *narodowościowy*.

4. Mikołajczyk quotation: Nitschke, *Wysiedlenie*, 41; see Naimark, *Fires*, 124. On Roosevelt, see Brandes, *Weg*, 258. On Hoover, see Kersten, "Forced," 78. On Churchill, see Frank, *Expelling*, 74. On the uprising, see Borodziej, *Niemcy*, 109.

5. See Brandes, *Weg*, 267–272.

6. Frank, *Expelling*, 89.

7. On Hungary, see Ungvary, *Schlacht*, 411–432; and Naimark, *Russians*, 70. On Poland, see Curp, *Clean Sweep*, 51. Yugoslav quotation: Naimark, *Russians*, 71.

8. On the incidence of rape in the earlier occupation, see Gross, *Revolution*, 40; and Shumuk, *Perezhyte*, 17. Worth considering are the reflections of a victim: Anonyma, *Eine Frau*, 61.

9. Quotation: Salomini, *L'Union*, 123; also 62, 115–116, 120, 177. The point about conscripts is made inter alia in *Vertreibung*, 26.

10. *Vertreibung*, 33. An admirable discussion is Naimark, *Russians*, 70–74. On Grass, see *Beim Häuten*, 321.

11. On the burial of the mother, see *Vertreibung*, 197.

12. On the 520,000 Germans, see Urban, *Verlust*, 517. On the 40,000 Poles, see Zwolski, "Deportacje," 49. Gurianov estimates 39,000–48,000; see "Obzor," 205. Still

more Poles seem to have been deported from Soviet Belarus; see Szybieka, *Historia*, 362. On the Hungarian civilians, see Ungvary, *Schlacht*, 411–432. On the mines, see Nitschke, *Wysiedlenie*, 71. For the 287,000 people taken as laborers and Camp 517, see Wheatcroft, "Scale," 1345.

13. For the 185,000 German civilians, see Urban, *Verlust*, 117. For the 363,000 German prisoners of war, see Overmans, *Verluste*, 286; Wheatcroft counts 356,687; see "Scale," 1353. Tens of thousands of Italian, Hungarian, and Romanian soldiers also perished after having surrendered to the Red Army. Regarding the Italians, Schlemmer estimates 60,000 deaths; see *Italianer*, 74. Regarding the Hungarians, Stark estimates 200,000 (which seems improbably high); see *Human Losses*, 33. See also Biess, "Vom Opfer," 365.

14. On the psychological sources of the evacuation problem, see Nitschke, *Wysiedlenie*, 48. Quotation: Hillgruber, *Germany*, 96. See also Steinberg, "Third Reich," 648; and Arendt, *In der Gegenwart*, 26–29.

15. On the Gauleiters and the ships, see Nitschke, *Wysiedlenie*, 52–60.

16. On Jahntz, see *Vertreibung*, 227. Quotation: Grass, *Beim Häuten*, 170.

17. Nitschke, *Wysiedlenie*, 135; Jankowiak, "Cleansing," 88–92. Ahonen estimates 1.25 million returns; see *People*, 87.

18. Staněk, *Odsun*, 55–58. See also Naimark, *Fires*, 115–117; Glassheim, "Mechanics," 206–207; and Ahonen, *People*, 81. The Czech-German Joint Commission gives a range of 19,000 to 30,000 fatalities; see *Community*, 33. Some 160,000 Germans from Czechoslovakia lost their lives fighting in the Wehrmacht. For Grass, see his *Beim Häuten*, 186.

19. Quotation: Nitschke, *Wysiedlenie*, 136; also Borodziej, *Niemcy*, 144. On the movement of 1.2 million people, see Jankowiak, *Wysiedlenie*, 93, also 100. Borodziej estimates 300,000–400,000 (*Niemcy*, 67); Curp gives the figure 350,000 (*Clean Sweep*, 53). See also Jankowiak, "Cleansing," 89–92.

20. On Potsdam, see Brandes, *Weg*, 404, 458, 470; and Naimark, *Fires*, 111.

21. Quotation: Naimark, *Fires*, 109. On Aleksander Zawadzki, the Silesian governor, see Urban, *Verlust*, 115; and Nitschke, *Wysiedlenie*, 144. On Olsztyn, see Nitschke, *Wysiedlenie*, 158.

22. On Public Security, see Borodziej, *Niemcy*, 80. Quotation: Stankowski, *Obozy*, 261.

23. For the 6,488 Germans who died at the Łambinowice camp, see Stankowski, *Obozy*, 280. Urban (*Verlust*, 129) estimates that, of the two hundred thousand Germans in Polish camps, sixty thousand died; the latter number seems high in light of the figures for individual camps. Stankowski gives a range of 27,847–60,000; see *Obozy*, 281. On Gęborski and Cedrowski, see Stankowski, *Obozy*, 255–256. On the forty prisoners murdered on 4 October 1945, see Borodziej, *Niemcy*, 87.

24. On the freight trains, see Nitschke, *Wysiedlenie*, 154.

25. On the robberies, see Urban, *Verlust*, 123; and Borodziej, *Niemcy*, 109. Nitschke (*Wysiedlenie*, 161) estimates that 594,000 Germans crossed the border at this time; Ahonen (*People*, 93) gives the figure 600,000.

26. On the November plan, see Ahonen, *People*, 93. For the figures cited, see Nitschke, *Wysiedlenie*, 182, 230. Compare Jankowiak, who gives 2,189,286 as a total for 1946 and 1947 (including only those in registered transports); see *Wysiedlenie*, 501. Death tolls in transports to the British sector are given in Frank, *Expelling*, 258–259; and Ahonen, *People*, 141.

27. Regarding the four hundred thousand Germans who died, see the original estimate in *Vertreibung*, 40–41; the agreement in Nitschke, *Wysiedlenie*, 231, and Borodziej, *Niemcy*, 11; the discussion and implicit endorsement in Overmans, "Personelle Verluste," 52, 59, 60; and the critique of exaggeration in Haar, "Entstehensgeschichte," 262–270. Ahonen estimates six hundred thousand deaths; see *People*, 140.

28. See the discussion of the difference between policies of deliberate murder and other forms of mortality in the Introduction and the Conclusion.

29. Simons in *Eastern Europe* introduces the geoethnic issues well.

30. On the relationship between the war and the communist takeovers generally, see Abrams, "Second World War"; Gross, "Social Consequences"; and Simons, *Eastern Europe*.

31. Secretary of State James Byrnes and the shifting US position are discussed in Ahonen, *After the Expulsion*, 26–27. See also Borodziej, *Niemcy*, 70.

32. Quotation: Brandes, *Weg*, 437. See also Kersten, "Forced," 81; Sobór-Świderska, *Berman*, 202; and Torańska, *Oni*, 273.

33. See Snyder, *Reconstruction*.

34. Documentation of the UPA's plans for and actions toward Poles can be found in TsDAVO 3833/1/86/6a; 3833/1/131/13–14; 3833/1/86/19–20; and 3933/3/1/60. Of related interest are DAR 30/1/16=USHMM RG-31.017M-1; DAR 301/1/5=USHMM RG-31.017M-1; and DAR 30/1/4=USHMM RG-31.017M-1. These OUN-B and UPA wartime declarations coincide with postwar interrogations (see GARF, R-9478/1/398) and recollections of Polish survivors (on the massacre of 12–13 July 1943, for example, see OKAW, II/737, II/1144, II/2099, II/2650, II/953, and II/775) and Jewish survivors (for example, ŻIH 301/2519; and Adini, *Dubno: sefer zikaron*, 717–718). The fundamental study is now Motyka, *Ukraińska partyzantka*. See also Il'iushyn, *OUN-UPA*, and Armstrong, *Ukrainian Nationalism*. I sought to explain this conflict in "Causes," *Reconstruction*, "Life and Death," and *Sketches*.

35. On the 780,000 Poles shipped to communist Poland, see Slivka, *Deportatsii*, 25. On the 483,099 dispatched from communist Poland to Soviet Ukraine, see Cariewskaja, *Teczka specjalna*, 544. On the one hundred thousand Jews, see Szajnok, *Polska a Izrael*, 40. For a discussion of Operation Vistula, see Snyder, *Reconstruction*; and Snyder, "To Resolve."

36. On the 182,543 Ukrainians deported from Soviet Ukraine to the Gulag, see Weiner, "Nature," 1137. On the 148,079 Red Army veterans, see Polian, "Violence," 129. See also, generally, Applebaum, *Gulag*, 463.

37. For further details regarding the 140,660 people resettled by force, see Snyder, *Reconstruction*; or Snyder, "To Resolve."

38. Snyder, *Reconstruction*; and Snyder, "To Resolve"; Motyka, *Ukraińska partyzantka*, 535. See also Burds, "Agentura."

39. Polian, *Against Their Will*, 166–168. In Operation South some 35,796 people were deported, on the night of 5 July 1949, from territories that the Soviets had annexed from Romania.

40. Polian, *Against Their Will*, 134.

41. See Polian, *Against Their Will*, 134–155, for all of the cited figures. See also Naimark, *Fires*, 96; Lieberman, *Terrible Fate*, 206–207; and Burleigh, *Third Reich*, 749.

42. On the eight million people returned to the Soviet Union, see Polian, "Violence," 127. On the twelve million Ukrainians, Belarusians, and Poles, see Gerlach (*Kalkulierte Morde*, 1160), who has examined these matters closely and estimates a minimum of three million displacements in Belarus alone.

43. Weiner ("Nature," 1137) notes that the Soviets reported killing 110,825 people as Ukrainian nationalists between February 1944 and May 1946. The NKVD estimated that 144,705 Chechens, Ingush, Balkars, and Karachai died as a result of deportation or shortly after resettlement (by 1948); see Lieberman, *Terrible Fate*, 207.

44. Survivors of the famine mention this in their memoirs. See Potichnij, "1946–1947 Famine," 185.

45. See Mastny, *Cold War*, 30. On Zhdanov's heart attack, see Sebag Montefiore, *Court*, 506.

CHAPTER 11: STALINIST ANTI-SEMITISM

1. On the murder, see Rubenstein, *Pogrom*, 1. On Tsanava, see Mavrogordato, "Lowlands," 527; and Smilovitsky, "Antisemitism," 207.

2. On the *Black Book of Soviet Jewry*, see Kostyrchenko, *Shadows*, 68. On the stars, see Weiner, "Nature," 1150; and Weiner, *Making Sense*, 382. On the synagogue used to store grain, see ŻIH/1644. On the ashes from Babi Yar, see Rubenstein, *Pogrom*, 38. See also, generally, Veidlinger, *Yiddish Theater*, 277.

3. Rubenstein, *Pogrom*, 35.

4. On Crimea, see Redlich, *War*, 267; and Redlich, *Propaganda*, 57. See also Lustiger, *Stalin*, 155, 192; Luks, "Brüche," 28; and Veidlinger, "Soviet Jewry," 9–10.

5. On the state secret, see Lustiger, *Stalin*, 108. On the decorations for bravery, see Weiner, "Nature," 1151; and Lustiger, *Stalin*, 138.

6. These figures were discussed in earlier chapters and will be again in the Conclusion. Regarding Jewish deaths in the USSR, see Arad, *Soviet Union*, 521 and 524. Filimoshin ("Ob itogakh," 124) gives an estimate of 1.8 million civilians deliberately killed under German occupation; to this I would add about a million starved prisoners of war and about four hundred thousand undercounted deaths from the siege of Leningrad. So, with both civilians and prisoners of war included, and very roughly, I

would estimate 2.6 million Jews and 3.2 million inhabitants of Soviet Russia killed as civilians or prisoners of war. If prisoners of war are reckoned as military casualties, then the Jewish figure will exceed the Russian one.

7. Franklin D. Roosevelt, Winston Churchill, and Josif Stalin, "Declaration Concerning Atrocities Made at the Moscow Conference," 30 October 1943. This was part of the Moscow Declaration.

8. On the "sons of the nation," see Arad, *Soviet Union*, 539. On Khrushchev, see Salomini, *L'Union*, 242; and Weiner, *Making Sense*, 351.

9. Thoughtful introductions to postwar Soviet culture are Kozlov, "Soviet Literary Audiences"; and Kozlov, "Historical Turn."

10. On the seventy thousand Jews permitted to leave Poland for Israel, see Szajnok, *Polska a Izrael*, 49. On Koestler, see Kostyrchenko, *Shadows*, 102.

11. On Rosh Hashanah and the synagogue, see Veidlinger, "Soviet Jewry," 13–16; and Szajnok, *Polska a Izrael*, 159. On Zhemchuzhina, see Rubenstein, *Pogrom*, 46. On Gorbman, see Luks, "Brüche," 34. On the policy turn generally, see Szajnok, *Polska a Izrael*, 40, 82, 106, 111–116.

12. On the *Pravda* article, see Kostyrchenko, *Shadows*, 152. On the decreased number of Jews in high party positions (thirteen percent to four percent from 1945 to 1952), see Kostyrchenko, *Gosudarstvennyi antisemitizm*, 352. The Grossman quotation is from Chandler's translation of *Everything Flows*.

13. On the dissolution of the Jewish Anti-Fascist Committee, see Kostyrchenko, *Shadows*, 104. For the train quotation, see Der Nister, *Family Mashber*, 71. For the MGB report, see Kostyrchenko, *Gosudarstvennyi antisemitizm*, 327.

14. Molotov quotation: Gorlizki, *Cold Peace*, 76. See also Redlich, *War*, 149.

15. Redlich, *War*, 152; Rubenstein, *Pogrom*, 55–60.

16. On the one hundred thousand Jews from the Soviet Union, see Szajnok, *Polska a Izrael*, 40.

17. This was true of most of the postwar regimes, including the Czechoslovak, Romanian, and Hungarian.

18. Banac, *With Stalin Against Tito*, 117–142; Kramer, *Konsolidierung*, 81–84. See also Gaddis, *United States*.

19. On Gomułka and Berman, see Sobór-Świderska, *Berman*, 219, 229, 240; Paczkowski, *Trzy twarze*, 109; and Torańska, *Oni*, 295–296.

20. On the exchange between Stalin and Gomułka, see Naimark, "Gomułka and Stalin," 244. Quotation: Sobór-Świderska, *Berman*, 258.

21. For the Smolar quotation and generally, see Shore, "Język," 56.

22. Shore, "Język," 60. All of that said, there were Polish-Jewish historians who did much valuable research on the Holocaust in the postwar years, some of it indispensable for the present study.

23. This was part of the slogan of one of the more striking propaganda posters, executed by Włodzimierz Zakrzewski.

24. Consulte Torańska, *Oni*, 241, 248

25. Gniazdowski, "Ustalić liczbę," 100–104 and passim.

26. On the Soviet ambassador, see Sobór-Świderska, *Berman*, 202; and Paczkowski, *Trzy twarze*, 114. For the percentage of high-ranking Ministry of Public Security officers who were Jewish by self-declaration or origin, see Eisler, "1968," 41.

27. *Proces z vedením*, 9 and passim; Lukes, "New Evidence," 171.

28. Torańska, *Oni*, 322–323.

29. See Shore, "Children."

30. This explanation of the absence of a communist blood purge in Poland can be found inter alia in Luks, "Brüche," 47. One Polish communist leader apparently murdered another during the war; this too might have bred caution.

31. Paczkowski, *Trzy twarze*, 103.

32. The Soviet Union did annex the Kuril Islands.

33. Weinberg, *World at Arms*, 81.

34. Quotation: Sebag Montefiore, *Court*, 536.

35. Service, *Stalin*, 554. On central Asia, see Brown, *Rise and Fall*, 324.

36. Kramer, "Konsolidierung," 86–90.

37. The argument about the difference between the 1950s and the 1930s is developed in Zubok, *Empire*, 77. See also Gorlizki, *Cold Peace*, 97.

38. On Shcherbakov, see Brandenberger, *National Bolshevism*, 119 and passim; Kuromiya, "Jews," 523, 525; and Zubok, *Empire*, 7.

39. On the Victory Day parade, see Brandenberger, "Last Crime," 193. On Etinger, see Brent, *Plot*, 11. See also Lustiger, *Stalin*, 213. Stalin's concern with medical terrorism dated back to at least 1930; see Prystaiko, *Sprava*, 49.

40. On Karpai, see Brent, *Plot*, 296.

41. Lukes, "New Evidence," 165.

42. Ibid., 178–180; Lustiger, *Stalin*, 264.

43. For the quotation and the proportion (eleven out of fourteen defendants of Jewish origin), see *Proces z vedením*, 44–47, at 47. On the denunciations, see Margolius Kovály, *Cruel Star*, 139.

44. For Slánský's confession, see *Proces z vedením*, 66, 70, 72. For the death penalty and the hangman, see Lukes, "New Evidence," 160, 185. On Margolius, see Margolius Kovály, *Cruel Star*, 141.

45. On Poland, see Paczkowski, *Trzy twarze*, 162.

46. Quotation: Brent, *Plot*, 250.

47. Kostyrchenko, *Shadows*, 264; Brent, *Plot*, 267. On the dance, see Service, *Stalin*, 580.

48. On Mikhoels as Lear, see Veidlinger, *Yiddish Theater*.

49. For "every Jew . . . ," see Rubenstein, *Pogrom*, 62. For "their nation had been saved . . . ," see Brown, *Rise and Fall*, 220.

50. Quotations: Kostyrchenko, *Shadows*, 290. See also Lustiger, *Stalin*, 250.

51. On Karpai, see Kostyrchenko, *Gosudarstvennyi antisemitizm*, 466; and Brent, *Plot*, 296.

52. On the drafting and redrafting, see Kostyrchenko, *Gosudarstvennyi antisemitizm*, 470–478. On Grossman, see Brandenberger, "Last Crime," 196. See also Luks, "Brüche," 47, The Grossman quotation is from *Life and Fate* at 398.

53. On Ehrenburg, see Brandenberger, "Last Crime," 197.

54. For the rumors, see Brandenberger, "Last Crime," 202. For the number of doctors, see Luks, "Brüche," 42.

55. Khlevniuk, "Stalin as dictator," 110, 118. On Stalin's nonappearance at factories, farms, and government offices after the Second World War, see Service, *Stalin*, 539.

56. On Stalin's security chiefs, see Brent, *Plot*, 258.

57. Stalin ordered beatings on 13 November; see Brent, *Plot*, 224. On the trial, see Lustiger, *Stalin*, 250.

58. For details on the "anti-Zionist campaign" of 1968, see Stola, *Kampania antysyjonistyczna*; and Paczkowski, *Pół wieku*.

59. Rozenbaum, "March Events," 68.

60. On the earlier Soviet practice, see Szajnok, *Polska a Izrael*, 160.

61. Stola, "Hate Campaign," 19, 31. On the "fifth column, " see Rozenbaum, "1968," 70.

62. Stola, "Hate Campaign," 20.

63. For the figure of 2,591 people arrested, see Stola, "Hate Campaign," 17. For the Gdańsk railway station, see Eisler, "1968," 60.

64. See Judt, *Postwar*, 422–483; and Simons, *Eastern Europe*.

65. Brown, *Rise and Fall*, 396.

CONCLUSION: HUMANITY

1. Compare Moyn, "In the Aftermath." The interpretations here arise from arguments that are documented in the chapters; the annotation is therefore limited.

2. Perhaps a million people died in the German camps (as opposed to the death facilities and shooting and starvation sites). See Orth, *System*.

3. Compare Keegan, *Face of Battle*, 55; and Gerlach and Werth, "State Violence," 133.

4. Most of the remainder of those who starved were in Kazakhstan. I am counting the deaths in Ukraine as intended, and those in Kazakhstan as foreseeable. Future research might change the estimation of intentionality.

5. This and the below quotation follow Robert Chandler's 2010 translation of *Everything Flows*, unpublished as I write. See also *Life and Fate* at 29.

6. A sustained discussion of the moral economy of land and murder is Kiernan, *Blood and Soil*.

7. Mao's China exceeded Hitler's Germany in the famine of 1958–1960, which killed some thirty million people.

8. For "belligerent complicity," see Furet, *Fascism and Communism*, 2. Compare Edele, "States," 348. Hitler quotation: Lück, "Partisanbekämpfung," 228.

9. Todorov, *Mémoire du mal*, 90.

10. Milgram, "Behavior Study," still repays reading.

11. Kołakowski, *Main Currents*, 43.

12. On international bystanding, see Power, *Problem*.

13. Fest, *Das Gesicht*, 108, 162.

14. As Harold James notes, theories of violent modernization actually fare badly in purely economic terms; see *Europe Reborn*, 26. Buber-Neumann quotation: *Under Two Dictators*, 35.

15. The most significant German crime in Soviet Russia was the deliberate starvation of Leningrad, in which about a million people died. The Germans killed a relatively small number of Jews in Soviet Russia, perhaps sixty thousand. They also killed at least a million prisoners of war from Soviet Russia in the Dulags and the Stalags. These people are usually reckoned as military losses in Soviet and Russian estimates; since I am counting them as victims of a deliberate killing policy, I am *increasing* the estimate of 1.8 million in Filimoshin, "Ob itogakh," 124. I believe that the Russian estimate for deaths at Leningrad is too low by about four hundred thousand people, so I add that as well. If Boris Sokolov is right, and Soviet military losses were far higher than the conventional estimates, then most of the people in the higher estimates were soldiers. If Ellman and Maksudov are right, and Soviet military losses were in fact lower, then most of these people were civilians: often civilians not under German occupation. See Sokolov, "How to Count," 451–457; and Ellman, "Soviet Deaths," 674–680.

16. On the deaths of 516,841 Gulag inmates, see Zemskov, "Smertnost'," 176. On the four million Soviet citizens in the Gulag (including the special settlements), see Khlevniuk, *Gulag*, 307.

17. Brandon and Lower estimate 5.5–7 million total losses in Soviet Ukraine during the war; see "Introduction," 11.

18. For an introduction to the memory culture, see Goujon, "Memorial."

19. Here as elsewhere in the Conclusion, discussions of numbers are documented in the chapters.

20. Janion, *Do Europy*. On Berman, see Gniazdowski, "'Ustalić liczbę.'"

INDEX